THE HEALTH
OF THE
COUNTRY

THE HEALTH

OF THE

COUNTRY

HOW AMERICAN SETTLERS
UNDERSTOOD THEMSELVES AND
THEIR LAND

BY

Conevery Bolton Valenčius

BASIC
B
BOOKS

A Member of the Perseus Books Group
New York

Designed by Reginald Thompson
Set in 12-point Fournier

Valenčius, Conevery Bolton, 1969–
    The health of the country : how American settlers understood themselves and their
land / Conevery Bolton Valenčius.—1st ed.
        p. cm.
    Includes bibliographical references and index.
    ISBN 0-465-08986-0 (hc); ISBN 0-465-08987-9 (pbk)
    1. Medical geography—Arkansas—History—19th century.   2. Medical geography—
Missouri—History—19th century.   3. Environmental health—Arkansas—History—
19th century.   4. Environmental health—Missouri—History—19th century.   5. Health
attitudes—Arkansas—History—19th century.   6. Health attitudes—Missouri—
History—19th century.
    [DNLM: 1. Attitude to Health—United States.   2. Environmental Health—
history—United States.   3. Climate—United States.   4. Geography—United States.
5. History of Medicine, 18th Cent.—United States.   6. History of Medicine,
19th Cent.—United States.   WA 11 AA1 V152ha 2002]   I. Title.
RA792 .V354   2002
614.4'2'09767—dc21

                                                                                            2002004400

First Edition

CONTENTS

INTRODUCTION:
"HEALTHY COUNTRY"

IN THE FALL OF 1815, Justus and Eliza Post and their young children arrived in St. Louis after a long, arduous journey from New York. They had spent months gathering supplies, and months on the actual trip. They traveled over corduroy roads in Pennsylvania, took a flatboat for long, weary days down the Ohio, then turned north at its mouth to make their way up the Mississippi to the small but growing river port of St. Louis. The Post family came to establish themselves in the Missouri Territory, early movers in a westward tide of American emigration that would by midcentury stretch to the Pacific Ocean.

All along their journey, and for their first few years in Missouri, Justus Post wrote letters back to his older brother, John, in their home state of Vermont. In letter after letter Justus described his hopes for his family's "remove." He sought farmland on which to establish his own and his extended family, and he also planned to profit from volatile land prices by purchasing tracts for later resale to other emigrants and investors. Speculator and farmer, Post looked to the bottomland of the Missouri with a calculating and hopeful eye.

His impressions are telling. Immediately after arriving in St. Louis, Justus Post reported back to John that "I see nothing to hinder its being an extremely healthy country." A year later, in August 1816, he wrote that he had found an attractive area near the city, "& as it is such a healthy section of the country I think probable I shall establish myself there." Again and again, urging his brother to emigrate, Justus emphasized that "this is a healthy country and you may with confidence say it is to all such as may enquire of you concerning it." His letters finally succeeded: after much urging, John and Elizabeth Post and their family moved to the region in 1821.

1

I first read Justus Post's letters not far from where he and Eliza (and Elizabeth and John) disembarked, in what had become the modern city of St. Louis. Reading through the delicate, slightly yellowed sheets under the beautiful vaulted ceiling of the Missouri Historical Society reading room, I could find much that was familiar and unsurprising about this family correspondence. As a historian of the nineteenth century, I knew that letters were the means through which literate American families kept in touch, especially families pulled apart by emigration. I knew that interlinked family emigration was a frequent pattern in American social history. I knew that the descriptions of farmland and community prospects that Justus wrote John were very similar to those I could find in many other collections—in fact, I knew that the stories traced through this carefully preserved stack of aging letters were common to many free families of the early United States.

I did not know what Justus Post meant, though, by his forthright and repeated insistence that Missouri was "healthy country." Family members were sometimes sick, and sometimes in good health, Justus was clear enough about that. But—like the writers of many other letters and documents I had read from this same era—Justus Post persisted in describing his very surroundings as also being "healthy," "unhealthy," or, in the language of his time, "salubrious" or "insalubrious."

How could land possess "health"? Why did nineteenth-century writers constantly describe places as being healthy or sickly? These characterizations mattered a great deal: people like Justus Post, heading to "new" territories beyond the Mississippi, often decided where to settle, where to buy land, or even whether to stay in a place based on how they evaluated its salubrity. Yet to me and to other historians—and to the common sense of the twenty-first century—this understanding of the environment was a mystery.

Though many scholars have written about American western expansion, and many people like me study it, I realized that we have not fully understood these matter-of-fact, plainspoken assessments, even though they filled nineteenth-century writings. We have somehow passed over descriptions of "sickly" countryside or "salubrious" valleys with little in the way of comment or explanation. I have come to see that in doing so, we have missed something important.

Descriptions of "the health of the country" belong to a world we have lost. They come from the common sense of another time, when the human body was understood differently and its functioning was believed to be linked in intricate and intimate ways with the similar balances of the surrounding world. To comprehend this geography of health is thus to discover a surprising holism in the worldview of the bustling, rapidly industrializing nineteenth century.

In this book, I explain why Justus Post's comments about "healthy country" make sense. To do so, I focus on newcomers to the present-day states of Arkansas and Missouri, what were then borderlands caught up in the continued process of American expansion, on the perceived edges of an American empire. I start when the United States claims areas west of the Mississippi, with lands of the Louisiana Purchase of 1803. Recognizing the radical effect of changes in medical understanding, in regional perception, and in the character of American self-imagining that would follow the bloody 1860s, I end with the Civil War (these are the antebellum, or prewar, years of U.S. history). Using the experiences of both ambitious and unwilling migrants, I explore the meaning of conversations taking place throughout the United States, wherever American claimants encountered land and peoples new to them.

Both environments and human bodies are extremely messy. So, too, is making sense of them. As I worked out the connections between health and place, I found that I had to figure out how nineteenth-century Americans understood their bodies. Their understanding turns out to be very different from our own modern knowledge and perceptions. I had to learn about plowing, farming, and ditching in order to understand what antebellum westerners did to their surroundings and what they thought their surroundings did to them. I had to delve into the history of medicine to explain the ancient roots of physicians' assertions, as well as the logic of everyday healing.

What I discovered in the process was a worldview in which people were influenced by their environments in direct and powerful ways, and the exterior world and the human body were not as separate as they are now. Good or bad, harmful or improving, terrain possessed health in the same language and for the same reasons that human beings did. Basic properties applied to self and to surroundings, from the struggle of a volcano to expel foul matter to the strain of a boil to release putrid fluids and the bodily essences called humors.

In Justus Post's universe, processes of transformation, release, and renewal governed equally the physical environs and the human form. Common sense saw in eruptions or oozings, whether from swamp or wound, the same expression of putrescence; in fertility of soil and of family the same often ambivalent blessing; and in radical and challenging changes—in sudden sickness, in the turn of seasons, in the emergence of green shoots from black soil—a single phenomenon, whether enacted through human bodies or through the fields they tilled. It is thus in the everyday places and everyday occupations of nineteenth-century Americans that some of their most profound beliefs and ways of understanding the world came to the fore.

People participating in the American migration into the Mississippi Valley drew on a reassuringly coherent set of beliefs to make sense of potentially bewildering environments. They insisted upon the intelligibility of newly encountered territory even as they marveled at hot springs, cursed swarms of mosquitoes, and struggled to conform agricultural patterns to new soils, latitudes, and weather patterns. Their assessments of terrain were rarely unanimous, and they were often self-contradictory, but nineteenth-century newcomers of widely differing backgrounds based their contentions on a shared geography of health that made sense of strange places as well as familiar ones. The people of the growing United States set out to "improve" new territory armed with a deep and abiding sense of union between themselves and the soils they tilled.

"Is It Thriving & Healthy?"

When newcomers like the Post family came to unfamiliar surroundings, they searched a common cultural vocabulary for ways of conveying the experience of place. Their language of "healthy" land, "sickly" places, and "salubrity" inhering in site was ubiquitous: it provided a structure for evaluating the natural world in terms that linked scientific discussions and popular wisdom. In subtle and not-so-subtle ways, it also expressed the anxieties associated with the process of settlement.

In the language of health and place, diverse participants in the American inrush expressed a shared geography of well-being. One Virginia farmer, Thomas Humphreys, who moved to St. Louis in 1835, recorded in his diary that he had decided not to offer a bid on one available plot "owing to the bad health of the place." The Irish immigrant Anthony Doyle, writing in 1819 to his brother in Carrick, expressed similar concerns, commenting, "I will in the course of this season go out to enter 320 acres of land in some healthy place where there is good land." The very terseness of many such brief references to "sickly" or "salubrious" land speaks for a shared set of assumptions and beliefs. Women also contributed to this geography of health: Cynthia Thrall, a missionary to the Cherokees in the 1820s, approved of a proposed mission site because it was "said to be healthy." Such assessments fill guidebooks and military reports, physicians' articles and private letters;

they form a little-noticed undercurrent in the flow of population across the Mississippi.

Encountering territory they found new and strange, travelers mused about what were to them obvious and unproblematic questions: how healthy the terrain was, what its effects might be on specific ailments or conditions, and how the nature of the environment, including its perceived salubrity, would shift with different kinds of inhabitants, vegetation, and usage. These observations were not unprecedented in American and European cultural experience: they were commonplace and commonly engaged in. Searching to understand American newcomers' perceptions of new places therefore reveals much of their everyday experience and matter-of-fact expectations of the world.

Widely shared worries reflected the realities of lives often plagued with illness. Before the germ theory of disease, before antibiotics, before many effective public health measures—before the revolution of medical theory and practice that began in the latter decades of the nineteenth century and has continued into the present day—injury and illness were the constant accompaniments of daily life. Maintaining health taxed heavily even the well. The Yankee emigrant Henry Merrell blamed the pervasive unhealthiness of central Arkansas for the failure of his own commercial ambitions. "All the year round and every year," he complained, "I had to keep about me quite double the number of hands that would have been necessary for the same works in a healthy region."

In the mobile antebellum world, emigration and resettlement in sparsely populated areas heightened already intense concern for personal and family health. Even common sicknesses were exacerbated by distance from friends, kin, and established patterns of care. Farm accidents, illness, nutritional deficiencies, and difficult childbirth could cripple the emotional strength and productive capacity of a family. What a Connecticut emigrant, Stephen Hempstead, in 1823 termed "afflictive providence" could strike without warning to injure, cripple, or even kill.

Business, government, and personal correspondence all reflect a preoccupation with bodily well-being grounded in the daily experience of challenges and threats to health. Personal letters were often packed with news of the health of family members and reports on the diseases of the region. This "health talk" played an important function in maintaining connection among families separated by migration. Worry about sickness, disease, and accident was part of the fabric of life for all manner of correspondents. John Henry, a businessman writing from New Orleans to his partner in Van Buren, Arkansas, in 1857, commented amid news of coffee prices and steamboat shipping that "for the last three days I done nothing as Mrs. H. has been very sick & I have been with her—She has the neuralgia of eyes & she has suffered terrably—She is much better to-day and I am going to work." Like plowing, harvesting, caring for livestock, or cooking for a family, the work of shipping and mercantile exchange could be disrupted and delayed by the common misfortunes of ill health.

The toll of new diseases was heavy. Endemic malaria, the dreaded "ague and fever," bedeviled newcomers and filled the often disparaging accounts of the Mississippi Valley, while cholera and other infectious diseases swept through in periodic outbreaks. Over 10 percent of St. Louis's population perished during the 1849 cholera outbreak; over half of those dead were young children. Chronic ills too marked daily life. Faces swelled, nursing nipples cracked, old aches got the "rheumatiz," and new wounds refused to heal. Even something as ordinary as a fungal infection could make life miserable: "obliged to leave Church on account of our feet itching very much," wrote a St. Louis schoolgirl, Mary E. Smith, in her diary in mid-March of 1836. (She and her schoolmate returned to their boarding school to bathe and grease their feet and wrap them in rags.) Maintenance of bodily well-being occupied time and resources on a constant basis.

Judging the health or sickliness of a place was complex. Observers were often emphatic, but seldom consistent. Regions of Arkansas and Missouri—or even the entire Mississippi Valley—were pronounced in one source to be healthy, sickly, or "miasmatic," and in another were just as resolutely claimed to be the opposite. Debates over diseases prevalent in a region, like debates over the relative fertility of tracts of soil or the likely patterns of future commerce, raged throughout the antebellum period. Boosters frequently found ways to explain away epidemics or minimize high mortality: commercial ambition shaped pronouncements about a place's health, as it did other aspects of settlement.

The stakes were high. Ambitious families moved to healthy places, not to sickly ones. In 1814, Henry Marie Brackenridge, a travel guide author, commented that the past year had been "uncommonly unhealthy throughout the western country." He observed: "This season did great injury to the commencing emigration to this county; many who had suffered, retired from it, and others who had determined to come, changed their minds." The perceived healthfulness of regions thus held profound meanings for community growth. Healthy sites meant thriving settlements; sickly situations brought problems both individual and communitywide. In the language of self and of terrain, newcomers wrote their concerns for the social and economic success of their risky venture of settlement.

Sources

Assessments of the health of places fill newcomers' letters and journals, the columns of local newspapers, the reports of physicians and scientific observers, the adventure stories of hunters and trappers, the tall tales of regional humorists, and the floridly written pages of the myriad travel and emigration guides that promised to interpret the Far West to American and European migrants. Understanding the geography of health and place means reading these sources in all their motley jumble.

Letters are one rich source on western movement. Free emigrants often tried to justify their move to family and friends and in doing so reveal much about their lives in a new place. Vesta P. Stevenson, a recently arrived schoolteacher in south-central Arkansas, wrote to her mother in about 1850. Though the letter is scrupulously polite, tensions between the two are clear. Her mother had apparently not approved of Stevenson's choice of husband, but Stevenson assured her that "as far as James is conserned you were certainly greatly mistaken. as the amount of work he has done since he has been here will bear ample testimony." Not everything was easy—"'Tis true we have not passed the *hard* place altogether"—but the family's prospects were good: "we are doing as well as could have been expected, as we commenced with so little." Proud of her own accomplishments, Stevenson reminded her mother that she was getting along without much help from her family. Stevenson's missive is also characteristic in the elision of certain important events: "say to Mary E," she wrote, "I congratulate her on the pleasing addition lately made to her household. Also say to her unles some sad mishap, I too will have something of which to boast, in about five months." Household stability, purchased by the hard work of husband and wife, was the Stevenson family harvest, and Vesta Stevenson's correspondence home was clear in its message. Independence from her family of origin—and news of a family of her own soon to come—was carried in letters like the "rose slips" that Stevenson's mother had once sent her for her garden, or the political news, family gossip, newspaper clippings, and homesick kisses enclosed by other correspondents.

Enslaved migrants' records are less direct and more complicated. Black residents of Missouri and Arkansas authored only a few written accounts of their lives in the antebellum period; most are freedom narratives written by escaped slaves. Other sources, like biographies of escapees written by Northern abolitionists, are highly mediated by white writers. To gain the widest range of experiences, I use accounts not only of Arkansas and Missouri slaves but also of slaves from other Southern states, just as I use accounts of migration from white families originally from many different locations. Taken together, such sources can indicate something of the perspectives and perceptions of black Americans in the period.

The ex-slave interviews collected by the Federal Writers' Project of the Works Progress Administration during the Great Depression are an invaluable repository for antebellum African-American history. They require, nonetheless, delicate handling. Memories of childhood sixty, seventy, or eighty years before are much different from impressions of the moment. The elderly Southern black interviewees, many of them hoping to receive government benefits, interacted in complicated ways with interviewers who were sent by the federal government, most of whom were white, all of whom were literate, and many of whom adopted a patronizing tone toward their interviewees. The ex-slave interviews have been faulted for including overexaggerated and demeaning dialect and for repressing material that depicted the brutality of life under the slave system. Yet the interviews are often rich, the Arkansas records particularly so. These documents provide at times counterpoint to, at times corroboration of the worldviews evinced by the white contemporaries for whom slaves worked and with whom they struggled.

Sources frequently blurred genre. Scientific reports also functioned as travel narratives; medical works offered social commentary; tall tales also told how to do everyday tasks or narrated rich geographic and topographic description; geographies gave emigration advice. The physician Daniel Drake's two-volume description of the diseases of the Mississippi Valley reprinted the account of an early-eighteenth-century French missionary making his arduous way up the Mississippi. In the course of preparing his medical account Drake came across a religious and descriptive account he knew would be of interest to his readers, so he simply included it. In antebellum works, authors ceaselessly stole from and quoted each other, not respecting the boundaries of intellectual ownership any more than they respected differences between kinds of texts.

In stories and reports popular throughout the nineteenth century, many authors described early Missouri and Arkansas as places where free men could fish, hunt, trap, and live a rough outdoor life. Such tales of outdoor adventure are often full of detail about the behavior of animals and their stalkers as well as the incidental aspects of everyday life. They can be a valuable source about life in the region, especially in the Ozark Mountains of northern Arkansas and southern Missouri. These stories give a masculine account of the natural world, one in which men move with independence through different kinds of terrain, learning about their environment not simply as a site of potential human habitation but as a home for myriad creatures—though these tall tales of the hunt have their limitations, notably when it comes to their accuracy about how big the "big bears" or bucks actually were.

Divergent sources contain some surprisingly similar observations about the connections between health and place. By using them, I aim to integrate the perspective of elite observation with that of everyday experience. Reading from accounts by politicians and geologists, by farm families and visiting Europeans, by former slaves and by many slave owners, we can uncover certain widely shared notions of the interactions between forces animating terrain and those mediating the functions of the human body.

Making American Territory

Driven by concerns about personal well-being, American newcomers were at the same time working through their ideas about the well-being and prospects of the nation. This story has important connections with other national histories, and yet it encompasses developments that—taken together—constitute something particularly American. The practices and intellectual structures brought by newcomers have important transnational roots, especially in the areas of western Europe and western Africa from which most American newcomers drew their cultural heritage. Even at the time, movement within North America was an international phenomenon. Emigration guidebooks that described new territories and how to reach them appeared not only in communities of the American East Coast but also in English towns, German villages, and cities throughout Europe.

The diverse upbringing, experiences, training, and background of many people involved in American migration meant that borderland areas were the site of cultural cross-fertilization. One German humorist, Friedrich Gerstäcker, parodied settlers from his country for their reliance on Old World tools rather than American axes and ingenuity. In his story "The

Young Schoolmaster," a newly arrived German family, already exhausted by the difficulty of traveling across the rough and muddy roads of their new country, grow desperate in the forests of Arkansas when using European saws proves laborious, when the cow breaks the last milk pot, and when wild hogs turn out to be too big to scald in any available vessel. They are rescued by the improvised solutions of a fellow newcomer, a young American, who teaches them how to fabricate tools, boil hogs in an earthen pit, and not only hew trees but whittle and shape delicate objects with the curved-handled, multipurpose American ax. In the end, the American neighbor, dressed in his "Sunday best" hunting shirt, asks for the hand in marriage of the eldest daughter of the family, Margarethe, who in the tradition of such frontier tales is robust, sensible, hard-working, and also very pretty. She, of course, accepts. Such cross-cultural exchange, even if exaggerated in Gerstäcker's fable, was common among borderlands settlers.

In their interactions in the American "Far West," migrants participated in an imaginative venture that would shape how the United States came to cast its own history. This perceptual stretch was deeply influenced by the environments in which nineteenth-century newcomers found themselves. Unlike people in Britain and continental Europe, migrants in the American West confronted what was to them an astoundingly abundant wilderness. They saw stretched out before them huge vistas of terrain that they regarded as untouched and new to agricultural—and therefore legitimate— use. They struggled to encompass and bound what they saw as vast wild spaces waiting to be put to ordered use.

How these environments would be shaped by Americans was a question of deep moral and political significance. From the nation's founding, the connection between farming and virtue had found clear expression in American thought and writing. Orderly fields of straight rows clearly delineated from the surrounding unshaped terrain implied orderly virtue in their free cultivators. Apparently unfarmed land was a moral as well as a physical challenge. The confrontation with unfamiliar territory that took place in the canebrakes, the fields, and the prairies of the middle Mississippi Valley thus marks one of the defining aspects of American self-imagination, for good and for ill.

Not only American migrants but also the many Europeans who thronged to the region saw themselves as participating in a process that was essentially *American*: taking over "new" lands and remaking them into American territory. This was a national as well as a personal project. Migrants to the trans-Mississippi western territories were participating in a series of arrivals at the "new" that had begun with European colonization of the Eastern Seaboard and would continue well into the latter part of the nineteenth century. Examining the creation of Missouri and Arkansas thus opens a window into the commonplace and intentional making American of territory and terrain.

In the overlapping processes of transformation that made up American migrants' confrontations with the new, the geography of health played an important part. In coming to understand and—they hoped—to command their environs, migrants repeatedly emphasized their physical connections with their surroundings. Discussions of the healthfulness of environments expressed a crucial moment of apprehension of the natural world—"apprehension" in its many senses, as understanding, fear, and appropriation. This book seeks to flesh out in the idiom of a later and very different age that physical and imaginative transformation of American geographical takeover.

It is my belief that large-scale narratives are needed for contemporary Americans often hungry for their own history, and that cultural and environmental historians should not cede the field of large-scale historical narrative to the political or military historians whose efforts at grand narratives we have so frequently—and rightly—critiqued for excluding all but literate and politically powerful white men. *The Health of the Country* thus offers larger narratives about Americans' western movement, a movement that turns out to be surprisingly complex, hesitant, and fraught with peril from within, as well as without.

All good history should have something to contribute to the historical scholarship that has come before. In this book, I try to bring together three areas of study that usually have only a nodding acquaintance: the history of medicine and science, environmental history, and the history of American westward expansion in the nineteenth century.

The history of medicine, science, and technology has in recent years been a field of conceptually rich scholarship. Recent work has focused not simply on *what* we know but on *how* we know it. Why, for example, do some observers have authority to speak on matters of scientific experiment? What role have externalities like court patronage or civic bureaucracies played in shaping the direction of empirical work? We can ask the same kinds of questions to understand how nonscientists gain understanding of their world. Applying some of the questions developed by historians of science to the environmental history of the nineteenth century can therefore reveal a great deal about how people came to *know* the feel of good plowland, or the smell of a healthy breeze.

American borderland experience also has something to say back. In this account, I do not respect the boundaries between professionals and laypeople, or between different professions, any more than their contemporaries did—and I find that the era's botanists, geologists, weather observers, and medical geographers can withstand this rough treatment quite well. I hope this book will push us to look harder through some of the porous boundaries between science and nonscience, finding in the swirl of everyday description of fields, river bottoms, and human well-being much that illuminates the history of scientific and technical knowledge.

Documents by nineteenth-century Americans have taught me that theirs was not a world in which the environment stopped at the seeming boundary of the skin. In the antebellum borderlands, the surrounding world seeped into newcomers' every pore, creating states of health that were as much environmental as they were personal. Territorial expansion came at a cost that was intimate and interior; medical and environmental history come together in settlers' bodies.

Environmental history has recently come into its own, offering a physically grounded way of understanding diverse kinds of historical change. One of the crucial insights of environmental history has to do with the instability between what humans call nature and humanity's own works, and with the inadequacy of the "natural" as an explanatory resource in historical inquiry. Humans have shaped what we think of as nature more than we know or are often willing to acknowledge, from the burning and clearing done by Native Americans to the re-created "nature" of climate-controlled shopping malls. Yet as the history of human disease makes clear, we also control less than we sometimes think we do: every one of us lives in thrall to microbes, parasites, contaminants, and genes whose tiny workings we can often only dimly intuit. People of the nineteenth century recognized this interconnection between self and nonself, this constant interplay between human agency and human lack of control, rather more frankly than we moderns. Giving voice to their perspective may help us find a vocabulary for coming to terms with the world, both inner and outer, toward which we reach in our imprecise but insistent searching after the "natural."

Finally, I hope to offer a better understanding of the costs of American westering. The struggle for what nineteenth-century wisdom would term "proper management" of both land and body was not always successful.

Very often, efforts to maintain appropriate and productive balances within oneself and within one's natural terrain ended in sickness, economic failure, family collapse, or death.

Justus Post, whose bold hopes set me onto the puzzle of health and environment in the nineteenth century, ultimately failed in his effort to found towns and create a fortune. The Posts lost much of their holdings in the financial crisis of the late 1810s, and Justus died much reduced in will and circumstances. For her part, Eliza Post lived through the death of her husband and beloved younger sons to endure loneliness and ill health in old age. Later in life she again took part in a long journey to little-known foreign territory, accompanying her sole remaining son, a physician named Augustus, on an ill-fated military adventure to Nicaragua. Eliza Post returned to New Orleans before the military expedition met its dolorous end, having once again experienced the failure of ambitious menfolk to conquer foreign territory. Like many of the stories that lie raveled through the letters and diaries of this bold and enterprising period of American history, the Posts' narrative is one not of boisterous success but of disillusionment and ultimate loss.

The process of settlement was never consistent, and the results were complicated and sometimes sad. Yet in the 1860s, when this account closes, Missouri and Arkansas were undeniably American, and the process of making them so does say something to us about the creation not only of American territory, but of American character.

Many emigrants to Missouri and Arkansas looked upon the land around them with a self-consciously triumphalist vision of American western movement. They saw themselves—as indeed later historians would see them—as part of a series of moves of American population, culture, and political, economic, and religious structures across the North American continent. While I will explore these hopes and imaginings, this book is not itself a triumphalist account. Instead, I am attempting to set down onto paper some of the complicated, idiosyncratic, and often contradictory ways in which people new to western territories shaped the gritty details of American territorial expansion.

To ignore the reports of boosters and regional impresarios, with all their romantic and unrealistic mythology of westward emigration and life in the Far West, is to miss a central driving force in antebellum American life. This account therefore takes as a starting point the almost self-obsessive quality of newcomers' reflections, their insistence on newness, on social malleability, on the *American-ness* of their process of claiming territory and resources.

Examining how and why those notions came to be expressed, and what anxieties clouded and permeated the rhetoric of American optimism, this project focuses precisely on how newcomers romanticized the process of "settling" land. Using the voices and the perspectives of those who saw themselves as confident conquerors (as well as many who came less willingly), this work tries to account for the sources, as well as the undertones, of their perspective. "Do the people in your quarter think I have gone out of the world?" inquired Justus Post of his New England brother in 1816; "If so then tell them that they mistake much, for I am in the center of it."

"NEW COUNTRY"

Chapter I

MOVEMENT PERVADED NINETEENTH-CENTURY American life. Calling themselves settlers and emigrants, "movers" and "improvers," households across the states and territories engaged in "removes" and travels that reshaped the American social and political scene. Euro-American newcomers came to Missouri and Arkansas intending to create order and ownership in what was to them vaguely empty space just past the Mississippi River, at the edges of their mapped terrain. Native American emigrants also came to these same regions seeking what they had formerly found in lands east and north: safety, game, and freedom from outside political interference. Slaves were forced to emigrate, in ways which often severed family ties. Confronted with the bodily consequences of their voyages into the new, American migrants embarked on a frustrating search for order in self and surroundings.

All of these overlapping migrations took place against a backdrop of cultural expectation. Behind the constant mobility of antebellum life lay a rhetoric of newness created by the free emigrants whose hopes it reflected. Newness held foreboding as well as promise, for new environments were understood in the nineteenth century to hold bodily threat, forcing migrants to accustom and acclimate their physical selves to foreign places. This bodily experience was an intimate in-reaching of hopes and fears about newness that affected many aspects of life.

"Wild" Land and "New"

At that time, Arkansas was a perfect terra incognita. The way to get there was un-known; and what it was, or was like, if you did get there was still more an unre-vealed mystery.

—**Cephas Washburn,**
recollecting setting out on
his mission to the Cherokees in 1819

Free emigrants often arrived in early Arkansas and Missouri with ill-chosen tools, few resources, confused plans, and too little money. But they almost always arrived with clear ambitions about their roles in this new country. (Of course this could not be said for enforced black emigration. See Chapter 9 for a discussion of differences in the experience and perceptions of free white and black emigrants.) One new emigrant, John C. Luttig, wrote that Arkansas was in need of being "organised," and, his tone implied, he was just the man to do it. The struggle to impose order and organization on new territories characterized white settlers' interactions with their physical environments, as with their own bodies. In each case, recalcitrant, un-wieldy, and complex systems defied easy mastery and demanded constant adjustment and recalibration. To both self and surroundings, however, many antebellum Americans brought an ambition born of their optimism about the new.

In the nineteenth century, the areas immediately beyond the Mississippi represented both the imaginative and the substantive "Far West" of Ameri-can settlement. "Two hundred miles west of the Mississippi River," ex-plained one British travel guide of 1820, "the arable soil of the country experiences a total change. Beyond that limit an extensive desert com-mences, which extends to the Pacific Ocean." Even the growing metropolis of St. Louis teetered on the edge of civilization.

European and American newcomers to this contested terrain—which many of his former neighbors, wrote Justus Post, "think at a greater dis-tance than the moon"—cast it as wild and new, in need of their "improve-ment." The newness of land formed the theme of the scheming and the improvident, the eloquent and the semiliterate. "Our land is of good quality and the country new," wrote an Arkansas immigrant, Kirkbride Potts, to his sister back in New Jersey in 1830, echoing the heady optimism of many newcomers. Arkansas's first territorial governor, James Miller, thought a "new country" was a "good one for a young persevering man." (Miller, a hero of the recent war with Britain, himself left the region after a short term, tired of heat, humidity, mosquitoes, and rough living).

Newness most of all connoted possibility. In an 1819 letter to his brother, a doctor, whom he hoped to convince to emigrate to Arkansas, Robert F. Henry wrote with passion of his hopes and ambitions:

> To come up to your ideas of a *new country*, unspoiled forests & uninhabited prairies are not the only requisites. It ought to be a country where society was in its infancy, where the population resembled Ovid's chaos, a rude & undigested mass; which the hand of genius & merit could shape to its own purposes. Where government was in its first grade; where offices were not filled; in short, where all the teeming possibilities of a new country were yet to be unravelled. The Arkansaw [Territory] opens an avenue through which all these things may be prefigured.

Henry's *"new country"* was young, unspoiled, and uninhabited; in it, a strong leader could shape and steady the "teeming" possibilities. Figuring the process of societal development like the workings of some monstrous digestion, Henry urged his brother upon the "undigested mass." Henry's fire ignores the possibility of failure: in new country lay the possibility for boldness to be transformative. Henry's somatic metaphors were typical of the ways in which even the political future of the region was figured in and through the body. Antebellum Americans understood the language and processes of the physical self to operate also in the very country around them.

Indeed, many free immigrants sought to re-create themselves physically and economically as they formed their new environments. Everard Dickinson's hopes represent those of many young movers. A bachelor of thirty-three when he left his job as a shop clerk in Hartford, Connecticut, Dickinson sought economic advancement and personal opportunity in the frontiers of the West. In 1848, he wrote his parents in Springfield, Massachusetts, about his experiences in northwest Arkansas, "a wild, romantic region of country [that] has been but little known abroad until within a few years." "In my Judgment," he assured them, "this is a healthy country." A year later, he declared that "This Wild and new Country suits me first rate, & it is a healthy region I think so [much so] as any part of the Union." Wildness, newness, possibility, and health bore a close and interdependent relationship. He reiterated in 1850 that "This is a healthy Country & the water is Good."

Dickinson found equality and self-reliance in the frontiers of Arkansas. Rather than working as a "a hireling and a slave, as all poor people are in those old thick settled countries" back East, he could be "an independent man—with a buckskin Hunting shirt on & leather breeches" (though he wrote his parents to please send him some percussion caps and "old *Kill Deer*," the family gun, so that he could make good on these dreams). "If I have my health continued for a few years," he assured his parents, "I will show you what E. B. Dickinson can do for himself in a New Country." He feared, or perhaps hoped, that "This is entirely too New & Wild a country to suit you," but hastened to promise that "if you choose to come here & live with me I will try & make a living for us all." A thinly settled land, where a pale store clerk could roam mountains and shoot at buffalo, offered sorely needed room for adventure, even as it promoted physical well-being.

Yet such hopes often ended in disillusionment. Dickinson ended his last remaining letter, in June 1850, with an ambivalent hint: "I may Go to *Calafornia*—(but [d]o not say I even think of it)." Across that letter, in different hand-writing, is scrawled a poignant notation: "read over by his Mother March 27th 1860 alone in her house." Everard Dickinson may have died in some accident near Buffalo Shoals, where he lived for two years, his later letters may simply have gone astray, or he may have succumbed to one of the illnesses endemic to the mining camps of California's gold rush: as with the stories of many who sought new opportunity in new country, the ending of this tale is unclear. Only the forlorn exchange of mother and son, a decade separated in time, on a piece of fading paper testifies to the failure of this shop-clerk's dreams.

Dickinson's praise for Arkansas reflected a desire for personal freedom and a healthy environment. Other characterizations of wilderness placed similar value on what it offered to the body politic. Nicholas Hesse, a German immigrant, asserted in 1838 a crucial function for American wilderness. "American republican constitution" would "very likely endure" so long as the population remained low relative to its available land, and "as long as the nomadic American still has space enough to move on to the west and so can follow his most cherished inclinations." Hesse's conclusions about the political function of American wilderness presage those that resounded through American historical scholarship in the following century in the "frontier thesis" of Frederick Jackson Turner. More importantly, they reveal the ways in which wilderness was seen in the early nineteenth century not simply as an economic, but as a political resource.

Yet this view of wild regions as a safety valve is ambivalent. Hesse implies that unpeopled "space" should always exist—but somewhere else, beyond civilization but within the reach of the "nomadic American." Except for a few hunters and trappers who relished "wild" lands (at least so long as they could buy coffee and butter when they wanted some), many of Hesse's contemporaries felt the same. Even praise of unsettled, uncultivated land relied upon the prospect of its ultimate taming and cultivation. In itself, unmanaged wilderness inspired dread.

Again and again in the writings of early travelers and settlers, wildness in landscape served to underscore the need to map, cultivate, and domesticate it. A journal kept by Ellen Stetson, an emigrant missionary, reflects her difficulty coming to terms with a natural environment strange to her. Stetson recorded her thoughts as she and a party of fellow missionaries made their long and arduous way in the fall of 1821 from the East Coast to Arkansas Territory to found the Dwight Mission to the Cherokees. Melancholy as she shivered by a fire in western Arkansas, Stetson felt a cold somehow deeper than any she had experienced in New England. Her bodily experience testified to the gulf separating her from home. In her journal, Stetson copied a poem about distance from family, friends, and known environment. Its stanzas lamented that Arkansas offered "no rural walk, in cultivated field / In orchard's shade, or garden's pleasant slope." A natural environment that was tamed, cultivated, and ordered meant familiarity and comfort—physical and emotional—for this homesick missionary.

Body and land were intimately intertwined in newcomers' search for order. In antebellum language, "settling" referred to a bodily and an environmental process, one national in scope and personal in meaning. Thus Owen Maguire, who had been in financial difficulties in the late 1820s and early '30s, moved with his wife, Mary Maguire from Kentucky to Missouri, and then finally emigrated south to Arkansas. After that last emigration, he wrote in 1836 to his sister and brother-in-law with evident satisfaction that "I have settled my self & got a valuable tract of land." From sowing wild oats, perhaps, to sowing wheat and corn, Owen Maguire had indeed settled both land and self.

At the same time, not just people but environments themselves were thought to be transformed with settlement. Tributaries of the White River, observed the author of an 1833 article in the *Saturday Evening Post* about communities in Arkansas Territory, "will become of importance as the country settles." Such language emphasizes the rhetoric of settling or calming wilderness—domesticating it in every sense—which accompanied the American westward move.

What mattered in the world of the American nineteenth century was not simply the actual wood and water through which early migrants made their way, but the perceptual environments in which they lived and moved. Settlers' bold hopes and depressed cautions both represent interpretive interactions with the world around them. In particular, their emphasis upon "new" land represents not a mirror of reality, but a forced insistence.

The physical difficulty of making one's way through the resistant terrain of early Arkansas and Missouri shaped the experiences and imaginations of newcomers like Owen Maguire, Everard Dickinson, and Ellen Stetson. Migrants traveled with river craft, on foot, on horseback, by mule, or with rough wagons. Mountains and swamps formed substantial barriers to their progress. Rivers and waters, by contrast, provided a means to enter land. In the first half of the nineteenth century, no railroads yet traversed the country's interior: ground was experienced as migrants moved across it, slowly, from no more than a few meters up. Dense underbrush in swampy lowland regions made travel strenuous and difficult. Roads would suddenly disappear under the feet of hapless travelers.

Sight lines and perceptions were further limited by rough terrain. Grasses on the Missouri prairies could be taller than an adult person, and hard for horses to push their way through. Canebrakes—stands of thick, high native bamboo that thrived in river bottoms—presented a swath of dense, unbroken verticality from every perspective, one in which even experienced trackers could find it difficult to gain their bearings.

Such environments resisted regularity and order. Directors of the unwieldy construction of the Little Rock–Memphis road in 1825 complained to their superior one wet, cold February, "The difficulty of hunting badly marked lines, run perhaps some ten or twelve years ago, if run at all, through Swamps, lakes, Bayous, heavy Cane breaks and at this inclement season, can only be estimated by those who performed it." The effort to run a straight road between Memphis and Little Rock, explained the exhausted managers, was frustrated by the demands of the countryside. Topography resisted surveyors' chains and thwarted American efforts to mark off territory into regular geometries of order.

In much the same way, newcomers' bodies experienced disorder and remained recalcitrant against all efforts to bring them into calm, smooth equilibrium. Disease, debility, and the life-cycle changes of the human form all proved the stubbornness of the flesh as of the surrounding terrain. In their attempts at healing as in their attempts to hack roads out of underbrush and drain bottomlands into fertile array, antebellum migrants attempted to force order on chaotic world.

The dynamism of their environments—like the dynamic qualities of their bodies—continually resisted them. Terrain itself proved unstable. Even as explorers, trappers, and prospective farmers surveyed, tested, described, and categorized portions of land, they knew that their environments were change-able—and had changed within recent human memory. Where they walked, as they neared any main river, could once have been waterway—and, in the next flood, could be again, as rivers reared up out of their old channels and found new ones. The very ground beneath one's feet could shift: the terrifying earthquakes of 1811–12, which were centered on what is now the Missouri boot heel, forced the Mississippi backward and caused church bells to ring as far east as Pennsylvania. Central to American apprehension of the early west-ern territories was dynamic and unstable bodily experience.

Newness of experience, great and small, met American cultivators in all the myriad details of their farms and surroundings. Justus Post, coming from the mountains and forests of northern New England, would have had little experience with the thick ooze of southern sloughs. Settlers from heav-ily forested regions were unaccustomed to the "prairies"—extensive sec-tions of tallgrass—they encountered nestled even among hollows of the Ozarks. The hot, humid afternoons of Arkansas and Missouri summers made their hands slippery against plow handles and left encrustations of salt on their coarsely woven, sweat-soaked clothing. Travel and work in the long hot season were laborious, slow, and uncomfortable. Changeable win-ter weather, in which balmy weeks could be followed by sudden cold snaps, challenged accepted patterns of farm and home. Even the foods of such wet regions were different: Germans coming to Arkansas pined for potatoes and were at a loss for how to prepare or appreciate rice.

Bright parrots (now extinct) flashed in the woods along the Mississippi; mountain lions roamed deep glens. The artist and naturalist John James Audubon reported during his tour of the Mississippi Valley that if enterpris-ing residents removed the glands from "pole-cats" (skunks), they could be stroked like a cat. Some newcomers kept deer—even buffalo calves—as pets. A Missouri storyteller named Theodore Pease Russell reported a par-ticularly effective technique for domesticating a captured fawn: he let it suckle on his earlobe. Strangeness both physical and cultural greeted those venturing into the realm beyond the Mississippi.

In September of 1827, Stephen S. Hempstead, an early Connecticut emi-grant to St. Louis, labored in his garden to rescue his crop of pumpkins. They had become infested with strange insects, bugs that "Eat up Evry green leaf on the pumpkins and Squashes and their Eggs Soon became a green worm about one Inch in lenght which took to all the pumpkins that were young and destroyed them." Awed by the thorough voraciousness of this new pest, which "in 24 hours . . . will Eat and Spoil a large pumpkin,"

Hempstead reflected that this was "a phenomenon, I had never before Seen." Struggling to render coherent a bewildering new country, American migrants confronted intractability both mundane and profound.

Acclimation

"Well, go on, but I can tell you, you will shake."

—Timothy Flint's record of roadside advice
given to an emigrant headed to the Boon's
Lick region of Missouri from a former neighbor
who was dejectedly moving back to "old Kentuck."

The shock of the new registered not only in the surrounding world, but in the most intimate experiences of one's own form. For people of the nineteenth century, the human form was steeped in its physical citizenship. Those who did not belong in a given terrain could expect to suffer for their temerity. Newcomers struggled through a process they regarded as both crucial and perilous, the changes through which their bodies would be "acclimated" to new climate and topography.

In 1815, Timothy Flint, a missionary who was to become a noted travel writer, wrote to ask Stephen Hempstead about moving from Cincinnati to St. Louis: "The object I have in view in writing this, is to enquire of you what prospects open to a missionary in your quarter? Whether he would be favorably received? And whether the [re]gion of St. Louis would, probably, be healthful to [nor]thern constitutions (for my family is resident with [m]e in this place)." Shaped by their "Northern" residence, the "constitutions" of Flint's family were appropriate for their life in Massachusetts and Cincinnati, not for the demands and conditions of life in the territories farther south and west. Flint's family could be endangered by their intrusion into lands to which they did not belong, for such a move threatened the mesh between people and their environment. Individuals who changed their surroundings were obliged to break their relationship with the old environment and remake it with a new and challenging one. Common wisdom warned white families of the fearful adjustment every migration demanded.

Change was possible—but at a cost. Moving out of one's accustomed environment required a process of gradual seasoning. One 1829 medical treatise emphasized, "In whatever latitude man locates himself, he assumes certain characteristic modifications." These changes forged a "relationship" with "that particular atmosphere, and the various objects which surround him." The "adaptive powers of the human constitution" allowed individuals gradually to accommodate themselves to regions as diverse and dangerous as the African coast or the Mexican plains.

Gottfried Duden gave a typical account of this process in his influential 1829 guide for German emigrants. An enthusiastic booster of American settlement, and especially of Missouri, Duden was nonetheless adamant about the dangers of change of place. He advised his readers, "The farmer who suddenly changes from the German farm life to the work of tropical plantations without intermediate stages exposes his physical constitution to the most dangerous disturbances. Settlements at the mouth of the Arkansas are perhaps already too far south."

Duden's caution reflected both medical understanding and views of the territory beyond the Mississippi. He linked the "mouth of the Arkansas" in present-day southeastern Arkansas with the tropical. Later generations might call Missouri "Midwest" and Arkansas, less assuredly, the "Mid-South" or "South-Central," but Duden's readership understood the area chiefly in terms of heat—dangerous southern heat. Sudden confrontation with this environment could create "dangerous disturbances" in immigrants' systems. To avoid this, Duden advised a process of "intermediate stages" of settlement so that immigrants' bodies would adjust gradually to their changed surroundings. Settlement from north to south—from the German states or from New England—would ideally take several years, giving travelers' bodies time to adjust gradually to each stage of the move.

Such cautions reflected the dangers inherent in change of place. Adjustment took a physical toll. First and foremost, people got sick. Medical understanding emphasized that a period of sickness was necessary to accustom each individual's body to the region's native ailments.

"Seasoning" diseases had marked Europeans' settlement of places in North America since the colonial era. The experience of migrants to the mid–Mississippi Valley continued a set of confrontations with new environments that had preoccupied successive generations of colonizers since the nobles running the Virginia Company stood aghast at the high mortality rates of their settlers, and eighteenth-century planters in the Chesapeake struggled to import enough indentured servants to make up for those who would die in their first year. The course of illnesses through which newcomers came to terms with a new place, and it with them, had a long history within moves across North America—which was of little help to anxious migrants seized with poorly understood ills that had no precedent in their personal experience.

"Emigrants generally suffer some kind of sickness, which is called 'seasoning,' implying that it is the summit of the gradual process of acclimation," observed Timothy Flint in his 1826 *Recollections*; "This sickness commonly attacks them the first, second, or third year, and is generally the more severe, the longer it is delayed." Once well seasoned, newcomers could bear their acclimation proudly, but getting through it drained resources, wore down stamina, and depressed spirits.

Even comparative newness could make an individual vulnerable. One longtime St. Louis resident wrote his family in 1835 of experiencing "a slight touch of the fever last fall after I moved to the country." Changing ground from urban streets to country fields, from the bustle of the St. Louis port to the still heat of nearby countryside, could bring on a "slight touch" of seasoning, a small but potent reminder of the forces binding person to place with grim specificity.

Often the "summit" or crisis illness that marked a newcomer's decisive acclimation was the "ague" or "chills and fever" usually identified by modern authorities as malaria. Having the chills and fever was an accustomed introduction to the western territories, and especially to the Mississippi Valley where (later investigators would realize) the mosquitoes that were its vector found their habitat. Whole families would undergo ague's acclimatizing "shakes" in miserable synchrony, their bodies coursing through alternations of piercing chill and exhausting fever in their first summer in the western borderlands.

Seasoning sickness was debilitating and disorienting. Timothy Flint's illness of acclimation left him utterly vulnerable, "preternaturally excited," unable to recognize friends and yet able with feverish imagination to "repeat . . . whole passages in the different languages which I knew, with entire accuracy." Flashes of light and ethereal music accompanied his delirium, rendering even more foreign the surroundings in which he found himself. All who underwent seasoning experienced some similar lack of control. Paroxysms of chill seized and controlled the sufferer, convulsing the body in violent shaking so strong that caretakers heard teeth gruesomely rattle and gnash. Thus rendered helpless and sundered from management of physical self and from any orienting sense of location—or sometimes even individual identity—newcomers were prostrate before the forces of a natural world that held them cruelly in their grasp. Only after losing volition in this dramatic way, only after being wrenched from health in demanding and exhausting illness, were migrants able cautiously to feel their way back not only to the land of the well but also to the new land to which they had come.

Seasoning was as dangerous as it was inexorable. Timothy Flint's 1826 guide was matter-of-fact about the New Orleans climate. "The chance for an unacclimated young man from the North surviving the first summer," he advised his readers with cool nonchalance, "is by some considered only as one to two." Only with time and experience would a person weather the changes and challenges of acclimation. What many nineteenth-century Americans termed "organization" might help. Everard Dickinson wrote in 1850 from the Arkansas Ozarks to his mother in Connecticut, praising her for raising him in a "wholesome—cleanly manner," so that he possessed "a healthy—sound Constitution & capacity Now to stand all changes of climate—diet & etc." Yet only the foolish or the foolhardy would ignore the imperatives of climate and latitude; those who did almost inevitably paid the toll of sickness and debility.

Common hope as well as boosters' rhetoric assured newcomers that those who had borne seasoning would thereafter enjoy their new environments' bounty without further physical cost. Modern medicine would offer some support for this belief. Intense spikes of fever and chill are characteristic of early infection with malaria, but not of subsequent bouts, and a person who has had malaria for some time experiences a subsequent partial immunity. She can go about daily life, though she will be weaker than someone whose body is not in a constant struggle to retain equilibrium with the parasite. Antebellum Americans' preoccupation with acclimation thus expresses some measure of immunological truth as we currently understand it—but was to an even greater extent a vehicle for the expression of the anxieties and hopes of migration.

Seasoning separated the proven from the "green." Though unacclimated newcomers might die in droves, those who felt themselves accustomed to an environment could feel a certain secure distance. Cholera might rage in St. Louis, as one emigrant wrote to his Connecticut family in 1849, but "there is not much sickness or cholera amongst the old & acclimated residents of the place"—himself among them. Thus local physicians reassured potential emigrants and their own clientele that "those long resident in the locality" were not at great risk, despite widespread mortality among the recently arrived. Our twenty-first-century perspective helps reveal the rhetorical insistence as well as the biological reality behind such reassurances: we recognize cholera as bacteriological, and thus not mitigated by acquired immunity, whereas at least some aspects of "seasoning" could come into play with malaria. Boosters' blandishments reflected what people wanted to be true. They were the outward expression of inner anxieties fueled by the unforgiving geography that bound health and well-being to place.

Newcomers experienced their bodily transformation with shock. Cephas Washburn, a founder of Dwight Mission who worked with the Cherokees, had barely entered Arkansas Territory with his fellow missionaries in 1819 when its fevers began to mark him. Meeting his fellows for the first time after several weeks of illness during his search for a mission site, Washburn recollected that "I was a frightful and squalid object to the sight. The blisters on my face and neck had dried, and the surface was covered with scabs. My face was so raw that I could not endure the process of shaving, and my beard was some three weeks old. My appearance was so disgusting that some of the brethren were nauseated, even to vomiting, on sight of me." When Timothy Flint returned to the Massachusetts town where he had been a minister before his western travels, he too found his experience etched into his bearing. His former parishioners and friends saw "my feebleness, in the traces of disease, and suffering, and travel, and sultry and sickly climate, worn so visibly into my countenance. . . ." The climate where he had lived (and which he extolled to great profit) had not only enfeebled him, it had impressed itself permanently into his visage.

Environments thus inescapably marked their people. Daniel Drake, a leading physician of the West, reported in 1850, "Doctor Farrar, of St. Louis, informed me, that in former years, he could distinguish, by their sallow complexion and languid aspect, the people of the American Bottom from those of the country back of the city." The American Bottom, that rich and swampy swath of fertile land along the Illinois side of the Mississippi, marked its people as deeply as their axes, plows, and surveyed roads marked it. Outsiders could read the features of terrain in the features of its inhabitants. Red cheeks, noted Friedrich Gerstäcker, showed that a man did not live in a swamp. The signs of place were not only wind patterns or temperature rhythms but also the characteristic attributes impressed upon inhabitants.

The body's own awareness underwent often startling change. Timothy Flint compared seasoning sickness to the effects of a strong drug. "My family had the ague," he wrote, "and the paroxysm creates a kind of poetical excitement, so that a person who is just rising from the fit, is in the highest degree capable of enjoyment, in a state of mind not unlike that produced by the agency of opium." Flint's reference to a heady drug known for illicit as well as common medicinal use evoked for his readers a world different and apart, at once alluring and full of danger. Flint's writings sketched the western borderlands of the Mississippi as a place of allure and threat, whose very essences worked within his frame like a potent opiate of sensuous excitement.

Like a child's growth or a developing pregnancy, acclimation had successive stages and could be completed only over a long period. Though some felt themselves to be accustomed to the vagaries of a new locale after one "sickly season," other observers asserted acclimation as an extremely drawn-out and painful process. Like the herb garnish that provided the flourish and piquancy to a steaming platter, or the crudely ground salt that gave frontier dishes their savor, seasoning was the complement and completion of a process of preparation long in the making.

Timothy Flint later explained of his family's decision to stay in New Orleans that "I had many friends . . . who judged that our acclimation was sufficient to give us confidence to reside in the city through the summer." Relying on the judgment of the more acclimated as a young wife might call on the knowledge of older women to assess the progress of her swelling belly, newcomers found themselves initiates in a system of understanding about the interaction of personal health with the natural world. Full knowledge was attained with the aid of others and was hard-earned through their own bodies' sensations.

Armed with extensive descriptions and due cautions, newcomers struggled to manage acclimation as they would any other bodily process. American and European sources abound in advice to be heeded for a successful seasoning. Most important was proper timing of the journey. Common wisdom advised migration only in cold months, past the sickly season of summer and early autumn. "Your family should come in the fall," Justus Post emphasized in an 1816 letter to his brother, as he urged John to join him in the West, "that the children may grow up with the season in the spring." The children would "grow up with the season" of their new home, the processes of their own physiology paralleling the readjustment of the natural world around them.

Heat was the most threatening aspect of new environments. Dr. Daniel Drake warned migrants that they should "in the heat of summer and early autumn, expose themselves as little as possible, either to the evening air, or the noon day sun." Movements within the calendar year and within the course of a day were alike crucial in shepherding the vulnerable body's energies through the rough assaults of a new climate. Transplanting themselves at auspicious times, and moving with care through the poisonous vapors of early evening and under the scathing sun of midday, emigrants tended to the process of bodily acclimation as they tended to newborn animals or fresh-sprouted crops. Managing the processes of growth and change required constant attention to the shifting balances of time, location, and bodily potential.

Because of the different initial conditions of diverse "peoples," migrants were told to be cautious in their destinations. Yankees would do well to choose different sites than Germans; those from the Ohio Valley faced different prospects than those from Maine. "[N]atives of New-England and New-York," Dr. Daniel Drake advised prospective immigrants to Ohio, should arrive in the fall, and secure "the most healthy situations which can be found." He urged rural settlers to seek high ground and "those who prefer the town, should choose the eastern and northern portions, which are more exempt from noxious effluvia."

Migrants were assailed with advice for managing their acclimation. Physicians advised flannel undergarments, bland and cautious diet, careful avoidance of all raw or undercooked food, sufficient sleep, cool houses and cool drinks (advice probably as out-of-reach as it was tantalizing), and temperance with respect to liquor and spirits. Keep to former habits, advised an 1837 work of medical counsel, and solicit the advice of native residents and prior migrants. Timothy Flint urged "Prevention" as a central adage, admonishing "avoidance of exposure to night air, to rains, and the direct and continued influence of the sun," "strict temperance in eating and drinking," and the preventive use of "cathartics, followed by the use of bark" (quinine, or "Peruvian bark," which alleviated the symptoms of ague). Acclimation proceeded like other illnesses: even when willful and in some ways out of control, the body could be at least partly interpreted, understood, and helped along in its changes.

In addition to the physical sicknesses of seasoning, change of place wrought numerous changes in the lives and perceptions of western migrants. All those coming to borderland territory, slave and free, experienced the transformation of practices and beliefs. Though white inhabitants of the American antebellum period tried to make sense of this experience through a variety of metaphors, acclimation remained a profound challenge to their sense of rootedness.

All manner of adjustments to the heretofore unknown were integral to a household's or an individual's condition of newness in a place. Local territory demanded new knowledge. Hunters had to learn to read the patterns of new game, and healers to utilize the properties of foreign herbs. The sun might rise or set more quickly in a different latitude. The sweep of clouds high in the sky might take on different characteristics before a storm. These experiences accompanied the physical ailments that were the most dramatic herald of new situations. This gradual experience of a place's diseases and of its environment more generally was summed up in what one German immigrant termed "the period of probation."

New weather patterned settlers' bodies as strong winds bent growing trees. Each new migrant's system had to become used to the burning summer sun of Missouri and Arkansas, and to changes of weather that could bring tornadoes barreling down with sudden fury, or could abruptly ice over streams after days of mild winter temperatures. Of the open-air St. Louis market, Henry Miller commented in 1838 that "truly none but our hardy sun burnt pioneers of the west would stand it, but they have been accustomed to it from their youth, & sun, cold, or rain makes not much difference to them." Seasoned by lashing rain, their white skins darkened by years of summer sun, the "hardy" folk who had been early American newcomers to St. Louis could flaunt a sturdy indifference to climate that in the eyes of outsiders marked their close relationship with it.

Every aspect of an unaccustomed environment demanded accommodation. The physician Joshua E. White reported of Savannah in 1807, "The water which is used for drink and culinary purposes within the city is pure, cool, and healthy." But forces beneficial to the acclimated could pose serious threat to unwary newcomers: "Sometimes, however, it produces diarrhœa in strangers from the upper country, if freely used."

The many-layered transformations innate to changing place were expressed and interpreted through a variety of metaphors. Some observers found in voyages by sea a metaphor for the bewildering ills experienced by strangers to the hot regions bordering the Mississippi. Amasa and Roxana Jones wrote from western Missouri in 1837 that "Persons coming here would have to be accustomed to the climate, who, like a person taking a voyage at sea, might suffer some sickness, but it is not usually of long duration." Seasickness aboard ship was like the seasoning experienced by newcomers to the waving oceans of grass that stretched from the hills of rolling western Missouri out to the broad grasslands few Americans had by the 1830s hazarded to settle.

Efforts to acclimate plants and agricultural crops to the strange climates of the middle Mississippi Valley filled the efforts of both early- and late-nineteenth-century farmers. Testing different seed varieties, crossbreeding promising lines, and trying out different regimens of care, the homesick and the ambitious attempted to transplant vegetation from other regions and other shores into the highlands, valleys, and prairies of early Arkansas and Missouri. Trees and crops that had become "naturalized" to the region were reported on by boosters and in family conversation. Small wonder that these efforts provided one imaginative resource for the understanding of the process by which human beings emigrated and accustomed themselves to places of hot days and steamy soil.

The deep-seated emotional challenges of "accommodation" were recognized by Timothy Flint in surprisingly gentle language: "But we well know, that love of country, like love of parents, is an innate and deeply rooted feeling; and when we leave our native country, like a tree torn up by the roots, it does not instantly flourish in another. A kind of desolation of heart, that results from feeling himself an alien in a strange land, long afflicts the resident in these new countries." Heartsickness was to Flint the emotional analogue of seasoning sickness. Desolating and long-afflicting, the yearning for reassuring and familiar home paralleled in its profundity and impact the bodily ailments of seasoning. Comparing the forlorn newcomer to an uprooted tree, Flint made real for his readers the perilous state of having no taproot. His metaphor called to mind the length of time necessary to transplant a long-rooted tree, as well as the riskiness of the attempt.

Their surrounding "country" itself echoed immigrants' feelings and physical experiences of disorienting disconnection. The desire for familiar, known environments on the part of human immigrants could be traced in the behavior of livestock: on emigrating journeys, they had to be tethered or might head back home. As one early-twentieth-century historian has observed, "Oxen have been known to travel one hundred miles and swim the Missouri River in an attempt to return. Ownerless horses were always to be found where the Missouri and the Mississippi joined, for they could go no further." The willfulness of stray cattle was a disorienting and even ominous reminder of migrants' own sense of rootedness in a home environment decidedly not *here*.

Many felt that the earth itself had to undergo transformation to adjust to new inhabitants. Justus Post, who like many Yankee emigrants decried the laziness of the Missouri folk about him, complained to his brother as he coaxed him to emigrate that "a set of northern & eastern people settled in this quarter would soon change the appearance of the country." Carrying with them the vigor of the Northeast, energetic newcomers could admirably transform the very landscape of east-central Missouri. A double parallel underlay such portrayals of the earth's cultivative acclimation. Body and land worked in the same ways; processes that were understood in the human body played themselves out in predictable ways in the natural environment, and vice versa. Consonance between the lived experience of human bodies and of natural terrain reinforced the understanding of each.

Even as newcomers suffered through the "shakes" of ague, learned the habits of new game, and named unfamiliar plants and land forms, they simultaneously caused ditches to be dug, trees uprooted, and crops planted. Draining swamps, burning prairies, cutting marshland vegetation, clearing forests, and planting domesticated seeds, they altered the terms of the process of acclimation even as they endured it. Cultivating the earth, they changed its very "health." They altered the face of the land as it altered them.

The possibility of failure clouded sunny promises of acclimation and brought with it fears about both the completeness and the consequences of the process. Accounts from early Arkansas and Missouri, as from other western regions, reflected ambivalence about how successful the process of seasoning could be, and about the ultimate consequences of adapting to a new environment. John Clendenin, a young and politically connected emigrant who came to Arkansas Territory in the 1830s to make a name for himself, cursed the heat and the backwardness of his chosen region. "Eduard Dunn died this day at two oclock after a short illness," he noted in his diary one Sunday late in September of 1836. "[H]e had been in this Country about 3 years, and thought he has acclimated, fatal delusion no constitution can become acclimated to this Country."

Elizabeth Ann Cooley McClure and her new husband, James, had been unable to find good affordable land near her family home in Virginia. Hope and ambivalence mixed in Elizabeth McClure's plans for emigration to the borderlands of the Southwest, and she worried about her own health and the future well-being of her husband. In her 1846 diary she wrote shortly after her marriage that "I have earthly love almost to perfection, and I am fixed to go to Texas, . . . and to leave my *dear* old native land for a new and untried place of residence, quit my *old*, *true* and long tried friends for new and untried love and friendship." The journey was indeed grueling—the couple traveled first to New Orleans, but then decided to turn north again to Missouri—and the prairies of western Missouri seemed to offer little. Ill health had plagued them along their long Mississippi journey and now it held tenaciously on. In the heat of July McClure lamented: "Mc. is sick and I feel low spirited indeed. It is such a pity persons should be raised in one climate, then be removed to another. They are so puny and so sickly." Journeying and "removal" were innately threatening, and this dispirited emigrant felt their consequences in her own body and in her marriage. "I really fear to stay here, I fear death," she wrote that fall, after the two had found work as teachers in western Missouri. She continued: "I fear Mr. McClure never will enjoy good health in Missouri." She and her young husband might succumb before they found the robustness to earn money and establish themselves in the new land they sought.

Difficulties dogged the McClures' move. They spent poverty-filled months on the prairie, during which both were often too sick to teach and were forced to board out, often separately, at pupils' homes. Though by December of 1846 their situation had improved, Elizabeth received news in April 1847 of the death of her far-off father, and sickness continued to plague the pair. They struggled with low spirits and regret about their move. In January 1848, James McClure recorded his thoughts in his wife's journal, as he did on occasion. "I want to teach school awhile and go to school one year," he wrote, "then myself and wife teach an Academy and live together in some country where we will not have to take pills all the time and the health of the country depend on the skill of the physicians." Little came of these hopes, however: "slow typhoid fever" brought an end to the couple's plans when it claimed the twenty-two-year-old Elizabeth late in March 1848. Though some emigrants found themselves able to thrive physically and materially in a new place, many other stories ended like Elizabeth Anne Cooley McClure's, in separation from family, dashed hopes, and mortal illness.

Such were the potential consequences of violating the profound environmental belonging in which people of McClure's era felt themselves soldered to places of long residence. Violating these felt relations of person to place meant bodily suffering. In August 1816, Justus Post admonished his brother that

> emigrations to this or any other country should always be made in the fall, especially when the distance is great, otherwise the arrival would be made in the heat of summer, when even the fatigues of travelling in the heat of the sun would of itself be sufficient to produce disease. You must not place your heart on a farm at the mouth of the Ohio—it will not do at present—You must come to that point by degrees—it is in too low a latitude (37°) for a man of 45° north to strike the first dash—You will find the country above the Missouri to suit you and the people of your country best.

John Post was a man of another "country" than his brother in the middle Mississippi Valley. His body, and the bodies of his family, must be given the proper time in which to change allegiances. Acclimation transformed physical citizenship: the process made a migrant *of* a different country.

The slow, even, step-by-step process Justus urged was meant to save John and his family from the drastic readjustment of arriving suddenly in the midst of a place and a season dangerously different from the cool summers of Vermont. Small, patient steps were necessary: small, patient steps that were both endlessly frustrating and financially impossible for families who had to race to get in a first crop before carefully saved stores gave out. As Justus Post cautioned his brother, sudden progress "will not do at present." Such healthy hesitation went right to the paradox at the heart of the process of transplantation: What family could afford such piecemeal progress, such carefully monitored arrival? What household could sustain such minute scrutiny and such modulated behavior amid the chaotic upheaval of a cross-continental or even transcontinental remove?

As with prescriptions for maintaining good health generally, adages about healthful acclimation laid out a near-impossible litany of care and restraint. Advice guides insisted that perfect timing and perfect vigilance were necessary to guide a family safely through the rough straits of environmental accommodation. Small wonder, perhaps, that despite voluminous, endlessly repeated advice, accounts of migration almost universally speak of wearying illness, disheartening disorganization, and the constant failure of prior plans. Becoming habituated almost invariably demanded more of newcomers than they had resources ready. Almost no one underwent the seizure of "shakes" or the frenetic exhaustion of high fever with any feeling of having retained proper governance or management. Guidance of the process of seasoning, though always advised, often attempted, and borne witness to in a thousand precautions, great and small, was necessarily partial and incomplete. Acclimation demanded surrender; well-prepared migrants hoped only to undergo it well enough to emerge on the other shore.

Advice like that of Justus to John Post, eager in tone and full of detail, reveals a central irony of American western settlement within the framework of struggles to acclimate. These ambitious men, so eager to remake their family configuration in the new lands of a new state, were bold in their ambitions with respect to the environment they coveted. They hoped to clear out trees and ditch hillsides, to plow and farm broad acreage, to change the kinds of vegetation prevalent in the environment and order large fields by the timing of their harvest schedule. Justus Post in particular came to Missouri to speculate in land, hoping to capitalize on inflated currency to swell his own fortunes. Yet Justus's realistic assessment of how his brother's children could safely adjust themselves to the terrain of Missouri reflects an enforced humility before the processes of a nature beyond either grasping brother's control. Bending themselves to the environment around them, knowing their own and their children's bodies to be in thrall to a climate powerful in its changes, the brothers Justus and John placed themselves with modesty in the very natural world they came also to change and remake.

Many historians have read counternarratives of tremulousness about the project of western migration in the narratives of women migrants. Such readings help identify many of the elements making free women's experience of borderlands different from free men's, but the less nuanced among them also tend to exonerate women from the historical burden of having carried out western conquest. But both men and women of early Arkansas and Missouri expressed heady ambition and anxious worry; wives and husbands both held bold dreams and uneasy doubts. This duality is a fundamental truth of western expansion. Interwoven directly into the fabric of textual appropriation of lands in the West are expressions of drastic limitation and acknowledgment of lack of control. Such language in the correspondence of the ambitious Post brothers is not unique, but rather entirely unremarkable: in the face of nature's powerful sway over the very fiber of their bodies, even scheming men were forced to acknowledge their own partial helplessness.

No booming frontier rhetoric could erase this vulnerability. Eager conquerors, both agricultural and military, whose records chart the process of family migration and whose words have shaped historians' understanding of American takeover of the western lands of North America, men like Justus Post left not only calls of confidence, but a quieter witness of resignation to forces outside their control. Wrapped within the scheming and the ambition of farmers, speculators, and colonizing settlers is the reality of accommodation of their own selves, on the most intimate level, to a "country" vastly and wildly beyond their mastery. Not simply within the domesticating narratives of westering women, but also in the seemingly confident plans of their husbands and brothers, is written an often-overlooked narrative of American western progress as humble as it is ambitious, as vulnerable as it is proud.

The Literature of Settlement

Newcomers in the American inflow into the Mississippi Valley did not come unprepared. Poring over emigration guides, they learned (often erroneously) which territories were the most valuable, what kinds of seeds and equipment to take with them, and how much to pack for their journey. Reading frontier novels and tales of backwoods adventure, they learned how to picture themselves as part of a westward progression across the continent. Almost all free migrants came into contact with at least some of the copious and creative material churned out by regional boosters and western promoters.

Among these was the peripatetic former minister Timothy Flint, who early in the process of American settlement turned his exhortatory skills to promoting the Mississippi Valley. His large and diverse literary output indicates the almost bewildering variety of forms in which new regions took shape in the American imagination. Flint was a Harvard-trained Congregationalist and Presbyterian minister in Massachusetts during the early years of the century, until he set out from New England with his family on a tumultuous period of travel and missionary work in varied parts of the United States. In 1816 Timothy, his wife, Abigail Hubbard Flint, and their children settled briefly in St. Louis, before moving for several years to nearby St. Charles, where Abigail ran a school. Timothy severed his connections with his missionary society and roved far in search of souls and income. Supported in part by Abigail's wealthy family connections, the family journeyed through upper Louisiana and Arkansas territory. Conditions were often rough: during one flatboat journey, after laboring through a terrible storm that tore open the roof of their boat cabin, Abigail delivered an infant. Like many babies in an era of high infant mortality, the newborn died soon after. The family lived for a time in 1822 in New Orleans, and in 1824 settled in Alexandria, Louisiana, on the Red River, where Timothy taught and preached. In 1825, the Flint household moved back to Massachusetts, where Timothy Flint began his career as interpreter of the American West with the publication of his *Recollections of the Last Ten Years, Passed in Occasional Residences and Journeyings in the Valley of the Mississippi* in 1826.

Over the next fifteen years, Flint continued to produce a wealth of fiction and nonfiction accounts of the borderlands and their inhabitants. His books included a wildly fictitious and widely influential biography of Daniel Boone, which created a long-lasting frontier mythology on its own, and provided grist for later writers and novelists. Flint's two guidebooks, *Condensed Geography and History of the Western States* (1828) and *History and Geography of the Mississippi Valley* (1831), provided many in the United States with relatively comprehensive information about the character and prospects of the Ohio Valley and the territories beyond the Mississippi. Flint was an early purveyor of information about the region; his accounts were endlessly quoted, rehashed, reprinted, and plagiarized throughout the antebellum period.

Few potential emigrants swallowed such renditions whole. Rather, dreamers pressed others for collaboration, read and reread letters from family members or former neighbors who had emigrated, compared various migration guides and promotional materials, and tried to construct for themselves a realistic picture of new lands. In November 1833, Hermann Steines, a German who had gone ahead to scout emigration possibilities for his extended family and community, wrote home from St. Louis to say of

Gottfried Duden's guidebooks: "Duden has written truthfully about this matter on p. 338," adding in exasperation, "If only prospective emigrants would follow strictly the directions and advice which he gives in his book!" Emigrants' guides constituted a kind of collective cultural text that those involved with emigration commented on, added to, revised, and annotated, making for themselves a reliable forecast (or so they hoped) of life in an unknown region.

Moreover, the literature of settlement flowed back from new regions as fast as new migrants could get there. Outright boosterism, chatty letters, regional humor, governmental reports, adventure stories, dry descriptions, newspaper accounts, medical geographies, and even truly awful poetry—many kinds of writings sketched the region. In diverse but important ways, these efforts contributed to the construction of Arkansas and Missouri as American territories.

The Arkansas author Charles Fenton Mercer Noland typifies efforts at regional promotion in the antebellum period. By turns bumptious and bucolic, he portrayed the state as a setting both for wild goings-on and, contradicting himself, for establishing a settled, civilized way of life. In the persona of "Pete Whetstone" (named for the knife-sharpening novaculite that was one of Arkansas's early mineral exports), Noland dispensed rustic witticism from the pages of the New York periodical *Spirit of the Times*. Whetstone kissed young women, hunted bears, and engaged in elaborate practical jokes, extensive whiskey drinking, and prolific personal violence with his backwoods cronies. Commenting on larger political developments through the small-scale politics of a rustic hinterland, "Old Pete" was an updated "Poor Richard," regaling urban New England readers with homespun common sense. The Arkansas he inhabited promised rough humor and adventure amid wilds far distant from the noisy cobblestones of Boston or the packed streets of Manhattan Island.

Yet Noland also wrote a series of county descriptions in 1830 and '31 that featured calmly fertile fields, rich pastureland, and commerce waiting to be developed. Published in a territorial newspaper, they were designed to be clipped and sent on, or reprinted by other regional newspapers in the borrowing so common of the journalism of the period. In another series, "Early Settlers of Arkansas," published in the *Spirit of the Times* in the winter of 1849–50, Noland attempted in some ways to undo the damage to the state's reputation he and similar writers busily produced in their backwoods satires, profiling instead the well-respected politicians of the young state. Noland's Pete Whetstone and his earnest regional descriptions were alternate sides of regional perception making. In broad caricature and polished promotion, many newcomers attempted to create, as much as to reflect, the environments into which they came.

"Movers" and "Improvers"

Ambition and disquiet commingled in newcomers' encounters with the territories beyond the Mississippi. Difficulties for many were heightened by the distance from home. "Movers" and "improvers" were diverse, and their paths of migration often long.

The American in-migration of the first two thirds of the nineteenth century mixed Yankees and upland southerners with a wide array of European newcomers and slave laborers. Many American emigrants came from the upper South and the lower Middle West, some from the Eastern Seaboard. As Justus Post observed in the fall of 1816, "It does appear as if all Kentucky are on the road for the country in the fork of the Mississippi & Missouri." Single men, families, and whole communities emigrating together flowed into the region through the Ohio and Mississippi river systems, settling first in clusters along the Missouri, Arkansas, and Mississippi rivers. In his memoirs of his youth in Arkansas, Sir Henry Morton Stanley made a reasonable assessment of migrants' home regions: "The Douglasses were from Virginia, the Crawfords from 'Old Georgia,' the Joneses and Smiths from Tennessee, the Gorees from Alabama. The poorer sort were from the Carolinas, Mississippi, Missouri, and Tennessee, the professional men and white employers from a wider area—which included Europe."

Immigrants entered the areas beyond the Mississippi from many regions of Europe, especially the British Isles and the German territories. Waves of German emigration were spurred both by political turmoil of the 1840s and by widely read emigrants' guides promoting the region (particularly those by the prolific, if not always accurate, Gottfried Duden). The emigration of people from the German territories had a substantial impact on the culture of Missouri and certain regions in Arkansas. Germans changed American customs and language and brought an emphasis on education and intellectual culture to rural areas. Especially in St. Louis, Germans were associated with antislavery movements and gave force in the prewar period to "free soil" sentiment—the movement to prohibit slavery from new regions of the United States.

Communities of immigrant groups created settlements of often sharply delineated cultural background. The author of one guide for German immigrants wrote of Missouri that "every town has its peculiar character, indeed greater differences and variations come about here because individual sects and national groups stay together and consequently they imprint a peculiar stamp upon their dwelling places." New residents marked their territory with their cultural practices, just as they marked it with hoes, shovels, and side-lot gardens, and just as the nature of the terrain in turn put its "peculiar stamp" upon them.

The experience of emigration for free people was usually embedded in family life. In June of 1830, Stephen Hempstead reflected, "This day 19 years ago I first came to St Louis and came to the house I now reside in[.] my Son Edwd lived in it at that time[.] I Stopted with my family untill Decr when I moved in a Logg Cabbin." The Hempstead family's experience was like that of many "movers." Born in 1754 and twice wounded during the Revolutionary War, Stephen Hempstead came in his later years to Missouri Territory with his wife, Mary Lewis Hempstead. In 1811, Mary and Stephen and their widowed daughter, her children, and their own youngest son and daughter joined three of their older sons, including Edward, who had already moved to the countryside surrounding the small town of St. Louis. This was characteristic of a pattern in which young single men, often working as surveyors, would search out land for their families and larger groups.

Stephen Hempstead's recounting of his family's experience was typical of the process of establishing the story of a move as a family narrative. What Timothy Flint with characteristic flourish termed "the patriarchal emigration for the land of promise" took on mythic qualities not only in later historical retellings but in the memory-making of individuals and families. Hempstead's account is representative, moreover, in its particularly patriarchal qualities: men frequently and volubly memorialized their moves, often on behalf of the whole family.

Many migrant families undertook a series of moves that might occupy three or four generations, or relocated a number of times over a period of decades. Planters who could obtain land with less expense than they could purchase labor would engage in intensive cultivation for a time and then, when the soil was exhausted, would move on to fresh fields. Less well-off families might squat on land in illegal but long-term and widely countenanced possession, moving on when newer land opened up. Whole planter families might plan a temporary emigration to a spot where they stayed long enough to make money from richer soil and then move back to a better-loved home. Even within a household, moves might be partial: some cautious eastern wives went west briefly, then traveled back to known society and familiar social circles when they became ill or neared childbirth.

Migrants often traveled in organized groups. Chief among these were the German "Emigration Societies" and bands organized by the Church of Jesus Christ of Latter-Day Saints (known colloquially, then as now, as Mormons). The removes of wealthier planter families also involved often massive households. Plantations would typically migrate in several waves, in the first of which a gang of workers would be sent under a son or overseer to build houses and get a first crop in, with more slaves and the free family coming later.

Many newcomers, especially in southern and eastern Arkansas and along the river bottoms of central and eastern Missouri, lived and labored in large plantation households. The journal of John Brown, a plantation owner who moved his household to south-central Arkansas (near present-day Camden) in the early 1850s, reflects day-to-day life on a substantial cotton plantation. Brown's frustrations were many: the health and upbringing of his many children, his efforts to work his way out of debt and secure legal title to his land holdings, state politics, the management of a slave labor force, and his struggles to promote the temperance movement. Brown was intimately connected with these events not simply as a head of household but as a local healer. Like the daybook of John Geiger, a Missouri farmer, judge, and practitioner also preoccupied with the related concerns of land and health during the antebellum period, Brown's journals reflect not only the successes of a local man of substance, but nights of anxious watchfulness during deliveries, epidemics, and the diseases of childhood. Through these writings—and through the contemporary comments of smaller-scale farmers and the later memories of former slaves—we can come to understand the challenges of agricultural and personal well-being that governed much of antebellum life.

At the same time, John Brown's detailed journal reflects the limitations on our access to his world. John Brown, not the slaves he directed, and not his wife, Clara, gives us the most detailed descriptions of a household in which those different participants surely had very different perspectives. Using narratives and oral histories by former slaves, we can piece together some of the rest of the picture, but gender is a gulf that the seeming precision of detailed documents like Brown's journal can obscure.

The vast majority of writings on the borderlands—and in this book—are by men. They tend to figure the earth as female, with all that that implied in the nineteenth-century world: celebrations of fertility as well as fears of wild generative capacity. Yet these men are, by their own accounts, not simply bold conquerors but also frustrated healers; not only successful plowers and harvesters, but also failed farmers, impotent in the face of weather and financial crisis. Their narratives give us hints about the more complicated dimensions of gender interactions unfolding even within what are frequently male stories.

Gender also influenced newcomers' experience of migration. Men and women took part in migrations for different reasons, and their experiences once in a new place differed, much as gender roles differed in "settled" parts of the world. "Men change their place of abode from ambition or interest," Timothy Flint mused in his biography of Daniel Boone; "women from affection." Stage of life also played an important and historically less acknowledged role in determining men's and women's attitudes toward migration. Women like Eliza Post, in established adulthood and with children to care for and an enmeshed social circle to rely on, were more reluctant to leave the communities they had established than younger or newly married women. Despite her husband's confident enthusiasm, Post dreaded leaving the East Coast to make her way in a "wilderness among the Indians."

Young, newly married women with few prospects back home reflected in their personal writings an eagerness to find better opportunity in new territory. These young women sound much like their husbands in their enthusiasm, as in their fears. Men expressed ambition about land more frequently than most women letter and journal writers, and, like Justus Post, men in a household were often the ones to urge friends and family members to emigrate. At the same time, many of their wives, daughters, and mothers expressed similar feelings. The ambitions of women and the anxieties of men that are revealed in the ubiquitous "health-talk" of settlement suggest further nuance to the story of American movers.

Early Arkansas and Missouri

Purchased under President Thomas Jefferson as part of the 1803 Louisiana Purchase, what is now Arkansas and Missouri had a tortuous legal and political history. These areas were first defined as part of the District of Louisiana, an immense region consisting of all of the Louisiana Purchase north of the present boundary of Louisiana, essentially an enormous swath encompassing the Missouri River and western Mississippi River watersheds. When Louisiana became a state in 1812, the region to its north became the Missouri Territory, with most of Arkansas as a county within that.

In 1819, a lower portion split off as the Arkansas Territory, which included most of the present state of Arkansas as well as regions to the west in what would become first Indian Territory and ultimately the state of Oklahoma. After those territories were sheared off, Arkansas ultimately become a state in 1836.

Missouri's path to statehood would be much more momentous. In 1817, Missouri Territory petitioned Congress to be admitted to the Union as a slave state. This request touched off a passionate debate in Washington and around the country: Missouri's admission as a slave state would mark Congress's acquiescence in the expansion of slavery as an institution and would threaten the precarious federal balance of eleven slave states and eleven free. From late 1819 until March 1820, Northerners and white Southerners argued fiercely over whether Congress had the right to extend slavery, or to curtail it (the enslaved Southerners with the highest stake in these matters presumably entertained few such constitutional objections). The bitter argument was regarded by all as significant for the future of the western territories beyond the Mississippi, as well as other thus-far-unorganized areas in the East.

The crisis was resolved in the spring of 1820 by what became known as the Missouri Compromise. Missouri would be admitted as a slave state, but it would be paired—as would subsequent territories seeking admission to the Union—with a free state, in this case Maine, created out of the northern reaches of Massachusetts. Furthermore, Missouri would be a geographic exception: no other portion of the Louisiana Territory that lay north of latitude 36°30', Missouri's southern boundary, would be allowed to admit slavery. The plan was blasted by many in the North because it allowed Congress to sanction the expansion of slavery, and by many in the South because it allowed Congress to limit it. Nonetheless, the Compromise patched over deep divisions and provided a formula by which new states could continue to be added to the Union.

The tenuous parity achieved by the Missouri Compromise was strained to the utmost by Congress in 1850, in another complex set of negotiations that became known as the Compromise of 1850. Like its counterpart thirty years earlier, this compromise kept the Union together—but only just. Much of the legislation similarly involved the fractious issue of new states, particularly those recently won from Mexico. The Compromise of 1850 added California as a free state, to the dismay of southern advocates of slavery, and jeopardized the Missouri Compromise by allowing the voting residents of New Mexico and Utah to accept or ban slavery in their proposals for statehood (Texas, too, was involved, relinquishing claims on what was to become New Mexico in return for federal assumption of Texas's preannexation debt). On the antislavery side, the slave trade, though not slavery itself, was banned in the nation's capital. But the main provision that rankled Northerners was the Fugitive Slave Act, which gave broad powers to federal marshals (or indeed, most anyone else) pursuing runaways, and mandated northern residents' cooperation in catching slaves. Enforcement of the Fugitive Slave Act proved deeply controversial, and the settlements of the Compromise of 1850 were short-lived.

In 1854, when Congress passed the Kansas-Nebraska Act, sectional tensions boiled over. This legislation finally voided the geographic provision of the Missouri Compromise by decreeing that popular sovereignty should decide whether those two territories, both north of the Missouri Compromise line, would join the nation as slave or free states. Northern voters furious at this reversal deserted the Democrats for the newly founded Republican Party, setting the stage for the essential conflict in party politics for decades to come. Three years later, amid terrible bloodshed in western Missouri and eastern Kansas accompanying struggles over the popular vote, in *Dred Scott v. Sandford*, the Supreme Court declared the Missouri Compromise unconstitutional, on the grounds that under the Fifth Amendment Congress could not deprive (white) individuals of their (human) property without due process of law. The Missouri and Arkansas region was thus in the thick of debates at once legal, political, and moral about the very nature of the "new" lands of the Louisiana Purchase and thus of the people in them.

Differing environments in Missouri and Arkansas influenced different economic and settlement patterns. Poor roads and broad swamps limited growth in the southern part of the region. Though Arkansas grew from a population of just over 14,000 in 1820 to nearly 210,000 in 1850, it was nonetheless a poor, rural state on the eve of the Civil War. Early in the nineteenth century, the culture and economy of Arkansas divided between the lowlands of the eastern Mississippi floodplain and the southern Gulf Plain, where slaves labored in a plantation cotton economy, and highland areas of the Ozark Plateau in the north and west of the state, where a predominantly white population typically worked single-family farms.

In contrast to Arkansas's slow and mostly agricultural development, Missouri boomed as a center of commerce. Government land grants to veterans of the War of 1812 encouraged settlement in Missouri (few actual veterans took up their grants, but speculators who bought up veterans' claims later resold them to an avid market). From just under 21,000 inhabitants in 1810, the territory's population tripled to almost 67,000 by 1820, as its bid to enter the Union as a slave state was fiercely and widely debated. This optimistic boom in migration was short-lived: reverberations from the Panic of 1819 and widespread economic depression subsequently slowed movement until the mid–1820s. By the '30s incomers once again took heart, and the state's population topped a half million during the population inflow of the 1840s. Immigration peaked in the four years immediately following the Graduation Act in 1854, a piece of federal legislation spearheaded by Missouri's energetic senator, Thomas Hart Benton, that drastically lowered the prices of still-unsold public lands. Well over a million people (more exactly, 1,182,012) were counted in Missouri in the 1860 census; with very few exceptions they or their families had arrived in the previous fifty years.

Under first the French and then the Spanish colonial regimes, Missouri had developed as part of the New Orleans market hinterland. Rivermen guided furs, lead, salt, and a variety of other items downriver to that commercial center in the eighteenth century, and ambitious colonials concocted schemes to exploit the mining sites of southern Missouri and the rolling grasslands west of St. Louis. Thus even before the Louisiana Purchase, Americans began to move to the region, encouraged by liberal Spanish land-grant policies. The central valley of the Missouri River was the first area to which Americans migrated in what was to become the state of Missouri, especially the "Boon's Lick" region in the southern dip of the Missouri River, which was settled by the Boone family early in the nineteenth century. Rich acreage in central and upper Missouri, especially bottomland along the Missouri and Mississippi rivers and their smaller tributaries, drew farmers frustrated by the rocks of New England, the soil exhaustion of tobacco country, and high land prices in the East.

Nonetheless, much of Missouri's growth was fueled by commerce, based first in the eastern river port of St. Louis and later in the western gateway towns at the start of the overland trails. Despite the rhetoric of rural life that pervaded the literature of settlement, city life shaped the experiences of many newcomers over the first two thirds of the century.

St. Louis was the main "provincial metropolis" of the region. It stood just below the mouth of the Missouri, at a point where the character of the Mississippi changes. Above this "break in the waters," the river was shallower, vulnerable to ice in winter, and had narrower curves and bends. Below St. Louis, the more generous river was usually open all winter and allowed for larger and deeper-hulled craft; after the teens, these were primarily steam-boats. Goods generally came up- or downriver as far as St. Louis in one kind of craft and then had to be loaded onto a different type of craft for the rest of the journey. St. Louis was thus an important trans-shipping point on this central riverine artery. In addition to linking the southern Mississippi Valley with the transportation and communication networks of the Ohio River and the river ports of the northern Mississippi Valley, St. Louis soon came to link the eastern and western parts of the United States, as cargo and commerce, mail and treaties, news and new migrants passed through it, bound in the early part of the century for Missouri and the Santa Fe Trail or, toward midcentury, for the spindly projections of western migration reaching out across the middle of the continent.

The 1840s were St. Louis's boom time: the city experienced tremendous expansion as migrants thronged into the growing entrepôt. Immigrants had already begun to enter the city in the thirties, but at a rate of less than 2,000 a year. Between 1848 and 1850 alone, 40,000 newcomers filled to bursting the increasingly crowded port city. In 1850, St. Louis was the largest city west of Cincinnati and boasted the eighth-largest population in the United States. By the late 1850s, though, St. Louis's growth had leveled off; the momentum of western migration had shifted to Chicago—an eclipse that has continued to rankle St. Louisans into the present day. In the story of western movement and the growth of the trans-Mississippi region, St. Louis is a crucial touchpoint. Throughout the antebellum period there were demographic differences between those who headed to St. Louis and those who claimed land in rural areas. Urban East Coast businessmen migrated to the city, whereas those originally from the countryside of the upland South—Kentucky, Virginia, Tennessee—generally moved to farms farther out.

Through the antebellum decades, both city and country were vulnerable to the vagaries of unstable markets and currency supply. Chronic economic woes in the region worsened during the depressions that gripped the country after the War of 1812 and again after the Panic of 1837, as well as in less extreme periods of economic decline. Currency was always tight, and sometimes strangulatingly so; the webs of transportation and exchange that linked Arkansas and Missouri planters and producers with the commercial hubs of New Orleans and the Hudson and Ohio valleys often proved flimsy. Nonetheless, both the planter families and the backwoodsmen who stretched themselves over terrain in the early decades of the century did so as part of networks of commercial interaction. Whatever their rhetoric of freedom, independence, and distance—and their rhetoric was very much a rhapsody on all those qualities—early free migrants to the trans-Mississippi West were bound to the growing commercial systems of the young republic in ways as subtly pervasive, though not as cruel, as were the slaves they brought with them.

Native Peoples

Despite their insistence and protestations, Euro-American newcomers did not arrive in "empty" territory. The Mississippi Valley was already the home of many indigenous groups, and it became the contested site of emigration for several other Native American peoples. Over the first four decades of the nineteenth century, smaller Indian groups like the Quapaws were pushed off land in Arkansas and Missouri. At the same time, the Osages, who had occupied parts of Missouri, fought to claim more land because of American pressures to the east and north, and the Cherokees from the hill country of the cotton states moved into northern Arkansas. Ultimately, the Cherokees and Osages would be overrun, dispersed, and displaced onto "Indian Territory" in what is now Oklahoma, but their interactions—with each other and with incoming Americans—make up a significant part of the social, economic, and environmental history of the middle Mississippi Valley.

As with every successive region of American territorial expansion, by the time Americans in any numbers arrived in Arkansas and Missouri, Native populations had already been affected by European and American commerce, culture, and pathogens. The thriving, settled villages encountered in the Ouachita River Valley by the Spanish expeditionary force of Hernando De Soto in 1541 had been largely abandoned by the time Arkansas Post was a small, but thriving French outpost in the eighteenth century. Their inhabitants had been killed off by diseases or forced farther west by Europeans and Americans as they expropriated land, created population pressures, and deleted game. Disease and ever-increasing and ever more hostile neighbors pushed the Tunicas, Caddos, and other tribes of the Ouachita River basin and southern Arkansas farther west and south, and forced a series of tribal mergers. By the time of American inflow in the early nineteenth century, the primary group in southern Arkansas was the much-reduced Quapaw Nation. In 1834, most of the remaining Quapaws were forced to a sliver of Indian Territory, but a small number of families and individuals remained in Arkansas, working their own farms or hiring out as cotton pickers.

Aside from these small groups, the situation of indigenous peoples in antebellum Arkansas and Missouri can be characterized in broad strokes by the conflict between a movement south and west of the Osages as they were pushed by eastern groups and declining buffalo yields, and the movement west of Native American groups from east of the Mississippi, led by the politically significant Cherokees. Even as Americans sought to claim western Missouri and Arkansas for themselves as new territory, Native groups sought to do the same.

The Osages had historically occupied a massive territory based in central and southwest Missouri, though hunting parties ranged out from summer base camps as far south as the Red River of present-day Oklahoma, southern Arkansas, and Louisiana; as far north as the Platte; and west to the Rockies. In the early nineteenth century, the Osages were convulsed by political, territorial, and cultural turmoil, as American pressure on tribes to the north and east pushed the originally Missouri-based Osages farther to the edges of their older hunting grounds. In the Ozark hills of what is now southern Missouri and northern Arkansas, Osages seeking more secure hunting and farming areas came into conflict with other indigenous populations and French and American settlers.

Conflict was particularly pitched with the Cherokee immigrants to northern Arkansas, who became known as "Western Cherokees." These people were themselves newcomers, part of a set of contentious emigrations from the Cherokee Nation of upland Tennessee, Alabama, and Georgia. Over the first thirty years of the nineteenth century, three waves of Cherokees migrated to Arkansas, and later to Indian Territory. Two groups were led by Cherokee factions and one was forced to migrate by troops of the U.S Army.

The first settlements of the "Western Cherokees" were small-scale and informal. Families and communities sought autonomy and freedom by removing west across the Mississippi. This displacement began in 1782, when the region was under Spanish control, but by the mid-1780s was a steady, if small, stream. Despite conflict with white immigrants interested in the same areas and disillusionment about the U.S. government's offers of protected land, these "old settlers," as they became known, were a potent social and mercantile force in early Arkansas. By 1816, over 1,500 Cherokees farmed and hunted in the rolling and hilly regions north of the Arkansas River.

But Cherokee takeover of these Ozark lands did not remain uncontested. Cherokee hunting and trapping, and that of white squatters, threatened Osages also claiming the region. Skirmishes and raids flared into open warfare over several periods from 1805 through the early 1820s. To staunch the bloodshed and prevent American settlement and unauthorized trading, the United States established Fort Smith, on the Arkansas River at the present-day boundary of Arkansas and Oklahoma. The fort was largely ineffective in those goals, as American pressures on Cherokee and Osage regions continued to mount. In 1828, Cherokee holdings in north Arkansas were abolished by treaty, and the Cherokees in Arkansas were officially dispossessed, pushed to lands in Indian Territory just to the west.

Meanwhile, the Cherokee Nation of the Southeast was under duress. Almost a decade of cultural revival, from 1819 to 1828, had given rise to prosperity, governmental reorganization, and greater political dexterity, as well as to the Cherokee syllabary created by Sequoyah (also known as George Guess). Yet by the late 1820s the Cherokee Nation faced political pressure, harassment, and terrorism, as white settlers and surrounding state governments (especially Georgia) strove to take over Cherokee land.

Amid political and cultural division within the nation, leaders of one Cherokee faction signed the treaty in 1835 of New Echota, which ceded all of their traditional lands for $5 million and assistance in resettling in new lands in what is now northeastern Oklahoma. "Treaty Party" members, many of them of mixed race, and a number of them affluent slave holders like some of the white planters moving to the region, emigrated to Arkansas in the second substantial Cherokee movement into Arkansas, in the mid-thirties. Their action played into the removal policy of President Andrew Jackson's administration. The collision of Cherokee Nation adherents, Treaty Party advocates, and formerly emigrated "old settlers" in the hills of north Arkansas and in the little-valued territory set aside in Indian lands was almost as violent as the simultaneous conflicts with the Osages. The leaders of the Treaty Party were killed by other Cherokees in a political assassination in 1839 for their perceived treason in signing away tribal land, sparking a long-running war of revenge.

Though the Treaty Party had acted without the approval of the Cherokee Grand Council, the United States argued that the whole nation was bound by the agreement it had made. The final and most wrenching of the Cherokee emigrations was the forced removal of the remainder of the Cherokee Nation in the bitingly cold winter of 1838–39. Their halting, ill-prepared, largely unsupported journey on several routes across the lower South, up the Arkansas River or over southern Missouri, to lands in Indian Territory made a mockery of governmental promises of protection and assistance, and became widely known as "The Path Where They Cried" or "The Trail of

Tears." Four thousand people—over a fifth of the Cherokee Nation—died in this removal, during which political dismay and personal loss exacerbated disease, exposure, and hunger.

Most of the Cherokees settled in areas of Arkansas were eventually forced in the late 1830s onto tribal allotments in Indian Territory, but some remained in the area or continued to have business links there. The Missouri Osages, meanwhile, gradually lost much of their former military and economic force and were maneuvered in a series of trading and treaty negotiations into smaller and smaller portions of their territory. They were officially consigned to an Indian Territory reservation after 1839, though Osage parties and Osage traders continued to interact with Missouri-area merchants and communities.

Against this backdrop of increasing demands by the United States and its insistent settlers, other Native American communities were moving in and through Arkansas and Missouri. Small groups of Indian travelers, hunters, and settlers came into the region informally. During a voyage of scientific exploration in south-central Arkansas, the scientist George Hunter encountered in the Ouachita River of 1804 a "Delaware Indian painted with Vermilion round the eyes," who "called himself Cap'. Jacobs"; in his 1818 diary, the traveler Henry Vest Bingham reported his impression of Sioux hunters he encountered in St. Louis. Central Missouri in particular provided brief respite for tribes of the Old Northwest (the upper Ohio Valley and present-day Illinois) pushed by American encroachment. Sac and Fox individuals, families, and settlements who had been encouraged by Spanish officials in the late eighteenth century to emigrate from north of the Ohio River to provide a buffer between colonial settlements and the Osages—continued to enter Missouri into the early nineteenth century. In 1816, a report by Governor William Clark listed nearly 5,000 Indians in Missouri, including Piankashaws, Shawnees, Delawares, Great Osages, and smaller groups of Peorias, Ioways, Sacs, and Foxes.

Though the Quapaws, Cherokees, and Osages were ultimately dispossessed as tribes, individuals continued to hunt, barter, and farm in the region. Notwithstanding these interactions, newcomers in the American incursion overwrote the physical presence of indigenous peoples imaginatively, legally, and with force, consigning to near invisibility an agricultural, commercial, and cultural heritage sustained by numerous Indian contemporaries.

American settlement often traced out older Native American paths and community sites. In making their homes and farms, nineteenth-century newcomers found marks on the land in the form of arrowheads, burial mounds, and traces of previous cultivative practices. Despite this, Americans' assertions of the newness of their land and the absence of any meaningful prior presence attempted to will into nonexistence visible traces of indigenous presence and ecological change: open woodlands created by burning, fire pits and established river fords, even the mortars hollowed out by premodern inhabitants of the Ozarks in the native limestone. "New" was an insistence, and it implied a context: new to whites, new to sedentary, Christian cultivators, new to people calling themselves Americans.

Emigration Stories, Black and White

The historical flexibility of newness emerges in the differences between white and black newcomers' perceptions of the region over the course of the nineteenth century. Free people entering the Missouri-Arkansas region saw it as new in the first half of the nineteenth century, after its purchase from France. Many black Americans, in contrast, regarded Arkansas in particular as "new" in the era of Reconstruction and into the later nineteenth century, when African-American families streamed into the state, attracted by a comparatively low population and still-available land. (This reflected the high mobility of recently freed slaves in the decades after the war, rather than a net population gain for the state. In fact, postwar Arkansas, like the whole South, endured a net loss of black families.) Victoria Sims, an ex-slave, told an interviewer about her experiences as a girl in the decades after the war, "We come to Arkansas with our parents. We heard the land was new and rich." White families, too, were still migrating to the two states in the later nineteenth century, but black emigration from other parts of the South was particularly marked.

Strikingly, freedpeople emigrating after the Civil War and into the late nineteenth century reflected many of the same impressions as white families moving seventy or eighty years before. Maggie Stenhouse remembered that her family had come to Arkansas in the late 1880s or '90s because her father felt the family would "do better" in a "new country." His ambitions echo those of the region's initial American settlers of fifty and sixty years before. The environmental perceptions of these black newcomers revolved around well-established themes. About her family's move to Holly Grove, Arkansas, in 1901, Laura Abromson was emphatic: "Wild, honey, it was!" The thick waters, high-kneed cypress, and sultry air of the swampy region were as "wild" to Abromson's family as they had been to white Kentuckians or Vermonters who moved west in the 1820s. Black families struggling to settle land and to settle into freedom sought country both "wild" and "new" in the late 1800s, just as white families from the eastern states had in the early part of the century—and in the same places.

Unlike the experience of African-American emigrants after freedom, former slaves interviewed in the 1930s cast the process of moving across country as slaves of white emigrants as a profound rupture in family relations and attachment to home. They emphasized the vast but unknown distances traversed, the sense of difficult labor without clear goal. "They rode in the fine carriages," recalled Mittie Freeman of moving before the war from Mississippi to Camden, Arkansas; "Us slaves rode in ox wagons." For these forced emigrants, memories of their remove centered less on physical surroundings and more on an unpredictable process over which they exercised little control: "Lord only know how long it tuck a-coming. Every night we camped. I was jest a little tike then but I has a remembrance of everything. The biggest younguns had to walk till theys so tired theys couldn't hardly drag they feets; them what had been a-riding had to get out the ox wagon and walk a far piece; so it like this we go on."

Disorientation and loss of sense of identity ever haunted the paths of slaves' migration. Children separated from their families lost parents, relatives, and even knowledge of their own names and ages when forcibly emigrated. One former Missouri slave, the 96-year-old Jennie Hill, recounted during an 1933 interview the many attempts made by separated families to find each other after emancipation. Most of these efforts were in vain, she recalled: "Some [family members] perhaps were killed in the battles but in the majority of the cases the children of slaves lost their identity when they were taken from the place of their birth into a new country." Hill's account of children "taken from the place of their birth into a new country"— phrases which sound as though they could open one of the swelling narratives of western progress popular throughout her adult lifetime—tells not of upward progression and cultural advance, but of family ties broken and familial and personal identity lost. The process by which newcomers were transplanted did uneven violence: for many emigrants to early Missouri and Arkansas, forced adjustment to "new country" left a loss that reverberated through later generations.

Former slaves often recalled with sorrowful precision how many of the children looked after by a central maternal figure were able to emigrate with her, and how many had to be left behind. One former slave told in the 1850s of her family's experience of emigration to Missouri: "I lived in Kentucky till I was about fourteen years of age, when old master moved off to Clay county, Missouri, carrying my mother with him, and all her children, excepting Millar, who had been sold to one of Mr. Campbell's cousins. She had thirteen children at that time, and had one more in Missouri. One daughter died on the journey." Whether the family's structure changed during the move was a central motif of slaves' recounted memories of the journey west. A slave family often centered on the mother or grandmother, for slave owners rarely tried to keep married couples together. Keeping a family from being separated usually meant letting a woman and her young children stay together. To be sure, white migrants also experienced the attenuation and fracture of kinship ties, but enslaved migrants had fewer resources for sustaining such ties. Few slaves could read or write; few later migrants could pass along news of those left behind, as white travelers constantly did for one another. In slaves' narratives, change of place is almost invariably linked to sudden, involuntary, and often permanent breakup of the family.

Lack of control, rather than ambition for the new, characterized the migrations of those in slavery. The patterns of their lives dictated not by family attachments but by the labor and skills for which they were valued, enslaved migrants experienced a reality as final as a comment by the child slave Josephine Ann Barnett: "None of the slaves liked it but they was brought." "Yankee mens immigrated us," commented one former slave of his experience during the Civil War, revealing with economy that emigration, rather than a choice full of hope and expectation, was simply something done *to*.

Understanding slaves' experience of migration as forced separation, over which they could exercise little control, is crucial to tempering the expectant and even triumphal tone of many white families' accounts of western movement, which have been so echoed and recapitulated in subsequent histories. Yet those in slavery also moved with agency in the world: though few were able to choose the paths of their own migration, some found in the less established social structure of growing communities—and especially in the river trades centered on St. Louis—degrees of autonomy. White people were not the only ones to seek to make over the region on their own terms. In the 1840s, a free black St. Louis resident named N. D. Artist attempted to recruit families for a colony in Liberia to be called Missouri. Artist and others sought a new creation of their hostile home on African soil, by retransplanted Africans. They attempted to resettle "Missouri" on their own terms.

Many African-American newcomers, in Missouri and Arkansas as else-where in the American South, sought a reconsecration of their own spaces in rituals that harked back to West African roots. Narratives of former slaves repeatedly mention the custom of praying or singing under an over-turned tub or pot. Lewis Brown, of Little Rock, explained, "If you wanted to sing at night and didn't want nobody [the whites, that is] to hear it, you could just take an old wash pot and turn it down—leave a little space for the air, and nobody could hear it." Some recountings make of this practice a practical trick: sound would not carry far inside a heavy metal pot. Yet an upturned pot also worked as a symbol that kept religious noise and fervor in a private and protected space. During prayer meetings, recounted a former slave, Austin Pen Parnell, slaves would "turn a pot down out in front of the door. It would be on a stick or something and raised up a short distance from the ground. . . . [It] would catch the sound and keep it right around there." An individual could "put her head under the pot and pray for free-dom," and groups could "set . . . the pot at the doors," perhaps to mark the site of a meeting, and perhaps to keep it private in a more symbolic manner. Washtubs and kettles, functional tools of cooking, cleaning, and carrying, were also symbolic vessels in which to convey devotion and hope to God, or to preserve the vulnerable community of worship in the slave quarters from prying owners' ears. Forbidden from claiming the new land that they worked, slaves nevertheless created religious space to mark as their own.

The African roots of this practice are many. Pots and concavities in the ground were associated with Yoruba worship rites involving river deities and the god of smallpox, and the use of washpots as sound catchers may be a symbolic inversion of their use as musical instruments. The practice could also be linked with African rituals of sanctification of a certain plot of earth. The everyday technologies of laundry and cooking thus became in the lives of the grandchildren and great-grandchildren of captured Africans a con-duit for the continuation and syncretistic adaptation of spiritual beliefs.

In ways as deeply personal as they were widely shared, newcomers to the borderlands of the "Far West" sought to make sense out of this unfamiliar terrain. Through description, promotion, and simply shared worry—and through the handed-down tales of migration that were illiterate peoples' records of their perceptions—migrants came to terms with places initially confusing and overwhelming. In their efforts to do so, they reveal many of the implicit assumptions they brought to making sense of their world.

BODY

Chapter II

IN A WORLD OF SUDDEN and threatening change, the body was no safe refuge. One's own physical self could undergo wild oscillation, overengorged by environmental surfeit or depleted by hard work, short rations, and the physical demands of new and bountiful earth. Nineteenth-century American migrants inhabited not simply the geographic surroundings we might easily, and wrongly, identify as the sum of their environment; they lived also in a complicated interior geography of sensation, movement, and flow. Keeping their roiled inner selves in check required delicate balance— of habits and emotions, but also of the forces and fluids that determined well-being. For us moderns, understanding their bodies, their inhabited and hidden selves, is a central task of understanding their more accessible, visible world of stream, swamp, mountain, and pasture.

Maintaining one's body in proper balance, like maintaining a household's fields in production, was a constant and not always successful struggle. Beset with disease and physical challenges, early- and mid-nineteenth-century Americans worked hard to push and pull their resistant forms back to the balances—between types of bodily fluids, between nutrition and excretion, between cold and hot temperature, between moist and dry texture, and between stasis and change—that defined good health. When well, they still had constantly to monitor and fret over their vulnerable physical selves. Health was dynamic and always precarious. Surrounded by forces of environmental health and disarray, early Americans fought off with powerful remedies the influences from their surroundings that could wrench their systems out of smooth functioning. This ongoing struggle defines the nineteenth-century sense of health and well-being.

Medicine and the Demands of Health

Common wisdom made sense of the myriad health experiences of the living body. Medical knowledge was understood to be accessible to all—books like *Gunn's Domestic Medicine, or Poor Man's Friend* asserted a by-your-own-bootstraps approach to healing that dovetailed with the boisterous political rhetoric of self-reliance in the Jacksonian period. Certainly, migrants to the antebellum borderlands did not all hold the same medical beliefs. Theoretical systems of medicine warred and clashed in the public arena. More quietly, though just as pervasively, communities of slaves developed belief systems and practices separate and often hidden from those of their white owners. Forms of magic were worked in the slave quarters, and many slaves attempted to assert their own ways of healing that ran counter to remedies undertaken by owner and overseer.

Yet agreement about fundamental aspects of well-being united many of the systems of healing and treatment of the first two thirds of the nineteenth century. That bodies had to expel harmful material or could be sickened by ill-managed change were truths accepted in slave cabins as in owners' houses. Documents of everyday life speak for a remarkably conservative and resilient common sense of the body, one in which flows of force and sensation, cycles of buildup and release, and tenuously achieved balance were central to both intellectual frameworks and ordinary experience.

The nineteenth century was a time of tumult in medical understanding. From the clinical centers of Europe (and to a lesser extent the United States) emerged several kinds of new tools. The development of the stethoscope, as well as the techniques of auscultation and percussion (tapping on and listening to a patient's body), sharpened physicians' understanding of the sounds of bodily spaces and organs. Along with the improvement and wider popularization of instruments like the microscope, these changes meant that those who kept up with such developments had more tools with which to probe the evidence provided by the body's interior. Physicians in Paris pioneered the quantification of medical data and the practice of drawing conclusions from large numbers of hospital cases. This "numerical method" promised to bring rigor to hazily imprecise disease definitions. Educated physicians thus had a larger array of conceptual resources and reference tools with which to diagnose many illnesses, though many of these methods still offered little in the way of treatment.

The demonstration of anesthesia in surgery in the late 1840s further opened the cavities of the human body to the imagination of innovative surgeons, though as with the elusive therapeutic promise of the numerical method, the actual practice of surgery on a widespread level would not be substantially altered until the late nineteenth century. Beginning in the late 1860s and accelerating throughout the following three decades and beyond, developments of laboratory science, especially the "germ theory" of Louis Pasteur, laid down a stark challenge to earlier medical truths. Accompanying such changes in ideology were the standardization of antisepsis and the reorganization and expansion of medical institutions like hospitals. Medicine in the late-nineteenth-century United States was transformed by these new elements, by the shift toward state regulation of medical education, and by the increasingly assertive and successful moves of "regular" practitioners to gain professional monopoly and standardize medical training.

"Regulars," almost all of them white men, were practitioners who generally styled themselves M.D.s, often, though not always, on the basis of their having received university training. Though an amorphous and contested domain, regular medicine was characterized by what were known as "heroic" methods: the use of bloodletting, blisters, chemical medicines, and other often dramatic therapies to force an illness to release its hold on a person's system.

Plenty of regulars drew on competing theories and therapies, and plenty of educated practitioners (notably homeopaths) opposed key tenets of regular medicine. Yet increasingly over the nineteenth century, regulars sought to anchor their professional standing in claims to scientific authority and professional forms. Modern physicians are largely the heirs of the fractious regulars of the nineteenth century, so historians of medicine have too often inflated the scientific orientation of their progenitors and underestimated the role of non-elite and competing healers. In medicine as in many other areas, the nineteenth century resists these neat definitions and tidy origin stories.

The period before the Civil War was marked by wide disagreement over the status and relative merits of types of medical practitioners and by profound and unanswered questions about many basic aspects of bodily functioning. Whether lay or professional, formal or informal, healers relied on many techniques and tools that would have been familiar to practitioners of the medieval era. Faced with ill health, people responded with alcohol and other depletives and stimulants, food and rest, botanical and chemical compounds, hot baths and poultices, many kinds of caustic or irritating substances with which to disrupt the skin, lancets and leeches to "let" blood, and other remedies and techniques from tradition and home health manuals. In this early-modern medical world, sick people were cared for in their own homes and beds, by family members and neighbors, as well as by those with particular claims to expertise.

Yet despite these historical continuities in therapeutic response to ill health, the first two thirds of the nineteenth century was also a time of theoretical challenge within medicine. Several important schools of medical thought questioned the theories and, more important, the therapies associated with regular medicine. Criticized as the creation of "eclectics," "irregulars," "sectarians," or even "quacks," these competing systems in fact characterized much of nineteenth-century thought and practice. In the eras before germ theory, standardized training, and medical institutions, it was not at all clear that the regulars would eventually prevail.

A primary challenge to regular medicine in the early nineteenth century was the botanicals-based regimen of Samuel Thomson. Thomson created an alternative medical system based on the notion that internal obstructions and insufficient body heat caused most ills. He notably employed the familiar domestic metaphor of cleaning out soot from a dirty stove to explain the workings of therapies within the human frame. Thomsonian therapies, outlined in his 1822 *New Guide to Health* and popularized through a patented system to which individual men, women, and families could subscribe, relied on botanical drugs and steam baths to clean out the body's blockages and restore its vital heat. When his ideas were at their height in the 1830s and early '40s, Thomsonian agents had sold over a hundred thousand patents and gained extensive adherents among the "backwoods" markets of the Ohio Valley and the western frontier. Ridiculed by the prominent regular Ohio physician Daniel Drake as "the steamers and the steamed," Thomsonians nonetheless reshaped much of contemporary medical therapeutics. For all that Thomson's system trumpeted its independence from the violently intrusive therapies of learned physicians, however, some of the basic principles of action, particularly its emphasis on clearing obstructions and the use of the emetic herb lobelia, were much like those of contemporary orthodox practice.

A similarly influential theoretical framework was the homeopathic system of Samuel Hahnemann. The late-eighteenth-century research of this German physician had resulted in two key principles of medical treatment: his "law of similars," which posited that anything that produced the symptoms of a disease in a well person would cure it in someone who was ill; and his use of infinitesimal doses, extremely dilute solutions of remedies. Infinitesimals took into account what Hahnemann saw as the extreme sensitivity of the sick body. Homeopathy was in direct response to regular medicine's allopathy, or insistence that medicines should forcibly counteract and be *different* from the illness against which they were directed (*allo* is Greek for "other"). As a system homeopathy was most influential among the more educated, but even less well educated people applied homeopathic notions as part of a mishmash of therapeutic possibilities. Practitioners were frequently willing to apply homeopathic remedies for some ills, but resorted to aggressive drugging and bleeding in others.

Such flexibility was commonplace. Contemporary medical regimes offered numerous alternatives to those leery of pukes and purges. For people with money and resources, hydropathy, or "water therapy," promised vigor and health. Popular particularly among well-to-do northeasterners, water therapy involved a set of bathing practices, from hot towel wraps to soothing soaks and stimulative regimens of cold or mineral waters. Perhaps even more important, water therapy resorts offered a respite from normal life. Invalids ate spare diets, went for long walks on groomed trails, and were relieved by spa residence from the usual grinding toil that characterized even affluent households. Not surprisingly, Yankee women who could afford it flocked to take the "water cure" in places such as Brattleboro, Vermont. Even those far from these refined establishments used water and bathing as an important therapy, taking advantage of the breadth of practitioners, treatments, and sites of health care in the antebellum period.

Dedicated proponents of specific medical systems defended their own cures with great energy and at high volume. Still, most Americans exercised an essentially pragmatic eclecticism about their health care. Drawing on a wide set of techniques and schools, they relied upon neighbors, relatives, and domestic health manuals. These manuals were especially important to western migrants. The rough conditions of many newly settled areas made catch-as-catch-can healing commonplace. Many practitioners made healing part of their social identity and income, whether as midwives or physicians, "root doctors" or bone-setters, but health and healing was in no way a professionally bounded domain. In 1841, Eliza Post's son extracted his mother's sore tooth, while in that same decade a neighborhood doctor charged John Geiger 25 cents for the same service. Physicians frequently performed procedures in which more informal healers had little practice: lancing, letting blood, administering the more powerful medicines, and sometimes amputations, simple surgeries, and fracture repair. Yet none of these was the province only of those who called themselves physicians. Most therapies involved the consultation and assistance of members of a sick person's family or household.

The physical conditions of personal health affected and concerned others in a person's circle. Individuals were constantly enmeshed in care for their own and others' well-being. Craftsmen, farm families, slave laborers, and merchants lived and worked within communities of people who needed nursing from one another. Conversations and household plans centered on the healing bones or impending confinement or seasonal ailments of neighbors and family members. Everyone in a house could hear the squalls of colicky newborns or teething toddlers, as well as the urgent struggles of women in labor. The normally restrained Missouri farmer Stephen Hempstead who shared a home with a daughter when he was in his seventies, complained in his diary that "our family consists of so large a number of Children it requires all the patience I am possessed of to bear with their noise & crying." When a baby was born, children in a household likely saw bloody linens and sheets of clean cloth being bundled into and out of the room; the urgent need of a brother with diarrhea for frequent trips to the woods or chamber pot was all too obvious to siblings sharing a pallet bed. No one was spared the work of health: plantation managers and family farmers had alike to plan around the injuries and ailments of the men, women, and children they directed. The smells and sounds and physical labor associated with illness were part of the texture of everyday life.

Force and Flow

Throughout the language and concerns of the early nineteenth century runs a sense of the body as fluid and in motion. The commonplace nature of animal slaughter and household accidents (and occasional stabbings and shootings) meant that most people were familiar with the shapes of dead or dying organs. Yet the body's interior was composed of much more than those collections of turgid tissue. Stomachs growled and gurgled; intestines churned; fetuses kicked; mysterious swellings bulged, and sometimes just as mysteriously disappeared; blood filled the faces of angry men and swelled the veins and muscles of women churning butter or chopping logs; feelings of heat or fatigue, prickliness or chill, traveled from one limb to another. Myriad sensations and experienced changes traversed the complex terrain of the body's interior. However named, these forces and flows created sickness or well-being.

Understanding the condition of the body called upon ancient classifications of the body's four humors: blood, phlegm, yellow bile (or choler), and the less clearly defined black bile. This nineteenth-century understanding of human health as a system of humoral balance had ancient historical roots. Contending theories about the number, qualities, and behavior of the body's fluids or essences emerged in the set of works associated with Hippocrates of Cos, from the fifth century before the Common Era (B.C.E.). The forceful synthesis and interpretation of the Hippocratic corpus by the Roman physician Galen of Pergamum, in the second century of the Common Era, served to coalesce these conflicting ideas into a coherent system of four fluids, or humors, whose balance determined each individual's health.

Hippocratic thought linked the four bodily humors with seasons and with times of life: blood was associated with spring and childhood; yellow bile was linked with Summer and youth; black bile with autumn and adulthood; and phlegm with winter and old age. Galen interpreted humors, moreover, not simply as the actual fluids of the body but as invisible, theoretical entities. Black bile, for instance, was not necessarily a specific secretion but an essence that influenced all the body's systems and fluids. Galen's influence on subsequent medicine of the Christian and Islamic worlds was far-reaching. Specific organs and organ systems became associated with certain humors, and eventually fit into the overarching theory of fluid balance. The four elements of the world—earth, air, fire, water—and the four fundamental attributes—hot, cold, wet, dry—soon found their place in this system. The notion of a balance of humors endured over the centuries as a powerful concept. As documents from the early American West make clear, the antiquity, flexibility, and simplicity of a theory of health based on maintaining the balance of a small number of bodily essences by regulating certain basic human functions proved both useful and reassuring to a people grappling with bewildering change.

The early and middle nineteenth century had its own sense of modernity, and some of these ancient classifications and explicitly humoral medical remedies were beginning to seem backward and unscientific to up-and-coming physicians. Yet the insights as well as the language of classical humoral theory continued to pervade common life well into the century. Thus, a widely read book like Mason Weems's *Life of Washington* explained action through an imbalance of both body and soul, blaming poor behavior on "a moral *cachexy* or *surcharge* of *bad humours*." In popular speech and writing, the usage associated with humors might be somewhat self-conscious, as in a diary entry of Mary E. Smith, a young Illinois girl studying at a girls' boarding school in St. Louis in the late 1830s, who wrote one January day that she "wanted to go home, and for it, shed a few drops of aqueous humor." Her stilted phrasing reflects the embarrassment of an adolescent diarist abashed, perhaps, to admit that she cried out of homesickness; old-fashioned words can be usefully distancing. Yet the fact that a girl of the 1830s could so easily call on the language of humoral theory is an indication that this language was part of the cultural background against which disease ideas of the early nineteenth century were being worked out.

As the century progressed, common usage moved away from humoral language and tended to emphasize sensations of fullness, heaviness, constriction, heat, or congestion, which moved and flowed within the body. Beneath a variety of expression, however, endured a sense of the body as composed of energies and forces that were subject to movement, collection, and release, and whose governance was the task of each individual.

Everyday ailments and complicated illnesses often involved forces flowing between parts of the body. One patient of John Geiger, a Missouri farmer and healer, suffered in 1836 with "pain in his leg, running up & down the front of shin bone." Fluids of the body held properties that were not simply academic, but were felt and experienced as important clues to one's well-being. Henry Morton Stanley, an English orphan who later achieved fame and knighthood for locating the British missionary and traveler David Livingstone in Africa in 1871, lived along the Arkansas River in southeastern Arkansas as an adolescent in the 1850s. (He fought for the Confederacy in the Civil War, after being sent a pair of women's undergarments in the mail as an anonymous taunt to his courage.) In his autobiography, Stanley described the attacks of "ague" that he suffered as being preceded by "a congealed feeling as though the blood was suddenly iced." Common reference to being "low" with illness or (in the words of an escaped slave, the novelist William Wells Brown) being "raised" to good health was similarly evocative of flowing movement, like that of change in the level of a river.

Movement between body parts—often without making explicit exactly *what* was moving—was of concern in many accounts. The Arkansas physician A. W. Webb, writing in 1844, emphasized flow and movement (probably, though not necessarily, of blood) in his observation that certain fevers are "attended with great determination to the stomach," whereas the morning paroxysms of intermittent fever typically involve "greater congestion, with more determination to the stomach, brain, and other viscera." A sense of the importance of intangible, circulating inner force is similarly evident in the advice of a St. Louis doctor who counseled during the cholera epidemic of 1849 that tourniquets be applied to the arms and legs of those who had collapsed, to limit circulation and thus "husband the vital power."

This notion of flow and flux provided structure for many kinds of understanding. One former slave described her spiritual experience of being "new born" in Protestant Christianity, after being brought up Catholic in Louisiana: "I tell you," she confided to her African-American patron, "that 'Merican religion makes any body feel happy all over; it runs all through you, down from your head to the very soles of your feet!"

Diseases and ailments moved within the body, and changed the individual's overall sense of energy or listlessness. As John Brown recorded in April 1854: "I feel reduced and of little force, my cold is shifting from my head to my breast." Illnesses thus traveling could take on different forms, moving from one kind of fever to another, or assuming the aspect of a related ailment. Sufferers recorded the movements of ills through a body whose own fluids and forces moved to compensate for or block, respond to or anticipate, this migration of disorders.

The tracking of the movement of disease, fluid, and sensation through the body reflects a localized sense of bodily spaces. Many ailments assailed specific body parts or locations, which were identified by an elaborate mapping of the body. Someone could be "ailing in his breast," while a former slave reported being struck with a "misery. . . in the chest." Medical reports of a variety of ailments frequently sited diseases within the organs or organ systems of the body. In the "inflammatory disease" prevalent in an area of Missouri, for instance, one physician observed in 1845 that "the lungs were but slightly affected, the bowels seeming to bear the principle onus of the disease." Prior weakness or injury could draw passing diseases to one location within the body. Worrying over the "deficiancy" in his wife's "left side," John Brown wrote in 1859 that he feared it would "by pressing on the lungs do them injury. That side is her weak point at any rate and when she takes cold it seems to settle there." Knowledge of the ways in which diseases traveled the body's interior geography was integral to a healing response that weighed the specific course of disease within an individual with her own constitution, climate, tendencies, and habits.

Blood

Medical professionals and laypeople alike often phrased concern for bodily flows as a problem of circulation of blood. Physicians attempted to equalize and regulate blood flow and on occasion removed excess blood from the body to calm it. A range of techniques influenced the distribution of blood within the body's interior. Vomiting was recommended by one Missouri physician in 1845 for its "tendency to equalize the circulation, forcing the blood from the centre to the circumference of the body." Blood concentrated too much in one area of the body could be a telling symptom of disorder, and could also itself wreak harm to the body's workings. An "engorged" brain or "congested" abdomen was both a sign and a cause of ill health.

Popular understanding also focused on the movement of blood within the body. Rebecca Butterworth, an English immigrant to the "Back Woods of America," wrote to her father in 1846 from her Ozark farm that a recent thunderstorm "scared me and threw the blood to my head." John Gunn's domestic health manual similarly warned that in severe ague, "the blood determines to the head," resulting in brief delirium. Imbalance in the distribution of blood within the body disrupted its many functions. A sudden surfeit in one location or lack in another imbalanced organs' ability to function properly. Equal distribution and calm flow—what John Geiger termed "equalebrium of circulation"—were the desired state of health.

Many therapeutic interventions thus addressed themselves to the drawing of blood from the body. Criticized by some irregular healers as symptomatic of the destructive harshness of regular therapy, bleeding was nevertheless an accustomed part of health maintenance. Many people expected blood to be drawn and experienced bloodletting as pleasurable; it relieved pain and drew strength away from gripping illnesses. Doctors employed ingenious spring-lock lancets and cleverly designed scarificators to minimize patients' fears of sharp blades and to ensure the maximum salutary blood flow. Yet domestic health manuals and emigration advice guides also encouraged ordinary citizens to draw blood using everyday knives and cups. To give in to squeamishness was to jeopardize the health of loved ones or valuable slaves. Just as bakers would score the surface of their loaves to let out steam and prevent the rising dough from splitting unevenly in the oven, healers sliced into veins to draw off built-up forces, keep the body's functioning in balance, and draw off malign humors along with the rich, warm blood.

Attention to the movement of blood in the body drew on insights into the circulation of blood that had been a major achievement of seventeenth-century medical understanding. The English physician William Harvey had in 1628 charted the body's circulatory system, showing that what had been seen as an amorphous or unidirectional set of flows was in fact a closed, constant system. Though Harvey's demonstration that blood circulated through the body was a dramatically new way of understanding blood flow, his insight was quickly assimilated into a preexisting sense of the body's waxing and waning forces. Despite its revolutionary implications, Harvey's work contributed to an older idea of the body as a personal landscape, knowable and manageable. Thus in the language and practice of the American nineteenth century, attention to blood and its circulating rhythm marked not a break with older, humoral notions of the body, but an adaptation of them. The flowing qualities of blood, its strengthening and tonic effect on each part of the body, and its rich symbolism as carrier of consciousness, vitality, and pain (those who were bled felt relief, but grew pale and could faint) transferred into modern physiological frameworks the fundamental insights of ancient ideas of bodily health.

Intake and Outgo

As with blood, so with bodily fluids and secretions more generally. The intake and waste products of the body provided access to its internal balance, and professional and domestic therapies alike focused on affecting what one New York medical guide termed "retentions and excretions." John Scoffern, a British author, cautioned feckless immigrants in 1857 against forcing up their appetites when in hot places "until the balance of excretion, and nutrition, is disordered, and some vital organs, usually the liver, succumb to disease." That which entered the body in strongest, rawest form was considered the most powerful. Cold winds, fresh fruit, green corn, alcoholic spirits, and passionate desires could all wreak havoc within the vulnerable human frame.

What came out of the body was intensely scrutinized. "We discovered that Ed had not urinated naturally for several days," John Brown wrote of his ill young son in 1858, "and is better since this has been corrected." Catheters and cathartics urged the body back to its normal and healthy patterns. Poor urination or "obstinacy of the bowels" were signals of obstruction or unnatural process within the body. If what came out of the body had too little potency, what remained inside it would be unduly powerful. Response to diverse ailments—like the cure for "rheumatism" copied by John Geiger in 1837—therefore involved pills and interventions "to keep the bowels regular." Stiff joints and aching bones could be eased by the regular passage of feces from smoothly functioning bowels.

An intuitive sense that the body had to throw off bad influences or flows within it was reinforced by myriad experienced and visible discharges. Unusual expulsions, rashes, oozings, or skin lesions, like the "strange eruption like chicken pox" that worried John Brown in 1860, could all signal ill health. Vomit, sweat, saliva, pus, feces, breast milk, mucus, blood, and other products and fluids from the body's interior could carry off malevolent excess of the bodily system.

Blockages of any type caused grave concern. In 1837, John Geiger recorded an autopsy that revealed the cause of a neighbor's death. "Amanday Herrington died a quarter past six this evening," he wrote, "& was opened by Dr. Tiffin and had a large knot of dead worms that could not pass down." Other blockages were invisible or of undetermined origin, but these, too, could be fatal: "Amenorehœa" was listed as the cause of death of one woman in St. Louis in 1845.

People regarded situations in which usual excretion or secretion was suppressed as moments of extreme danger. Solomon Northup, a slave who escaped from a Louisiana cotton plantation, wrote that "When the slave ceases to perspire, as he often does when taxed beyond his strength, he falls to the ground and becomes entirely helpless." Drastic action was required: "It is then the duty of the driver to drag him into the shade of the standing cotton or cane, or of a neighboring tree, where he dashes buckets of water upon him, and uses other means of bringing out perspiration again." A body unable to expel salty water was a body in danger. Water thrown over the exhausted person shocked the system, cooled it, and sympathetically pulled more water out of it. But rather than being able to rest and recuperate after such a crisis, continued Northup, the overheated worker was subsequently "ordered to his place, and compelled to continue his labor." Slaves' bodies were valued only insofar as they could produce.

Anything that stopped the body up, obstructing release, was harmful. (Costiveness, or constipation, was a frequent nineteenth-century worry.) Suppressed menses could reflect either a positive transition in which bodily energies would be drawn to the developing fetus, or a harmful interruption of the body's rhythm of release. Such suppression of the body's inclination to cast off harmful matter impelled the matter inward, where it might have worse effects.

A missed period thus held multiple meanings. It could be a sign of illness as well as pregnancy. Menstrual flows that proved "stubborn" or irregular demanded intervention. A Cherokee woman, Mary Swimmer, failed to experience her period and was stricken with fainting and spasms while emigrating to Indian Territory in 1837 after the Treaty of New Echota. In response Dr. Lillybridge, a white physician accompanying her group, had her bled. Regularity in menstruation and vaginal outflow was closely allied with the body's overall balance. The death of one Missouri woman after childbirth in the summer of 1836, for instance, surprised John Geiger, since at first, "She was as healthy and as Natural in her Discharges as Common." The body existed as a system of material coming in and material being expelled. When discharges were regular and of appropriate volume and kind—"healthy and . . . Natural"—an individual existed in health.

Just like steam in a boiling pot, bodily energies like menstrual blood needed periodic release, especially when challenged by strain or change. As young Arkansas immigrant Hiram Whittington wrote to his brother in 1832, "The bile had been stirred up in me, and, like Banco's ghost, it would not down." The naturalist Thomas Nuttall, journeying through Arkansas Territory in 1819, commented in his journal repeatedly on his need for emetics and purges. During one severe sickness he reported a fever so high that he "felt ready to burn with heat," a heat that reinforced the dangerous potency of the environment through which he traveled. But "by forcibly inciting a vomit, I felt relieved." Strong action was at times necessary to relieve an overexcited and pent-up body of dangerous "bile" or "heat."

Violent expulsion could be salutary to a "stirred up" system. Many treatments reflected interest in promoting "operations from the bowels," visible, smelly, redolent expulsions of matter from the body. A sense of relief is evident throughout records from nineteenth-century families when an ill person "passed off a great portion of fetid matter." Medicines that promoted the vomiting or fecal excretion of intestinal parasites were potent proof of the sick body's need to expel harmful matter or organisms ("Charles better," noted Stephen Hempstead in 1823, "had Several Worms come from in the Course of the night"). Jars of huge worms preserved in dispensary windows satisfied fascination with the morbid details of pathological body functioning even as they reinforced a sense of the necessity of periodic purges or cathartics. Who knew what hideous creatures curled lurking in one's own bowels?

Disruptions of the body's surface, though unpleasant or painful, could be a sign of health, evidence of bodily processes working as they should to cast off negative influences. Daniel Drake, who was not only a prolific medical author but an enthusiastic promoter of western settlement, commented in 1815 that children in the Ohio region frequently suffered rashes in the summer, but mused, "There is even reason to believe these affections salutary, as they frequently appear on the healthiest children." Caretakers often created blisters by smearing caustic pastes, pressing irritating plasters, or binding salve-drenched bandages on an area of skin. Though performed with a variety of irritants, "applying a blister" was an all-purpose remedy. Inflammation drew material within the body to the surface, relieving pressure or congestion around afflicted organ systems and "exciting" redness and heat. Commonly applied to the extremities (and in drastic circumstances even on the head), blisters, caustic plasters, and other surface prickings or irritants evened out circulation and drew material away from the vulnerable torso. In many people's experience, such treatments worked. "Blistered Harriett & it drew & gave ease," wrote John Geiger of his daughter in the late summer of 1835.

In other cases, "ease" proved more difficult to grant. In January 1828, a Mr. Giddings, a neighbor of the Missouri farmer Stephen Hempstead, lay dangerously ill. He was unable to respire freely, despite multiple bleedings and a "blister on his breast . . . to help his Breathing." By drawing blood out from his body and irritating an area of his chest, Giddings's friends and family members tried to loosen the hold of his disease on his pulmonary system. Pulling the body's energies toward other locations and toward the body's surface, they struggled against the ailment's increasing hold on his lungs. In this case, however, the inflammation continued, and Giddings's health continued to fail. Health was the subject of struggle between family and friends attempting to pull ailments out into the visible, smellable, touchable world, and harmful influences that buried themselves in the body's interior and shifted elusively within it.

"Risings" and Release

Common wisdom read abscesses, boils, pustules, ulcers, and similar swellings and disruptions of the body's surface as manifestations of unwanted, harmful material from the body's interior being extruded through its surfaces. The perceived necessity of such buildup and release is reflected in nineteenth-century preoccupation with "gatherings" and "risings."

These evocative terms, so enigmatic to us now, reflect the frequency of inflamed, knobby, swollen, sometimes suppurating tissue in nineteenth-century experience. Improved hygiene and contemporary medical treatments have relieved us moderns of many of these afflictions. Some were undoubtedly tumors, cysts, infected abscesses, calcifications, and tubercular skin lesions, but many were likely the result of more prosaic irritations and infections of the skin. For early modern people, these experiences had physical and nosological coherence. What we might separately understand as acne, hemorrhoids, and cancer, nineteenth-century people grouped as a common manifestation of miserable swollen-ness, evidence of the body's upwelling and excrescence.

Various episodes of the concentration of fluid, swelling, and various kinds of tissue inflammation (often accompanied by painfully discolored, taut skin) were common complaints. These experiences reinforced a sense that what the body gathered up, it must also want to expel. The nineteenth-century map of the body paid great attention to all such bumps, boils, swollen tissue, and unusual extrusions. Anything that changed the body's topography had to be read and interpreted. Emergent chancres and turgid boils were, after all, the visual and palpable result of the body's constantly changing inner truths. "Risings" were thus intensely scrutinized, and their changes could reflect not only the bodily state of one individual but the life changes of a household or family.

In the family life of Stephen and Mary Hempstead, such swellings accompanied many of the family's health problems. Their skins' surface bore witness to the ill health of once-vital but then aging grandparents, the hoped-for but sometimes lost potential of subsequent generations.

Early immigrants, Mary and Stephen Hempstead lived through tremendous change in their new home region. The pages of Stephen Hempstead's diary record the changing society and politics of St. Louis. Territorial officials and state opinion makers supped at the family table; Creole servants and black slaves alike proved recalcitrant, and seemed to Hempstead to require his constant care. As a result of the increasing immigration of the late 1820s, Hempstead and other civic and religious leaders were caught up in efforts to minister to the orphaned immigrant children, cholera widows, and helpless families who found the "Far West" unequal to expectation. The Hempsteads watched their family grow and change even as the region itself did. Their daughter Mary married a leading fur trader, Manuel Lisa, succeeding the Indian common-law wife with whom he had two children. One son went off to sea as a merchant sailor, was captured "on the Spanish main," and never returned to his grieving family. Some children and grandchildren sickened and died, while others went on to build families and businesses within the expanding commercial networks of the Missouri and Mississippi rivers. The complicated ailments and changing fortunes of the Hempstead family represent many of the problems and hopes of similar households in the early American inflow to the Mississippi Valley.

Throughout their years in Missouri, many in the Hempstead family were beset with painful, drawn-together eruptions that held serious health consequences. "My wife complains of some thing gathering on her back and right Shoulder," Stephen Hempstead wrote in 1814. The family's physician made repeated deep incisions to discharge "much matter" and bring out of the body all that was gathered into the abscess. Though it was "a *Shocking* Sore," the ulcer was ultimately resolved and Mary Hempstead returned to health. She lived another six years, dying of a sudden illness during the "sickly season" of fall 1820. ("She was Sixty three years Six month and Twenty days," noted her grieving husband; "we had lived together Forty three years and five days in love and Unity.")

The year after her mother recovered from the gathering on her back, one of Stephen and Mary's daughters-in-law, Cordelia Hempstead, "had her Breast gather and brake by cold taken some weeks since." The pulling together and violent expulsion of putrescent material, pus or other discharge was painful—"She hath suffered much"—and yet it signaled the end of the long process—her body's reaction to a cold, or perhaps a missed menstrual period ("taking a cold" was a common euphemism). Ordinary and yet fraught with danger, these episodes indicate both the frequency and the painful threat of mysterious swellings through which the body would express some deeper unease.

In May of 1829, Stephen Hempstead's grandson, Christopher Keeney, a young physician, came to visit "sick with a rising on his back Very dangerous." A month later Keeney was still afflicted, "in great body pain with an abisces or rising on his back bone." The treatment given the young man was meant to aid the body in its struggle to consolidate the putrid material. A week later the family doctor was busy "polticeing the abciss a trying to bring it to a head." Despite the poultice, however, the rising refused to give up its essence. When lanced, it "discharged no matter." Dejected, Stephen Hempstead wrote that "the abses hath been more then one year a growing, and I am fearful the young man will never get well he is continuel in pain and . . . much Emaciated in Body and his leg & foot debilitated." The longer an abscess had developed, the more it had gathered to itself and the more it had gathered from the body, emaciating and debilitating it. Unless human intervention could force such a rising to give up its loaded material, it continued to work its harm. The failure of medical intervention to bring out and expel the fluids filling Keeney's back abscess meant his prognosis was very grave, and indeed he died a brief time later. Unlike the gatherings on his grandmother's back or his aunt's chest, Christopher Keeney's festering ailment consumed too much of him for his body to survive its depredations. Unable to expel the harmful matter, his body fell victim to it.

Risings could thus herald significant passages, and indeed they marked the end of the family's patriarch. In 1831, as an old man, Stephen Hempstead remained afflicted with the painful skin eruptions that had plagued him throughout his adult life. His physician, he wrote, "Sayes I have much boil is the cause of my Complaint." Hempstead's doctor attributed his aches and chest pain, his increasing weakness and fatigue, to the boils that were the most visible symptom of a malfunctioning body. Though he tried to maintain his busy errands of care for his large family and for the lost and forlorn of St. Louis's burgeoning population, Hempstead was rapidly weakening. His final diary entries reflect the familiar gathering of neighbors and family around an ailing relative that Hempstead himself had so often recorded, and in which he had so often participated as a source of healing and consolation. Family members finished his diary for him, recording Hempstead's death on October 4, 1831, as he had recorded almost two decades of family and community life in his daily records.

Gathering inflammation was like the mounding in the sky of a far-off thunderhead or the maturation of a field's crops, a long, slow process of potentially critical importance to individual or household. To report the growth and resolution of pustulent swellings was to narrate the well-being of the person from whose hapless body such energies drew together. The gradual drama featured slow development and sudden intervention, as angry, lumpy cysts or putrescent risings would ultimately coalesce in a vulnerable, loaded portion, which healers could remove or drain.

Such a process featured significantly in the 1843 account by Leonard Stephens of his wife Caty's death. He wrote from Kentucky to his brother and sister-in-law, far off in Missouri, to tell them of his wife's last days. Her long illness was first marked by difficulty breathing and swallowing. Over time, those internal blockages were expressed as externally visible manifestations of fluid, severe swellings that at first signaled the disease's accessibility to treatment: "There were two tumors or risings out on each side of her neck that showed themselves for a considerable time. I had strong hopes that when they came to perfection or were ready to be opened that they would relieve her & that the disease would pass off in that way." Reaching the height of intensity, such inflammations "came to perfection" like pimples or like the firm, pale ears of corn that rose up over long seasons from tended soil. Risings that were "ready to be opened" were like grain ready for harvest or a field prepared for plowing: they followed a progression that led over time to the moment of appropriate intervention. Done at the right time, opening inflamed skin could pull out putrid, harmful matter and give vent to the malevolence of internal disturbance.

In Caty Stephens's illness, however, propitious signs were misleading. When her debility seemed fatal, and drastic action warranted, the family's physician agreed to lance the swellings with the help of another doctor. When the two cut with sharp metal into the sides of her swollen neck, "there was a copious discharge of yellow matter, & she became very much relieved. She could breathe much freer & with considerably more ease." The release of "copious" matter whose color indicated that it was unusual and harmful at first held out the hope of successful outcome to the frantic husband: "I then indeed had strong hopes that through those tumors the disease would exhaust itself & that her recovery would be the consequence." In the violent rising up of discharged material, the disease, localized around her lungs and throat, might have spent itself, depleting all its ability to harm. In the thick, yellow, serous pus that poured out from his wife's neck, Leonard Stephens saw the destructive potential of her long illness. Removing it might be to remove the disease's further capacity to wreck her body.

"But alas," concluded the mourning husband, "how vain are all our calculations." Weakened and still sick, Caty Stephens lived but a few more days before losing control of her neck muscles and her ability to breathe. Yet she died surrounded by her family, "without scarcely strugling at all." The medical interventions into her tumors had given her time to admonish and encourage her family and "shout . . . glory several different times."

A conviction that negative essences build up and strain for release fills the imaginative realm of popular literature of the era, as well as the day-to-day records of family life. In Harriet Beecher Stowe's antislavery novel *Uncle Tom's Cabin*, the slave dealer Haley explained why he refrains from beating female slaves who weep and act distraught when their children are sold away from them: "'It's natur,' says I, 'and if natur can't blow off one way, it will another.'" "Natur" might be temporarily constrained or directed, but would "blow off" in unwanted ways—like a slave's violence or suicidal despondency—unless more wholesome release was permitted. Washington Irving similarly commented in his *Tour Through the Prairies* that "A Frenchman's vivacity . . . if repressed in one way, will break out in another, and Tonish [his Creole assistant] now eased off his spleen by bestowing volleys of oaths and dry blows on the pack-horses." Like a bodily engorgement that could expel itself healthfully or, remaining in the body, lead to further pathological buildup, the emotions of Irving's caricatured companion normally came out as "vivacity"; when "repressed," they forced a venting good for his own body (lest his spleen be overengorged by negative emotions) but not so helpful to the packhorses.

Derangement and Proper Management

In the evocative language of the period, illness or strong emotion "deranged" the human system. Derangement was a powerful concept, applicable to the human body, to one's mental state, to the economy, and even, according to one frustrated correspondent, to the mails. Derangement was internal and invisible but was made manifest in observable symptoms. Feverish sweating, labored breath, or inflamed rashes were all clues to the state of the body's interior. "Boughton remained deranged & very restless," wrote John Geiger of a laborer in 1837; "Fever high, the urine small & sharp with signs of strangury, the bowels acted a little." Scrutinizing the body's external signs, Geiger sought insight into what would bring the "deranged" system back into ordered normality. Swollen gums in a teething infant, warned medical authorities, were not merely a local inflammation but the painful, angry symptom of a "disordered state of the system" that could "aggravate" a disease like cholera.

Health was the result of the regulation and moderation of the forces of the body's interior. Encouraging or drawing out fluid or other energies could maintain well-being. Starving, stimulating, heating, or cooling a sick person could change the internal imbalances creating the illness. Thus sassafras tea, recalled one former slave, was a good spring drink; it purified the blood at a time when it was sluggish and thick.

Heeding the evidence of the sick body, healers helped along what they perceived as the body's natural processes of illness. Therapies replicated the heat and sweat or the draining exhaustion of high fever, the surface irritations or rashes of pox, and the profuse and liquid bowel movements of intestinal ills. Rubbing the chest with a strong-smelling, heated concoction might lead congestion in the lungs to the skin and then out of the body. Blistering an extremity could "counterirritate" and draw out a fever. Smelling salts, camphor, or other stimulatives could pique a sluggish body into response. "Internally exhibited" medicines might force imbalanced humors out toward the body's surfaces, where they could be dealt with.

Because the body was a well-balanced whole, visible symptoms from one bodily region could indicate health or illness in another. John Geiger's 1835 assessment is typical of common understanding of health: "Mrs. Galatin's mouth futched with the mercury," he wrote, "& the chills abating & stools mending." Drawn tissue of the mouth could signify a diminishment of the forces wracking the body with chills and diarrhea. Moreover, overall health depended not on any organ but on the body as a whole.

Domestic healers acted powerfully and decisively in response to profound derangement, to redirect roiled bodily forces and force the body into "reaction" against disease. Medicines "broke" fevers and paroxysms, shattering their hold on the system. Nineteenth-century therapeutics relied heavily on treatments whose action was visible and unambiguously experienced. Mercury in particular produced dramatic effects, especially the profuse salivation and loosening teeth that the early modern world welcomed as salutary signs but that modern medicine would recognize as a sign of potentially lethal mercury poisoning. Mercury was often dispensed in the form of calomel (mercurous chloride), given by itself or as one ingredient in everpresent blue pills. Its action was immediate and unambiguous. When his young son Dick fell ill in 1857, John Brown wrote that "I gave him my old remedy, small doses of calomel and opium. It prostrated him greatly." The next day, satisfied, Brown concluded that "I am much relieved by the success of my medicine with Dick." The "prostration" produced by the calomel and opium combination in his young son also leveled his disease. Strong ailments demanded strong treatments; effective medicines had to be powerful agents within the human form.

Pain from a treatment was one sign of its potency. Of a shipmate recovering from scurvy in the late 1830s, the Harvard student turned sailor Richard Henry Dana wrote: "The strong earthy taste and smell of this extract of the raw potato at first produced a shuddering through his whole frame, and, after drinking it, an acute pain, which ran through all parts of his body; but knowing by this that it was taking strong hold, he persevered, drinking a spoonful every hour or so."

Just as raw abscesses and grossly swollen risings signaled important events within the body, the felt pain of one's own reaction to a healing regimen could be a sign that the medicine was taking the requisite "strong hold." Medicines felt to be effective were also recognized to be destructive. As the Mississippi Valley authority Timothy Flint observed of the "intermittents" so common to Missouri, both the "frequent returns" of these periodic, probably malarial fevers "and the course of medicine necessary to check them, soon break down the constitution."

Forceful or subtle, long-lasting or sudden, remedies were meant to match their diseases. "I dare not give strong medicine," fretted John Brown about his infant daughter Clara, sick with "flux," or diarrhea, "which in this disease is almost certain death." Doctors warned that emetics should be used until they worked to help the body expel harmful matter, but should not "operate unkindly." Medicines had to be finely calibrated to the ailment against which they were aimed. Each individual body also had a particular relation to its medicines. A newcomer to Arkansas, Cordelia Hambleton, wrote to family members in 1854 that one ill relative was still sick, but was improving somewhat, since "the medicine has a good effect which it has not had before." The effectiveness of medicine gave an indication of the strength and condition of the body that received and reacted to it.

Such tendencies were read not only as personal but also as national attributes. One German homeopath and travel guide author ascribed the common preference for dramatic therapies to Americans' sense of their own robustness. Nicholas Hesse explained in the late 1830s, "The western inhabitant does not want to accept homeopathic treatment, because he cannot comprehend how such little doses could cure him." Brash settlers needed big doses to operate in their bodies and to fight the powerful ills of their new country.

Nineteenth-century Americans lived in an intricate matrix of interacting flows and balances, many of which could be perceived only with difficulty but all of which were important to the preservation of well-being. Inhabiting a shifting, often uncertain physical body, living within a world of many and varied threats, each individual was forced to govern and manage his or her own health. Regularity in mental and physical habits was considered necessary to maintain a healthy system in balance. "My mode of life is now very regular in my meals, my sleep, my business hours and my mind is commonly on or near an equilibrium," wrote the self-satisfied John Brown in the summer of 1856, concluding, "I think cooly, act cooly and live thankfully." His behavior accorded with medical advice to keep regularity in life patterns like rest, nourishment, and labor. Steadiness of habit led to inner "equilibrium" as well as good business decisions. Regulating diet and drink (moderating or giving up alcohol, and eating no more than was necessary to satisfy hunger), maintaining habits of regularity and predictability, and modulating activity and location to adjust for the threats of the external world were the responsibility of each family and each person. Diligent habits and good morals were as important as pills and salves for those who hoped to preserve their health and well-being.

The steadfast attention and constant calibration demanded by the effort to remain well was summed up in what antebellum Americans termed "management." Reporting widespread sickness among nearby lowland slave laborers in Arkansas in 1836, Thomas A. Bennett ascribed it to "bad Management and want of Medical aid." Many white observers held that when overseers paid attention to slaves' clothing, diet, hours of sleep and rising, and type of work, even diseases endemic to lowlands could be avoided. Better-managed plantations, with better-managed bodies in them, would have a healthier workforce. Illness in oneself or in one's slaves signaled a lack of control.

The need for management was just as intense within the individual body. John Brown commented on his wife Clara Brown's sickness in 1860 that "The use of a preparation of iron, and a little stimulus seems to have measurably given her command of the action of the liver." An individual in "command" of her own internal organs kept in harmony the delicate balances of influence, intake, and excretion that kept them functioning without complaint. Let the reins slip, and the wild body could veer out of control toward harmful and difficult-to-remedy extremes.

Change

In this carefully registered world, moments of sudden change were times of intensity. Shifts within the body, whether of heat or of intense emotion, could create or intensify illness. New habits and new situations were alike challenging and suspect. Antebellum Americans felt the jealously guarded balance of their bodies to be intimately tied to the natural world. Steady and predictable transitions—whether shifting winds, the aging of the human body, the agricultural cycle of planting and harvest, or the cyclic disappearance and reappearance of the moon—formed the backdrop to nineteenth-century life. Unaccustomed or extreme changes, however, could be deeply threatening. Autumn storms, spring seeding, and late-summer illness were anticipated. Farm households could expect periodic alternations of strain and ease, relaxation and difficult marshaling of resources. Within these patterns, the irregular visitation of seasonally related crisis was most disruptive, whether it was from summer swarms of locust, devastating spring tornadoes, or the epidemic cholera that came upriver with steamships during summer's longest days.

People eyed unusual seasonal shift with well-grounded apprehension. Dr. William J. Goulding's 1840 "Medical Topography of Central Arkansas" attributed the prior year's heavy toll from fevers to "winds coming upon us during the hot season from an unusual or unfavorable quarter—and also . . . the fact that the great annual or June rise in the Arkansas river occurred some four weeks later in the season than is common, and the overflow in central Arkansas was unusually great." Flooding water and water acting in unusual ways were both cause for concern. Winds were to be expected.

Winds from "an unusual . . . quarter," though, could sicken and harm. Goulding's emphasis upon the atypical qualities of winds and waters reveals an abiding suspicion of any but the most regular change in the environments of central Arkansas.

Temperature variation was an important source of extremely harmful change. Nicholas Hesse charged the climate itself with being fickle and therefore adverse. Temperature changes from winter to spring were "too striking . . . to be wholesome." Differences between daytime and nighttime temperatures made July and August dangerous, without "care taken to defend the system against these changes," observed the south Arkansas physician A. W. Webb in 1844. Webb's language of a "system" zealously "defended" against impinging "changes" is typical of the concerns and the efforts of people of his time.

The body as a whole, its interlacing organ systems and tissues seen not individually but as a integrated system, was vulnerable to outer changes, as to the temperature of the skin's surface, which brought about alterations in its internal forces. The body had therefore to be guarded and protected by counterbalancing measures. On the simplest level, cool drinks—taken in moderation, and not *too* cold—could work to balance the increased temperature of a hot day, allowing an individual to remain healthy and productive during a sweltering afternoon. In more complex moves, rest, poultices, stimulants like spices or alcohol, or soothing measures like warm baths could quiet, fill, deplete, or gently excite systems whose flow was disrupted or pulled out of balance by transitions like those of dusk or dawn.

"Changes in the weather" were regarded by common consensus as by medical authorities to be the cause of a host of ills. This frequently used phrase encompassed day-to-day and seasonal changes, which all registered specific effects within the human body. As Dr. Lillybridge worried in March of 1837, "The weather the last two days has been very warm & dry, and the transition from the late cold and humid atmosphere has produced considerable appearance of Bilious affections among the Emigrants." Other people found themselves with colds that same spring after a series of "frequent & sudden changes" to which their bodies were hard-pressed to adapt. Anyone exposed to rapidly changing weather conditions—as all immigrants to Missouri and Arkansas were—had either to be blessed with a powerful capacity to endure or to bolster internal systems accordingly.

Families had to protect themselves against changes in the natural world through careful management of dress, exertion, food, and rest. "I am doing little else but guarding my family in their diet and movements," wrote John Brown during an early summer's period of sickness in 1857. Small miscalculations had severe consequences. Fretting over his wife's worsening illness in May of 1860, Brown noted in his diary that "Clara had another slight attack from an imprudent change of a garment." Putting on the wrong shift, or putting aside a heavy coat too soon, could expose a person's body to the disorganization of the outside world.

The turning of seasons brought about pervasive change within the human system as within natural terrain. Different balances of temperature and light, the lengthening or shortening of days, the various kinds of winds, cloud formations, precipitation, humidity levels, weather patterns, and the general feel of the air and climate associated with successive times of year worked corresponding changes within the human body. Qualities of light were like qualities of nutrition: types of air were felt in much the same way as types of medicines. The lightness and energy experienced by even jaded modern observers during bright days of early spring were registered much more strongly by nineteenth-century Americans keenly aware of the constantly shifting matrices of air, climate, weather, soil, water, elevation, and latitude within which they moved.

Springtime brought vigor. "I have not been in good health this winter," the humorist and Arkansas booster C. F. M. Noland wrote his father in March of 1841, "but as summer approaches, I improve." Yet spring was an unpredictable, changeable season, one that brought mounting potential to both field and person. Physicians warned of the "rousing of sensibilities which had been, in a measure, dormant through the winter"; as chill torpor gave way to restless breezes, bodies were unusually receptive, senses heightened, and responses primed for stimulation. Fresh colors from buds and shoots, new textures on trunks and hides, coatings of pollen and sap, tantalizing smells of winds from further-off places and unknown environments, even the animal odors of abandoned winter nests and the scat of young deer or fresh broods—all evoked responses in human beings as in the wild things and domestic animals around them. People experienced a rebirth like that of their environment; their juices flowed like sap.

Heightened sensation and aroused potential, warned medical professionals, meant that skin eruptions, "[g]out and apoplexy, excessive mental excitement, and madness itself," various manifestations of surfeit and excess within the human form, "not unfrequently mark the vernal equinox." The richness of sensation and potential brought about by the transition from winter's lull to spring's excitement had to be judiciously managed, leaping impulses governed by careful limit.

Seasons quickened or dulled the pulse; bleeding had therefore to be adjusted to the time of year. Generous "bleeds" during the warmer months reflected the body's increased energy and potentially congesting fluid, whereas winter "letting" would be more conservative. The combination of processes that constituted seasonal shift were experienced in the body's own adjustment. Those committed to heroic therapies would seek a "spring bleed," a bloody version of the spring housecleaning that marked the transition to a new season.

Even when transitions were beneficial, the process of change within climate, weather, or season was regarded as intrinsically dangerous. John Brown worried in February 1856 that his family had "all suffered from colds since the weather became more mild." The weather had changed, suddenly and unusually, and was therefore harmful, even though "mild" temperatures were generally regarded as healing and healthful. John Brown's worry continued into the following week. Fretting that his family had been ill "since the cold weather relaxed," Brown further reflected in his diary that "So long as the constant freeze continued the system seemed to be braced up, but as the natural elements relaxes the human frame seemed to take in cold and disease as it was suddenly let down and most generally settled on the lungs of my family producing cough."

Like a strong worker carrying a heavy weight, the body could adjust to accustomed loads. Sudden "relaxation" in the weather, however, left the body struggling against an adversary no longer there. "Suddenly let down" like someone pushing hard against a door abruptly opened, the individual's system was left vulnerable to "cold and disease," which entered the body and "settled" on specific organs.

Fear of the irregular, unpredictable changes of "variable climates" reveals connections between the geography of health and the economic and familial concerns of people who were closely dependent upon agricultural labor. Predictability was valued and safe; surprising change was threatening. Early frosts, sudden storms, or unseasonable weather—what Stephen Hempstead in 1814 crustily termed "a cold backwards Spring"—could all be devastating to a successful crop cycle. Fields as well as people suffered from changeable weather. As John Walker, a St. Louis farmer, complained in 1834, a recent "cold, hot wet & dry" spring, one incorporating changeable and contradictory elements, was "a very unpromising one for Crop[p]ing." Just as such unusual seasons imperiled a family's financial future and livelihood, they could threaten a family's physical state. The well-being of workers and field were similarly bound up in one another. Healthy laborers could care for their crops and animals with vigor, whereas those shaking with the chills and fever of "ague" needed care themselves. A hearty harvest meant strong field hands, while a paltry yield left the household less defended against the next winter's blows.

Even in their regular progression, seasons bore threats to health. Recurrent bouts of illness made the character of seasons themselves a subject of discussion. "The last fall and winter has been very Sickly in this State," wrote Kirkbride Potts from Arkansas to his New Jersey sister in April 1852, "and a great many persons have died." Whether the season was "sickly" or "healthy" was a meaningful and important question. The presence or absence of prevailing illness formed the basis for most such evaluations. Aaron S. Fry, a Missouri farmer, noted with pleasure in his journal in November of 1835: "No Epidemick diseases this fall a very Healthy fall."

An 1840 letter from an Arkansas Post resident, B. W. Lee, reflected the dual vision in which the absence of disease was such a benefit that it colored more general appraisals. "We have suffered here a little with cold and wet," he wrote a St. Louis friend, "but it has been a remarkable healthy winter, a great number of cattle have died but I believe principally from poverty, the winter range here abouts is pretty well exhausted." Cattle might die of "poverty," and "cold and wet"—used not as adjectives but pervasive forces in themselves—could make residents of a region "suffer," but when disease was absent and mortality was low, the season was "healthy" and inhabitants thankful.

Residents of early Arkansas and Missouri in particular discussed, expected, and lamented the "sickly season" which generally set in during the long, sweltry, late-summer days of August and September. Its duration or intensity could vary, but the spread and prevalence of a set of ailments headed by "ague and chills" was as much a part of community life as the civic speeches of Independence Day or the ubiquitous planting of early spring. Epidemics of typhoid, whooping cough, scarlet fever or yellow fever, or the fast-moving and distinctive cholera could also grimly mark the sickly seasons of some years. Yet even without those ills the endemic diseases of a region seemed to its inhabitants to advance as long summer wore down bodily endurance, holding communities in their grasp until checked by the crisp nights and sparkling frosts of fall. The primary and potent marker of seasonal shift was the "ager" or "ague" that greeted new inhabitants to the Mississippi Valley and returned regularly to visit their households.

Chills and Fevers

The "chills and fever" that was the primary illness of humid western country was commonly called ague. (The term, which dates back to the fourteenth century, comes from the same root as "acute." Historians of medicine tend to pronounce it "aaag," but people of the time seem to have called it "a-gew" or "ager.") Ague was characterized by alternating seizures of very low and very high body temperature and repeated and violent "shakes." On muggy late-August evenings, those wracked with this ailment would huddle around roaring fires in an attempt to drive away the piercing chill no outer heat could combat. "Ague" referred not only to the bouts of chills but also to the feelings of dissipation and weakness, the gaunt carriage and sallowness of skin, and the mental and emotional exhaustion that accompanied this late-summer illness.

Modern scholars have generally regarded classic chills and fever as malaria. Other fevers—dengue, yellow fever, typhoid fever—likely were also present, and retrospective diagnoses are necessarily hazy. Yet much of how people described ague fits what we now understand about the impact and transmission of malaria. Malaria is caused by a microscopic parasite, a protozoan of the genus *Plasmodium*, that spends part of its life cycle in a female anopheles mosquito and part in a vertebrate host. Injected as the mosquito feeds on the vertebrate, the plasmodium matures, spreads, and then is taken up again by another mosquito to infect other host animals. In humans, four different species of *Plasmodium* cause four different types of malaria, but only two were substantial problems for residents of North America. Vivax malaria, the more geographically widespread, is less fatal, killing only about 5 percent of its victims, whereas falciparum malaria, which struck only the regions of North America below about the 35th Parallel, can kill as many as 20 to 40 percent of its victims. Malaria in all its forms is a problem not simply in the most dramatic chills and fever of new infection, which can be fatal, but also as a chronic illness. Infected people can reach an accommodation with the plasmodium such that they can go about their daily lives despite its continued residence in their bodies, but they are liable to be anemic, weak, and more vulnerable than noninfected people when coping with additional physical stresses like pregnancy, nursing, and illness.

There are important differences in how African-American and Euro-American newcomers' bodies resisted this disease. Most Americans descended from Africans were immune to *P. vivax*, and many possessed (and possess, in the present day) hemoglobin and other traits that made it significantly harder for *P. falciparum* to infect their bodies. Black Americans certainly contracted malaria, but less often than their white contemporaries, and they died of it less frequently. Slave owners saw in this difference, which was an evolutionary adaptation to a disease native to West Africa, a powerful argument for the naturalness and appropriateness of black labor in the southern regions where "ague" was endemic.

Modern epidemiology would relate at least some of the nineteenth-century "sickly season" to the usual outbreaks of falciparum malaria. For reasons we still do not fully understand, it tends to hit in the late summer and fall, whereas vivax malaria tends to be a disease of the planting season and early summer. Yellowness of skin—the sallowness cited by many nineteenth-century travelers to swampy and lowland regions—can be produced by the jaundice of malaria. The regular alternation between spells of fever and of chills, the most striking characteristic of ague, fits modern understanding of malaria. What antebellum people experienced as three-day cycles of shivering and fever (which they called "tertian fever"), present-day researchers would explain as the cycle in which the malaria parasite infects, reproduces within, and then explodes human red blood cells. Such predictability brought a certain grim familiarity with the disease. One bit of 1845 regional humor held:

> How would you like to live in a place where a man's salutation to his neighbor of "good morning, sir," is immediately followed by the query, "is this your day for shaking, sir?," and "no, bless the Lord! I don't shake till to-morrow," or the day after, as the case may be, it being periodical in its attacks, amusing some every day at a certain hour, others on every second or third day.

"Amusing" antebellum households, especially the white people in them, the ague was an ever-present burden.

The geographical specificity of malaria also buttressed nineteenth-century ideas about health and place. Anopheles mosquitoes do not fly far from the pools of stagnant water in which they come to larval life. Working or living near sources of still, algae-filled water thus makes someone much more likely to contract malaria. Nineteenth-century distrust of low, wet bottomlands bore out the universal experience that disease was associated in powerful ways with moist, swampy places.

We cannot simply reduce the geography of health to any one illness, however widespread, nor is it a sufficient explanation of early modern perceptions simply to cite twenty-first-century science. Older ideas were based upon a complex set of interrelationships that rarely depended on any single factor, and to understand them fully we have to approach them in their totality. At the same time, because of the prevalence of malaria in the Mississippi Valley, its characteristics—as we now understand them—can help make a bridge for us moderns to some of what might otherwise be puzzling notions.

Common names for ague reflected its association with new settlement and with wetland areas: "Arkansaw chills," "swamp fever," and simply "seasoning." To the Cherokees, it was "the great chill," reflecting its primacy in their experience of health. Swollen spleens produced "ager cakes" or "fever cakes," hard tumescent abdominal swellings carried around by many of the region's residents. "The ague" or "an ager" pursued early Americans like a feared frontier beast, its ferocity that of a bear or "painter" (panther), its malevolence and persistence almost willful.

The alternation of chills and fever typified the experience of ague. It was often known as "intermittent fever" for the way in which it would suddenly grip—and then just as suddenly release—a sufferer. Yet both chills and fevers were categories of ailment that might have many variations. "Chills" could be a part of many diseases; there were diverse kinds of fevers, not all of which were based primarily around temperature. Being "chilly" was itself a description for the state of the whole body.

Fever indicated an excess of excitement or energy, a superfluity of intensity, which could be the product of emotional or physical problems or could produce them. Fever could be triggered by other ailments: A. W. Webb observed of southern Arkansas that "The predisposition to bilious River[?] fever is so strong that all other diseases prove exciting causes." A "fever" produced excitement within the body, followed by an exhausted debility. It could have both generalized and highly specific effects. Silas Bent, writing from St. Louis in 1812, chronicled a family sickness in which "my wife has recovered from a fever but with the loss of her right hand which has perished." Ague usually afflicted the whole body, but occasionally observers wrote of having, for instance, "ague in my head," or used the more specified language of "*an* ague and fever," which suggests a potential difference between types of agues or fevers.

Different kinds of fevers—"inflammatory," "intermittent," "bilious"—could combine, as Webb observed, especially when "kept up by local inflammation." Fever was seen in some accounts almost as feeding on the bodies of sufferers: the more body, the more fever. Thus Justus Post complained to his Vermont brother in 1820 of the fevers he had experienced from the beginning of his late June harvest until mid-September, adding that "were not my habits temperate and my body always thin in flesh, I should have had a real trimmer, but my fever substance is light."

Little could be done against the ague. Only quinine reliably reduced its symptoms. Known as Jesuit or Peruvian bark, or cinchona, for the South American tree from which it was derived, quinine had been recognized as a potent remedy against ague's vertiginous oscillations of chills and high fever since the seventeenth century, and it was available in the United States beginning in the 1820s, both in coarse form and as premade pills. Especially in the western territories, many people reached for "Sappington's Anti-Fever Pills," a widely used patent remedy. These were produced by John Sappington, an enterprising physician from rural Missouri who quickly realized the commercial potential of this remedy for the agueish settlers of the borderlands. In the 20 years after he began production of his quinine pills in the early 1820s, Sappington sold nearly 6 million boxes containing 24 pills apiece. Thus despite its bitter taste and side effects of ringing ears and queasiness, quinine formed an often-used staple of heroic therapies against fever and chills. Yet "bark" was sometimes hard to obtain and was often expensive, and premanufactured pills could be diluted or misleadingly labeled. Quinine was seen as one strong remedy among many, and as a probable, but never certain, cure.

A "fever-doctor," as one immigrant, Henry Merrell, called the successful medical practitioner, could prescribe calomel or other purgatives like rhubarb or castor oil to "break" the fever and disrupt the hold the disease had on the system. In addition to these, healers could also employ quinine to combat the ailment itself, and they made use of other therapies as preventive measures: a "shower bath of cold water," gulps of cod-liver oil, cups of steaming coffee, or, better yet, tumblers of coarse whiskey. Despite these ministrations, however, recurrent fevers sapped energy and made bodies weak and faces haggard throughout bottomland regions.

Ague and other seasonal illnesses were central to antebellum life. Theodore Pease Russell emigrated to Missouri from Connecticut with his family as a child in the early nineteenth century. Sickly as a child in New England (his parents dressed him in skirts long after other boys were wearing short trousers, and kept him about the kitchen, fearing to let him play outdoors), he grew to robust and healthy manhood tramping the ridges and valleys of the Arcadia Valley in the mineral-rich mining region about 80 miles south of St. Louis. His family did well, and his many siblings settled nearby, the brothers going back East to bring home wives, as did Russell himself. As an old man, Russell reflected back on a youth spent before the pressures of overflowing immigration and the rupture of the Civil War had irrevocably changed the safe, bounded world of hunt and family he had known. His reminiscences, written for a newspaper children's column, dwell lovingly on the details of life in an earlier and seemingly more abundant time. About sickness, however, he was not so romantic. The stamp of illness marked Russell's memory of the season of early fall. His description of ague reveals the ways the body's experience mirrored the year's turning.

September, he wrote, was the "most disagreeable" of "all the months of the year." Its qualities were both unpredictable and insufferable:

> The dead heat of the sun: the cold breath of the air, makes one feel chilled outside while burning up inside and such a feeling of lassitude, no account feeling. Days of cold winds and nights with thick blanket to cover and to lie and shiver. Nights of hot sultry air, not a breath of fresh air, a feeling of unrest. No sleep until near morning, and oh, so sickening and woe begone a feeling. A feeling of "it's just as well to die and be done with it."

September was the month of changeability, of sultriness next to chill breezes, of stuffy rooms alternating with "cold breath of the air." Disquieted and discomfited, restless sleepers felt the creeping in of the season's ague. Within the terrain of their bodies, nineteenth-century people felt sensations that mapped seasonal shift and weather changes. Their inner geography changed along with the outer world.

For Russell, a bout of illness in September of 1840 was particularly memorable in its emotional and physical toll: "I had had the shakes until I was shook pretty near out of myself. I got so I did not have strength to shake any longer: just lay and shivered outside and was burning up inside. O so thirsty! I felt as if I could lie and let a good sized spring branch run right into my mouth." The violent shaking of an attack of ague wore out its sufferers, and its alternating fits of high fever and deep cold forced them through tumultuous and unsettled seasonal shift within their own frames. The desperate thirst and weariness of the September illness spoke of systems out of balance, needs disproportionate, bodily hungers grown improbably ferocious. The whole body mirrored the season's lack of reason, and in its wild shifts and improbable twinnings—victims "shivered outside and . . . burn[ed] up inside"—tried desperately to respond to the wild variations between heat and cold of a transition time at its worst.

The yearly nature of the worst bouts of fevers and illness inscribed themselves into the patterns of personal life and community. As one physician commented of St. Charles, Missouri, in the 1830s, "the inhabitants expect a sickly season every year, as much as seed-time and harvest." The routines of sickness were as much a part of daily life as the yearly rhythms of cultivation. Ague and other ailments defined and limited activity during the sickly season. Hiram Whittington, a Yankee emigrant and sometime invalid, was characteristically debonair: "It is fashionable to be sick in the summer in this town," he wrote his Massachusetts brother about his adopted city of Little Rock, "and most of the people engage a physician by the year. I expect to have the fever, if nothing worse." Families put off travel or emigration during the "warm and sickly season," and wealthy planters engaged in a seasonal migration back East, to the comparatively robust climates of Kentucky, or to other regions of the upland south.

The expected and dreaded sickly season had a similar effect on the patterns of civic life. One German traveler observed in October 1838 that St. Louis was much livelier than when he had last visited, when the diseases of the hottest time of the year had shuttered shops and restricted public activity. During colder months, street life was more active and "the most carefree enjoyment of life had taken the place of deathly anxiety and precaution."

Surrounding "country" was not external to American and European newcomers to the forests, prairies, and swamplands of early Missouri and Arkansas. Every alteration of tempo in weather and season pulled along the human body in an often unwilling dance. Documents of the antebellum nineteenth century reveal pervasive concern for the kinds of spaces through which people moved. Elements of the world of nature were categorized, named, and described, their probable influences upon human health surmised and argued over. Those areas of argument and attention, those observations, quibbles, and measurements, indicate how Americans of another era created their own environments of perception and belief, even as they felt their environments inescapably shaping them.

PLACES

Chapter III

SLOGGING THROUGH THICK VEGETATION and over rocky outcroppings, making their way through dense tallgrass and deep morasses, newcomers to the nineteenth-century American West struggled to make sense of territory strange to them. The resources and possibilities of early Arkansas and Missouri were suggested by trappers' reports and re-told Indian stories, by explorers' and missionaries' tales and by the emigrants' guides and family correspondence that beguiled and beckoned newcomers. Yet even as the "Far West" became populous and "settled," much remained unknown: How fertile would this acreage prove? How did that stream taste? When would the nearby river flood? In ways both collective and personal, incoming migrants attempted to map the lived realities of terrain, much as they might probe, feel, listen to, and record the experiences of the body of an ailing family member.

Interacting with their terrain, those working fields, gathering plants, and hunting game came to know a place in specific and interconnected ways. Farm families saw how a wetland changed with heavy rains, how hillside vegetation shifted with seasons, how the animals, birds, and parasites of a region made their nests or bore their young. Slaves came to intimate knowledge of a place through labor in sloughs and fields. Almost every resident of antebellum Arkansas and Missouri, excepting only the most urban St. Louisans and the most privileged planter offspring, had to learn to judge the many complex signs of what one medical advice guide termed "the nature of soil, water, and situation."

Their environmental imagination is foreign to our twenty-first-century world. In places where many of us might describe a beautiful vista or a steep climb, or where those with more specialized training might speak of mineral

85

types or underlying soil strata, bird and animal habitat or tangled forbs, nineteenth-century people experienced healthy breezes, favorable or threatening water sources, sickly emanations, and a whole network of influences likely to be either "salubrious" or "unhealthy." The many and varied environmental factors in personal health made the character of one's surroundings a crucial and immediate question to the farm families and ambitious entrepreneurs seeking to establish themselves in the new airs, waters, and places of the western borderlands.

"Place"

Nineteenth-century Americans were preoccupied with trying to find surroundings that would keep them healthy, and avoid places that would make them sick. Letters, newspapers, stories, and common conversation were filled with nonstop environmental appraisal. These worries were widely shared because people of that era regarded environment as a crucial and yet extremely flexible concept.

"Place" could stretch—as in Daniel Drake's midcentury treatise on the people and diseases of the "Interior Valley of North America"—to encompass the hundreds of square miles of the Mississippi Valley. Reports could meaningfully be made of "the West," "Missouri," or "the Arkansas River territory." To newcomers concerned about where to settle themselves and locate houses, fields, outbuildings, and mills, the sites of interest could also be limited to one creek over another, a location on a hillside instead of the top of the hill or the bottomlands beneath. The geography of health formed so broad and so powerful a framework that statements about huge swaths of territory and queries about a half-section alike constituted valuable knowledge.

Knowledge about place was many-layered, composed of observations from the broadly general to the keenly specific. The area of questioning might narrow, but the same types of questions and conclusions remained valid. In 1805 Major James Bruff reported on the resources and health of the Mississippi River area above the mouth of the Missouri:

> from 1. to 3. miles back for about 30. miles when the river washes the hills the interval or prairie has in places a narrow border of woodland along the River; but it is esteemed unhealthy . . . about 20 miles above this bay, is the Indian Boundary or river Jofflone, when the Country rises &cc—at and about that point there are Several considerable Streams, boat harbors, good water, plenty of timber, pleasant and healthy situations.

Bruff's language reflected hesitancy: he was not sure whether to call a large swath of grassland "interval" or "prairie," any more than other newcomers were certain whether to hunt in the tall grasses, burn them, or plow them under. Observations on "a narrow border of woodland"—a thin, defined portion within the immense blank contours of newcomers' geographic understanding of North America—served to fill in, with delicate detail, a territory yet unknown. Healthfulness, political frontiers (especially the "Indian Boundary"), and potential resources for navigation and settlement were all part of what bureaucrats in Washington tried to piece together about their newly acquired Louisiana Territory.

Boosters forced to acknowledge areas of unhealthfulness urged the wider public toward greater sophistication in understanding "new" regions. "The shores of the Arkansas river as far up as Little Rock are decidedly unhealthy," admitted one 1833 piece of regional promotion in the *Saturday Evening Post*, yet the authors were unwilling to lose advantage so quickly. "[B]ut this fact," the article urged, "should by no means stamp the character of this vast district." Little Rock itself was "healthy and pleasant," and its "celebrated warm springs," mineral resources, and fertile soils recommended the region to prospective emigrants. Few observers were willing to blithely endorse the swampy bottomlands encompassed within Missouri and Arkansas, but few were willing to cede too much to ague and fever.

Insistence on variation in health environments therefore marked many of the detailed reports of the region. "It is a very absurd idea," wrote Timothy Flint in 1832, "that a country of the extensiveness of [Arkansas Territory] should be all alike sickly. In this territory there are many positions, but a few miles apart, one of which may be as sickly as the shores of Surinam, and the other as healthy as any country in America."

Flint's comment knots together several strands in the geography of health. The hearty tone of his prose was typical of much of the reporting about the health and also the agricultural and social environments of the West. His enthusiasm was also shared. Except for some disillusioned (often European) travelers who wanted no part of miasmatic countryside and hog meat three meals a day, many travelers to the West quickly began to encourage and recruit others to join them.

Flint's comparison to "the shores of Surinam" was also telling. The early nineteenth century witnessed an upsurge of interest in exotic lands. Adventurers' reports from foreign places filled scientific and popular journals in the United States and western Europe, and whetted hunger for knowledge about the strangeness and danger of unknown locales. Linking the West with travels to the tropical coast of South America was not merely Timothy Flint's conceit, but a part of broadly popular imagining. Like the fearless European and American geographers who scaled peaks, braved mountains, and haggled with baffling tribes in their attempts to further scientific knowledge, Americans of the early republic participating in the move west saw themselves as players in their era's apprehension of fascinating and untried regions. Breaking the bounds of their own tenuous nation—moving outside of "any country in America" to territories whose political status continued to be in flux—western immigrants saw themselves as one flank of a general movement into the wild and unknown.

As travelers came into new places, they found in specific aspects of environments the basis of good or poor health. Their reports made up a finely spun and sometimes contradictory net of assertions and belief, one diverse in specifics but held together by the fundamental notion that human well-being was determined by a dynamic, interactive relationship with a complex and changing world.

Telling the "Health of the Country"

Specific aspects of place were associated in popular understanding with healthfulness or sickliness. Elevation in particular was regarded as crucial to a region's impact on its inhabitants. Higher elevations were generally held to be more salubrious than lower ones. In 1814, for example, one newcomer remarked to the surveyor for Missouri that the western part of St. Genevieve County was "remarkably high and healthy." Such praise was commonplace. Settlements with a "high, healthful position," situated near but above rivers, were considered ideal. In contrast, low elevation was closely related to ill health: as the governor of Arkansas complained to the secretary of war in 1820, land given to displaced Choctaws was "too low & sickly, they cannot stop there."

The geography of health thus created a racial topography. Most slave owners situated their own families as much as possible on higher ground, while sending their enslaved workforce to carve fields out of insalubrious bottoms (only a few slave owners kept their slaves from working in low-lying river areas). White Americans mapped differences in class and race onto elevation in a telling striation of disease potential.

Such choices had important consequences. As one new Arkansan explained in 1836, "Some Plantations in the bottoms have from 15 to 25 Negroes sick at once, while others on the Hills with as many Negroes ar perfectly healthy." The miasmatic influences of low-lying territory could sicken plow-hands and cripple a plantation's output. Fevers associated with bottomlands affected not only individual health but the economic endeavors central to American emigration. Low areas in streams' floodplains were, however, easy to plow and often extremely good for crops. Mortal disease and fertile soil both came of such terrain; prospective settlers did their best to be prepared for both.

Elevation was closely related to the wetness and moisture of an environment. Frequent references to "low, marshy grounds" reveal the perceptual links between low land and land overrun by water, as indeed much low-lying territory was. Yet simply moving uphill from soggy bottomlands was not enough to ensure good health. "It is not so generally known to the public," mused the southern Arkansas physician A. W. Webb in his medical notebook in 1844, "that elevated situations in the vicinity of marshes or land subject to inundation are not always an effectual security against disease." Multiple environmental factors interacted with one another; proximity to dangerous areas could make even otherwise healthy sites dangerous.

Comments like Webb's underscore that environmental concern was never related to only one aspect of the surrounding world. Elevation was but one aspect of environs lived and experienced in their totality. In 1833, Captain John Stuart reported that Fort Smith in western Arkansas Territory, on the border with Indian Territory, was unhealthy, since

> the point itself is about Fifty feet above the level of the river at low water and it is nearly . . . surrounded by bottom or Swampy land . . . and that portion of the land considered highlands is almost as unhealthy as the low lands, from the circumstance of its being flat . . . land, and a great portion of it is in small basins or Pools in which the rain water stands continually from the commencement of the rainy season in the fall, until it is evaporated by the sun in the Months of July, August, and September.

Flat land on which water could pool and stagnate was "almost as unhealthy" as low-lying land. Proximity to river bottoms and "Swampy land" overrun with seasonal floods compromised the otherwise beneficial effects of elevation. Stuart's complaints, however, did him little good: he died in 1839 in the Cherokee Nation, not far from the site which he found so insalubrious, "after an illness of five weeks."

Waters were often regarded as having power to overcome healthier influences. The influential Ohio physician Daniel Drake reported in 1850 of the Jefferson Barracks, a few miles from St. Louis, that they were meant as "a

healthy asylum for troops broken down by service in the hotter climates."
Unfortunately for the broken-down troops, Jefferson Barracks' location was
compromised by "the contiguity of the American Bottom [a notoriously
swampy lowland] on the opposite side of the river." To evaluate the healthfulness of a site was thus to balance numerous factors against one another.
Swamplands like the American Bottom held particular potency—the noxious
influences of a boggy morass could more than counteract the tonic effect of
a high situation or a regular, fresh breeze—but no one factor, however powerful, ever overrode the need to evaluate the environment as a whole.

Change was perilous. As one western medical journal observed in 1854,
during the spring season, "great changes of temperature, and in the direction and force of the winds . . . are attended by corresponding mutations in
the activity of the functions of the living body." Variation and sudden transformation within the natural world called forth alteration within the human
form. The body experienced the world around it in profound ways, "living"
a fate as much environmental as individual.

Distrusting sudden transitions, many new westerners—lonely or homesick even in their ambition—named the familiar as healthful. In 1828, the
Yankee emigrant Hiram Abiff Whittington yearned, like many of his fellow
newcomers, for the ocean he had left behind. "If I could only smell the seas
once more," he wrote his brother plaintively, "I have no doubt that I should
be a different kind of fellow in a short time." Failing in that, he instead
moved to the region's hot springs.

Farmers, merchants, and even roving scientists were all subject to the lure
of the familiar. The English geologist George Featherstonhaugh was relieved to reach the prairies after trekking through the Ozarks in the early
1830s, a journey he undertook for the U.S. Congress. He remarked that "It
was with sincere pleasure I found myself upon geological grounds, with
which I was well acquainted." Emigrants commonly moved to regions
whose topography reminded them of home: settlers from the upland South
were said to follow the Boones to the Boon's Lick region of Missouri not
only because of the fame of the pioneer family, but also because the area resembled Kentucky.

Familiarity was intertwined with "wholesomeness." George Engelmann,
a German emigrant who was a noted physician and naturalist, in 1837 described the plight of a family in southeastern Missouri:

> The previous nights we stayed with a very poor family from South Carolina.
> Here among the hills they had been stricken by the fever. They complained

much about the cold and unhealthful country, and also wanted to go on to Texas. These people had picked out land that was overgrown with pine trees, since they had been accustomed to that kind from their youth, and since they believed it was most wholesome to live in such an environment.

Suspicion of change and desire for the accustomed had resonance within the understanding of health. Such feelings could justify and even determine important settlement choices. Implicit in such accounts is an ascription of salubrity to the prior or home environment. This nostalgia reveals both the relational, comparative nature of evaluations of healthfulness and the often severe emotional consequences of westward migration. A widely shared geography of health gave voice to migrants' yearning for home and validated their visceral sense that transcontinental migration was threatening in profound and pervasive ways.

Particular aspects of places could hold disease-specific tendencies. These properties of environs were not necessarily well understood, but were given wide credence. John Brown puzzled over the environmental causes of disease in a diary entry for May of 1854:

> There seems to have been some peculiarity in the state of the atmosphere this whole winter and spring to have kept up colds, of a peculiar kind, mostly have a tendency to muscular effects, pain in the neck, enlargement of the glands sometimes sorethroat and shifting from the head to the lungs and from the lungs to the head, etc.

Such conviction harked back to earlier investigations into relationships between environments and human well-being, especially the research into atmospheric "epidemic constitution" of the seventeenth-century English physician Thomas Sydenham. Sydenham correlated particular kinds of weather and outbreaks of disease, applying refined diagnostic and quantitative methods to widely shared environmental intuition. His research—part of the energetic investigation we often call the scientific revolution—galvanized inquiry into medical environmentalism. In John Brown's diary musings, we can see these scientific insights played out in South Arkansas cotton fields. Specific kinds of "atmosphere" placed certain parts of the body most at risk. With keen precision, if not a scientist's vocabulary, Brown recorded his observations that the state of the surrounding world mapped onto the human form, its changes and influences writing a topography alternately of pain and debility or strength and wellness.

Environmental influences also affected the natural history of disease types. Under the logic of the geography of health, terrain could exacerbate tendencies of a disease, bringing out certain manifestations more strongly or suppressing others. What one physician termed "locality" was, he felt, critical in causing different forms of fevers in one county of Illinois. In 1846, Dr. James Maury observed, "the typhoid modification prevail[ed] in the eastern part of the county, *the most highly malarious*, whilst the bilious, remittent, and intermittent forms prevailed, in the southern and middle portions, *the least malarious*." Certain sections of the country were not simply "unhealthy," they were "*malarious*," and that character of locale meant that while fevers were common throughout the county, people in unhealthy regions experienced very different types.

Elements of natural terrain had histories, just as did the lived human form, and were described in ways that echoed the processes of the human body. Healthy environments also evinced humoral balance. The author of one American medical tract aimed at a popular audience observed that "a moderately warm and moist atmosphere of uniform temperature is the one most appropriate to those suffering from disease of the lungs." Slightly "warm" and slightly "moist" had been considered the ideal state of the human form since antiquity. Insofar as an environment possessed those qualities, it could help bring back into balance bodies racked with pulmonary ailments.

Describing the changing balances of the surrounding world was much like describing the body's journey through illness. John Geiger wrote of a severe illness suffered by his 23-year-old son in 1837:

> at ten o clock in the Morning the Patient Complained of Chylly and Stiff feeling which Continued until Near Night with Puls Rather Low but Quicker than in health then the Puls Increased with Considerable heat and Remained the Most of the night. In the Morning the Patient Able to Go about with Tollerable Comfort & ate some Breakfast at 6 o clock.

The progress and prospects of this young man were only to be understood in a narrative of illness that detailed its every course, its changing intensities, sensations, and myriad symptoms. Fevers would rise and fall, and certain ills might tend to excite or subdue the body at characteristic times of day. In the same way that those nursing the sick might scrutinize this natural history of illness, they would also look across the fields they worked—theirs or their owners'—and estimate from the patterns of winds, the smell of the air, and the level of nearby streams the course of the environment in which they would labor that day. People brought to the observation of local landscapes the same attention and the same vocabulary they brought to sickroom bedsides.

Though the geography of health was pervasive, it affected people differently. Many antebellum observers perceived environmental influences to be felt unequally by men and women. Women died more in the Arkansas swamps, wrote the German adventurer Friedrich Gerstäcker, but overall he felt that women enjoyed better health—widows were so common that "there was almost no household that didn't have at least one, and some farmsteads were veritable nests of them." (Single men were in fact far more common than single women in borderland households of his era, but Gerstäcker kept a keen eye on women generally.) He attributed this perceived difference in mortality to men's exposure to the "unhealthy land" outdoors. "Always out in the open while hunting in the swamps and marshes, lying at night in the wet and heat, constantly breathing the poisonous swamp gases," he explained, "the men did not fare as well as the women, who stayed in the house more." Gerstäcker thus attributed women's comparative health to the traditional divisions of labor whereby free women were occupied within cabins and houses.

Other sources attributed problems of women's health to the violation of norms of behavior. Henry Rowe Schoolcraft, a geologist and ethnologist, concluded during his trip through the Ozarks that the women and children of the first struggling settler families often died—probably, he felt, because the women were exposed to the elements doing what was properly men's work. Morality and mores were thus commonly tied to questions of well-being. Dr. J. E. Thompson, a Missouri physician, recorded the history of a female patient in 1856 with similar concern: "Being much exposed to the winter weather, from an open house and an indolent husband, she was attacked . . . with cough, chill, and pain near the left clavicle and under the left nipple, extending round to the same point in the back." The weather was indeed one cause of the woman's distress, but even more to blame was her husband's indolence. Thompson's account drew a direct connection between a husband's lack of attention to family welfare, exposure to a harsh environment, and specific, highly localized physical affliction. Winter weather brought on physical ailments; shiftlessness brought searing pain.

Such descriptions reflect the importance accorded to dwelling spaces and each sex's role in them. Schoolcraft's commentary is telling. Women of early Arkansas and Missouri did extensive work outside in fields and woods, slave women often as full-time laborers, and free women occasionally as primary agricultural workers, but more often as keepers of extensive garden plots and as supplemental field hands during periods of heavy demand. Even when occupied mainly with chores related to the house, women carried water, gathered and chopped wood, collected plants (herbs, nuts, bark, berries, mushrooms, and so on), and did numerous other outdoor tasks. The gender roles of refined society placed men in the larger world and women within domestic environments, but for large families living often in small houses, and in close and continual contact with the meadows, forests, and fields about them, such distinctions were sometimes not easily drawn. The permeability of boundary between women's and men's space is echoed in the permeability of interior and exterior spaces in the conceptual imagination of antebellum Arkansas and Missouri.

Indoors and Out

The built environment established by newcomers on newly cleared forest soil or newly drained marshland drew much the same scrutiny as did the natural surroundings. The makeshift quality of many structures was often regarded as unhealthful. Praising the endurance of American women, Friedrich Gerstäcker described a difficult situation: "In a lean-to of rough-hewn logs, protected on only three sides from wind and rain, the woman lives . . . months or sometimes even years under conditions that would destroy the health of a European. The cold damp earth is her floor, the wide, lonely forest her domicile." Rough homes and hastily made buildings provided only dubious shelter for many in early Missouri and Arkansas. Physical conditions mirrored social constraints. For Gerstäcker, the loneliness endured by settler families was as destructive as the exposure to harsh elements; and yet, in his optimistic and admiring account of early Arkansas society, Gerstäcker insisted that many women endured enforced self-sufficiency and primitive conditions with robust cheer.

Other observers were more critical. "Fort Smith," reported one early official in disgust, "is entirely too small to accommodate my Command, and its Construction is such as not to promise a suitable Security for Health to the Troops." Whether flimsy or rotting (and subsequent Fort Smith officials charged that the buildings were both), the built environment of the frontier outpost itself jeopardized its defenders' well-being.

Sickening rot and creeping foul air were thought to pervade many homes and buildings. Every prosperous household needed a cellar to store fruits and vegetables during winter frosts and long, hot summers, but such necessity brought peril. Dark, often damp, sometimes with standing water, and in direct contact with the soil and its creatures, underground spaces beneath homes rendered intimate and domestic many of the most feared elements of

the natural world. The *St. Louis Medical and Surgical Journal*, eager to as-
sign to the community's diseases a remediable, nonintrinsic cause, decried
"the thousand (at least) local marshes—dens where the evil genius of death
and decomposition manufactures the agents of destruction—*the cellars of
St. Louis!*" Buildings did not always shield their inhabitants from the natural
world. In some cases, they were thought to conduct the destructive influences of environment to the people.

The recollections of a former Georgia slave, John Goodwin, of a torrential rainstorm reflect the power of weather experienced by many antebellum settlers, as well as the heightened vulnerability experienced by those
living in slavery. Goodwin's mother, forced to leave her youngest child,
Jim, alone in their earth-floored cabin all day while she worked the fields,
rushed back to check on him when a heavy rainstorm broke. Not finding
her baby, she "went down toward the creek as fast as she could, and there
she found little Jim being rolled over and over by the rain. Mammy said Jim
was almost to the creek when she took him up." Rains could wash a young
child from his cradle, coursing unhindered through a slave cabin as down
an open hillside.

Newcomers experienced the porousness of boundaries between indoor
and outdoor, private and unenclosed, in everyday ways. The clay, mud, and
woodchips that chinked together the spaces between hewn or round logs in
many cabins let through icy air drafts in winter, especially in the first year,
when unseasoned logs would shrink and settle. Fireside stories told of bears
breaking into cabins and of jokesters able to fool a merchant into paying
them over and over for a single deer hide: they sold the skin, collected their
draught of whiskey, and then, when one of the group got thirsty again,
snuck around back to the hewn log storeroom and carefully extracted the
hide once again through a gap between the logs. Such tall tales held truths
not only about frontier interaction, but about the nature of dwelling spaces.
An adult bear was more than equal to a wooden door, while the gaping
spaces between logs in a hastily built cabin could be large enough to pull a
supple deer hide through.

The missionary Cephas Washburn's recollection of a dramatic story from
early-nineteenth-century Arkansas reveals the vulnerability created by an
architecture of necessity. Washburn's account centered on an Osage girl
captured by Cherokees during the two groups' conflict over lands in the
Ozarks in the early 1820s. The girl had been raised as an adopted daughter
by a Cherokee family. Then, while she was still quite young, her foster father was tricked into giving her over into the care of a slave trader. A call for

the girl's rescue went out. Spiriting her down the Mississippi, the would-be slaver made the mistake of hiding out in a deserted cabin. Rivermen alerted to the child's description were able to sneak up to the cabin and peer easily through its walls to identify and rescue the girl, whom they returned safely to the Dwight Mission. Indoor and outdoor were not effectively blocked from each other. A "solid" wall could allow groups of people to see into and out of dwelling-places. Privacy and stealth might be found in wild terrain and thick canebrakes, where runaway slaves could sequester themselves at will, but could be frustrated by the built environment.

Indoor and outdoor thus blurred when it came to evaluating the health effects of an environment. The threats of environs could not be evaded simply by stepping inside one's home. The influences of the earth, like the inquiring gaze of passersby, entered built environments, just as they did forest glade or shadowy marsh. Harmful vapors emanated from dirt floors, sickening inhabitants who had no buffer between their bodies and the thick-stamped clay. On his 1819 journey through Arkansas, Henry Rowe Schoolcraft commented: "Mrs. H. tells me, she has not lived in a cabin which had a floor to it for several years; that during that time they have changed their abode several times, and that she has lost four children, who all died before they reached their second year."

Dirt floors carried the stigma of low, wild living in the early nineteenth century. They also brought occupants that much closer to the source of potentially harmful or even lethal emanations. Their privacy compromised and their health threatened, early-nineteenth-century westerners had few defenses against the influences of the outside world.

This lack of distinction between outer world and inner house mirrored the relationship of the body's interior to its surroundings. Elements of place literally permeated the body. According to Dr. Daniel Drake, abdominal fluids from miners in the region could be heated to reveal globules of lead. Such was the felt experience of life in the borderlands. As one German observer wrote of immigrants from his homeland in 1855, "try as [a newcomer] might to bar windows and bolt doors against American life, nothing avails; it forces itself in through countless cracks, and continues to sting and buffet him." Miasmas that seeped up from floors, waters that coursed unobstructed through cabin doors, and winds that found their cruel way in between inadequate chinks were only the most physical manifestations of powerful dangers not easily avoided. Forces of the outer world—dropping cotton prices on the New Orleans market, warfare and political unrest over Indian removal, and the pulsing force of "American life" itself—permeated the self irrespective of skin or clapboard, muscle or barred window, sinew or mud chinking.

Climate and Constitution

Early migrants to the Missouri and Arkansas regions read their future in the whole of environment. Natural terrain was experienced as a diverse set of influences whose interaction imbued a place with health or sickliness. The sum of these factors of place was what contemporary observers termed climate. "Climate" encompassed temperature, seasonal changes, and weather events, but also implied a broad connection between all the varied aspects of terrain. In their concern for the influences of a region's climate, nineteenth-century Americans attested their conviction that different sites had different pervasive and permeating essences that carried important consequences for human life.

Weather was of critical importance to early American inhabitants of the Far West. Good or foul weather determined the kinds of work that could be done, the physical spaces into which a household might be cramped, the condition of roads and rivers, and, crucially, the success or failure of a season's crops. Observing weather conditions was therefore an integral part of daily life. The conditions of the weather were noted in official records of military surgeons, in the private records of industrious scientist-physicians, in the diaries of farmers who relied on previous years' journals to time planting and harvest, and in the private notes of settlers whose daily lives were affected by rain clouds or clear vistas.

The state of the skies and winds was described in evocative language. Characters in an 1847 humorous sketch traveled through a *"pea-green climate"*, an 1820s emigrant guide touted the "Charming" climate of Missouri Territory, and John Geiger in 1835 experienced "soft . . . , rather smokey" weather. The tempers of the surrounding world had their own attributes, smells, colors, and textures. All were scrutinized by early Americans who read in the shape and rate of clouds, the shifting of winds, and the thick or heavy air of different seasons an augury of their own futures.

Not simply crops, but laborers' bodies were in thrall to the conditions of temperature, barometric pressure, and precipitation. The effects of the "sickly southern clime" ranged from the particular to the pervasive. "The weather is cloudy and uncomfortably warm," recorded John Brown in the fall of 1854; "I fear it will produce sickness." The many conditions that were summed up as "the weather" could bolster or imbalance the human form.

The enervating sultriness of New Orleans could create passivity in its inhabitants, as a German author, Karl Postl, warned potential immigrants, while other immigrants reported that Little Rock's "delightful climate" soothed a "broken down" constitution. The Yankee immigrant Hiram Abiff Whittington was characteristically sardonic. Advising his brother on emigration, Whittington consoled him that "So long as you behave yourself, you shall neither be shot, dirked, or gouged; the only danger, then, you would incur will be from the climate." Quite apart from the pervasive violence of the backcountry, climate could be in more general ways "not congenial to health."

Yet climate could also function as a medicine. One early traveler noted that a "mild, warm, and agreeable day acted as a restorative" to those who had been indisposed. Indeed, the climate of Missouri was seen to bring to health those with certain ailments. A party of missionaries to the Osage Indians felt that Missouri's climate cured consumption (or, as modern observers would likely name this ailment, tuberculosis). Every aspect of the external environment had potential consequences for the inner workings of the human body. With the same intensity with which they scrutinized bowel movements or symptoms of fever, western migrants observed the interrelated aspects of the natural world that they named "climate."

The notion of "climate" was a broad one, implying that terrain possessed a diffuse but essential character modulated by vegetation, soils, and waters, as well as by the prevailing weather and winds. Trees could affect temperature and precipitation, so describing a region's rain clouds was intrinsically related to describing its forests. As one 1828 Western medical account observed, "Climate may be defined to be that peculiar constitution of the atmospheric fluid, modified as it is by the amount of heat, humidity, aridity, electricity and quality of soil, which immediately invests the earth, and in which all animals move and breathe." Groping for a way to express a deeply shared conviction that the essence of locale imparted itself to living creatures in important ways, medical professionals found in climate a way of talking about the essences of place.

Such interrelationship largely characterized the scientific world of the early and middle nineteenth century. To investigate a disease, scientists and physicians would not simply prod and feel a person's body, but would inquire after his family's tendencies, his recent passions, his favorite foods. Surrounding weather was of course part of this mix: How could sharp winds not threaten the travelers into whose clothing they knifed? Or sweet-smelling spring rain not help strengthen worn-out bodies enervated by the bland diets of winter? In this interconnected world, the reduction of disease to microscopic pathogens or of contagion to isolable parasites came not simply as revelation, but as rude shock. To reduce well-being to test cultures, petri dishes, and unseen mites meant to ignore all the influences that people plainly experienced: How could prognosis be divorced from a person's mental state? How could her susceptibility to disease not be related to strong drink or recent pregnancy? The introduction of germ theory and its microscopic world sharply fractured (though it did not destroy) a much more organic and holistic understanding of health and disease. Early-nineteenth-century people encapsulated in their notion of climate a whole worldview that was soon to come under sustained attack.

As they described the world around them, so too did early Americans describe themselves. The use of "climate" to describe interrelated aspects of an environment paralleled the common phrasings of "organization" and "constitution" with which nineteenth-century people referred to a complex of attributes of the individual person. "Organization" implied physical structure as well as moral and mental make-up. The novelist James Fenimore Cooper, in his original "Leatherstocking Tale," the 1823 novel *The Pioneers*, used language familiar to his readers in describing the feelings of one particularly obtuse and unctuous figure as "the kind of self-satisfaction that a man of his organization would feel, who had really, for once, done a very clever thing." "Organization" allowed for compact allusion to the many habits and tendencies—moral, mental, and physical—intrinsic to a person's character and physical embodiment.

Of even more protean usefulness was the notion of "constitution." An 1843 medical text asserted that "Each man is primarily endued with a particular constitution, distinct from temperament. . . . The constitution may be modified by regimen, but not destroyed. In a word, the constitution is the foundation of the individual being." A person's individual constitution, or basic bodily tendency, was set early; it expressed itself throughout life in actions, emotions, and speech, no less than in good or poor health.

Children were often characterized by their health and behavior as infants. A "puny delicate and irritable child," as one Missouri father characterized his newborn in 1844, might not be expected to live long, probably as the result of a weak or flawed constitution. A "sickly" child was deemed more susceptible to the prevailing diseases of a "sickly country," and more likely to cry and fuss. A "robust" infant, on the other hand, would likely express inner heartiness not only through later good health but through activity and enthusiasm.

A person whose constitution was "injured" or "broken down" might never be profoundly ill, but was also never completely well. In-born constitution, however, could be altered or strengthened in subsequent life. Explaining his failure to appear in a timely way in Arkansas, the soon-to-be-former territorial governor James Miller pleaded to the Territorial Assembly in 1820 that his "Constitution was impaired by privation and exposure to the inclement seasons of the North during the late war," thus making it even more difficult for him to endure the bugs, ague, and oppressive heat of "the warm and unhealthy season of the South."

Antebellum Americans commonly examined many aspects of the world—surrounding terrain, family members, one's own body and mind—for their innate, underlying, imbuing essences. Constitutional differences between people had myriad ramifications. As the physician William Hillary had stressed in the late eighteenth century, those treating the sick had to perceive "the difference between one who has a viscid, sizy, or buff like blood, from the one who has a lax, putrescent dissolved state of blood." The contents of one's veins told the nature of one's being. Moreover, constitution was more than body alone. Features emotional and physical interacted to determine a person's constitution. "You say Betsy has been quite ill," wrote Justus Post in 1807 to his brother John. Confessing "great doubts of her health," Justus explained that "she has been so long in a melancholy state, and this is as fatal to the constitution as the consumption." Indeed, the mind itself had a constitution that governed and affected the constitution of the whole self.

Like the internal being, the external world was composed of similarly resilient patterns, tendencies, and capacities. Daniel Drake could refer easily to "the geological constitution" of the Ozark Mountains. Seasons, too, had different constitutions that were determined by prevailing diseases. Atmosphere in particular, that fluid matrix of winds and airs, possessed in times of great sickness "an epidemic constitution" like that described by Sydenham. Essential, underlying being, which people sought to perceive in its various interactions and developments, was as characteristic of soil and season as of the human body.

An individual's experience of illness thus represented an interaction between the underlying essences of the disease-bearing surroundings and those of the very person. Finding this appropriate mesh between constitution and climate guided the quest for health. "This is a delightful climate," pronounced Amos Wheeler of Little Rock in 1820, "and suits my constitution broken down as it is."

Climate was an important tool in American migrants' struggle to understand and apprehend unknown territory. Naming a potentially protean set of factors, the nineteenth-century term "climate," like the early-twenty-first-century term "nature," was at once descriptive and evocative, eliding some forms of discussion while allowing for others. Under its rubric, newcomers to Arkansas and Missouri could express their concerns and hopes and discuss influences that seemed at times both overwhelming and indecipherable—if always vitally important.

Movement

Discussions of health and environment tried to pin down the external conditions that produced well-being or sickness, but the people's surroundings were rarely still. The organic world was perceived to undergo alteration beyond human influence. "[T]he whole of this country," reported Dr. George Hunter of one area of the Red River in 1804, "appears to be newly formed & forming & growing gradually more & more elevated, dry & healthy." A notice in the *Western Medico-Chirurgical Journal* in 1851 similarly concluded that "our malarious fevers appear to be every year diminishing in the West, and others of a continued character taking their place." Observers of western sites saw themselves in a dynamic world demanding constant vigilance.

The healthfulness of terrain could be radically affected by human intervention. In particular, draining marshes would "prevent as much as possible exhalations from putrified vegitable matter" and thus cleanse the air of its sickening miasmatic influences, A. W. Webb admonished in 1844. The "improvements" made by farm families and new communities were aimed at improving the very health of the environment itself.

Making a place more salubrious, however, was as challenging as making a sick person well. The upper reaches of the Red River in southwestern Arkansas had been rendered impassable since the earliest days of European exploration by what one engineer termed a "Grate raft" of fallen timber lodged in the river's course. Perhaps initially created by a mammoth flood, the raft continued to catch and hold further debris. William Dunbar, an explorer and naturalist charged by Thomas Jefferson with exploring the lower Mississippi and Ouachita rivers in 1804–5, reported that the raft supported "trees of considerable size," with such a dense vegetative cover that "the river may be frequently passed, without any knowledge of its existence." In 1833, the mass was so thick that "the whole width of the river may be crossed on horseback." Stretching for over 70 miles, the Red River Raft resisted for decades the federal engineers who attacked it with snagboat crews and dynamite. It proved a stubborn obstacle to free traffic on the river.

Furthermore, the raft acted against the health of the surrounding area. The geologist George W. Featherstonhaugh predicted, "When the great work of cutting the raft out is accomplished, an immense quantity of rich lands will be brought to their true value, and the salubrity of the country much improved." Yet until well after the Civil War, the raft remained a tremendous, creaky, marshy obstruction that hindered commerce and worsened the health of the surrounding area. Wrestling with dynamic terrain was like wrestling with the complex and ever-changing balances of the self. Each struggle could be transformative.

When environmental challenges proved too daunting, or the costs to health too high, migrants to early Arkansas and Missouri were willing to relocate themselves. Many antebellum Americans, like their European peers, embarked upon both temporary journeys and permanent moves when the remedies of family and physicians failed to stem chronic illness. Recounting his own emigration from Massachusetts, Timothy Flint explained that "You remember the miserable state of my health, and the hopes I entertained, that in a milder climate and a new order of things, I might regain my health and cheerfulness." Change of place was tied up with a "new order of things" more generally—and with the hope that change in life-situation would also effect a change in the body's own well-being.

Changing elevation, moving uphill or down to the bottoms, was one way to preserve well-being. In one district of Arkansas, for instance, where Timothy Flint found fevers to be strangely powerful in the "high country," he noted that "they, who ascend in the season of fever from [nearby] low plains, have the course of their disorder precipitated." Potential engendered in "low plains" was triggered by the change to highlands living. Flint's comments are typical of those by literate whites in the early nineteenth century. Records of postwar black life indicate that similar environmental thinking may have held currency among slaves. A former slave who moved to Arkansas to farm in Drew County in the 1880s recalled getting "down sick with slow fever. When I got over that I decided that I would move to higher ground." Faced with a variety of health environments, those who had control over their own movements used mobility as a therapeutic response.

Newcomers to Missouri and Arkansas promoted their regions as healthful destinations, hoping to convince family or friends to join them in emigration. "I think that were you to settle in Missouri—which you ought to do," wrote Anne Biddle from St. Louis to a male cousin in 1835, "the travelling and change of air would no doubt be of considerable benefit to your health." Many indeed moved west to Arkansas and Missouri "in search of health," and immigrants frequently did find their health improved, or at least they so boasted in their correspondence. Reverse migration also took its cue from prevailing environmental ideas about health. When the southern climate proved too much, the regional booster Timothy Flint admitted, "the last resort in such cases is a journey, or a voyage to the North."

Despite the perils that could be involved, people often regarded journeys themselves as beneficial, especially for men. Sea voyages were held to be particularly healing, usually for the combination of salt water, fresh air, new sights, and, for young men who shipped as sailors, hard labor aboard a ship. Richard Henry Dana's *Two Years Before the Mast* was perhaps the most widely read testimony to such voyages. It is an autobiographical account of Dana's life aboard a merchant vessel in 1836–38, on which he shipped out as a deck hand when ill health kept him from pursuing his studies at Harvard. The sea cure was recommended and tried by many, but not always with success. People understood the rigors of travel as integral to its health effects. Weak individuals would rise to the challenge, strengthened by the stimulus of hard pallets, fresh air, and a simple, unrefined diet of bracing meat. Tonic to moral as well as muscular fiber, long trips were a dramatic and difficult—but sometimes efficacious—remedy for the desperate.

For women, too, voyaging was recommended by medical texts and common wisdom. Certainly the active life of a sailor was only available to men, and few white women ventured overland to Santa Fe or the Rocky Mountains before the late 1840s, but there is a great deal of evidence that women did undertake travel, often lengthy or difficult travel, out of health concerns. When in 1819 Mary Hempstead's physician recommended riding horseback as a curative for her chronic complaints, she and her husband duly rode out to visit family and friends. Stephen Hempstead noted happily in his diary that "my wife hath received much Benefit from her complaint the Dropsey by the Journey." The process of a trip—the physical effort of the body, the stimulating conditions that travel entailed—was a therapeutic regime employed by a wide variety of travelers.

Correspondence surrounding one midcentury slave's use of healing springs reveals the many considerations that could inform such therapeutic visits as well as the complex set of negotiations affecting slaves' health. Though no written record remains from "the negro Richmond," held as a slave by a Memphis-area owner, B. B. Eskridge, his well-being is a central theme of correspondence between Eskridge and a prominent Little Rock politician and newspaper publisher, William E. Woodruff, in the tension-laden months of 1860–61. In a not uncommon arrangement, Woodruff managed Richmond for his far-off owner, hiring him out in Little Rock and relaying to Eskridge offers for his purchase.

In the fall of 1860, Eskridge wanted Richmond back in Tennessee, if his poor health would permit him to be sent back over the difficult Memphis–Little Rock road. Responding perhaps to a suggestion by Woodruff, or perhaps to Richmond's own request, Eskridge wrote, "I am Confident that the waters of the Hot Springs [in Arkansas], will effect no permanent good." Reflecting the commonly held sense that mineral and thermal springs had specific properties that operated most effectively on certain ailments, Eskridge continued, "I now intend to send him to Baileys Springs in Ala[bama] as the place from all I . . . understand, most suited to persons in his Condition." Though Richmond was apparently not well enough to travel, by December he was "improving in health," and the two slave owners consulted about how much to charge others for his hire.

Yet Richmond never bathed in Baileys Springs. By May of 1861 he was instead in Hot Springs, Arkansas, under the supervision of Hiram Abiff Whittington. Eskridge wrote Woodruff that Richmond could not be brought "home because his Swellings & complaint seemed to increase without the Heating at Hot Springs." Moreover, "*his wish* is to be again at Hot Springs where he says with the use of the waters he can keep in very good health." Like many of his contemporaries, Richmond attributed therapeutic properties to the thermal springs. He apparently made arrangements to hire out his labor while he stayed near the springs, arrangements that evidently persuaded his owner: if at Hot Springs, Eskridge continued, Richmond would "bring me at least $10 per month, average, the year round." Thus convinced, despite the "heavy travelling bills" over which he grumbled, Eskridge agreed to his slave's desire to remain at the springs—over, perhaps, Eskridge's own prior plan to send him east to Alabama. Only in December of 1861 did Eskridge write Woodruff, enclosing a letter to Richmond (who was apparently literate) calling him home, "as he seems without benefit in any way at the Springs."

Though evidently summoned back to Memphis in the end, Richmond's preferences with regard to treatment and his ability to find employment remunerative for his owner had kept him where he wanted to be. And, as a worried mention in Eskridge's correspondence implies, where he perhaps had more freedom than under the watchful eye of his owner. "I have ever regarded him as a reputable well behaved negro," Eskridge exclaimed in a letter of late May 1861, and noted that two acquaintances, Mr. Peay and Mr. Hammond, had also spoken well of Richmond's behavior, presumably at Hot Springs. But, he added, "Probably the present excitement general amongst us may at this time induce more criticism of him there—as one of uncertain occupation." In other words, the racial and social fears inspired by the critical 1860 election and the crisis over Fort Sumter, which had decisively broken open the long-simmering hostilities between North and South a bare few weeks before, meant that an unaccompanied black slave, however "reputable" and "well behaved," was increasingly viewed by the white residents of Hot Springs with suspicion or fear. His actions were too free, his attitudes, perhaps, too "uncertain." The freedom of spirit other observers found at Hot Springs was also to some extent reflected in this slave's experience. Two white slave holders wrote back and forth about his care, and others participated in keeping watch over his actions and character, but Richmond's story, as outlined in their letters, reflected therapeutic behavior substantially of his own volition.

Others attempting to preserve or regain their health made a variety of pilgrimages. Most people regarded high country as particularly restorative, especially for those with lung complaints. "I thot a trip to the mountains would be of service to Eliza," wrote John J. Walker from St. Louis in 1830, "but we could not accomplish it." When epidemics or sudden sickness struck a region, flight was an ancient response. "I go to the Merrimac [River] to Son Gratiots," wrote Stephen Hempstead in 1822, "and find the family all sick and removed from the Selean [a bottomland area] to Richard Wells a healthy place 2 or 3 miles distant." Struck by the lethal fever epidemic which swept through the St. Louis area in the "sickly season" of 1822, Hempstead's extended family fled the region that had imparted their fevers for a "healthy place" not far away, in a desperate bid to recover.

Like any medical treatment, such moves were laborious and took time. Like other regimens, they sometimes worked: "Son Gratiots wife & Children left their in the forenoon to return home, haveing been there Several weeks and the children Sick, who had recovered their health So as to return to the Merrimac," Hempstead wrote with relief two and a half months later. Even local "removes," like that of the Gratiot family, or visits of only a few days, could provide the necessary respite for an ill person to "recruite" his or her health. Traveling within a county or visiting a friend whose home was better situated was, like moving to the top of a ridge or from a swamp, a way to transform one's personal geography of health.

Chronic illness was considered especially susceptible to changes in place. Long-lasting ills thought to be the result of pervasive influences could potentially be affected by changes in the overall environmental situation entailed in long travel. When a coughing, wasting illness began to make incursions into John Brown's prosperous family, the Arkansas farmer, judge, and domestic healer turned to travel in hopes it would revive William, his oldest son and the darling of his father's hopes. William Brown had trained as a doctor with a local medical practitioner and had attended lectures first in Philadelphia and then in New Orleans. (Like many ambitious Southern men, William reoriented his training away from traditional medical bastions like Philadelphia and toward Southern medical schools as the nation's sectional conflicts became more heated over the course of the 1850s.) When he returned from his out-of-state training, his proud papa gave him slaves, bought him a buggy and office furniture, and set him up for a comfortable country practice. Even as he made his preparations, however, William was weakening and beginning to cough up blood. In the fall of 1859 he started a "Southern trip" through Texas and parts of the Plains, in hopes, his father wrote, that the "camping out, being in the open air, etc." would ease his ill health. Despite some optimistic reports, it became clear by the spring that he was no better, and in March of 1860 William's brother Hugh was sent to bring him home to die.

The course of William's illness was like that of many invalids struggling against the ravages of consumption. The disease took a larger toll in this family, as in many others. During the fraught presidential campaign and increasing sectional tensions that marked the electioneering of the fall of 1860 Hugh Brown in turn began to sicken. In July 1861 he marched off at the head of a column of local Confederate recruits, but he returned home a week later, too weak to lead them into battle. Soon other brothers and sisters and John Brown's wife, Clara, showed the now-familiar signs. The early 1860s brought devastation to John and Clara's family just as it did to the region as a whole.

Traveling for health was closely allied with the practice of traveling for consolation. Friends and family members might visit the recently bereaved to offer help, reassurance, and comfort, or those in grief would travel to those who could ease their troubles. Many of these visits were by women. In 1829, Stephen Hempstead recorded that neighbors went to stay with a widow after her husband's death (they saw this as particularly important because she had no "neighbors" within several miles). After these visits she went to stay with families in turn, keeping involved in other households' routines after the profound disruption of her own. Men, too, engaged in nurture and consolation. In 1827, Hempstead "spent the day at Mr Earls our next door Neibor whose Brother had died." Visiting could help with healing of spirit as well as body, with travails of the heart as well as of the physical system.

Most travelers employed journeys in conjunction with other medical therapies. The combination of travel with specific remedies and the effects of new places more generally was seen as a potent cure. "His trip, change and Dr. Ruffins treatment has had apparently a fine effect," wrote John Brown in 1861, temporarily satisfied at the return of his consumptive son Henry from a several-month stay in El Dorado, Arkansas. The effects of "trip, change and . . . treatment" reinforced each other. Medical understanding emphasized the positive mental as well as physical aspects of change of site: wellness was an integrated and constantly balanced state of body and mind.

"[T]his post is *intrinsically* unhealthy," concluded the Army doctor C. B. Welch in an 1834 assessment of Fort Smith, "and will continue to be so as long as like causes produce like effects." Welch's forthright summary speaks volumes not only of the disease etiology but of the environmental understanding of his time and of his peers in East Coast offices as in a poorly established military outpost at the western edge of a borderland state. Factors of surroundings—the sodden vegetation of local bottomland, the rot and "scum" atop a nearby stream, the winds that blew over swampland as over soldiers' fortifications—affected the health of environments as they would the health of people within a locale. Place and person were swayed by the same kinds of forces; sloughs and forests underwent the same processes as did lagging recruits and ambitious farmers. "Like causes" might be baleful and unwanted, but their action was not untoward. They produced consistent and mutually intelligible effects on terrain and on the human beings struggling within it.

Complex arrays of environmental forces impressed themselves upon the human form. Balance or maladjustment in surrounding fields, weather, season, or pond could force "derangement" within the person, or could promote strength and good health. As John Brown observed in early August 1857: "A fine rain has greatly revived animate as well as inanimate nature in this neighborhood." "Nature" of many kinds responded to the succor or punishment of a complexly acting world.

"Place" in the antebellum nineteenth century was thick. It was not simply grass over which people strode, or the waters through which they pushed unwilling mules, or the air that sometimes caressed and sometimes punished them, but an amalgamation of sense and essence filling the whole perceived world, a unified experience of external reality that mightily constrained, through it never fully circumscribed, the efforts and will of its inhabitants.

AIRS

Chapter IV

SURROUNDING AND FILLING the human body, air was a palpable presence for those who described early Arkansas and Missouri. Planters, travelers, and field hands; merchants, speculators, and observant children all took note of the winds through which they moved. "Free mountain air" was to the Connecticut shop clerk Everard Dickinson a symbol of the economic and personal possibility he felt in the Arkansas Ozarks. "Airs" could invigorate and strengthen, imparting the beneficial aspects of the surrounding world to the people who moved within it. The influences of environment, moreover, were not bound strictly to a certain place. Air currents carried the essences of one region into another.

Winds and breezes embodied the mobile and infusing qualities of the natural world. Contemporary reports delineated many positive qualities in "good" air: it came from a region that was itself perceived as healthful, it partook of freshness and purity, and it was soft or refreshing, but not too harsh. A gentle balm, it brought life and healing.

If good airs imparted health, foul airs were filled with threats no less real for their intangibility. Through the malevolent airs called miasmas the atmosphere could take malevolent action. The protean and diffuse qualities of miasma make it difficult to define, but also rendered it formidable. All-permeating and ubiquitous in effect, miasmas emanated from rotting, filthy, or unfinished things and brought essences of disease into the human body. With every breath of miasmatic air, American migrants respired the very stuff of illness.

Though their power was exclusively harmful, miasmas reveal the ways in which airs, good and bad, could imbue people with their qualities. Miasmas' appearance, action, and consequences are central to the perceived causal relationship between environmental "sickliness" and human ill health. They entered the body as breath or fluid, and they operated within it just as they did within terrain. They carried the environment's imbalance, disturbance, or putrefaction into the depths of the body, expressing within the individual the sickly tendencies of the locale. Produced from nature, they worked within a person like the humors that governed the body's health.

Perhaps because air is always necessary and always around us, it is paradoxically central to environmental discussions, but often invisible in them. It is our task to call into visibility the complexly different airs of the antebellum United States, making knowable in twenty-first-century terms what was intuitively apparent in the early and mid nineteenth. For us, appreciating these nuances of air is central to understanding that era's geography of health and place, for air currents connected body and land in bonds both unseen and sure.

Reading the Air

Describing the air was integral to describing a place in the antebellum United States. Like soils or tree types, swamp creatures or game animals, cleared fields or acres of canebrake, an area's atmosphere was particular to it. Air could be "heavy" or a "light breeze," "bracing" or "languid." "Atmosphere" could be "clear" or "poor." Such variety held consequence. Hot air, warned one British health guide, dissipated the blood, whereas cold air "obstructs perspiration," and air too moist destroyed the elasticity of organs and tissues. Air currents and air qualities carried the essences of disease or health.

The air of a place was thus primary to travelers' and newcomers' experience. October on the Missouri prairies, commented an English traveler, William Faux, around 1820, was a month of "a dark blue hazy atmosphere caused by millions of acres . . . [of] blazing, smoking fire." Prairies could be categorized by their distinctive skies as by their oceans of grass. During the weeks when new settlers or Native Americans burned the prairies to clear land for farming or better hunting, the "dark blue hazy atmosphere" was in many ways the most important element of the environment. Attuned sensibilities discerned different characteristics in different air currents. Wind could be "variable and thawey," as the Missouri farmer Stephen Hempstead recorded in 1815, on a "smoaky foggy day." Day-to-day experience of a place was shaped by the qualities of surrounding air. In cities or on country homesteads, by campfires or behind a plow, the residents of the Mississippi

Valley were subject to a prevailing atmosphere tempered only by the small-scale interventions of waving fan or roaring fire.

Airs not only touched human beings, they infused them. The airs of Arkansas, proclaimed the rustic tall-tale-teller in T. B. Thorpe's short story "The Big Bear of Arkansas," were potent and invigorating; "just breathe them, and they will make you snort like a horse." Since airs of different places held different qualities of healthfulness, maintaining well-being could entail the search for more healthful air. In 1848, a Missouri immigrant, Flora C. Byrne, wrote her eastern foster sister Eliza Blackwell Mayer that her daughter Annie was "far from well . . . I would give a great deal if I could take her away on to Baltimore to breathe another atmosphere." Connecticut emigrant Mary Lisa and her husband, the Missouri fur trader Manuel Lisa, similarly brought a daughter with "the hooping Cought" to the rural farm of her parents, Stephen and Mary Hempstead, in 1818, "to receive the Benefit of the Country air." Though in this instance the "Country air" proved insufficient—the girl, Mary, died three days later—through the worry of Manuel and Mary Lisa, Flora Byrne, and their contemporaries, as through the exaggeration of Thorpe's backwoodsman, ran the certainty that the atmosphere imbued its people with something elemental, whether for good or ill.

Positive qualities of air were often related to purity and freshness. The airs of "new country" thus held promise. Good "atmosphere" was in the words of an 1850 medical brief about St. Louis "pure, and . . . free from all predisposition to disease." Indeed, one 1837 medical advice book argued that pure air could actually revive the sick. Visual cues indicated purity; the more clearly air could be seen through, the better. "Transparent atmosphere—pure breeze" commented Washington Irving of Governor William Clark's residence near St. Louis in 1832. In contrast to the air of close, indoor, and often urban quarters, fresh air stimulated the body. Medical observers as well as common wisdom recognized the potency of fresh air. The presence of oxygen was necessary to human conception, argued an 1807 article in the *Medical Repository*, attributing the "astonishing number of births to the South, among the negroes," to "their copulating in the day, exposed to the sun, on the sides of hills, where the air is uncommonly pure." Vital energy, racial and sexual primitiveness, and unsullied air were combined in this argument in a literally potent mix.

Some of the effects of air were produced by the action of temperature or breeze on the surface of the body. Cold air brought on chills, hot air inspired sweat, "rough" air made the body stiffen in response to biting cold or nipping breeze. "Clear & hot but the air bracing," noted the naturalist S. W. Wood-house of a good day's travel up central Arkansas from the steamboat port of Napoleon in June of 1849, reflecting the ways in which air could act as a stimulant when temperature would otherwise be oppressive.

The temperature and texture of air brushing the body's surfaces prompted sharply different responses. Air along the Ohio River, thought the missionary and travel writer Timothy Flint, was of "a delightful temperature . . . more easily felt than described." Such an atmosphere was fundamentally different from northern air: "A slight degree of languor ensues; and the irritability that is caused by the rougher and more bracing air of the north, and which is more favourable to physical strength and activity than enjoyment, gives place to a tranquillity highly propitious to meditation." Varied emotional, physical, and mental activities followed from the stimulus of a languid or a "bracing" state of the air.

The motion of air was also important to human health. Freely circulating air was healthy air, argued medical sources and conventional wisdom. Emigrants' guides advised newcomers to scrutinize a region's winds. Healthful areas, after all, were characterized by healthy breezes. In the language of the nineteenth century, "air" was action as well as object: to "air" or "ventilate" a room or a garment rendered it less offensive and less dangerous. The environment itself could be cleansed by the action of wind. Timothy Flint assured "planters, who prefer raising cattle to cotton" that Arkansas prairies "swept by the winds" had fewer "musquitoes" and were "healthier than the bottoms." The action of wind was that of a cleaning broom, sweeping away the plaguing insects of the bottoms.

Winds carried many qualities of place. Observers frequently commented on the particles and odors borne by breezes. "A very warm uncomfortable day," as Stephen Hempstead characterized November 5, 1818, in his diary, could be marked by "high wind & dust flying. . . ." Few winds traveled empty-handed: they flung dust and debris at unprotected settlers. Other qualities borne by air currents could be more welcome. A young woman staying at a western military outpost in 1845 wrote a friend, "Every wind on the prairies comes laden with sweets & our beaux bring us bouquets every day." Enjoyment of the climate merged with the charms of an army encampment. Beaux and prairie winds brought pretty flowers and agreeable odors—pleasures at once perfectly licit and pleasurably stimulating. To describe a place's winds was to describe one's sensual experience.

"Refreshing breezes," commented an 1860 meteorological work on southwest Arkansas, "render the climate pleasant and healthful" during the summer. Mild currents of air were refreshing to body and spirit alike. A European observer in the 1850s commented that "what to the European is especially agreeable" about Portland, Missouri, was that "a gentle breeze nearly everywhere drifts coolingly towards him." Wind that was quiet, "gentle" and breeze-like, that "drifted" rather than roaring piercingly out of the north, was experienced as pleasurable and reviving. "The soft breezes of the south" were welcome; a harsh, cutting wind was not.

The attention paid the different varieties of wind reveals a sense that their essences differed. Wind carried something of the land or water over which it traveled. "A complete Rocky Mountain breeze" brought the cold air of craggy peaks, and perhaps an accompanying sense of invigoration or adventure, to the door of John Brown's flatland Arkansas plantation one November morning. For the Missouri-based immigrant naturalist George Engelmann, the different breezes in Hot Springs, Arkansas, marked its regional identity: "we are in another land; the breath of the South blows over this valley." Airs were *of* a region, and carried its essential nature with them.

John Brown noted in his diary in the summer of 1857 that "We have had a north and northeast wind much more than usual, which accounts for sickness." The following fall he complained about the ill effects of another kind of wind: "Pestilential East wind still occasionally prevailing, and some deaths." Brown's concern was widespread: John Geiger commented in July of 1841 on the "southeast sickly wind" characterizing his region. Winds of different directions had distinct names and properties. "I hope you will be very careful in the month of March and not expose yourself in any way to the bleak spring winds," wrote Flora Byrne to her foster sister in 1840. "Bleak" wind not only was cold, damp, and unpleasant but also conveyed ominous threats to health. A "sickly wind" was likewise possessed of pervading qualities of ill influence. The "East wind" about which John Brown complained was itself "Pestilential," and would tend to produce or encourage pestilence generally, even if a traveler took shelter from the abrupt strength of its buffeting blows.

The language of wind suggests much about the operation of "airs" in environmental understanding, but it does only that: descriptions of sites make clear the potency accorded airs, but do not trace that power's source or means. The lack of explanation of airs' influence over the human body, however, is itself telling. Silence about *how* airs imparted the nature of surrounding terrain to the human body was indicative of the completely unremarkable nature of that transfer. Airs' action on the human frame was part of the common sense about the functioning of the world that was shaped by shared experience and expressed through shared language. Central to this understanding of the relation between self and surrounding are the foul vapors known as miasmas.

Miasma

"The fluid which we breathe is inodorous, invisible, insipid, colorless, elastic, possessed of gravity, easily moved, rarefied and condensed," explained Noah Webster's *American Dictionary* in 1832. When air transgressed these foundational attributes, when it became smelly, thickly visible, darkly colored, or oppressively still, it held potentially malevolent power. Miasmas epitomized these harmful aspects of air: they were composed of dampness, odor, haziness, and clinging impurity. Their nature, however, is difficult to capture. The word itself varies, even by the standards of idiosyncratic nineteenth-century spelling. People wrote of "miasm," "miasma," and, less commonly, "miasthma" for the singular; "miasms," "miasmas" or "miasmata" for the plural. During the early decades of the nineteenth century, medical authorities were beginning to use the newer term "malaria"—*mal-aria*, or quite literally, "bad air"—for the emanations from lowland waters and rotting sloughs. Only in the 1880s and '90s did "malaria" become the name for the disease itself, not for the vapors that had been thought to be its cause.

In many ways, the concept of miasma functioned usefully precisely because it was so flexible and protean. As twentieth-century Americans would fear "germs," so antebellum Americans feared "miasmas": they were the useful catch-all for disease worries. Acting a number of ways, made manifest in multiple signs, miasmas could be accommodated into many experiences of the surrounding world. Indeed, their ubiquity was nearly complete. People of the nineteenth century from varied ethnicities, walks of life, and countries of origin lived in daily fear of miasmas' harmful effects.

Like malevolent sprites, miasmas were at once wispy and possessed of great power, ethereal in nature but chillingly tangible in effect. Miasmas emanated from harmful or degraded places or things, infiltrating their surroundings with illness. They carried the essence of decay and putrefaction. Like fog or mist, they moved in and through air. They could emanate from stagnant water, from earth, and from rotting objects. Transferring imbalance and ill health from the surrounding world to the interior of the human body, they were the causal mechanism whereby elements of the environment affected individuals' health.

Fear of miasma registers in many early-nineteenth-century admonitions concerning what one Missouri traveler, Henry Vest Bingham, in 1818 termed "unhealthy fog." Accounts are unclear about whether the visible moisture of fog *signified* miasma or *was* miasma, but the presence of fog was strongly indicative of the presence of miasmatic influences. When Justus Post wrote his brother in 1818 with instructions on how to make the journey from Vermont to Missouri, he warned his brother to "bring along medicine for the children & mind they do not get sick on the road—When on the Ohio keep them close in the boat whenever there is a fog, else they will have the ague & fever."

Miasmas behaved like smoke or mist, blown with air currents, wafted by winds, and rising from earth, vegetation, or water. Yet miasma was more than any of these. Just as the writer T. B. Thorpe could suggest that a bear was supernaturally powerful by describing how it loomed "like a *black mist*," descriptions of miasma as mist and fog evoked supernal origin and power.

Miasmas were particularly related to stagnant water. Just as air, unmoving, transgressed its healthful state, so too still, boggy, corrupted water represented the antithesis of all that was life-giving about pure, fresh, sweet waters. Widespread opinion as well as medical argument saw in "stagnant marshes" a source of "pestiferous effluvia." Dreaded miasmas emanated with great harm from algal ponds and slow-seeping sinkholes.

The writings of Benjamin Rush open one window into perceptions of miasma. Rush was a highly influential physician of late-eighteenth- and early-nineteenth-century Philadelphia whose work provided much of the systematic basis for regular medicine's aggressive "purging and puking" as well as copious bloodletting. A staunch opponent of the notion that disease passed easily from person to person, Rush focused attention on the state of the individual within his or her surroundings. Miasmas were a crucial aspect of Rush's understanding of disease. They bore sickness to people who came into contact with them, and were therefore to be avoided or attacked at every turn. Rush's descriptions of miasma (like his medical treatments and outlook on life generally) tended to be particularly opinionated and forceful, but his was to a large extent a more robustly articulated version of common belief.

Miasma appeared in many accounts as an actively entwining, almost filamentous, essence reminiscent of other aspects of hot, humid terrain. Benjamin Rush criticized the bags of camphor or rags wetted with vinegar which apprehensive citizens hung around their necks during Philadelphia's epidemic in 1783. Far from offering protection from yellow fever, he inveighed, these smell-charged packets could increase people's contact with the disease "by entangling, in their volatile particles, more of the miasmata of the fever, and thus increasing a predisposition to it." Rush saw miasmas as long, potentially "entangled" strands, like the hanging Spanish moss that newcomers identified so strongly with the moist atmosphere of southern swampland.

Noah Webster termed miasmas "infecting substances floating in the air; the effluvia of any putrefying bodies, rising and floating in the atmosphere." In Webster's definition, miasma was particulate and free-floating. Other descriptions concur. Trees on the brow of a hill stopped the "diffusion of Miasmata," argued A. W. Webb in 1844, relying on a notion of discrete particles that could be filtered or blocked. When winds blew over bottomlands and picked up miasmas, they carried them to people beyond. A change in the wind's direction could therefore afflict one side of a mountain with fevers, leaving the other healthy.

Common language, however, implied that miasma did not simply travel *on* air; it changed the nature of the air through which it propagated. A recent emigrant, Anderson Wilson, explained in 1835 that a summer overflow of the Missouri River would cause sickness because it filled with water "the ponds & hollows which will Stagnate and infect the air this fall." Like a diseased person, atmosphere was infected by miasma. The air itself became sick. Not passively transported, but noxiously transforming, miasma charged the very atmosphere with sickness.

Miasmas were a flexible category. Though often free-floating strand or particle, they could be figured in many ways to reflect their multiple forms of influence on the human body. Accounts frequently referred to miasma as fluid, something people would move through or draw into their bodies. Hapless emigrants, cautioned Timothy Flint, carelessly sleep in open cabins and "drink in the humid atmosphere of the night." Feeding on the thick liquid of moist, close atmosphere, a region's inhabitants took it into themselves.

The effects of miasmas were as powerfully diffuse as were their descriptions. Miasmas conveyed not simply a particular disease but a tendency toward disease in general. The miasmatic product of marshy bottomland east of Kansas City, explained one local doctor, was not "confined to the immediate locality where it is generated, but is carried over the brow of the low hills to the North, and gives character to the diseases that prevail through the hill country." All of the ills of a region were shaped by miasmas' influence, just as all the persons within an environment could be influenced by them. As the human constitution could be characterized by general attributes—vigorous, bilious, phlegmatic, splenetic—a region could come to be indicted as miasmatic. "All this low flat country is defective in salubrity, the whole of the Mississippi Basin being tainted with miasm atmosphere," concluded one 1839 guide for British emigrants. Not one specific failure of healthfulness was at fault, but what the guide termed the "fever and ague character of the territory." Myriad fears of environmental ills could be summed up in the telling condemnation, "miasm atmosphere."

Many accounts used miasma as an overall indicator of the health of a local environment. Edmund Flagg's *The Far West*, published in 1838, was both adventure story and migrants' guide. Flagg used his own journey as a narrative structure to record the agricultural potential and social conditions of the regions through which he traveled. Flagg dramatically shaped his readers' reactions to and understanding of the bottomland along the Kaskaskia River in lower Illinois:

> a weary plod through the deep black loam, and the tall grass weltering in the night-dews, and the thickets of the dripping meadows, was anything but agreeable.... As I wandered through this region, where vegetation, tower[ed] in all its rank and monstrous forms . . . I thought I could perceive a deadly nausea stealing over my frame, and that every respiration was a draught of the floating pestilence. I urged onward my horse, as if by flight to leave behind me the fatal contagion which seemed hovering on every side; as if to burst through the poisonous vapours which seemed distilling from every giant upas [a fabled poisonous tree] along my path. That this region should be subject to disease and death is a circumstance by no means singular. Indeed, it seems only unaccountable to the traveler that it may be inhabited at all.

The whole environment worked in concert against Flagg's health. "Dripping" moisture and "floating pestilence" pressed themselves against him. He was helpless to avoid their malevolent influence. Trapped within towering vegetation, "rank and monstrous," he was forced to inhale "poisonous vapours" emanating from all around. The entire scene arrayed itself against him.

Despite Flagg's somewhat overwrought tone, his environmental fears were widely shared. Not one isolable element, miasma was rather a defining characteristic of the natural world. It was symbol no less than sign of an environment both hostile and toxic.

Smell

Miasma was not the same as smell, but miasmas were strongly correlated with stench and foul odor. Experience underscored etiology. Unpleasant odors that prompted recoil and disgust were taken as signs of harmful miasma penetrating the human body. Bad smell itself helped create disease, as a German emigrant's description of the Pinkney Bottom in Missouri in the late

1830s makes clear: "The many trees that have fallen down and are partly or wholly decomposing, disseminate with the rotting leaves an odor which often is oppressive to our nostrils, and this in union with the noxious vapors of the so-called sloughs—puddles of calm foul water which are present everywhere in these bottoms—cause chills or ague and gallsicknesses." The odor of trees' rot spreading into the surrounding atmosphere, and into the human body, not only signaled but actively conveyed "noxious" putrefaction.

Odors had a range of meanings and consequences for health. Good smells were commonly regarded as good for the body. In the pine woods of Alexandria, Louisiana, Timothy Flint noted that "the air has an aromatic and terebinthine odour, that is deemed healthy, and at least is grateful." Far from being harmful, the distinctive "terebinthine" pungency of the pine resin was regarded as restorative. Smells indicated underlying well-being of people as of sites—and were thus an important diagnostic aid. Some diseases produced specific odors in the body, like the "peculiarly offensive odor arising from the patient" which one southern physician, W. H. Gantt, argued was diagnostic of typhoid fever. Both producing and produced states of well-being, smells were an important element of the geography of health.

Odors were recorded and interpreted with interest. The experienced world was a smelly one. Cooking meat made juices flow; jocular exaggeration held that the smell of roasting game would "make a lean man fat." Even different peoples might be experienced as possessing particular smells. Among white observers, what one St. Louis slave-holder mincingly termed "the peculiar *odour* of our 'colored brethren'" was the subject of interest, investigation, and coarse humor. The smells of sickness and death were common and familiar.

Furthermore, a sense of the potency of stench crossed racial boundaries. One 89-year-old former Arkansas slave commented of his work cleaning "water closets" at a hospital after the Civil War, "After a while I took down sick from the work—the scent, you know." Yet some concerns with odors were undeniably different in the black experience of the antebellum South. Every slave knew the baying yell of the bloodhounds whose long, keen noses tracked runaways. The particularity of each person's scent was not an innocent diagnostic aid but the means of pursuit—and often capture. Though all nineteenth-century Americans might try to overwhelm or counterbalance bad odors to prevent, combat, or hide disease, only escaped convicts or enslaved workers like the successful runaway Archer Alexander knew, as he put it, the desperation of racing for water "so as to kill the scent" and throw off pursuing hounds.

The powers and properties of bad smell were often conceptually linked with disease and with fog, which in turn bore strong associations with miasma. One Tennessee freedwoman's account of nursing those struck with yellow fever during the epidemic of 1878 reveals this set of associations: "The odor was terrible. When whole families died and a house been closed up and then be opened seemed like a fog come out. It would knock you down." Smell, thick color, and heavy weightiness were related and harmful properties of air. Odor, like fog, was a manifestation of foul air. Stench would "knock . . . down" those forced to endure it, like a powerful gale or an exhausting illness. Each sensory experience reinforced the qualities they all shared.

The conviction that foul smells wrought personal harm endured well into the latter part of the century. The reeking smell of John Busby's "stink boat," a floating steamboat-turned-rendering-plant anchored at the foot of St. Louis's Barton Street in 1873, generated great agitation among residents of the nearby German immigrant neighborhood. A local newspaper agreed with frantic crowds that the malodorous boat was "a festering sore, breeding sickness and death in our neighborhood." Contemporary medical theory, which was beginning to reject foul odor as a cause of disease and search instead for microscopic "germs," might argue against the protesters, so long as no animal byproducts were actually being dumped in their neighborhood. Yet these St. Louis crowds drew on widespread and deeply rooted common sense in their perception of the harmfulness of rancid stench. Though Busby tried to quell the disturbances by insisting that a new "Chicago patent" would consume the offensive and harmful smells, distrustful St. Louisans eventually forced him to move his boat across the Mississippi to the Illinois shore, where downwind communities immediately took up the complaint. It would take many decades to dissociate the visceral experience of extremely bad smell from ideas of disease causation. Well into the post-Civil War period, the body's perceptions were implicitly trusted.

Counteraction

Yet smell was not solely threat, but weapon. Many prophylactic measures produced powerful smells to counteract miasmatic influences. During the 1849 cholera outbreak, the St. Louis Commission on Public Health advised members of the public to burn resinous tar, coal, and sulfur to fill the air with smoke and odor and thus counteract the miasma of illness. One of Benjamin Rush's methods for combating miasmas suggested human operation on the atmosphere parallel to the operation of strong medicines within the body: when confronted with powerful action, oppose it with a force equally strong. He proposed "impregnating the air with certain effluvia, which act either by destroying miasmata by means of mixture, or by exciting a new action in the system." The air over fermenting wines, for instance, could be helpful; likewise smoke, ammoniac vapors, the fumes from burning coal, or even putrefying carcasses. Material usually loathsome could take the place of miasmas in air, or inspire a counteraction within the human body. Like "salutary pus" and a healthy "puke" working to expel harm from the body, Rush suggested that bitter air or rotting stench could work against the equally pungent miasmas of illness.

This method of eradicating miasma was like techniques for dealing with more visible pests. Richard Henry Dana's account of life aboard a merchant vessel in the 1830s describes the practice of clearing a ship's hold of vermin by "smoking" it. Removing all the cargo from the hold, the ship's crew

> made a slow fire of charcoal, birch bark, brimstone, and other matters, on the ballast in the bottom of the hold, calked up the hatches and every open seam. . . . The next morning, we took the battens from the hatches, and opened the ship. A few stifled rats were found, and what bugs, cockroaches, fleas and other vermin there might have been on board must have unrove their lifelines before the hatches were opened.

Perhaps smoking out bedrooms or living quarters suspected of harboring malignant miasmas worked similarly. In addition to provoking counteraction like the work of strong medicine within the body, stench and smoke could smother or drive away the particles of miasma as sailors' fires did infesting insects and rats.

Smell could even defend one's person. Domestic manuals recommended hanging a bag of strong-smelling asafetida around the neck. Such talismanic "assafiddity bags" were a common sight on farms and plantations during feared epidemics. Most extreme was the practice of placing strong-smelling or preventative herbs in the mouth as a barrier to miasma's action. When the earnest missionary and new emigrant Cephas Washburn fell ill during an 1818 journey to scout a mission site, he was all but deserted by his would-be hosts in northwest Arkansas. "Mrs. L," at whose house he collapsed, feared that his sickness (thought to be the dreaded yellow fever) would be communicated to her or her household. She immediately ended all personal contact with her sick visitor. For two weeks, recalled Washburn, "Morning and night she would send her servant, her mouth filled with tansy, lest she should *catch* the fever, to ask if I wanted anything." Stopping up a vulnerable orifice with a strong-smelling herb that would purify the contaminated respiration and stench of the sick missionary, "Mrs. L's" slave registered the potency of odor, breath, and shared air in the communication of illness.

Everyday experience was crucial to the understanding of miasmas, and to fighting them. In his suggested "means of destroying the morbid miasmata," Benjamin Rush drew on commonplace imaginative as well as physical resources to combat a pervasive, entangling, proto-fluid that he could neither see nor fully define. He cited historical precedent to suggest covering "putrid matters [with] water or earth," and suggested that miasmas would have difficulty crossing ditches of water. Rush brought to bear the cleansing power of water, whose spiritual manifestations would be familiar to his Christian readership from the rite of baptism. Washing and rinsing houses and streets and placing "tubs of fresh water" in gross places, he suggested, could stem or slow the onslaught of miasmatic ills. More simply, Rush proposed fastening doors and windows against miasmatic wind. Miasmas were accessible to human perception, and, Rush insisted, vulnerable to everyday interventions.

Combating airborne threats to health placed great responsibility on each individual. Proper clothing and diet, always crucial to health maintenance, were especially critical when going near known sources of miasma. Those who did sicken sometimes held themselves to blame. Qualifying her report of household illness in an 1844 letter, Flora Byrne insisted to her foster sister, "You must not think this place sickly." Byrne's ill husband, Edmond, she explained, "got his attack by riding through the prairie in the hot sun with James Smith, who wished to kill a deer, & my attack was from being exposed to the night air." Byrne insisted that "The place is so well protected from the miasma of the rich bottom of the woods, that no one would get sick unless they exposed themselves wantonly to that miasma—which Edmond certainly did, and I was not quite prudent enough." Headlong chases after game or reckless enjoyment of the early evening could expose the vulnerable system to the workings of wetland miasmas. Keeping well demanded cautious management of impetuous behavior and almost impossibly constant vigilance in the details of domestic life.

Disgust

Emotional and aesthetic perception as well as physical sensation revealed the harmful operation of miasmas. In their many guises, they evoked disgust. To one young Maryland surveyor, sweating through the heat of a Mis-

souri summer, "noxious vapors" were symbolic of a host of harmful relationships besetting the environment. Joseph Shriver exclaimed to his
brother in 1829: "A *new, unsettled country* will always be found to contain
more poisonous animals than an old one. They seem necessary to inhale the
noxious vapors that are constantly rising and therefore *they* may be a chief
cause of the health of a new region!"

In Shriver's understanding, the country's newness and unsettledness were
directly related to its threats to human health. Poisonous animals thrived on
the miasma exhaled from the intrinsically unhealthy *"unsettled"* country.
Shriver's vehemence reflects a common understanding of miasma as existing
in close relationship with things awful, poisonous, slimy, and venomous. Giving an account of central Arkansas in the 1850s, Henry Merrell, a Yankee industrial entrepreneur, complained of "fallen and decayed timber, which bred
insects by millions, and tainted the air with a sickening vapor." A variety of
repulsive and physically difficult elements were produced by the same cause.

The matrix of associations enfolding miasma made it a rhetorically as well
as intellectually useful concept. Poison, disgust, and venom were powerful
concepts of social criticism as well as of bodily and environmental understanding. In reformers' prose, pervasive societal ills were "miasmatic." Ad-
dressing them aided the health of the body politic as destroying
miasma-filled sloughs of rubbish helped physical well-being. The symbolism of miasma underscored an 1858 "Warning to Slave-holders" written by
an escapee, Edmund Turner, formerly of Petersburg, Virginia. Like a latter-
day Moses, Turner urged slave owners to "Let my People go," and be-
seeched them for the sake of their souls to end their participation in chattel
slavery. A note at the close of the letter reflected on his own hard-won freedom: "This signature bears the name of one who knows and felt the sting of
Slavery; but now, thanks be to God, I am now where the poisonous breath
taints not our air. . . ." Identifying those who would enslave others with the
hissing vipers and slithery things feared by contemporaries like Joseph
Shriver, Turner emphasized the sweetness of freedom's air in a passage rich
with physical analogy and emotional resonance.

Expertise and Common Knowledge

The many connections between miasma and other disgusting and disturbing
elements of the world meant that the observer was both empowered and endangered. One's self was a good guide to the qualities of an environment;
the body's sensations accurately registered peril. Air that stank of rot could

in fact be harmful. The rich stench of manure indicated its potential as fertilizer, just as the disgusting odors associated with miasma warned of their infective potential. An "oppressive" smell might join with "noxious vapors" to cause illness. The matter-of-fact reporting of miasma's effects reflected widespread faith that the world spoke in signs that all were equipped to interpret. Miasmas were equally intelligible to nearly illiterate subsistence farmers and to trained physicians; foul smell and clinging fog were interpretable by any farm woman or planter who encountered them.

Scientific explanations of miasma reinforced common perception. One source quoted in an 1839 medical work argued that campfires destroyed miasmas "for the moisture being evaporated by the heat, the poison is either dispersed with the vapor, or, if separated from it, falls innoxious, and probably inert." Hunters drying out mildewy clothing demonstrated common sense consistent with medical recommendation.

Educated observers nonetheless employed scientific rigor to discern the principles of miasmatic action. A few made miasmas almost mathematically calculable. Dr. W. H. Gantt, writing in 1853, explained that the more people who breathed a "pestilential atmosphere" in a given area, the less "violence" each individual attack would have. Gantt's miasma was an entity of quantifiable potency: when divided up among many, its force was lessened. Benjamin Rush similarly argued that rain diluted miasma and therefore rendered it less effective. Such calculations attempted to bring rigor to a horror of looming fogs, but were likely of little comfort to anyone sickened in smelly marshland.

More detailed analysis tried to probe the secrets of miasmas. Army doctor C. B. Welch, at Fort Smith, Arkansas, explained in 1834 that miasma tended to rise because its specific gravity was less than that of air; high ground could therefore in some instances be less healthy than low. In addition, he observed, humid air carried miasma more effectively than dry, "in consequence of the particles of miasmatic poison attaching themselves to the humidity of the air and thereby being carried by the wind." Another 1843 medical author similarly noted that a region's healthfulness was dependent upon "the admixture of terrestrial emanations dissolved in [the atmosphere's] moisture." Such nineteenth-century scientific interest in the relationship between miasma and air was a continuation of earlier seventeenth- and eighteenth-century explorations into the chemistry and composition of air.

Yet though the mechanisms might be mysterious to their less educated contemporaries—and though learned observers might argue over the specific explanations—these and similar speculations about miasmatic action concurred in certain fundamental respects with widespread notions: miasmas, all agreed, were harmful substances that propagated through moist air and could be fought with heat. Whether as attached particles or as "dissolved" emanations, miasma inhabited air in ways that were consistent with broader understanding of the natural world.

Miasmas could also be specific to certain illnesses. Editors of the *St. Louis Medical and Surgical Journal* were unsure why cholera was appearing in the summer of 1850: "With this exception our city is, and has been, unusually healthy." Their supposition was that "the peculiar poison which gives rise to [cholera], still lurks in the atmosphere, and only requires to be developed by some one of the exciting causes." The "peculiar," disease-specific nature of atmospheric "poison" was somewhat speculative, more tenuous than the existence of miasmatic influences in general. The tentative distinction made by the journal, however, speaks to an implicit recognition of different disease types.

Certain illnesses, notably smallpox, were observed in popular sources to spread in distinct, recognizable form, often from person to person, while others, like ague or "biliousness," were understood not to be transmissible between individuals but instead to reflect each person's reaction to the surrounding environment's "constitution." One "bilious" person might experience cramps in the belly, while another could suffer sick-headache. Every person stricken with smallpox, on the other hand, would have distinctive and painful pustules. Environmental causes and bodily predispositions had to converge to produce both kinds of illnesses—a strong constitution could reduce the severity of smallpox, while a weak person would be all the more affected by strong winds or virulent miasmas. The distinction between these disease types was therefore flexible rather than absolute. It is nonetheless significant that miasmas were perceived to play a role both in the illnesses generated by the effects of internal imbalance and in the specific manifestations of identifiable ills. Miasmas could act to make infants "sickly" or "agueish," and could also produce the unmistakable rice-water vomit and shaking blue paroxysms of cholera.

The precise role of miasma in causing or precipitating disease was the subject of heated debate within the elite nineteenth-century medical world, in part because of these disputes about whether disease was transmitted from person to person or caused by environment. Some medical theorists concurred with the widespread understanding of the person-to-person contagion of certain diseases (especially smallpox), arguing that miasmas conveyed illness directly from one individual to another. Most physicians and learned observers of the early part of the century, however, tended to view direct contagion with skepticism and instead blamed generalized atmospheric forces and individual predisposing conditions. These medical authorities denied the role of direct human contagion, arguing instead that overall *environmental* influences, formed of smells, rot, temperature, winds, and other variables, caused disease, and that miasmas simply conveyed these environmental characteristics into the human form.

Debates over contagion versus environmental transmission held great consequences for public health activism throughout the United States and Europe. Heated conflicts animated the pages of learned journals as leading physicians defended the cleanup of garbage or the quarantining of suspect commerce as the most effective way for municipalities to curb disease. Environmental pollution or person-to-person contagion: Which was to blame for the epidemics that ravaged nineteenth-century cities?

Beneath such seemingly intractable disagreement, however, ran undercurrents of theoretical accommodation. Many physicians, like their lay contemporaries, were willing to acknowledge overlapping and interacting forms of disease causation, in which miasmas played multiple roles. As the Missouri doctor J. E. Thompson commented in 1856 in the *Boston Medical and Surgical Journal*, two different epidemics of puerperal peritonitis in western Missouri were "undoubtedly propagated by contagion: *first*, through the medium of a tainted atmosphere; and *second*, through the medium of the accoucheur [midwife]." Clearly, "contagion" was a broad concept, stretching to include many kinds of contact—some still familiar to us moderns, but others more particular to Thompson's world.

Thompson went on to spell out a tripartite structure for the causation of disease in his comments on pertussis: "Some contend that it is *unconditionally contagious*; others ascribe it exclusively to *atmospheric* influences, wholly independent of contagion, either in its origin or its propagation; while another class, taking a middle ground, contend that it may arise from *meteoric* causes, and afterwards become contagious." Sidestepping endless debate through etiological compromise, many practitioners, like their patients, accepted multiple possible causes of disease. Miasmas could act between individuals, as well as between people and their environments, and other environmental causes could always be at issue.

This flexibility about disease causation was of particular utility for commercial elites who hoped to avoid epidemic quarantines that isolated cities and shut down business. If multiple causes, not diseased bodies, were at fault for yellow fever or cholera or other fast-racing diseases, then commerce could continue even as death tolls mounted. Thus for anxious merchants, as for medical professionals and Americans generally, the agency of miasma was a powerfully flexible explanatory resource in the understanding of disease and ill health, one that preserved a certain maneuvering room at city council meetings as at patients' bedsides.

Many medical observers stressed therapeutic action over abstract theorizing. Dr. A. W. Webb traced the constraints on contemporary science when he acknowledged that "The origins and nature of miasmata, their mode of operations, and the influences of exciting causes, are so little understood that they open a wide field for conjecture and speculation."

These limits on scientific apprehension did not, however, blunt his work. Though Webb remained agnostic about how miasmas operated, he wrote for pages about how planters could try to counteract miasmas by retaining uncultivated soil near their houses to absorb miasmatic vapours, and by not doing field work when they or their slaves were hungry, tired, or poorly clothed against damp vegetation. His therapeutic advice was predicated not on a theoretical understanding of miasmas, but on what Webb emphasized was "Ten years practice" in the region where he saw their effects.

Lived experience shaped the ill-defined identity of miasma. Chemical and other investigations had as yet not identified or named the fundamental essence of miasmas, Benjamin Rush acknowledged in 1805, "but their effects are as certainly felt by the human body as the effects of heat, and yet who knows the nature of that great and universal principle of activity . . . ?" Indeed, Rush insisted that the lack of scientific identification of miasmas rendered them no less potent. "It is to no purpose to say," he argued, "the presence of the peculiar matter which constitutes an inflammatory or malignant state of the air has not been detected by any chemical agents." By the *effects* of miasmas their existence was demonstrated, and Rush assembled evidence from around the globe: sick inhabitants near marshes by "the river Vateline," unhealthy cattle in certain regions of the island of Minorca, "morbid appearances" of the livers of diseased cattle in Holland, and sick cows in the United States. These demonstrable physical signs revealed the power of miasmas and obviated the need to isolate miasma itself in the air.

The everyday experiences of his contemporaries bore out Rush's emphasis. Cattle did indeed grow sick without obvious external causes, just as people living near marshes fell prey to diseases that left untouched their neighbors living on higher ground. Miasmas had demonstrable and visible effects on people and livestock. The centrality of miasma as an etiological construct reveals the importance of *experience* in understanding of place in the nineteenth century. Through miasmas, human beings named the myriad ways in which the essential nature of a region could reach out to entangle and sicken them. The action of miasmas tied human health inextricably to the health of the country surrounding them.

Change and the Perils of Human Action

Miasmas were exuded from in-between places and incomplete processes: bottomlands sometimes dry, but periodically flooded, shaded by overhanging trees but still hot with the sun of summer, and full of trees rotting but not yet fully decayed into rich humus. What Dr. G. M. B. Maughs, a Kansas City physician, in 1860 termed "sloughs and foul marshes" provided "fruitful laboratories for the production of *miasma*." Rotting mulch, half-inundated vegetation, and debris warmed by summer heat created and sent into the atmosphere infective miasmatic matter. Miasmas were produced by rot and decay of all kinds. Anything decomposing—no matter how innocuous in its uncorrupted state—was potentially harmful. Such horror of objects in a state of decay or putrefaction reveals nineteenth-century fears of uncontrolled change. Like a human body vulnerable during a moment of transition, matter changing form, losing material integrity and becoming slime or mulch, could exude foul and harmful essences as a byproduct of that shift.

Like the generative energy of the human body, positive forces, if suppressed, could be perverted into putrid miasmatic exhalation. The more potency something possessed in its original state, the more harmful its corrupted energies. Fertile soil, cautioned Edmund Flagg, sent forth a "mephitic vapour" when shaded from the sun. Its powerful energies prevented from working to germinate seed or ripen stalk, the potential of agricultural earth was corrupted by shade, producing harmful emanations instead of life-giving crops. Like a mounting disease, miasma had to be channeled into productive release; otherwise it would remain trapped, hidden, and pathological. A unified logic of change and transformation made sense of foul miasmas as of smelly, pus-laden risings.

Many people held humans themselves responsible for interrupting a dynamic balance in the environment, thus producing miasmas. In his *History and Geography of the Mississippi Valley*, Timothy Flint argued that "deep and grand forests feed their foliage with an atmosphere, that is adverse to the life of man." When forests were cleared, therefore, "the noxious air, that used to be absorbed and devoured by the redundant vegetation and foliage of the forests, and incorporated with its growth," was "inhaled" by cultivators and clearers to cause disease. Flint's argument is revealing on many levels. His implicit natural history of the environment omitted any reference to Native

American fire-clearing and agriculture. In Flint's logic, American settlers were the initial disturbers of an environment previously in equilibrium. In Flint's account, miasma actively fed vegetation, being "devoured" by foliage and "incorporated" into its organic development. Miasma was like manure, air, or water, a potent ingredient of life. This system of nature had a certain balance, until settlers intervened to fell trees and force clearings. Only with human—that is, *American*—action did miasma become extraneous, unconsumed, and without purpose. Entering into plants, it nourished them. Entering human bodies, it brought sickness and even death.

American newcomers thus recognized the dangers as well as the potential of altering their environments. They intuited some of the hazards of their own transformations of the environment even as they thrust their way forward. Henry Marie Brackenridge's 1814 emigrants' guide listed miasmas as one of many interlinked threats to health generated by American settlement:

> Much depends on the care which the settler takes in avoiding whatever may tend to produce sickness. The scorching heat of the sun is universally agreed to be unfavorable to health. Night dews and exhalations are not less so. The food of most of the settlers, is calculated to generate bile; great quantities of fat pork, seldom any fresh meat, or vegetables, and large quantities of milk and coarse corn bread are used. The mephitic exhalations from putrid vegetables, and from enormous masses of putrefying trees, in the new clearings, also contribute to this insalubrity. The fields of corn, with which the settler surrounds his cabin, are thought by many, to be another cause; the foliage of the corn is so rich and massy, that it shades the earth, and prevents the action of the sun from exhaling unwholesome damps.

Not just one aspect of settlement but an association of practices and processes brought disruption and danger. Fieldwork and food preparation alike could threaten harm. The newness of settlement was itself to blame: labor in high heat, consumption of the rough meat and cornmeal that were a new homestead's initial foods, the decay of recently girdled or felled trees, even the surging growth of a corn crop all produced danger. "New clearings" brought a host of changes to an environment, and the resultant processes of decay and putrefaction could sicken the newcomers whose labor was the cause.

Not only wild environments but long-settled cities testified to human culpability in producing miasmatic poison. The cotton mills of Massachusetts produced "a heated and an unnatural air," argued Timothy Flint, "an atmosphere, if I may so say, of cotton." Such an atmosphere had ill effects both moral and physical on the young people who labored to turn the South's bales of white cotton into bolts of processed cloth. Denouncements of "asphyxiating coal gas that covers the green meadows like a toxic blight" became a staple of mid- and late-nineteenth-century travel writing. Such creeping blight was the industrially tainted miasma of an ever more commercial and industrialized frontier.

Geology and population patterns rendered St. Louis particularly susceptible to foul airs. The karst, or porous rock, underlying the city was easily eroded by rain into subterranean caves that could suddenly collapse. These sinkholes collected water and hampered swift drainage, and despite innovative early efforts to create a sewer system that would wash the city's storm water and waste out into the Mississippi, as late as the 1890s, foul masses of sewage would regularly back up in low-lying areas of the city. Such pollution led to urban agitation, and those who could afford to moved away. Urban spaces, like those of undeveloped or transitional swampland, could be abundantly unhealthy and impure. An environment characterized by oozing trash piles, industrial smoke, and raw sewage running down gutters in the city's streets produced "vapours" and "exhalations" as toxic as the rot of newly cut trees or partially drained swampland.

Accounts such as Flint's fit with a Jeffersonian rhetoric of the healthful wild and the diseased city, the baleful influence of human development as opposed to the cleansing power of the uncorrupted landscape. Yet common perception, unlike political argument, viewed the natural world with a somewhat more jaundiced eye. Miasmas could indeed be the product of human intervention mishandled or misapplied, but the "natural" itself held similarly lethal potential. The forces of undisturbed surroundings included healthful air and cooling breezes, but also roaring flood, tearing earthquake, and "noxious" miasma. The downed trees whose rot bred stench, grubs, and disease could have been toppled by woodcutters or by a lightning strike. Many medical observers viewed towns as being more salubrious than rough, frontier settlements. Though the ideal of the innately healthy countryside held power as a political and artistic trope, few accounts of American borderlands expansion reveal such a simple dichotomy—or such ease with a surrounding world manifestly threatening and dangerous.

Yet human agency could bring order as well as harm, health as well as danger. William Switzler, a Missouri settler and lifelong booster of the trans-Mississippi West, reflected on the condition of Arkansas in 1836, the year it became a state. While acknowledging Arkansas's present abundance of harmful miasmas, he affirmed migration and cultivation as "cures":

> [Arkansas] is now as all other newly settled countries are, subject to the irresistible vapour called by physicians "miasthma," supposed to arise from dis-

tempered, putrefying or poisonous vegitation or bodies in its nature insalubrious, & produces wherever it rises, ague & fever. From this fact it is plausible
to suppose that when the vegitation (which springs up & grows spontaneously
over the vast prairies and plains) is destroyed . . . when the country becomes
more densely inhabited, that the state of Arkansas will prove as healthy as any
other state in the Union, but so long as the country remains in its present state,
the surface veiled with fragments of trees and vegitation that spring up, flourish & decay without molestation, it will prove insalubrious. When these impediments are removed (and emigration is all that is requisite to remove them)
there is no reason to doubt but that Arkansas will present as many healthy
neighbourhoods, towns & villages, as any other state of the same dimensions.

Carried to completion, settlement would quiet a "distempered" environment as a cool wash could quiet a raging fever. Breaking up "impediments"
as cathartic medicines might internal blockages, the process of settlement
released terrain into a "healthy" state. Human action, Switzler argued,
cleansed the "veiled" surface of the countryside, destroying the "spontaneous" outgrowths that erupted from land's wildness, and covered it instead
with the congressionally mandated and geometrically ordered "neighbourhoods, towns & villages."

Blurred Boundaries

The stinking cesspools dreaded by prosperous midcentury St. Louis merchants and the miasma-laced exhalations of thick grassland of the 1830s
might seem to us modern observers to have little in common: they were
from radically different kinds of environments, and though we recognize
sewage as a real danger in our present day, few of us would fear new-plowed
soil as a threat to health. Yet behind these and other environmental anxieties
of the American western borderlands, slipping on- and offstage like a barely
glimpsed thief whose surreptitious actions nonetheless propel the drama,
was invisible but amply felt bad air. Miasmas flouted distinction between
people and their land, blurring the boundary between self and surroundings.

Miasmas were breathed back and forth by people and their organic world,
connecting and binding together person and place. An 1839 emigrants'
guide typically referred to "exhalations from the soil" in describing factors
of sickness in the Mississippi Valley. The naturalist and artist John James
Audubon warned in identical language of the debilitating effect on squatters
along the Mississippi of "exhalations arising from the swamps and
morasses." Soil and trees, particularly, were seen to "breathe out" miasma.
The imagery of embodiment enlivening these descriptive passages under-

scores the interrelationship between humans and the places they struggled to make theirs.

Miasmas operated in and through human bodies just as they did waters, vegetation, or earth. Once inside a person, many observers argued, miasmas could be given off as they were from inanimate matter. They existed and preserved their essential characteristics in the human body as in a body of water or land. Furthermore, environmentally created miasma could be discharged from an individual's body along with excretion, exhalation, or other bodily emanations. Thus diarrhea could have a salutary effect, as Benjamin Rush made clear in the rhetorical question he posed in his 1811 annotation of William Hillary's 1759 account of yellow fever in Barbados: "Were not some of the infectious miasmata, or of the morbid matter, discharged and carried off by those loose stools, which rendered the above symptoms more moderate and milder after?" Like land, water, and vegetation, the human form was a potent source of noxiously infective miasmatic material.

Another medical work reprinted in the aspiring *St. Louis Medical and Surgical Journal* reported with distaste and suspicion on the effects of "highly putrescent organic matter, mingled with the expired air." Its effects were absolute: "Wherever, either from the presence of numbers or the absence of ventilation, you have the fetid sickening air generated by human effluvia, there assuredly you will find fever." As disease essences generated from terrain or water subsequently passed through individuals, breath carried the essence of disease. This action of miasma in and through the human body blurred the boundaries between self and environment.

Reproductive potential further united the environment and the human body. Air could be a productive force within the environment: "The wind laid & produced a frost," commented the Missouri farmer and healer John Geiger in October 1836. In other accounts, disease-bearing miasma was the generative agent acting upon air. Audubon, using phrases typical of travelers to the thickly vegetated morasses of the South and West, made reference to "one of those sultry days which render the atmosphere of the Louisiana swamps pregnant with baneful effluvia." His offhandedness implies the ease with which his readers would connect miasma, parturition, and the power of moist heat to nurture the growth of noisome "effluvia" as well as highkneed swamp cypress and thick lowland cotton.

Air itself could be fecund with disease. In an 1857 account of his experience of smallpox, a Missouri traveler, Peter Carr, recounted that he journeyed in a train with a feverish man, and a "current of air impregnated with the accursed virus, may have been wafted to me." Innocent but fertile, air currents were the unwitting agents of miasmatic reproduction, in language closely allied with that of the human body.

The fertility of the human body was forced and unwilling. In his 1805 *Inquiry into the Various Sources of . . . Summer & Autumnal Disease*, Benjamin Rush warned his readers of a visitor to Philadelphia who carried away "the seeds of the yellow fever in his body" and subsequently sickened his wife, and of another "who left Philadelphia when highly impregnated with the miasmata of the same fever." Each individual was at once vulnerable and fertile. Stealing into the human frame, miasma raped the human soil, causing it to bear illness rather than health. Weakened and made womanly by the power of their surroundings, even masculine bodies could bear this monstrous progeny. Like the natural environment, the human form could be acted upon in the most intimate of ways; the fertility of human and that of terrain were both encompassed in one structure of understanding.

In a later passage, Rush cautioned that "In leaving a place infected by miasmata, care should be taken not to expose the body to great cold, heat, or fatigue, for eighteen or twenty days, lest they should excite the dormant seeds of the disease into action." Rush's comments presented the body as soil planted with miasma's deadly "dormant seeds." The language as well as the mechanism of such descriptions spanned the human and the agricultural: in the nineteenth century, "seed" could denote either semen or a plant's generative kernel. Just as farmers and makers of kitchen plots mulched, plowed, planted, watered, and tended the earth, they themselves were acted upon by the generative potential of the surrounding world. Unlike the wholesome preparations of a farmer, however, or the normal development of a growing child, foul and harmful forces excited the poisonous seed of miasma. This noxious agriculture would in time manifest itself as illness and disease.

Through the action of miasma, bodies experienced their environments directly and dramatically. Human beings shared essential characteristics with their surroundings. Trees and rotting vegetation exhaled miasma; human soil nurtured miasmatic seed into growth; fecundity in the external environment was matched with human procreation. This blurring of language was neither coincidental nor vestigial. The potential and vulnerability of the individual were those of surrounding terrain. The human body registered miasmatic action the same way the world of nature did. In familiar and reassuring ways, common notions of health and place explained lived experience. The good airs and baleful miasmas of the Mississippi Valley created a fundamental identity between human and environment, one that antebellum Americans lived with every breath.

WATERS

Chapter V

WATERS WERE THE LIFEBLOOD of early Missouri and Arkansas. Just as warm blood coursed through trunk and limbs, pooling at times in harmful ill-adjustment, needing occasional release from plethoric flow, but in its normal course dispersing strength and vitality throughout the body, watercourses sped transit and commerce, connected people with markets and far-flung families, but threatened periodically to become congested, to overflow, and even lethally to overwhelm. Water in proper flow nourished each individual's system, bringing health, news, and products into and out of the Mississippi Valley. When water failed, crops withered, and with them, settlers' hopes. When water overflowed and coursed in wild imbalance, it brought miasmas lapping at cabin doors and ate up lowlands in overengorged sprawl.

To an extent foreign to us moderns, the waters of a place defined and characterized it for nineteenth-century people. Perhaps only present-day sailors, or those who inhabit areas of extreme aridity, have a similar sense for the ways in which the presence or absence, the taste, flow, and color of water could define the world in practical terms. What most of us experience as a clear rush from our faucets bears little relationship to the environmental force earlier Americans encountered when they forded streams, took shelter from rainfall, or gulped from metal cups water stained brown by the tannic acid of autumn's leaves, steeped in alkaline soils and mossy rock growth, animated by the quick flash of minnows and the sudden flick of crayfish. Waters were experienced in many ways like airs: they were necessary to life, they existed in many different forms, and though people could harness and use them, they were never fully under human control. Unlike airs, waters could be poured, touched, put into containers—and their role in

133

health was less theoretically pliable. They nonetheless represented a range of influence on human affairs, affecting work, commerce, and well-being in their varied on-rushing flow.

Conduit

Water was not only the primary entry into environments for early American observers and settlers, but a way to structure understanding of new terrain. Exacting descriptions specified the degree of wateriness of a region, from "dry, airy, and eligible" sites that "will command many advantages for mercantile purposes," to "pondy" bottoms, to a river "swimming for a mile" (in this last it was *travelers* who had to swim it to cross it). Official maps, emphasized an anxious Land Office official, were to "accurately indicate" the "extent of land" occupied by particularly notorious swamps, for water-laden places constrained travel and shaped other uses of terrain.

Daniel Drake epitomized the attention to waters within "new" American environments, as he epitomized so much else about the American western movement. Drake structured his entire mammoth 1850 treatise on medical understanding of the West, the two-volume *Systematic Treatise, Historical, Etiological, and Practical, on the Principal Diseases of the Interior Valley of North America,* as an investigation into major rivers' drainage systems. His was a "hydrographical method," he explained, through which he explored the human geography of American territories by tracing streams to their sources and observing both "alpine and marine borders" of the Mississippi valley. In framing his research within the continent's "Interior Valley," Drake represented both the ways in which river systems bounded land—especially in the period before American political boundaries of town or county were firmly established in theory or surveyed on the ground—and the ways in which they were central to popular perceptions of terrain.

Waters and waterways were also crucial to the economic and social well-being of growing American communities. Streams and rivers were always described in detail in boosters' accounts of Missouri and Arkansas. Where there were good streams, prospective emigrants knew, they would enjoy cheaper transport, more frequent mail, and more easily plowed bottomland. Waterways represented exchange and contact. "[S]ending this to the river" was the way northern Missouri correspondent Flora Byrne termed her mailing of a letter. The Mississippi carried not only thickly roiling water, but communication between two foster sisters separated by marriage and migration. Even for those living in slavery, rivers represented possibilities for greater autonomy and freedom. The noted novelist William Wells Brown, an escaped Missouri slave and abolitionist, narrated in his autobiography the relative freedom of Missouri slaves who worked for hire in the river trades. Taking work or booking passage aboard steamboats (whose captains were often too urgently in need of labor to be very careful about checking free papers) was an avenue of escape for some.

Yet the sinuous rivulets of summer rain that nourished crops and slaked thirst were kin to the crowding, sinister waters of torrential floods and the brooding, silted ponds that bred mosquitoes and foul "corruption." Water could impose as well as grant, threaten as well as bless. Multiple kinds of waters coursed through the accounts of early Arkansas and Missouri, waters good and bad, sweet and baleful. Though in documents of the period these many waters lay intertwined and interflowing, like the many streams rushing into the course of the thick, wide Mississippi, carefully separating them and accounting for their differences reveals some of the metaphoric and spiritual meaning, as well as the many aspects of physical necessity, granted by the waters of bottomland and high country.

Blessing

Clear, fresh, reliable waters were avidly sought, described, and celebrated (though not always shared) by newcomers to Missouri and Arkansas. Those moving through terrain found water to be one of their most pressing needs. Thirst was a theme of countless descriptions. Migrants' accounts stressed the aching disappointment when springs or pools were fouled or had run dry. Racked with thirst by fever and the heat of travel, the Arkansas missionary Cephas Washburn resolved to drink from a small pond, though his companion attempted to dissuade him and "its color was almost that of milk." His story follows every movement of desire: "I had just brought my parched and blistered lips to the water, when a large moccasin snake plunged into the pool directly under my mouth. I could hardly restrain my tears, so great was my disappointment." A "drink of first rate cold water," on the other hand, could be welcome enough to warrant including in a travel diary, as did the naturalist S. W. Woodhouse in 1849.

Locations were valued in direct proportion to their nearness to what one 1839 Danish report on Missouri termed "good running water." Fresh, potable water was an immediate and universal need. Settlers were delighted when water was easy to attain, where it was "no trouble to git," where "no rock in this country" hindered the digging of wells. Wry realism pervaded the advice of an Arkansas farmer, Silvester How, to his Uncle Jo, who contemplated emigration in 1860: "tell him," he wrote his cousin Jane Pursley, "if he ever comes to this part of Arkansas—Bring his well with him for if he [doesn't] he will have to go Back after it." The search for good water was in some ways always ephemeral. "[N]ext fall if i live i intend to go to the Colorado River in Texas where there is good water they say," How continued, chasing the elusive promise of "good water" that was always over the next boundary, perhaps on the Colorado, perhaps further west, or perhaps just on better land within one's own territory or state.

Once located, waters were evaluated by smell, taste, aspect, temperature, and color. That the Arkansas River had a similar color to the Missouri was for one 1819 settler a positive recommendation for family emigration. Above Alexandria on the Mississippi, another remarked that "The water is red and tastes like lye." Many travelers noticed that the water streaming from the Missouri River was visibly separate well after it joined the Mississippi. The colored waters of the Missouri—milky, light-brown, gray, and in some lights even crimson or silver, from the sands, clays, gravels, and limestone that leached into it along its journey—would keep to the west bank, visually maintaining its identity. Color told the origin and character of waters as it might betray the anger or choleric temper of a person's countenance. "The river on the rise," wrote the judge and farmer John Geiger of the Mississippi in 1839, "and very muddy as if the Missouri predominated."

Aspects of water embodied and reinforced perceived salubrity of land. "This is a healthy country & the water is Good," wrote Everard Dickinson to his parents from northern Arkansas in 1850. Descriptions of new territories consistently linked "fine Clear Spring and well water" with "the appearance of Being a healthy place." Hermann Steines, a young German sent as a scout for family emigration, wrote home in May of 1834 to describe farms near Washington, Missouri: "The soil is very good, the location healthful and the water excellent." Waters conveyed the healthfulness considered to inhere in sites to the people using them.

In the medical understanding of the time, water occupied a middle ground between food and air. It was at once an aspect of nourishment and a more general influence. That water was necessary to the whole strength and functioning of the "human organism" was abundantly clear. Individuals deprived of water weakened in both body and mind, and went mad with features pinched and darkened by dehydration before dying a painful death. Fresh water was therefore seen to act like food or air, a necessary ingredient to be brought into the body. The flowing of water into the individual system was, moreover, helpful or harmful in the same ways as the flow of air: both airs and waters carried something of the essence of the natural world, infusing those qualities into the bodies into which they were taken. A profound sympathy operated through water; ingesting healthy waters rendered the body healthy.

Even the most ordinary water could bear with it balance, restoration, or harm. A "change of waters" could "set . . . right" an ill family member, hoped John Brown, echoing a conviction shared by many of his contemporaries. Bringing a new region's waters into the system could help bolster the body against the ravages of illness or the ill effects of some other environmental influence. On the other hand, the power of waters was such that healers sometimes feared they could strengthen a disease that held a sick person in peril. Silas Turnbo recalled that his grandfather, during his mortal illness in 1827, was forbidden by attending physicians to have anything to drink. Though a "fine spring of living water was in forty yards of the house," "[h]e died begging for water."

"Strong" water could be effective in the same way as a "strong" medicine— "a powerful cathartick and . . . a purifier of the blood!" was how one traveler described the water of the Mississippi in 1814. Though "clear" water was highly prized, many people also regarded water with a high degree of mineral content or sediment as healthful. Such was the case with water of the Mississippi near St. Louis, which one German emigrant reported in 1842 was "said to be healthful," despite the fact that in the summer it was "of course, tepid, and besides so muddy that a glass-full has a muddy deposit a quarter of an inch thick when it has stood for half an hour." Similarly, a Milanese nobleman traveling through the area in the late 1830s commented that the Missouri river water was "wholesome" despite its turbidity: "it only requires a little courage to swallow it for a few days, and then one has the habit." Health seekers regarded such muddy waters as healthful precisely because they were so intimidating: the manifestly roiled and impure water held potency, with respect to newcomers' bodies as well as the lands they sought to claim.

Threat

In 1819, the beleaguered surveyor William Rector sought to explain to his superiors in Washington the nagging delays in completing a survey of the region between the St. Francis and Arkansas rivers in east-central Arkansas Territory. His explanation, which touched on several important threats to health that bedeviled his crews, betrayed his frustration: "Every one of the Surveyors as well as their hands were greatly afflicted with sickness, produced I suppose by working very hard in the midst of summer, drinking bad water &c, by which they lost much time." "Bad water," along with hard labor in summer's heat, was to blame for serious illness that hampered communication and community development. That early settlement was slow and cumbersome in the delta regions in the east of Arkansas, where midcentury planters would later grow rich from acres of cotton, was due not only to the unstable swampland hindering roads and blocking transit but also to the sickening effect of ingested water.

Noxious water, like noxious air, inverted the properties of healthful fluid. Rather than strengthening the human form, it left people weak or ill. "Everything going to destruction, drinking the worst kind of water, breaking our constitutions," fretted the newly married Virginia emigrant Elizabeth Ann Cooley McClure as she nursed her sick husband through a bout of Missouri ague and fever. Harmful water was often dark, still, smelly, and foul-tasting. It carried green or slimy growth and was hard to see through. Confronted after a long day of hot travel with another small, shallow pond whose "whole surface was covered in a thick green scum," Cephas Washburn and his missionary colleagues were "compelled [by their thirst] to drink it, surcharged as it was with malaria." Unequipped to comprehend the microscopic world that at times assailed them, Washburn and his contemporaries relied on clues manifest in their surroundings. The appearance and texture of the water signaled its potential harmfulness. Water and air shared consistent qualities: "thick green scum" was the visible sign of permeating miasmatic "malaria" which corrupted and degraded the pond.

Disgust and harm were linked in the effects of water as of air. In 1834, Captain John Stuart of Fort Smith in the Arkansas Territory described sickness arising from the sensually unpleasant and materially harmful products of stagnant and rotting water:

> one greate cause to produce Sickness here arises from the Porteau [River], which empties itself in the Arkansas immediately at the Fort, It is frequently backed up by the Arkansas to the distance of twenty miles, and when that happens in the Summer its Water becomes Stagnant and is covered with a Green or Yellow Scum, and emits at times a very offensive Effluvia.

Effluvia rising from the stagnant, backed-up waters of the river were offensive to the body's health as well as to its senses. The bright "Green or Yellow" of the "Scum" contrasted vividly with the normal colors of free-flowing water, and its smells perverted the qualities associated with clear-flowing streams. The color, odor, and effects of "bad" waters were foully and mutually consistent.

The straightforward logic of sense perception meant that peopled environments were as intelligible as "wild" ones. Henry Kayser, St. Louis's street commissioner, complained in the 1840s of the stopped-up sinkhole outlets left by the combination of the city's porous limestone topography and its copious wastes. In particular, a late-nineteenth-century city history complained, drainage problems created on Biddle Street "a very ugly body of water, which in summer changed to a yellow-green, and emitted vapors freighted with chills, fever, and death." Nearby residents agreed, calling the reeking pond "Kayser's Lake" and agitating to have it once and for all drained. "Choteau's Pond" was a similar combination of industrial effluvia and topographic happenstance that for decades stank up the southern portion of downtown. With water as with air, harm could flow from pollution seen as natural or as arising from human interventions. City manufacturing plants or rivers running by a frontier outpost could be equally indicted under the rubrics of geographical well-being.

People viewed stagnant water in particular with alarm. Any fluid that did not flow freely was a potential source of harm analogous to the "stoppage of . . . courses" in the human body. Gently flowing water was generative and productive, nourishing people and crops, but if its flow was stopped, this potential could become grossly perverted. Even the usually pure rainwater of storage cisterns could, as the traveler Henry Miller feared, "bring forth" grubs or other noisome insects if dirtied with fallen leaves or sullied with the dust of the roofs from which it was collected. Stagnant water was harmful both in itself and as an element of an environment. It was detrimental to drink, and it also gave forth essences that wrought harm in and through its surroundings.

Early Americans perceived a close connection between water and miasmatic ills. The telling names of Sick Creek in the swampy districts of eastern Arkansas and the Fever River mentioned by the Missouri farmer Stephen Hempstead were typical expressions of this long-standing and threatening relationship. "Over the sluggish waters of [slow-moving] streams," complained an 1835 Arkansas petition from the territorial legislature, "disease and pestilence are ever brooding." Though Congress did not approve their request for funds to build a hospital near the mouth of the White River, the legislators' appeal spoke eloquently of the malevolent effects of miasmatic waters on ever-threatened immigrants.

Bottomlands were regarded as sickly for those working and living on them. Yet at the same time, antebellum people recognized that "the land of good quality . . . generally is confined to the different streams." This created a dense paradox for would-be settlers: "I was thinking of setting my cabin on the rocks that line the Missouri," mused one French emigrant in 1837, reflecting the need for both fresh-running water and transportation, "[but] I was told that fevers are more to be feared at the edge of waters." Settlers confronted the irony of good situations: proximity to waterways, so necessary for economic well-being, meant proximity to miasma and deadly ills.

Many reports of illness and good health focused on how contact with water could affect the body. One former Missouri slave reported that jumping into a "deep and cold hole in the river" was the only way his father found to fight off a bout of chills and fever that medicines had failed to cure. In contrast, being caught in rain or soaked by "damp dews" could engender "protracted cases of intermittents," which could be countered only by strong action or "broken up by emetics." Wet bodies were cold bodies, dangerously out of balance. Stephen Hempstead noted the grim consequences of getting thoroughly drenched in his 1820 diary notation on the death of his brother and sister-in-law: "They took cold by being wet, that Brought on a Bilious fever of which they Servived but a few days." A chain of inattention began with allowing oneself to be soaked, led to a besetting fever, and ended in mortal illness. Water was one of the many grave threats against which individuals and families had to guard.

Distrust of thoroughly immersing the body was cultural as well as physical. The sacramental rite of complete submersion customary among Baptists "causes coughs and colds," reported the suspicious German emigrant Nicholas Hesse. Being in water was also dangerous to nonswimmers. The ex-slave Solomon Northup reported of his twelve years in bondage that slaves "are not allowed to learn the art of swimming, and are incapable of crossing the most inconsiderable stream." This enforced ignorance was crucial to slave holders' ability to control slaves: in the swampy Bayou Boeuf area of northern Louisiana where Northup was held, inability to swim meant that slaves had few opportunities for flight. A shock to one's system or outright death by drowning could both be the unhappy consequences of being overcome by water.

The combined effects of heat and water were particularly dangerous. The simultaneous experience of heat and of slogging, muddy, watery labors was common to many in early Missouri and Arkansas. Given the area's hot, humid summers and many streams and swamps, physical labor in both fields and engineering projects often meant being uncomfortably hot and wet. These two potent properties magnified each other. "I have now about 25 men on the sick list," reported the supervisor of the project to clear obstructions from the Red River in 1833; "the labour is severe and exposes near the whole force to the heat of the sun and constantly in the water."

An 1853 editorial in the *St. Louis Medical and Surgical Journal* expressed the ways in which both heat and moisture nourished noxious properties in the environment, particularly through the agency of miasmatic airs. Commenting on the recent epidemic of yellow fever in New Orleans, the editors reflected that "For some time previously rain had fallen almost daily, and this added to a hot, burning sun, seemed to give strength to the poison, and lent intensity to the disease." This skepticism about rainfall contrasted strongly with the common perception of the health-giving properties of "frequent and refreshing rains." John Brown noted in his journal in 1855, "A heavy rain this morning. Great rejoicing." Yet even showers of rain, which gave life to fields, damped the dust of dry roads and fields, and lifted spirits in the hot months of summer, could foster harm within the environment. Summer rains and burning summer sun gave rise to miasmatic "poison" just as they gave energy to planted fields. Water was an ambiguous force: powerful in many ways, but never securely and unchangeably welcome.

Flood

Flooding was a chronic problem for the American settlers who based their agriculture on the rich soil created by river floodplains. What the river had given it could well steal away. Unavoidable, unpredictable, and catastrophic, "freshes" (floods) took away livelihood and threatened prospects just like grave illness or other calamity. Serious floods struck the Mississippi region throughout the antebellum period, with especially destructive overflows in 1826, 1844, and 1856. The state of nearby rivers was thus the subject of individual record and community discussion—when they "riz," when they were "on a stand," and when they "fell."

Floods were terrifying and disorienting. Second Lieutenant Lancaster Platt Lupton, sent east from a border post to Nashville in 1833, was forced to travel by boat through "boiling floods" in Arkansas Territory. He wrote in his journal: "The Arkansas when high boils up from the bottom like a pot of boiling water—owing I believe to the rolling of the sand with which the bottom is covered—these boils as they are called, are sometimes so violent as to upset small boats."

Such frenetic water rose quickly, lapping at doorways and pulling cattle under, killing families who failed to escape to higher ground. The roiling up of normally placid water could cause riverbanks suddenly to collapse, creating what Lupton called "a most tremendious crash which lasted more than a minute." The frightening sounds of a "booming flood" signaled great danger—the falling in of many acres of heavily timbered riverside could easily capsize a small craft the size of Lupton's—and were but one aspect of waters running riot. When rivers rose to overflow their banks, landscapes were transformed: high places became islands, the stench of rotting flesh and vegetation blanketed huge areas, the normal noises of woodland or field were silenced, and even fierce predators became cowed in the ceaseless damp.

Floods transformed familiar places, chaotically rearranging homes and farms. Boys in a White River family had to harvest corn during an 1824 rise by bravely riding their horses into the water covering the family's small field and reaching down under water to feel for the tall shocks. One resident of early Arkansas later recalled a flood in February 1834: "Many persons were drowned in their beds, so sudden was the rise, while others were rescued, more dead than alive, by passing steamboats, after having been imprisoned in tall trees for several days and nights." An environment could be turned upside-down by the ever-encroaching onrush of water out of control.

The long-term consequences of flooding could be profound. Rivers changed course; fields were wiped out; whole settlements were swept into disarray. As Mark Twain observed of the constant silt deposition and channel-shifting of the frequently flooding Mississippi: "Nearly the whole of that one thousand three hundred miles of old Mississippi River which La Salle floated down in his canoes, two hundred years ago, is good solid dry ground now. The river lies to the right of it, in places, and to the left of it in other places." Waters created changes profound and individual, re-making environments throughout their powerful flow.

Floods brought a conjunction of economic and bodily harm. B. W. Lee, a farmer and physician suffering inundations and flooded fields at Arkansas Post (along the Arkansas River in the southeast part of the state), lamented to a St. Louis friend in 1844 that "I almost envy you your locality, above all over flow, and in a salubrious helthy atmosphere, whilst we are surrounded by water, and threatened at altimes with disease." The "over flow" suffered by many such river towns during that flood year effected many kinds of injury: it washed away topsoil, forced people into close contact with the broad stagnant waters productive of miasmas, and blocked travel and communication with a sometimes impassable moat that "surrounded," hemmed in, and in many ways controlled the lives of flooded-out farmers. The commercial torpor of water-logged districts was like that of a body distended by a gross imbalance of humors. Simultaneously barrier, conduit, and destructive force, preventing human movement while sweeping away fields and conveying miasmatic influences, overflowing, uncontrollable water was destructive and "insalubrious" to economic hopes and personal health alike.

The sudden chaos of flooding waters disrupted the stable relationship between self and surroundings which nineteenth-century Americans hoped fervently to establish and maintain. Despite the clack and roar of mills and manufactories, despite the commercial hubbub of crazily expanding cities like St. Louis, people of this era moved and breathed in profound connection with their environments. The terrible changes wrought by floods temporarily broke those connections and disrupted the balance of self with surroundings toward which so much antebellum energy was directed. Such disruption underscores the threat posed by the dynamic and ill-understood influences of an ever-changing world.

When terrain was flooded, the consequences of environmental imbalance were made manifest in human ill health. Reflecting on the floods of 1844, John Geiger recorded that "as [the water] commenced to fall then commenced a sickness which was very great." The resultant congestive fever "was very common untill the summer & fall of 1846." The health consequences of overflow were not merely local and limited in duration but characterized the disease environment of a region for some time after. Apart from the ill effects of the water itself, floods represented an instance of radical change that could also harmfully affect the human body. "This season with us has been remarkably sickly," remarked the missionary Cephas Washburn in 1833, explaining, "This is doubtless to be attributed to the great fresh & the peculiarities of the season." Clear water nourished health; flooding waters brought miasmas and illness. Moreover, anything that disrupted or made "peculiar" the usual patterns of season and year was intrinsically unhealthful: when floods disrupted the rhythms of life, people sickened and even died.

As accounts of flooding suggest, bodies of water could conduct or they could block. The Mississippi's strong current allowed hollow logs tightly packed with valuable bear grease and steamboats heavily loaded with precious cotton to travel quickly down to market at New Orleans, while unexpected flooding raised a barrier to human crossing as sure and effective as a massive wall. This dual function of water operated within the natural world as well as in human affairs. Sicknesses, like the people they beset, could be transported or frustrated by an environment's waters.

The rushing power of a large river served to protect nearby communities, even as it threatened periodic overflow. The *St. Louis Medical and Surgical Journal* argued in 1847 against the notion (widely held both in the area and beyond) that the city was "by virtue of its location and other uncontrolable circumstances necessarialy more unhealthy than other cities in the same latitude." Instead, the editors insisted, St. Louis's location actually contributed to good health: "According to the best authorities, marsh miasmata cannot pass over a body of water so large as that afforded by the Mississippi." Such arguments stemmed, perhaps, from common perception of the ethereal and airy nature of miasmas: malign spirits in European folk tradition had similar difficulty crossing bodies of open water.

Water's power in terrain raised anxieties like those related to personal well-being. In southwestern Arkansas the balky obstruction of the Red River Raft acted within the growing state polity like the internal obstructions against which domestic therapies were directed. Blocking the river, unyielding even to the strongest of attacks and treatments, the raft was an expression in the greater physical world of the internal blockages of forces and fluids that so concerned early Americans. To a people plagued with constipation and outfitted with a series of remedies designed to loosen various obstructions and release stubborn menstrual flow, the raft was another reflection of the ways the natural world and the human body were subject to a consistent set of properties, functions, and problems.

The language of river and waterway reinforced a sense within the perceptual world of the nineteenth century that an underlying identity united bodies of water and human beings' bodies. The geologist George W. Featherstonhaugh, in a report on Arkansas excerpted by the *Arkansas Gazette* in 1835, termed the Arkansas a "noble, but too uncertain stream." Featherstonhaugh was concerned about the "constant change" in the river's course and obstructions like "snags" or "sawyers"—trees that lurked under the surface of the river, threatening steamboats and smaller craft. High flow meant that rivers could carve out new bends or curves, swallowing farmland with smooth and devastating ease. Featherstonhaugh's language, however, was that of character evaluation. Even in his cool scientist's prose, environment was personified and made human.

The qualities of waters affected all aspects of well-being. The "bad waters" confronted by frustrated settlers and floodplain engineers were at once injurious to personal health, frustrating to their work plans, and harmful to the planned political and economic development of the swampy territory. Nowhere were these obnoxious qualities of water more in evidence than in the many swamps that plagued early Americans in their attempts to travel and farm on solid, predictable ground.

Swamp

Frustrated travelers and farm families frequently found themselves and their ambitions held fast by muck in the antebellum Mississippi Valley. Mire, bog, swamp, marsh, slough, backwater, bayou, morass—many different words named unpleasantly watery terrain. Swamps ranged from the Mingo Swamp in the Missouri boot heel, deceptively covered in thick vegetation, to the occasional boggy meadow, flooded in high water, to the "quaking prairies" over which people could only tremulously cross as the quasi-solid mass of vegetation shook beneath them, to lake-like areas bounded by high-kneed cypress that could be navigated only by boat.

Waters in these places were still, and mineral and vegetal material from surrounding soils and plants seeped into them. Descriptions of the greenish color and oozing texture of swamp regions reflected travelers' fascination with the gross and abhorrent qualities they represented. Swamps were the abode of multiple agents of harm—miasmas, alligators, hanging moss, poisonous snakes, and ill-defined buggy and slimy things. These many forms of threat came together in intermixture in a "sloo," in a fluid matrix of scummy water and floating swampgrass.

What one 1836 traveler called "swamps and miry bayous" were not new to Americans' and Europeans' experience, but they were certainly new as a defining element of the natural world. Swampy areas hindered migrants throughout the bottomlands of Louisiana, Missouri, and Arkansas, and the "great swamp," or "Mississippi Swamp," extended across much of what is now the cotton and soybean country of eastern Arkansas, just west of the Mississippi, substantially limiting migration into Arkansas. It was a boggy barrier that profoundly affected roads, communication, and territorial business.

Friedrich Gerstäcker knew that his German readers would not be familiar with the environments in which he set so many of his Arkansas hunting escapades. He therefore described the region's swamps in detail:

> A swamp in America . . . isn't soft marshy ground, but rather nothing more than a very low-lying area that is quite susceptible to flooding but that dries out quite quickly as soon as the flooding recedes. Drier, higher strips of land intercross the swamp, and even when the flooding is at its peak they provide protection for the fairly numerous game that lives there. The swamp is covered by the most wonderful, luxuriant primeval forest one could imagine. . . . Under these trees the rich soil sends forth a veritable sea of vines that can drive a hunter to distraction, making the forest impenetrable in places. Above all, the greenbrier and its officinal [medically useful] sister, the sarsaparilla, grow so thickly that for bear hunts on horseback, the horses have to be supplied with leather leggings so the skin isn't torn off their bones. . . . And finally there are the poisonous vines with leaves that look like oak, but with a milky sap that makes the hands and face swell up if one is careless enough to touch them while trying to break through the entanglement.

Even in his appreciation for the abundance and bountiful game of the Arkansas swamps, Gerstäcker described a place both entwining and dangerous. Difficult to pass—or, as other sources emphasized, to see through or perceive the safest way across—swamps represented an environment at once challenging and opaque. Rich in vegetation and in animal life, from bears to vexing vegetation, they were unwelcoming to all but the most energetic and intrepid of hunters.

Travelers in swampy regions haplessly watched wagon axles disappear into clinging mud and felt their dresses become heavier with every step, as clods and thick muck coated their petticoats until dragging them exhausted their wearers. What Daniel Drake termed "small miry and lagging rivulets" tugged at the pant legs of travelers and the hooves of their horses. "I have seen no man who has traveled through the swamps from Memphis to little Rock," wrote a weary Arkansan in 1849, "that ever expects to Try them again."

Wet regions were not only difficult, they were intrinsically unhealthy. Laborers refused to work in the "Mississippi Swamp" during the summer months, and road contractors complained that "it is so unhealthy in the swamps in the summer season that we could Calculate on little benefit from the labour of our hands." Swamps were dangerous in the same way as other situations prone to flooding or encompassed by water: the overabundance of water in an environment was like the overabundance of humors within the human form, rendering it imbalanced and dangerous. What Friedrich Gerstäcker called the "noxious climate" of swampy areas drained life from those who lived near them, rendering them "pale and haggard as if they were wasting away."

Miasmas lurked in many aspects of swampland: the low mists moving across water surfaces in the early morning, the smells of rot and mulch associated with morasses, even the draping Spanish moss that newcomers identified so strongly with the hot, moist atmosphere of southern swampland. The moss had much in common with miasmas, and by some accounts it could produce them; travelers' fascination with the moss reveals the associations linking the two. The missionary and travel writer Timothy Flint called it "parasitical" and "beautiful." The gray-green knotty tendrils made trees they covered "look as if they were dead," he mused, "yet the moss will not live long on a dead tree." Miasma and moss clung to live trees and active human bodies, yet were closely related to death. They embodied an environment both hostile and engrossing.

Alien and threatening, the animals inhabiting swamps were symbolic of their pervasive and clinging dangers. Thwarted by illness and a "sickly southern clime" in her and her husband's quest to find better land in Texas, Elizabeth Ann Cooley McClure dreaded the journey up from Louisiana and Missouri on a "nasty sickly alligator river." Others' experience of swampy areas echoed McClure's conjoining of swampland beasts and swampland threat. "Wherever there is a basin of stagnant water, it is full of alligators," recalled the ex-slave Solomon Northup of the swamps of northern Louisiana. Things that lived half in water and half out of it were both transgressive and powerful, symbolic of terrain multifarious in its dangers.

Sloughs of the Spirit

In addition to their physical threat, swamps also held a set of powerful social meanings. The experience of being "bogged down" was frequently understood by inhabitants of the American nineteenth century in spiritual terms, though it had different meanings for the free and the enslaved.

Travelers attempting to cross the region's swamps and sloughs experienced in literal terms the trials of the character Christian, whose travels to the "Celestial City" form the central allegory of John Bunyan's *Pilgrim's Progress*. Many in the early republic were familiar with the labored seventeenth-century parable, which was retold in numerous nineteenth-century American editions.

A crucial moment in *Pilgrim's Progress* concerns the miring power of spiritual morass. Fleeing the chaotic secular city, which promised damnation, Christian falls in with a companion, Pliable, on his journey to the holy realm. The two begin to talk carelessly, and as they do so they "drew nigh to a very miry Slough . . . and they, being heedless, did both fall suddenly into the bog; the name of the slough was Despond. Here, therefore, they wallowed for a time, being grievously bedaubed with dirt; and Christian, because of the burden that was on his back, began to sink in the mire." The spiritual pitfalls of Christian life were eloquently represented in the mucky dangers of swampland travel. Saved only by the strong arm of Help, who intervenes to assist him and set him back on his way, Christian's fall into the slough, weighed down by his burden of sin and material care, underscores his dependence on holy aid and the necessity for humility and disciplined attention on his journey.

Readers of *Pilgrim's Progress* found in Christian's difficulty a model for their own experience. When the traveler John Glover called the Missouri swamps he laboriously crossed in 1826 "purgatory," or when an Ohio settler, Caroline Kirkland, used Bunyan's image of a "slough of despond" to describe her travels, they cast slow, muddy, difficult, smelly, frustrating travel in familiar terms. Elizabeth McClure's complaint that a Tennessee swamp was a "dark, gloomy desert" called upon similar spiritual imagery. Though the close, humid morass through which she traveled could not be more unlike the arid, sun-parched regions we call desert today, McClure used an older sense of the word: deserts were where the Old Testament God left his people to wander when they disobeyed, where wild beasts threatened, and where permanent human habitation was impossible. They were areas of physical and spiritual desolation.

The anxieties of borderlands travelers stymied and confused by swampland are well represented in "The Lost One," John James Audubon's 1821 tale of a man "bewildered" in east Florida while making his way from his cabin to a swamp where he cut wood. It is not so much a story of a specific person as it is a parable of lostness in which a nearby environment of wet hummocks and moist mists, though it should be familiar, is rendered strange and foreign.

In Audubon's recounting, a confident woodsman loses his way in a sudden fog. Tall grass and twisting game trails confuse him—he experiences the disorientation common to many who pushed their way into the dense growths of cane that lined bottomland valleys. Even experienced travelers who stumbled into canebrakes could wander disoriented for hours. Indeed, something like this fate befalls Audubon's nameless wanderer. The story follows the man as he realizes his predicament and spends not only all day, but that night, and the following day, and days and weeks to come in the solitary woods, unable to find his way home. He is overwhelmed and cowed by his surroundings: "The huge gray trees spread their giant boughs over him, the rank grass extended on all sides, not a living being crossed his path, all was silent and still and the scene was like a dull and dreary dream of the land of oblivion." Audubon's woodsman wanders in dreariness, hunger, and thirst for a biblical 40 days as he searches fruitlessly for his cabin and family.

In this bewildering slough, Audubon's "Lost One" is reduced to wild nature, eating raw animals he can kill with his ax and feeding "now on cabbage-trees, then on frogs and snakes." Finally, barely alive and almost bereft of hope, he reaches a river where he encounters other settlers in a canoe: "On his knees did the eye of God see that poor man by the broad still stream that glittered in the sunbeams."

Purgatory endured, "the Lost One" returned to his family, having wandered over 400 miles in his quest to walk between his cabin and a live-oak hummock eight miles away. Audubon's parable struck at the quick of fears of lostness and bewilderment in foreign and confounding terrain. In swampland strange to them and threatening, Audubon's contemporaries feared the alienation of society and soul experienced by his nameless protagonist.

Yet even in the darkness and confusion of his 40 days in the swamp, Providence provides for Audubon's character. When he is about to go mad from confusion and thirst, he encounters a turtle that he smashes open and eats raw. His faithful prayers sustain him through terrors and isolation. Audubon's moral is clear: "Nothing but the great strength of his constitution, and the merciful aid of his Maker, could have supported him for so long a time." Like Christian, the woodsman was forced to recognize his need for Help. Swamps created vulnerability and reliance on God.

Free white Americans labeled swamps sickly and fearful. Yet in a narrative of moral journeying, they represented the challenge necessary to reach symbolically and literally firmer shore. For those living in slavery, the meanings of swampland were even more complex. The narrative descent by the kidnapped freedman Solomon Northup into a north Louisiana swamp, during his attempt to escape from the cotton plantation where he was held in bondage, conveyed to his antebellum abolitionist readership a visceral and moral connection to the trials of Bunyan's Christian.

Northup was born a free black man in upstate New York, but was kidnapped into slavery in 1841. In one particularly chilling episode of his autobiography, which he wrote with a Northern journalist and published in 1853, he is pushed to flee to the surrounding bayous by the brutality of the man who owns him. Unjustly punished, Northup fights back. As the two men struggle, his owner threatens to murder him. Northup is strong, though, and a good fighter: he overpowers his tormentor and has the opportunity to kill him, yet he knows that if he does he will swiftly be lynched. Facing death if he stays, and death if he kills his owner, Northup runs to the surrounding "Great Pacoudrie Swamp" in a desperate attempt to seek the house of a former owner who still has a partial mortgage on him and who therefore has reason to protect him from his current owner's violence.

Racing to escape pursuing bloodhounds, exhausted by exertion and fear, Northup plunges into the bayous. He forces his way all afternoon and all night through the marshy, resistant terrain, plunging and swimming through an environment in which each "human footstep" is foreign. His clothes tattered, his body "covered with scratches," his feet full of thorns, Northup's physical condition, like that of the pilgrim Christian, speaks his despair: "I was besmeared with muck and mud, and the green slime that had collected on the surface of the dead water, in which I had been immersed to the neck many times during the day and night."

Northup is menaced by dangers—"monster" alligators, "hundreds of moccasin snakes," "the bear, the wild-cat, the tiger, and great slimy reptiles"—and is deeply afraid. Yet for him the swamp is not simply an obstacle to be pushed through; he is safe from the keen noses of pursuing bloodhounds only as long as he is in the water. Furthermore, he is in the swamp of his own volition—and his ability to swim means that he can move in and through deep water. Indeed, unlike Audubon's "Lost One," Northup is not disoriented, even in his exhaustion and fear. He makes his way deliberately and successfully to his former owner's, where he is cared for.

A duality, an ambivalence, mark the symbolism of the swamp in this story. In Northup's account, no figure of Help appears to lift him out of the swamp and set him on his way to salvation. Northup's painful ordeal ends with him back in slavery, in only slightly mitigated circumstances. In Northup's autobiographical narrative, his desperate night in the swamp underscores the *lack* of Help, the dearth of resources available to slaves in his position. Even a physically powerful, literate, formerly free man, a man of strength, talent, and stamina who yearned to return to his family and could swim through the swamps that were an impassable barrier to his fellow slaves, was unable to escape by himself from his cotton-plantation bondage. Echoing through Northup's narrative is an indictment of the horror from which he was rescued only by a chance whispered message, the intervention of his family, and the work of a white lawyer whose family had once owned Northup's family. For the black "Christian," unlike the white, the Slough of Despond was cruelly deep.

But for Northup the meanings of the swamp do not end there. Swampland provides not only confounding barrier and mortal threat but refuge and succor. Surrounded by fear and danger, he finds himself also in the midst of bounty. In the dead of night he encounters the rich life of the swamp:

> My midnight intrusion had awakened the feathered tribes, which seemed to throng the morass in hundreds of thousands, and their garrulous throats poured forth such multitudinous sounds . . . that I was affrighted and appalled. All the fowls of the air, and all the creeping things of the earth appeared to have assembled together in that particular place, for the purpose of filling it with clamor and confusion. . . . Even in the heart of that dismal swamp, God had provided a refuge and a dwelling place for millions of living things.

The phrases of Genesis fill this evocation of abundant life. Swamps threatened, but also spoke of the larger freedoms of God's creation. Bayous could be terrifying and dangerous, but they were the last refuge of the runaway, a place where black slaves could move of their own volition, escaping the human laws of the white South for a deeper stage of Creation.

Northup's real experience and his autobiographical retelling were echoed by the literary use of the swamp in Harriet Beecher Stowe's 1856 antislavery novel, *Dred*. In this work, the Great Dismal Swamp between Virginia and North Carolina provides the place where an escaped slave named Dred, a fierce prophet who is the son of the rebel Denmark Vesey, lives in freedom and connection with God.

These two portrayals—one a memoir largely based on fact and one a highly symbolic novel—point to the complexity of the experience of the swamp, as of other liminal spaces, for those in slavery. "Unwanted" environments could function as places of opportunity for slaves and others at the edges of free white society. Swamplands were frequently the base for both temporary and long-standing communities of runaways. In the tidal wetlands of low-country Georgia, slaves could move with freedom, gain skill and expertise, establish knowledge of land not held by their owners and overseers, and create economic and therefore social opportunity for themselves. Hunting and trapping, maneuvering in small craft they made themselves, slaves made territory "beyond the banks" of rice plantations into their own. The watery regions of French colonial Louisiana similarly offered sites of interaction for different cultural groups. Escaped slaves could join communities of Native Americans in the canebrakes or dense swamps of the countryside, where they traded food and equipment with hungry colonial soldiers and created small, contingent, safe spaces.

This interstitial nature of swampland functioned on the symbolic as well as the physical level. For both slave and free, swamps were in-between places. To free Americans and immigrants, they represented the arduousness and necessary reliance on outside help of an important process, a process of journey *through* the swamp, to God, or to inexpensive, available land. For slaves, swamps were also places to escape *to*, places that offered solace precisely because they were physically insecure, teeming with dangerous animal life and creeping sickness.

Being trapped in a bog represented many kinds of threat. Those who ventured into swamps could drown, be attacked by wild or poisonous creatures, or become lost. They could grow sick from the unhealthy emanations from a world of rot, putrescence, and damp moisture. Less tangibly, they could experience the sickness of the spirit that came from being bewildered, abandoned, and without recourse. Yet at the same time, hunters could find plentiful game and those in flight could take succor from a terrain others wished to avoid. Audubon's and Northup's stories convey these multiple meanings of swampland for the well-being of American newcomers.

For escapees as for free travelers, swampy mires represented the trials of an unforgiving environment, one that for many of these pilgrims offered little hope of aid. For slaves and free people, the labors of travel and settlement were spiritual and physical, and on both levels they were profound. Yet in the wearying landscape of gloomy swamp and thick-mudded desert, many early American newcomers to the region found also solace and refuge. In the surprising and much-sought gushes of water from natural springs, terrain was imbued with spiritual promise as well as material aid.

Wondrous Waters: Healing Springs

Feelings of wonder and marvel associated with hot and mineral springs expressed many newcomers' understanding of the order of the natural world.

Springs reassured grime-encrusted, mosquito-bitten travelers that their God had endowed the world judiciously with resource as well as threat. In what they perceived as Native Americans' appreciation of these sites, moreover, American and European observers read an underscoring of the underlying Christian truths toward which even naked savages reached. White migrants created narratives in which native peoples expressed reverence and peace at springs in order to emphasize Indians' underlying educability and the potential for converting them to worship of the bountiful Creator to whose works they were instinctively drawn.

Springs were a selling point in the many varieties of boosterism that animated nineteenth-century discussions of borderland territory. Freshwater springs bestowed a continual source of water that was unlikely to erupt in destructive deluge. Springs were also less likely than wells to run dry during times of drought. One Arkansas booster in 1830 asserted that travelers would find in the territory "not only first rate land, but an elevated country, abounding with springs inferior to none in the world." Salt springs, too, were valuable for luring wildlife and for manufacturing edible salt. Yet of the many types of springs, people particularly valued mineral or "*Warm Springs* [for their] supposed *Medical Virtues*," as one citizen emphasized in a letter to the official federal Missouri surveyor in 1814.

The stink of sulfur springs promised to many antebellum Americans a powerful medicinal resource. Stephen and Mary Hempstead went to visit relatives south of St. Louis in the late 1810s and early 1820s in part to be near "Sulpher Water" they both drank. Stephen Hempstead recorded his and his wife's hopes that the dark, oily water of the sulfurous springs would "help her Dropsy complaint." Such therapy was worth great effort: Hempstead and his son-in-law's "hands" spent sweaty days in June 1818 building "a Camp at the Sulpher Spring for my wife to Stop in while taking the water."

As the medical use of odorous, rotten-egg-tasting, sulfur-laden waters suggests, the healing properties of springs' water could be related to their potency. Like almost any therapy or remedy of the nineteenth century, spring water was thought to injure if taken in excess or injudiciously. One 1804 report of central Arkansas commented that "There is a spring of Cold water not far off which by its Killing one of the people that went with them they thou' a poison spring but probably he only drank too much being very warm & thirsty." That which could force a body back into balance or "break up" an internal blockage could be terribly harmful if misapplied, overindulged, or used when in a state of health.

The abundance of free-welling springs in many areas of Arkansas and Missouri meant that the use of reputedly healing springs was a commonplace domestic therapy. John Brown commented in 1855 at "Cantrell's Springs near Pine Bluff" that he "Drank some of the water which I think is useful water." Brown's phrase denotes the prosaic satisfaction of a farm manager and sometime healer. The spring water was "useful" in the same ways as a strong mule, a well-made saddle, or a hard-working slave. Not dramatic or radical in effect, but possessing solid, workaday virtues, the water of Cantrell's Springs was one more resource in a world full of forces that could either pull astray or strengthen the individual constitution.

At times this resource could disappoint. Beset by ills, Justus Post's wife, Eliza Post, visited her eldest son in 1836 in an attempt to find relief from an illness. "I went out to Augustus', again, for the benefit of cold Spring water," she wrote in her diary, but to little avail: "I still have chills, & fever." No more infallible than any other remedy, but one available within the sphere of many households' care, springs were part of an everyday world of healing.

For many who brought injured limbs or chronic conditions to bathe in their waters, healing springs became retreats for both body and spirit. People sought refreshment and play as well as strengthening waters. When, as Stephen Hempstead recorded in late July of 1830, "daughter Beebe left here in a gig for Herculanum Springs to Stop Some time for the benefit of the water from the Springs with widow Riddick," she left behind dusty fields and hot, close living quarters for the hope of cool, healing water and the pleasures of companionship. Sociability and comfort as well as therapeutic regimens soon came to characterize many spring sites.

A few areas were developed as spas. This was particularly true of the upwellings centered at Hot Springs, Arkansas. One valley of the Ouachita Mountains of south-central Arkansas is interrupted by a profusion of thermal and mineral springs, some of them remarkably hot, which drain into a small creek flowing ultimately to the Ouachita River of southern Arkansas and upper Louisiana. The site, known as the "hot" or "boiling springs," was used by Native American groups and early European settlers. When traveling on their voyage of exploration, William Dunbar and his colleague, the Philadelphia physician George Hunter, in 1804 encountered in a canoe "a consumptive person . . . on his way to the hot Springs for the recovery of his health." Another early visitor recorded that "in 1815, the number of persons at these Springs at one time was about 500 some of whom . . . came from the South Carolina upwards of 500 miles." Official knowledge of the region thus trailed behind popular knowledge: health seekers were already exploiting the therapeutic properties of a region that observers in Washington had not yet fully mapped.

Ceded to the American government by the Quapaws in August 1818, the area surrounding the springs subsequently existed as a common resource with a hazy legal status, while avaricious American claimants threatened to lay private title to the commercially promising spots. Meanwhile, the area continued to develop a substantial folk reputation. The springs, recorded the visitor Joseph Meetch, were "said to possess considerable Virtue in curing certain diseases perticularly the Consumption and the rheumatic aff[l]iction." The "healthfulness of the region" was itself a draw: relative elevation gave the area a reputation as a haven from summer's fevers. After years of dispute, the hot springs and surrounding regions were declared a reservation for public use in 1832 (though rancorous debate over ownership of the valuable springs continued well into the late nineteenth century). Starting in the 1890s, the town of Hot Springs became a fashionable high-society resort and gamblers' haven. Now fallen on quieter times, it is a national park trying hard to market its quaintness: carloads of American visitors and busloads of curious foreign tourists throng Victorian-themed gift shops, fill gallon jugs with drinking water from the springs, rest tired feet in an open-air catch basin of warm, reputedly therapeutic water, and purchase soaks and massages at one of the few spas remaining on the once-bustling "bathhouse row." The region has continued as a health resort through almost two centuries of change in etiological theory and therapeutic regimes.

Springs generated considerable scientific interest on the part of professionals and laypeople. The Arkansas hot springs fascinated the geologist George W. Featherstonhaugh, who undertook a mapping journey for the U.S. Congress during his 1832 visit. He too exclaimed at the "beauty and salubrity of the country." His interest was shared by other scientifically trained visitors. The German emigrant and naturalist George Engelmann noted that the waters of the hot springs seemed to heat and cool more slowly than normal water: "The warmth seems to be bound up in the water, as if it were a part of it." The physician and explorer George Hunter spent almost a month in 1804 investigating the springs, measuring their temperature, pressure, geology, and vegetation, and testing the acidity of the waters.

Such investigations, though focused on Hot Springs because of their renown and the intensity of their heat, were undertaken in other sites as well. John Geiger recorded in his diary in 1840 that "Mrs. Lansford's spring in Illinois, about six miles east of Kihokia, ebs and flows every 24 hours as the sea." The mysterious relationship of this Illinois spring to far-off ocean waters was part of the mystique of spontaneous and healing waters. Springs were marvelous sites, their waters carrying unusual properties and providential powers into mountainous wilds and mule-plowed fields.

Scientific and lay observers alike were impressed not only by the useful properties of the Arkansas hot springs, but by their beauty and spiritual power. George Featherstonhaugh reported approvingly that "these waters annually perform very admirable cures of chronic complaints incident to southern climates," and thus "seem providentially placed . . . for the use of the inhabitants of the low lands in the vicinity of Red river." The springs were intelligible not only in scientific understanding, but in a narrative reading of nature as God's word writ large. They were but one manifestation of a widespread conviction that the cures of a place fitted its ills. Cinchona bark, the source of quinine, was a primary example: found in hot places, it cured their characteristic ills. Like manna provided with the morning dew and quail that came with rushing wind to feed God's hungry people in the wilderness, healing springs were one part of a long history of God's beneficent and appropriate provision.

Springs, moreover, provided spiritual solace. They were to George Engelmann in 1837 an "oasis in a mountainous desert," one he welcomed with "wonder." Engelmann recounted the varieties of vegetation with a botanist's eye and investigated the temperatures of the springs and their geologic formations, as had other scientific observers before him. Yet he emphasized too the "glorious colors!" the "majestic foliage," and the natural beauty of the narrow footpaths and simple baths that gave invalids access to the springs. "How wonderfully the warmth affects things!" he sighed, recounting the powerful influence of the "valley of peace, as the red people call it," which generated unique plant specimens as well as human harmony. Engelmann's marvel reflected and broadcast the multiple meanings of the site: Americans saw the steamy, redolent waters of mineral and hot springs as a source of physical refreshment and spiritual balm.

Such interpretation of springs was widely shared. To enslaved blacks as to free whites, biblical imagery spoke of sweet waters and gushing springs. To slaves as to masters, a "soul athirst," in the line of one former slave's favorite hymn, could be answered by the "spring of joy" "Gushing from the Rock" of God. Like the biblical waters that gushed forth when the prophet Moses struck desert rock with his staff at his God's command, sweet water and spiritual water flowed to a variety of souls.

To American and European observers, the hot springs of the Ouachita Mountains manifested the grace of God. This spiritual meaning, moreover, was enmeshed with their perceptions of former Quapaw, Caddo, and other Native American practices. Throughout early Euro-American reports of the hot springs, a variety of Indian groups were said to make use of their healing properties.

Furthermore, Native Americans were thought by many whites to recognize the spiritual as well as physical meaning of the springs by treating them as neutral territory. Hiram Abiff Whittington reported that natives "always considered [the springs] as sacred ground. Hostile tribes on meeting here, (no matter how inveterate they were towards each other) embraced as brothers, the tomahawk was buried, and the pipe (emblem of peace and love) was passed from a member of one hostile tribe to that of another." Sacred by nature, and recognized as such by nature's children, the springs soothed tribal warfare as they did individual ills. "Even the raw natural man feels himself close to god," mused George Engelmann, "and lays his tomahawk down in awe before he enters this place."

The homage paid by "raw natural man" to these places of wonder underlay their message to peoples who saw themselves as more civilized. As one enthusiast testified, "Every intelegent and scientific Traveler both foreign and native, who has visited these salubrious and efficacious Springs, which the bounty of Providence has bestowed on the invalids of the southern & western States, unite" in the opinion that "the Hot Springs is destined by Nature to be the most celebrated & the most frequented watering place in North America!" Behind the superlatives of this account was the widely shared conviction that the springs held goodness that was evident to all. God's providence was immanent in the world. Both untutored native and "intelegent and scientific Traveler" could sense the moral and bodily healing power of the mineral-laden freshets, as they could sense the rightness of divine revelation. Constructing divine will, nineteenth-century Americans constructed a usable past. History played an important but subtle symbolic role, creating precedent for Americans' use of territory.

Lessons about the rightness of human activity inhered in every aspect of water's interplay with the lives and travels of early Americans in the region. Through waters, settlers found in wild and new terrain that which would strengthen and nourish them. They confronted threats to body and to spirit—but those threats were interpretable in religious allegory that urged enmired pilgrims to reach for Help, and to continue stalwartly on their journey. Nature echoed their own perceptions: fearsome crocodiles lurked in places dangerous to soul as well as body, and Indian tribes revered places deserving of hallowed reflection. In the host of experiences and influences of myriad waters, free American and European migrants read intelligible and encouraging meaning. Beset by drowning, flood, and sickening fluids, they traveled, too, in a land that offered healing and spiritual comfort and in which the varied aspects of the natural world spoke a familiar and yet apparently universal spiritual language that validated their own material pilgrimage.

LOCAL KNOWLEDGE: MEDICAL GEOGRAPHY AND THE INTELLECTUAL HINTERLAND

Chapter VI

AMERICAN POPULAR WISDOM HELD that personal health and environmental surroundings were linked in close and ever-changing relationship. In documents public and private, newcomers to the regions beyond the Mississippi fretted over the effects of lowlands, hillsides, prevailing winds, humid heat, and variable weather on themselves, their spouses, their slaves, their children, and their economic future (few slaves presumably worried on behalf of their owners). Folk knowledge about the relationship between human body and natural world was not everywhere uniform, but certain fundamental concepts and concerns were widely shared.

This common sense of the body and its lived relationship to its environs was also basic to scientific and medical investigation during the period. Intuition about the ill effects of a smelly wind or one that blew over rank marshland informed the questions of leading scientific investigators as well as ordinary people; both everyday conversation and careful scientific study endorsed an implicitly environmental medicine. Research into the connections and correlations linking peoples and places formed a significant part of scientific discussion during the early and middle nineteenth century in Europe and the United States. In its most explicit form, such investigation was known as medical geography. Involving both meticulous detail and wild speculation, informed by both scientific curiosity and booster enthusiasm, medical geographies of specific locales covered a seemingly bewildering array of topics: geological formations, topography, weather patterns, mineral and other resources, climate, humidity, plants and animals, prevailing diseases and ailments, and the area's indigenous and immigrant peoples. Yet in nineteenth-century terms this dizzying variety made sense. In medico-scientific observation as in popular understanding, human well-being was integrally related to a host of factors great and minute, intensely localized as well as broadly general, that were understood as intrinsic to the surrounding world.

Physicians and natural scientists reported on many different places, but scientific curiosity was particularly intense with regard to sites previously unknown to Europeans and Americans. Describing the characteristics of places in the exotic, unknown world was a primary mission of nineteenth-century science. Off in the American borderlands as well as high in the Alps and deep down South American valleys, observers struggled to apply the insights (and take the measurements) of the keenest science of their day. What they created was a knowledge at once local and expansive.

It may be difficult for many of us to see past the parochial nature of this mode of science. The methods and conclusions of medical geography can seem curious and quaint, like the elaborate hinged wooden boxes with which nineteenth-century physicians carried their gently clinking glass vials of medicine. We smile at such artifacts, comfortable at how distant they seem from the vast and complicated resources of modern medical science. Yet those wooden boxes were meant to be thrown hurriedly into leather saddlebags and hauled over rutted muddy tracks; they were designed for rough and frequent use. Only in our museums do the glass stoppers glisten pristinely, wiped clean of the smudge of dirty fingers and the smears and stray powder of hasty preparation.

The science of local knowledge of the nineteenth century was similarly robust and practical. Though filled with rhetorical flourish and steeped in regional boosterism, medical geography was in deadly earnest. The diseases it sought to understand killed infants and sickened laborers; the laws of health and place it sought to interpret governed human endeavor around the globe. This form of knowledge—an exacting study of seemingly insignificant places—was thus particular in its means but ambitious in its scope. Armed with detailed study of diverse regions, scientific and medical investigators could answer questions of the broadest scale about how people could live, and where. Through medical geography, the local could become the universal.

This process of knowledge gathering had both intellectual and political ramifications. Through detailed research into new environments, natural scientists assimilated them into the already-comprehended territory of the United States. Mapping the interaction of place and person, medical geography and the many associated exercises of environmental investigation brought unknown terrain into Euro-American intellectual frameworks, enacting discursively what the many merchants, frontier riflemen, military expeditions, and plantation households of the borderlands effected through conquest, trade, and settlement.

Investigations into the character and health prospects of local territory link exploration in North America with similar efforts mounted by Europeans all over the globe. Yet in the United States these investigations held particular meaning. Emphasis on the "new" qualities of land was central to how American settlement was insistently (and unrealistically) imagined. This insistence had scientific as well as political consequences. The rhetoric of American expansion made exploration of new, unknown, wild territory a vital enterprise, and the science created from such observations carried the excitement of untapped national potential. In the young United States, frontier knowledge was good knowledge. A relentless emphasis on the supposedly unused and unexplored—new lands, new observation of them—thus marks this as an *American* story. Understanding medical geography's linkage between forms of knowledge and national and regional self-definition helps us grasp the political ramifications of scientific study in the nineteenth-century United States, and the depth and resonance of American claims to be a people of restless movement and new claiming.

"On the Medical Topography of Saint Charles County, Mo."

In his "Medical Topography of Saint Charles County, Mo.," published in the first volume of the *Missouri Medical and Surgical Journal*, Dr. Leo Twyman, a physician in the county, discussed the environment—physical, geographical, even geological, and human—he encountered in medical practice between 1829 and 1841. The structure of his observations was familiar not only to the audience of regular physicians likely to subscribe to the fledgling journal, but also to a potentially broader audience of those engaged in the medical and scientific trades beyond the state's borders.

Twyman's essay is typical of works of medical geography, a scientific endeavor that captured the interest and energy of many borderlands physicians and scientific observers in the antebellum United States. Medical geography offered a framework for understanding health, diseases, and human well-being as intimately connected with the surrounding world.

Twyman began with a description of the county. It lay in the "point of land formed by the junction of the Missouri and Mississippi Rivers," north and west of the emerging center of St. Louis, east of the rapidly settling Boon's Lick region that drew settlers from Tennessee, Kentucky, and the upper South, and northeast of the mineral-rich areas of the Ozark Mountains. Twyman gave the latitude of the county and described its borders, mapping the region for his readers. Sources of water figured importantly in Twyman's description, as they did in American settlement generally. He noted the proximity of parts of the region to the two main rivers, the Missouri and the Mississippi, and traced the paths of smaller streams. Twyman observed that the "bottom abounds in sloughs, or strips of land lower than the common level, in which the water collects after heavy rains, and remains during the greater portion of the year." Observed distinctions between bottomland, prairie, and highland were important to his account, as they were to farmers in the area (floods inundated regions around the town of St. Charles several times during the 1820s and '30s).

These descriptions reveal main features of a genre of medico-scientific investigation that was influential for Twyman and his contemporaries. Medical geographies introduced and described a specific region in scientifically legitimate but also widely accessible terms. The territory of a region of study could be vast or very restricted: all of the Mississippi Valley or one county of Missouri. A drainage basin or a few acres of land each held coherence as a "geography" to be studied. Like Twyman, many borderlands authors took rural regions or countryside as their subject, but medical geographers also studied cities and urban areas.

In underscoring the role of waters, and particularly marshes, Twyman drew on scientific and common knowledge. His attention to waters echoed common associations of malignant water with harmful diseases. He carefully detailed the proximity of the town of St. Charles to the Missouri bottom, since "in dry seasons the water on the bottom is dried up, leaving a large surface of mud, filled with vegetable and animal matter in a state of decomposition, exposed to the action of the sun." In Twyman's account as in popular imagining, sources of putrefaction and heat hung heavy over the landscape.

Like descriptions of land by nonscientists, Twyman's medical geography sought to discern the multiple interrelationships of his environment. He reported on the "rich alluvium" and "black loam" that made up the area's soils, as well as the mix of winds that blew over them: "pleasant" in the higher grounds but "cold and damp" in the bottomlands at night. He characterized the available well water ("good"), vegetation ("exceedingly luxuriant"), and topography ("undulating"). His concern for local place was predicated on the practical problems of human habitation. "The streets of the town," he commented, "are generally so muddy as to render it difficult to pass from house to house in wet weather." Medical geography focused on the interaction of person and place, not on uninhabited terrain. Twyman's careful reporting on the particular details of the St. Charles environs rested on environmental understanding held in common with his readers. "It will be perceived," he concluded after describing seasonal wetlands thick with moist, rotting matter over which winds blew toward white settlements, "that there exists in the county of St. Charles abundant material for the production of what is considered the cause of fever."

Twyman went on to draw sharp conclusions from these observations. Homes near local bottomlands were potentially at risk because "continued exposure to the deleterious influence of miasma" could lead to the "enlargement or structural derangement of the abdominal viscera," which left its victims vulnerable to organ inflammation and the dreaded chills and fever. He avoided grand theorizing, writing that he would "simply state some of those facts, leaving the reader to draw his own inferences from them"; but argued, like his more famous contemporary, Daniel Drake, for "marsh miasm" as the root cause of "autumnal fever."

Medical geographies, like other European and American reports on "new" regions, usually ignored completely the existence of prior Native American settlements. In other ways, though, they were deeply historical. Examining a place as a healer would examine a patient, medical geographies detailed a narrative of illness or well-being among credible (that is, usually white) recent settlers. Thus, after outlining for his readers the nature of his surroundings, Dr. Twyman turned his narrative to a "history of the diseases in this county." He noted that varieties of "inflammatory disease" were common in his early years of practice, whereas by the middle 1830s diseases tended to manifest themselves more as "diarrhoea and cholera morbus."

Twyman's record of one case of "Asiatic cholera" layered environmental and personal history in ways typical of medical geography. The victim, "a German girl, twenty years of age, and of nervous temperament, [had an] attack . . . brought on by great fatigue and mental excitement" created by the family's journey from Europe and the young woman's care for her ailing mother. Significantly, "in consequence of the smallness of the house," a hastily built structure, she had spent the night before her attack "on the ground, under an arbor of bushes." In Twyman's account, as in broader understanding, racial constitution and bodily predisposition could be reinforced by individual temperament and the physical stress and family disruption of emigration, and in this case had left his patient vulnerable to the noxious influences of direct contact with earth and vegetation during the night. Her sickness was entirely comprehensible as the product of her personal history and specific environment.

Dr. Twyman's medical geography relied on widely shared precepts of folk knowledge but was couched in contemporary scientific language. From a small town in eastern Missouri, Twyman participated in a larger set of exchanges about the characteristics of the American borderlands and other places new to Euro-American expansion. Articles like his, in publications like the *Missouri Medical and Surgical Journal*, added to the stock of knowledge about places little known to American science, while simultaneously bringing forms of scientific inquiry into the homes of small-town and country practitioners of the Mississippi Valley. Such reports were also an important aspect of regional self-definition and promotion. Twyman's was one contribution to a practice of mapping disease and health environments important both to nineteenth-century scientific understanding and to American western expansion.

Works like Twyman's could have many labels: "medical geography," "medical topography," "medical etiology," "medical geology," or simply the study of weather, climate, and health. All of these projects fell along a spectrum of concern for perceived relationships between health and locale. Medical geographies could include narrative descriptions of particular portions of land or incidents of disease, as well as charts, graphs, or numerical data. They filled nineteenth-century scientific and medical journals in the United States and in Europe, and were the subject of governmental as well as popular interest. Intense curiosity surrounded borderland areas, where the "newness" and foreign nature of environments invited intellectual investigation as well as burgeoning settlement. In the United States, investigations of the relationships between the health of human beings and the places they occupied was a significant area of medical and scientific research from the early nineteenth century until after the Civil War, and especially in the late 1840s through the '50s.

Such research reached an apex with Daniel Drake's mammoth work, *A Systematic Treatise, Historical, Etiological, and Practical, on the Principal Diseases of the Interior Valley of North America, as they Appear in the Caucasian, African, Indian, and Esquimaux Varieties of its Population*, which appeared from 1850 to 1854. This two-volume project represented an important summary of work in the field. It was widely read and often cited. Drake's impressively substantive but also occasionally chatty work was an introduction for many people, not just medical professionals, into the character and prospects of the territories in their country's West.

Works of medical geography interwove medical observation with comments on iron ores, recent shipping patterns, newly observed flora, fossil and geologic remains, and the habits of recent immigrants. In Daniel Drake's *Systematic Treatise*, peoples, social and natural histories, disease descriptions, and etiology combined in his title as they did in his book. Rather than narrow monographs, medical geographies were broadly based reports about areas that few of their intended readers had experienced. They made foreign places intelligible as subjects of natural scientific inquiry. Medical geography was a technique of American colonization, as ambitious as mercantile exchange and as quietly pervasive as the surveyor's chains that divided into congressionally mandated squares ever more of the North American continent.

Investigations into the "salubrity" of place extended Euro-American classifications and frameworks of analysis to places previously unknown to Americans and Europeans. Making a place intelligible, medical geographies represented the intellectual dimension of a takeover at once political, military, cultural, and environmental. Imposing a familiar discursive framework onto new territories, work like that of the small-town Missouri physician Leo Twyman wrote foreign terrain into the intellectual mapping of the ever-expanding United States.

Science of the Local

The science of environmental observation to which Leo Twyman and his peers contributed was a messily defined endeavor. Work in medicine, observation of rocks and minerals, knowledge of plants and animals, familiarity with tide tables and agricultural rhythms, and insight into climate and weather were all part of a unified effort to make sense of the surrounding world. Science of the era searched for broad correlative insights in the minute exercises of local inquiry. Medical geographies like Twyman's account of his home county were thus squarely embedded in the science of his day. They were part of a larger project that sought to construct global descriptions of the interrelation of humans and the nature they occupied by collating observations from distinct and often restricted zones. With a political emphasis inherited from European early modern and Enlightenment state builders, American observers sought to measure, quantify, represent, and thereby assimilate key elements of new territory. Exploring places familiar and exotic, bustling and backwater, natural scientists of the period helped construct an overarching scientific edifice in which their work held meaning and significance.

Medical geography was one expression of a more general move in late-eighteenth and nineteenth-century European and American science toward integrative description and investigation. This movement drew particularly on geography, but also encompassed other techniques of description and measurement. Led by the colorful Alexander von Humboldt, whose widely read journals made scientific exploration both popular and heroic, geologists of the era aimed at systematic study of varied environments, with the goal of uniting diverse observations into global geographies revealing associations between geologic, climatic, and organic forces. Other natural sciences assimilated many of the techniques of quantification and visualization being popularized in geography. Improvements in instrumentation and measurement, particularly in the portability of smaller and increasingly more precise instruments, equipped workers in the sciences to observe more closely and quantify in more detail aspects of the human body and its environment. Beginning in the late Enlightenment, European practitioners were thus able to integrate skills related to the earth and physical sciences into the practice of medicine, as they began to quantify and map elements of the natural world.

In medical geography as in allied investigations, attention to precise measurement was closely linked with a more prominent role for numerical quantification and statistical compilation. In the early nineteenth century, leading European scientific researchers into environments and populations increasingly reported their conclusions in tables, graphs, and charts. Many antebellum Americans began to regard statistics as a matter-of-fact language of description of the natural world. By the 1840s and '50s, those writing on science and medicine in the United States had begun to use statistical comparison in innovative ways to illuminate problems in the relationship between site and well-being, combining, for instance, measurements of dew point and information on mortality in specific epidemics to test the relationship of atmospheric humidity to disease.

The sciences of geography, exploration, and environmental medicine relied not only on quantified data, but on its visual representation. By midcentury maps and charts became a common feature of medical geographies and affiliated investigations. Argentina's flora and New Orleans' diseases were alike rendered into numerical and geographic comparison through elaborate fold-out charts, diagrams, and maps.

In particular, the American Medical Association's *Transactions* featured densely packed and carefully composed graphs, charts, and maps in its studies of health and place in the late 1840s and through the '50s. Vivid colors, filled in by hand, dramatized the relationship of temperatures in the shade to temperatures in the sun throughout southern regions' hot summers; related lines (often graphed on the same diagram) indicated the fluctuating depth of nearby rivers, the time of sunrise, the changes in humidity, and the disease-specific mortality for the region. Articles would feature state-by-state maps that showed mountains, swampy areas, and rivers and streams, and used color-coded shadings to represent the yearly mortality of each county. Accompanying charts employed census data to tabulate the deaths in each county from a wide variety of ills and ailments, while others compiled observers' records on wind direction and speed, humidity, atmospheric heat, cloudiness, and other meteorological data. Medical workers combined and compared information about political divisions, topography, human populations, and weather conditions in these compelling visual and statistical representations. Through them the increasingly professionalized medical practitioners of the United States made the territory they traced their own.

The Politics of Local Knowledge

The intricate mappings and diagrams of illness and environments that filled publications like the AMA's *Transactions* charted more than technical triumph and statistical virtuosity. Innovative technologies for mapping space and presenting data reflected the ever more detailed and integrated scrutiny that accompanied and accomplished border regions' absorption into the American union. Even as these complex and often beautiful representations brought data into a compelling and powerful whole, they granted each set of observations or measurements significance as one component of a unified, coherent, global science of nature. In the same way, local and even parochial

investigations contributed to a grand vision of what was—or would become—American.

Medical geography emphasized local inquiry in ways that had long historical roots but took on particular meaning in the antebellum United States.
As early modern European states increasingly attempted to capture information about places where they wanted to capture markets and territory,
they used study of local regions as the basis for overarching frameworks.
Expanding European states, from Sweden to the German territories, investigated their own resources and attempted to carefully catalogue those of
colonies and outposts. Mapping, enumeration, and statistical chronicling
served commercial as well as intellectual purposes.

Scientists and physicians in North America learned from a substantial European scholarship on the value of local investigation to the consolidation of
both knowledge and markets. Even as they drew on European models and
history, however, their work served the political expansion of the United
States. Efforts in the nineteenth century to knit together environmental observations of specific areas into an overarching whole were inextricably
linked with the project of making American the lands they chronicled. Investigating local phenomena, scientific observers brought them into a structure at once political and intellectual. Classifying the natural resources of
the lands they observed, antebellum scientists forwarded a program of national development: lands assimilated into American understanding were
available for its enrichment. Taking the mission, as Daniel Drake phrased it,
"to amalgamate the foreign with the indigenous," busy hinterland quanti-
fiers trekked through muddy paths and struggled with difficult terrain to
"amalgamate" what they saw and experienced with the expectations of the
expanding republic.

Physicians and natural scientists slogged through early Arkansas and
Missouri to describe with great labor and varying degrees of precision the
various potential of recently acquired American territory. William Dunbar,
charged by Thomas Jefferson with exploring the lower Mississippi and
Ouachita rivers in 1804–5, was accompanied by the mineralogist, chemist,
and physician George Hunter of Philadelphia. Hunter's journals of the
Ouachita River expedition, written at Jefferson's express request to ensure
accurate descriptions of the region, incorporated observations about the
minerals, soils, wildlife, hunting patterns, colonial settlements, Native
American habits, water currents, and native plants of the swampy Ouachita
bayous, as well as remarks on the attractions of the Arkansas hot springs for
French and American invalids. Hunter's observations expressed the many

dimensions of governmental interest in new territory—interest largely shaped by the demands of American settlement.

Other environmental investigations similarly reflected the intertwining of scientific, governmental, and popular concerns. George W. Featherstonhaugh, the influential English geologist, undertook a congressionally authorized examination of the country between the Missouri and Red rivers in the mid-1830s. His *Excursion Through the Slave States* was at once an attack on the region's social structures and a detailed description of the main features of land. Extracts of his report were front-page news for the *Arkansas Gazette* in the summer of 1835. Featherstonhaugh's conclusions about the mineral resources to be gathered from the state's Boston Mountains and his earnest pleas for a "system of levées" to control flooding coincided with commercial and agricultural interests. The geologist and ethnologist Henry Rowe Schoolcraft and the botanist Thomas Nuttall similarly wrote reports of Missouri and Arkansas that were widely read both as scientific texts and as descriptive narratives. Even the missionary writer Timothy Flint touched on scientific as well as religious and social themes in his many popular publications about the Mississippi Valley. Much as the geologic and climatic forces they tracked had formed it physically, the descriptions published by these mosquito-bitten categorizers formed the land in common perception.

If environmental medicine was one thread in an informal web of practices that enfolded "new" regions and made them part of the United States, it was also a formal tool of American expansion. Keen observation of weather, climate, and environs was included in the official role of the many medical and scientific practitioners stationed in the borderlands as part of the U.S. military, as well as specific expeditions like Dunbar and Hunter's or Lewis and Clark's.

Such official reports often focused on the health influences of place. In 1834, the assistant surgeon of Fort Smith in northwestern Arkansas, C. B. Welch, wrote to the surgeon general of the armed forces at the request of his commanding officer. Summing up a litany of environmental threats, from the nearby "sluggish stream" to the area's "sickly and variable" weather changes, Welch condemned the fort as conducive to debility and disease. His was one of a series of damning reports on the environmental and medical situation of the fort (complaints that were widely shared by those posted there but that did nothing to change their dismal situation), and it was written at the request of his commanding officer. Rather than being one forlorn camp doctor's protest, Welch's letter was an example of the duties of a medical practitioner stationed in a little-known area. Beginning in 1814, the surgeon general had directed all hospital surgeons, mates, and post surgeons in the Army Medical Department to keep a diary of weather, which was to be reported quarterly. Similar efforts were undertaken in the General Land Office, run by the Department of the Treasury. Fort Smith physicians began to keep weather records in 1821 and continued to do so for much of the next half century. Even before the 1814 order, military physicians and officers were often careful observers of the natural histories of the regions to which they were posted. Medical geography was a basic task of the physician as military observer and medical practitioner.

American expansion was contingent on local observation. Knowing land through a formal survey was one component of this larger project—one that makes clear the credence given those with direct experience of the places they described, whether as explorer, army doctor, or raconteur. The Territorial Assembly of Arkansas, for instance, petitioned Congress in 1823 for their own surveyor general. Continuing a litany of complaint about neglect by St. Louis–based authorities, the assembly's petition cited the "six or seven hundred miles" that separated St. Louis from "a large portion of the public lands which are yet to be Surveyed." The petition argued that "a Surveyor general resident at St. Louis, cannot possibly possess that knowledge of our local Situation, and of the character of the lands yet to be Surveyed, which is necessary to enable him to do justice to the government. . . ." To mark off, label, bound, and sell the land of a new territory, its leading citizens demanded someone based there. For proponents of this growing region, making known their "local situation" was fraught with political intensity.

Local knowledge was valid because it read "the book of nature"—an *American* nature often wild and challenging. In *The Last of the Mohicans,* James Fenimore Cooper's sturdy hero Natty Bumppo says of the lore of the hunt and the close observation of nature that he learned from his adoptive Indian family: "This is my schooling . . . and if one neglects the book, there is little chance of learning from the open hand of Providence." What Cooper elsewhere called "experimental knowledge"—not because it took place in a laboratory but because it was based on the experience and observation of Providence's open book and "open hand"—was a knowledge truer, more valuable, and, most important, more localized than the grand philosophical schemes Cooper and other authors increasingly dismissed. Uniting the plaintive complaints of territorial representatives and the heavy-handed instruction of romantic novelists is the credence given those with experience of American places, and especially the American frontier. Yet gaining that experience, particularly as a medical or scientific observer, proved to be a challenge.

Professional Anxieties of the Periphery

In 1819, Robert F. Henry, a new and even more than usually optimistic settler, wrote to his physician brother with calculating ambition about the role of a professional in the western territories, as well as about the prospects of the region overall. "And let me tell you," he urged, stressing the benefits of emigration, "the time will surely come, when to be the first physician or lawyer, of Arkansaw will be no mean station." Betting on growth, hoping to better their "station," those in the medical trade moved into Missouri and Arkansas to cultivate the social prospects of the area, just as they and their neighbors sought to cultivate its soil. Many found barriers as steep and rocky as an Ozark hillside.

In cultural background, place of origin, and motivations for westering, the physicians of early Arkansas and Missouri closely resembled their contemporaries who chose to move to the region, and their struggles were similar: disease, drought, flood, fire, and chronic economic woes. Like other migrants, many came from states of the upper South, notably Tennessee and Kentucky. Those moving to St. Louis found a cosmopolitan atmosphere and a fair degree of professional organization and specialization. In the rural regions of both Arkansas and Missouri, by contrast, medicine was much more informally practiced, and the difficulties of travel and payment in muddy areas with poor roads and poorer inhabitants were often substantial.

Particularly in lowland regions where the use of slave labor was common, many physicians worked on both black and white patients in their practice, though generally in ways that recognized the social, economic, legal, and medical distinctions drawn between them. William Armour Cantrell, a young practitioner of means and ambition whose Tennessee planter family had moved to Jefferson County in south-central Arkansas, is typical in his professional trajectory. Sent to the East as an adolescent for his education, Cantrell received a degree from the University of Louisville Medical School in 1848 and returned to Arkansas to practice. He began work as a healer on his father's plantation before moving to Little Rock in 1852 for what would be a successful medical career in Arkansas. The medical work of this prominent physician began among a plantation population consisting mostly of enslaved black workers. Only later, his technique practiced, did Cantrell move to make his way among a larger, and presumably whiter, community.

Many physicians immigrated to the Missouri and Arkansas borderlands carrying with them credentials and training from "back East." Aspiring practitioners could also "read medicine" with an established physician, as did "Thornton, a Cherokee who is studying medicine" in the Arkansas-based Cherokee Nation of 1828, according to curious traveler Hiram Abiff Whittington. Despite the frequency of this local training, the prejudices and standards of "Northern" medicine proved influential in the American borderlands. Even as regular medicine was contested by sectarian therapies and more individualistic regimes of healing, the centers of Boston, New York, and Philadelphia (and, farther afield, Edinburgh, London, Paris, and Berlin) were lodestones for the interest of professionally aspiring practitioners of the hinterlands.

Most farmers also worked intermittently at other trades—as blacksmiths, chimney builders, honey finders (or bee liners), coopers, merchants, or furniture makers. Being a physician was another one of the many ways free men might earn money as they ran a farm. The novelist William Wells Brown, an escaped slave, wrote of his former owner, who emigrated from Kentucky to a farm 30 or 40 miles north of St. Charles, that "in addition to his practice as a physician, he carried on milling, merchandizing and farming. He had a large farm, the principal productions of which were tobacco and hemp." Such diversification was demanded by the economics of medical work. Even for practitioners with degrees from elite institutions, "doctoring" was on again, off again. Though less predictable than the seasonal cycles of farms and livestock, medicine was like farming in the wide variation in the time demanded of the practitioner: spates of illness in the community could mean extra work and the possibility of greater income (*if* clients actually paid their bills), while poor economic conditions or "healthy" seasons left physicians reliant on other prosaic skills.

Earning a living was a constant struggle. In towns and cities, healers faced substantial competition, while in rural areas hardscrabble economies often left little over for paying doctors. Hermann Steines, a hopeful young apothecary dispatched from Prussia to serve as a scout for a larger family migration, reported back disconsolate from St. Louis in 1833. Attached to "an empiric, or in common terms a quack," he found himself reduced to mixing "wonder balsam and healing balsam" (even *he* had to guess the ingredients)—a far cry from what he had imagined it would be like to "learn the secret and methods of American physicians and American medicines." Despite his pessimism, however, his family was undissuaded; a party of 153 Steines relatives and associates formed the Solingen Emigration Society and came to Missouri in 1834.

Professional, personal, and agricultural difficulties could hinder or end a borderland physician's medical career. B. W. Lee, a doctor in Arkansas Post, wrote in frustration to his St. Louis friend and colleague in 1844. His crops ruined by severe flooding that "washed off" his fields, his family's health weakened by a harmful environment, his reputation tarnished by his fondness for "ardent spirits"—which he claimed finally to have renounced— and his finances debilitated by years of failure to "make collections" from his clients or make profits from his crops, Lee felt himself mired by debt in the marshy Arkansas countryside. He sought advice from his better-connected friend on the possibilities of commencing practice and opening a drug store in St. Louis, but acknowledged that "it requires years in a city to establish a stranger in the practice of my profession." Awash in repeated failures and inundations, Lee watched the Arkansas River strip away his professional aspirations just as irrevocably as it had his topsoil.

Social and educational constraints as well as financial difficulties limited regular physicians' ability to define themselves as a professional group. In Arkansas, very little formal codification, recognition, or organization of medicine took place until after the Civil War. Not until the 1860s, '70s, and '80s did concerned community leaders and physicians establish substantial hospitals, a state medical society, state oversight of medicine, or significant action on public health. Outright hostility to regularized forms of medicine found expression in ridicule and in legislative action, and occasionally in both: John Pope, governor of Arkansas Territory, vetoed an 1831 bill for the licensing of physicians, which would have favored those with college degrees or out-of-state licenses, declaring, "I know, and so does every man of experience and observation, that many who have gone through a regular course in medical schools are grossly ignorant of the theory or practice of medicine."

The urban atmosphere, wider economic base, and greater educational opportunities of Missouri's cities, especially St. Louis, provided the basis for the development of a more professionalized medical elite. Two medical colleges were founded in St. Louis in the 1840s. The schools used the city's hospitals for clinical instruction, offering this innovation at a time when medical education at most institutions consisted only of identically repeated lecture series. Ambitious practitioners in the 1840s and '50s inaugurated a series of medical journals in Missouri, mostly published from St. Louis. Four journals—both regular and homeopathic—began during the 1840s, and eight more, encompassing homeopathy, regular practice, and dentistry, were founded in the following decade. By 1820, informal groups of physicians had begun to meet in St. Louis, and in 1835 the 20 regulars of the city formed the Medical Society of Missouri in the best tradition of early-nineteenth-century associations and convocations. In 1850, the Missouri State Medical Association published the proceedings of its organizing convention, taking care to present itself with the same formal ritual as medical organizations in bigger cities on the Eastern Seaboard. A group of St. Louis physicians in 1829 began publishing "fee bills," in which they collectively advertised agreed-upon charges for given services; similar fee bills were put together in 1845 by doctors in St. Joseph, in the western part of the state. Organization and joint standard setting characterized Missouri regulars at an early era.

Connections with outside developments and professional forms did exist in more rural areas, but usually required substantial personal effort. The leading Arkansas physician A. W. Webb, who established himself in practice first in Chicot County and then in Little Rock, collected a valuable library of several hundred medical and other scientific works by the time of his death in 1866. In his personal notebook Webb recorded items from the *New York Journal of Medicine* and various British medical texts, as well as many other medical authors. In one passage he discussed the principles governing use of the stethoscope, developed by a French clinician, René Laennec, in 1819. Through personal resources and wide reading, Webb kept himself abreast of current medicine, but neither his diligence nor his financial resources were typical. Most of the region's skeptics would have found reasonable accuracy in one 1843 send-up of "The Swamp Doctor": "The city physician, compelled to keep up appearances, deems a library of a hundred authors a moderate collection; the swamp doctor glories in the possession of 'Gunn's Domestic Medicine,' and the 'Mother's Guide.'" Armed with the same domestic guides that occupied the shelves of their lay neighbors, many physicians drew more on common knowledge than on any particularly rigorous training.

Arkansas and Missouri physicians labored under a self-conscious awareness of their region's frontier status. Lack of facilities and financial support prevented many kinds of medical or scientific investigations. Professional status, moreover, was unsteady, destabilized not only by the limitations of therapeutic intervention but by popular mistrust and ridicule.

Arkansas medical practice—like its people—provided an almost endless source of humor for early- and mid-nineteenth-century satirists (as for those of the twentieth and twenty-first). Marcus Lafayette Byrn's 1851 *Life and Adventures of an Arkansaw Doctor* featured Dr. David Rattlehead as an irresponsible practitioner and clever trickster who traipsed through a benighted Arkansas. In these stories Dr. Rattlehead dispenses equal portions of medicine, braggery, and tall tales. He feeds hot peppers to hounds that bay at him, and digs up bodies for dissection in late-night "resurrections" that terrify the superstitious slaves who assist him. The cruel humor of these exploits combined medical satire with regional parody and racist stereotype. Like the violent ignoramus already beginning to emerge in other humorous fiction about the Ozarks, the "Arkansaw Doctor" fed—and fed on—the insecurities of the region.

Critics particularly skewered the American tendency to apply military and medical honors in a loose and informal fashion. Charles Dickens enlivened his 1844 *Martin Chuzzlewit*, in which his British heroes find themselves owners of worthless swampland in Missouri, with the profuse pomposity and overconfidence of a series of emphatic generals. In one American boarding house his protagonist observed that "There seemed to be no man there without a title: for those who had not attained to military honours were either doctors, professors, or reverends." The author's disdain for American aggrandizement, like his disdain for American society generally, raised hackles but also anxieties among those he skewered. Washington Irving brought a similarly biting wit to his trip through Indian Territory in the mid-1830s. His journal for the return through Arkansas notes meeting at one small community "the usual number of Judges, Generals, and Colonels, not to speak of lawyers and Doctors." Inflated titles, and the American "Doctors" who bore them, were routinely ridiculed by Europeans and cultured Northerners traveling through the South and West.

Practitioners regarded the title "doctor" very differently. It stood not for formal education but for one's place in the world. Taking it up was, in effect, a declaration of one's intention to practice. William A. Falconer, for instance, explained to his mother in 1848 that he had begun to style himself an M.D. after years of being called upon by his neighbors for healing. Arguing that he had neither time nor need for "old school" training, Falconer insisted that "the confidence of my fellow citizens" and his familiarity with "diseases peculiar to the South" amply qualified him to be a physician.

Other American newcomers railed against such complacency. From St. Louis, William Cooke, a young Virginia lawyer pushed by economic pressure to new territories across the Mississippi, vented his ire to a friend back home:

> It is bad enough for a *lawyer* to practice without being prepared . . . but it passes my understanding that the laws of Christian & civilized communities should permit ignorant men with the title of *Doctors* (which can be bought at any institution in the United States for $200 to $300) to practice upon the lives of their fellow-men. The ignorance of the regular medical faculty has been the great cause of empiricism in our day & generation; and especially here in the West.

To William Falconer, his styling himself a doctor was justified by his local experience and local expertise. To William Cooke, that easy assertion of competence was criminally irresponsible. Such ill-trained practitioners drove the public toward the "empiricism" of quacks and irregulars.

Cooke's pessimism was widely shared. Antebellum Americans indeed held well-founded reservations about regular physicians. Many would have agreed with the somber assessment of one Missouri settler who wrote to her aunt from the Grand Prairie of Missouri in 1838: "In the medical skill of this country I have little confidence."

Would-be regular physicians in early Missouri and Arkansas occupied an uneasy position. They faced financial pressures, distrust, and difficulties connecting with the larger world of medical practice. In this situation, medical geography helped provide both connection and validation, linking the activity and concerns of borderlands physicians with those of leading scientists and medical observers.

Aspiring doctors in the canebrakes of Missouri, far from the research centers of Edinburgh, London, and especially Paris, were creating an image of what it meant to be a man of science in ways quite separate from the new sciences of clinical observation and postmortem diagnosis. As they did so, the techniques and practices associated with environmental observation became inscribed over the course of the antebellum period as a fundamental and everyday part of practice for a scientifically informed practitioner, in the boondocks as in Boston or Baltimore.

Medical geography legitimized practitioners besieged by unpaid bills and their contemporaries' skepticism. Over the first two thirds of the nineteenth century, research into health and place became part of the fabric of medical life for those who saw themselves as doctors. It helped define, day-to-day, what it meant to be a physician in the borderlands.

Somewhat paradoxically, part of what was appealing about medical geography was its connections with common belief. In an 1853 article investigating "the Meteorological Causes of Climatic Diseases" in the St. Louis area, the botanist George Engelmann listed a number of traditional observations about the relationships linking the natural world and human well-being. The dictums were simple but potent: "A wet summer is a healthy summer"; "A wet fall is a healthy fall." Rather than distancing himself from such folk knowledge, Engelmann acknowledged his own debt to common wisdom. "All my ambition here," he emphasized, "consists in substantiating these old maxims by precise statistical and meteorological observations." These texts of medical practice reflect confluences between the concerns of medical practitioners and those of their fellow farmers. Even elite observers like Engelmann drew on folk knowledge of agriculture and healing to inform their observations of surrounding terrain. In an era characterized largely by diversity and disagreement in medical approaches, the precepts of environmental medicine represent an instance of agreement on health issues between regular medical practitioners and the general public.

Everyday concerns permeated physicians' thoughts and musings about the intricate relationships between health and place. Through the observations and descriptions of medical geography, hinterland practitioners asserted themselves as scientists and physicians. Observing the local, they delineated their own competence in ways understandable to their skeptical neighbors and peers. Engaging with the study of place and human health shaped the ambitious practitioner not by marking him out as removed from his contemporary situation, but by giving him particular mastery to observe it.

Regional Boosterism and Southern Medicine

Medical geography was one expression of a regional definition and regional promotion in which medical professionals were as deeply engaged as any of their fellows. Observers like Twyman wrote not simply as medical men but also as leading citizens—boosters, promoters, people proud of their adopted regions, putting them forward as useful and worthy objects of study. Twyman's prose was measured and reasoned, and he did little to minimize the diseases of his region, but other medical geographies sounded a clear call to prospective immigrants.

In his "Medical Topography of Central Arkansas" (1843), Dr. William Goulding combined medical observation with forthright civic boosterism. Publishing in the *Western Journal of Medicine and Surgery*, Goulding hoped not only to describe his new home region but also to convince others to emigrate (Goulding himself had come from Worcester, Massachusetts, by way of Oswego, New York, in part seeking a better climate for his health). In describing features like latitude (35°40'), longitude (which he put at 15°20'), weather, winds, soil types, and topography, Goulding took care to characterize Little Rock as an "eligible" site with "many fine public and private buildings," concluding that "being near the centre, and the capital of a large and growing state [although with a present population, he admitted, of only 2,400], its future destiny can hardly be mistaken." His analysis of mortality from fevers during 1839 acknowledged their heavy toll, but he insisted that those sickened were newcomers; "those long resident in the locality" were not at great risk. Resting his faith that the environment would become healthier the longer and more thoroughly it was settled, Goulding testified to the civilizing effect of culture and commerce on the very terrain itself. He concluded that within a short period central Arkansas would "be noted for its salubrity as it is now for its beautiful and commanding location." Like many other hopeful town improvers of the period, Goulding cast his characterizations and hopes in terms of medical changes to be wrought through settlement. As a physician, he expressed his ambitions for what was then a buggy, marshy, culturally limited settlement in a tone of scientific certainty and medical authority.

Goulding's personal history provides a poignant coda to his medical geographic enthusiasm and his efforts at boosterism. Already sick, probably with consumption, when he arrived in Arkansas and wrote his essay, Goulding did not live to see it published. He died in late November 1841, in New Orleans, of a long-standing illness. As it remained for many of his contemporaries, Goulding's quest for healthy place was an elusive one.

Essays like Goulding's promoted the health benefits of their local areas. They also helped create—and shift—regional identity in subtle ways. Physicians' attention to medical geography reveals a change over the course of the antebellum period. What had been "West" began to become "South." Americans' concerns relating to these two amorphous areas were in some ways similar: lack of civilization, difficult living conditions, late-summer epidemics, and illnesses from swampland were all hallmarks of "western" territory and of "southern" places. In the literature of health and place, one began to shade into the other, as medical authors increasingly framed the borderland regions of Missouri and Arkansas as being of the South. This redefinition has much to do with the rise of Southern regionalism, and ultimately Southern nationalism. In particular, the politics of being "South" meshed with the concerns of medical geography.

Environment-specific illness and environment-specific treatment required practitioners to be *of* their regions in powerful and lasting ways. Such a call to belonging resonated particularly in the increasingly embattled and self-conscious slave states. South of the Mason-Dixon Line, intellectuals drew on the logic of environmental health to argue that physicians' techniques should emerge from experience gained in the South and knowledge acquired in Southern institutions. Interest in regional medical specificity dovetailed in the 1840s and '50s with an increasingly vocal Southern nationalism insisting upon the distinctiveness—medical as well as political and economic—of the South. Medical and scientific observers in Missouri and Arkansas came increasingly to participate in this push for Southern-ness in medical practice as their regions became more and more identified with a beleaguered and belligerent South.

Environmental medicine reinforced the latent anti-intellectualism with which Southern and backwoods practitioners defended and defined themselves. Medical geography gave credence to localism and experience—the central tenets of a "Southern medicine" based on observation, not intellectual constructs. As Leo Twyman advised in 1845, "He who would be a successful practitioner, must prescribe for the symptoms which present themselves, and not for the name of a disease."

Immediate and local experience, not abstracted knowledge, armed physicians against the creeping illnesses of the heat-soaked South. No matter if learned authorities attacked the use of emetics on a theoretical basis, argued A. W. Webb in 1844, their use "is confirmed by the universal experience of the most experienced of the southern physicians." The Alabama physician and Southern medical advocate W. H. Gantt argued that the "witnessing" of disease was essential to treating it: "I have seen the Northern medical man, of deep learning, but not the learning of Southern men, and with no Southern experience, stand by the bed-side of his patient, and let him die from congestive fever; all the time, doing as his Northern teachers had taught him."

Gantt's condemnation of the intellectual but impotent Northern "deep learning" forcefully linked Southern-ness with effectiveness and experience. And experience, he and others pressed, could only be gained *in situ*.

Southern advocates made understanding a disease in its local context crucial to its proper treatment. Dr. Webb argued: "I have certainly never seen a treatise on the subject [of intermittent fever] which would qualify a stranger to treat it with success." According to the Yankee emigrant Henry Merrell, a "great fever-doctor" would quickly "learn the right methods adapted to the diseases of the country," and therefore adjust the series, dosages, and combinations of treatments that would correctly mesh constitution and climate.

As the broader political crisis of sectionalism widened, such arguments for localism, experience, and knowledge of the region soon turned to calls for Southern medical education. Over the middle third of the nineteenth century, medical writers hotly contested the site and style of medical training. Southerners grew increasingly restive at being forced to go north and east for training—and they were in fact increasingly resented in the ever more polarized centers of the Northeast. The editor of the New York *Sun* commented acidly in 1860,

> The Southern medical student is well known in the neighborhood. . . . He is a long-haired, lantern-jawed, verdant youth, afflicted with chronic salivation and inveterate profanity. Reared in the semi-savage solitude of a remote plantation, and deriving his ideas of morals, grammar, and behavior from his negro nurse and picaninny playmates, he becomes in New York a puzzle to professors, a terror to landladies, and a munificent patron of grogshops. Having finished his so-called course of study . . . he returns to his native wilds to commence practice on a pretentious stock of medical ignorance, calomel, and quinine. Next to his taste for tobacco and grog comes his taste for Disunion. . . . his stock of political ideas consists wholly of hatred of the people to whom he is obliged to come for instruction.

A Southern medical student's skills were at one with his demeanor, argued such screeds; neither was worthy of the profession. Racial taint, cultural predisposition, and unrefined therapies all demonstrated the unfitness of such candidates for medical learning.

In this context, the powerful urging of medical geography for a locally informed medicine merged into calls for Southern therapeutics and Southern medical institutions. "Remember that if you wish to become familiar with the treatment of Southern diseases," one representative of Southern medical colleges admonished prospective medical students in 1859, "*you must be educated at the South*." Notions of health, disease, and location were tied to the movement for Southern medical education that led to Southern students' exodus from Northern medical schools in the winter of 1859–60. Arguments about locale and well-being were thus linked with larger arguments about the standing and coherence of the South.

Environmental medicine drew legitimating impetus from the movement for Southern medicine, even while providing a broader argument for it. Medical geography justified a localist medicine in which practitioners from a specific area were uniquely fitted for certain kinds of natural scientific investigation. At its extreme, medical geography gave pride of place to the parochialism that became the retreat of prewar Southern intellectuals.

Medical geography and arguments for Southern medicine were mutually reinforcing trends within medical practice. A growing sense of the South as a region compelled practitioners toward a local knowledge based in and of the South. In ways both obvious and indirect, investigations into health and place served the politics of sectionalism.

The Uses of History

Amid what was a diverse and widespread medical literature on environment and health in the early and mid-nineteenth century, the perceived history of medical thinking played an important role. Practitioners in the medical mainstream and in the aspiring cities of the borderlands actively invoked figures and themes from the history of medicine. This search for ancestors reveals important characteristics of medicine in the period.

The quantifying measurements of Thomas Sydenham were in particular a touchstone for antebellum observers. A late-seventeenth-century London physician, Sydenham drew detailed correlations between measurements of climate and of disease. His positing of an "epidemic constitution" of surrounding atmosphere during outbreaks of sickness was the mainstay of a new science of medical meteorology, one based on quantification and statistical thinking.

Sydenham's mantle was eagerly claimed by later researchers engaged in their own speculations about the connections between human environments and human well-being. One passage in Leo Twyman's topography of St. Charles County argued: "The physician, by attentively observing the vicissitudes of the weather, and carefully studying, according to the custom of Sydenham, the constitution of the season, may, very early in the commencement of an epidemic, be able to detect its nature, and thereby save himself much trouble, and his patient much suffering." Twyman urged the adoption of a quantitative, observational attention to the qualities of environment very much in keeping with the emphasis on exact measurement and tools of understanding meteorological phenomena that characterized the legacy of Sydenham.

Yet the historical self-fashioning of antebellum physicians stretched much further back than the seventeenth century. In their thinking about health and environment, physicians of Arkansas plantations and Missouri hamlets self-consciously drew upon a textual tradition rooted in antiquity. The fifth century B.C.E. Greek healer Hippocrates of Cos held particular intellectual and professional significance. Many nineteenth-century observers traced the formal genesis of medical geography to the Hippocratic treatise *Airs, Waters, and Places*, a text written within the humoral tradition that held so much meaning for the settlers of Arkansas and Missouri.

Airs, Waters, and Places instructs physicians to closely observe local characteristics, on the premise that disease is a product of specific locales. It treats elements of the environment—changes in seasons, direction and force of wind, the type and source of waters, the level of heat, the directions in which towns face, and the overall climate of an area—as important factors in human illness and well-being. Nineteenth-century studies of healthfulness and site were punctuated by calls on the authority and legitimacy of this text as a guiding beacon for contemporary endeavor.

In what was seen as a direct response to Hippocratic imperative, works of American medical geography often included statistics on the direction and force of wind, the type and source of waters, the level of heat, and the overall climate of an area. Hippocratic thinking reinforced arguments for regionally specific Southern medicine. According to many Southern physicians' arguments, only those in warm climates—in what was framed as Greek latitude—could put to use the Hippocratic medical therapies created in the hot Mediterranean.

The credence given Hippocrates in antebellum American medicine is consistent with a broader use of classical texts and figures. Reference to the glories of classical civilizations—especially the democracy of ancient Greece—characterized much of the self-conscious early national political culture of the United States. In the South, such references had a particular resonance. As George Engelmann and other immigrant observers often noted, among the seemingly peculiar naming habits of Americans—such as giving children surnames as first names, or bestowing on them old-fashioned biblical names—was slave holders' penchant for giving slaves names from Greek and Roman antiquity. Men named Plato, Horace, Cicero, Cato, and Romulus labored to build plantation empires under the Southern sun, in strange and ironic echo of the intellectual and political labors performed by their namesakes in other empires long faded but long remembered. Citation of Hippocrates was thus one of a series of rhetorical links between past but glorious civilization and the national project of the young United States.

Claims to continuity with the thought of classical antiquity had an important bearing upon the professional dynamics of American medicine in the first two thirds of the nineteenth century. The Hippocratic canon was used as an important professionalizing resource by regular physicians, especially those trained in European medical centers or influenced by their teachings. Physicians cited Hippocrates as part of a rhetorical strategy contrasting their "rational" practice with the unnecessarily "ornate" explanatory systems of competing practitioners. Regular practitioners portrayed knowing the local environment according to the Hippocratic imperative as part of their commitment to careful observation rather than anchorless theory. Accessible to men of dedication and acuity, free of the theoretical commitments of competing medical systems, local knowledge was democratic knowledge. Allegiance to a medical geography inspired by and continuous with Hippocratic tradition was thus part of the professional as well as intellectual struggle characterizing early American medicine. There were tensions, however, in this recruitment of heroes. Both supporters and opponents of regular medicine used Hippocrates as a rhetorical resource: historical ancestors are easier to raise up than to control.

The Hippocratic rhetoric of antebellum medical geography taught medical practitioners a usable, if contested, past. Medical geography simultaneously asserted regional coherence and specificity and established continuity with classic works of Western civilization. It helped create a legitimizing and stabilizing professional history for the practice of medicine while asserting local informants' unique competence to come to terms with new territories of the United States.

Models for Hinterland Practice

Medical geography provided practitioners in Missouri and Arkansas a bridge to a history rich in political and intellectual resonance. It brought the reassurance of tradition well maintained, of classical heritage preserved. Investigations into the relations between health and environment further connected local practitioners with scientific developments in other parts of the country and, indeed, the world. Location-based medical investigations provided a model for how to engage in scientific investigation. Pedagogically as well as rhetorically, study of local environments helped create a professional role for physicians of the antebellum borderlands.

In the context of weak, ineffective, and repetitive systems of medical education, medical geography offered the chance for innovative work. At medical teaching institutions in the South, students writing theses on the particular diseases, climate, weather, topography, geology, and ethnography of their home regions managed original work refreshingly unlike the stilted, often plagiarized essays churned out by most medical students.

Medical geography could also provide a means of self-enrichment for isolated practitioners. In July of 1844, Dr. A. W. Webb recorded in his massive medical notebook a handwritten, 70-page treatise on local fevers and their relation to climate and habits of life. It is not clear whether Dr. Webb intended his "Account of the Intermittent and Remittent Fevers of Arkansas from Observations Made during Ten years practice in the County of Chicot" solely as a way to organize his own thoughts, or (more likely) meant it for eventual publication. Yet the work indicates the ways local observation offered doctors an intellectual outlet.

Ambitious local practitioners used environmental medicine to cultivate connection with larger scientific and professional networks. Physicians of the borderlands eagerly read reports on medical geographies produced elsewhere. The experience of doctors in other places with warm climates held particular interest for area physicians, who struggled to come to terms with diseases associated with long, hot summers. As Americans reached out to Europe to stay current on new developments, so area physicians reached out to learn of other regions facing similar challenges of weather and humidity.

Yet hinterland practitioners did not simply accept or absorb such environmental knowledge; they took an active role in its creation. In producing local medical geographies and medical topographies, Arkansas and Missouri physicians took part in a larger intellectual endeavor that earned them legitimacy and recognition. Daniel Drake reprinted in his *Systematic Treatise* a portion of George Engelmann's detailed temperature and barometric readings at St. Louis. In his description of the Mississippi River's "Southern Basin," Drake also thanked "Doctor Borland of Arkansas" and physicians in Memphis, Tennessee, for materials for his map of diseases, and he mentioned the work of Leo Twyman and other Missouri physicians. Similarly, an 1856 medical topography of Bates County, Missouri, by Dr. J. E. Thompson appeared in the *Boston Medical and Surgical Journal*. Through the medium of medical geography, the activities of hinterland observers gained validity and audience.

Those situated to observe natural phenomena unavailable on the East Coast parlayed information into social and intellectual connection, operating as connective links between scientists in the borderlands and those back East. In 1853, for instance, George Engelmann wrote to a prominent natural historian on the East Coast for copies of scientific publications and tables to distribute to his Missouri-area colleagues. Scientific observers in remote regions could barter their observations for professional status.

Their efforts parallel those of specialists in other fields. When the editor of *The Horticulturalist*, the leading American horticultural journal of the day, expressed interest in hearing about the effect of the winter of 1851–52 on flora of different parts of the country, a north Arkansas nurseryman, Jacob M. J. Smith, took up the invitation and relayed a detailed account of how his nursery had fared. Smith contributed several other letters over the next few years, reporting to the cultured and fashionable audience of *The Horticulturalist* (its editor, A. J. Downing, was a leading arbiter of taste) on the fate of his fruit trees, flowering vines, and commercial flowers. Smith not only made a success of a commercial nursery in the Arkansas Ozarks but also made his plants relevant subjects of discussion in a publication of national scope and high culture.

Hinterland practitioners like George Engelmann and Jacob Smith maintained and built connections with professional and intellectual communities in the leading centers of the United States by capitalizing on their knowledge of backwater regions about which few other skilled observers could report. In recent years, historians of science have observed the crucial role played by courtly or gentlemanly status in determining the legitimacy of scientific observers in the early modern period: not all who were present at an event, they have argued, could bear credible testimony to its occurrence. Social place, these scholars have demonstrated, was an important aspect of early modern scientific observation. Environmental investigation in the American borderlands similarly makes clear the crucial role played by *geographic* place in determining the credibility and importance of scientific observers in the American nineteenth century.

Research into medical geography took place in the context of other scientific investigations that demonstrated the unique potential of science in the American borderlands. A main figure in the success of frontier science was William Beaumont. A military physician in Michigan Territory in the 1820s, Beaumont embarked on a series of experiments on the functioning of the digestive organs when a French trapper was wounded in a way that left a gaping hole through his skin and stomach. Cajoling and bribing his often recalcitrant subject, Beaumont dangled bits of food tied to a string through the fistula, testing how long it took for substances to be digested, and timing how long it took for food the man ate to show up in his stomach. The methodologically simple but unprecedented experiments were heralded worldwide and were seen as a triumph of practical American science. To the great delight of the St. Louis scientific and medical community (though not without a great deal of complaining on his own part), Beaumont was transferred to St. Louis in 1834, where he became a leading physician. His rough-and-ready, enterprising scientific research brought the sheen of successful scientific observation to the struggling practitioners of the city.

In a similar way, though with less drama, medical geography taught borderlands observers how to fit medical and scientific investigation into their experience. It provided models for practitioner behavior. The observations and publication of Dr. Nathan D. Smith make a powerful case for the pragmatism and impact of "frontier" science, as well as the subtle rhetoric of rustic simplicity that validated it. Smith was a typical antebellum physician: a medical graduate from New York, he worked first as an apprentice physician in New York and then—work as a doctor was hard to find—as a journeyman printer in New Orleans. Around 1820, he and his family moved to southwestern Arkansas Territory, near the county seat of Washington. There they established a farm and informal hospital of rough log cabins, where Smith and his daughters ministered to patients from nearby white settlements.

In 1840, Smith began his major life work: he started taking an astounding but by no means unique series of detailed weather measurements at appointed intervals every day for over 20 years. A professional acquaintance recommended Smith's work for publication by the Smithsonian Institution, and his "Meteorological Observations Made Near Washington, Ark." appeared in 1860 in a thick, leather-bound volume of weighty scientific essays. (Immediately after Smith's is the essay by the physician S. Weir Mitchell on rattlesnake venom that helped establish Mitchell as a prominent medical authority.) Like A. W. Webb, Nathan Smith performed his original research, as he claimed, "for the satisfaction of myself and family, without the expectation of its being appreciated beyond my household circle." Stamped—quite literally—with the approval of an official scientific body, Smith's rows and columns of observations carried knowledge produced in the Arkansas countryside into print and into institutions around the country.

Smith's regimen of observation was extreme, but his interests in weather and climate were widely shared. Observing and recording the weather was standard in the daybooks kept by many farmers, who often referred to them in subsequent years to determine the timing for clearing, planting, and harvesting. Details of the weather similarly fill personal correspondence of the period. By the mid-nineteenth century, English, continental European, and American observers (religious and secular, scientific and untrained) were at work gathering numerous kinds of weather data, and efforts were focused on both the accumulation and the interpretation of such information. Medical associations and agricultural societies alike looked to untangle complex relationships between the weather and the human and natural environment from page after page of crabbed tabulations of dew point, temperature, wind strength, and humidity. Smith's activities thus linked academic culture and common concern, scientific practice and agricultural commonplace.

Smith's weather observations were determinedly prosaic. He explained that

> My thermometer has hung all the time in the same place, in the open air, in the window-frame, outside of the sash, on the north side of the house, eight feet above the ground. . . . My rain-gauge is a deep tin cup, set on the ground, in an exposed spot in the garden.

Smith's plain prose matter-of-factly acknowledged the technological constraints of a region in which travel and transportation could still be slow and unreliable, and instruments hard to obtain. His technical preamble was similar to caveats made by other scientific observers in the region. George William Featherstonhaugh was frustrated in his 1834 attempt to investigate the mineral content of the Arkansas hot springs because he was unable to transport his scientific equipment across the swampy and rough terrain of southern Missouri and northern Arkansas. He had arranged for his gear to be sent downriver, but it had not arrived when he needed it. Instead, Featherstonhaugh used an ordinary thermometer to measure the temperature of the springs and employed commonsense descriptions in his geologic commentary. "I always found the water hot enough," he reported, "to make my tea without any further boiling, as well as wash my clothes." Thomas Nuttall similarly commented in 1819 that the main stream of the Arkansas hot springs was "hot enough to boil eggs or fish." Like them, Smith framed scientific endeavor as a pragmatic venture, in which domestic technologies had to be implemented when more robustly scientific means failed, and in which household implements could yield valuable data.

In the very structure of his account, Smith's meteorological report reflected his domestic and agricultural setting. His tables not only detailed the "observed temperature at sunrise throughout the year, and at 2 P.M. in the winter and 3 P.M. in the summer; amount of rain, and remarks on the weather" but also noted some of the interrelated aspects of the agricultural world he inhabited. On the 14th of January, 1840, for instance, on a day when the temperature had risen a degree, from 59° to 60° Fahrenheit, over the course of the afternoon, and the weather was cloudy and full of rain, Smith's tables also reveal "Oaks in bloom; vines in leaf." Later that spring, on a cloudy April day free of precipitation, with temperatures in the low 70s, another cycle of production was beginning: "Silk-worms spinning."

The laconic commentary of his tables alludes to, though it does not dwell on, agricultural experiments in silkworm production and other details of an agrarian world in which both Smith and his patients waited anxiously for rain, scrutinized the qualities of soils for productive value, and had to time their labors with the changing seasons. Smith's records were not divorced from the agricultural and domestic context of his life but interwoven with it. They bespoke a scientific understanding in which elements of one's surroundings, though they could profitably be quantified and registered, could not fully be understood out of relationship with each other.

Combining the domestic attentions of an almanac with the fabulous specificity of dedicated routine, repeated day after day for decades, Smith's account is a fascinating testament to the compelling power of observation of the natural world to capture and structure a scientific imagination. It is a testament, moreover, to the ability of science in the borderlands to be, effectively, science. The assumed modesty of its practitioner—a modesty serving to reinforce the dedication that produced his measurements, even as it provided a shield from potential critics—belied the importance of Smith's claims. Rainfall measurements made with a "tin cup, set on the ground," became part of the valuable knowledge to be gained about the country.

In his records, Dr. Smith took advantage of the rough conditions of the borderlands to do whatever science presented itself. His work was at once the product and the validation of science in the hinterland. As a text, it taught others how to be a physician–scientist far from the centers of medical learning or the new clinical pathology.

Nineteenth-century environmental medicine and natural scientific observation emphasized the place and position of local informants. They were, as Daniel Drake boasted of his work, "not dependent on the written archives of the profession, but copious in its acquisitions from co[n]temporary observers." Observers in small river towns and hidden among the area's canebrakes, observers often with little formal education but always with a sharp eye for natural detail, put themselves forward by means of medical geographies as legitimate and credible contributors to scientific knowledge.

Works like Smith's also indicate subtle strategies of professional positioning, in which successful physicians used "frontier" experiences as a way of validating their own success—much as contemporary politicians did. Many in the American public regarded having a rough and ready childhood as indicating something important about a man's character, and the character of his knowledge, in the increasingly urban, potentially effete world of the industrializing nineteenth century. Daniel Drake recalled being sent in his Kentucky boyhood to take corn to the gristmill, which provided, he wrote, "fine opportunities for seeing the world." In the course of long rides to the mill, he noted "the influence of soils on the character of the forest" as he passed out of a diversified wood into "a forest of white oak, supported by argillaceous soil." Such sophisticated observation by a boy still too young to lift the heavy bags of corn onto the family horse by himself may represent as much the adult Drake as the child, but the rhetoric is revealing: in Drake's account of life in the West, running errands in wild lands taught him to read nature's book with insight and accuracy. What had been a liability, in the rough ridicule of "Doctor Rattlehead" and similar regional humor, he trumpeted as an asset.

Engaging in environmental reports and observations in far-flung regions was a bid for intellectual relevance by antebellum physicians very much on the periphery. Study of health and environment provided a way to participate in intellectual culture while at the same time struggling to run a farm and build a practice in the hinterland. Medical geography gave intellectual structure and professional validation to mid-nineteenth-century Missouri and Arkansas physicians. It provided a means for ambitious local doctors to say, with one Arkansas settler, "I am pretty well reconsiled to the back woods."

Local observation and the construction of local knowledge created a science of localities—one in which being on an ill-defined frontier or in the swampy backwaters of a distant American territory could be turned to advantage. Moreover, as the sectional crisis of the questionably united States deepened, medical geography slid easily into an argument for Southern nationalism. Not only within the community of medical and scientific professionals but also in debates over the substance and meaning of the nation, environmental medicine served to help define the character as well as the understanding of new American lands.

Just as medical geography considered numerous factors as part of an interlinked whole and as part of a grander scheme of natural scientific knowledge, the projects and practices of environmental medicine linked individual medical and scientific practitioners in the American borderlands of Missouri and Arkansas with a larger scientific endeavor. Such work simultaneously built connections between far-flung places and the larger, already-possessed and already-known nation whose savants, merchants, and public rushed to take advantage of the resources, peoples, and potential of new territory.

CULTIVATION

Chapter VII

IN THE WINTER OF 1854, the southern Arkansas planter John Brown recorded in his diary that "the women are grubbing and cleaning up the new ground." Several years later, one of those women, a slave named Courtney, fell ill with a fever. Brown noted with satisfaction that "a dose of oil and turpentine . . . had a fine effect, after the calomel and dovers powders [a patent medicine] cleaned her out." Digging out roots and stones from a fallow field was effectual in the same language and with the same process as cleansing the body of inner imbalances. Strong action "cleaned . . . out" or "clean[ed] up" sites and bodies alike. John Brown worked the land he owned, just as he worked the people on it, managing their bodies with techniques that resonated with the labors of coaxing cotton to rise from the earth.

Like the rippled kiss of a smallmouth bass disturbing a calm stream surface, the pragmatic relief of this plantation manager tells us who are watchful on the banks of a larger body unseen beneath. Brown's casual vocabulary reveals a larger truth: bodily and environmental processes worked in the same ways, observed the same logic, and demanded much the same care. As observant fishers, we can learn from these surface signs. What people *say* isn't always what they *do*, and isn't the whole of what they think or feel, but the net of language offers us a tool with which to scoop up, at least for a time, the swiftly wriggling vitality of a larger identity of self and land.

Fundamental to the connections people felt with their surroundings were the labors of planting and harvest that shaped everyday life. The work of "settling" land—work that involved plants and animals, fire and axes, streams and far-off centers of commerce—expressed an intimate relationship between self and soil. This ongoing and lived relationship gave reassuring consistency to new environments that threatened often to bewilder and overwhelm.

Nineteenth-century language indicates some of the depth of meaning of labors on farm or plantation. Though in modern usage "cultivation" usually refers to the process of eradicating weeds and keeping soil loose near growing plants, in antebellum writings the notion of cultivation has a broader resonance. To cultivate land was not simply to hoe or plow it but to bring it to its full potential, much as one might cultivate aspects of oneself. More than physical labor, cultivation represented moral and spiritual engagement.

To cultivate land was to work healing upon it. Not a soothing and restful healing, but the painful, violent, wrenching healing of powerful emetics, bitter cordials, and desperate bouts of shaking and sweats. Working the land, like healing the body, was usually neither comfortable nor serene. Change to terrain and change to body were difficult, dangerous, and fraught with tension. Both were utterly necessary.

Understanding the everyday reality of a far-off and distant world demands from us a contradictory set of labors. Very few people (then or now) muse about the self-evident, and they rarely wax eloquent about the obvious. That which is most taken for granted may require the greatest conceptual leap for us of a very different time. We must be both earthy and imaginative in our efforts. From gritty details and commonsense advice, enigmatic rituals and down-to-earth customs, we can begin to piece together fundamental assumptions that nineteenth-century people (to the great frustration of historians seeking to understand them) almost never directly explained. As a patient angler scrutinizes the evidence of wind and weather but also consults his own intuition about where to cast a line, we can peer with imagination between the most prosaic details of ordinary life to make out truths at once metaphorically resonant and physically profound.

John Brown's journal of daily life through the 1850s and '60s gives us a set of clues into the complex of ideas that simultaneously made sense of inhabited body and inhabited terrain. Brown's efforts to produce cotton and other crops through the labor of his two dozen slaves, his concern for the health and welfare of the large household he managed, and his reflections on the agricultural year weave together many interrelated aspects of farm life in early Missouri and Arkansas. As domestic healer and agricultural manager, Brown was preoccupied with the linked concerns of bodily well-being and agricultural process which surface repeatedly throughout other sources. In these connections lie the meanings of cultivation for the health of newcomers to the early American Far West.

Agriculture as Material and Moral Imperative

Agricultural labor was the central theme of American borderland experience. A young man could map out a whole life's worth of intentions in his comment that he would soon marry and "go to farming" on the White River. Agricultural potential was fundamental to all assessments and evaluations of early Missouri and Arkansas, like "new" regions of the United States generally. As one Missouri man wrote to his mother, from Memphis, Tennessee, "I know [Mr. Daniel, a relative] wil be pleased with this contery it is a great stalk countery and can rais any thing that grows in the ground."

On the most basic level, a household's crops and livestock provided its primary sustenance. Families would augment their stores with some essentials (the Brown plantation laid in coffee, molasses, salt, flour, sugar, and tools every year from New Orleans), but corn and pork, augmented by garden produce and game, fed most of the region's households. Without the minimal care households gave domestic animals, without the more rigorous labors of cultivating a crop of corn, without expertise in hunting and trapping, bad seasons could be lean and hungry. Many farms, even small ones, quickly began to produce some items for trade, including bear oil, tobacco, cotton, honey, cordwood, and butter. Yet for most newcomers, early years were marked by the struggle to eke out subsistence. Households large and small relied upon their own slaughtered hogs, shucked corn, rough-ground meal, and carefully stored vegetables. The failure of a crop or herd might not wipe out a larger plantation, but it could dramatically alter its economy and at least short-term prospects. No one in early Missouri or Arkansas lived far from the realities of the year's crop. The search for what John Brown, in a contented moment, termed "mild plenty" filled the thoughts and workdays of cotton growers and small farmers. Sizable estates and squatter families alike lived by the rhythms of seeding and harvest.

"Settling" meant, in all practical terms, cultivating. The lack of industry of a "Spaniard" and his five family members encountered by the explorers George Hunter and William Dunbar living in a bark cabin along the lower Ouachita disturbed Hunter's sense of the proper order of things: "although they said they had been settled these five years," he observed skeptically, "there was no appearance of any crop or any store of any kind of vegetable produce." Much as the ragged family might insist on the fact of their "settlement," to Hunter their inability or unwillingness to coax regular sustenance from the earth meant that their "settling" was only titular.

Hunter's comment reflects the close relationship in popular understanding, and, increasingly over the period, in governmental regulation, between agriculture and legal ownership of land. Squatters who cultivated land— "improved" it, in the common and legal language of the time—were seen throughout the early part of the century as having informal rights to it. Their precedence, long felt and at times enforced with threat or violence, was ultimately codified in law. Over the early nineteenth century, several limited pieces of federal legislation, notably the 1814 Missouri Preemption Act, essentially legalized squatting by giving squatters first righ to purchase land they farmed. In 1841 the Preemption Act gave this right full sanction: when land came up for sale, those who had "improved" it had only to appear at the local land office and pay at least the minimum price of $1.25 an acre to purchase up to 160 acres. (The 1862 Homestead Act took this idea to its logical progression: settlers had simply to pay a small filing fee and live and "improve" land for five years in order to come into legal possession.) As Everard Dickinson explained to his parents, "any body can have a farm who will select an unoccupied place & settle upon it—build a log cabin & clear an acre or two to raise corn—then . . . he has the first right to Enter the land whenever it comes in market." Raising "an acre or two" granted land rights as well as a season's yield. To farm a piece of land meant taking it over; agriculture yielded not simply crops, fruits, meats, and grains, but also the social, and then legal, prerogatives of ownership.

Americans insisted on their own precedence because they did not regard the environments they came to claim as having been in any meaningful sense used before. Native American agriculture simply and profoundly failed to register with most American newcomers. This willful blindness was in part due to ingrained ideas about Indian racial inferiority, but it was reinforced by Americans' equally deep but subtler conceptions of land use and ownership.

American immigrants rejected the common fields and woodlots of their scattered French predecessors in favor of individual homesteads. Individual men owned land; with rare exceptions, communities did not. Though scores of slaves might harvest wheat or plant cotton—and construct buildings, wash clothes, cook food, shoe horses, and do all the other work of a large plantation—American legal systems and social rhetoric viewed American ownership of land as vested in the rights and resources of one individual: the owner. The language of American farming likewise excluded many of the people who did the actual work on the nation's fields, orchards, and pastures. A "farmer" was a white man, regardless of the free women and children and the black slaves who also cared for "his" crops and livestock.

Native American agricultural systems entirely eluded American understandings of farming and ownership. Americans viewed agriculture as a year-round process, one intrinsically related to the repeated use of specific plots of ground under the supervision of a male owner. Osage and other Native American agriculture in the region, in which groups of women raised squash, corn, and other crops in small meadows, moving garden sites from year to year, was to American observers something more haphazard than true cultivation.

Gender roles profoundly influenced perceptions of agriculture. For older Cherokees of the early nineteenth century, farming was the work of women, children, and old men—not something in which self-respecting hunters would engage. Many Cherokees and other Native Americans resisted the inversion of gender roles in agriculture and other activities pushed by American missionaries, U.S. officials, and accommodationist factions within their own nations. Many Americans in turn refused to acknowledge as farming the work done by Indian women. The botanist Thomas Nuttall observed that the French Creoles in central Arkansas "are entirely hunters, or in fact Indians in habits, and pay no attention to the cultivation of the soil." In other places in his account, Nuttall recounted the elaborate cultivation rituals of the Quapaws, particularly the women, who were primarily responsible for the community's crops, yet despite this evidence he persisted in arguing that to be "Indians in habits" was to disdain cultivation. The only farming that counted was that done by males.

For American newcomers, settled farming held moral as well as physical meaning. Unlike banking, land sales, gambling, soldiering, or city odd-jobs, cultivation was, in the words of a territorial official of Arkansas, "an honest livelihood." What the land received it gave back, supplying what one Arkansas planter termed *"good generous living."* Agriculture's "honesty" was related to a sense of duty. Steady and thorough farming was a free man's obligation as well as a way of life. Owen Maguire insisted emphatically in 1836 that Arkansas farms responded with abundant yields "wher people does ther duty by ther crops." The process of cultivation implied a relationship between farmer and land, in which each held responsibilities to the other, and steady attention would be rewarded with fruitfulness.

It is tempting to look back from a much more mechanized and less agricultural society—one in which tomatoes arrive shrink-wrapped in our supermarkets and jet fuel propels crisp apples around the globe for the benefit of American consumers—and mistake much of the nineteenth-century characterization of agriculture for the literal truth. Certainly raising crops and livestock was much closer to almost everyone's experience in much of the American nineteenth century, but not all those waxing rhapsodic about the value of farming had much intention of carrying it out. Some of those who talked of the virtues of agriculture were wealthy planters who directed labor while joining in it as little as possible; plenty of others, like the ever-optimistic Justus Post, saw farmland as one variable in a complicated equation of financial speculation that also involved interest rates, currency supplies, and preemption policies. Yet the importance of commerce and larger-scale markets to discussions of land in the Mississippi Valley does not negate the idealization of agriculture everywhere reflected in nineteenth-century life. Valuation of land for reasons of character, spirituality, and fertility did not push aside valuation for commerce, avarice, and gain: rather, each added more depth to the other. A work ethic that accumulated wealth was also demanded by land that needed cultivation to be complete and healthy. The many meanings of agricultural labor underscored each other.

Americans were, in the words of Timothy Flint, a "people whose object it was to make farms, and live by agriculture." The work of farming and the centrality of crops and livestock in everyday life was not at all unique to the United States, yet Flint's comment reveals the importance of agriculture as ideal in the self-imagination of Americans of his era (and even, if fierce debates over farm subsidies are any indication, to our own). The work of cultivation marked not only each person, but a *people*: to be American was to be a planter of rows, a harrower of fields.

Those who failed to cultivate the land represented the failure of civilized hopes and norms. Immigrating to Missouri, Henry Vest Bingham stopped by a small settlement in eastern Tennessee. "[H]ere is a Cabbin & two or three Ill looking men In It In a verry Merry humor," he recorded in his journal, adding that "there is not a spot of Earth Cultivated at this Cabbin or Near it & there people Must Subsist In a Misterious Manner." Bingham's dark suspicions of "Ill looking men" and ill-begotten subsistence convey the primacy of agriculture in many Americans' self-imagining.

Boosters and enthusiasts characterized agricultural improvement as easy and swift: the natural result of the earth's own urgings. "The soil is free from stones," Timothy Flint wrote of St. Charles, Missouri, reassuring New

England readers like his Massachusetts cousin James Flint, who were only too familiar with rocky fields; it is "loose and mellow, and needs no manure, and it is very abundant in the productions natural to it, the principal of which are corn, fruits, and wheat." The land's fertility had political consequences: Flint was sure that "speculation and wealth" would never shape the prospects of the West, whatever ambitious platters might plot. "Nothing" Flint concluded, "will grow vigorously in our land from artificial cultivation"; only settlements resting on its natural products, those of farm and field, would continue to blossom and grow. Farming in new lands of the West was not a traumatic process of demanding from the country a grudging product, observers like Flint assured potential migrants, but facilitated the land's own natural proclivities.

Despite Flint's confidence, though, other accounts emphasized the difficulty of imposing deep furrows and straight roads on a landscape that seemed to swallow and resist them. A. W. Webb characterized the "natural state" of southern Arkansas as "covered with forests." Friedrich Gerstäcker's description of variably cultivated homesteads reveals wilderness similarly hostile. Though the sixteenth section of each township was set aside by congressional mandate for education and was therefore usually used for the schoolhouse and teacher's plot, only the teacher's constant vigilance would maintain it in habitable state. If one short-term teacher failed to succeed the other fast enough, "before long the place becomes overgrown by such a tangle of brush and vines that it is virtually impossible to clear a second time. It is almost as if the land were furious at being wrenched out of its natural condition even for so short a time." Full of an abundance and fury embodied in twisting, tripping vines and sharp-thorned, resilient brush, wild nature could be forced into regimes of garden or field only at great effort and cost. Webb's and Gerstäcker's land resisted the plow as surely and naturally as Flint's welcomed it.

Further pessimism emerges in retrospect, when people looked back on once-abundant natural resources that had since disappeared. One former slave reflected back on her childhood near Wattensaw, Arkansas (formerly known as Pigeon Roost—presumably before the extermination of the flocks of passenger pigeons that once swept through the country's woodlands). Earlier it had been "the richest land you ever seen in your life." In particular, the "whole washpot full of stewed pigeon" she once enjoyed was "fine eating." Still, "It was a shame to waste up all the pigeons and clear out the place." For most American settlers, clearing out the place was the explicit goal and the ultimate mandate.

"Melodious seemed to me the constant cracking of root," rhapsodized the German immigrant Frederick Muench, describing the difficult initial plowing of his land in Missouri, "for it was a song of victory, it meant the end of the primitive state of nature." Similarly, Henry Morton Stanley took "extraordinary pleasure in laying low with a keen axe the broad pines" of land he worked in southern Arkansas in the early decades of the nineteenth century. As the "fierce joy" of Stanley and Muench in the success of their work makes clear, agricultural labor was not merely labor. It was an engagement with the natural world in which cultivators imposed their own will, putting an end to "the primitive state of nature."

Farming was a spiritually resonant act for early Missourians and Arkansans. To claim land for civilization was to claim it for Christian life. Savagery, violence, heathenism, and lack of the knowledge or will to cultivate were interlinked concepts for white Americans of the nineteenth century. Such lessons had a long history. Agricultural metaphors fill the Bible, and many parables of Christ are framed in allegories of planting, seeding, tending, and exercising stewardship over land and resources. Religious labors were often described metaphorically as agricultural work. "We were clearing away the rubbish," wrote Cephas Washburn of the early years of Dwight Mission, "breaking up the fallow ground, and scattering broadcast the good seed, and preparing for the precious harvest season we afterwards enjoyed."

Agricultural practices held distinct spiritual meaning not only in the experience of white newcomers, but also in the lives of Arkansas and Missouri slaves. People in slavery used song to impart meaning, exchange messages, and keep time in rhythmic, repetitive tasks. Rows of enslaved workers picking cotton, singing as they worked, would "swing low" to reach the cotton bolls as they sang about the coming of Elijah's sweet chariot, experiencing as bodily discipline what they simultaneously expressed as redemptive hope.

Within the Native American groups of the region, agriculture and agricultural plenty held religious significance. In the "green corn dance," which Cephas Washburn described as "their annual feast of First-fruits," an entire Cherokee village would fast, purge and cleanse themselves, and offer ritual thanksgiving before a collective feast of beans, early corn, and venison. The first sweet peaches were similarly recognized in community ritual before any were eaten. Marriage ceremonies among the Cherokees and the Quapaws included a public and formalized exchange in which the man offered the woman a leg of deer, and she gave him an ear of corn, symbols of the hunting or cultivation that each partner would contribute to the family.

In multiple ways, laborers and farmers of early-nineteenth-century Missouri and Arkansas conjoined community ritual and community harvest. Spirituality, moral virtue, and the cultivation of the soil were closely bound in symbol, as they were in daily life. Callused hands grasping a "whole-note" hymnal to sing and fingers marked with red Arkansas clay lifting up a kitchen pot to "holler" both bore testimony to the intimate and everyday intertwining of religious devotion and agricultural work.

Yet to understand the metaphorical weight carried by notions of agriculture is to understand only partially the importance of farming and husbandry for early Americans. The meanings of cultivation were carried out and inscribed by the rhythmic and the repetitive, the sweaty and the soggy labors necessary to effect it.

Farm Work

Cultivation was not a monolithic enterprise in the middle trans-Mississippi region. In the early decades of the century, a variety of crops filled the fields of Missouri and Arkansas settlers. "Shoe-top cotton," so called because the straggling bolls never grew higher than settlers' boots, vied with tobacco, corn, and even wheat in the Ozark plateau. Flatlands gave root to grains and cotton, while everywhere gardens produced vegetables and herbs for the table. Especially in the Ozarks, some farmers tended fruit orchards, and in Missouri's German counties, even vineyards. By the 1850s, larger plantations had enthroned cotton as king in the rolling lowlands of Arkansas, steel-edged plows had proved the fertility of the Missouri prairies for wheat, and drovers had made both states substantial producers of livestock. Arkansas's lowlands were dominated by cotton plantations like John Brown's, which were usually smaller than those of the Deep South, but similar in organization and culture. Missouri, too, was a slave state, but slave labor only figured large on tobacco or hemp farms along the state's two principal rivers, the Missouri and the Mississippi. Even as holdings became more consolidated, and commercially oriented plantations and larger farms dominated the better growing lands of both states, a variety of cultivative practices occupied Missouri and Arkansas farmers. Chronicling the forms and labors of the area's agriculture thus traces the bodily motions and the patterns of life which formed the touchstone of common experience and common life.

Though crops varied throughout the region, a typical small farm might grow two or three staples: corn, almost always (to eat fresh or dry on the cob, to make into meal, to feed hogs, and on occasion to produce home-distilled whiskey), and often wheat or another grain. Larger farms and plantations grew crops with an eye toward the New Orleans markets: cotton predominated in the river bottoms of southern Arkansas, while wheat, hemp, and tobacco, augmented by rye, buckwheat, and other grains, were the standard cash crops of Missouri.

John Brown's holdings are representative of plantations in south Arkansas at midcentury. Fields were mostly given over to cotton, but the plantation also raised corn, several kinds of potatoes, and turnips as winter feed for the cattle. The Brown household ate peas, onions, cabbages, lettuce, mustard and collard greens, and sweet potatoes, while warmer months brought raspberries, watermelon, peaches, figs, and plums (apples, too, ripened in the fall). On plantations like Brown's, slaves usually ate much less fresh food than their masters. Theirs was often a diet of cornmeal and fatty salt pork. At least for the slave-holding Browns, ducks, pigs, and beef and milk cattle provided food and eggs; the Brown plantation must have had chickens, and at least in one year they kept guinea hens. People on the Brown plantation probably sweetened food with both honey and molasses. Despite this seeming variety, in many seasons the Brown household—especially the slaves—likely relied on cornmeal and hog meat to a degree most of us would find both wearisome and nutritionally unwise.

Many newcomers were unprepared for the demands of livestock and field. Though drawn by the prospect of agrarian success, English immigrants frequently arrived with little experience of farm labor. Immigrants from German-speaking territories, many of whom had been educated members of small-town and city bourgeoisie, wrestled endlessly with new realities of borderlands life. They sought relief from political tyranny in the free soil of the United States, but were often unfamiliar with the rudiments of agricultural practice. Emigrating Americans were more likely to come from farm families, yet those from urban areas needed advice and help on how to split wood, build and repair tools when theirs broke or wore out, weed a garden plot while keeping small children away from open fires or boiling vats, and prepare food without the usual complement of household pots, pans, bins, and storage space.

"Movers" settled first in river bottoms and partially wooded areas. An initial step in the settling of forest regions was to clear underbrush, grub out roots, haul off the larger rocks and boulders, and "girdle" or "deaden" trees by stripping off a ring of bark to kill them as they stood. After the upper parts of the tree were dead (usually a year or more after the field was initially established), trunks had to be burned or dug out of the ground. Farmers working in haste merely plowed around the "deadenings." Along with planting came a plethora of activities, by women and men, adults and their children, needed to establish a farm household. Cutting trees, fitting a kitchen, hauling rocks, feeding the family from the carefully managed supply of cornmeal, burning out stumps, "ditching," making implements for house and field, breaking paths to water source and fields, establishing a garden plot, and plowing land—these and other labors of settlement were both the practical and the symbolic appropriation of terrain.

Few farms of the borderlands followed the disciplines of careful manuring and crop rotation recommended by agricultural authorities and eastern journals. Households struggling to establish themselves were concerned with demanding the maximum immediate return from the land (their methods of slash-and-burn farming have a certain environmental brutality, but in the short term, at least, made sense: for a few years many soils could give good or even prodigious yields without the expensive fertilization recommended by Yankee experts). On larger plantations, and later into the century, fields might be alternately planted in clover or in a corn/wheat rotation, or even let to lie fallow as pasture for a year, but for many immigrants cultivation was a race to capitalize on the land's fertility before a growing family, mounting debts, or impoverished soils forced another move.

To sow fields, workers broke up the soil with heavy plows. They then used harrows, rake-like implements made of pegs mounted usually on an A-shaped frame and drawn by domestic animals, to break apart the heavy clods of dirt and smooth out the ground. On smaller farms, seeds were frequently spread broadcast, although corn was often planted "Indian style," in small mounds with legumes nearby, and with melons or squash planted among the cornrows. After planting, farmers might harrow again to cover the seeds. Through the period of intense cultivation, fieldworkers might plow several more times, to kill weeds and cast dirt onto the growing roots of the crop. Such care was particularly given to cotton: slaves planted it in long lines, placing seeds down the middle of furrows, often in "drills" (holes or trenches dug with a sharp tool). Then they would harrow the furrows over with care, beginning a process that would proceed for several months of cultivation as they used plows and hoes to cover weeds and "chop" the crop, killing unwanted vegetation.

Planting involved rhythmic labor done on small holdings by a farm couple or a few laborers and on larger plantations by field gangs of dozens of slaves used to working closely with one another. On plantations as on smaller farms, labor was organized by ability: the strongest adults guided or pushed plows, "broke" land, and performed the back-aching seeding and picking, while older people and young children would assist with those tasks, bring out water, clear away debris, weed, and do other small chores.

Many slave women did heavy fieldwork, rolling logs and plowing fields, picking cotton with quick fingers while pulling along sacks that bulged to the ground. In white families of fewer resources, women similarly engaged in fieldwork. With progress in the family's fortunes, free women were more likely to tend the garden plots and milk cows, which were understood to be women's domain. As Selina Seay wrote her mother from Camden, Arkansas, in February of 1859, "The weather cleared off into regular spring, & every Lady is gardening." Yet even among urban slave-holding families, a "Lady" might perform grueling physical tasks. Matilda Fulton, whose husband, William, was an important political figure in early Arkansas, wrote him in 1832 while he was away in Washington that she had worked all day with a slave to slaughter and cut up nine hogs just before going into labor and delivering their son.

In the early years of American occupation, common wisdom held that "corn won't grow where trees won't." Many settlers thus shunned prairies, which were known evocatively as "the barrens." By the 1830s, adventurous farmers had begun to establish that prairies actually yielded extraordinarily fertile soil. To prepare prairie land for cultivation, would-be farmers had to break up the thick, tangled roots of the grasses and flowers making up the tall, waving vegetation of the grasslands. In 1831, it cost two dollars an acre to break the Missouri prairie using hired plow teams equipped with the durable and expensive metal blades needed to cut through matted root systems several feet thick.

The changes wrought by cutting and rolling trees, digging out rocks, breaking prairie sod, tearing down brambles, bounding land with rough fences, and building and maintaining the tools, houses, and outbuildings necessary to keep up this work on the land were described in a series of evocative phrases. Land was "cleared up," "cleared off," or "taken up." Long-developed and long-settled regions—where clearing and girdling and initial plow-cuts had given way to landscapes of comfortable farms—were characterized as "a high state of cultivation," or simply "in high cultivation."

The different qualities of agricultural terrain, like different levels and kinds of cultivation, gave rise to a detailed vocabulary of agricultural description. Like a tired farm worker, heavily used land would become "worn out." James Gill, a former slave who had been taken to eastern Arkansas when his plantation moved from Alabama, remembered that "it sure was rich lan' den," in contrast to the fields they had left home in Alabama, where "de lan', it was gittin' poor an' red and mought near wore out." Land could be "strong" and easily cultivated, or "poor," yielding little even to hard work. "[M]y land is a dark molatto," commented one Arkansas farmer in 1860, "and the groth is Pine." Like a "strong" woman, a "poor" family, or a "mulatto" slave, terrain bespoke qualities reminiscent of the human condition.

Farm life was yoked to the seasons. Spring was the beginning of the agricultural year. During these cold, wet months, cattle would be "brought out of the cane," driven from the canebrakes where they found winter forage into fields closer to home. Only in April would owners discover how many calves their cows had borne over the winter. Planting was performed in the spring: plantations growing cotton would usually begin planting corn in February or early March in order to leave the main part of the spring (usually April through early May) for sowing the all-important cotton. May and June brought the important work of tending the new crops. Rows of corn and cotton had to be "chopped" and cultivated—the rows weeded with plow and later with hoe, and the cotton plants carefully thinned by hand. By mid- to late July, corn and cotton would be "laid by," the stalks and plants growing strong enough on their own that they required less intensive work with the hoe and plow. Late summer was thus a brief respite after the months of planting and care of the young shoots. July and August were often a time to "cellar" potatoes and "pull fodder"—take the broad leaves of corn to dry and store as winter feed. Harvesting the main crops of cotton, grains, and corn usually started in late summer and early fall, when the burning sun still lay heavy across wide fields. Harvest was a race against the coming of autumn's rains, but on ambitious holdings whose plantings outstripped the available labor supply, it could last into December. During times of harvest whole communities were energized around efforts in the field.

Social interaction was shaped by agricultural cycles. In the early nineteenth century, May and June were trading months when Native American groups from up the Missouri would gather in St. Louis to trade furs for other valuables, and to reinforce political ties through ritual and gift exchange. Fall was the time for neighborhood gatherings—corn huskings, dances, or children's "play-parties" for those whose religion did not allow dancing to music (at such parties, young people sang their own music to get around proscription). Religious revivals were held in the heat of summer, when the crops were "laid by" but harvest not yet begun.

In the autumn, households harvested root vegetables and some varieties of wheat, stored bushels of fallen nuts, hurried to hunt bear and deer to smoke sides of rib or venison before the animals went into hibernation or began to lose weight, preserved and dried fruits and vegetables, and slaughtered hogs to "put up" meat for the coming months. In Missouri, agricultural fairs brought scattered farm families together with the "neighborhood."

Cold months were the time for what one Arkansas overseer termed "doing various things about the plantation." Fences, outbuildings, and equipment needed repair, white families' children received more steady instruction, women of the household (slave and free) worked spinning wheels, and field hands might plant early wheat or potatoes. Slaves often were put to work during winter months clearing land. The seasonal rhythms of crops strongly marked everyday life. Resources and people would be exhausted in the spring and autumn, but winter lulls left time for some free families, as one emigrant enticed his family, to "set round the fire and do Nothing but go to frolicks."

The demands of the agricultural year were overlaid and intensified by seasonal patterns of sickness and disease. The "sickly season" was perilously close to the period of highest physical demand. Harvest coinciding with the season of ague and fever could bring hunger in January to a farm family or a village. As Henry Merrell reflected of his experiences in southwestern Arkansas, "the uniform sickliness of every fall season of the year prevented the gathering of such crops as were made, until the frost and rains had nearly ruined them for market." Merrell did not note a further irony: the hard frosts that killed vegetables were usually credited with ending epidemics or community bouts of illness. The needs of cultivators and field were in some ways at odds.

Throughout the farmlands of early Arkansas and Missouri—on the holdings of earnest subscribers to agricultural journals as on the small, hastily cleared plots of small farmers from the hills of the upland South—a common sense based on bodily experience governed human interaction with terrain. Every plow hand knew that different soils had different colors, tastes, and smells, and that these were indicative of different kinds of "strength" or fertility. Trees and vegetation indicated qualities of agricultural land. One emigrants' guide noted that "the timbered land is covered with tall canes, a sure indication of a warm and productive soil." The qualities of environments were interpretable through the feel of sandy loam, the sensation of passing winds, and maxims that translated the characteristics of a new environment into agricultural wisdom.

A range of practices and types of agriculture were practiced in the high slopes and the curving river floodlands of early Missouri and Arkansas. Seasonal rhythms strongly tied to agricultural labor governed everyday life. Underlying the agriculture of Missouri and Arkansas was the basic fact of slavery: the distinction between free white labor and black slaves' work permeated the entire society. Uniting the personal experience of the region's inhabitants, however, was the intimate process of cultivating the natural environment and dependence on its products. The physical effort of plow, rake, hoe, and hand gave a depth of lived experience to the myriad figurings of agriculture in the language and the imagination of the time.

Cultivation and Sense of Self

Cultivation was central to identity, for all those engaged in working the land. The demands and disciplines of agriculture shaped Missourians' and Arkansans' sense of their own physical presence and of the lands they farmed. Land merited description in the language of bodily experience, just as settlers' own bodies could be quantified with reference to the work done out in the fields.

Slaves undoubtedly found meanings in cultivation different from those of the white families who claimed to own both them and the land they worked. What one former Mississippi slave called "hard work, field work" was the starting point and fundamental cause of slaves' imprisonment. Lives were regimented around the seasonal rhythms of the household's crops. Workdays in summer's intense period of cultivation began as soon as the sky was light enough for laborers to see to work the fields, and ended when darkness hindered labor. Slaves put in long days away from their children and their family quarters. As a number of former slaves phrased it, they worked "from can 'til can't," measuring work time by their own bodies' perceptions of rising sun and fading light.

Slave labor often "settled" land, whether through slaves' work in large fields or their own garden plots. Henry B. Miller, a young traveler from Illinois who recorded in his diary his observations on life in Missouri in 1838, commented that slaves kept "small lots or patches, which they Plant with corn and cultivate on Sunday & by moonlight." Though slaves made money by selling the crops to their owners or at market, Miller noted how even this labor was used to owners' advantage: "These patches are usually such spots as are newly cleared, the negroes making the first crop; . . . this plan is encouraged by many of the planters as a way of getting their land cleared and under cultivation, the negro clearing a new patch every year."

Yet despite the many levels of exploitation that went with chattel slavery, agricultural prowess was also a valuable skill, for slaves as well as masters. Black Southerners of the early twentieth century boasted about their youthful ability to work hard, plow straight, and quickly plant or pick a row. For blacks seeking escape from bondage just as for whites seeking land and economic opportunity, agricultural labor could be a step toward emancipation.

James L. Bradley, who was born in Africa, captured as a boy into slavery in South Carolina, and forcibly emigrated with his owner's plantation to territorial Arkansas, recorded in 1835 an account of his tumultuous life. Determined to win his own freedom, Bradley slept only three or four hours a night after working the fields in his mistress's Arkansas plantation, waking early to plait horse collars out of corn husks for his own profit. After several years of this small-scale entrepreneurship, he was able to buy hogs which he fattened and sold. Bradley also grew tobacco and corn on "wild land in the neighborhood that belonged to Congress." Each harvest fed more pigs and increased his herd. After encountering a group of missionaries in 1828, he "longed to be able to read the Bible!" and managed to learn to read from "an old spelling-book, which I carried in my hat for many months." He persuaded the young child of his owners to help him learn to write. After almost nine years of labor, Bradley fought his way to literacy and to freedom. For seven hundred dollars he bought himself out of slavery. He subsequently entered the Lane Seminary in Cincinnati, where he worked with other antislavery activists. For Bradley, working the land meant working toward his liberation. Coaxing corn and tobacco from the earth, Bradley came to possess his own body—and the tools to shape his soul. Its mix of meanings like that of the Christianity which slaves learned from white owners but then made over in their own services, cultivation was a central and complex fact of life for Missouri and Arkansas slaves.

The ubiquity of agricultural work led to an intimacy with the earth for laborers both black and white. Body and land were related in measure and in value: one was only worthwhile in the presence of the other. Agricultural labor was quantified and compared in the conversations of nineteenth-century Americans as a common and deeply personal referent. The amount of work an adult man could do in a day—epitomized in the "task" system of labor on many plantations—provided a way of speaking about one's capacity for toil. A "task" would be assigned to a slave as a day's labor. When it was complete, the slave could work his or her own land. In the "gang" system increasingly common on cotton plantations, a driver would direct a whole group of people together; individuals thus had much less control over how or when to complete their work, and often had less time to cultivate their own plots or spend with their families. Tallying tasks was a measure of strength, effort, and stamina, as well as a way of quantifying the value of a field hand.

The disciplines of quantification were harsh ones: if the weight of their basket of cotton failed to measure up at the end of a long day's picking, wrote former slave Solomon Northup, field slaves would be beaten. If they had more than usual, their expected pick would be raised. Doing either too little or too much labor could bring slaves to harm. Yet even within a system of such extreme external control, blacks, as well as whites, compared and counted their own labor. Older African-American women of the South, interviewed in the 1930s, sometimes spoke proudly of having been able to do the work of a man when young, just as leading physician Daniel Drake took pride in his later years in having been able to do " 'half a man's' work with the sickle and . . . the scythe" as a boy in his early teens. The number of rails that a man could split in a day was a convenient and frequent reference-point, one uniting the experiences of men in the Appalachian regions, the plantation South, and the Ozark hills (though in most instances local qualifiers were necessary: the number of rails depended greatly on whether the wood was pine, beech, hickory, or oak, and no one could split straight rails of twisting gum).

The amount of sustenance the earth would yield for the labor put into it was a similarly crucial measure. The emigrant Kirkbride Potts wrote to his family with satisfaction, "nothing could induce me to live in jersey now for I can make more in one year here than I can there in five with the same labour." Stephen Hempstead similarly evaluated the fertility of the nearby American Bottom in his economical comment, "Saw 32 men in one field reaping." Western lands rewarded work and were quantified by it. Measuring labor against oneself, and oneself against the labors of a homestead, expressed the many relations of person and environment which filled the experience of early Missouri and Arkansas.

Parallels between environmental and human processes underscored the intimacy of relations between planters and planted, farmers and farm. "[I]t appears to be an improving place," commented the military naturalist S. W. Woodhouse of Pine Bluff, Arkansas, in 1849. Woodhouse used language commonly applied to town, plantation, or person: all could be "improved" when in poor condition, and all could be classified in the progressive tense as "improving." When Timothy Flint commented in 1832 that the White River region held "some of the . . . healthiest soil for planters in this country," his praise mixed human body and agricultural crop: the soil was healthy for farm-holders both because they could raise good harvests on it, and because their bodies would remain healthy while they worked it.

Fundamental unity between person and environment functioned on multiple levels. Mourning the loss of a daughter to scarlet fever, one St. Louis father wrote his brother in 1832 that he was attempting to remember spiritual consolation, but "the stroke is severe. She was a tender plant, and was closely intwined around our hearts." The metaphors of a deeply agricultural world slid easily between a much-loved child and the delicate tendrils of a young vine.

The same developmental processes were seen to govern people and the nature they inhabited. The former St. Louis slave Lucy A. Delaney observed in the 1880s of her mother, who refused to move from Missouri to Toronto to be near her daughter, "old people are like old trees, uproot them, and transplant to other scenes, they droop and die, no matter how bright the sunshine, or how balmy the breezes." Land was understood and interpreted as bodies were: the earth and its associated vegetation behaved like a person.

Fertility and Generation

Day-to-day life revolved around fertility and generation. When the "red sow took boar," when the "young black sow piged," or when "One of [the] ewes droped 2 lambs" were important and noted events. Those piglets and lambs fed and clothed families, their wool or meat turned to use or turned into commodity for sale down the river in New Orleans. The multiple values attached to agriculture extended to every aspect of the growing world. Seeds, shoots, cuttings, and roots in particular held a wealth of association. People discussed them intently, revealing an attention to newness, both potent and frail, of the living world.

Seeds and seedlings were precious commodities in the agricultural world of the early American Mississippi Valley. Bottomland farmers vied for good-quality cotton seed, but purchasing the right seed lines required perception and savvy. Itinerant dealers might mix or confuse varieties, while the multiple and often overlapping names for lines of cotton made judgments difficult. Expertise in cotton seed was the mark of an astute planter. Excess cotton seed, culled out of the white boll by the long teeth of a gin, was only gradually recognized as a commodity in its own right. By the 1840s, some Southern farmers had ceased simply dumping it in marshes or bayous, and had begun using the seed as fertilizer. In the following decade some operations began milling cottonseed oil. Seeds were the object of investigation and scrutiny as owners struggled to make farms pay and grow.

Widespread belief held that "thanking" for seeds—expressing gratitude when given them as a gift—would spoil and ruin them. Theodore Pease Russell, who as a young man returned to southern Missouri to set up a household with his Connecticut bride, thanked a neighbor for supplying him with a portion of seeds from her garden. She responded with anger and disappointment. By thanking her out loud he had ruined all the hard work she had put into gathering and storing the seeds and carefully instructing him in their cultivation. Her frustration speaks of a sense of regional perception bound up in the important ritual of obtaining local seeds: "You Yankees may do as much thanking as you please way down where you come from," she scolded, "but it won't do in this country."

This suspicion of courtesy or gentleness around plants reflects a long-standing folk belief that vegetative growth was a difficult and demanding struggle, testing people's mettle. Weakness could betray a cultivator. "Got to hard cuss gourd seed, they say, to get it up out of the ground," recalled one man of the "grudgin' land" he farmed near Nameless, Tennessee, in the late 1970s.

Exchange of new plants and reports about their progress connected former and present environments. News of how gardens fared—when shoots began to show, how the snap-peas were adjusting to the moist air of the Far West—connected far-distant correspondents. Newcomers to Arkansas and Missouri valued crops, flowers, and fruits brought or sent from "home" as physical reminders of family and friends, and also as a means of making the new environment look, smell, and taste reassuringly familiar. Sending seeds and seedlings in the mail, and by traveling friends, formed tangible connections between loved ones' gardens. Women in particular treasured seeds sent or carefully carried from the original family home and sent seeds of Arkansas and Missouri plants in return as gifts from the new country.

Emotional connections were made manifest in the exchange of seeds, slips, and seedlings. Neighbors customarily presented to a young married couple the startings of a garden plot. "Mrs Mattock gave me something of all she had, and Mrs Dr. Viser two . . . trees," Selina Seay wrote her mother, "And soon, if Bro[ther] Tho[ma]s sends me some of Mrs Webb's roses, I am quite rich." A family's garden could grow unfamiliar seedlings as well as long-cherished plants. To a couple newly settled in a small town on the banks of the Ouachita River in southern Arkansas, "Mrs Webb's roses" and neighbors' vegetables represented not only decoration and sustenance, but the nurturance of social ties both old and new.

Migrants often placed value on tracing the history of their seeds and their plants. The lineage of a specific seed line could trace generations' successive moves. "I have about 60 bareing Trees of Grandfather Howisons fine white plumb peach," J. W. Calvert wrote a cousin in 1851, adding, "The seed was braught to Kentucky by uncle John Howison in 1790 and I have them in Arkansas." The spring blossoms of the Howison hybrid, opening every year in the St. Francis County countryside, carried the history of the family's emigrations. The number and fertility of the "fine white plumb peach" developed by his grandfather were for Calvert the symbol of his own immediate family's success as well as its link with an extended family removed in both place and time. Calvert's pride in his 60 trees is made the more poignant by the circumstances of his letter. He wrote with eagerness to catch up his long-lost cousin on all the events of his adult life. Like the letter itself, chronicling a generation of marriages, births, deaths, financial troubles, and eventual solid footing, Calvert's "bareing trees" bespoke a history complex and long.

"New country" held promise that linked family and farm. Owen Maguire could buy little in his native Kentucky "unless it was some pore place." His choice was clear: "I concluded that I had better go to some new Country where land was Cheap & I could have a chance of geting that was good." Maguire hoped to "get" land, but his language was evocative: one of the meanings of "get" was to father a child. His "chance of geting"—his prospects for a number of futures—hinged for Owen Maguire on his and his family's move to a country of more open prospects.

Other sources concurred on the centrality and intermingled nature of reproductive potential. Fertile land needs fertile people, advised Anderson Wilson, a Missouri settler, to eastern relatives wondering whether to emigrate: "But if you want to know how Old I think a man Should be to be to old to leave Carolina I will tell and that is when he is to Old to Get Children or his wife to old to bear, then he is to old to move & had better Stay, But not til then." His advice was at once pragmatic and metaphorically resonant. Children's labor was economically vital to most farming households. At the same time, land demanded not simply labor but also matching energy from its inhabitants and cultivators. People must mirror the terrain they cultivated. They must be fecund, able to "get" and "bear," in order to take full advantage of their environment. The generative qualities of the environment demanded and echoed those of the human form.

Folk beliefs reinforced these connections. Early-twentieth-century folklorists documented traditions in which a couple would sow their seed naked, under a full moon, the man walking behind the woman and casting the seed onto her bare buttocks, where it would then fall onto the fertile soil. Naked or clothed, many nineteenth-century farmers timed the sowing of seed to particular phases of the moon, linking the potential of their fields to women's little-understood monthly cycles of fertility and blood. Modern readers may be forgiven for wondering whether such late-night bare-naked planting involved simply walking up and down rows, and in fact other folk tradition makes clear the logical progression of such practices. Some Ozark farmers interviewed in the early twentieth century talked with the pioneering folklore collector Vance Randolph of how successful farmers "fucked over" their fields, making love in new-plowed dirt and alongside growing crops. "It takes fucking and loud grunts to raise big melons," explained one farmer of a prize-winning specimen. While not all people would have believed in or acted out these beliefs—probably some who talked of this practice did so only sheepishly, or perhaps tongue in cheek—they carry out in the most direct form a set of connections to which tamer reference also testified. Sexual union made gardens respond; human reproduction evoked parallel responses from the generative world.

In the world of Owen Maguire, Anderson Wilson, and lusty Ozark farmers, bodies shared important characteristics with their natural environment. Nature's fecundity matched and might even be prompted by human procreation. In fact, the people as well as the plains of early Missouri and Arkansas reproduced prodigiously. A large portion of the women Anderson Wilson saw about him at any time would have been pregnant, nursing, or otherwise caring for young children. Clara Brown gave birth to three children in the late 1850s and early 1860s, in addition to the seven she and her husband John already had. She and her eldest daughter, Margaret, each bore two children during the same several years; during the spring of 1857, John Brown worried in his diary about the "delicate condition" of both wife and daughter. At 57, John Brown had infants and toddlers as both children and grandchildren. Fertility and generation were not poetic goals, but facts of life for farm families struggling to raise both crops and the children to work them.

Common speech often enfolded in metaphor the generative nature of new places. American towns, reported one recent German immigrant, are "rapidly blooming." George W. Featherstonhaugh, traveling south from the Missouri mining districts toward the White River valleys, commented that "the country bore the appearance of being still more pregnant with metallic matters." Writings about the Mississippi Valley region figured the land as fertile in multiple ways, pregnant with possibility and meanings. Even contrasting observations used fertility as the governing metaphor. Traveling to the Gasconade River, his party on the trail of Cherokee removal passed "through a barren and sterile country," recorded the accompanying physician, Dr. W. I. I. Morrow, in 1839. Fertile or barren, productive or sterile, environments held generative qualities made manifest in a variety of ways.

The generative potential of new environments was in some cases seen as overly promising, superabundant in ways difficult to harness. Missouri prairies were *too* productive to grow good wheat, explained Nicholas Hesse to a German readership yearning to leave behind worn-out topsoil and surely bewildered at the idea of overfertile land which had to be exhausted by other crops before wheat plantings could begin. Similarly, John Brown was delighted by the prospects in garden and field one spring, commenting in his diary on "vegetation swelling out so fast as to be almost visible to the eye," but his unaccustomed exaggeration implies an abundance somewhat disconcerting.

T. B. Thorpe's tall tale "The Big Bear of Arkansas" celebrated the rough manners and wild prospects of the new territories, and its caricatured humor amplified some of the concerns of actual farmers like Nicholas Hesse or John Brown. As Thorpe's effusive Arkansan protagonist recounts a long story about a preternaturally powerful bear, he impresses on his steamboat companions a sense of his land's fertility, insisting that he owned "Such timber, and such bottom land, why you can't preserve anything natural you plant in it unless you pick it young, things thar will grow out of shape so quick." Beets turn to heavy stumps, and potato hills grow to the size of Indian mounds: "As I expected, the corn was overgrown and useless: the sile is too rich." The stunning development of corn, potatoes, and beets reflected the fundamental essence of the terrain: such alarming growth was the land's rebellion against the imposed constraints of agriculture. As the storyteller contentedly concludes, "I don't plant any more: natur intended Arkansaw for a hunting ground, and I go according to natur."

The cost of overweening and sometimes overwhelming development might be systemic exhaustion. One German immigrant to Missouri observed that "fruit trees grow much faster here than in Europe but are not as long-lived." The American environment sped up growth, but such profligate abundance met its reckoning. Timothy Flint similarly found "something . . . almost appalling in this prodigious power of vegetation." Though he found himself hard-pressed to explain why, he found the fertility of western lands to be ominous and dangerous. There was "an association of this thing with the idea of sickness." (Perhaps this was a reflection of his own roots in the hard glaciated landscape of unforgiving New England.) Too much was made manifest in the lush insistence of long-limbed trees and swaying grasses. Flint's economy of balance was rendered off-kilter by the eager, hungry growth of an environment "prodigiously" ripe. In the very plant life farmers sought to succor, in the processes of fertility and generation toward which all farm labor was directed, something profound and disturbing took place.

Such fears echoed perceptions of human growth. Dorothea Klein, a German traveler writing home from St. Louis in 1859, commented in puzzlement, "The climate here lets everything ripen much quicker, but equally quickly everything deteriorates much faster. A felled tree trunk will not have new shoots like in Germany, it rots immediately." The fast growth and rapid decay of the moist and fertile Mississippi Valley ominous echo in the condition of the human form: "The same has been found to apply to human beings; American ladies are matured and eligible for marriage at 15, at 26 they are already faded. One seldom or hardly ever encounters old people."

Educated Europeans were not the only ones to express these fears. Charles Williams, an Arkansas freedman who wrote a remarkable autobiographical account in the early twentieth century, detailed a similar concern for his son, who was born in 1882. "When my Boy was 13 year old," he recounts, "He had full sets Whisker black & shiny. He was a stout built young negro & I surpose he was a short liver. I did not expect to raise him." His fictional interlocutor asks him why he thought that. Williams explains, "I jest had that idea. He grew too fast For Me. Never seen a Boy Grow so fast in all my life." This intuited sense of limits on the body's vitality points to the parallels between human and plant life in long-standing traditional belief. Anything that underwent growth and development was subject to a conservation of energy whereby rapid shooting up presaged early dissolution or death. Tall weeds, like fast-growing children, would reach a natural limit more quickly than slower-growing organisms. In the act of cultivation and processes of growth were important lessons about generation and abundance.

Changes Wrought by Cultivation

Cultivation represented a harnessing of environmental potential to profound effect. Common sense saw in the making of straight furrows and ordered rows a thoroughgoing alteration in terrain. Agricultural domestication was not a moment, but a process, one that involved multiple aspects of the environment. This conviction that cultivation altered its surroundings reveals the power accorded to agriculture, as well as its intimate connections with the human form. Ultimately, the diverse changes created by plowing, planting, weeding, and harvesting came together in the diffuse but powerful understanding that natural environments underwent the same transformations as those that convulsed human physiology.

Agriculture was understood to change myriad environmental features. Morris Birkbeck, an English emigrant who fitfully attempted to set up an English manor on the prairies of Illinois (his project was a dismal failure, in part because no one, with land so inexpensive, was willing to play peasant to his manorial lord), asserted that cultivation even "altered the character of the soil: where the plough goes it is no longer a marsh, but dry sandy arable." Nor were these changes limited to the moisture and composition of the earth. He insisted that blackflies "go away altogether as soon as cultivation begins." Birkbeck's steady refusal to bow to the conditions of American life was ridiculed by his contemporaries—it is unlikely that many would have believed his claim about the flies, although certainly many would have wished it were true!—but his depiction of agriculture as a singularly transformative process is typical of many western accounts.

American cultivation changed new land to ordered terrain, made of wild places settled farmland. Every blow of an ax, every rearrangement of stones, every groan of red oak suddenly uprooted was a radical reworking of the natural world. Such change was visible on the most domestic of scales. "The rose-slips you sent me have all died," wrote Vesta Stevenson from Jefferson County, Arkansas, in 1850 to her mother; "I suppose the reason was the grownd was so wild, never having been cultivated." As well try to pet the wolves whose howls frightened children huddling in new-built cabins as propagate domesticated and ornamental cuttings in land not yet farmed and tamed. Only the wrenching process of agriculture could make land over in a way that would welcome rose slips—or, by implication, the new residents who so carefully tended them.

Many people shared the conviction that agriculture would change weather patterns. Thus one German visitor to Missouri in 1838 complained about the winter weather, lamenting that "there is no such thing in Missouri as a winter which approaches the rainy season of the tropics. There will be no change in the climate of the state until clearings and tilling of the soil have done their work." Some migrants' experience apparently bore out this immigrant's hopes. Theodore Pease Russell wrote in 1890 of his Missouri boyhood that "The climate has changed wonderfully since then, as all countries will when cleared up and brought under cultivation." As farmers worked the land, changing its nature, they trusted that their transformation of the soil would ameliorate and soften an initially foreboding environment.

These assumptions regarding humans' ability to affect weather through their labor prefigured later assertions about the Great Plains that "rain follows the plow." Under this banner, farmers were urged to cultivate the dry grasslands of the continent's interior, trusting that their labor would help create a climate perfectly suited for familiar patterns of agriculture. In a culture in which the Christian God was given frequent and public thanks and prayers, American frontier rhetoric preserved a radically powerful notion of human agency: American cultivators participated with their Creator in granting form to the natural world.

The writings of the promoter western Charles Dana Wilber from the early 1880s stress the mystical process whereby cultivation created rainfall in the American prairies:

> Not by any magic or enchantment, not by incantations or offerings, but, instead, in the sweat of his face, toiling with his hands, man can persuade the heavens to yield their treasures of dew and rain upon the land he has chosen for his dwelling place. It is indeed a grand consent, or, rather, concert of forces—the human energy or toil, the vital seed, and the polished raindrop that never fails to fall in answer to the imploring power or prayer of labor.

Wilber's initial clauses are deceptive. American farmers, like Old Testament priests, offered up prayers to their God, but their implorings traveled upward not on the savory smoke of burned flesh but in the steaming sweat of plowmen, the heavy grunt and strain of laborers straining muscles in unyielding toil for hours on end. Working their supplications in the earnest, unspoken "prayer of labor" that came naturally to the free, Protestant yeomen who Wilber hoped would people the Great Plains, American settlers at once implored and compelled their God, in thrall to the natural environment even as they coerced it.

A similar sense of vulnerability even in optimism, of worry conjoined with hope, touches also the conviction that farming affected the salubrity of soil in various ways. In the mix of notions about the healthfulness of unplowed and cultivated land lies a central conviction that cultivation was healthful, if long and thoroughly pursued. Both the certainties of agriculture's benefits and ambivalence about how to create them point the way toward the underlying process that bound together human body and natural world.

Most agreed that new-broken earth had pronounced physical effects, though they might disagree about what these were. Some, like the Philadelphia surgeon Benjamin Rush, ruminated that breaking up soil released effluvia not noxious but beneficial. "The vapour which issues from fresh earth," he explained, "has been supposed to destroy the miasmata which produce malignant fevers, by entering into mixture with them." Rush's optimism added a new dimension to the understandings of miasmas: just as sickening vapors arose from putrefactive matter, health-giving ones were released by fresh, new soil. Example as well as argument bolstered his case. Rush reflected that gravediggers and men digging cellars during the yellow fever outbreak of 1793 were untouched by the disease. He also cited folk wisdom in support of the positive effects of newly turned earth: "In the new settlements of our country, it is said, the poison of the rattlesnake is deprived of its deadly effects upon the body, by thrusting the wounded limb into a hole, recently made in the earth." The vitality of fresh earth could energize forces of nature to grow or to heal.

Yet others portrayed "new" environments as intrinsically liable to produce ill health. The Arkansas physician William J. Goulding assured the readers of *The Western Journal of Medicine and Surgery* that the central portion of the state would prove more health-giving as soon as the "local causes [of fevers] incident to all new districts" passed away. Newness was not only wild, it was sickly. Cultivation of land would thus clear away the causes of disease along with tangled underbrush.

Like newness, the fertility and the health of land were often linked in the literature of settlement—but sometimes in uneasy ways. Many descriptions spoke straightforwardly of "productive and healthy" lands, or "pleasant, healthy, and fertile country," or, in contrast, country that was "level, poor and I think sickly." Climate was frequently seen to be good for health and crops or bad for both. Like was linked with like.

In the nineteenth century, people like this man, poling a slender canoe on Arkansas's White River, often accessed land through waterways. They came to know terrain through the work they did farming or simply making their way through it. (Bernie Babcock Picture Collection, image 2577.63. Courtesy of Arkansas History Commission.)

Many American farmers, like these proud Arkansas growers, copied Native American cultivation techniques and planted legumes, melons, or squash among their corn. Cultivating or "improving" land was a central mission of those streaming into the Mississippi Valley in the nineteenth century. In their labors of farming, nineteenth-century people enacted some of the same processes with which they tried to keep their own bodies in productive health. They let out bad essences, encouraged proper growth and development, and strove for a settled, ordered balance that all too often proved elusive. ("$30 Corn from $10 Land in Arkansas along Cotton Belt Route," Photograph Collection 53, image 14. Courtesy of University of Arkansas at Little Rock Archives and Special Collections.)

A farm couple cuts their corn in a field not long hacked out of the forests that surround it. Their nineteenth-century parents or grandparents would regard nearby woodland as an economic resource but also a threat to health. Trees cut down and vegetation left to rot were seen as sources of potentially lethal miasmas, and winds that blew from thickly covered, flat terrain were considered much less salubrious than those that came from open, high places. (Loyd Matthews Collection, Kalen and Morrow papers, Jefferson City, Missouri. Courtesy of Lynn Morrow.)

Though this photograph probably dates from the early twentieth century, many of its elements are consistent with those of the antebellum period: African-American workers pick cotton, overseen by white men on horseback. On plantations, tasks were usually divided by age and ability, but during times of high demand such as the harvest season, all available hands, even the smallest, could be out in the fields. Many of these people are warmly bundled: cotton picking could extend into the winter, when yields were heavy or the labor force limited. Enslaved and free Americans had different experiences of farm labor, yet agriculture was central to the lives of both black and white people. (Bernie Babcock Picture Collection, image 2577.25. Courtesy of Arkansas History Commission.)

Men reap wheat, likely in Missouri, in new fields still crowded with "deadened" trees. Clearing terrain as these workers have done—baring land, opening it to the sun, scoring and changing its surface to make it grow ordered crops, not "wild" forests—had important consequences for health. Nineteenth-century Americans regarded these interventions with ambivalence. Though ultimately producing settled, healthy countryside, the imposition of agriculture meant disturbance and change, stirring up imbalance that could also affect people living and working on that terrain. (Loyd Matthews Collection, Kalen and Morrow papers, Jefferson City, Missouri. Courtesy of Lynn Morrow.)

Many in the nineteenth century saw steamboats, as in this *Harper's Weekly* illustration of the Arkansas River near Little Rock, as graceful and majestic, a triumph of engineering. Steam power allowed people to travel upstream without the laborious and frustrating work of poling, pushing, rowing, or cordelling (towing a boat from a long line). Yet steamboats were still vulnerable to snags and "sawyers" like the ones shown here, and their massive boilers were not only prone to violent explosion but required immense amounts of wood. Even as they enjoyed the benefits of their era's technical mastery, antebellum Americans were enmeshed in the environments in which they lived and traveled. ("Big Rock on the Arkansas," *Harper's Weekly*, 26 May 1866, image 3785. Courtesy of Arkansas History Commission.)

Farming rich bottomland meant taking a yearly gamble: rivers in a "fresh" might rise up out of their beds and spill over nearby floodplains. Crops could be ruined, animals stranded, fields scoured away, and people endangered when nearby waters chose to reassert themselves over the lands through which they ran. In addition to the immediate physical threat, floodwaters spread rot and mud, which nineteenth-century settlers understood to be sources of dangerous and disease-producing miasmas. ("Mississippi Floods," *Harper's Weekly*, 22 March 1890, Photograph Collection 32, image 53. Courtesy of University of Arkansas at Little Rock Archives and Special Collections.)

Belching black smoke, this heavily loaded steamboat carries bales of cotton from rich Arkansas fields to faraway markets, most likely in New Orleans. Rivers were essential to these commercial connections: even after the arrival of rail lines, waterways were often the most economical and efficient way to transport this much heavy freight. (Photograph Collection 70, image 102. Courtesy of Huddleston Collection/University of Arkansas at Little Rock Archives and Special Collections.)

Despite the labor-intensive efforts of snagboat crews of the U.S. Army Corps of Engineers throughout the early- and mid-nineteenth century, the Red River Raft in southern Arkansas remained a persistent obstruction to travel and commerce until 1873. As soon as crews would clear portions of the raft (formed by wood borne on floodwaters or fallen into the river when swift current undermined upstream banks), it would re-form, becoming once again a vegetative, marshy, near-solid mass. In places, travelers could ride their horses across the raft, barely aware they were crossing a river. Such a rotting mat of wood and plant matter was in nineteenth-century terms a dangerous source of miasmas, but it was also an obstruction to free flow that resonated with the concerns of people preoccupied with all manner of internal blockages, from "stubborn" menstrual flows to constipated bowels. (Undated newspaper engraving, Photograph Collection 100, image 1230. Courtesy of J.N. Heiskell Collection/University of Arkansas at Little Rock Archives and Special Collections.)

Invalids utilize a crude shelter to bathe their limbs at the Arkansas Hot Springs. The region became an early center for health travel, as people with a variety of ailments visited the area or took up residence there, hoping that the hot mineral waters of the springs would soothe and cure them. (From Bernie Babcock, *Yesterday and Today in Arkansas: A Folio of Rare and Interesting Pictures from Mrs. Babcock's Collection of Stories and Legends of Arkansas*, 2nd ed. Little Rock: Jordan & Foster, 1917. Courtesy of Arkansas History Commission.)

At the Arkansas Hot Springs, shown about 1860, steam fills the upper part of the image. By the middle and late nineteenth century, Hot Springs was a place of fashionable refuge as well as a health retreat. Genteel bathers like the well-dressed man in the center could take advantage of complicated wooden aqueducts running up and down the steep hillsides to channel water into bathhouses; other structures (like the wooden platform leading off to the right) were built directly over particularly therapeutic upwellings. (Image 1372.4. Courtesy of Arkansas History Commission.)

This illustration from Friedrich Gerstäcker's memoir *Wild Sports in the Far West* demonstrates common fears of swamp travel, particularly in the wetlands of Arkansas in which this German adventurer traveled and hunted. Though trackers often found game in wetlands, and farmers drove their livestock into the canebrakes of swampy bottomlands to overwinter, swamps and bogs were nonetheless regarded as perilous places. Travelers feared becoming lost, being sickened by miasmatic vapors, getting stuck, or being attacked by poisonous or toothy creatures like the approaching alligator. ("The Alligator," in Friedrich Gerstäcker, *Wild Sports in the Far West*, trans. by Harrison Weir. London and New York: Geo. Routledge, 1894. Courtesy of Arkansas History Commission.)

An African-American family navigates a cypress swamp in a dugout canoe. Particularly during slavery, swamps and sloughs—often unwanted and dangerous areas that were nonetheless rich in animal and plant life—could be a resource for black Americans (as well as Native Americans) who made use of them for hunting, fishing, trapping, travel, and long-term or temporary refuge. Similar environments could be experienced in very different ways. (Bernie Babcock Picture Collection, image 2577.34. Courtesy of Arkansas History Commission.)

This engraving of St. Louis in 1857 shows the black smoke from steamboats and from the factory smoke-stacks visible on the right that characterized the bustling waterfront of this river port. The environmental influences within which nineteenth-century Americans lived came not simply from countryside, streams, and farmland, but from the smells, smokes, breezes, and often-polluted waters of crowded city areas. (View of St. Louis in 1857, from *Harper's Weekly*. Courtesy of Missouri Historical Society, St. Louis.)

By 1854–55, the reeking, polluted basin called "Chouteau's Pond" had been almost drained. Once a serene retreat, the pond had become a stinking cesspool as St. Louis swelled with newcomers. City-dwellers feared the disease-bearing miasmas of urban sewers and runoff just as they feared the miasmatic emanations from swampland and newly-cleared fields. Both "natural" and human-produced environments were indicted under the logic of health and place. (*View of Drained Area of Chouteau's Pond with Cows*. Half plate daguerreotype, c. 1854, by Thomas Easterly. Courtesy of Missouri Historical Society, St. Louis.)

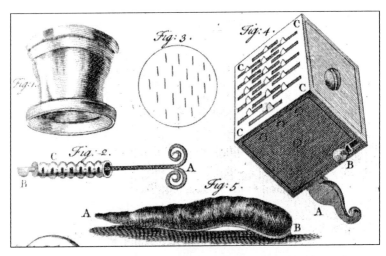

This plate, from an eighteenth-century surgical guide, illustrates common equipment for blood-letting. *Fig. 1* is a cup for catching blood; *Fig. 2*, a lancet for cutting small veins. *Fig 4* shows a scarificator, a boxy device whose blades snap forward when the cocking mechanism is released, making shallow, parallel cuts in the skin. *Fig. 3* demonstrates the pattern of incision created by a scarificator. *Fig. 5* shows a less complicated blood-letting tool: a leech, applied externally and, at times, in orifices of the body. All of these, in various forms, were in use in the United States well into the nineteenth century. Such interactions with the body's surface recapitulated in visually apparent form the scoring and striation American agriculturalists created in their fields with hoe, harrow, and plow. (Plate 12, from Laurence Heister, *A General System of Surgery, in Three Parts*, 4th ed. London: W. Innys, 1750. Courtesy of Bernard Becker Medical Library, Washington University in St. Louis.)

These unpleasant-looking devices, from an 1889 medical catalog, illustrate the longevity of blood-letting techniques and technologies. The basic principles of these various sharp implements would have been familiar to medieval and Renaissance practitioners. (*American Armamentarium Chirurgicum.* George Tiemann & Co, 1889, San Francisco & Boston: Norman Publishing & The Printers' Devil, 1989, p. 115. Courtesy of Bernard Becker Medical Library, Washington University in St. Louis.)

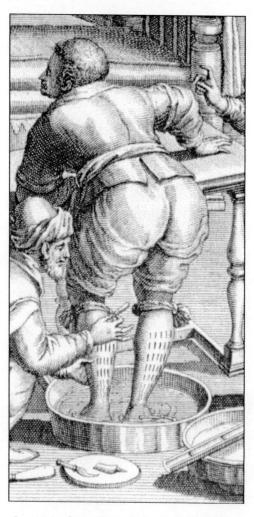

An engraving from a 1719 medical guide illustrates the
parallel stripes created by letting blood with a lancet or
scarificator. Here, the man being bled stands in a basin of
probably warm water, to promote salutary flow and catch
the blood. (Prosper Alpinus, *Medicina Aegyptiorum*, and
Jakob de Bondt, *De Medicina Indorum*. Lugduni
Batavorum [Leyden]: Ex Officina Boutesteiniana, 1719.
Courtesy of Bernard Becker Medical Library, Washington
University in St. Louis.)

An 1899 photograph shows a man tilling in new ground, amid girdled and deadened trees. The striations of soil echo the stripes etched in the skin through blood-letting, in a visual underscoring of parallels between self and soil that nineteenth-century Americans experienced in myriad ways. (Loyd Matthews Collection, Kalen and Morrow papers, Jefferson City, Missouri. Courtesy of Lynn Morrow.)

This engraving from a book of regional tales illustrates a character from one short story: a surly and sallow-faced woodcutter, a ruffian sort who made a living peddling high-priced fuel to steamboats that plied the Mississippi River. This fictionalized representation, like other aspects of the literature of settlement, represented many Americans' fears about the environment—both physical and social—of new terrain beyond the Mississippi. (Title page, *The Big Bear's Adventures and Travels*. Philadelphia: T.B. Peterson & Brothers, 1846. Courtesy of Arkansas History Commission.)

By modern standards, nineteenth-century living was close, crowded, and uncomfortable. Building homes was often secondary to the effort to clear fields and bring in a crop. Members of this household are wearing probably most of the clothing that they own, in an effort to keep warm in the mountainous districts of northern Arkansas in a cabin not very well chinked against the elements. Indoor and outdoor were often not as separate as they are for climate-controlled moderns; winds, miasmas, rain, animals, and insects could easily permeate such dwellings, bringing inside the health effects of surrounding terrain. (Bernie Babcock Picture Collection, image 2577.31. Courtesy of Arkansas History Commission.)

Political rhetoric bolstered this common wisdom. In Mason Weems's biography of George Washington, which was widely read in numerous editions after its initial publication in 1800, Washington's return to his farm after victory over the British was a telling sign of his personal greatness (one of many identified by the indefatigable Parson Weems). Weems explained: "To breathe the *pure healthful* air of a *farm*, perfumed with odorous flowers, and enriched with golden harvests, and with numerous flocks and herds, appeared to him a life nearest connected with individual and national happiness." That the Father of the Country would seek healthful air, sweet odors, and rural bounty was only natural to his hagiographer. That he would find all those aspects of happiness on his farm, among "golden harvests" and "numerous flocks and herds," was equally preordained.

Yet land could be deceptive, at once fertile and insalubrious, its abundance promising good yields but also threatening individual health. One Missouri surveyor reported in 1814 that "The Land between Saint Francis and Black River . . . is principally a low, Flat Country, interspersed with many marshes and Cypress Swamps, and occasional Ridges or Islands of rich and excellent Land, covered with Cane &c. well qualified for raising Stock—This tract of Country cannot be healthy." Phrases of praise came to an abrupt and thudding halt in his concluding remark. The rhythms of description, like the rhythms of work and family life, were disrupted by the grim finality of illness.

Similarly, James Clemons, Jr., a St. Louis resident, reported to a friend in Kentucky in 1816 that nearby bottomland was "one of the most desirable places a farmer could wish—but—Fever & ague is prevalent in it." Clemons's dashes slid quickly from the enthusiastic first half of his sentence to the grim reminder of the second, in the same way that his and his contemporaries' perceptions encompassed at one quick glance both rich lowland soil and lurking miasmatic threat. These passages reveal a deep ambivalence in relationships to terrain: farm families needed rich, well-watered, "excellent land," but that soil could also produce sickness. Settlers frequently noted these contradictions, and to some they even seemed axiomatic. One 1823 Missouri immigrant sadly reflected, "The best and richest land is most sickly, poor high land more healthy than low bottom land."

The potency of new and fertile terrain could harbor threat as well as promise. Transforming land through cultivation was the crucial intervention. Nineteenth-century Americans firmly believed that whatever the original health of the land, it became more healthy when settled and farmed.

A. W. Webb contended that "sections of country which originally were very much infested with Intermittent fevers become healthy as a regular system of agriculture is introduced and a considerable portion of the cleared land is keep up in a regular state of cultivation." Webb's concern for the harmony, rightness, and healthfulness of "a regular system of agriculture," "a regular state of cultivation," and the planter's duty to "keep up" his "cleared land" plays upon notions of regularity within the human frame. Popular wisdom and works of medical advice regarded regular times of eating and sleeping; regular, predictable seasonal changes; and regularly repeated periods of exertion, rest, contemplation, and worship as integral to a healthy body.

Casual asides make clear how obvious was the power of agriculture. Newly posted to Arkansas Territory's Fort Smith in 1820, Captain John R. Bell (like most others who arrived at the Fort) found the site unhealthy. But when he wrote to his superiors assessing the "causes of the acknowledged sickliness of the recent settlements," he reassured them that "by the increase of settlements, and the progress of cultivation, they will be in part removed." Bell offered no specific causal mechanism, nor was one needed. His brief reference drew on widely shared common sense.

The initial stages were dangerous—healing was a process fraught with peril and often accompanied by risk and pain. Thus an 1848 *Emigrant's Hand-Book* warned that when "The forest is levelled, hundreds of trees moulder and putrify about the cabin." What had been coolly shaded pools would be "exposed now to the burning rays of the sun, and rendered more deleterious by being filled with trunks and branches of decaying trees, and all kinds of putrid vegetation." Seething with the sources of illness, once-innocent ponds would become "laboratories of miasma, and generate on every side the seeds of disease."

But despite all this threat—to the environment and to the weary bodies of those working it—settled agriculture would ultimately bring manifold well-being. Successful resolution of the transition depended on the civilizing influence of population and plow. The *Hand-Book* continued:

> Yet, where the forest is cleared away, and the land has been for a sufficient time under cultivation, and is sufficiently remote from stagnate waters, [it] may be considered as healthy as any other country. . . . in proportion as the country becomes opened, cultivated, and peopled—in proportion as the redundance and rankness of natural vegetation is replaced by that of cultivation, the country becomes more healthy.

Cultivating land released harmful essences associated with the tumult of change of state from wilderness to arable plot. It did so because both body and land operated under the same logic of perilous, necessary crisis.

Crisis

Agriculture appears in these and other accounts as a process of fundamental transformation. Threatening and yet potentially productive, its changes affected all aspects of the environment. It could alter weather, it could transform the healthfulness of environments, and it could change the very nature of land. Change of this significance, watched with high anxiety and managed with great care, occupied a particular place in nineteenth-century medical imagination. Such important and transformative change was a "crisis," a turning-point when the body was both vulnerable and resilient, in danger and in flux. The passing of crisis could mean the difference between life and death, but in no case was a sick person subsequently the same. In going through cultivation, land endured a crisis that paralleled that of disease: when accomplished, crisis changed the entire state of the body or site; when blocked or only incompletely unfolded, it resulted in harm.

Crisis was a moment of dynamism, rife with anxiety. A crisis was the period in which one stage succeeded another, or when the course of a disease shifted radically, and health dawned. Childbirth was a critically important and dangerous "crisis" in the life-history of both body and family. Even weaning, as John Brown fretted about his ninth child, was a "crisis in the history of mother & child." Colloquial language expanded the notion to include pivotal moments in many domains. Brown called a move to a new household "an important crisis in my life, and in my family, and affairs, and I have an abiding confidence that it will greatly benefit me and family." Crises were periods of high risk. One's body and mind were gathered up to undergo change for good or ill.

A crisis of health could "give . . . the death blow," or it could resolve disease and "bring the fever to a perfect solution." Critical moments in an illness were occasions for heightened vigilance and medical attention. Misreading or failing to interpret a coming crisis could have fatal consequences. John Brown regretted not being present to offer further medical care at the deathbed of a family matriarch in 1852. "I thought her case dangerous," he reflected in his diary, "but had not supposed her case would so suddenly come to a crisis." Unanticipated and therefore unmanaged, the old woman's crisis ended in death.

Crisis was not in itself necessarily bad. Though dangerous, successful pregnancy and weaning were both vital to the growth of a child and a household. Crises were the inevitable result of the body's maturation, growth, and aging. Still, even a seemingly productive crisis could be pathological if it took place too suddenly. John Gunn's *Domestic Medicine* advised that those with "ulcerous sore legs . . . if of long standing, should be cautious how they heal them suddenly, without purifying and preparing the system for the change;—because the sudden suppression of a habitual discharge, without this previous purification, almost invariably seats some new disease on a vital organ, or produces death by APOPLEXY." Crises must be managed and prepared for, lest they wreak unintended consequences. Gunn's urgent capitals highlighted the anxiety produced by crisis gone awry.

Resolution of crisis meant the drawing out of destructive essences or the passing of potent material. A series of interventions, in home therapies as well as in professional medicine, was geared toward producing a crisis in which the body would let off built-up and harmful forces. Draining pus, lancing a boil, vomiting, experiencing diarrhea, letting blood, sweating, and salivating were commonly recognized as ways to "draw off" and draw out of the body the sources or effects of imbalance. Piled-on blankets, hot wraps, enemas, herbal infusions, caustic plasters, and bitter teas created or supported productive crisis, encouraging the body to gather up and let off that which was out of place.

Suppressing the body's urgent outflows was intensely dangerous. The physician William Hillary described elephantiasis as an "imperfect crisis" in which "morbid matter" was "cast upon the leg" rather than being properly worked through and expelled by the body. He amplified his understanding of the logic of the body in a description of the deceptions practiced by slave traders hoping to get a good price for Africans afflicted by the gruesome skin lesions of yaws:

> upon the first appearance of the yaws, . . . [slave traders] apply some strong repellents to [the sores]; such as the juice of roasted limes mixed with the rust of iron, and sulphur or gunpowder; by which they repel the morbid matter into the blood, where its acrimony is increased, though they thereby render their skins clean for a short time, and then rub them with palm oil, which makes them soft and look well; . . . but in a few days or weeks . . . the virulency of the morbid matter being increased by the retention and heat of the body, the yaws break out again much worse than ever, and are then very difficult to cure, or sometimes incurable.

Traders who frustrated the crisis of yaws—not from a desire to help the afflicted person, but out of greed—cast the disease back into slaves' bodies, where it intensified rather than dissipating harmlessly. Interrupting the crisis of release harmed the individual in whose form conflicting forces battled. To manage ill health, healers had to recognize when to counterbalance the body's forces and when to reinforce them. Healing a grave illness required crisis and successful resolution. So too did making barren land fruitful.

Images of land undergoing cultivation employ the same language and call upon the same explanatory framework as depictions of bodies in thrall to illness. Such identity underscored the many relations between body and land in everyday language and practice. In process and in product, in the management required and in the grave consequences contingent, healing the body and husbanding land called upon the same structure of understanding.

The virulence of that which was released was in both cases similar. Many accounts emphasized the ways in which cultivation could release sickening factors. Writing in the 1830s, Louis Cortambert attributed disease plaguing white settlements in Missouri and the unorganized western territories not to an innately unhealthful environment but to "clearings" that promoted vegetable decay and "cause harmful mists to arise from the ground." A century later, Mary Staton Jones, an elderly African-American woman in North Carolina, expressed a similar fear to her white WPA interviewer. "I'm scared to let in air a-comin' over new-plowed ground," she said, explaining why she sat by an open fire on a warm day in June; "It's agin good breathin'." Sparking a crisis within the environment, cultivation provoked reaction from it, a reaction in many ways like the human body's. Newly cleared fields could in their potency exude moist mists and harmful airs.

Like humors, miasmas were at once vague and powerful. Both were force as much as fluid, seen to obey clear physical laws of movement in some ways (miasmas could blow like a mist; humors could accrete to cause visible swellings) but to act in other ways as a more enigmatic, ubiquitous presence. The same fundamental insight was involved in raising blisters or raising a crop: potentially harmful essences were drawn to strong action and could then be surfaced or let out, allowing health and generative processes to flourish.

The process of cultivation, like the process of undergoing a crisis of health, was accompanied by peril. Initial clearing not only drew out dangerous forces from the natural world but was in itself a dangerous activity. The cautious Dr. Webb inveighed against "the fatigue and exposure attendant on clearing and cultivating new lands," which he maintained "must of themselves frequently prove an abundant source of disease among new settlers." Such depictions reveal a paradox with regard to human action upon the land. Clearing swamps and plowing land was necessary to the improvement and planting of land, but could also gravely impair the health of those laboring.

Within the ringing endorsements of cultivation as healthy improvement, ambiguities creep in when observers attempted to quantify exactly when cultivation became conducive to good health. Many observers suggested a period of transition during which lands being worked for agriculture initially held ill effects before they became more salubrious. One 1852 article in a St. Louis medical journal held that "land that has been in active cultivation for fifteen or twenty years" was healthier than that recently cropped; there was "less clearing up of fresh lands" so "there must necessarily be less decay of vegetation." Dr. A. W. Webb felt that a shorter time was necessary—he acknowledged that many regions might be "more unhealthy within the first five or six years after they are cleared than they are at any subsequent period"—but he, too, placed emphasis upon the improved health of land that had a history of being cultivated.

Equivocations like Webb's quietly acknowledge the potential failure of this vital process toward which so much energy was directed. Just as healing could be incomplete or unsuccessful, just as the transitions of birth or aging at times could prove lethally difficult, so too the promise of settling land could remain elusive. Health, balance, and productivity were desired outcomes not always reached.

Stop midway, give in to the insistent wildness of terrain and disorder of the body, and dire imbalance would triumph. Diseases half cured meant redoubled danger; cases of intermittent fever, warned Dr. Webb, could be complicated when "the intestines are imperfectly evacuated." Normally efficacious emetics, he explained, "are injurious in all cases in which the reaction is incomplete." Applying the same logic, the physician William Currie warned that fevers and fluxes were widespread in "lands in an imperfect state of cultivation." Processes that were interrupted or incomplete ended only in sickness or death.

While in transition, "being cleared up," land was like a patient moving from disease to wellness; in an in-between state, the environment itself held properties of imbalance and disease that were conveyed to human inhabitants. Once thoroughly imbued with the attributes of agriculture, however, environment again exerted beneficent influences. After it had been wrenched from its wild state, stable land in a state of high cultivation promoted good health as well as sustenance and profit.

Observers' unease with the initial periods of agriculture points to a discomfort with matter changing state. "The most dangerous period," Timothy Flint warned prospective settlers, "is, after the trees have been leveled a year or two, and while they are still decaying about the dwelling." The trees had not yet been "cleared up;" they remained on and in the environment, not living but not yet returned to the earth. Their liminal state could have pathological effects on terrain and on those working it. Like a baby in the birth canal, trees cut down but not yet gone represented the midpoint of change and therefore danger. It was crucial to minimize the time spent in transitional moments or near transitional elements. Human form and natural terrain both required watchfulness and guidance to move as swiftly as possible to a new and more classifiable state.

During the crisis of cultivation, land was threatening to the people working it, just as transition moments in disease were particularly perilous to the sufferer. Ichabod Sargeant, the Yankee emigrant turned Missouri physician cautioned that "In a country not cleaned so as to admit the sun to the ground a man may enjoy good health, but as soon as the ground is opened so that the sun can act with force he is sickly untill it is cleaned and cultivated." Obscene exposure of what Benjamin Rush termed "fresh earth" and the soil's "moist surface" to the harsh penetration of the sun's rays conjured sickness and peril. Assaulted by burning daylight, "opened" fields were irritated or injured like the skin beneath a mustard plaster or a caustic compress. Sickness arose to those points like the clear serum of a friction blister. A crisis had been forced. At this point in the process, cultivation—like any therapy of drawing out or encouraging eruptions or other gatherings of fluid or force—was indeed perilous. Angry matter had been impelled to a single place. The slashed stumps of a hard-won clearing and the raw skin of a successful blister alike testified to the violence that created them. Concentrated and potent, miasmas from earth and fluids from the body waited under the surface, lurking threat.

But in clearing land, as in bodily therapeutics, the crisis did not stop at the moment of highest tension. It was carried through and resolved. As a blister would be drained, pus drawn off, blood let, or hot skin cooled, so too the miasma of former swampland would be released by the operation of the sun. Initial sickness resulted. No one could deny the chills and fever associated with initial bottomland settlements, any more than the pain caused by a compress of hot pepper. Yet once through the dangerous unbalance of initial settlement, once past the pain of the lanced boil, the offensive odor of festering pus and feverish sweat, the drawing out of harm meant that a new balance could be found.

That which effected transformation was in each case parallel. The body became healthy in the same ways that land became productive. Cultivation worked on soil as medicine worked on the body; cutting into land with a plow functioned with the same properties as cutting with sharp knife or keen lancet into an inflamed nodule or turgid "rising." Farming, like domestic healing, was disruptive, risky, and painful—but both processes could produce life and bounty. Creating fundamental change and rearranging the balance of undisturbed regions, agriculture worked on the natural environment like a powerful "puke," a tonic purge, a salutary "bleed," or an effective blister within the human form. It worked, moreover, in the same ways and for the same reasons as these often-employed therapies.

Leveling forests and draining swamps released their miasmatic, disease-bearing potential in a manner resonant with the "letting" of bad humors associated with nineteenth-century medicine. The crisis of cultivation and the crisis of sickness unfolded the same way because miasmas and humors functioned with the same principles, producing the same changes in earth or in body. In both human form and terrain, forces exuded from sick or decaying matter could cause disease and ill health, but their release allowed the body or the land to readjust and become once again healthy or fertile. Sensual similarities link the two processes. The release of miasmas and foul smells from land and water would be familiar to people for whom emetics and purges were part of both medical pharmacopoeia and domestic therapeutics. Stink and fetor unmistakably marked the passage of a crisis; the putrefaction of diarrhea as of rotting mulch could herald release and rebalance. Human body and surrounding world mirrored each other, responding to similar stimuli in similar ways.

In both human bodies and bodies of land, protean essences below the surface could be aggravated by localized disturbances. In certain respects, these operations were visually parallel as well as functionally identical. Clearing land changed the surface of terrain. Cutting trees and burning away surface vegetation bared and disrupted discrete patches of previously well-covered soil. Like plastering or blistering the human body, these disruptions created areas in which negative forces were drawn to the surface and released. The burning rays of the sun acted on previously unexposed areas to draw out bad essences, just as heat acted on the human body, whether through warm wrappings or Thomsonian steambaths.

Similarly, the long, parallel furrows produced by harrow and plow scored the surface of the land in ways that looked and functioned like the striations of a blood-letter's lancet or the parallel bloody stripes of a scarificator, a hand-held device of boxy efficiency whose curved metal blades snapped together to slice open the skin. Every spring, as they prepared fields for planting, farmers and farmhands sliced, disturbed, and re-arranged the earth's surface. As they drove through clinging clods with the smooth board or cool iron of a plow, they willed and enacted a springing to new life of brown, faded fields. Cutting through soil, turning it, smoothing it out over small seeds, the workers of a farm household devoted their attention and labor to disrupting a surface in order to draw out and draw up forces of regeneration. Is it any wonder that at the same time, and for similar reasons, many planters sought a "spring bleed"? Even the "Click! click!" of a physician's scarificator mimicked the brisk cut of sharp metal on yielding vegetation, the efficient noise of shears or sharp hoes working their way down an orchard row or long furrow. Establishing themselves upon the land and working it to make it productive, nineteenth-century households employed techniques recapitulating therapies of professional and home-based health care. They wrought a domestic, and domesticating, medicine upon the land.

In the environmental logic of the antebellum era, farming "cured" wilderness, managing a transformation between states. Yet just as healing could require either violent remedies or therapies of comfort, the processes of cultivation demanded a range of action and passivity. Farmers worked strenuously to lift, turn, and mark their soil, but had also to master patience during the long wait for seed to flourish, cows to bear, or seasons to shift. John Brown tracked rain clouds along with his harvesting neighbors each fall and anxiously scrutinized the first sprouts of green seedlings every spring. He waited beside the bedside of his sick children and ailing slaves with similar attention and similar emotions; his plantation's health depended on the outcomes of all crises, whether of torrential flood or painful menarche, late-blooming spring or difficult teething, paltry harvest or prolonged childbirth.

The fundamental sameness of cultivation and domestic healing reflects images of power and control, but also nurturance and care, vulnerability and powerlessness. Resonances between the two processes reflect nineteenth-century Americans' many levels of relationship with their bodies and natural environments. The forces governing both body and place were only incompletely understood, and they were never fully mastered. Lack of control and acknowledgment of dependence—on others, on weather, on the will of God—marked the experiences of sickness and of agriculture. Understandings of cultivation reflect the power felt by those who successfully established a household, cultivated the soil, and created of the land sustenance for their families. They also reflect the less powerful aspects of the process of settlement. Accounts of the early American settlement of Arkansas and Missouri place the human self in the position of land: fertile and full of potential, but requiring active intervention and careful ministrations to go through desperately sought transformations. The geography of health offered a double identity, that of powerful cultivator and of vulnerable land, to the men and women who worked and cleared the wild terrain around them.

Profound identification of self and soil was daily enacted in the cultivation of garden plots and rows of hemp, in water-paths laboriously broken down and near-wild cows once again milked. An old pattern of Ozark folk speech, in which people referred to their land as themselves—"guess I need plowing," one farmer might muse to another—speaks the truth of an older system of understanding in which fundamental insights had multiple sites of action, and identical processes operated on varied substrates.

When John Brown wrote of the "good health" of his region, he called upon a host of associations shared with other American and European immigrants streaming into the Great Valley of the Mississippi. Health in land implied an ongoing relationship with the human bodies that farmed and managed it; in the language and imagination of the nineteenth century, relationships between self and environment centered on the work of cultivation. Understanding of terrain altered radically once it was no longer *new*, once it was "cleared off," and "used up." Multiple connections linked the lived human body and the land it worked. Similar categories of analysis applied to each: fertility, goodness, strength, poverty, and the will to wildness could be attributed equally to neighbor or field. Riches spiritual as well as agricultural, fecundity of family as well as field intertwined in discussion and in concern.

These multiple layers of mutual influence and interrelationship came together in the connections between cultivating land and cultivating personal health. The practices and processes of agriculture drew upon and in turn reinforced ideas of how the body functioned. These connections had power because they were based on widespread and everyday experience. Any laborer or farmwife could experience the itchy discomfort of the suppuration of a wound, or walk long furrows on a drizzly April morning to plow and seed fields. Parallels at the most foundational level of understanding worked because they drew on widely shared activity and bodily sensation. The *feel* of working the land and the workings of the body rendered the connection between healthy land and a healthy person self-evident. Agriculture's many meanings built each other. Cultivation could not be healthy without also being good and honest, could not wreak transformations in new soils if it could not draw out all that was potentially harmful in them, could not be separated from the understanding of other aspects of everyday life precisely because it was integral to day-to-day sensations and day-to-day survival.

Tracing out a web of associations rich with meaning, we must take care not to tear each strand too far apart. Beliefs about agriculture and health gave shape to a geography of health and place because of their multiple and minute points of contact. Spun together, interconnections between pregnancy and germination, the fertility of fields and the prospects of a farm household, the letting of miasmas and the breaking of a fever, created a worldview at once resilient and powerful, one that made sense of everyday experience while simultaneously giving range to imaginative play and wonder.

Farm labors of the nineteenth-century borderlands were enfolded within a matrix of associations. Their very richness and multiplicity is instructive. Not all of the meanings of working the land can be easily reconciled with each other. Yet within those many meanings, images coalesce around certain attributes. Cultivation was powerful, significant in both presence and absence and able to imbue all manner of practice and belief with meaning. It was transformative, a process of graduated aspects and differing degrees. Making fields productive was a crisis that demanded management and held out the hope of resolution. The cultivation of land functioned in ways that were fundamentally identical with processes of the human body experiencing illness. Most of all, despite its necessity and its power, cultivation was ambiguous. As with crises in the body itself, its workings were only partially comprehended, and no outcome was guaranteed.

Precisely because cultivation held great potential, it was simultaneously possessed of great threat. Agricultural work was strong and potent, able to raise up crops so large they were deformed, to render outsized and grotesque all that was meant to be domesticated, subdued, and quietly generative. Images of cultivation reveal an environment that could be unexpectedly barren—or surprisingly powerful. The many meanings underlying the cultivation of antebellum Missouri and Arkansas reveal the vulnerability of men and women who worked with fierce energy to heal sick relatives and to establish families upon new land, but who in neither case could be sure of understanding and balancing all the factors related to these parallel crises. In their cultivation of the soil as in their treatments of the body, Americans of the nineteenth century attempted to control and manage that which they knew to be intrinsically outside their governance. Pronouncements about the "health" or "insalubrity" of land relied on a complex web of interactions between the human body and its lived environment. Their sharpest point of contact was the cutting edge of a plow.

RACIAL ANXIETY

Chapter VIII

IN 1830, THE ARKANSAS IMMIGRANT Hiram Abiff Whittington wrote to his brother Granville in Boston about the expected immigration of a young New Jersey woman to Arkansas Territory. Hiram commented, "She will think she has got among the Indians when she sees our sallow faces. I suppose you think we are white people here, but you are sadly mistaken; there is as much difference between us and the people of the Eastern States as there is between us and the Indians."

This warning, facetious though it may be, betrays a larger cultural unease. Hiram Whittington's remarks reveal two central worries of the American borderlands: concern for the arduous process of acclimation through which their new environments transformed immigrants, and concern about the consequences of that acclimation for the stability of race.

In the world that Whittington inhabited, environments shaped the health of those in them, and human beings in turn shaped the health of their environments. The geography of health demanded that newcomers investigate what the influences of place might be, and do their utmost to mitigate or improve them. Yet medical environmentalism held a further threat: a profound linkage not only between person and place, but between race and environment.

Many Americans traveled to healthier regions to improve their states of health or, conversely, feared going to sickly areas because of their ill effects. Moving across long distances, especially from northern to southern latitudes and from cooler to hotter places, took this effect of place on person to its logical extreme. New surroundings remade inhabitants' bodies, forcing them to become "seasoned" or "acclimated." That process was intricately related to how white newcomers defined themselves as different from black people and Indians. As Hiram Whittington's remarks suggest, whites in particular saw themselves as altered by residence in areas of new climate and surroundings. Such alteration especially threatened the "people" and "race" to which white newcomers understood themselves to belong.

Change of place—that dangerous source of radical instability—created change of person in the inchoate borderlands. In health, in skin color, in countenance, in modes of life and habits of being, even in political allegiance, the process of acclimating to a place was irrevocably and unstoppably transformative. For many migrants, coming to a radically new place meant becoming sick. Having survived the new and strange illnesses confronted in a foreign environment, however, they felt themselves able to stave off or live with them. Yet acclimation also meant coming to terms with a whole system of weather, elevation, seasons, and temperatures, as well as the actual diseases of a new place. A sense of becoming accustomed in the very fiber of one's being to the conditions and constraints of a new environment was expressed through the notion of acclimation.

In this process, racial and individual identity were vulnerable: the changes unleashed in new territory threatened the coherence and clarity of physical differentiation demanded by the racial economy of antebellum America. "Whites" became brown in the sun of the Far West, while the violence and rape of the slave system created "blacks" whose skin, hair, and features failed utterly to speak that identity. Common language assigned the differing gradations of racial identity different labels, in linguistic attempts to set right what was so visibly amok.

Yet race-based labels for skin tone and physical appearance did not solve the ultimate failure of racial categories, particularly the crossing over of the crucial white/black boundary, when "black" slaves looked "white," and "white" children were sold as "black." Notions of race themselves suffered slippage even as did individual bodies. What category would hold "white" people who moved west and turned copper in the sun, of "white" children who could not be told apart from "black" servants?

This account of how American newcomers felt environment to challenge racial identity is largely a story about white anxieties. Previous chapters looked at commonalities underlying many Americans' ideas about new territories, but this chapter focuses on an area of divergence. There are far fewer records of emigration by slaves than by free whites, and they are much more limited in scope. Most accounts of emigration by former slaves are removed in time and (often) in place: former slaves struggled to recall events of their childhood, rather than writing down their own adult experiences at the time. In these abbreviated accounts of emigration, acclimation does not figure. The only hints of a process of acclimation undergone by these writers come with reference to emancipation and moving to cities. In free people's narratives, by contrast, acclimation assumes enormous importance. It is a process about which white people worried endlessly. Yet their concern was for their own bodies and families, not for their chattel. Shaking with fever and changing intimate habits of life, white newcomers felt themselves not only individually but racially vulnerable to the environment of the middle Mississippi Valley.

Like all conversations about race in America, this discussion also attempts a complicated double dance. While unraveling the construction and questioning of racial categories, we must simultaneously fall back upon them to describe and distinguish individuals and groups. It is impossible to speak meaningfully about those in the country's past borderlands (of racial identity as of natural terrain) without using some of the same racial categories whose twisting and turning we are trying to trace. This shimmering back and forth of analytic categories is one manifestation of the lack of safe resolution of political, social, and economic issues from the American past. The dearth of vocabulary for stepping outside of race in talking about historical interactions in the United States is one indication of the present centrality of racial identity and racial difference in our own time.

Many scholars have tracked the racial beliefs and prejudices among white Americans of the nineteenth century, as well as the violent acts that accompanied them. In this respect, the Arkansas and Missouri borderlands are typical of the kinds of tensions that increasingly preoccupied the United States in the decades that lead to the Civil War. Particular to this story are the environments in which people were arriving, and the ways those environments figured in white Americans' anxieties. The "tropical" climate of the middle Mississippi Valley heightened many migrants' attention to the effects of change of place, since they feared the enfeebling effects of hot climates. Furthermore, the "newness" of the territories to which they came—a newness that had to do with contemporary beliefs about settlement, about agriculture, and about Americans' role in transforming nature—forced people to confront the drastic extent of their own transformation, and opened the larger question of how stable their hierarchies of race and "people" really were. Racial fears sprang from what many Americans understood as physical truths about human beings and their surrounding terrain. Looking at the environmental logic of individual transformation thus reveals the physical underpinnings of legal and political debates over the status of race in the antebellum world.

Peoples and Places

The logic of white Americans in the antebellum period was simple. They did not belong in hot places; black people did. Whites were thus in danger when they moved into regions of southern heat—a danger that threatened not simply each individual person, but the structure of racial differentiation. The backdrop for this set of anxieties was the widely shared preoccupation with human "races," or, as they were often termed, human "peoples."

"Race" and "people" were powerful concepts. Each implied a historic integrity, geographic specificity, and cultural particularity to a group of human beings. Thus Timothy Flint could characterize his family's impressions at the beginning of their western travels: "To us, West Pennsylvania appeared to be peopled with a tall, hard, lank-looking race of men." The concept of inherent distinctiveness was far-reaching. Migrants could expect to come in contact with "peoples" fundamentally different from themselves, of foreign attributes, characteristics, and physical composition. These might be encountered, moreover, not simply in the entrepôt of St. Louis or the exotic Osage trading posts of Missouri Territory, but along the public highway of long-settled Pennsylvania.

"White" was a powerful category in the American nineteenth century—white people were, after all, exempt from slavery, a freedom that grouped them together much more powerfully than derisive comments about "Yankees" or "Germans" could divide them. Yet whiteness was ambiguous, its coherence seemingly always vulnerable to fracture. Its meaning was unstable, and changed over the antebellum period. "White" was most powerful in opposition to "black"; it could, however, be regarded as less important than other, more clearly defined "races." Annoyed at an 1854 dock workers' wage strike, which slowed down the shipment of his cotton, John Brown deplored "These Irish, the lowest of their race." Beginning in the 1830s, apologists for Southern slavery began more vehemently to defend the category of whiteness as one that included the rowdy Irish dockhands Brown regarded with such distancing disdain. Yet as Brown's comment makes clear, throughout the antebellum period one striking feature of discussions of people considered "white" in the broad sense is the attention paid to differentiating between them.

National character provided one starting place for judgments about human difference. Observations were drawn in broad strokes (many of them stereotypes still familiar to us today). In 1838, Henry B. Miller, an emigrant from Illinois, described fellow passengers on a Mississippi River steamboat journey to New Orleans:

> the Germans sit and smoke their hug[e] pipes (rolling it out of their mouths like a house on fire) with the greatest gravity and apparent composure; give a German a Pipe about the size of a Teapot with a stem about three feet long, let him have his pipe well filled with tobacco & handsomely light up, and he will then appear to notice nothing more around him. . . . The Irish, when they get the whisky in motion & themselves in order, are the very reverse; all is noise & agitation, tumult & disorder; nothing of composure and gravity.

Serious Stuttgarters and boisterous Dubliners together churned downriver, their individual characteristics blurred into national caricature.

Many travelers insisted that national origin was reflected in how families kept their households. Germans had neat farms; French people might be lackadaisical about their agriculture but always planted pretty flowers near their cabins. Those emigrating from within the United States had no time for manure or winding trellises: instead, their rough homes and rougher fields signaled a people out for the main chance, hacking farms out of wilderness only to move soon again.

Behind such stereotypes lay some actual cultural differences, especially with respect to farming techniques. Beneath them also ran a much deeper sense of national character. Common conversation easily cast those of different national origin as "different races," as Timothy Flint called the French and the Americans of the Mississippi Valley. Such groups were innately different, each possessing its own attributes and characteristics. What Flint called the "strong features of nationality" were usually regarded as being significant and long-enduring. As he reported of New Madrid, Missouri, "The Germans, the French, the Anglo-Americans, Scotch, and Irish, all retain and preserve their national manners and prejudices."

Common wisdom agreed that heritage gave rise to temperament and feeling. Davy Crockett could write in 1834 about his prospective mother-in-law, with every confidence of being understood by the readers of his autobiography, that "her Irish was up too high to do any thing with her, and so I quit trying." Though conversations about race were in particular directed by white people against black contemporaries, notions of racial heritage were also shared by black Americans. "I had a terrible temper," observed a former slave, Richard Bruner, of Nelson, Missouri, to a 1930s WPA interviewer, adding in explanation, "I'm part Choctaw Indian."

Such differences were seen to be borne out in physical characteristics. "The Germans," noted Flint, "are large, stout, and ruddy-looking men and women. The poorer French are spare, thin, sallow, and tanned, with their flesh adhering to their bones, and apparently dried to the consistency of parchment." The bodies of those Flint described in the American borderlands spoke their cultural and historical differences. That they were all now making their way in the earthquake-rent, heat-soaked, river-threatened districts of the Missouri boot heel created similarities in their present concerns, but these were played out against the telling evidence of their fundamental heritage. Just as the earth itself gave forth intelligible and interpretable signs of its nature and tendencies, just as the environment existed to be read for signals of Christian purpose, so too the individual human form reflected honestly and intelligibly the influences that had shaped it and accurately revealed "what is for disposal within."

Before the end to the importation of slaves mandated by the Constitution in 1808 (a legal change that drastically curtailed, though it did not stop completely, the African slave trade in the United States), slaves were marked by distinctive African heritages, depending on their specific place of origin. White agriculturalists of the Eastern Seaboard were interested in purchasing Africans of particular countries and races for particular skills. Plantation owners valued those from Sierra Leone and Gambia for their knowledge of rice culture, while they thought "Mohammedan" slaves made good managers and record keepers. These distinctions had their basis in experience: many natives of Sierra Leone and Gambia were originally rice farmers, and likely brought rice culture to North America. Captured Muslims tended to be people from coastal trading cities; many were multilingual and literate in Arabic. Accustomed to participating in cosmopolitan and cross-cultural trade, they stumbled bewildered out of slave ships chained in coffles with men from quiet villages in the African interior. These kidnapped Africans brought with them their own sense of ethnic and class identity, which historians have only recently begun to uncover.

In the economy to which they came, their origins told potential buyers of valuable skills and predilections. As a household manager would judge the yield of a strain of cotton seed, as a drover would estimate the breeding capacity or milk quality of cattle up for sale, so purchasers of slaves estimated the potential of people not only by the evidence of their bodies but by the "people" and "country" to which they belonged.

Environmental Belonging

"Race" and "people" were strongly tied to the influence of place. In the same way that the geography of health produced ill health or well-being, it also marked the intrinsic belonging of a region's inhabitants. As Timothy Flint observed in a revealing litany of perceived human difference, "We never mistook the German for the Frenchman, the inhabitant of the South for him of the North, the morose for the social, nor the stupid for the intelligent." As intrinsic as intelligence, as observable as the signs of nationality, innate capacity and tendency were shaped by one's geographic place—including the increasingly important differences between the American South and North.

Antebellum Americans inhabited a world in which people belonged innately in certain types of places—and not in others. Climate, with all its myriad meanings, insinuated its way into every element of personhood, determining racial belonging as well as personal well-being. How this happened was the subject of debate by learned men by the middle part of the century.

In the early decades of the United States, most intellectuals in the Anglo-European world followed the main current of thought of the Enlightenment in understanding humankind to be one basic entity, differentiated by long residence in diverse conditions. All humanity had, after all, begun with Adam and Eve, but over many generations climate and differing conditions had created human races. (Some theologians looked to the curse on Ham, Noah's youngest son, as the creation of African peoples.) As with arguments about the connection between cultivation and the transformation of a region's health, details of mechanism were much less important than the basic fact. Places simply made people different.

This thesis, later known as monogenesis, allowed for racial change. Slow, gradual racial change, in ways that were left extremely vague, but racial change nonetheless. Such was the background for white intellectuals' hopes that Indians could be "civilized," or black Africans gradually raised to a more cultured form of life. This optimism, however, was clearly no match for the racial prejudices of a slave society, which demanded a more entrenched and less forgiving notion of human difference.

In the 1830s and '40s, a few influential Southern ethnologists and medical observers—prominent among them Josiah Nott of Mobile, Alabama—began to challenge the widely held notion that climate had created different races with different traits. Instead, they argued, different races of humankind had been separately and differently created. These proponents of "polygenesis" also came up with scriptural basis for their history of humankind, arguing that the biblical account of Creation referred only to white people, to whom they granted a complicated Indo-European history. Side references to other communities and civilizations in the Bible, they contended, showed that other races of humanity had also been created, but offstage, as a kind of afterthought by the Creator. Human races were immutable. Indians could not be civilized, nor black people raised above their god-given station. Racial characteristics were divinely ordained and permanent.

This argument made inherent race, not environmental influence, the central means for explaining human difference. Rather than environments shaping races, races were instead created for particular environments. What the biologist Louis Agassiz had termed "zoölogical provinces" explained not simply the distribution of varying kinds of animal creatures but the different aspects of humanity: races were placed where they were to mesh with varying climates. The assertions of polygenesis turned acclimation from the cause of racial differentiation to its effect. The defenders of intrinsically distinct races thus represented a considerable challenge to the contemporary environmental logic that made sense of personal well-being and collective belonging.

As with many theoretical debates over matters of widespread concern, however, the stark differences in these two histories of humanity changed few people's behavior. Scientifically minded slave holders and those more hostile to traditional Christian biblical interpretation took up this new polygenist ethnology, yet they supped at the same tables and were served by the same slaves as defenders of slavery who held to a more environmentalist view of racial differentiation. White dominion and black degradation were the overwhelming denominators of these varying theories of difference. And no matter how they posited racial origins or environmental causality, few in the white majority questioned the main conclusion that human peoples intrinsically belonged to the locales for which they were suited.

Physical citizenship, not surprisingly, justified for many white Americans the economy and hierarchy of race-based slavery. People whose origins lay in Europe were made for (or perhaps made by) calm, cool climates. African bodies belonged in hot African places. An 1848 *Emigrant's Hand-Book* warned that in the slave states "the climate is unsuited to the European constitution. . . . To raise cotton, tobacco, sugar, and other tropical products, is the peculiar employment of the African, and could not be attempted by those indigenous to temperate regions." Hot sun and sweltering humidity were as racially inappropriate as they were unpleasant for those of European descent.

In the worldview of slave owners, the appropriateness of African-descended individuals for the "peculiar employment" of North American slavery was multifaceted. Heat and cold were powerful governors of human ability and human races. Black slaves were regarded by white observers as uniquely fit for work in scorching heat and sultry humidity. Timothy Flint, like many of his white contemporaries, concluded resoundingly, "The African constitution can alone support labour under such circumstances." Black workers were also held to suffer in extreme and untoward ways from cold temperatures. What the historian George Fredrickson has termed "thermal laws" were enlisted in arguments that black people should be excluded from colder regions (like the free North), and subjugated in the "tropical" regions of the cotton belt.

Such environmental assertions had bearing not only on notions of race but on perceptions of region. Arguments about race and place continued to shift conceptions of the Mississippi Valley from "West"—as they had been resoundingly characterized in the literature of settlement of the early part of the century—to "South." The politics of region were underwritten by the geography of health.

Black immunity to disease, real and perceived, was a powerful argument for white Americans about the rightness of black servitude. African-Americans possessed what white observers firmly believed to be resilience against some of the most threatening diseases of new American territory. It was clear to many slave owners that their chattel withstood the "seasoning" of ague much better than they themselves did. White owners also understood black slaves to be more able to withstand and survive yellow fever; though this disease was rare in the middle Mississippi Valley, earlier colonial history of yellow fever and its continuing ravages in port cities like New Orleans reinforced racial arguments about disease. On the other hand, African-Americans were thought by many whites to be much more susceptible than they to the fearsome cholera, as well as to respiratory illness and chronic eye, bone, and skin ailments like leprosy and yaws.

Again, cultural stereotype has some basis in fact. People of West African heritage are more likely to possess genetic traits that protect against falciparum malaria (and which are also tied to potentially crippling and even fatal sickle-cell anemia). Those born in regions where malaria or yellow fever are prevalent are likely to have gained maternal immunities during fetal development and breastfeeding; they are likely also to experience yellow fever as young children—when it is mildest—and acquire their own immunity to it.

Yet white imagination ranged far beyond epidemiological truth. Black bodies, argued defenders of slavery, were fundamentally different from white ones. As the Southern physician W. H. Gantt explained, "Their internal organization is as different from the white man's as is their external conformation." Some even asserted that slaves felt less pain. Brute strength came from brutish sensibilities; beatings and punishment had to be severe to even register.

Such anatomical conclusions held clear consequences for the fit between blackness, southern climates, and servitude. Under the rubrics of health and place, Africans belonged in the slave South. Change of place therefore held little challenge for them. Unlike delicate and more vulnerable white people, slaves had no need to undergo acclimation. They already belonged where they were.

True, slave owners did report illness in their slaves during the first seasons or years after emigration. Henry Merrell recalled his household's prolonged seasoning to Arkansas, including one slave's: "The servants all got the better of their chills. . . . Tabby the Cook suffered most because of her exposure to extra heat over the stove." Some also noticed that recently emigrated slaves expressed malaise and unhappiness, and seemed "dissatisfied."

Despite this medical recognition of black acclimation, however—despite the abundant evidence that change of place was a physical as well as emotional upheaval for all of those involved, including those in bondage—the antebellum literature of settlement nonetheless focused on physical acclimation as a problem for free people faced with choices in their migrations. In part, this reflects the environmental logic that held little difference between the American South and the presumed homelands of American slaves. Any necessary acclimation was assumed to have taken place during the first years or the first generation of transportation from Africa. The Middle Passage was the implied site of bodily adjustment, if any was needed.

Instead, slave owners tended to regard slaves' acclimation as a process of *social* adjustment and discipline. "In regard to unacclimated negroes," explained Samuel Cartwright, a noted Southern physician, the overseer should "make it a part of his business to make the whole lot of new negroes as comfortable, as contented & as happy as possible & to prepare the way for their gradual incorporation with the others." Carefully tallying and observing their own ailments with grim anxiety, emigrating Euro-Americans saw their seasoning ailments as physical effects of the environment, but they regarded black ill health as primarily a problem of household management.

Emigrating slaves did not have access to as many ways of telling us about their experiences. In their more abbreviated accounts of emigration, change of place was primarily a social, not a physical, ordeal. For white migrants, migration was also a social rupture—they too left behind friends and family. Crucially, though, voluntary migrants held many more options for keeping in touch and bringing loved ones with them. For blacks forcibly emigrated, the rupture that registered most had to do with family ties, not with physical adjustment to a new place.

To the extent that slaves' accounts of migration involved a sense of change to oneself (beyond the wrenching change to one's family), it involved getting used to new disciplines and a new order. Becoming accustomed to a different authority structure, to a different overseer's temper, and to the new duties or new punishments of a place—rather than to the environment itself—was a transition for slaves fraught with anxiety and peril. Solomon Northup gave a chilling account of his "habituation" to slavery after he was kidnapped, as he was forced to learn a new name, a new age (younger field slaves were more valuable), and a new demeanor in his condition as a slave. Northup documented the process of owners' and overseers' demonstration of mastery over newly purchased slaves that was the focus of black Americans' concerns of acclimation. The former slave Mary Armstrong recorded a cruel echo of whites' conversations about "seasoning" in her description of her St. Louis owner, William Cleveland: "He'd chain a nigger up to whip 'em and rub salt and pepper on him, like he said, 'to season him up.'" Tortured by the burning pepper and searing salt, the slaves assaulted by Cleveland were becoming acclimated, perhaps, to his brutal management.

Accounts of postwar life contain some hints that ex-slaves entering freedom had to undergo a change of self similar to whites' acclimation. One former South Carolina slave's account of Reconstruction bears witness to a sense that black migrants had physically to adjust to radical change, and could be harmed by its suddenness. Telling of being taken to a larger city by his mother, Warren McKinney recalled widespread sickness and death: "People died in piles," he told his Depression-era interviewer. "I don't know till yet what was de matter. They said it was the change of living." Emancipation was like menopause, a change of life that was in itself challenging to well-being. Freedom brought danger because it was so different from what had come before.

The shift from slavery to freedom was the crucial change awaited and yearned for by those enslaved. That transformation was momentous. Other changes—of site, of state, of "old" land for "new"—registered with much less importance than the paramount fact of a family's existence or destruction. Contemporary silence about the physical process of black slaves' acclimation reveals a central paradox of beliefs about change of place. Acclimation, a process of involuntary change and often unwelcome transformation, was integrally related to choice in one's own movement.

Acclimation was primarily a concern of free, white migrants concerned with their own physical experience and those of their families and children. In profound and important ways, they felt themselves to belong elsewhere than the new and lush territories of the Mississippi Valley. White newcomers were thus preoccupied with their own acclimation to a place in which they felt they did not belong.

Vulnerability of the Racial Self

Even when they had safely weathered the physical adjustments of acclimation, the process held problems for white emigrants. The logic of racial change meant that they had much to lose. If indeed they became seasoned in places of long sun and moist heat, and if the people most intrinsically suited for those places were the black slaves that they directed, what did that mean for their own subsequent status? What of their vulnerable children, raised amid environments of intrinsic threat? Whites had cause to fear the consequences of their own acclimation to new places: Would they become more black?

The sense that seasoning, like other attributes, could be passed down to future generations struck at the heart of contemporary credence given to race as a seemingly fixed attribute. Some sources depicted acclimation as operating within families or bloodlines. Henry Miller observed in 1838 that in the American Bottom "There are a number of French settled in this valley . . . who have stood the Ague Shakes for several generations, and appear to be well naturalized to it." Acclimation was accomplished over generations as well as over the life of the individual.

Such a process, however, brought with it nagging ambivalence. Was it progress that a family celebrated in its "naturalization," or a process of steady degeneration into debility and weakness? In becoming fitted for a climate, were they becoming less than they had originally been? Was acclimation a positive change, or a fundamental weakening?

B. W. Lee (the depressed southeastern Arkansas planter and physician) reflected the fears for family line shared by many white settlers to the Mississippi Valley. Despondent at his own failures, in 1844 he wrote his St. Louis friend that "I have a wife, and a very promising son, not quite two years old, he is not as healthy or as stout as I should desire, and it causes me great uneasiness on his account, knowing that but few persons are raised to manhood in this climate, with strong and vigorous constitutions." Lee saw an enervating climate as sapping manhood and strength, transforming and weakening the family line. Lee's plaintive passage resonates with a powerful anxiety that the ambitions that led this farm family to settle in the area would end up sabotaging future generations.

Black Americans of Lee's era left many fewer records of their own anxieties. Yet later scholars have recovered some sense that slaves, too, worried over the fate of their progeny. The historian Michael Gomez has argued that the experience of raising children was a pivotal challenge for the first generation of enslaved Africans, who in their American-born progeny saw both their further commitment to what Gomez calls a "sorrowland" and the attenuation of their own ties to the homeland for which they yearned. The fate of the family was thus central to the fears of many working the soil of the Mississippi Valley.

A sense that races could change or degenerate over time represented everyday sense to people who themselves engaged in routine—if usually small-scale—animal breeding. It was abundantly apparent that prize lines would drift back into common stock if not sustained by breeders' watchfulness and intervention. Indeed, documents indicate a similar sense of potential hereditary drift within human populations. In 1826 Timothy Flint mused on changes he noticed in the people of the Boston-area countryside, lamenting that he "looked in vain for the plump form, the round, ruddy, pretty, but unthinking Saxon face of the farmers' daughters of other days." This people, he realized, had been supplanted: employing the bug-based metaphors peculiar to his prose, he reflected that "in lieu of them we have insect forms, long and pale visages, covered with calash bonnets, a race apparently an importation from Italy." The tall ships of the Boston merchant trade brought in new fashions, in feminine form as in the shape of "bonnets"; the robustness of Flint's romanticized, pastoral ideal had given way to a more affected and physically refined country society. Yet the women he saw greeting his coach as it swayed through the farm villages of eastern Massachusetts were not simply themselves transformed; in Flint's warning prose, they represented a new "race," one with unaccountably foreign influences and, he implied, domestic consequences. Such fears of destructive racial change were intensified by the social, economic, and ethnic chaos of the early American Mississippi Valley.

White Americans' fears about acclimation were grounded in a long history of concern over racial change or "degeneration" in the European colonization of other parts of the world. Through the colonial era, Europeans had feared that the climate and geographic conditions of their New World could sap hereditary potential as creatures slid back into lesser forms. Beasts and people would become smaller and less potent as they served out generations on North America's hostile soil. Europe had the elephant, insisted natural philosophers like the Comte de Buffon; the Americas could boast only the comparatively tiny tapir. And so on through the list of creatures in Old World and New: scornful European *philosophes* observed that in each case Europe's animals, like its native peoples, were larger, more numerous, and more vigorous than those to be found in the enfeebling Americas. (Thomas Jefferson reached furiously for the fossilized bones of woolly mammoths to rebut such ideas: these animals were not extinct, he argued—since that would make his adversaries' point only too well—but might indeed yet be found, thundering through forests presumably yet to be discovered.)

In the environmental understanding of this early modern world, hot places registered with particular danger. The vitality of vegetation held deceptive threat. Parallels between person and place spelled out the consequences for emigrants of the lush growth of the Mississippi Valley. Many American newcomers feared that hot places would produce faster-growing but less nourishing crops and quickly maturing but soon debilitated inhabitants. In the same way, they would produce peoples who would ultimately fail in vitality.

Degeneration away from true type proved a lasting fear. European thinkers of the middle and late nineteenth century drew on older notions of degeneration in their concern with criminal types and the animalistic tendencies of the laboring masses. After Charles Darwin elucidated his theory of evolution by natural selection in 1859, scientific thinkers and social leaders expressed fears of degeneration in new scientific language. Well into the twentieth century—with terrifying consequences, both in the United States and in Europe—proponents of eugenic arguments pressed the need to prevent the further debasement of society's potential by weeding out its "unfit."

In the conversations of the antebellum Mississippi Valley, concerns for racial degeneration similarly expressed social fears. These were not, though, fears of a "type" or "mass" distant from elite observers. Instead, degeneration represented white Americans' anxiety for *themselves*. The forces of degeneration in the American nineteenth century were those of an environment that seized without exception the free migrants making their way across the Mississippi or down to lower latitudes.

The process of acclimation threatened to change the core essence of civilized, white bodies. As appearances changed—as ague sapped rosy freshness, producing the sallow faces so characteristic of places where the chills and fever were endemic; as pale skin darkened and became rough—white observers feared change in their very selves. No longer one with their former "people," emigrants from the East Coast would discover their own race shifting with their ailments and life habits.

Recent historians have identified shifts in this era in medical and scientific thinking about race fixity. In the early nineteenth century, scholars have argued, white peoples were urged to adapt to new places by imitating local practices. Later in the century, medical advice and widespread thinking slid into pessimism: not adaptation, but racial degeneration would result from whites' continued habitation in places for which they were intrinsically unfit. Yet in documents of the common life of the American antebellum borderlands, the axis of change appears somewhat different.

Sources suggest no such clear change in perceptions of acclimation. Throughout the antebellum decades, observers expressed a mix of beliefs about whites' ability to "naturalize" to foreign places. Accounts of successful acclimation and of permanent "sickliness" are both common. Fears of degeneration of the family, the individual, and the race coexist with optimistic accounts of the successful acclimation of emigrants.

Nevertheless, attitudes about the proper place of peoples did shift in crucial ways in the course of the nineteenth century. Many sources demonstrate a hardening of the link between blackness and slavery, reflected in attention to the consequences of race mixture and distrust of those so mixed.

Blurred Boundaries

The failure of racial vitality and the degeneration of one's "people" threatened white newcomers to the trans-Mississippi West because of the manifest blurriness of racial markers. The possibility of racial change was threatening because white people often had difficulty telling the difference between races, yet felt always compelled to do so. Such anxieties were not unique to early Arkansas and Missouri. Instead, the changes wrought to the human form by emigration heightened fears common in the United States throughout the nineteenth century. They bring into clearer focus the fault-lines in the concept of racial demarcation.

In regions ruled by the system of race-based slavery, skin tone and the physical characteristics of race held immense importance. In American political, economic, and legal systems, the inheritance of so-called "blackies" was slavery, whereas the inviolable heritage of white individuals was freedom. To slaves, whiteness could stand for freedom itself. According to his biographer, the escaped slave Archer Alexander exulted at his freedom with the cry "Now I'se a white man! Now I'se free!" Crossing the line between slave state and free transformed his symbolic race: he changed "color" when he crossed that crucial political divide. Differences between light or dark skin, smooth or kinky hair, narrow or broad noses—even in what were alleged to be the different smells of different bodies—were related in antebellum writing and thought not only to the essences of the underlying person but to the external political freedoms enjoyed in connection with regions specified as "slave" or "free."

Slaves' skin color was similarly a symptom of bodily well-being. Thomas Beckwith, a longtime Missourian born to a white settler family in 1840, reminisced in his old age that "When negroes were well fed on by hot meat they looked black and slick, when poorly fed they looked ashy." Gray skin, flaky with dryness, signaled slaves in poor health, ill or depressed, not taking care of themselves or being properly cared for. The state of a "black" slave's blackness was a sign not only of family line but of household management and individual well-being.

White inhabitants of the region noted their own changing colors, their own sun-burned or browned skin, as they did the skin tones of their free black and enslaved contemporaries. "Swarthiness" could be a sign of ill health: "whites" who were not "white" were either sick or suspect. One Arkansas woman, writing to her sister in 1843 about the well-being of her family, commented, "Frank is a tall mischievous Boy and almost as white as Bill." The pigmentation of one's servants and one's sons could alike be of interest to a slave-holding woman.

Complicating white anxieties was the stubborn flexibility of the human form. What it meant to be "black" or "white" was not self-evident. Again and again, definitions proved problematic, characteristics malleable, appearances deceptive. One 1853 conviction of a slave for the attempted rape of a white woman was overturned by the Arkansas Supreme Court, primarily on the grounds that the alleged victim had failed to prove that she was white. Her apparently white skin did not in itself demonstrate her race. Authorities groped for systems of racial adjudication. In a suit for false imprisonment brought by Abby Guy, an Arkansas woman, and her four young children, the family won the case—and their freedom—by exhibiting their bare feet to the jury. The state Supreme Court upheld this test of whiteness, agreeing that feet could indeed bear the telling evidence of race.

The obscure quality of such tests of race reveals the lengths to which antebellum observers were forced to go in their search for unambiguous signs of racial belonging. The evidence was often confusing. At times "black" slaves could be taken for free "whites." In 1839, the children of the politically prominent Arkansas family of Matilda and William Fulton mistook a new slave for a "poor white man." Such "mistakes"—failures of the cultural definitions of race fully to shape visual perception—were not uncommon. To some living in slavery, mixed-race status meant that they could try to "pass" as whites and escape. To many of their white contemporaries, people or practices that represented what one Illinois traveler in 1830 termed the "White man niggahafied" posed a danger to a system based on maintaining clear demarcations between the two races.

Racial confusion was heightened by occasional everyday experiences like the change in the apparent race of a slave mother's newborn reported by a former slave named Henry Green. The baby was born with very light skin, indicating it had been fathered by a white man. Soon, however, the infant's skin darkened, a process common to African-American and other ultimately dark-skinned babies. In Green's account, the infant's change from "white" to "black" indicated the deep conflict smoldering beneath Southern domestic arrangements. The initial lightness of the baby's skin enraged the wife of the slave-owning family, arousing tensions among slaves who knew that a household mistress's jealousy and anger could be expressed not only at her husband—the presumed father—but at the more vulnerable slave community. As the infant began to look "black," the white mistress's anger abated, and with it the immediate danger to the household.

This incident from Henry Green's life as a slave indicates a primary fear of many white Americans: the sexual and reproductive entwining of putatively separate peoples. In body as in habits of life, profound adjustments took place when people moved long distances, and these changes were echoed in the changes to "people" heralded in new societies of the borderlands. The dramatic alterations, social and physical, demanded by western migration threatened to change the nature of races and nations.

Some observers looked forward to change in the American people as a positive consequence of American growth. The German immigrant Nicholas Hesse insisted in the late 1830s that Americans "must be considered as the superlative of the British, from whom they are chiefly derived." This kind of characterization stressed the superiority of latterly formed peoples, in terms intelligible from the plant and animal breeding that was commonplace at the time. A "derived" line could be refined to evince specific attributes more strongly than the parent breed. Such a perspective expressed in racial form Hesse's optimistic political vision of U.S. western expansion.

Like Hesse's, other accounts of racial shift offered visions of the strength of "hybrid" peoples. Daniel Drake viewed with characteristic heartiness the emergence of a "compound" people from the swirling mixture of "varieties and races" he saw about him. Chemical and metallurgical metaphor provided reassuring images of an amalgamation in which staunch "Anglo-Saxon" qualities would stabilize and shape the surrounding mass. He concluded the first volume of his treatise on the Mississippi Valley in 1850 by heralding

> a new national constitution—physical and mental—of which the Anglo-Saxon, itself a compound, will be the basis and the governing element. The physicians of a future day will see, what we cannot now, a prevailing temperament, a stature, form, complexion, and physiognomy, characteristic of an indigenous, but greatly compounded race; with its own physical, intellectual, and moral constitution; its special liabilities and exemptions from disease; its national idiosyncrasies, and the required peculiarities of hygienic regimen, and therapeutic treatment.

Drake looked forward with medical curiosity to the hybrid vigor of a new American race, accepting matter-of-factly and optimistically what many of his contemporaries feared as social catastrophe.

Drake's blending, however, had strict limits. Elsewhere, his writings make clear that the "compounding" of races he foresaw was to take place between *white* peoples. In 1851 he proposed that free states no longer permit "negroes, or their descendants of mixed blood, citizens of Liberia excepted, to reside in, pass through, or even visit them; and the slave States should forbid emancipation, except a guaranty be given that the liberated should not seek the free States." Drake was one of series of intellectual leaders in the second third of the century to express an increasingly militant desire for an all-white free population. Black Americans would remain slaves in the carefully bounded South. They played no part in the new and strong amalgam Drake imagined would be melded in the cultural interactions and geographic adjustments of the Mississippi Valley.

Many writers shared a sense that a new race might emerge from the chaotic intermixture of cultures on the American borderlands, but worried that it would be a race of rough and predatory outcasts. Washington Irving's rendering of this possible future for the Great Plains was typical of many observers' purple rhetoric and racialist fears. Beyond civilization's limits, Irving wrote,

> may spring up new and mongrel races, like new formations in geology, the amalgamation of the "debris" and "abrasions" of former races, civilized and savage; the remains of broken and almost extinguished tribes; the descendants of wandering hunters and trappers; of fugitives from the Spanish and American frontiers; of adventurers and desperadoes of every class and country yearly ejected from the bosom of society into the wilderness.

Not a hardy, well-shaped cross-breed, but a snarling "mongrel" cur would in Irving's imagination emerge from the careless throwing together of racial undesirables. Wild lands, he thought, might give rise to a wild people, a composite of the cast-offs of stable society.

To antebellum travelers who pushed their way along the crowded docks of St. Louis, such a future seemed already near. New Orleans river men eager for their leave, slave laborers carrying cargo to smoke-belching boats, embarking passengers anxious for their parcels, free black merchants struggling to make next month's rent, travelers, wharf boys, and hustlers of all kinds jumbled together in a milling mass. The chaotic crowd spoke a patois of bastardized French, accented English (from Dublin, from the Atlantic Seaboard, from the American backwoods), and a smattering of other tongues—Shawnee, Osage, Hungarian, Spanish, emphatic German. As huge throngs jostled one another amid stacked bales, crates, and the ever-present smell of rotting fish, the rolling syllables of West Africa and the twangy singsong of Kentucky were alike foreign to observers who looked in vain for delicate white skin or gentle refinement. In fashion and in speech, in manners and in progeny, such a society seemed to many white Americans to be combining pell-mell into a frightening and unwanted miscellany.

Proper Place: Free Black Identity

One reaction to cultural and racial combination was hostility expressed by white people toward those who represented to them an unacceptably blurred boundary. White inhabitants of the American South and the American borderlands attempted to enforce the logic of person and place when it seemed in danger of violation. Hostility to mixedness came to a head in hostility against free blacks: those who failed to mesh in a system that tied people to their proper places.

Hostility toward the very existence of free black people dramatically intensified throughout the South in the 1840s and '50s. Many white Americans increasingly found free black people in odious violation of the conceptual, legal, and social links connecting black identity, slave status, and the slave South. Through the doctrines of acclimation, the "fit" of place and person could be remade to accommodate "European" whites in the sultry South. Yet white Southerners, including those of the borderland slave states, began to question free blacks' future place in the hot regions of slavery.

In a system demanding a match between self and land, white imagination could make room for black Africans toiling in well-controlled rows under the hot southern sky, and for whites whose racial origins lay in cooler, northern Europe, but who had acclimated through fearsome processes to the new world of the slave territories. Free black Southerners, though physically formed for southern climates, were *socially* unacclimated: *in* a place but not *of* it, unfit by virtue of their race to move freely and of their own volition in the dichotomized world of the slave South. In their proper social role, and in the proper geographic region—that is, as slaves, in the American South—blacks fit neatly into the conceptual frameworks of white racism. When black people violated this linked natural and social order, when they were mobile and free in a slave state but not in the state of slavery, proponents of the slave system used the logic of medical environmentalism to find them not physically but socially out of place.

Free black people were a small but significant social presence in colonial Missouri, and in the first decades of American presence in Missouri and Arkansas. Their legal and social status changed significantly over time. With the intensification of antislavery rhetoric in the North, with American expansion into areas like Missouri, where climate and topography rendered plantation-style slavery problematic, and with the concomitant rise of vehemently antiblack sentiment in the South, in the 1840 and '50s freedpeople were met with ever more hostile action and rhetoric from the white population. Tensions came to head on the national level with the Kansas-Nebraska Act of 1854, but had been intensifying in localities around the South for years before. Laws in both Arkansas and Missouri restricted free black residents' ability to enjoy freedom of movement, exercise basic legal rights, or even hold legal residence. Influential whites called for the expulsion of the area's free blacks (moderate whites advocated colonization back to presumed African homelands).

The fall in status of free black Arkansans and Missourians in the decades of tension culminating in the Civil War was most evident in the trades in which black workers represented an economic threat to white labor. A significant mark of this broader trend was the attack on both free and slave black artisans, who were fundamental to craft work and the building trades in cities. As a result of this upswing in persecution, a few freedpeople with sufficient resources undertook a characteristically American response: they moved west. Yet for most black people such measures were unavailable. Those who fell between monolithic categories of place and identity represented an intractable challenge to the logic of belonging that governed so much of nineteenth-century life.

Mixedness and the Problem of Color

White Americans feared mixedness. They feared those who mixed legal, social, and environmental categories, who lived with dark skins but without white ownership. They also feared those who in their very selves embodied the blurring of racial boundaries.

In the early decades of the antebellum period, Indianness was a key element in white Americans' fears of mixed identity. Unlike the colonial French, Americans of the Mississippi Valley had no use for people of partial Native American heritage. Many Americans saw in the racial intermixture of white and Native American groups a sign of inevitable and inalterable passing. It was only to be expected that lesser peoples would vanish beneath the force and vigor of the mightier.

Common perception sought the dominant strain that would shape racial cross-breeding, much as horticulturalists might search for the delicate buds of a crossed line or farmers assess the weight of a carefully bred hog. Weaker white peoples were seen as more prone to racial amalgamation. Though Americans did not blend well, Timothy Flint noted, he was impressed with the "facility with which the French and Indians intermix. . . . The French settle among them, learn their language, inter-marry, and soon get smoked to the same copper complexion," he told his American readers. In American perception, the very countenances of the "inter-marrying" French changed to match their social, familial, and sexual connections with this more primitive and darker people. According to Flint, the intrinsic weakness of the French line that would allow for this possibility was evident in the consequences of such racial blending: native characteristics—"[t]he lank hair, the Indian countenance and manners"—dominated the physical appearance (and, he implied, the moral constitution) of later mixed-race generations.

Welcoming "a spirit of improvement and industry brought by the Americans settling here," prospective English immigrant Henry Bousfield was thankful in 1819 that in Missouri such an energy was "taking [the] place of the apathy and indolence of the mongrel race who have till lately solely occupied this place." Specifying his scorn more carefully, he continued: "they are not French"—that would, in English eyes, likely be bad enough—"but half Canadien French and half Indian." The degradation of a European people long resident in North America, the "Canadien French," had been further accelerated by relation with the area's Indian denizens. American robustness would soon set aside the half-hearted efforts of such a lessened people. Bousfield's long tour of Missouri convinced him to move from Cumberland, England, to the Boon's Lick region of central Missouri to share in the American infusion of "improvement and industry," replacing, according to his logic of bloodline, a flawed line with a better.

White Americans' fears for racial intermixture underlined and reinforced environmental anxieties. In the mixing of black and white many thinkers of the middle nineteenth century feared for the deterioration of the white race. Amalgamation could mean the weakening of a once-vital line—much as it had proved for the French of the Mississippi Valley.

Despite the common presence of mixed-race individuals in antebellum Arkansas and Missouri, their identity—and the intimacy of individuals and cultures that created them—was regarded by most white American newcomers to the region as a profound threat. Children of mixed black and white parentage formed the most dramatic testimony to the violence and internal contradictions of the slave system. Though a few white men with slave or black partners gained some semblance of social recognition for their racially mixed children, in almost all cases these liaisons, often forced on the woman, ended with the enslavement of children recognizable as their "master's" own. Abolitionists drew back in horror, and genteel slave holders publicly denounced such extreme perversion of benevolent family life. Yet identifiably mixed-race people, especially slaves with white or Native American heritage strongly visible in their appearance, were a fundamental part of the slave system, the region's labor force, and the multiple and overlapping frameworks of racial understanding.

A mesh of conflicting views enwrapped mixed-race people. Fertility in particular was regarded with ambivalence. The many "mulattos" inhabiting plantation slave quarters and serving slave-owning families amply testified to the viability of human racial intermixture. Yet cultural fears were not to be so easily silenced by experience and evidence: tortured arguments by white experts claimed the eventual infertility of mixed-race people. Proponents of polygenesis argued that different races were in fact altogether separate species; mixed-race humans, like the product of any other crossing of species lines, would therefore be infertile. Mulattos, like mules, would have no heritage to pass down.

Unlike in the lower animals, this process was held to be gradual. Racist arguments acknowledged that the first few generations might be fertile, but insisted that mixed-race people would eventually die out. In the face of evident mulatto fertility, white observers struggled to assert that what they feared simply could not be. They expressed what one 1860 writer for *De Bow's Review* called an *"aversion to hybridity"*—in social as well as biological forms. Such assertions are echoed in the subsequent beliefs of at least some African-Americans. One former slave originally from Georgia recalled wistfully in the 1930s, "I never had a child. They tell me now if I had married dark men I would maybe had children. I married very light men both times." The snarls of racial unease trapped many in anxieties about fertility.

White inhabitants of the mid-Mississippi borderlands consistently attempted to keep the lid on the confusing racial array around them. They sought to enforce difference when it was not self-evident. Just as the language of farming can reveal deeper parallels of understanding, so too the language of race indicates the ways cultural contact led to fears about change to race as well as person.

With careful and even obsessive attention to racial differentiation, many attempted to restrain the conceptual cacophony of blending that was all too evident. A young New Orleans resident, Caleb Cox, described race-based wordplay characteristic of antebellum language in an encounter with a local farmer during his 1819 steamboat journey to St. Louis. The farmer stated that his wife was "Dutch"—a common term not for those from the Netherlands but for people who said they spoke "Deutsch," that is, German. When asked whether she was "High" or "Low Dutch" (implying a class distinction based on the kind of German spoken by immigrants), the farmer responded that she was "Black Dutch." Cox was then introduced to the woman, whom he derisively described as a "Venus of the West. She appears to be about five feet two inches high and something more in circumference, a squalid Indian face, jet black hair, heavy eyebrows which almost concealed a pair of piercing black eyes that too plainly spoke the ability to exercise the cruelties of her tribe."

The husband's attempted banter about his wife's ethnicity was probably his attempt to stave off such prejudice with humor, or provide at least some sort of alternative racial label for her. That the attempt was such a failure (at least, judging by Cox's scorn) had much to do with the searching examination of race characteristic of his society. The many varieties and combinations of person in the borderlands gave rise to complex and contested racial naming.

Characterizations of Indian identity tended to fall into the terms commonly used to describe blacks and whites. In part this reflects the vulnerable legal standing of Native Americans: many mixed-race and even full-blooded Indians lived in slavery. Stephen Hempstead noted in the summer of 1822 that "my Daughter Mary Sent her Squaw melato to the trading house up the Missouri. Named Terris." This brief allusion gives no hint of the complexity of the racial and familial relations in the Hempstead household in that year. Mary Hempstead Lisa, one of the two widows of Manuel Lisa, was living with her father after losing her fortune at her husband's death. She also had living with her Manuel's daughter Rosalie from his concurrent marriage with an Osage woman named Mitain, whom he had married first. As borderlands society shifted away from the more accommodating policies of the French Creoles to the racially unforgiving codes of American settlers, families like the Hempsteads attempted to distance themselves from tellingly in-between members like Rosalie, or likely Terris herself.

In larger terms, the relative invisibility of any separate category of "redness" is itself a symptom of the increasing bifurcation of the social and political life of the slave South into two worlds, black and white. Conflation of Native American "mulattos" with black slaves or "black Dutch" women prefigures the two-race configuration of the later South. Physical diversity was reduced to a racial dichotomy.

An elaborate language of racial intermixture served to define or hide evidence of mixed-race heritage. Common language developed an intricate system of identifying the different pigmentation of those deemed "black." Their contemporaries carefully evaluated mixed-race individuals along a spectrum of tinge. Timothy Flint recorded that the "yellow women" of New Orleans, mixed-race women of both white and black heritage, were regarded by many Americans and Europeans as particularly beautiful and graceful. James Thomas, a former Tennessee slave who became a noted St. Louis entrepreneur, similarly noted in his memoirs that an elaborate language defined the complexions of those put up for sale in New Orleans. "Griffe" slaves were lighter than "blacks" but darker than the progressively "whiter" levels of "mulatto, quadroon, Octroon." New Orleans' social stratification represents the apex of attention to racial differentiation: in much of the Mississippi Valley, racial vocabulary was more coarse and general. Common to the culture of the slave South, however, was the basic differentiation between black and mulatto.

Former slaves and the children of slaves applied similar care, though not the same language, in describing their own and their families' colors. Her mother was "a dark woman," recalled one early-twentieth-century Arkansan, and "Papa was a ginger cake colored man." One former slave's grandmother was "a regular Indian color," while other family members were "bright," light-skinned in a way produced by white, not Native American, heritage. Occasionally, those on the bottom win. Though the vocabulary for skin tone used by whites and slave traders—mulatto, quadroon, octoroon—has not survived into common use, many of the terms used by slaves and free black people themselves survived into the modern era. When I was in school in Arkansas in the 1970s and '80s, my schoolmates teased each other for being "dark," "light," "yellow," and "bright," using language handed down from their great-grandparents—not mine.

Yet again and again, despite such seeming linguistic precision, fractured vocabulary indicates the failure of attempts to keep careful track of *who* was *what*. Multiple labels overlapped. Reflecting common preoccupation with the race of those around him, Stephen Hempstead recorded in his diary in June of 1826 that someone had been killed in a brawl between "a Yellowman" and an actor in a traveling circus. Six months later, he noted one Sunday that "Mr Giddings preached in the forenoon and an Yellow man Nicholas in the afternoon." Unlike Flint's comment about yellow women,

however, Hempstead's diary entries about these yellow men are quite ambiguous.

Hempstead may well have been employing the usage of 1826 to refer to
mixed-race "black" men of light skin color. On the other hand, he was 72
years old when he wrote these notes. Hempstead was already middle-aged
when he immigrated to Missouri in 1811, and his formative experiences had
been of the colonial and Revolutionary era. Indeed, his several Revolutionary War wounds were increasingly painful as he navigated old age in the
1820s. In his youth, not "mulattos" but Native Americans could be referred
to by white Americans as "yellow." In 1782, for instance, Daniel Boone,
later to become a neighbor and afternoon story-swapper of Hempstead's in
Missouri, encountered what one of his fellow fighters called "yellow" Indians in the lands they were attempting to colonize in Kentucky. As a Missouri
resident in the second decade of the nineteenth century, an elderly Boone reflected changing racial perceptions in talking of the "red men" with whom
he had negotiated territory and hunting grounds. Over the 50 years between
Hempstead's Revolutionary War service and his life as an old man in a community along the Missouri River, language had shifted: Americans had
learned to see Native Americans as "red" and light-toned blacks as "yellow." With the further western spread of the United States, they would subsequently come to use "yellow" for the Chinese men laboring to lay
railroads across the broad expanses of the American West in the 1860s. It is
hard to know where on this changing framework to place Steven Hempstead's recordings of "Yellow" men in St. Louis: many eras' racial perceptions were at work in the public conversations and private documents of the
early Mississippi Valley borderlands.

The further failure to stabilize race and hold it constant resonated in the
horror stories of the antebellum era of whites who were taken for black. Accounts abounded of white children—that is, children who did not simply
look fair-skinned, but who in fact had no black ancestry—being sold into
slavery. In his autobiography of life as a slave in Missouri and then as a free
escapee, the writer William Wells Brown told of meeting a young man in
New Orleans whom he had known in St. Louis. The boy was the son of an
impoverished, hard-working free white widow. He was hired on as an assistant by the storekeeper who was his mother's employer, taken downriver on
the pretext of business, and then treacherously sold as a light-skinned slave,
to the storekeeper's profit. Other accounts told similar tales of white children kidnapped and sold into slavery. A former slave, Isaac D. Williams, reported that because of this practice, one potential "purchaser would not buy

until he was perfectly convinced beyond all doubt that the party was a legal slave"; only the displayed (and presumably grieving) mother, summoned "from a long distance," was adequate to give proof of the essential blackness of one "beautiful child, as white and delicate a featured boy as I ever saw." Legislators might try to regularize racial boundaries, but the blue eyes and fair skin of many "black" slaves told the searching truth about the sanctity of race in the slave-holding South.

Frustrated owners, like careful buyers, attempted to clarify the manifestly blurred status of their human property. In a horrifying anecdote in the appendix of William Wells Brown's freedom narrative, he quoted a report in the *St. Louis Gazette* that "A wealthy man here had a boy named Reuben, almost white, whom he caused to be branded in the face with the words 'A slave for life.'" When complexion failed to testify to this enslaved child's status, his face was made to.

Many of the fears of white Americans came to a head in the possible erasure of whiteness. That "white" children could be bought and sold was, along with the rape of white women by black men, the consequence of racial interaction most feared by white Southerners. Such exchanges marked the failure of racial boundaries as impermeable vessels of social meaning. They marked, further, the changeability of race itself. Whiteness was a volatile agent within a changing landscape, no longer self-evident but needing constant redefinition and even violent enforcement.

In coming to terms with race in the context of chattel slavery, newcomers to Arkansas and Missouri before the military rebellion of the Southern states brought together anxieties, hatreds, and complexities facing the nation as a whole. Race continued to be a well-defended category of social oppression well past the war that reforged the Union and ended legal slavery. Yet discussions of acclimation and race in the antebellum period reveal the fissures threatening that solid wall. Undermining the separation between whites who were by definition free and potentially enslaved blacks was swirling conceptual confusion. The demonstrated interaction of various races in the Mississippi Valley threatened to collapse white racial stability just as the experience of acclimation threatened white Americans' individual and collective identity.

The Failure of Order

The lived human body was not constant in the antebellum United States, any more than terrain itself was. The very self changed as a product of life in places strange and distant. Change of place threatened multiple kinds of transformation: change of person, in whites' bodily transformation and blacks' loss of family; change of "people," as individuals and whole households became *of* the Mississippi Valley; and change of race, as "black," "white," and "Indian" were revealed as manifestly impermanent and unfixable types. The alterations of health, skin tone, and daily practice summed up in acclimation were as deep and unavoidable as the fundamental changes undergone by "wild" land tilled by American plows. Challenge at a profound level awaited the inhabitants of "new" territories, as it did the soil they broke.

The geography of health reveals the vulnerability of race as stable system. Newcomers to the American borderlands had to figure out their own "peoplehood" because of the fit between place and person demanded in the logic of environmental health. Confronted by change in themselves that was brought about by their change of place, migrants had also to confront challenge to the easy determination of "race" and "people." Taking seriously antebellum newcomers' concern for the intimate ties between personal and environmental well-being thus provides skeptical modern observers a way to understand the experienced physical dimensions of slippery racial definitions and white preoccupation with them.

The changes created by new territory—especially hot, sunbaked new territory increasingly allied with the culture and environment of the South— heightened attention to the existing hierarchy of race. White newcomers were confronted in their bodies and their sense of themselves with the logic of health and environment. The worries of migrating Americans reveal the medical and environmental underpinnings of racial anxiety and violence.

In these anxieties, too, are visible the limits of Americans' reach for stability, their failure to create order. Environments seeped into human experience in ways as myriad as they were uncontrollable: through miasmas, winds, smells, dirt, food, water—and through change to one's own self and to white people's safe, reassuring conception of their own race. Much as white newcomers might try to make sense of race, it remained stubbornly complex. The conceptual dissonance in accounts of color and race is telling. Not the actual categories established by a race-based society but the tensions between categories, the many contradictions they encompassed, created the conceptual space for the powerful amalgam that is race in America.

Such disputes, questions, and violent conflict over change to person and race give further insight into the rhetoric of the American frontier in the period. The essential qualities granted "race" and "people" came into conflict with concurrent discourses about putting down new roots, and that conflict formed an important countervailing voice within confident assertions of American empire. Concerns over race—especially the race of various "whites"—also reveal white newcomers' sense that those from different regions were different in fundamental ways. This development of a consciousness of race articulated by American region was to be one governing factor in divisions between North and South. In that long-simmered war, notions about the core differences between "peoples" of different regions were mapped onto political divisions within the United States.

Further, the tight binding of race and region explains some aspects of the singular hostility directed at free blacks. Rather than articulating deeper pessimism with respect to their own regional acclimation, white Missourians and Arkansans of the middle nineteenth century reacted vehemently against those who did not fit into a neat topography of "people" and place: those whose skins were "black" but whose lives were their own.

Discussion of race and of acclimation reveals the tension of a powerful framework of common understanding for nineteenth-century Americans and Europeans. Set notions went spinning: people as bound to land, or people as changeable over generations; race as an enduring characteristic, or race as potentially improved, degraded, or mongrelized. Competing but significant ideas about blood and essence seeped through American anxieties of the borderlands.

Lived experience told—to slaves as to masters, to all who walked along town streets or rode the region's traces—of the complex products of human interaction across all lines of race and people. Nineteenth-century Americans mustered an increasingly complex vocabulary in their efforts to bring order to motley hue. They stretched a hierarchy of naming over the unquantifiable variety of physiognomy, in an attempt to preserve and protect the boundaries between and within races. Yet the undeniable blurring of set racial characteristics thwarted this effort, and threatened to blur the categorical differences white Americans sought so clearly to enforce. The language of health and place leads not to widely shared basic insight, but to a coiled mass of conflicting ideas whose venom would become more and more deadly as the nation lurched toward disunion.

That the system of racial economy persisted well after the Civil War—and in many important respects persists still—is historical fact. Confused and blurry, and at the same time overpoweringly dominant, the framework of racial definition encompassed both threat and internal contradiction. The challenge posed by beliefs about the power of place perhaps best reveals the strength of this racial framework. For all that white Americans lived the

contradictions of racial unclarity, they found in the environment-bound notions of race and peoplehood a structure for their own experience, not least
as they came to terms with a terrain for which most felt themselves manifestly unfit. In the changing of diverse peoples to a people *of* the central
Mississippi Valley, as in the changes within white and black race of the antebellum period, nineteenth-century Americans lived an ideology that,
though it might tremble, would not of itself fall.

CONCLUSION

Chapter IX

But the basin of the Mississippi is the BODY OF THE NATION.

—**Mark Twain**, preface to
Life on the Mississippi

WHEN AMERICANS OF THE NINETEENTH CENTURY asked about the "health of the country," they phrased with great economy a mass of related questions. Is this a place in which good health inheres, and in which, most important, good health will come to *me*? Is this a place possessed of balanced forces that will yield not only fertile crops but a good crop of children? Is this a region that is "thriving," a place whose economic and social prospects are good and where networks of commerce and communication are at least promising? Is this a place whose goods, products, and produce will support commercial exchange, where hard labor—in store, factory, mine, or farm—will return a profitable income? Does this site have all the many factors that go into making a good life for me and my household?

Divining the salubrity of settlement sites, those who possessed freedom of movement expressed their foremost anxieties: their own well-being and that of crops and household ledger. Correspondence from emigrating families spoke of "healthiness" or "insalubrity" inhering in site. Emigration guides from a variety of countries glowed with praise for the hearty healthfulness of American farms and American life. Scientific and medical works attempted to trace the diverse strands of environmental well-being. These varied conversations, conducted in similar terms, though often to dissimilar ends, constituted the answer to a larger question: What were the present realities and future prospects of "new" lands beyond the ragged edges of mapped settlement? What was, in the vocabulary of the period, the "situation" of borderlands territory?

The broadness of such questions, like the broadness of the language used to convey them, hints at the almost overwhelming complexity of what American migration and American expansion meant for individual "movers" and for the American republic. Well-being—of nature, body, and nation—was a central preoccupation and governing metaphor in the expansion of American political and agricultural economy across the North American continent in the nineteenth century. An emphasis on health and healthfulness pervaded the personal experience of numberless migrants as it did the rhetoric of American expansionism. Antebellum discussions of site and self, and of the intimate and many-layered connections between them, resonated up and down levels of meaning. That a stretch of land was "healthy" held significance not only for the future of the household that claimed it but for the future of the nation dependent on such successful settlement.

Imagining and describing the human body provided nineteenth-century Americans with a means to think through and express their place within larger economic and political arrangements. Great pressures of population and popular excitement pressed against the older boundaries of the nation, calling to mind commonsense notions of crisis and release. Just as the bursting through of settlement across the Cumberland Gap had in American imagination brought healthful release and a wholesome cultivation to the middle South and upland regions of Tennessee and Kentucky, the continued outflow of emigration to the new lands of the Louisiana Purchase would result in a two-fold condition of well-being: health for the older parts of the nation, which would rid themselves of a surfeit of uncomfortably restless energy, and health for the wild and unclaimed territory that would be brought under systems of agricultural and social order.

Such felt connection—connections forged by practical observation that melded knowledge of forest and field, bone and body, pregnancy and economy—opens for us a new understanding and appreciation of American political debates. The metaphors of strain, release, buildup, nutrition, exhalation, and exhaustion that marked political speech and political worry take on a new meaning when we can understand them as grounded solidly in lived experience. Our political history may be enriched and deepened if we begin to take seriously the physical dread people of the mid-nineteenth century felt at the prospect of breaking apart and breaking away.

The logic of the body and of its land meant that the healthy release of Americans from constrictive boundaries, the extension of systems of regularity and management to unordered terrain, the passing away of vitiated peoples before robust and heartier ones were natural developments. Political processes, like those of fever or soil, called on a common sense made abundantly manifest.

The body's fragility was the nation's own: expend too much energy, stretch too far, fail to monitor proper intake or balance, and the system could collapse. Flaws and failings could be writ onto the national future as onto terrain. Despite these threats, the processes at work in environs and in the human form could also bring reassurance. Strengthened with the healthy flow of commerce, coursing as blood in the body or as water in the region's streams, maintained in regular order by the dispersal of groups of fractious immigrants, growing through the absorption of territory as fitting and appropriate to its needs as was food to a healthy person, and releasing and forcing from itself the refuse of those who could not appropriately be taken in, the civil body flexed and flourished.

As newcomers to the middle Mississippi Valley gazed out over meadowlands or down from ridges or into sloughs dark even at midday, some saw a land they sought to work or to possess; others saw a land whose fields of cotton or wheat, tobacco or hemp were the reason they themselves were bought and sold. Antebellum Americans were eager learners of the lessons taught them by changes of season and changes of self. The common language through which they explained, discussed, and assimilated processes of body and of cultivated field was also a powerful tool in comprehending, phrasing, and shaping the future of the state.

From body to terrain, to nation and back again, the literature of American borderlands settlement passed quickly and easily between levels of meaning. The almost limitless multiplication of sites for metaphor, the rangeless flexibility of patterns of understanding, and the blithe sliding back and forth of imaginative play between the details of spleen and kidney, the concerns of farm and planting, and the scope of "country" and nation can baffle modern observers who prefer our metaphors constrained and our categories neat. Yet posing the question "Why did antebellum Americans describe and think about outer terrain and inner body in the same imagery and language?" does violence at the outset to the worldviews of those it interrogates. Starting from a distinction between the operations of self and those of nature bifurcates a nineteenth-century vision that was seamlessly integrated.

In an 1895 memoir of his long life, the Arkansas politician William F. Pope recalled a play about Napoleon performed by a traveling troupe in the Mississippi Valley in the early part of the century. The likeness of the primary actor to the soldier and future emperor was so remarkable that "whenever he appeared in the New Orleans theatres, cries of '*Vive l'Empereur*' would rend the air and the old French soldiers in the audience would mount the stage and, taking him upon their shoulders, would parade around and around, singing French songs until their enthusiasm cooled."

Such a scene is uncomfortable to us later readers in a number of ways. The crowd seems duped by the show, unable, like "primitives" recorded in some early anthropology, to distinguish between theater and event, between spectacle and actual happening. The man they trundled through the galleries was not, after all, the real Napoleon; he was a representation, a man able through makeup and posture (and a snuffbox prop) to bring verisimilitude into hinterland playhouses. We tend to think, too, of such blending of audience and players as a coy trope of the twentieth century, the stuff of subversive playwrights unsettling the complacent.

But the boisterous crowds rousting about their Napoleon quite apparently saw the world in a different way. They knew, of course, that this was not Napoleon; they also saw, quite rightly, that he would stand in. They understood that they were audience; they also understood that their participation in acting out a celebratory procession was not simply tolerated but was in a certain sense necessary for the success of the show. It had been designed precisely to invite the revelrous celebration of the New Orleans crowds. Their seizing upon the moment of symbolism and making it *theirs*, in rough and colloquial ways, was not a failure to judge the reality of the situation but a triumph. The show was meant as an occasion for this reexperiencing of patriotism and pride. The permeability of audience and stage in this early-century tableau, like the interpermeability of dirt floor and miasma, of chill wind and human being, of human intervention and natural balance, is— precisely in its awkwardly foreign nature—a singularly important clue to how people experienced things through most of the nineteenth century.

It is for us, observers of the twenty-first century, that the meaningfulness of phrases like "healthy land" or "sickly country" has become unclear. The overlapping and mutually informing meanings of those judgments were as unselfconscious in the antebellum United States as they are strange to us now. This is not to say that our era has somehow emptied metaphors of meaning or fails to use language and structural frameworks for many different and often only loosely related kinds of work. It is to say that for us to talk of hummocks or ponds possessing and being possessed by "health" in the same ways as the human body is to venture an almost unthinkable cognitive leap. Oneness of process and product made sense in the world of the nineteenth-century American borderlands because common sense and everyday experience ratified and reinforced each other. We live in a world in which these relationships have been utterly transformed, not only by dramatic changes in science, medicine, and technologies but also by cumulative revolutions in everyday life, by most Americans' distance from agricultural practice, by our collective creation of vastly different environments. Our common sense thus acts on different substrates; our understanding functions by different metaphors. People of the nineteenth century saw things differently because theirs was a different world. This book has aimed not to use their understanding, but to describe and work within it, to give it sense and shape against the skeptical common sense of a differently informed era.

I hope to have sketched for us moderns a sense of this world we have lost. We are profoundly estranged from the ways people of not so many generations ago, inhabiting land many of us now think of as ours, felt and saw and spoke about the world around them. This book is an attempt to make their vision of the world intelligible, to animate it with the robustness and coherence it once possessed. The preceding chapters have traced a set of beliefs, practices, and ways of understanding certain fundamental processes that linked health with the places where human beings moved, worked, loved, bickered, schemed, and made their lives. The task of understanding this cosmology of the past is to realize—that is, to *make real*—a felt, lived unity of sensation and experience that was as calmly extended to many related aspects of the world in the nineteenth century as it is abruptly foreign now.

This book has traced the imaginative geographies trod and worked by early Americans encountering places new to them. Their worlds were at once coarsely physical and composed of ideals and dreamings. Settlers who penned grand visions of political or economic success home to worried parents and aunts made the region in words even as they framed the region as polity, developed it as an economy, and shaped its waters and earth into more or less fruitful farms.

In the mappings of self and space that shaped American use of terrain, land had meanings political and economic, social and deeply personal. Implicit recognition of fundamental sameness between nature and human body created ownership and intelligibility of what was "new" and unknown. The geography of health helped make *American* an environment perceived as unknown and potentially harmful. American settlers understood that which was wild and feared in similar terms as they did the everyday, lived reality experienced within their bodies. This very link to the familiar signals the many meanings of the natural world.

The fundamental connection between actions of body and environment revealed in nineteenth-century geographies of health expresses the destabilizing potency of the partially understood. The language of health and land centers on the private experience of the human form, a body dependent upon forces both interior and exterior. Yet bodies themselves were only incompletely comprehended, the forces besetting them only incompletely catalogued, just as land was never completely brought under control. Bodies could be watched, shepherded, treated, and often restored to health when thrown into sickness's disarray. They were also easily "deranged," subject to myriad influences from within and without. Understanding the environment and the body through the same foundational principles expresses both dominance and vulnerability, linkage and lack of control. "Healthy" land, like a "healthy" body, was in dynamic tension, never fully at rest, and never fully mastered.

The geography of health expressed a volatile mix of vulnerability to land and to bodily ills, and power over them. It expressed the possibilities of both balance and disarray, dread illness and robust health, success and economic failure. When Arkansas and Missouri emigrants like the farmer John Brown, the missionary Cynthia Thrall, or the speculator Justus Post pronounced the land they wished to settle "healthy," they not only revealed important aspects of how they understood their own bodies to work but also drew on a powerful set of resources for understanding and interpreting land. Taking it into their conceptual framework, seeing land and body as operating in the same ways, American settlers transformed a landscape they experienced as wild and inchoate into the familiar and understood. Employing a resonant language of healthfulness, they expressed their relationship with the natural world as simultaneously intimate and tenuous. The worldview on which they drew reflected the ambiguous and always freighted passion of the attempt to "settle"—in experience and in imagination—the early American "Far West."

AFTERWORD

Almost fifteen years ago I started work on this project as an undergraduate honors thesis. It has grown, with many changes, into this book. As a mountain climber might be thankful for rest houses and company along the way, I am grateful for all the many institutions and people who have made this a valuable and worthwhile journey.

My undergraduate work was supported by a 1988 History of Medicine Research Award from the University of Arkansas for Medical Sciences and a 1988 Golden Grant for Undergraduate Research from Stanford University. The major research for my doctoral dissertation was made possible by a 1994 Research Fellowship from the Missouri Historical Society, St. Louis.

Several major fellowships supported me through graduate school. I am grateful for a 1992 Jacob K. Javits Fellowship from the Department of Education; a 1992 Mellon Fellowship in the Humanities from the Woodrow Wilson Foundation; the 1992 Strominger Prize in the History of Medicine from the Department of the History of Science, Harvard University; and a 1997 Graduate Fellowship from the Dibner Institute for the History of Science and Technology. More recently, I have been supported by faculty research funding from Washington University in St. Louis. I am deeply and lastingly thankful for the financial support which both encouraged and made possible this intellectual pilgrimage.

I appreciate the help of the staffs of the many libraries and archives from which I gathered material: the archives of Duke University, the Missouri Botanical Garden, the University of Arkansas at Little Rock, and the University of North Carolina–Chapel Hill; the Arkansas History Commission; the Bernard Becker Medical Library and Olin Library of Washington University in St. Louis; the Historical Research Center of the University of Arkansas for Medical Sciences; and Widener Library at Harvard University. In particular, I applaud the staff of the Missouri Historical Society, St. Louis, for consistently excellent help during my initial research visit and in the years since. Lynn Morrow, director of the Local Records Division of the Missouri State Archives, graciously supplied photographs from his private collection.

Writing and research are only seemingly individual enterprises. I am glad to have this chance to acknowledge the many communities by which I have been sustained and supported, challenged and invigorated, throughout the creation and writing of this book.

I would like to acknowledge the people of Central City Hospitality House and Compass Community Services, two extraordinary organizations of San Francisco, for assisting me in my journey toward teaching and historical research. I did not know during my several years of work with those two institutions that I was figuring out the skills that I would need as a historian, but I was. They have helped me even as they help so many others who come to them day in and day out.

During my training in the Department of the History of Science at Harvard University, I learned as much from the bright and kind people about me as I did from the books that fill my shelves. The administrative staff consistently eased pragmatic challenges and made intellectual work a pleasure. For conversations, advice, citations passed back and forth, and insights and struggles shared, I particularly wish to thank fellow students Peder Anker, Richard Beyler, Hasok Chang, Alix Cooper, Karen Flood, Lara Freidenfelds, Michael Gordin, David Kaiser, Nicholas B. King, Michelle Murphy, Carl Pearson, Matt Price, Rena Selya, David Spanagel, and Nick Weiss. I am grateful to the staff and residents of Dudley Cooperative House at Harvard University, whose company I was very fortunate to share for two years.

At Harvard, I was guided by able and generous mentors. I would like to thank Gerald Holton, Barbara G. Rosenkrantz, and Sylvan S. Schweber for helping create valuable intellectual community. Everett Mendelsohn has spent many hours and conversations shepherding this project, as he has those of countless flocks of graduate students. I am grateful for his diligent care.

In my final year of graduate work, I benefited enormously from the quiet collegiality of the Dibner Institute. I appreciate the staff and directors of the institute for creating a place in which good work and invigorating conversations can take place, and I would like to thank also the colleagues with whom I shared a productive year, particularly Noah Efron, Diane Greco, and Rachel Laudan.

The last three years in the Department of History at Washington University in St. Louis have been a wonderful experience. I am grateful for the friends, colleagues, staff members, and students who have shaped and enabled my work.

Through my teaching, I have come to know and understand my historical material far better than I ever could have otherwise. I appreciate very much the insights and questions of the people it has been my privilege to have taught. In particular, Julia Fowler and other members of the seminar "Peoples and Places: Race and Environment in North America," Harvard University Department of the History of Science, spring 1999, pushed me to sharpen and reinterpret key parts of one chapter. Members of the History Writing Seminar "Sickness and Society" in the Department of History, Washington University in St. Louis, spring 2002, gave me extremely helpful suggestions on a final draft of the introduction. To them and to other students who have offered their questions, enthusiasm, and suggestions, I give my lasting thanks.

At several crucial moments, I was fortunate to share and discuss my ideas in extremely invigorating conferences. I am grateful to Nicolaas A. Rupke for the chance to contribute to the conference "Medical Geography in Historical Perspective," convened in June 1996 at Georg-August-Universität, Göttingen, and for his and other participants' suggestions, arguments, and encouragement. A number of people gave me valuable comments on two articles that I contributed to *Medical Geography in Historical Perspective*, the book that emerged from that conference. Their critiques have, I hope, been evident in much of this larger study. My particular thanks go to Jody Callisen Bresnahan, Alix Cooper, Michael Dorn, Barbara Duden, Wilbert M. Gesler, Sara Gronim, Rachel Laudan, Robert L. Martensen, Everett Mendelsohn, Michelle Murphy, Ronald L. Numbers, Charles E. Rosenberg, Vincent Vinikas, and Richard White. In 1998, I was fortunate to participate in a conference on "Body and Place," organized by Christopher Sellers at Rutgers University/New Jersey Institute of Technology. I benefited greatly from comments by Arthur F. McEvoy, Mart Stewart, and Joseph E. Taylor, III, as well as other conference participants.

I very much appreciate the suggestions and comments I have gained from presenting pieces of this project to audiences at the American Association for the History of Medicine; the American Historical Association; the American Society for Environmental History; the Department of History, Stanford University; the Department of the History and Philosophy of Medicine at the University of Kansas Medical School; the Environmental Sciences Reading Group, Harvard University; the History and Philosophy of Science Brownbag Series, Washington University in St. Louis; the History of Science Society; the Missouri Historical Society; the Nature and Culture seminar at the Hall Center for the Humanities at the University of Kansas, Lawrence; the Sciences and Cultures Workshop at Harvard's Center for Literary and Cultural Studies; and the University of Arkansas, Fayetteville. I would particularly like to acknowledge the comments and questions of the History of Medicine Working Group in the Department of the History of Science, Harvard University, to whom I presented several early chapters. I was also privileged to participate in the conference "*Naturgeschichte*/Nature's Histories," sponsored by the Max Planck Institute for the History of Science, Berlin. I am grateful to these groups and institutions for giving me the chance to present and work on the ideas in this book.

A number of scholars have contributed information, intellectual connections, and commentary. My thanks to Mario Biagioli, Charlotte Borst, Michael Brodhead, Leslie Brown, Theodore Feldman, Anne Harrington, Margaret Humphreys, Vladimir Jankovic, Alan Kraut, Jeffrey Moran, Linda Nash, William R. Newman, Katharine Park, Karen Reeds, Steven Shapin, Werner Sollors, Keith Wailoo, and George Yatskiebych.

Individual chapters have been shaped by the comments, criticism, and suggestions of colleagues to whom I am pleased to offer my thanks: Katherine Anderson, Harriet Deacon, Rebecca Herzig, Nicholas B. King, Lisa Lynch, Barbara Rosenkrantz, David Spanagel, Richard White, and Donald Worster. A number of my Washington University colleagues have read and given me valuable comments on this manuscript in its entirety. I have benefited greatly from detailed and very helpful comments by Iver Bernstein, Richard Davis, Derek M. Hirst, David Konig, and Kenneth Ludmerer.

From initial drafts to final polishing, Deborah F. Weinstein has lent a discerning eye and good sense to many parts of this book. My father, S. Charles Bolton, has read every chapter (several times over!) with care and enthusiasm. With unlooked-for generosity and unflagging insight, Ari Kelman offered a detailed reading of a penultimate draft of the entire manuscript. His comments not only strengthened the substance of this work but gave me energy for the final lap.

I have a lasting debt to the labors, counsel, and sustaining friendship of Lisa M. Herschbach. I am grateful for her readings of many drafts over many years, as well as for all the other ways in which she has helped me and this project. As both colleague and close friend, Corinna Treitel combined careful and constructive criticism about this entire project with goodwill that knew no bounds. Corinna's thoughtfulness and imagination about history, her humor and perspective, her enduring friendship, and her plain good sense mark this work throughout.

David S. Barnes read and advised my Ph.D. thesis with a fine attention to language and writing, and with a well-honed perspective on historical argument and historical work. In similarly pervasive ways, Warwick Anderson's critiques, advice, and beautifully literate scholarship have profoundly shaped my thinking and this book. Peter L. Galison advised the undergraduate thesis that brought me to the work of history, and many years later he helped devise the final title of this book. Those are fitting bookends to many years of sustaining interest, argument, and mentorship for which I am enduringly grateful.

I am honored to offer great thanks to my graduate adviser, Allan M. Brandt. I deeply appreciate his guidance as my adviser and his example of engaged intellectual life. His comments on my arguments and on my writing invariably go to the heart of the matter: with discerning care, he has helped hone and refine the essence of this work. Allan Brandt sets a model of well grounded and humane scholarship which it is my hope to sustain and follow.

In the final stages of this project, it has been my immense good fortune to work with editors of rare insight at Basic Books. Don Fehr took on this project, shaped it, and pushed me to write in ways slightly more open and flexible than usual academic prose. To the process of editing and revising the final manuscript, Sarah McNally brought a gracious sensitivity of language, a generous sympathy for the arguments and goals of this book, and an unerring sense for the flow of prose and arguments. I am grateful for the chance to have worked with such fine people.

Outside my academic world, friends and relatives have enabled this project and taken very good care of me. Generous friends David and Angela Melson opened their home to me during my research trips to St. Louis, introducing me to a city I have come to love. For conversations, adventures, good meals, and all the essential stuff of life, I am thankful to a host of friends. Chief among them are Paulo Frank, Véronique Mauron, and Laura Frank; Jennifer Fraulo; Adam and Mara Goldman; Edward A. and Margaret C. Handy; Anja, Holger, Hannah, and Esther Kappe; Ashish Karamchandani, Vibha Krishnamurthy, and Kabir and Karun Karamchandani; Pauline Kleingeld, Joel Anderson, and Jonah and Esther Anderson; John and Irene Kochevar; James Mokhiber; Magnus Nordborg; Elizabeth A. Oyler; Mark S. Weiner and Stephanie Kuduk; and Lilla Vekerdy.

I am blessed with wonderful family. My siblings Jesse D. Bolton and Rebecca May Judge have been for me a continual source of encouragement and perspective. Though Becca is no longer willing—as she was at age eleven—to photocopy archival materials all morning in exchange for a cheeseburger and fries at lunch, her interest and praise, and Jesse's, have at every turn helped along this project. I am grateful for the unfailing support and encouragement of my extended Bolton, Hughes, May, Sullivan, and Valenčius families, and especially Janet E. Bolton, Catherine F. Conway, Sally Hughes (my dear Grams), Paul and Marilyn Valenčius, and Shannan Venable. I am honored to acknowledge John Valenčius, Sr., whose many recollections of a long life well lived are a constant reminder to me of the power of telling stories about the past. Most recently, I am delighted to welcome Lillie Jean Bolton—and look forward to seeing how her story unfolds.

For many years I have relied upon the steadfast care and supportive partnership of Matthew Gregory Valenčius. Among all his other labors, Matt always insists on our living a full life, no matter what lectures have to be written or footnotes researched. For all this—and most of all, and most simply, for bringing a constant joy into my life—I offer my great and glad thanks. Ilan Valenčius is not yet old enough to understand what the fuss is all about when he tries to gnaw through the power strip of my computer, but he is a blessing beyond measure.

Finally, I owe my parents my deepest and most lasting gratitude. Charlie Bolton has nurtured me and this book with good advice, careful reading, numerous citations, constant support, and his own scholarly work. I am proud to be following in my father's craft. Susie May has sustained me throughout this project with her unstinting encouragement, her characteristic ebullience, her pragmatic perspective (and excellent cooking!), and, in recent months, her cheerful baby-sitting. I see her creative energy in my own efforts, and am grateful for that inheritance. Cleve May's praise for an early article was a pivotal moment as I began work on my Ph.D. thesis: hearing his interest, I knew I could do this, and I knew it was what I wanted to do. From late-night math lessons in junior high to support and good humor more recently, he has helped forge the interest and discipline that have produced this project. In these and so many other ways, my parents have launched and sustained me throughout my life. It is to them that this work is dedicated.

St. Louis, Missouri
February 2002

ARCHIVAL INFORMATION AND ABBREVIATIONS

―――――――――

Archives

AHC   . . . .Arkansas History Commission, Little Rock

DUA   . . . .Duke University Archives, Durham, N.C.

MBG   . . . .Missouri Botanical Garden, St. Louis

MHS . . . . .Missouri Historical Society, St. Louis

UAMS   . . .University of Arkansas for Medical Sciences Historical Research Center, Little Rock

UALR . . . .University of Arkansas at Little Rock Archives and Special Collections

UNC   . . . .University of North Carolina at Chapel Hill, Archives, Southern Historical Collection

Abbreviations

The following abbreviations are used in the Notes.

ASFN   . . . .Aaron S. Fry Notebook (1833–45), MHS

AWW . . . .A. W. Webb (1844), "An account of the Intermittent and Remittent Fevers of Arkansas from Observations Made during Ten years practice in the County of Chicot," in "Medical Notes and Reflections" (original unpaginated, page numbers added), UAMS

AWWN   . .A. W. Webb notebook (undated) of "Medical Notes and Reflections" (original unpaginated, page numbers added), UAMS

BFP   . . . . .Ball Family Papers, Small Manuscripts Collection (box 2), AHC

BeFP . . . . .Belcher Family Papers, MHS

BP   . . . . . .Baker Papers, UNC

CFMN . . . .Charles F. M. Noland Family Correspondence, Heiskell Small Manuscripts, UALR

CFP . . . . .Cordell Family Papers (1849–50), MHS

CGC . . . .Caleb Green Collection, MHS

CoxFP . . .Cox Family Papers (1818–72), MHS

EGBP . . . .Edwin G. Baker Papers, UNC

EGPMB . . .Eliza G. Post Memorandum Books (1815–58), MHS

ESJ . . . . . .Ellen Stetson Journal, Small Manuscripts Collection (box 18, file 2), AHC

GDKAF . .Gottlieb and Dorothea Klein Alphabetical Files, MHS

GEP . . . . .George Engelmann Papers, Correspondence with Daniel Drake, MBG

HBD . . . . .Henry Bousfield Diary (transcript), Journals and Diaries Collection (box 1, 1775–1839), MHS

HSM . . . . .Heiskell Small Manuscripts, UALR

int. . . . . . .interviewed by

ISMN . . .Ichabod Sargeant Medical Notebook (1816; original unpaginated, page numbers added), Jules F. Valle Collection (1773–1918), MHS

JCBP . . . .John C. Barrow Papers (1854–62), AHC

JDC . . . . .Journals and Diaries Collection, MHS

JFVC . . . .Jules F. Valle Collection (1773–1918), MHS

JJB . . . . .Journal of John Brown (1852–62, original and typescript), Heiskell Small Manuscripts, UALR

JJCDAB . .John J. Clendenin Diary and Account Book (1829–60), Small Manuscripts Collection (box 3), AHC

JJG . . . . .Journal of John Geiger (original and transcript), Journals and Diaries Collection (box 1, 1775–1839), MHS

JJWL . . . .John J. Walker Letters, MHS

JJWP . . . .James Josiah Webb Papers, MHS

JLTC . . . .John L. Trone Collection, UNC

JMD . . . . .Joseph Meetch Diary, Heiskell Small Manuscripts, UALR

JMJP . . . .John M. Jarrell Papers, DUA

JPP . . . . . .Justus Post Papers (1807–21), MHS

JTAC . . . .James Trooper Armstrong Collection, UNC

JWS . . . . .Journal of William Switzler, UALR

KC . . . . . .Knight Collection, AHC

MESD . . . .Mary E. Smith Diary, Journals and Diaries Collection (box 1, 1775–1839), MHS

MFJPP . . .Mary Frances Jane Pursley Papers, DUA

MFP . . . . .Mullanphy Family Papers, MHS

MLC . . . .Miscellaneous Letters Collection, UALR

NDAD . . .N. D. Allen Diary (1834–88), MHS

PFL . . . . .Potts Family Letters (1823–52), Small Manuscripts Collection (box 43), AHC
PRC . . . . .Philip Rainey Collection, UNC
RWTC . . .Robert Wilson Trimble Collection, AHC
SFM . . . .Scarborough Family Manuscripts, DUA
SFP . . . . .Sappington Family Papers, MHS
SHC . . . . .Southern Historical Collection, UNC
SHP . . . . .Stephen Hempstead Papers, MHS
SMC . . . . .Small Manuscripts Collection, AHC
SSWFC . . .Samuel Spotts Wassell Family Collection, AHC
StFP . . . . .Stephens Family Papers, MHS
SwFP . . . .Switzler Family Papers, MHS
TKHD . . .Thomas K. Humphreys Diary, MHS
TWC . . . .Thomas Wheat Collection, UNC
WBSS . . . .W. B. Stevens Scrapbook, MHS
WC . . . . .Washburn Collection, AHC
WEWP . . .William E. Woodruff Papers, AHC
WFSP . . . .William F. Switzler Papers, AHC
WLC . . . .William Ludlow Collection (1838–60), AHC
WSFP . . . .William Savin Fulton Papers, AHC

NOTES

Abbreviations used in the Notes are listed on pages 271–73.

Introduction: "Healthy Country"

1 . . . . **Justus Post's hopes:** Foley, "Justus Post," especially 25–26; and Justus Post, St. Louis, to John Post, Addison, Vt., 19 Aug. 1815, and ibid., 11 Aug. 1816. Journals left by Eliza G. Randolph Post say much less about why she moved or what she thought of Missouri, though a few comments imply that it was her husband's optimism, not her own, that pulled the family west (EGPMB).

1 . . . . **"I see nothing to hinder":** Justus Post, St. Louis, to John Post, Addison, Vt., 26 Nov. 1815. **"a healthy section":** ibid., 19 Aug. 1816. **"this is a healthy country":** ibid., 7 Oct. 1817 (similar assertions, 23 Aug. 1816). **John and Elizabeth Post's emigration:** See the biography of their son Erastus Post in Thomas, 208.

2 . . . . **letters connecting families:** See "The Lowell Letter," a similar letter between an emigrated brother and one back in northern New England. **letters in nineteenth-century life:** Hedrick, 77–82; Zboray.

2 . . . . **historical works on prior eras' understanding of health:** Historians have recognized travel for health as a powerful force in many eras of American life (see sources for Chapter 3), yet few have examined the underlying logic that made places "healthy." Some who have: Cassedy, "Medical Men"; Dobson, "Health and the Environment in Early Modern England," in Wear.

2 . . . . **common sense:** As the anthropologist Clifford Geertz has insightfully argued ("Common Sense as a Cultural System," in Geertz, *Local Knowledge*), common sense is a kind of knowledge whose main characteristic is to deny its own construction. James Keefe and Lynn Morrow observe about a nineteenth-century story about hunting in the Ozarks that "not everyone knew or participated in all aspects of folk culture, any more than everyone knew about the techniques of making and setting live traps." To say that something was "common sense" or "common belief" is not to argue that it was ubiquitous in an absolute sense. It is, rather, to identify that belief, that practice, or that way of imagining and speaking about the world as something widely shared by many people. Keefe and Morrow, *White River Chronicles*, 301, n. 63.

3 . . . . **borderlands:** The term is vague by intention, suggesting the amorphous and flexible conceptions of region and nation within which antebellum Americans lived and moved. **Civil War:** I end there, but ideas linking person and place certainly did not. Anderson, *Cultivation of Whiteness,* discusses these environmental ideas in the very different medical world of the late nineteenth and twentieth centuries.

4 . . . . **"health" in evaluations of land:** Cleary, 71; M. O. Jones; Merrens and Terry. **"owing to the bad health of the place":** TKHD, 17 Dec. 1835. Another potential emigrant seeking advice about whether he should move to Missouri asked, "Is it thriving & healthy?" L. D. Pitts, Westmoreland, Va., to Meredith M. Marmaduke, Jonesboro, Mo., 6 Dec. 1831, box 2, 1830–38, SFP. **"320 acres of land in some healthy place":** "Meet Me in St. Louis—1819," 182. **"said to be healthy":** Cynthia Thrall, Dwight Mission, Ark., to Lydia [Shinn], 29 Sept. 1828, Cynthia Thrall Correspondence, 1828, box 23, number 16, SMC.

5 . . . . **newcomers' perceptions:** These are only one part of a larger story; health fears have also frequently been directed *against* new immigrants. See Kraut.

5 . . . . **health challenges of "new" regions:** One useful overview is Faragher, *Sugar Creek,* Chapter 10. **"All the year round":** Skinner, 262.

5 . . . . **nutritional deficiencies:** Kiple and King, 117–33 (many of their conclusions would also apply to white people of the era). **perils of childbirth:** High fertility brought risks. In Arkansas in 1840, the number of children under ten for every thousand women aged 16 to 44 was 43% higher than in the U.S. as a whole. S. C. Bolton, *Territorial Ambition,* 80–83. **"afflictive providence":** Jensen, Part 7, 27 Sept. 1823, 75. Hempstead was referring to a farm accident that killed a neighborhood boy.

5 . . . . **governmental concern:** For example, secretary of war, Washington, D.C., to Daniel Bissell, 24 April 1804, in Carter, vol. 13, 20. **"For the last three days":** John Henry, New Orleans, to Les Williams, Van Buren, Ark., 24 Feb. 1857, series 2, file 14, MLC.

6 . . . . **diseases:** Patterson (See also sources for Chapter 2.) **malaria:** Ackerknecht, *Malaria;* Humphreys. **mortality during 1849 cholera outbreak:** Adler, 99. The previous cholera epidemic, in 1832, had killed 5% of the city's population. Corbett, *In Her Place,* 43. **cholera epidemics:** See Rosenberg, *Cholera Years.* **in Arkansas and Missouri:** "Cholera Epidemics in St. Louis," 1936; Joan Cooper, "The Cholera Epidemic of 1849," in Corbett, *In Her Place,* 52–54; McLear; Roth. **"obliged to leave Church":** MESD, 13 March 1836. This may not have been so bad a day: Mary Smith and her best friend commonly used any excuse to get out of attending services—especially when that meant they could stay in their boarding-school parlor and read novels while pretending to peruse religious tracts.

6 . . . . **diseases prevalent in a region:** "Sore eyes may be mentioned as a prevailing disease of the western states. . . . Dyspepsia, and liver complaints of a chronic kind, are troublesome maladies in the Mississippi states, especially in the cities" (Baird, *Valley of the Mississippi,* 86). **debates over healthfulness:** The historian M. H. Dunlop (182–84) has noted that arguments over "which landscape markers spoke of disease and which of health" invariably marked American incursion into regions with which they were unfamiliar.

6 . . . . **"uncommonly unhealthy":** Brackenridge, 112.

7 . . . . **"as far as James is conserned:** Vesta P. Stevenson to "Dear Mother," ca. 1850, series 2, box 1, file 9, MLC. **Homesick kisses:** Like the inked-in smooch sent by James J. Webb, Santa Fe, to Lillie Webb, Cornwall Bridge, Conn., 8 June 1856, JJWP.

7 . . . . **sources on slave life:** Useful reflections on our sources on the region's enslaved people include Katherine Douglass, "Elizabeth," in Corbett, *In Her Place,* 36–37; McLaurin; Seematter.

8 . . . . **Federal Writers' Project ex-slave interviews:** George Rawick thoughtfully discusses these issues in his introduction (Rawick, *American Slave,* vol. 1). Other sources from the 1920s and '30s, including regional folklore collections like the pioneering work of Vance Randolph in the Ozarks and the WPA state guides, provide some context for the reports of former slaves collected in those same years (Randolph, *Ozark-Mountain Folks,* Randolph and Wilson, *Down in the Holler;* WPA, *Missouri;* and ibid., *Arkansas*). **stereotyped dialect:** I give quotations directly as rendered. Deleting all stereotyped vocabulary might also bleach out some of the rich use of language that makes the interviews both compelling and complex narratives. The inclusion of writings by nineteenth-century white migrants, many of whom spelled phonetically, demonstrates the ubiquity of regional accents. **Arkansas records:** More interviews were conducted there than in any other state, and they offer less evidence of selective suppression than in other states. George Rawick, who collected and edited the WPA interviews, notes that Irene Robertson and Bernice Bowden transcribed interviews without exaggerated and stereotyped dialect. Two Arkansas interviewers, Samuel S. Taylor and Parnella Anderson, were themselves African Americans and were also active workers in the Little Rock Urban League. The program director, Bernie Babcock, despite her own prejudices, was an active supporter of black civil rights in Arkansas, and she worked to get private publication for the autobiography of Charles Williams, quoted in Chapter 9. See Rawick, *American Slave,* Supplement 1, Part 2, liv–lv and xli, and Supplement 2, Part 1, i–iii.

8 . . . . **account of French missionary:** "Voyage of du Poisson," from *Early Jesuit Missions in North America,* trans. Rev. W. J. Kip, Part 2, 232–52, in Drake, *A Systematic Treatise,* 111–21. Copyright laws were extremely weak, so reprinting passages—or, indeed, whole books—was unlikely to result in any legal action.

8 . . . . **hunting stories:** For instance, Gerstäcker; Keefe and Morrow, *A Connecticut Yankee;* ibid., *White River Chronicles;* J. Miller; Noland, *Pete Whetstone of Devil's Fork;* Pike. **Hunting:** Slaves also hunted in the woods and marshes of Missouri and Arkansas. See McNeilly, 148.

9 . . . . **Transnational roots:** Carney; D. Hall; Stewart, "Rice, Water, and Power"; Tyrrell.

10 . . . . **"The Young Schoolmaster":** J. W. Miller, 166–200.

10 . . . . **wilderness and American self-imagining:** See R. Nash. This concept is still slippery; see Cronon, *Uncommon Ground,* especially his introduction, for trenchant critiques of the "wild." **land "unused" for agriculture:** Much of the land they took had, of course, been farmed for centuries. I write this not far from the mounds of Cahokia, Illinois, where the largest urban center north of Mexico City, nourished on corn and at the center of vast, intercontinental trade routes, flourished during the European Middle Ages (see Iseminger). Nonetheless, both European and American migrants thought that territory in the vast middle of North America had not been used agriculturally as they intended to use it, and their

perceptions of land as new to settled cultivation are an important element of their territorial capture.

10 . . . . **political virtue of farming:** As exemplified in Jefferson, *Notes on the State of Virginia*.

10 . . . . **process that was essentially *American*:** I therefore include as "American" both people born in the United States and those who had recently immigrated. Their projects, too, were bound up with what they saw as an "American" destiny.

11 . . . . **scientific authority and scientific work:** Biagioli; Galison; Shapin, *Social History of Truth;* Shapin and Schaffer. **applying questions developed by historians of science to environmental history:** This approach is also influenced by recent moves in the history of science toward a recognition of the importance of physical environments in understanding how scientific work is done and scientific knowledge made (especially Ophir and Shapin, "The Place of Knowledge,"; ibid., "House of Experiment.").

12 . . . . **surrounding world seeped into newcomers' every pore:** The mutual porosity of people and the places they inhabit has begun to be developed by environmental historians, especially Sellers; Murphy, "Sick Buildings and Sick Bodies"; ibid., "The 'Elsewhere within Here' and Environmental Illness"; ibid., "Toxicity in the Details"; Nash, "Disease."

12 . . . . **environmental interventions of Native American groups:** Cronon, *Changes in the Land;* White and Cronon; Key. **Shopping malls:** Price, Chapter 4. **interpenetration of "natural" and created worlds:** Cronon, *Nature's Metropolis;* Fiege; J. Taylor; R. White, *Organic Machine*.

13 . . . . **Justus Post's demise, Eliza Post's lonely old age:** Foley, "Justus Post"; "Eliza G. Post," 26 Dec. 1876, probably from the Missouri *Republican,* WBSS, 25.

14 . . . . **"Do the people in your quarter?":** Justus Post, St. Louis, to John Post, Addison, Vt., 3 June 1816, JPP.

Chapter I: "New Country"

15 . . . . **"movers":** Pope, 207, 210. The term was apparently such a typical Americanism that Nicholas Hesse retained it in his descriptive guide for German immigrants. Bek, "Nicholas Hesse," Part 1, 34. **"improvers":** Flint, *First White Man,* 103.

15 . . . . **overlapping migrations:** Westward migration was just one among many across North America, including movements south to north, by displaced Native Americans, and north to south, by those in the Spanish Empire. On these often conflicting movements, see West.

16 . . . . ***"Arkansas was a perfect terra incognita":*** Park, 70.

16 . . . . **"organised":** "Documents: John C. Luttig, Pork Bayou, Ark., to Christian Wilt, 16 April 1815," 154.

16 . . . . **"Far West":** Embodied in the title of Gerstäcker's title, *Wild Sports in the Far West.* **"Two hundred miles west of the Mississippi":** Blowe, 665. **Even St. Louis on the edge of wilderness:** Adler, 47.

16 . . . . **"the moon":** Justus Post, St. Louis, to John Post, Addison, Vt., 24 Dec. 1815, JPP. **"Our land is of good quality":** Kirkbride Potts, Galley Creek, Pope Co., Ark., to Ann

Potts, Bordentown, N.J., 1 July 1830, PFL, 1823–52. **"new country":** James Miller, Post of Arkansas, to Mrs. Ruth Miller, 20 March 1820, box "A-O," file "Miller," RWTC.

17 . . . . **"your ideas of a *new country*":** Robert F. Henry to J. F. Henry, 12 Sept. 1819, box 2, file 64, HSM.

17 . . . . **"a wild, romantic region"; "In my judgement":** Everard B. Dickinson, Buffalo City, to Mr. and Mrs. Philo Dickinson, Hartford, Conn., 22 Sept. 1848, box 1, folder 54, HSM. **"This Wild and new Country suits me first rate":** Ibid., North Fork, Izard Co., Ark., to Mr. and Mrs. Philo Dickinson, Springfield, Mass., 22 June 1849. **"This is a healthy Country":** Ibid., 21 June 1850. After this letter, both Dickinson and his parents stayed put.

17 . . . . **"a hireling and a slave" and subsequent descriptions:** Ibid., 22 Sept. 1848, HSM.

18 . . . . **"I may Go to *Calafornia*":** Ibid., 21 June 1850, HSM. For a fascinating fictional account of Dickinson's experiences, see Harington, 150–56.

18 . . . . **"republican constitution":** Bek, "Nicholas Hesse," Part 7, 242. **Turner:** Faragher, *Frederick Jackson Turner.*

18 . . . . **Hunting and "wild" lands:** See, for example, Gerstäcker; J. W. Miller.

19 . . . . **Need to domesticate "wilderness":** Kolodny, *Land Before Her.* **"no rural walk":** ESJ, 11 Dec. 1821. Stetson's determination was apparently equal to her occasional discouragement: she remained with the Dwight Mission until her death in 1850. Ross, "Letters of Hiram Abiff Whittington," 55, n. 27.

19 . . . . **"I have settled my self":** Owen Maguire and Mary Maguire, Washington Co., Ark., to Samuel and Sally Clark, Montgomery Co., N.C., 18 Sept. 1836, SFM. Mary and Owen Maguire went on to establish themselves as a prominent family in their northwest Arkansas county. Sizemore, 164, 177.

19 . . . . **"will become of importance":** "Arkansas Territory."

19 . . . . **"perceptual environments":** I take that evocative phrase from Merrens and Terry. Other insightful investigations of the perceptual environments of the nineteenth century: Dunlop; Heat Moon, *PrairyErth;* Nash, "Changing Experience of Nature"; Schama; Winsor.

20 . . . . **no railroads in country's interior before midcentury:** In 1859, the Hannibal & St. Joseph line reached St. Joseph, on the western edge of the state. Schneiders, 58.

20 . . . . **Sight lines limited:** Even in the late twentieth century, "in the Arkansas Ozarks one generally experiences limited visibility and a sense of enclosure by woodlands, hills, mountains, and above all, ever-encroaching vegetation" (Sizemore, *Ozark Vernacular Houses,* 133). **Grasses taller than a person:** Christisen, "A Vignette of Missouri's Native Prairie," 172. In this sense, many current renditions of land—bird's-eye views and aerial photographs which present to the eye a constructed, coherent overall plan—are a historical artifact from our time, and are not representative of how people of the early nineteenth century could envision land.

20 . . . . **"difficulty of hunting":** Joseph Paxton and Thomas Mathers, Little Rock, Ark. Terr., to John C. Calhoun, 12 Feb. 1825, in Carter, vol. 19, 771. **topography resisted surveyors' efforts:** Near present-day Magnet Cove, Arkansas, deposits of lodestone near the soil's surface made compass needles frenetic. WPA, *Arkansas,* 328; Featherstonhaugh, "Geology of

Arkansas," 11 Aug. 1835. **Geometries of order:** Nobles; Stegner, 81–85 and 97–99; Stilgoe, 99–107.

21 . . . . **earthquakes:** M. Ross, "New Madrid Earthquake."

21 . . . . **prairies:** Christisen; Foti, "The Grand Prairie"; Peacock. **foods:** The *Arkansas Gazette* in 1834 published a list of recipes because "[s]o little seems to be known about the various methods of cooking rice." "Rice Delicacies," *Arkansas Gazette*. On Germans' yearning for the potato, see Bek, "Nicholas Hesse," Part 1, 38.

21 . . . . **parrots:** Lottinville, 67. **local fauna generally:** L. Hall; Sealander; Shepherd; Sutton. **"pole-cats":** Audubon, 67. **wild animals as pets:** Ellen Briggs Thompson, Little Rock, int. Samuel S. Taylor, in Rawick, vol. 10, Part 6, 313; Bek, "The Followers of Duden, Fourteenth Article," 221; Keefe and Morrow, *White River Chronicles*, 72. **suckling-the-ear-lobe trick:** Ibid., *A Connecticut Yankee*, , 207–8.

21 . . . . **"Eat up Evry green leaf":** Jensen, Part 8, 1 Sept. 1827, 191. Staffers at the Missouri Botanical Garden helpline inform me that it's not certain which pest this is; a number of very hungry caterpillars continue to plague Missouri gardeners.

22 . . . . **Acclimation:** Though most historians have used "acclimatization," common reference in the American nineteenth century was most frequently to "seasoning" and "acclimation" (also "naturalization," "acclimatization," "habituation," or "climature"). Webster, s.v. "acclimated." "climature": Caldwell, 361.

22 . . . . **"Well, go on":** Flint, *Recollections*, 207.

22 . . . . **The shock of the new:** I take the phrase from Hughes, *The Shock of the New.*

22 . . . . **"object I have in view":** Timothy Flint, Cincinnati, to Stephen Hempstead, St. Louis, 29 Dec. 1815, box 2, SHP. **notion of region-based constitution:** Monette, 89.

22 . . . . **experience of seasoning:** To date this concept has been dealt with primarily in terms of Europeans' experience in tropical colonies and military theaters, especially in the latter nineteenth century. See Anderson, "Climates of Opinion," "Disease, Race, and Empire," "Immunities of Empire," "Geography, Race and Nation," and "The Trespass Speaks"; Kennedy, "Climates of Concern" and "Perils of the Mid-day Sun"; Livingstone, "Human Acclimatization"; Renbourn, "Seasoning Fluxes and Fevers"; ibid., "Solar Topi." Contemporary historians continue to use "seasoning" as an explanatory tool even as they situate the notion historically. Kupperman, 220–21; Savitt. **"In whatever latitude":** Collins, "Further Thoughts on Climate," 458. **"adaptive powers":** Scoffern, 181.

23 . . . . **"The farmer who suddenly":** G. Duden, 246.

23 . . . . **"Seasoning" and European settlement:** Morgan, 158–59; Kulikoff, 33.

24 . . . . **"Emigrants generally suffer":** Flint, *Recollections*, 128.

24 . . . . **"a slight touch of the fever":** John J. Walker, St. Louis, to Thomas H. Walker, Brownsburgh, Rockbridge Co., Va., 18 Feb. 1835, JJWL.

24 . . . . **"ague" and "chills and fever":** The seasoning illnesses borne by newcomers to the Mississippi Valley undoubtedly represented a wide assortment of ailments, but malaria was certainly chief among them. Acclimation could also be identified with a number of other specific ailments. Dr. George Hunter noted that in New Orleans, "my Son was violently attacked with an Ardent Bilous fever commonly called the seasoning to the Country" (McDermott, "Western Journals," 62). **malaria as introduction to the frontier:**

Humphreys, *Malaria*, 30–36. **family experience of "shakes":** Keefe and Morrow, *A Connecticut Yankee*, 87.

24 . . . . **"preternaturally excited":** Flint, *Recollections*, 129. **separate countries of wellness and ill health:** Sontag, 1.

25 . . . . **"The chance for an unacclimated young man":** Flint, *Recollections*, 300. **"wholesome—cleanly manner":** Everard B. Dickinson, North Fork, Ark., to Mr. and Mrs. Philo Dickinson, Springfield, Mass., 21 June 1850, box 1, file 54, HSM.

25 . . . . **partial immunity to malaria:** Humphreys, *Malaria*, 19. **acclimation and modern immunology:** Even if modern understanding of immunology coincides with certain aspects of nineteenth-century people's reports, we still need to explain in their terms why those people thought something was so.

25 . . . . **"not much sickness or cholera amongst the old & acclimated:"** William H. Belcher, St. Louis, to Nathan Belcher, New London, Conn., 21 May 1849, BeFP. Another account of the 1849 epidemic similarly stressed that "the whole number of deaths reported from Cholera was 4905. . . . probably Seven Eights of all were foreigners." NDAD. **"those long resident in the locality":** Goulding, 327.

26 . . . . **"I was a frightful and squalid object":** Park, 82. **"my feebleness":** Flint, *Recollections*, 374.

26 . . . . **"Doctor Farrar, of St. Louis":** Levine, 138. **red cheeks:** J. W. Miller, 173.

26 . . . . **"My family had the ague":** Flint, *Recollections*, 274.

27 . . . . **"I had many friends":** Flint, *Recollections*, 307.

27 . . . . **"Your family should come in the fall":** Justus Post, St. Louis, to John Post, Addison, Vt., 3 June 1816, JPP, MHS.

27 . . . . **"in the heat of summer":** Drake, *Natural and Statistical View*, 181.

28 . . . . **"[N]atives of New-England and New-York" and subsequent advice:** Ibid., 181.

28 . . . . **recommendations for successful acclimation:** See, for example, Caldwell, 367–72. **Keep to former habits; solicit advice of residents:** Ticknor, "Climate and Season," 262. This recommendation of heeding "native" inhabitants was also characteristic of broader discussion of acclimation. See Anderson, "Disease, Race, and Empire," 64. **"Prevention":** Flint, *History and Geography* (1833), 39.

28 . . . . **"period of probation":** Bek, "The Followers of Duden," 492.

29 . . . . **"truly none but our hardy sun burnt pioneers":** "Journal of Henry B. Miller," 252.

29 . . . . **"water which is used for drink" and warning:** J. E. White, 355.

29 . . . . **"Persons coming here":** A[masa] and R[oxana] Jones Harmony, Mo., to Timothy Stearns, Ashburnham, Worcester Co., Mass., 23 May 1837, in Bronaugh, 391. **Grasslands as ocean:** Dunlap.

29 . . . . **plant (and animal) acclimation:** Anderson, "Climates of Opinion"; Dunlap; Koerner, "Linnaeus' Floral Transplants"; Koerner, *Linnaeus: Nature and Nation*, especially 113–39; and Osborne, "A Collaborative Dimension of the European Empires." On the Colonial-era conviction that plants, like people, change their characteristics when moved, see Kupperman, 229. **"naturalized" vegetation:** Goulding, 324.

30 . . . . **"But we well know":** Flint, *Recollections*, 236.

30 . . . . **"Oxen have been known to travel":** Anderson, "Missouri, 1804–1828," 172.

30 . . . . **"a set of northern & eastern people":** Justus Post, St. Louis, to John Post, Addison, Vt., 19 Aug. 1816, JPP.

30 . . . . **earth underwent transformation:** This idea is in sharp contrast with later portrayals of acclimation in the American Philippines. There, it was tied to the refinement and therefore vulnerability of educated, advanced, and thus sensitive whites and depended on their maintaining distance from potentially lethal "native" bodies and "degenerate" habits of life. Anderson, "Immunities of Empire" and "The Trespass Speaks."

31 . . . . **"Eduard Dunn":** JJCDAB, 25 Sept. 1836.

31 . . . . **"I have earthly love" and subsequent diary entries:** Jervey and Moss, 173, 193, 195.

32 . . . . **"I want to teach school awhile":** Ibid., 205. **"slow typhoid fever":** Ibid., 206. James McClure finished Elizabeth's diary on the day of her death, as Stephen Hempstead's kin finished his (see Chapter 2). Families frequently ended such journals with an often eloquent notation about the time and manner of the diarist's death.

32 . . . . **"emigrations to this or any other country":** Justus Post, St. Louis, to John Post, Addison, Vt., 23 Aug. 1816, JPP.

33 . . . . **Justus Post's ambitions:** Foley, "Justus Post." **Land speculation in westward movement:** Adler, 19–22; A. Taylor.

33 . . . . **tremulousness:** Schlissel.

34 . . . . **tales of backwoods adventure:** Works like James Fenimore Cooper's "Leatherstocking Tales" thus appear throughout this work, as literary background to the activities described in the text. **regional boosterism and promotional literature:** Adler, especially Chapter 3; Boorstin, 124–34 and 296–98; Dunlop; P. Gates, 188–92; Merrens; and Schnell and Clinton.

34 . . . . **Timothy Flint:** C. Hartley Grattan, introduction to Flint, *Recollections*, vi–xii; Frapp, 500–501. **Abigail Flint:** On her school, see Jensen, Part 3, 12 April 1817, 63. She was a relative of Joseph Peabody, a wealthy Salem merchant (Grattan, introduction to Flint, *Recollections*, vi). **delivery of child amid storm:** Flint *Recollections*, 275–77.

35 . . . . **Boone biography:** Flint, *First White Man*. **Impact:** Final chapter of Faragher, *Daniel Boone*. **Rehashing of Flint's guidebooks:** Adler, 54 and 202–3, n. 106.

36 . . . . **"Duden has written truthfully":** Hermann Steines, letter, 8 Nov. 1833, in Bek, "Followers of Duden: First Article," 60; see also Steines's letter from Baltimore, 16 July 1833, in ibid., 52. Joan D. Hedrick observes that women's letters and parlor literature functioned as women's emigration guides, making intelligible new places for travelers and migrants (see Hedrick, Chapter 8).

36 . . . . **truly awful poetry:** For instance, Cottle.

36 . . . . **Noland's writings as typical:** Bolton, *Remote and Restless,* Chapter 5. See the bibliography for a listing of Noland's writings. Noland's style of sometimes bawdy, sometimes buffoonish regional humor would later cut with a sharp edge in the works of Mark Twain. See Boorstin, 334–35, and Hauck. **prolific personal violence:** As a young child, the Cherokee

emigrant John Rollin Ridge wrote to a family friend that in Fayetteville, in northwest Arkansas, "the people sometimes fight with knives and pistols, and some men have been killed here, but the people do not seem to mind it much" (quoted in Parins, 35). **in regional perceptions:** Cochran, "Hanged by His Friends"; ibid., "'Low, Degrading Scoundrels': George W. Featherstonhaugh's Contribution to the Bad Name of Arkansas"; C. F. Williams.

36 . . . . **Noland's writings:** In addition to his listed works, he may well also have written "Arkansas—Her Products—Inviting Emigration." The varied accounts in eastern newspapers represented a battle over the development of the borderlands waged where it most counted, in the opinion of the eastern public most likely to move or send their dollars there. Adler, 43.

37 . . . . **"It does appear as if all Kentucky":** Justus Post, St. Louis, to John Post, Addison, Vt., 20 Nov. 1816, JPP. **"The Douglasses":** Stanley, 154. Examining early American trans-Appalachian movements, Malcolm J. Rohrbaugh has argued that institutions, especially military posts, were established first, and settlers filled in around them (*The Trans-Appalachian Frontier*). Sources from early Arkansas and Missouri, however, reflect more informal, *ad hoc* settlement by bands of migrants connected by kinship or former place of residence, and the subsequent building up around them of governmental structures: it is much more the kind of process recognized by John Mack Faragher in *Sugar Creek*, his study of an Illinois town over the same period.

37 . . . . **German immigrants to Missouri:** Gerlach; Nagel, *Missouri*, 95–100; Rafferty, *Historical Atlas*, sections 33–39.

38 . . . . **"every town has":** Gregory, 117.

38 . . . . **"This day 19 years ago":** Jensen, Part 9, 13 June 1830, 430. **Young men emigrating first:** "In 1833 My Mother moved to Arkansas and lived with me until her death." J. W. Calvert, St. Francis Co., Ark., to John L. Trone, 29 July 1851, JLTC. **surveying and American apprehension of "new" places:** Faragher, *Sugar Creek*, 39–40. Joan Cashin (*A Family Venture*) has argued that emigration in the nineteenth century often increased the autonomy of younger male family members; for a counterargument about the importance of male kinship ties, see Baptist.

38 . . . . **"the patriarchal emigration for the land of promise":** Flint, *First White Man*, 106. Flint was characterizing the Boone family emigration across the Cumberland Gap. Late-nineteenth-century "pioneer societies" and handed-down family histories like the one Stephen Hempstead set in motion in this passage would later create historical and political coherence for what were at the time chaotic family events.

38 . . . . **serial emigration:** Samson Gray came to Bayou Meto, north of Little Rock, in the winter of 1820–21, with his parents and a family of his own. One grandfather had emigrated to North Carolina in 1766, and his parents had subsequently moved to Tennessee in 1804. For families like the Grays, forging a place in a strange environment was a familiar family activity. Little, 3. **plans to move back east:** Adler, 97–98; "Go into the Wilderness," in DeBlack. **wives traveling back East:** See correspondence between spouses in EGBP and JTAC.

39 . . . . **German group emigration:** Hermann Steines's letters reporting on Missouri were distributed to his neighbors and relations as a collective report on the West, one which prompted and guided the 150-person "Solingen Emigration Society" in the late 1840s. Bek, "Followers of Duden, First Article," "Second Article," and "Third Article." **planter house-**

hold emigration: When the Bullock clan emigrated from Tennessee to Arkansas, the group included more than a hundred people: nearly thirty white family members (from four nuclear family groups) and almost eighty slaves. Bolsterli, 15. **plantation emigration in shifts:** McNeilly, 37–38; account by Blanche Edwards of the stories of Emmeline Waddille, Lonoke Co., Ark., in Rawick, vol. 11, 13 and 13A, 13B. Waddille was 25 when she was migrated. **"plantation":** The term is often used by historians to refer to an estate of 20 or more slaves. Borderlands usage was more flexible. One 1833 traveler in Arkansas noted, "We arrived that evening at Col. R's farm, or rather plantation as all farms are called in this country" (Lupton and Lupton, 226; see also Rohrbaugh, 139). Here, "plantation" generally means a large holding worked by slaves, and "farm" refers to a smaller holding, whether worked by slave or free labor.

39 . . . . **Journal of John Brown:** In 1853, Brown counted 31 family members ("towit 22 blacks, seven children and we, the old folks," he and wife Clara). Brown held just over the median number of slaves compared to plantations in nearby cotton-growing counties; Gray, vol. 2, 535. The period 1852–62 saw the births of three children to John and Clara Brown and of several slave children, visits by numerous relatives and boarders; also, the marriage of the Browns' two older daughters, the travels for health or education of his oldest children, and the deaths of two older sons and at least one slave (a young runaway). **Arkansas plantation life:** See Bolsterli; DeBlack; McNeilly, 128–35; Whayne, *Sunnyside*. McNeilly (72) argues that many who held only a few slaves were connected through kinship and other ties to larger slave holders and would have interests in common with them.

40 . . . . **"Men change their place of abode":** Flint, *First White Man,* 30. **men's and women's experiences of emigration:** Faragher (*Women and Men on the Overland Trail*) has argued that the experience of migration essentially confirmed gender roles. One compelling analyst of women's experience is Annette Kolodny, who has chronicled both the textual ways successive "new" lands were taken into American understanding (*The Lay of the Land*) and the ways women sought to domesticate wild places by making them into the more familiar, ordered, and useful spaces of garden plot (*The Land Before Her*). See also Armitage; Baptist; Cashin; Schlissel. **gender ratios:** In the early periods of American development these were strikingly skewed. In 1840, women of childbearing age made up only 17.3% of the white population of Arkansas—less than in any other region in the U.S. S. C. Bolton, *Territorial Ambition,* 82. In St. Louis in 1850, men outnumbered women 185 to 100. Corbett, *In Her Place,* 48. **"wilderness among the Indians":** Quoted in Foley, "Justus Post," 20.

40 . . . . **experiences of younger vs. older women:** These have been noted by, for example, Schlissel, 115.

40 . . . . **political flux of the mid-Mississippi region:** The grave marker for John Patterson, during whose lifetime the territory belonged to Spain, France, and the United States, bears a riddle he used to tell: "I was born in a Kingdom, Raised in an Empire, Attained manhood in a Territory, Am now a citizen of a State, And have never been 100 miles from where I now live" (WPA, *Arkansas*, 342). **Even the language of region has its disputes.** Outsiders might pronounce the state "Mis-sour-y," but true locals knew it as "Miz-zour-a" (WPA, *Missouri*, 131). Written history can fortunately sidestep this matter of cultural definition, but others remain: "Ozarkers" are proud of that title (especially since the other option is likely to be

"hillbilly"), but what to call residents of Arkansas is more problematic. "Arkansawyer"—occasionally used in the nineteenth century, as was "Arkansian"—has advocates still among some state boosters, but I will settle for the more gentrified "Arkansan" as befitting a state currently promoting film sites and presidential libraries along with soybeans and cotton. Elliott West's introduction to WPA, *Arkansas*, xx, n. 2; "Change the Name of Arkansas—Never!" in G. Stewart. **political history of Arkansas:** Bolton, *Remote and Restless*, 24–25.

41 . . . . **Missouri controversies and debate over extension of slavery:** A useful précis of an immense literature is Boyer, 508, 149–50, 417, 693–94.

42 . . . . **creation of the Republican party:** Foner, 125–27.

42 . . . . **historical geography of the region:** Foti, *Arkansas;* Rafferty, *Historical Atlas of Missouri,* and ibid., *Missouri: A Geography.* **emigration to Arkansas:** "To Arkansas," in McNeilly. **Arkansas census figures:** De Bow, 548. Even by 1860, fewer than 0.5% of Arkansas's population worked in industry; it remained an agricultural state throughout the nineteenth century. WPA, *Arkansas,* 68. **Arkansas in the nineteenth century:** Bolton, *Remote and Restless* and ibid., *Territorial Ambition;* Moore; Woods, "A Promise Unfulfilled." **highland and lowland cultures:** Bolton, "Economic Inequality in the Arkansas Territory"; ibid., *Territorial Ambition,* 42–46; Whayne and Gatewood; Otto and Banks; "The Ozarks as a Geographical and Cultural Region," in Sizemore.

42 . . . . **early Missouri:** Foley, *Genesis of Missouri;* Hurt, *Agriculture and Slavery;* Morrow; Nagel. **in-migration:** There were also out-migrations. Traders and entrepreneurs left Missouri after 1822 for the Southwest via the Santa Fe Trail, and beginning in the 1840s settlers set out on the overland trails to Oregon (after 1843) and California (after 1849). Missouri's border with Kansas was substantially *de*populated during the 1850s partisan warfare. Not until the era of Reconstruction were many of the swampier bottomlands of Missouri and Arkansas and the areas along the Missouri-Kansas border in private hands. **Missouri population figures:** De Bow, 665; J. Kennedy. **Immigration following the Graduation Act:** Shortridge, 73, 83–84.

43 . . . . **French and Spanish regimes:** France ceded the regions west of the Mississippi to Spain in 1763, to regain them briefly at the turn of the century. This little affected French families and traders still active in Missouri in the late eighteenth century. **Spanish land-grant policies:** Generous Spanish land grants were later to become the occasion for widespread fraud. Bolton, *Remote and Restless,* Chapter 1, and Shortridge, 79. **"Boon's Lick" region:** Hurt, *Agriculture and Slavery.*

43 . . . . **"provincial metropolis":** The phrase is Steven Shapin's ("Nibbling at the Teats of Science"). Little Rock was the political and cultural capital of Arkansas after the mid-territorial period, but it played a much more minor role than St. Louis in the development of the trans-Mississippi region as a whole. **St. Louis as transshipment point:** Schroeder, 32–33.

44 . . . . **the 1840s:** The number of inhabitants more than doubled, from 35,930 to nearly 80,000, from 1840 to 1845. Adler, 62. **growth rates:** Corbett, *In Her Place,* 48.

45 . . . . **Native Peoples:** I generally use "Native American" but I also reflect our contemporary unsettledness of language in occasionally using "Indian." To Europeans, names like "Osage," "Cherokee," or "Indian" were *ethnic* labels, but to Native groups they were *cultural* and *political* designations. For example, someone not born into the Cherokee tribe could become Cherokee

through marriage or adoption. Yet to Americans, white children adopted by Cherokees were still white. Someone in 1830 who had three white grandparents but had lived all his life among Cherokees would be called Cherokee by some people I quote, but white by others.

45 . . . . **native populations affected:** When the French exploring party of Jolliet and Marquette reached the Peorias in present-day Iowa in 1673, they found the native people already wearing garments made of French cloth. Foley, *Genesis of Missouri*, 3. A good overview is M. Green. **Ouachita River Valley villages:** Dickinson, "Historic Tribes." **Quapaws:** This group called themselves the "Gappa" (Bizzell, "A Report on the Quapaw," 71). The Quapaws suffered decimation from European-borne diseases. In 1600 the estimated population was 20,000; there were 6,000 in 1682, and about 1,500 in the late 1690s, when, Jesuit explorers reported, villages were being combined to make up for the terrifying mortality. For much of the 1820s, one faction remained on land in south-central Arkansas, while another attempted to make a new home with the Caddos of central Louisiana. During the period 1818–24 the roughly 500 remaining Quapaws were confined by American policy and population to a bounded region within east-central Arkansas. Baird, *The Quapaw Indians; The Quapaw People,* and "The Reduction of a People"; Dickinson, "Quapaw Journey to Red River." **A few individuals remained:** Quite a few Native Americans remained after "Indian removal." See Calloway, 227–30. Almost the sole reminder of the tribe in present-day Arkansas is in the name of a historic district in downtown Little Rock, the "Quapaw Quarter."

46 . . . . **Osages:** Baird, *The Osage People*; Rollings. **Osage territory:** American officials negotiated a territorial cession from the Osage in 1808, but this treaty was regarded differently by its various signers. Osage groups still claimed hunting rights on lands they had sold in northwestern Arkansas. Baird, *The Osage People*.

46 . . . . **first settlement by Western Cherokees:** Dale, 96; Huddleston, "Some Indian Incidents"; McLoughlin, 56, 94, 166, 170, 209, 262–65. In 1816, an Indian agent, William Lovely, negotiated a formal Cherokee reservation spanning much of northwest Arkansas, on land initially ceded by the Osage.

46 . . . . **pressures on Arkansas Cherokees:** McLoughlin, 217–21. **Cherokee-Osage warfare:** Ibid., 218; Park. **Fort Smith:** S. C. Bolton, *Territorial Ambition*, 24–25. **1828 abolition of Cherokee holdings:** McLoughlin, 264–65, 413–14.

47 . . . . **cultural revival:** Ibid., Chapters 14 and 17. **pressures on Cherokee Nation:** Ibid., Chapter 20.

47 . . . . **1835 treaty and assassinations:** Ibid., 450–51; Ridge.

47 . . . . **Cherokee Trail of Tears:** Calloway; Howard and Allen; Lightfoot; Ridge. Many members of the other "Five Civilized Tribes"—the Choctaw, Cherokee, Chickasaw, Creek, and Seminole—were to recapitulate all or part of the soon-infamous Trail of Tears during the U.S. government's further removal of indigenous groups in the late 1830s and '40s. M. Green, 519–33.

48 . . . . **early-nineteenth-century Osage removal:** Foley, *Genesis of Missouri*, 248; Rollings.

48 . . . . **other Native American emigrations:** Lankford; Usner, "An American Indian Gateway." **"Delaware Indian painted with Vermilion":** McDermott, "Western Journals,"

98 (he was likely there as a hired hunter; see Dickinson, "Historic Tribes," 9). **Sioux hunters:** Bingham, 183–84. **report by Governor William Clark:** Foley, *Genesis of Missouri*, 247. In one of the many ironies of American expansionism, the much-recorded emigrations of the extended Boone family from the Carolinas to Tennessee and then Missouri paralleled that of Shawnee tribes who left because of British and American territorial encroachment. Faragher, *Daniel Boone*, 145.

48 . . . . **intercultural interaction:** Faragher, "More Motley than Mackinaw"; Foley, *Genesis of Missouri*; McNeilly, 31; Usner, "An American Indian Gateway." The first few pages of Aaron S. Fry's notebook describe races and shooting matches with various Indians in the 1830s Mississippi River town of Hannibal; see ASFN.

49 . . . . **patterns of settlement:** Keefe and Morrow, *The White River Chronicles*, 4–5; Morrow, 241; WPA, *Arkansas*, 268. **roads and trails:** Pope, 86; WPA, *Missouri: A Guide to the "Show Me" State*, 98. **ecological impact of Native Americans:** Key; White and Cronon. **evidence of previous quarrying in southern Arkansas:** Featherstonhaugh, "Geology of Arkansas," 25 Aug. 1835. **Indian arrowheads and other stone artifacts:** Keefe and Morrow, *White River Chronicles*, 69. **burial mounds:** Widely noted throughout Arkansas and Missouri, they were plowed under or their closely packed dirt used for levees. They are the reason for an old nickname for St. Louis, "Mound City." **mortar stones:** Carey, 89. **"Indian Hieroglyphics":** McDermott, "Western Journals," 95; Keefe and Morrow, *White River Chronicles*, 9.

49 . . . . **emigration, black and white:** Holley, 246; Stewart, 194. **"We come to Arkansas":** Victoria Sims, int. Irene Robertson, in Rawick, vol. 10, Part 6, 109. **Freedpeople emigrating:** Shortridge. Planters' anxieties about controlling free black labor led to efforts to recruit white immigrants, particularly Germans. Holly, 249.

49 . . . . **"do better" in a "new country":** Maggie Stenhouse, int. Irene Robertson, in Rawick, vol. 10, Part 6, 222–24. **"Wild, honey, it was!":** Laura Abromson, int. Irene Robertson, in Rawick, vol. 8, Part 1, 109. In October 1935, 75,000 acres of land that had been cut over by timber companies was forfeited to the state for tax liabilities. Hungry city-dwellers streamed onto the land to claim some portion of it under homestead legislation. To these members of a semi-urban working class devastated by the Great Depression, "new" land held out the promise of agricultural redemption much as it had to settlers hamstrung by the financial crashes of 1819 or 1837. WPA, *Arkansas*, 281–82.

50 . . . . **rupture in attachment to home:** Stewart, 178, 180. Anthony Kaye (8) argues that slaves "defined solidarity in terms of a profound sense of place." **slaves' emigrations:** McNeilly, 44–52. Schlissel (112–15) argues that white women on the overland trails would find markers of time and distance with which to make narrative sense of a trek from known to unknown. Schlissel argues that these tallies represent and convey women's resistance to and resentment at the dangerous remove. In the memories of slaves' migrations appears no similar structuring metaphor. **"They rode in the fine carriages":** "Aunt" Mittie Freeman, int. Beulah Sherwood Hagg, in Rawick, vol. 8, Part 2, 346–47. **Other brief emigration accounts:** Dock Wilborn, "a mile or so from Marvell, Arkansas," int. Watt McKinney, in Rawick, vol. 11, Arkansas narratives, 1–2; Fil Hancock, no interviewer given, in Rawick, vol. 11, Missouri narratives, 147. **exercised little control:** Many people in slavery did certainly attempt to influence their own moves. Two Missouri women asked their owners to sell

them so they could remain where they were, near their husbands, rather than being taken to Texas. Blassingame, 13.

50 . . . . **profound family rupture:** A "Lost Friends" column in a Methodist-Episcopal newsletter helped reunite those separated by slavery and war. Albert, 117; Foner, *Reconstruction*, 82–84. **"taken from the place of their birth":** Interview with Jennie Hill, in Blassingame, 593.

51 . . . . **"I lived in Kentucky":** Autobiographical account of Malinda Noll, in McKivigan, 258.

51 . . . . **"None of the slaves liked it":** Josephine Ann Barnett, De Valls Bluff, int. Irene Robertson, in Rawick, vol. 8, 1–2. **"Yankee mens immigrated us":** Henry "Happy Day" Green, near Barton and Helena, Ark., int. Irene Robertson, in Rawick, vol. 9, Part 3, 87.

51 . . . . **urban slaves and free blacks:** Bellamy, "Free Blacks"; Lack; Seematter. **Liberian colony of "Missouri":** Bellamy, "Persistency of Colonization," 18.

52 . . . . **"If you wanted to sing at night":** Lewis Brown, Little Rock, int. Samuel S. Taylor, in Rawick, vol. 8, Part 1, 295. A former slave from Georgia recounted that workers would "put a big washtub full of water in the middle of the floor to catch the sound of our voices when we sung." Albert, 12. **sound doesn't carry far:** Michael Gomez (260) emphasizes this aspect of the practice. **"turn a pot down out":** Austin Pen Parnell, Little Rock, int. Samuel S. Taylor, in Rawick, vol. 10, Part 5, 270. **"put her head under the pot":** Rachel Fairley, int. Samuel S. Taylor, in Rawick, vol. 8, Part 2, 258, and vol. 8, 28.

52 . . . . **Use of pots for prayer:** Rawick, vol. 1, 39–45; E. Ball, 248. **African roots/sanctification:** Genovese, 236–37.

Chapter II: Body

53 . . . . **conceptions of disease and the body:** This exploration is greatly indebted to the work of Charles E. Rosenberg, particularly *Cholera Years* and "Therapeutic Revolution." John Harley Warner's *Therapeutic Perspective* is also basic to historical understanding of the medical world of the American nineteenth century.

54 . . . . *Gunn's Domestic Medicine:* Gunn. **medicine of self-reliance:** Gevitz, "'But all those authors are foreigners'"; Rosenberg, introduction to Gunn facsimile edition, and ibid., "John Gunn: Everyman's Physician" and "Medical Text and Social Context." **slave health:** Fox-Genovese, 169–71; Genovese, 62, 225–29; Kaufmann; Keeney; Kiple and King, Chapter 11; Savitt; Stampp, Chapter 7; O. Taylor, Chapter 9. **forms of magic:** Gorn; Stewart, *"What Nature Suffers to Groe,"* 138–46.

54 . . . . **agreement about bodily functioning:** On the fundamentally similar metaphors uniting sectarian and "regular" medicine, see Haller, *Medical Protestants*, 43. John Harley Warner, in *Therapeutic Perspective* and "From Specificity to Universalism in Medical Therapeutics," has argued that significant shifts in the therapeutic ideas of educated physicians took place over the period 1820–80, but these shifts are obscured by the subtle ways institutional therapeutic practice gradually changed, toward less drastic bloodletting and a decreased use of mercury-based compounds. At the level of common practice, however, change was even slower to register. Indeed, Warner's evidence suggests this; see *Therapeutic Perspective*, 134.

54 . . . . **developments in nineteenth-century medicine:** These are well encapsulated in Bynum and in Cassedy, *Medicine in America,* Chapter 2. **stethoscope, auscultation, percussion:** Bynum, 33–41; **instrumentation:** Bynum, 99–101; Cassedy, *Medicine in America,* 40–41, 60. **movement toward quantification:** Cassedy, *Medicine and American Growth.* **Paris-based "numerical method":** Bynum, 42–44; Warner, *Against the Spirit of System;* ibid., *Therapeutic Perspective,* Chapter 4. **changes in pharmacy resulting from the influence of the "Paris school":** Shryock, *Medicine and Society in America,* 126–31.

54 . . . . **anesthesia:** Pernick. **ascendancy of germ theory and laboratory:** Cassedy, *Medicine in America,* 76–123; Numbers and Warner. **consolidation of authority of medical "regulars":** Starr, Book 1. **medical education:** Ludmerer.

55 . . . . **"regular" physicians:** They were also termed "old school," "majority school," "allopathic," and "orthodox" by their irregular peers. Haller, *Medical Protestants,* 34. Excellent introductions to medical practice in the period include Cassedy, *Medicine in America,* 25–44; Haller, *American Medicine in Transition;* and Warner, *Therapeutic Perspective.*

55 . . . . **professional role of medical practitioners:** Rosenkrantz; Shryock, "Medical Practice in the Old South"; Starr. **therapeutics:** Shafer, Chapter 4. **domestic environment of medical care:** Abel; Bolton, "'A Sister's Consolations'"; Keeney; Leavitt, "'A Worrying Profession'"; Ulrich.

56 . . . . **"eclectics," "irregulars," "sectarians":** Gevitz, *Other Healers.*

56 . . . . **Thomsonianism:** Gevitz, "Unorthodox Medical Theories," 612–14; Haller, *Medical Protestants,* Chapter 2; Jordan. **"steamers and steamed":** Haller, *Medical Protestants,* 56.

56 . . . . **homeopathy:** Gevitz, "Unorthodox Medical Theories," 604–11.

57 . . . . **water therapy:** Hedrick, Chapter 16; Sklar.

57 . . . . **domestic health manuals:** For example, Buchan, *Domestic Medicine;* and *The Domestic Physician* (1814?). **as important tools of emigration:** Flint, *Recollections* (1826), 198; Bek, "Followers of Duden: Second Article," 225. **health in newly settled areas:** Faragher, *Sugar Creek,* Chapter 10; Dickinson, "Health and Death in Early Arkansas"; Ekberg, *Colonial Ste. Genevieve,* Chapter 8; Lanser; McMillen; Moffatt. **healers:** Particularly on smaller plantations, owners and overseers often administered care (JJB; DeBlack, 135). On other plantations, women were more central—either the woman of the owner household, or a respected slave healer (Bolsterli, 40; Baxandall and Gordon, 49–50). **tooth extractions:** EGPMB no. 5, 21 Sept. 1841; Geiger account book, apparently for 1847, JJG, 149.

58 . . . . **everyday experiences of health and disease:** See Dobson; Hedrick; Porter and Porter; Rothman; Ulrich. **"our family":** Jensen, Part 8, 4 Sept. 1827, 192. **sharing beds:** MESD, 27 Jan. 1836.

58 . . . . **Force and Flow:** My conception of humoral theory as expressed in the notion of flow and shifting force is indebted to the work of Barbara Duden (*Woman Beneath the Skin,* particularly Chapter 2) and Charles Rosenberg ("Therapeutic Revolution"). Though Duden's work is based on the records of a seventeenth-century German physician, her insights are extremely helpful in clarifying nineteenth-century American primary sources.

58 . . . . **humoralism:** Nutton, "Humoralism," provides a cogent review of a complex history. See also Porter, *Greatest Benefit,* 57–58.

59 . . . . **relationship between ancient practices and later ideas about the body:**
See Kuriyama. **humoral notions in nineteenth-century U.S.:** Rosenberg, "Catechisms of
Health," 189; Stilgoe, 141. **historical continuity of humoral notions:** Helman; Rippere.
On the long duration of many nineteenth-century disease notions, see also Humphreys, Chapter 6.

59 . . . . **naming nineteenth-century notions:** Older disease names lived on in common
language. In 1837, John Geiger went to visit a girl with "the King's Evil." JJG, 9 Feb. 1837. **language of humors alive and well into the early twentieth century:** Henry "Happy Day"
Green, Barton, Ark., int. Watt McKinney, makes reference to "bilious" white patrollers, in
Rawick, vol. 9, Part 3, 94. **"surcharge of bad humours":** Weems, 34. **"aqueous humor":**
MESD, 13 Jan. 1836.

60 . . . . **"pain in his leg":** JJG, 6 Feb. 1836. **"a congealed feeling":** Stanley, 156. **Doctor Livingstone, I presume?:** Driver. Stanley followed his American military service with
exploration and conquest in Africa. He explored Lake Tanganyika, traced the Congo to the sea,
founded the Congo Free State, and brought troops to the aid of the Emin Pasha in the Sudan.
Attacks of ague apparently did not deter his interest in places tropical. **"oppression":** JJB, 27
May 1857. **"raised":** W. Brown, 45–46.

60 . . . . **"attended with great determination":** AWW, 1, 14. **"husband the vital
power":** Quoted in Primm, *Lion of the Valley*, 162.

61 . . . . **"I tell you":** Albert, 68–69.

61 . . . . **"I feel reduced":** JJB, 2 April 1854.

61 . . . . **disease mapping:** As one Missouri physician observed, "No disease is equally distributed throughout the system." ISMN, 13. **"ailing in his breast":** Noland, *Pete Whetstone of
Devil's Fork*, 77. **"misery . . . in the chest":** Boston Blackwell, North Little Rock, int. Beulah
Sherwood Hagg, in Rawick, vol. 8, Part 1, 173. Blackwell was 98 years old during the Great
Depression, when he was interviewed, and had lived in Arkansas since the age of 3. Blackwell's
understanding of disease and body functioning was presumably shaped to some large degree by
the culture and practices of Arkansas in the mid-nineteenth century. **"Misery":** A common
phrasing; see Gorn, 313. It may have been a euphemism employed because "pain" was strongly
associated with childbirth. Randolph, *Down in the Holler*, 105. **"the lungs were but slightly
affected":** Twyman, 27. **"deficiancy":** JJB, 19 Nov. 1859. **doctrine of therapeutic specificity:** Warner, *Therapeutic Perspective,* Chapter 3; ibid., "From Specificity to Universalism in
Medical Therapeutics."

61 . . . . **bodily typologies of blood and its diffusion:** Kuriyama. **"tendency to
equalize the circulation":** Twyman, 31; **"engorged" and "congested":** Ibid., 30.

62 . . . . **"threw the blood to my head":** Rebecca Butterworth, [Outland Grove, Ark.],
to W. W. Barton, Rochdale, Lancashire, England, 5 July 1846, in Erickson, 176. **"the blood
determines to the head":** Gunn, *Domestic Medicine*, 133. **imbalance in distribution:** J. W.
Calvert, St. Francis Co., Ark., to John L. Trone, 29 July 1851, JLTC. **"equalebrium of circulation":** JJG, 25 Nov. 1836; similarly, 14 Sept. 1835.

62 . . . . **bloodletting techniques:** Davis and Appel; Shafer, 96–99. **theory and practice of bloodletting:** Warner, *Therapeutic Perspective.* **pleasure associated with having
blood let:** Milledoler, 47. Physicians sometimes bled "to syncope"—until the patient

fainted—as Dr. C. Lillybridge did with his patients Big Corn and Water Dog in March 1837. Foreman, 242, 243. Scoring skin and drawing blood were part of traditional Cherokee medical and spiritual practices (Mooney, "The Cherokee Ball Play"), and many Cherokees had blood let, although they resisted other American practices. (See also Mooney, "Cherokee Theory and Practice of Medicine.") **lay administration of bloodletting:** Gunn, *Domestic Medicine*, 197 (but see warning, 246). **scoring loaves of bread:** My thanks to Madeline Mullen, Countway Library Rare Book Room, for this insight.

62 . . . . **Harvey:** Leake, *Exercitatio Anatomica*. **nineteenth-century syncretism:** Rosenberg, "Catechisms of Health," 189–90.

63 . . . . **Intake and Outgo:** Ibid., "Therapeutic Revolution." **"retentions and excretions":** As expressed in Ricketson's long title. **"until the balance of excretion, and nutrition":** Scoffern, 182. Providing appropriate food was part of a practitioner's attention to both healing and comfort. When a Cherokee man named Turtle Fields fell ill with dysentery on the removal from Cherokee Nation, Dr. C. Lillybridge had him moved to a more comfortable bed, and "brought him a cup of Coffee & Navy bread, which he said made him feel better." Foreman, 237.

63 . . . . **"Ed had not urinated naturally":** Ibid., 23 Aug. 1858. On 5 July 1861 Brown noted that bad signs about a sick person included that he "Has lost flesh and his secretions irregular and inactive." **"obstinacy of the bowels":** Foreman, 239. **"keep the bowels regular":** JJG, 14 March 1837.

63 . . . . **"strange eruption like chicken pox":** JJB, 1 Feb. 1860.

64 . . . . **blockages:** Gevitz, "Unorthodox Medical Theories," 612–14. **"large knot of dead worms":** JJG, 12 November 1837. **"Amenorehœa":** Mitchell, 271.

64 . . . . **"slave ceases to perspire":** Eakin and Logsdon, 171–72.

64 . . . . **Costiveness:** Rafferty, *Rude Pursuits and Rugged Peaks*, 70. The final remedy for "costiveness" was the rectal scoop; see ISMN, 115–16.

64 . . . . **Menstrual flows:** B. Duden, 46–47, 70–71, 110–35; Klepp, "Lost, Hidden, Obstructed and Repressed," 77–83; Smith-Rosenberg. **Mary Swimmer's missed period:** Foreman, 235. **"as Natural in her Discharges":** JJG, 19 July 1836.

65 . . . . **"bile . . . stirred up in me":** H. A. Whittington, Little Rock, to Granville Whittington, [Boston], 20 Nov. 1832, in Ross, "Letters of Hiram Abiff Whittington," 31. **felt ready to burn," "vomit":** Lottinville, 204, 225.

65 . . . . **"operations from the bowels":** Maury, 267. **purgation:** Another area of overlap between American and Cherokee beliefs; Park, 179. **"portion of fetid matter":** JJG, 13 Aug. 1837. Flatulence, however, was a matter of constant concern to some, like the unfortunate John Brown (see JJB, 14 July 1860). **"Charles better":** Jensen, Part 7, 17 Sept. 1823, 74. **jars of worms:** Moffatt, 91–92.

65 . . . . **"reason to believe these affections salutary":** Drake, *Natural and Statistical View*, 187. **blistering:** "I ordered a sinapism [an irritating mustard plaster] to [a companion's] abdomen and gave him a bottle of Chalk mixture with Kino," noted S. W. Woodhouse in 1849. Tomer and Brodhead, 83. **On ankles:** EGPMB no. 7, 16 Oct. 1845. **On the head:** Jensen, Part 8, 11 April 1827, 185. **typical course of treatment:** Ibid., Part 7, 13–18 Sept. 1823, 74–75. In this case, the sick person died. **"Blistered Harriett":** JJG, 19 Aug. 1835.

66 . . . . **Mr. Giddings:** Jensen, Part 8, 19 Jan. 1828, 196–97.

66 . . . . **boils:** These were thought to be manifest within the body as well as on its surfaces. When John Geiger's son died, his father wrote, "I believe some internal bile or ulcer broke as he passed matter by all the main passages, even by urine." JJG, 16 July 1837. **"gatherings," "risings":** JJB, 12 Jan. 1860; JJG, 26 Jan. 1842; Jervey and Moss, 202; Sarah Potts to Ann Potts, N.J., 23 Jan. 1849, PFL, 1823–52; J. E. Thompson, especially 270–73. An older man like Stephen Hempstead, born in 1754, might talk of "risings," while his younger contemporaries might more readily refer to "tumors," but the treatment was the same.

67 . . . . **Stephen Hempstead:** Hempstead's diary and family correspondence are in the Stephen Hempstead Papers. His diary was edited by Mrs. Dana Jensen and appeared in nine parts; quotations from his diary are from Jensen. Hempstead was something of a busybody, often involved with the comings and goings of those about him. Faragher, *Daniel Boone*, 292–95. **Mary Hempstead Keeney and Manuel Lisa:** Corbett, *In Her Place*, 28–32; Foley, *Genesis of Missouri*, 119. In October 1827, the Hempstead family received word that "Son Thomas," long absent at sea, was being held at Cadiz, Spain, after being caught engaged in illegal trade. Thomas had not returned by 1831, when his father's diary ended. Jensen, Part 8, 23 Oct. 1827, 194. Cordelia Hempstead eventually petitioned for a legal divorce. In September 1831, as he lay sick, Hempstead wrote in his diary that "Son Tho' wife that was came out to See me with her little daughter Cordelia I was exceding [glad] to See her. She professed the Same parentel affection for me as She always had in her husbands time whom we conclude must be dead having been absense in the Spanish Country 4 or 5 years & have never heard anything of him. The year past She took a divorce from him." Jensen, Part 9, 14 Sept. 1831, 444.

67 . . . . **"my wife complains of some thing gathering" and subsequent interventions:** Jensen, Part 1, 20 Sept.–14 Oct. 1814, 52–53. **"She was Sixty three years":** Ibid., Part 5, 9 Sept. 1820, 48.

68 . . . . **"had her Breast gather and brake":** Ibid., Part 2, 24 Dec. 1815, 300. **"taking a cold":** Losing the humoral heat necessary to produce excess blood was one explanation for a missed menstrual period. Klepp, "Lost, Hidden, Obstructed, and Repressed," 78–79. **Not all inflammations resolved so well:** A Michigan relative wrote to one Arkansas resident in 1858 of his father, explaining that "the Doctor said that an ulser broke was the reason of his dying so sudden." Margaret R. Dean, Lyons Ponid Co., Michigan, to William Ludlow, Laconia, Desha Co., Ark., 28 Nov. 1858, WLC.

68 . . . . **Christopher Keeney's medical practice and marriage plans:** Correspondence 1826–29 in the SHP. **"Sick with a rising on his back" and course of illness:** Jensen, Part 9, 11 May; 13, 17, 30 June; 2 July 1829, 415, 417–19.

68 . . . . **Stephen Hempstead's plaguing boils:** Jensen, Part 1, 20 Aug. 1813, 40; Ibid., Part 9, 14 Sept. 1831, 444. His doctor's diagnosis was perhaps made out of kindness, since boils were fairly easy to cure, unlike the more general pains of a war-scarred, long-worked body. **Stephen Hempstead's death:** Ibid., Part 9, entries for September 1831, and, after Hempstead's final entry on 24 Sept., the final notation: "Those are the last lines ever penned by our beloved and departed father Stephen Hempstead."

69 . . . . **Caty Stephens's death:** Leonard Stephens, Beech Woods, Campbell (later Kenton) Co., Ky., to Elizabeth Stephens and William Stephens, Middle Grove, Monroe Co., Mo., 27 Aug. 1843, StFP: "I have been thus minute, because I thought you would like to know all the particulars." His narrative interlaced the physical details of Caty's disease with her spiritual preparation of herself and her family for her own death.

70 . . . . **"copious discharge":** Those writing about "risings" often commented on the amount of liquid released from them, as in the case of "a healthy man who had the Rising opened with the Lancet Said to be a Rising from the Mammary Glands said to Run two Quarts." JJG, 30 March 1836.

70 . . . . **"'it's natur,' says I":** Stowe, *Uncle Tom's Cabin*, 48. **"A Frenchman's vivacity":** Quoted in introduction, McDermott, *Western Journals,* 52.

71 . . . . **Derangement:** Gunn, *Domestic Medicine*, 19, 49; Sprague, 3; AWW, 10. **of the mind:** Jensen, Part 9, 15 Oct. 1829, 424; John J. Walker to Thomas H. Walker, Brownsburgh, Rockbridge Co., 15 Feb. 1834, JJWL. **of the mails:** Charles F. M. Noland, Batesville, Ark., to Maj. William Noland, Washington City, D.C., 7 April 1838, CFMN. **"Boughton remained deranged":** JJG, 19 April 1837. **teething as "disordered state of the system":** Gunn, *Domestic Medicine*, 348; Drake, *Natural and Statistical View*, 186. **disease as disorder:** Rosenberg, "Cause of Cholera," 332. In the anthropologist Mary Douglas's terms ill health was a kind of dirt—matter out of order. M. Douglas, *Purity and Danger*.

71 . . . . **sassafras tea:** Charlie Vaden, Hazen, Ark., int. Irene Robertson, in Rawick, vol. 11, Arkansas narratives, 77.

71 . . . . **therapies help along body's processes:** Gunn, *Domestic Medicine*, 133; Rosenberg, "Therapeutic Revolution," 46. **nineteenth-century regular therapeutics:** Shafer, Chapter 4, is a good review; see also Howard-Jones. **underlying philosophy of such treatments:** Warner, *Therapeutic Perspective*. **sectarian therapeutics:** Haller, "Eclectic Materia Medica," in *Medical Protestants*. **camphor:** Jervey and Moss, 186. **counterirritation:** R. Porter, *Cambridge Illustrated History,* 125. **"internally exhibited" medicine:** Park, 127.

71 . . . . **"Mrs. Galatin's mouth futched":** JGG, 12 Sept. 1835.

72 . . . . **"reaction":** J. E. Thompson, 53. **"broke" fevers:** Park, 85. **salivation:** ISMN, 26. **calomel:** R. Porter, *Cambridge Illustrated History,* 266. **praise of calomel:** Skinner, 262. **"I gave him my old remedy":** JJB, 8 and 9 June 1857.

72 . . . . **Pain:** The ability "cheerfully" to "submit" to painful remedies like cupping, blistering, and purgation was praised as moral virtue. Park, 127. **pain as a diagnostic aid and professional marker:** Pernick. **"The strong earthy taste and smell of this extract":** Dana, 329.

72 . . . . **"frequent returns":** Flint, *Recollections*, 232.

72 . . . . **"I dare not give strong medicine":** JJB, 8 Aug. 1857. **"operate unkindly":** AWW, 46. **"the medicine has a good effect":** A[lexander] Hambleton and Cordelia Hambleton to John Compton, Owensboro, Ky., 4 Sept. 1854, series 2, file 24, MLC.

73 . . . . **"The western inhabitant":** Bek, "Nicholas Hesse," Part 6, 146.

73 . . . . **"My mode of life is now very regular":** JJB, 4 June 1856. **regularity:** Levine, 654.

73 .... **careful attention and "management":** William H. Belcher, St. Louis, to Nathan Belcher, New London, Conn., 21 May 1849, BFP; William Fulton, Washington, D.C., to Matilda Fulton, [Little Rock], 2 June 1840, box 1, file 14, WSFP. **"bad Management":** Thomas A. Bennett, Spring Hill, Ark. Terr., to Philip Rainey, Boydton, Va., 18 June 1836, PRC.

74 .... **"The use of a preparation of iron":** JJB, 12 Dec. 1860.

74 .... **"winds coming upon us":** Goulding, 327.

75 .... **Temperature variation causes disease:** Dana, 326; Ricketson, 9. **"too striking ... to be wholesome":** Bek, "Nicholas Hesse," part 7, 245. Hesse included this in a list of cautions for German immigrants. He also warned them against "Negro slavery," "poisonous snakes," and the various animal pests associated with "rural life"; along with these moral and physical dangers, he further listed "willful street urchins in the cities, who, with extraordinary pertinence, throw their little fire crackers into the window of their neighbors." **"care taken to defend the system":** AWW, 9.

75 .... **"transition from the late cold and humid atmosphere":** Foreman, 243. **"frequent & sudden changes":** John J. Walker, St. Louis, to Thomas H. Walker, Brownsburgh, Rockbridge Co., Va., 13 March 1837, JJWL.

75 .... **"I am doing little else but guarding my family":** JJB, 26 June 1857; **"Clara had another slight attack":** Ibid., 12 May 1860.

76 .... **"I have not been in good health this winter":** C. F. M. Noland, "Batesville Arks.," to Major William Noland, Washington D.C., 4 March 1841, CFMN.

76 .... **"rousing of sensibilities," "[g]out and apoplexy":** "Cautions for the Season," 1854, 113.

77 .... **seasonal bloodletting:** AWW, 42.

77 .... **"all suffered from colds":** JJB, 17 Feb. 1856; **"constant freeze":** Ibid., 22 Feb. 1856, typescript copy.

77 .... **"variable climates":** Drake, *Natural and Statistical View,* 180. **"a cold backwards Spring":** Jensen, Part 1, 14 May 1814, 48. **"cold, hot wet & dry" spring:** John J. Walker to Thomas H. Walker, Brownsburgh, Rockbridge Co., Va., 9 June 1834, JJWL.

78 .... **"the last fall and winter has been very Sickly":** Kirkbride Potts, Galley Creek, Ark., to Ann Potts [Bordentown, N.J.], 13 April 1852, PFL. **"healthy" seasons relative:** "My command cannot be regarded Sickly for the season," reported Matthew Arbuckle from Fort Gibson, late in July of 1826, "yet I have still an unusual proportion of Officers sick." Matthew Arbuckle, Cantonment Gibson, to Lieut. E. G. W. Butler, Cincinnati, 29 July 1826, in Carter, vol. 20, 277. **"No Epidemick diseases this fall":** ASFN, 28 Nov. 1835.

78 .... **"we have suffered here a little with cold and wet":** B. W. Lee, Arkansas Post, to James H. Lucas, St. Louis, 15 March 1840, KC.

78 .... **"sickly season" of summer:** James Trooper Armstrong to "My dearest Ladie" (Matilda [Green] Armstrong), probably in Tennessee, 17 Oct. 1852, JTA; and Preston Y. Bloyed, to his uncle Eli Bloyed, 25 Nov. 1865, "Bloyed Family Letters," 32. Indeed, the recurrence of seasonal illness made it a useful marker of the time of year; northern lakes in 1826 had "fever and ague blossoms" much as later-nineteenth-century gardens had the early-blooming "graduation rose." Flint, *Recollections,* 304.

79 . . . . **etymology of "ague":** *Oxford English Dictionary.* **pronunciation of "ague":** Noland, *Pete Whetstone of Devil's Fork,* 129.

79 . . . . **malaria:** an elegantly concise history is Humphreys, *Malaria,* upon which I rely for much of what follows (on types and spread of malaria, see 8–10); Ackerknecht, *Malaria in the Upper Mississippi Valley,* also remains a classic. See also Dunn; on Arkansas in particular, Lancaster; and on the cultural impact of the disease, Merrens and Terry.

79 . . . . **racial differences in susceptibility to malaria:** Humphreys, *Malaria,* 14–20. Black slaves were also apparently more resistant to yellow fever, but African Americans were regarded by many whites as being much more susceptible than white people to cholera and eye, bone, and skin complaints. Kiple and King, 41–49, 146–47, 78. **as an argument for slavery:** See Chapter 8, 236–38. Most of these physical arguments had no basis in what we now understand to be scientific fact. In such politics-based assessments, both cultural perception and biology are at work.

80 . . . . **malaria's seasons:** Humphreys, *Malaria,* 12; jaundice, 9; cycles of chill and fever, 9. **"How would you like to live in a place":** "Health of the Country," 1845. Because people could be infected with more than one form of malaria at a time, not all episodes of chills and fever fell into the classic clinical three-day pattern.

80 . . . . **Anopheles mosquito ranges:** Humphreys, *Malaria,* 10.

81 . . . . **malaria as disease of the frontier:** Humphreys, *Malaria,* 30–36. **"Arkansaw chills":** Skinner, 261. **"the great chill":** Howard and Allen. **"ager cakes":** Noland, *Pete Whetstone of Devil's Fork,* 129; with the less phonetic spelling "ague cake," Skinner, 251 and 262 and Stanley, 154. **"fever cake":** Humphreys, *Malaria,* 138. Modern diagnosis would relate this swelling of the spleen to the life cycle of the malarial parasite. **"an ager":** Porter, *Big Bear of Arkansas,* 26. "A fellow can live in Arkansas if the chills dont com in contact with him," wrote S. V. How in 1860, adding, in a comment revealing his own success at evading them, "But i hope . . . that i will get clear of them this spring." Silvester V. How, Bayou Metou, Pulaski Co., Ark., to Jane Pursley, 6 March 1860, MFJPP. Black Americans who had lived through much of the nineteenth century similarly personified the ever-pursuing "chills." Humphreys, *Malaria,* 134.

81 . . . . **efforts to differentiate among previously generalized fevers:** P. Allen.

81 . . . . **"The predisposition to bilious River[?] fever":** AWW, 36. **"my wife has recovered from a fever":** Silas Bent, St. Louis, to Jared Mansfield, surveyor general of the United States, Cincinnati, 30 Jan. 1812, in Carter, vol. 14, 517. **"ague in my head":** Jensen, Part 3, 27 May 1818, 85. **"an ague and fever":** Alfred Finney and Cephas Washburn, Journal of the Arkansas Mission, 3 Jan. 1820–3 June 1821, in file 4, HSM. (emphasis added)

81 . . . . **kinds of fevers "kept up by local inflammation":** AWW, 18. **"were not my habits temperate":** Justus Post, Bonhomme, to John Post, Addison, Vt., 1 Oct. 1820, JPP.

82 . . . . **quinine:** Modern medicine recognizes quinine's power to prevent malarial symptoms. Before the Civil War, however, it was generally used as a treatment for ague and other fevers, not as prophylaxis. Ackerknecht, *Malaria,* 122–23; Humphreys, *Malaria,* 36–38. For one use as a preventive measure, see Flint, *History and Geography* (1833), 39. **quinine pills:** Isaac T. Roark, Fayetteville, Ark., to "Dear Sim," Oct. 1860, file 108, HSM; Shryock, *Medicine*

and Society in America, 131. **Sappington's pills:** Humphreys, *Malaria,* 36. **therapies against southern fevers:** Monette. **expense of quinine pills:** Park, 82.

82 . . . . **"fever-doctor," calomel and castor oil to break the fever, a "shower bath of cold water" and cod-liver oil as preventives:** Skinner, 261–62. **calomel and rhubarb:** Coolidge, 449. **coffee and whiskey:** Ackerknecht, *Malaria,* 123.

83 . . . . **"The dead heat of the sun" and description of ague:** Keefe and Morrow, *A Connecticut Yankee,* 122–23.

84 . . . . **"the inhabitants expect a sickly season every year":** Twyman, 29. **"It is fashionable to be sick":** H. A. Whittington, Little Rock, to Granville Whittington, Boston, 21 April 1827, in Ross, "Letters of Hiram Abiff Whittington," 2. **"warm and sickly season":** Hartwell Boswell, Cynthiana, Ky., to Josiah Meiggs, Washington, D.C., 3 June 1820, in Carter, vol. 19, 188. **Delaying travel:** Bek, "Followers of Duden: First Article," 67; DeBlack, 78; "Journal of Henry B. Miller," 1931, 232.

84 . . . . **"the most care-free enjoyment of life":** Bek, "Travel into Missouri," 33.

Chapter III, Places

85 . . . . **slaves' lived sense of place:** Stewart, *"What Nature Suffers to Groe,"* 178–79. **"the nature of soil, water, and situation":** Ricketson, 17.

86 . . . . **airs, waters, and places:** The Hippocratic treatise "On Airs, Waters, and Places" formed both a substantive and symbolic background for nineteenth-century concerns of environmental health. Its title thus provides an organizing principle for this and the following two chapters.

86 . . . . **Daniel Drake's treatise:** Drake, *A Systematic Treatise.* **the other extreme of geographic reporting:** The French explorer de Gruy noted a region within the lead district of Missouri where "the land produces nothing but a few oaks that seem to grow only reluctantly," and where, more remarkably, "the snow which sometimes lies on the ground for six weeks or two months [elsewhere], melts immediately in this spot." This interest was typical of the intense attention to particular parts of new territories. Ekberg, "Antoine Valentin de Gruy," 144. **house siting:** Sizemore, 134–35. Unlike houses in New England and colder climates, houses in the Ozarks were generally not positioned to limit exposure to winds; main concerns were to be near a water source (but higher than floods), above miasmas, and, if possible, on a rise.

86 . . . . **"from 1. to 3. miles back":** Copy of letter from Maj. James Bruff, St. Louis, to Genl. James Wilkinson, Massac, 28 May 1805; enclosed with letter from James Wilkinson, Massac, to Henry Dearborn, secretary of war, Washington, D.C., 15 June 1805, in Carter, vol. 13, 136. **naming sweeps of tallgrass:** "Meadow" soon seemed inadequate for the broad western grasslands. Eventually the French term "prairie" won out. G. Stewart, 151–52.

87 . . . . **"The shores of the Arkansas":** "Arkansas Territory."

87 . . . . **"as sickly as the shores of Surinam":** Flint, *History and Geography* (1832), 281.

87 . . . . **allure of adventurous exploration:** Dettelbach; Terrall.

88 . . . . **fundamental cohesion of health geography:** In 1848, a Missouri medical journal reprinted reports originally from Berlin that barometric pressure affected mortality rates

("Influences of the Weather Upon Health," reprinted in the *Missouri Medical and Surgical Journal*). The observations of a German physician were judged relevant to practitioners struggling to advise patients in the burgeoning urban environment of St. Louis and the prairieland of surrounding communities. Details of specific regions might vary, but the framework of thinking about health was globally encompassing.

88 . . . . **"remarkably high and healthy"**: William Russell, St. Louis, to William Rector, surveyor for Missouri, 20 April 1814, in Carter, vol. 14, 753. **"high, healthful position"**: Bek, "Nicholas Hesse," Part 1, 30. Hesse was describing Jefferson City, the state capital. **"too low & sickly"**: James Miller, Fort Smith, to William H. Crawford, the secretary of war, Washington, D.C., 11 Dec. 1820, in Carter, vol. 14, 246. Some authorities held that higher regions were free of certain kinds of diseases, since air closer to the earth was "more contaminated with noxious exhalations," as one medical advice book put it. Other medical professionals held that the *kinds* of diseases in areas of varying elevation did not differ, but their *frequency* did. Ticknor, 271. For a contrasting view, see Twyman, 29. Modern medicine would relate many of these differences to the ecology of malaria; anopheles mosquitoes do not fly far from their birthplaces. Humphreys, *Malaria*, 10.

88 . . . . **slaves working unhealthy lowlands**: Scarpino, 29–31. Planters in the Georgia low country tried to site slave quarters in locations that would produce the least sickness, but also put slaves closest to the fields. Stewart, *"What Nature Suffers to Groe"*: 308–9, n. 121.

88 . . . . **"Some Plantations in the bottoms"**: Thomas A. Bennett, Spring Hill, Ark. Terr., to Philip Rainey, Boydton, Va., 18 June 1836, PRC.

89 . . . . **"low, marshy grounds"**: Cornet, 228. **"It is not so generally known"**: AWW, 12.

89 . . . . **"the point itself"**: Capt. John Stuart, Fort Smith, Ark. Terr., to Col. R. Jones, adjutant general, Washington, D.C., 19 Sept. 1833, in Carter, vol. 11, 794. **"after an illness of five weeks"**: *Arkansas State Gazette*, 2 Jan. 1839.

90 . . . . **"a healthy asylum"**: Levine, 138.

90 . . . . **"great changes of temperature"**: "Cautions for the Season," 112.

90 . . . . **"If I could only smell the seas"**: H. A. Whittington, Little Rock, to Granville Whittington, [Boston], 2 July 1828, in Ross, "Letters of Hiram Abiff Whittington," 5. Whittington later journeyed back to Boston, married Mary E. Burnham, and then returned to open a hotel, which he ran until 1849. In 1856 he opened a quarry exporting whetstones. He was able to turn the resources of Hot Springs to his advantage in a number of ways, and he died an upstanding citizen in 1890. Scully, *Hot Springs, Arkansas*, 29 and 403–4.

90 . . . . **"geological grounds"**: Featherstonhaugh, "Geology of Arkansas" 25 Aug. 1835. **following the Boones**: Anderson, "Missouri, 1804–1828," 159, quoting Brackenridge, 109. **Familiarity**: McNeilly, 16, 22. Regions of Arkansas Territory, the New York *Saturday Evening Post* reassured readers in 1833, were "as healthy as any country of Pennsylvania or New England." "Arkansas Territory." **the lure of the familiar**: As an old man in 1830, the Connecticut emigrant Stephen Hempstead bought some oysters that had been shipped up from New Orleans by steamboat—"the first that I have seen sense I came to the country [Missouri]." Sadly, "They were not good as many of them were dead having a long passage"—a passage from sea-country not unlike that of Hempstead himself. Jensen, Part 9, 23 Feb. 1830, 427.

90 . . . . **"The previous nights"**: Bek, "George Engelmann," Part 3, 526. **George Engelmann:** A prominent collector, botanist, and natural scientific observer, Engelmann was enlisted by a local magnate, Thomas Shaw, to develop a botanical garden. Shaw later donated it to the city of St. Louis. Opened to the public in 1859, the Missouri Botanical Garden has become an international center of botanical research. Bek, "George Engelmann"; Elliott, *Biographical Dictionary*; Goldstein, especially 584; Jansma and Jansma; WPA, *Missouri,* 319–20.

91 . . . . **"some peculiarity in the state of the atmosphere"**: JJB, 19 May 1854. **"epidemic constitution"**: Hannaway, 296–97.

92 . . . . **"*the most highly malarious*"**: Maury, 267.

92 . . . . **"moderately warm and moist atmosphere"**: Ticknor, 257.

92 . . . . **"at ten o clock in the Morning"**: JGG, 18 June 1837.

93 . . . . **"there was almost no household"**: J. W. Miller, 82. **gender imbalances:** see notes for p. 40.

93 . . . . **Schoolcraft on mortality of women and children:** Rafferty, *Rude Pursuits,* 74. **"Being much exposed":** J. E. Thompson, 270.

94 . . . . **"In a lean-to of rough-hewn logs"**: Romantic though he was, Gerstäcker was astute about the priorities of the larger society. "As much as has been written about the backwoodsmen of the West," he observed, "it is hard to find much information about the women who share the loneliness of the forests with their men" (J. W. Miller, 49).

94 . . . . **"Fort Smith":** Matthew Arbuckle, Fort Smith, Ark. Terr., to John C. Calhoun, secretary of war, Washington, D.C., 16 May 1822, in Carter, vol. 19, 417.

95 . . . . **"the thousand (at least) local marshes"**: "L.," "The Causes of Disease in St. Louis," 535.

95 . . . . **"found little Jim being rolled over and over"**: Albert, 63–64.

95 . . . . **chinking between logs:** McRaven, 42–43; Faris, 91–92. **lack of barrier between indoors and outdoors:** Dunlop, 34–35. **invading bears:** Keefe and Morrow, *White River Chronicles,* 76–77 and 99–101; Rosa Simmons, int. Bernice Bowden, in Rawick, vol. 10, Arkansas Part 6, 157. **trading post trickery:** Keefe and Morrow, *White River Chronicles,* 42–44 (the merchant eventually noticed that each successive hide was exactly the same weight and color and was worth, coincidentally, exactly a quart of whiskey). **gaping spaces in cabin walls:** "At breakfast time," reported George Hunter of his 1804 exploratory trip up the Ouachita River, "stopped at a Bark cabin inhabited by a Spaniard; it seemed to need no windows nor had any, but what light passed thro the joints was fully sufficient for every purpose." McDermott, "Western Journals," 90.

95 . . . . **rescue of Osage girl:** Park, 135–37. **"Solid" walls:** Ladurie (37, 40) notes that in the fourteenth-century Pyrenees hamlet of Montaillou, villagers could walk over and lift up the roof of a neighboring cottage to see who was at dinner. Ladurie contrasts the "flimsy and fragile construction" of the house with the "notional durability" of the household, or *domus*; in early Missouri and Arkansas, the household was a notion of similar social resonance but physical permeability.

96 . . . . **blurring of indoor and outdoor:** A scandalized Gottfried Duden reported to his German readers that not only did Missouri settlers leave their cabins whistling with wind,

but "In any season the children run, half naked, from their bed or from the blazing fireplace into the open." Quoted in Lanser, 32. **"Mrs. H. tells me"**: Rafferty, *Rude Pursuits,* 74.

96 . . . . **physical household mirroring larger social relations of the self**: St. George. **globules of lead**: Drake, "Traveling Letters," letter 9, 543. **"try as [a newcomer] might"**: Trautmann, 375.

97 . . . . **climate affects health**: These ideas had deep roots. See Sargeant.

97 . . . . **weather**: Fleming; Stewart, "Let Us Begin with the Weather?" **weather records**: Eliza Post recorded close to 50 years of Missouri weather in her memorandum books; Stephen Hempstead's diaries, too, carry almost daily weather notations. Journals by John Geiger and John Brown reflect farmers' ever-present concern for weather; the diary of the Little Rock politico and sometime farmer John Clendenin places weather in daily life. George Engelmann's observations are representative of conjoined scientific and popular interest (Bek, "George Engelmann," Part 1). **"pea-green climate"**: Thorpe, 155. **"Charming" climate**: Blowe, 686. **"soft . . . , rather smokey" weather**: JJG, 24 March 1835.

97 . . . . **"sickly southern clime"**: Jervey and Moss, 187. **"The weather is cloudy"**: JJB, 27 Sept. 1854. **sultriness and passivity**: McDermott, "A Warning," 244. **"delightful climate"**: Amos Wheeler, Little Rock, to Amos Wheeler [Sr.], N. Stonington, Conn., 21 May 1820, file 131, HSM. **"So long as you behave yourself"**: H. A. Whittington, Little Rock, to Granville Whittington, [Boston], 25 June 1831, in Ross, "Letters of Hiram Abiff Whittington," 25. **"not congenial to health"**: John [Welborn?] to "My Dear Brother and Sister," [Lucinda Smith and husband?], 5 May 1854, BFP.

98 . . . . **"mild, warm, and agreeable day"**: Jefferson and Dunbar, *Documents Relating to the Purchase and Exploration of Louisiana,* 59. **Missouri climate cures consumption**: A[masa] and R[oxana] Jones, Harmony, Mo., to Timothy Stearns, Ashburnham, Worcester Co., Mass., 23 May 1837, in Bronaugh.

98 . . . . **trees thought to affect climate**: Thompson, "Forests and Climate Change"; ibid., "Trees as a Theme." **"Climate may be defined"**: Collins, "A Dissertation on the Remote Causes of Fever," 492.

99 . . . . **"the kind of self-satisfaction"**: Cooper, *The Pioneers,* 319.

99 . . . . **"Each man is primarily endued"**: Royer-Collard, 141.

99 . . . . **"irritable child"**: NDAD, 24 Jan. 1844.

100 . . . . **"injured"**: H. A. Whittington, Hot Springs, to Granville Whittington, [Boston], in Ross, "Letters of Hiram Abiff Whittington," 50. S. W. Woodhouse noted of a sick soldier that "his constitution is broken down having had Syphalis 6 times and has it now" (Tomer and Brodhead, 81). **"Constitution was impaired"**: Message by Governor Miller to the Territorial Assembly, 10 Feb. 1820, in Carter, vol. 19, 138–40, 139.

100 . . . . **"viscid, sizy, or buff like blood"**: Hillary, iii. **"You say Betsy has been quite ill"**: Justus Post to John Post, 16 Dec. 1807, JPP. **mind has constitution**: Drake, "Anniversary Address," in Shapiro and Miller, 60.

100 . . . . **"geological constitution"**: Levine, 165. **Seasons have "constitutions"**: Twyman, 28. **"an epidemic constitution"**: Reed, 11. Such notions of innate tendency were tied to Christian teleology through the widely shared faith in what Daniel Drake termed "the

plan of nature." Underlying meaning was immanent in the material world, and could ultimately be made accessible to sustained observation. Levine, 654.

100 . . . . **"This is a delightful climate"**: Amos Wheeler, Little Rock, to Amos Wheeler [Sr.], N. Stonington, Conn., 21 May 1820, file 131, HSM.

101 . . . . **"[T]he whole of this country"**: McDermott, "Western Journals," 20 Oct. 1804, 82. **"our malarious fevers"**: "Health of the Season," Sept. 1851.

101 . . . . **altering environments to change their healthfulness**: Nash, "Disease"; Riley, *Eighteenth-Century Campaign*. **"prevent . . . exhalations"**: AWW, 69. A "dry culture" ordinance passed in Savannah, Georgia, in 1817 conversely specified that the switch to dryland crops from rice cultivation was necessary because the areas near the city would therefore be "sweated" of their miasmatic waters. Stewart, *"What Nature Suffers to Groe,"* 143.

101 . . . . **"Grate raft"**: Henry M. Shreve to Brig. Genl. C. Gratot, Washington, D.C., 5 June 1833, in Carter, vol. 21, 730. **"trees of considerable size"**: William Dunbar, American State Papers, Indian Affairs, in WPA, *Arkansas*, 322. **"the whole width of the river"**: "Arkansas Territory." Captain Shreve directed the efforts of 150 laborers and four snag boats over a five-year period to destroy the raft; when they were done, in 1838, a flash flood immediately caused debris to clog up the channel once again. The federal government spent over a quarter of a million dollars in efforts to keep open the channel, but the raft wasn't finally cleared until 1873. Shallat, 147–48; WPA, *Arkansas,* 322; U.S. Army Corps of Engineers, 43.

102 . . . . **"great work of cutting the raft out"**: Featherstonhaugh, "Geology of Arkansas," 1 Sept. 1835.

102 . . . . **health travel**: Barbour; Baur; Hedrick; B. Jones; Long; Rothman; Thompson, "Climatotherapy"; ibid., "Wilderness and Health"; Wrigley and Revill. Traveling to improve health was such an expected and routine part of medical therapy that it could prove useful for those not wanting to divulge details about their journeys; medical reasons were premise enough for any trip. Dunlop, 181. **"You remember the miserable state of my health"**: Flint, *Recollections* (1826), 8. As Charles Noland lamented, "My health has been decidedly worse this winter than ever before, and I am determined on abandoning Arkansas—I have fool like stuck here, until my constitution is all but ruined and my money in a great measure exhausted." Charles F. M. Noland, Batesville, Ark., to Maj. William Noland, "Washington City," 2 Jan. 1846, Noland family correspondence, file 67, HSM.

102 . . . . **"ascend in the season of fever"**: Flint, *Recollections*, 258. **"down sick with slow fever"**: Amsy O. Alexander, Little Rock, int. Samuel S. Taylor, in Rawick, 25–26.

103 . . . . **"were you to settle in Missouri"**: Anne Biddle, St. Louis, to Dennis Delany, M.D., 19 Feb. 1835, box 1, MFP. **"in search of health"**: Julia Barnard Strong to "My dear Aunt H.," 15 Feb. 1838, in McClarty, 339. **claims of improved health**: For instance, letters from an Arkansas plantation manager, James Trooper Armstrong, Woodstock, Ark., to his apparently dubious wife, Matilda (Greene) Armstrong, [Tenn.] 27 Oct. 1851 and 3 Oct. 1852, JTAC. **"the last resort"**: Flint, *Recollections*, 360.

103 . . . . **recommendation that men travel for health**: ISMN, 121–22. **Sea voyages as a way to improve health**: Jonathan M. Dow, Augusta, Ark., to Charles G. Dow, Dover, N.H., 8 Sept. 1837, box 1, file 43, HSM. **Dana**: Dana returned to Boston after spending two years in the cattle-hide trade along the California coast in good health, though appalled at the condi-

tions of common sailors aboard ship. **salutary challenges of travel:** Drake, *A Systematic Trea-tise*, vol. 1, 175. As G. Penn, St. Louis, wrote to Meredith Marmaduke, in March 1849, "I have no doubt travelling would be of service to her provided she has suficient strength to stand it." Box 5, SFP.

103 . . . . **women traveling for health:** Sheila Rothman (*Living in the Shadow of Death*) has argued that men were seen as benefiting from journeys, particularly under rough conditions, but women were typically expected to stay within the domestic environment, the health ben-efits of travel notwithstanding. Sources from the Mississippi Valley do not bear this out. **"my wife hath received much Benefit":** Jensen, Part 4, 4 July 1819, 280. As Susan Klepp ob-serves ("Lost, Hidden, Obstructed and Repressed," 78–79), because of the links between "cold" humors and the absence of metaphorically "hot" menstrual blood, women suffering from ailments associated with the common cold (including rheumatism and pleurisy) were given some of the same treatments as for obstructed menses, including horseback riding.

103 . . . . **slaves' hopes for health benefits of travel:** Prince, 18. **"the negro Rich-mond":** B. B. Eskridge, Memphis, to W. E. Woodruff, [Little Rock], 7 Sept. 1860, WEWP (Es-kridge wrote variously from Memphis and from nearby Wassanka, in Arkansas). Identifying this slave only by a first name, while calling the two slave holders by their last names, uncomfort-ably recapitulates the racial and economical differences of power at the time. The other option would be to call him "Richmond Eskridge," but since many slaves rejected owners' last names after emancipation (or even during slavery), that seems even more inaccurate. **Woodruff's management of Richmond:** Eskridge to Woodruff, 7 Sept. 1860. Urban slaves—often those skilled at artisanal work or in the building trades—frequently hired out their own time; many even lived independently in their own households, remitting periodic fees to their owners. This practice was made illegal in Little Rock after 1832. Bellamy, "Free Blacks"; Lack, especially 263; B. L. Green; Hunter, especially 244–45; McGettigan, Part 2, 272–78; Seematter, 41; Scarpino, 37–43.

104 . . . . **Little Rock–Memphis road:** Though it had been improved since the territorial period, travel between the two cities was still not easy. **"I am confident," "I now intend":** Eskridge to Woodruff, 7 Sept. 1860, WEWP. It was not unprecedented for slave owners to send their chattel to hot springs and other places of healing, especially Hot Springs, Ark. Kiple and King, 169. **"improving in health":** Eskridge to Woodruff, 12 Dec. 1860, WEWP.

104 . . . . **"his Swellings & complaint":** Ibid., 21 May 1861, WEWP. *"his wish"* (Eskridge's emphasis), **"bring me at least $10"; "heavy travelling Bills":** Ibid., 6 May 1861. **"as he seems without benefit":** Ibid., 9 Dec. 1861.

105 . . . . **"I have ever regarded him":** Ibid., 21 May 1861, WEWP. **white hostility to "loafers" among urban slaves:** Lack, 272. Slave owners also feared "lurking" runaways who would escape from plantations to urban areas where their relatives lived. B. L. Green, 160.

105 . . . . **"a trip to the mountains":** John J. Walker, St. Louis, to Thomas H. Walker, Brownsburgh, Rockbridge Co., Va., 5 Sept. 1830, JJWL. **"I go to the Merrimac":** Jensen, Part 6, 5 Sept. 1822, 240.

105 . . . . **"Son Gratiots wife & Children":** Ibid., 27 Nov. 1822, 245. **"recruite":** Ibid., Part 1, 2 Feb. 1813, 33. Travel—like all remedies—sometimes failed, leading to another mournful journey. Stephen Hempstead wrote in January of 1829 that the corpse of a neighbor

had just been brought back from "Pensacole"—no easy task in an era before embalming—after "she went their last fall in quest of health." Ibid., Part 9, 17 Jan. 1829, 411.

106 . . . . **William Brown:** His bright future and subsequent illness are chronicled in JJB, 11 March, 6 April, 28 June, and 19 Sept. 1858; and 13 Jan., 22 March, 10 April, 23 April, and 10 May 1859. John Brown wrote of his efforts to send William on his "Southern trip" 2 Oct., and worried about William's journey throughout the fall. William died 30 March 1860.

106 . . . . **Hugh Brown:** He marched off in battle dress 11 July 1861 and returned 17 July, and though he and his new wife continued with their plans to have a house built and went visiting in mid-August in hopes it would improve his health, he was hemorrhaging blood in late September. By October 1861, Hugh was dying and his older sister Margaret was sick.

106 . . . . **neighbors visit widow, and she them:** Jensen, Part 9, 23 Jan. 1830, 12 June 1830, 426, 430. **"spent the day at Mr Earls":** Ibid., Part 8, 27 Sept. 1827, 193.

107 . . . . **"change and Dr. Ruffins treatment":** JJB, 5 July 1861. **well-being a balance of body and mind:** Scoffern, 185–86.

107 . . . . **"this post is *intrinsically* unhealthy":** C. B. Welch, Fort Smith, to Jos. Lovell, surgeon general, Washington, D.C., 28 Feb. 1834, in Carter, vol. 21, 916–18.

107 . . . . **"A fine rain":** JJB, 1 Aug. 1857.

Chapter IV, Airs

109 . . . . **"Free mountain air":** Everard B. Dickinson, Buffalo City, Ark., to Mr. and Mrs. Philo Dickinson, Hartford, Conn., 22 Sept. 1848, box 1, folder 54, HSM.

110 . . . . **"heavy" air:** JJG, 15 Jan. 1836; **"poor" atmosphere":** Jervey and Moss, 178. **"obstructs perspiration":** "Of Air," in *The Domestic Physician*, especially 128.

110 . . . . **"a dark blue hazy atmosphere":** William Faux, account of travels in 1819–20, in Reuben Gold Thwaites, *Early Western Travels 1748–1846* (Cleveland, 1905), in Christisen, "A Vignette of Missouri's Native Prairie," 175. **"variable and thawey":** Jensen, Part 2, 2 Jan. 1815, 284.

111 . . . . **"just breathe them":** T. B. Thorpe, "The Big Bear of Arkansas," in W. T. Porter, *The Big Bear of Arkansas,* 17. **"breathe another atmosphere":** Flora C. Byrne, Byrnham Wood, Clark Co., Mo., to Eliza Blackwell Mayer, Baltimore, 6 Aug. [1848], "Byrnham Wood in Missouri," 99. **"hooping Cought":** Jensen, Part 3, 13 Aug. 1818, 90.

111 . . . . **"pure, and . . . free":** "Health of St. Louis." **Pure air revives sick:** Ticknor, "Climate and Season," in *The Philosophy of Living,* 268–70. By the latter nineteenth century, exposure to outside air was proclaimed as part of the West's "wilderness cure." Thompson, "Wilderness and Health," 153; Jones, *Health-Seekers in the Southwest.* **"Transparent atmosphere":** McDermott, *Western Journals,* Sept. 13, 81. **"astonishing number of births":** Ewell, "Speculations Concerning the Agency of Oxygene in Promoting Conception," 132. Ewell further speculated that couples could prevent conception "by embracing only in vessels filled with carbonic acid or azotic gas."

112 . . . . **"the air bracing":** Tomer and Brodhead, 81.

112 . . . . **"a delightful temperature":** Flint, *Recollections,* 28.

112 . . . . **Freely circulating air healthy:** Ticknor, "Climate and Season," 266–67. The prospective English immigrant Henry Bousfield observed that Franklin, Missouri, was "a most healthy district," not least because of "the free circulation of air over its extensive yet undulating plains." HBD, 21 Jan. 1819. His tour of reconnaissance was evidently satisfactory: Bousfield moved to the Boon's Lick region surrounding Franklin shortly thereafter. **Emigrants' guides advised scrutiny of winds:** Flagg, *Far West,* 202. **to "air":** "To ventilate," "to expose to the air," "to expel dampness." Webster, s.v. "air." **Airing makes things less harmful:** Park, 81. **"swept by the winds":** Flint, *Recollections,* 255–56.

112 . . . . **"A very warm uncomfortable day":** Jensen, Part 3, 5 Nov. 1818, 94. **"Every wind on the prairies":** Emily Mason, Fort Gibson, to Catherine Rowland, 1 March 1845, in Scully, "Across Arkansas in 1844," 48.

112 . . . . **"Refreshing breezes":** N. D. Smith, iv. **"a gentle breeze nearly everywhere":** Gregory, 121. **"soft breezes of the south":** JJB, 16 Jan. 1860.

113 . . . . **"Rocky Mountain breeze":** JJB, 12 Nov. 1859. **"the breath of the South":** Jansma and Jansma, 232.

113 . . . . **"a north and northeast wind":** JJB, 26 June 1857. **"Pestilential East wind":** Ibid., 16 October 1857. **"southeast sickly wind":** JJG, 10 July 1841. **"bleak spring winds":** Flora Byrne, St. Louis, to Elizabeth Blackwell Mayer, 23 Feb. [1840], in "Byrnham Wood in Missouri," 73.

114 . . . . **"The fluid which we breathe":** Webster, s.v. "air." **Damp air dangerous:** AWW, 70; Flint, *Recollections,* 291. **still air unhealthful:** Flint, *History and Geography* (1832), 281; Bek, "Nicholas Hesse," Part 2, 180; Hannaway; Nutton, "Seeds of Disease"; Rupke, "Humboldtian Medicine"; Temkin. **naming miasma:** John Bell referred in 1825 to contemporary interest in "marsh miasmata or effluvia, or, as it is now more fashionably called, malaria." Bell, "On Miasm as an Alleged Cause of Fevers," 275. **shift in meanings of "malaria":** Humphreys, *Malaria,* 46.

114 . . . . **miasma:** This concept survived for so long because it expressed something useful: people's intuition that air that looked funny and smelled bad could hurt them. Modern medicine has taken away this reassuring continuity between felt experience and disease causation, but suspicion of "bad air" continues into the present day, with "sick buildings" and now mold reconfirming the connection between bad air and sickness. Belkin; Murphy, "Sick Buildings and Sick Bodies"; Ibid., "The 'Elsewhere within Here.'" **miasma as near-universal worry:** Solomon Northup recorded his dread of "the poisonous miasmas" of the Louisiana swamps among which he was enslaved (Eakin and Logsdon, 179). Northup was a free-born man from New York state, so his impressions may have more in common with those of the New Englanders Stephen and Mary Hempstead or Everard Dickinson than with those of the Southern slaves with whom he labored. Yet much of what made miasmas compelling—their relationship with dangerous and repulsive environments, their capacity to function both as mist and as particle, and their ability to connect natural terrain and human body in functionally powerful ways—was common to the lifeworlds of North and South.

114 . . . . **preoccupation with putrefaction:** This continued into later-nineteenth-century etiology; see Hamlin, "Providence and Putrefaction."

115 . . . . **"unhealthy fog":** Windell, 46. **fog creates illness:** Bacon. **"medicine for the children":** Justus Post to John Post, Addison, Vt., 1 Feb. 1818, JPP.

115 . . . . **miasma as smoke:** Drake, *Natural and Statistical View,* 183. **miasma wafted:** Coolidge, 442; Twyman, 27. **"like a *black mist*":** W. T. Porter, 30.

115 . . . . **"stagnant marshes":** "L.," "Causes of Disease in St. Louis," 535. The correlation of miasmas with low, wet places facilitated subsequent acceptance of the mosquito vector theory—which, after all, agreed with folk knowledge in identifying stagnant water as a source of disease, if not for exactly the same reasons. Humphreys, *Malaria,* 46.

115 . . . . **Benjamin Rush and "heroic" therapeutics:** Shryock, *Medicine and Society in America,* 67–72; Sullivan. Rush ("An Enquiry"; An Inquiry) was perhaps the most prolific authority to argue against person-to-person contagion and for miasma as the transmitter of disease. See also Hillary.

115 . . . . **"by entangling":** Rush, *An Inquiry,* 33.

116 . . . . **"infecting substances floating in the air":** Webster, s.v. "miasma." **"diffusion of Miasmata":** AWW, 12. **winds carry miasmas from bottomlands:** Coolidge, 442. **one side of mountain "healthy":** Twyman, 25–32.

116 . . . . **"which will Stagnate":** Anderson Wilson Clay Co., Mo., to Samuel and Ann Wilson Turrentine, Orange Co., N.C., 6 July 1835, in Stokes, 500.

116 . . . . **"drink in the humid atmosphere":** Flint, *History and Geography* (1833), 37.

116 . . . . **not "confined to the immediate locality":** Maughs, 5. **"miasm atmosphere":** Matthew, 59–61.

117 . . . . **"a weary plod":** Flagg, *Far West,* 201–2. **"upas" tree:** *Antiaris toxicaria,* a Javanese tree with poisonous sap, was thought in the nineteenth century to be so virulent that it killed all other living things for miles.

117 . . . . **smells sicken:** See Barker. **But there was some debate:** Chisholm. **"many trees that have fallen down":** Bek, "Nicholas Hesse," Part 1, 27.

118 . . . . **odors and health:** Corbin; Dobson, 10–18. **"terebinthine odour":** Flint, *Recollections,* 340. **"peculiarly offensive odor":** Gantt, "Medical Topography," 197. **odors and geography of health:** Naysayers of the Boone family migration into Kentucky "scented in the air of the country, deadly diseases." Flint, *First White Man,* 79.

118 . . . . **"make a lean man fat":** Noland, *Pete Whetstone of Devil's Fork,* 87. **different peoples have different smells:** To visiting Native Americans in 1725, women of the French court smelled like alligators. Foley, *The Genesis of Missouri,* 23. **"the peculiar *odour* of our 'colored brethren' ":** Thomas C. Reynolds, St. Louis, to George Payne Rainsford James, a British novelist visiting Norfolk, 20 June 1853, in Drumm, "Letters of Thomas Caute Reynolds," 26.

118 . . . . **smells of sickness and death:** J. W. Calvert, St. Francis Co., Ark., to John L. Trone, 29 July 1851, JLTC. **"After a while I took down sick":** Boston Blackwell, North Little Rock, int. Beulah Sherwood Hagg, in Rawick, vol. 8, Part 1, 173. **"so as to kill the scent":** Eliot, *The Story of Archer Alexander,* 52.

119 . . . . **"The odor was terrible":** Rose Mosley, Brassfield, Ark., int. Irene Robertson, in Rawick, supplement series 1, vol. 2, 15. Mosley was probably working in Memphis.

119 . . . . **smells considered dangerous into later nineteenth century:** Henry Morton Stanley later recounted the horrors of a Union prisoner-of-war camp, describing severely ill

prisoners who fell near the latrine ditches "and made their condition hopeless by breathing the stenchful atmosphere." Stanley, 210. **"stink boat" and popular suspicion of disease-bearing smell:** Hurley, "Busby's Stink Boat," 145, 147, 151. **"a festering sore":** *St. Louis Globe-Democrat*, 19 July 1873, in ibid., 146. On the legal collision between commonsense notions of the harmfulness of stench and the commercial interests of emerging industries that produced bad smells as well as thick smoke, see Golan.

119 . . . . **burning substances against cholera:** McLear, 176–77. **"impregnating the air":** Rush, *An Inquiry*, 45–48.

120 . . . . **"made a slow fire":** Dana, 243–44.

120 . . . . **asafetida bags:** Keeney, 290; WPA, *Arkansas*, 101. **"assafiddity bags":** Ideas about disease are long-lasting. Children in the Ozarks (and likely elsewhere) in the 1950s still wore drugstore-purchased "assafiddity bags" to ward off flu. I learned this in conversation with L. Scott Stafford, Little Rock, 28 Dec. 1997; on this practice (and pronunciation) see also "Oh, the Smell of It!" **"her mouth filled with tansy":** Park, 81.

121 . . . . **"means of destroying the morbid miasmata":** Rush, *An Inquiry*, 45–50.

121 . . . . **clothing and other measures to combat miasmas:** AWW, 70; Rush, "An Enquiry"; Rush also admonished people to wash frequently, and of course to be bled. **"You must not think this place sickly":** Flora C. Byrne, Byrnham Wood, Clark Co., Mo., to Eliza Blackwell Mayer, Baltimore, 7 Aug. [1844], in "Byrnham Wood in Missouri," 80. **cautious management:** Such ceaseless caution was laced with delicate regret. "Methinks I should tempt fortune a little too far in exposing myself to the night air at this season of the year," mused Henry Bousfield in the winter of 1819. HBD, 24 Jan. 1819.

122 . . . . **"A new, unsettled country":** Joseph Shriver, "Camp Osage," Mo., to his brother in Maryland, July 1829, in Klein, "Letters of a Young Surveyor," 75. **tales of disgusting and fascinatingly huge centipedes and monster snakes:** Keefe and Morrow, *White River Chronicles*, 205–22.

122 . . . . **"fallen and decayed timber":** Skinner, 252. **small insects and disease:** Daniel Drake advanced what has been termed the "animalcular theory" of disease contagion, arguing that tiny, winged, invisible, airborne insects were the actual bearers of miasmatic poison. The medical historian Charles E. Rosenberg has noted that this theory, so attractive to historians searching for antecedents to modern "germ theory," was simply a variant on standard ideas of miasma as particulate matter mixed with air. Rosenberg, "Cause of Cholera," 336.

122 . . . . **"the poisonous breath taints not our air":** "Warning to Slave-holders" sent by Edmund Turner, Hamilton, Canada West, to the abolition activist William Still, 1 March 1858, in Woodson, 572. Association between poison and slavery was a common metaphorical strategy; see Charles Peabody, 1846 Journal, 7, in box 2, 1844–1870, JDC.

123 . . . . **"for the moisture being evaporated by the heat":** Usher Parson, Boylston Prize Dissertations (Boston: 1839), Chapter 5, 227, quoting from an unnamed original source, in P. Allen, 496–97.

123 . . . . **"pestilential atmosphere":** Gantt, "A few Reasons," 212. In another article ("Medical Topography," 319), Gantt warned that those suffering a relapse from intermittent fever in north Alabama were in danger when "kept within the range of the malarial emanations

of the low lands," implying a measurable distance of miasma's reach. **Rush on rain and miasma:** Rush, "An Enquiry," 208.

123 . . . . **"particles of miasmatic poison":** C. B. Welch, Fort Smith, to Jos. Lovell, the Surgeon General, Washington, D.C. 28 Feb. 1834, in Carter, vol. 21, 918. Other observers concurred. Timothy Flint (*History and Geography* [1833], 38) remarked, "It is said, that the miasm . . . is specifically lighter than atmospheric air; . . . and that, were it colored, it would be seen overlaying the purer strata of air beneath it." **"terrestrial emanations":** "C.C.," 145. **early modern science of air:** Hannaway. Indeed, miasmatic theories were often explained in the vocabulary of the emerging chemical investigations, for instance, "Why Epidemics Rage at Night," 1850?.

124 . . . . **"the peculiar poison":** "Health of the City."

124 . . . . **smallpox as ideal-type of contagious disease:** Rosenberg, "Cause of Cholera." **popular notions of contagion:** Rosenberg, "Cause of Cholera" (see 337, 350) and *Cholera Years*. He argues for a gradual shift in medical thought over the course of the century, toward the acceptance of disease specificity and contagion.

124 . . . . **medical skepticism about miasmatic theories of disease:** "Medicus," 509; Collins, "A Dissertation."

125 . . . . **contagion and disease causation:** Ackerknecht, "Anticontagionism"; P. Allen; Barnes; Coleman; Hamlin, "Predisposing Causes"; Pelling, "Contagion/Germ Theory/Specificity"; Rosenberg, "Cause of Cholera."

125 . . . . **"undoubtedly propagated by contagion":** J. E. Thompson, 269.

125 . . . . **"Some contend that it is *unconditionally contagious*":** Ibid., 329. Such a structural division is common to many medical writers (see Drake, *A Systematic Treatise*, 1).

126 . . . . **"The origins and nature of miasmata":** AWW, 6.

126 . . . . **"but their effects are as certainly felt":** Rush, *An Inquiry,* 82; **"It is to no purpose to say" and subsequent examples:** Ibid., 97–98.

127 . . . . **"sloughs and foul marshes":** Maughs, 5. **Rot produces miasma:** In his cataloguing of the many causes of miasma, Benjamin Rush listed examples of both animal and vegetable matter in a state of putrefaction: "the canvas of an old tent," damp cotton, "old books, and old paper money, that had been wetted, and confined in close rooms and closets," "the entrails of fish," or, more ominously, "Human bodies that have been left unburied upon a field of battle." Rush, *An Inquiry,* 6–10.

127 . . . . **"mephitic vapour":** Flagg, *Far West,* 202.

127 . . . . **"deep and grand forests":** Flint, *History and Geography* (1833), 37. **relationship between plants and miasmatic vapors:** The subject of wide study. Rotting plants, all agreed, could give off or encourage miasmas. Live vegetation, by contrast, was suggested by some observers to have a positive effect; one physician-scientist proposed colonizing the entire Mississippi Valley with a swamp plant that he concluded absorbed miasmas and rendered marshy districts healthful. Ricketson, 3; Cartwright.

128 . . . . **"Much depends on the care":** Brackenridge, 111–12.

128 . . . . **"an atmosphere, if I may so say, of cotton":** Flint, *Recollections*, 369. **"asphyxiating coal gas":** J. W. Miller, 64. By the 1850s, urban pollution—especially the highly pol-

luting coal brought over from Illinois—was an offensive and widely discussed problem of the St. Louis city streets. Tarr and Zimring.

129 . . . . **sewers and drainage in St. Louis:** Corbett, "Draining the Metropolis"; Schroeder, "Environmental Setting of the St. Louis Region," 18–19. **flight from urban pollution:** WPA, *Missouri,* 390.

129 . . . . **skepticism about healthy countryside:** "In the State of Ohio," concluded Daniel Drake in 1840, "we have ascertained that the towns have been more healthy than the country." Drake, "Summer and Autumn Diseases of 1840," 399. **medical opinion on comparative health of cities:** Humphreys, *Malaria,* 30–31.

129 . . . . **William Switzler:** Conard, s.v. "Switzler, William Franklin"; Gentry; Hurt, *Agriculture and Slavery,* 280–81, 297. **"[Arkansas] is now as all other newly settled countries":** Switzler, "My Second Tour in the South" (transcript), 13–14, WFSP.

130 . . . . **"exhalations from the soil":** Matthew, 59–61. **"exhalations arising from the swamps and morasses":** Audubon, 139.

131 . . . . **"some of the infectious miasmata":** Hillary, 43.

131 . . . . **"highly putrescent organic matter":** "On the Influence of Noxious Effluvia," 556–57.

131 . . . . **"The wind laid & produced a frost":** JJG, 2 Oct. 1836. **"one of those sultry days":** Audubon, 117.

131 . . . . **"current of air impregnated":** Peter Carr, Jefferson City, Mo., to James O. Broadhead, probably Pike Co., Mo., 4 Feb. 1857, in "Fragments of Broadhead Collection," 45.

132 . . . . **"the seeds of the yellow fever":** Rush, *An Inquiry,* 19.

132 . . . . **"In leaving a place infected by miasmata":** Rush, *An Inquiry,* 21. Similar language about the "seeds of disease" flourishing in human "soil" prepared well by jailhouse filth and poor nutrition can be found in Hunt, 343–44. Imagery of human beings as soil that could be seeded would also have been familiar to Rush's audience from the New Testament parable (Matthew 13:19–23) in which God is a sower scattering seed on different kinds of soil.

Chapter V, Waters

133 . . . . **crucial role of waterways in American settlement:** Schneiders, Chapter 4. **and the environment of the western U.S.:** Reisner; Worster. **cultural, technological, and scientific meanings:** Nash, "Changing Experience of Nature"; White, *Organic Machine.* **spiritual meanings:** Mooney, "Cherokee River Cult."

134 . . . . **"dry, airy, and eligible":** Rafferty, *Rude Pursuits,* 119. **"pondy" bottoms:** Drake, *A Systematic Treatise,* vol. 1, 169. **"swimming":** Park, 85. **"accurately indicate":** Elijah Hayward, General Land Office, to James S. Conway, surveyor, Ark. Terr., 17 June 1835, in Carter, vol. 11, 1050–51.

134 . . . . **Drake's "hydrographical method":** Levine, 2.

134 . . . . **Waterways in booster accounts:** "Arkansas Territory"; "Arkansas—Her Products—Inviting Emigration." **"sending this to the river":** Flora Caldwell Byrne, Byrnham Wood, to Eliza Blackwell Mayer, Baltimore, 12 May 1845, in "Byrnham Wood in Missouri," 85.

waterways and autonomy of slaves and freed people: W. W. Brown, 6–11; Seematter. **steamboats as potential avenue of escape:** Schafer, 97–115; Franklin and Schweninger, 118, 133–4, 168.

135 . . . . **Thirst:** For instance, Stanley, 150. **"its color was almost that of milk":** Park, 79–80. **"drink of first rate cold water":** Tomer and Brodhead, 83. When water was not particularly potable, other options might be found. A considerate host in 1833 packed for a traveler "a bottle of good old whiskey, which I found very acceptable as the water was not the very best in the world." Lupton and Lupton, 226.

135 . . . . **"good running water":** Nelson, 268. Water was crucial not only for drinking, bathing, and cooking, but for keeping things cool: households used springhouses, wells, or simply large containers of fresh water to preserve dairy products. Sizemore, 125. **"no trouble to git":** Martin Camp and M. A. [?] Camp, [Saline] Co., Ark., to Mary and L. H. Williams, 2 March 1860, series 2, box 1, file 21, MLC. **"tell him":** Silvester V. How, Bayou Metou, Pulaski Co., Ark., to Jane Pursley, 6 March 1860, MFJPP.

136 . . . . **taste and temperature:** Levine, 661. **color of the Arkansas:** Robert F. Henry, Hopkinsville, Ark., to Dr. J. F. Henry, "On the Wing," 12 Sept. 1819, seventh page, Box 2, File 64, HSM. Creeks in one part of Crawford County, by contrast, were "inclined to be red and muddy." Noland, "Crawford County." **"The water is red":** Jervey and Moss, 185. **colorful waters of the Missouri:** For example, Levine, 141. Robert Schneiders (29–30) points out that the Missouri River, the "Big Muddy," was not actually muddy for most of the antebellum period; instead it was silty with leachates. The mud came when farming caused prairie topsoil to run off into the river. The Red River, by contrast, stained the Black River red; McDermott, "Western Journals," 114. **"The river on the rise":** JJG, 3 July 1839.

136 . . . . **"This is a healthy country":** Everard B. Dickinson, North Fork, Ark., to Mr. and Mrs. Philo Dickinson, Springfield, Mass., 21 June 1850, box 1, file 54, HSM. **"fine Clear Spring and well water":** Bingham, 187. **"The soil is very good":** Bek, "Followers of Duden, Third Article," 442. Hermann Steines's family later emigrated as a large group to Franklin County, Missouri.

136 . . . . **nutritive qualities of waters:** Levine, 661–68.

136 . . . . **Even ordinary water powerful:** "Cold water causes many diseases, injures the teeth." ISMN, 22. **"change of waters":** JJB, 9 May 1861 (see also 26 June 1861). **"died begging for water":** Keefe and Morrow, *White River Chronicles,* 26.

137 . . . . **"a powerful cathartick":** Zadok Cramer, *Navigator,* 1814, in M. Allen, 257. **"said to be healthful":** Bek, "Followers of Duden, Twelfth Article," 488. **"it only requires a little courage":** Arese, 62; also B. M. Jones, 35. Water from the silty Missouri was often regarded as health-giving; those drinking it just had to be sure to sip only the top portion so as not to swallow thick sediment. Schneiders, 39–40. Waters that stank or that acted with force within the digestive tract worked on the same principles as the "strong and very bitter decoction" with which an early scientific traveler through the region staved off "a slight attack of the intermittent fever" in 1819. Lottinville, 204.

138 . . . . **"Every one of the Surveyors":** William Rector, Surveyors Office, St. Louis, to Josiah Meigs, Washington, D.C., 18 Oct. 1819, in Carter, vol. 19, 116.

138 . . . . **"Everything going to destruction"**: Jervey and Moss, 195. **"thick green scum"**: Park, 76.

138 . . . . **"one greate cause to produce Sickness here"**: Capt. John Stuart, Fort Smith, to Lewis Cass, secretary of war, Washington, D.C., 7 Feb. 1834, in Carter, vol. 21, 898.

139 . . . . **"Kayser's Lake"**: J. Thomas Scharf, *History of St. Louis City* (1883), in Corbett, "Draining the Metropolis," 111.

139 . . . . **stagnant water**: C. B. Welch, Fort Smith, to Jos. Lovell, Washington, D.C., 28 Feb. 1834, in Carter, vol. 21, 917; Lottinville, 254; J. E. Thompson, 49. **"stoppage of . . . courses"**: Gunn, 297. **"bring forth" grubs**: H. Miller, 284.

139 . . . . **Sick Creek**: Edwin T. Clark, Washington, D.C., to the secretary of war, 18 April 1832, in Carter, vol. 21, 499. **Fever River**: Jensen, Part 7, 13 July 1826, 83. **"Over the sluggish waters"**: Memorial to Congress by the Territorial Assembly, 24 Oct. 1835, in Carter, vol. 21, 110.

140 . . . . **"the land of good quality"**: Richard D. C. Colins, "Camp on the road near the Saline," Ark. Terr., to Major Thomas S. Jesup, in Carter, vol. 21, 435. **"I was thinking of setting my cabin"**: Cortambert, 209.

140 . . . . **"deep and cold hole"**: Ed Craddock, in Rawick, vol. 11, Missouri narratives, 97. **"damp dews"**: AWW, 67. **"They took cold by being wet"**: Jensen, Part 5, 15 July 1820, 45.

140 . . . . **"causes coughs and colds"**: Bek, "Nicholas Hesse," Part 3, 302. **"not allowed to learn the art of swimming"**: Eakin and Logsdon, 101. Bayou Boeuf was named for the beef cattle that were the area's first colonial industry.

141 . . . . **"about 25 men on the sick list"**: Henry M. Shreve, "Red Rever Raft," to Brig. Genl. C. Gratot, Washington, D.C., 5 June 1833, in Carter, vol. 21, 731.

141 . . . . **"rain had fallen almost daily"**: "Health and Mortality of New Orleans," 558. **Sun makes water dangerous**: Rush, *An Inquiry*, 57. **"frequent and refreshing rains"**: "Health of Our City," 166. **"A heavy rain this morning"**: JJB, 13 May 1855.

141 . . . . **floods and flood control**: Barry; Daniel; Pabis. Periodic threat of deluge prompted a certain dry humor. One Ozark resident remembered a flood in 1824 as the "Pumpkin Freshet." Keefe and Morrow, *White River Chronicles*, 272, nn. 14, 15. **"riz"; "on a stand"; "fell"**: John Geiger thus described the nearby Mississippi. JJG, 5, 6, and 7 June 1835.

141 . . . . **"boiling floods"**: Lupton and Lupton, 224.

142 . . . . **"a most tremendious crash"**: Ibid., 225. **"booming flood"**: "A Flood," in Audubon, 29–35.

142 . . . . **harvesting corn under water**: Keefe and Morrow, *White River Chronicles*, 19–21. **"Many persons were drowned in their beds"**: Pope, 176. See also "The Inundation," 276–78 in Drake, "Traveling Letters," letter 4.

142 . . . . **flooding transforms terrain**: An 1826 map of the New Madrid area notes a "Fort part of which is already carried off by the waters." Foley, *Genesis of Missouri*, 126. Similarly, in 1828 the town of "Franklin simply slid into the water." Nagel, 61. **"Nearly the whole of that one thousand three hundred miles"**: Twain, *Life on the Mississippi*, 15 (Twain's original is in italics).

142 . . . . **"I almost envy you your locality"**: B. W. Lee, Arkansas Post, to James N. Lucas, St. Louis, 30 April 1844, KC. **floodwaters' consequences for commerce**: McNeilly, 112.

143 . . . . **"then commenced a sickness":** JJG, 143. **"remarkably sickly" season:** Cephas Washburn, Cherokee Nation, to James Moore, Little Rock, 5 Sept. 1833, WC.

144 . . . . **"by virtue of its location":** "L.," "Causes of Disease in St. Louis," 535.

144 . . . . **"noble, but too uncertain stream":** Featherstonhaugh, "Geology of Arkansas," 1 Sept. 1835. Similarly, "water does not rest on these prairies," observed Henry Bousfield in 1819, drawing an image of restless water that fit well with the sudden formation of rivulets and storm-streams during a summer's downpour on the mid-Missouri prairie. HBD, 6 Feb. 1819.

145 . . . . **swamps, marshes, bogs, and wetlands:** See Dobson, Chapter 6; Meanley; Vileisis; Wilson and Moritz; Winsor. **their myriad names:** G. R. Stewart, 61, 63. A particularly boggy region was referred to as "swampeast Missouri." WPA, *Missouri*, 93.

145 . . . . **"sloo":** Keefe and Morrow, *White River Chronicles*, 5.

145 . . . . **"swamps and miry bayous":** Switzler, "My Second Tour in the South," typescript, 40, WFSP. **historical constancy of encounter with swamps:** Braudel, 67. **"Mississippi Swamp":** An area "thirty or forty miles in extent, and annually subject to inundation." Petition to Congress by Samuel Dickins and others, 6 March 1832, in Carter, vol. 21, 467. As Arkansas schoolteacher and songwriter Jimmy Driftwood wrote about the 1825 frontier, "I never would've made it through the Arkansas mud if I hadn't been ridin' on my Tennessee stud."

146 . . . . **"A swamp in America":** J. W. Miller, 143–4. See the evocative brief description in Lupton and Lupton, 221. **difficult places also bountiful:** Theodore Pease Russell's childhood memories of winter hunting camps along the St. Francois and Black rivers centered on the delight of abundant food in animal-rich canebrakes during the winter. Keefe and Morrow, *A Connecticut Yankee*, 129. Darnton ("Peasants Tell Tales," in *The Great Cat Massacre*) focuses on a similar fascination with food in the folk tales of hungry Europeans. **vexing vegetation:** It's not clear what plant Gerstäcker meant. George Yatskiebych, botanist at the Missouri Botanical Garden, explains that twining milkwood has milky sap but is usually innocuous; poison oak's leaves look like white oak leaves but it is uncommon in the region; poison ivy—the most likely culprit—twines in trees and can have thick vines, but has a clear, not milky, sap (personal communication, 19 April 2002).

146 . . . . **"small miry and lagging rivulets":** Drake, *A Systematic Treatise*, vol. 1, 171. **"I have seen no man":** J. M. Jarrell, Rockport, Ark., to Mr. and Mrs. William D. Kelly, Rockford, N.C., 12 Nov. 1849, JMMP.

146 . . . . **wet regions unhealthy:** "Westward Along the Boone's Lick Trail in 1826," 196; J. W. Miller, 206, 227. Charles Dickens structured the American portion of his 1844 novel *Martin Chuzzlewit* around the land speculation and frustrated settlement of the deeply insalubrious bottomlands of the Mississippi Valley (see also Humphreys, *Malaria*, 32–33). Some Illinois boosters successfully linked wet environments with "salubrity," but this rather radical rhetorical move was not taken by the Arkansas-Missouri area's otherwise energetic and creative promoters. See Winsor. **"it is so unhealthy in the swamps":** Anderson Carr and Irvine to Brig. Genl. Thomas S. Jesup, 18 December 1826, in Carter, vol. 20, 334–35. **"noxious climate":** J. W. Miller, 172.

147 . . . . **"parasitical" and "beautiful":** Flint, *Recollections*, 253. One medical observer reported that a region of South Alabama "is emphatically that of long moss, and mosquetoes." Harris, 464. **miasma and moss:** Henry, 302.

147 . . . . "sickly southern clime": Jervey and Moss, 187. "Wherever there is a basin": Eakin and Logsdon, 114.

147 . . . . *Pilgrim's Progress:* Southey. Stephen Hempstead's 1826 notation on being "now in the 73^d year of my Piligrimage," and, four years later (on the day he turned 77), on "my Pilgramage from youth to old age," were structured at least in part by Bunyan's tale. Jensen, Part 7, 29 May 1826, 81, and ibid., Part 9, 6 May 1831, 438. The young girls in Louisa May Alcott's *Little Women* act out the story of Christian, moving from the cellar of their house out onto the brilliant sunshine of the roof; see "Playing Pilgrim" in Alcott.

148 . . . . "drew nigh to a very miry Slough": Southey, 17.

148 . . . . "purgatory": "Westward Along the Boone's Lick Trail in 1826," 190. "slough of despond": Caroline M. Kirkland, *A New Home: Who'll Follow?*, ed. William S. Osborne (New Haven, Conn.: College and University Press, 1965), 40–41, in Vileisis, 62. "dark, gloomy desert": Jervey and Moss, 179.

148 . . . . "The Lost One": in Audubon, 124–29. On Audubon's own swampland experiences, see Vileisis, 58–59.

149 . . . . Even experienced travelers vulnerable to disorientation: Reflected in a (possibly apocryphal) response by the elderly Daniel Boone in 1819. Asked if he had ever been lost in the woods, Boone replied, "No, I was never lost, but I was bewildered once for three days." WPA, *Missouri,* 363. "The huge gray trees": Audubon, "The Lost One," 125. The time he spent condemned to wandering recalls Jesus Christ's 40 days of temptation in the desert, which echo the 40 days and 40 nights of Noah's flood and the 40 years the Israelites wandered in the desert before they could enter the promised land of Canaan (Matthew 4:1–7, Genesis 7 and 8, Numbers 14:33–34).

149 . . . . "now on cabbage-trees"; "On his knees": Audubon, 128.

149 . . . . 400 miles: Ibid., 128–29.

149 . . . . "Nothing but": Ibid., 129.

150 . . . . "human footstep"; "covered with scratches"; "I was besmeared": Eakin and Logsdon, 104–5.

150 . . . . "monster": Ibid., 103. By "tiger" Northup may mean a cougar, or this may simply be the florid and inaccurate phrasing of his ghostwriter. ability to swim: He emphasizes (101), "In youth I had practised in the clear streams that flow through my native district, until I had become an expert swimmer, and felt at home in the watery element." The "clear streams" of a free state contrast strongly with the murky, grossly rich waters of Southern morass.

151 . . . . "My midnight intrusion": Eakin and Logsdon, 105. swamps as refuge: Vileisis, 103–5.

151 . . . . Harriet Beecher Stowe, *Dred:* George Fredrickson (112–13), however, notes that the main character goes mad largely because of his long periods in hiding amid grotesque and "fantastic" swamps.

151 . . . . swamps as base for runaways: Franklin and Schweninger, 100–103. Georgia: Stewart, *"What Nature Suffers to Groe,"* Chapter 4. French Louisiana: Usner, *Indians, Settlers, and Slaves.* Usner makes this argument not only of bayous and swamps but of rivers and waterways.

153 . . . . spas, healing springs, and water resorts: Bridenbaugh; Bullard; Crets, 183–85; Geores; Gesler, "Bath"; ibid., "Lourdes"; Harington, *"Let Us Build Us a City,"* Chapter 1; Hedrick,

Chapter 16; Little; Silber, Chapter 3. **springs and boosterism:** Drake, *Natural and Statistical View,* 192–97. A late-nineteenth-century history of Missouri (see Swallow) listed numerous salt, sulfur, chalybeate, petroleum, and fresh-water springs in the state. **"not only first rate land":** Noland, untitled article on Arkansas Territory, *Arkansas Advocate.* **salt manufacture:** Dickinson, "Historic Tribes," 2. **economic value of salt springs:** Blowe, 673. **Salt springs in the American imagination:** Cooper, *The Last of the Mohicans,* 122–23. **"Warm Springs":** William Russell, St. Louis, to William Rector, surveyor for Missouri, 20 April 1814, in Carter, vol. 14, 757.

153 . . . . **"Sulpher Water":** Jensen, Part 3, 19 May 1818, 84; **"a Camp at the Sulpher Spring":** Ibid., 30 June 1818, 88. Hempstead added that they "(Made a very comfortable residence) and Slept very well."The Hempsteads were probably at Sulphur Springs in what is now in Jefferson County. See map in Bullard, 7.

153 . . . . **"There is a spring of Cold water":** Thomas Rodney to Caesar Rodney, Washington, Miss. Terr., 20 Oct. 1804, in S. Gratz, "Letters of Thomas Rodney," *Pennsylvania Magazine of History and Biography* 44 (1920): 62–64; in McDermott, "Western Journals," 101.

154 . . . . **"Cantrell's Springs":** JJB, 3 Aug. 1855. Others, too, found the Arkansas hot springs "useful"; see Carter, vol. 15, 180. **"I went out to Augustus'":** EGPMB, no. 1, 21 Oct. 1836. The fever only left her in early November.

154 . . . . **"daughter Beebe left here":** Jensen, Part 9, 21 July 1830, 431.

154 . . . . **Hot Springs, Arkansas:** Dickinson, "Health and Death," 32–37; Malone; Scully, *Hot Springs, Arkansas;* WPA, *Arkansas,* 153–63. **"boiling springs":** McDermott, "Western Journals," 66; **"a consumptive person":** Ibid., 94. See also Macrery. **"in 1815":** JMD, 13 Nov.[?] 1826. French colonists early adapted Quapaw steam bathing practices in the region. Dickinson, "Health and Death," 32–33.

155 . . . . **legal status of Hot Springs:** "Memorial to Congress by the Territorial Assembly," 15 Feb. 1820, in Carter, vol. 19, 148–49; Scully, *Hot Springs, Arkansas,* especially 30–32. **"said to possess considerable Virtue":** JMD, Nov.[?] 13, 1826. George Engelmann disagreed: "The sicknesses for which people come . . . are largely the various types of rheumatism, ills which derive from the misuse of mercury, chronic skin conditions, and above all lower body ills, which are after effects of the chills and fevers and gall fevers or of the yellow fevers, such as dyspepsia, constipation, edema, and the like. Consumptives and such, who suffer from any kind of illness that causes a fever, do not come here, and fear harm if they use the waters." Jansma and Jansma, 230. **"healthfulness of the region":** Ibid., 242–43.

155 . . . . **"beauty and salubrity":** Featherstonhaugh, "Geology of Arkansas," 11 Aug. 1835. **"The warmth":** Jansma and Jansma, 240. **George Hunter:** McDermott, "Western Journals," 101–3; Malone. Scientific interest in the springs continued into the late nineteenth and twentieth century: Scully, *Hot Springs, Arkansas,* 145–47.

155 . . . . **"Mrs. Lansford's spring in Illinois":** JJG, 31 May 1840.

156 . . . . **"these waters annually perform":** Featherstonhaugh, "Geology of Arkansas," 11 Aug. 1835. **cures of a place fit its ills:** Of the Michigan hinterland of the 1830s and '40s, the novelist Caroline Kirkland in *A New Home, or Life in the Clearings* (1843) observed, "The opinion that each region produces the medicines which its own disease require, prevails extensively." In Faragher, *Sugar Creek,* 92. **manna and quail:** Exodus, Chapter 16.

156 . . . . "oasis in a mountainous desert": Jansma and Jansma, 230; "glorious colors!" and other descriptions: Ibid., 232–35.

156 . . . . "soul athirst": Albert, 45; biblical waters: Exodus 17:1–7.

157 . . . . Indian use of Hot Springs: Pope, 187 (see also 89). Nearby Caddo and Quapaw Indians did use the Hot Springs. Dickinson, "Health and Death," 32–34. springs as neutral territory: [Blowe], 674. "always considered [the springs] as sacred ground": Hiram Abiff Whittington, Hot Springs, to Granville Whittington, [Boston,] 3 March 1833, in Ross, "Letters of Hiram Abiff Whittington," 33. Whittington concluded, "I wish I could say the same of the whites since they have settled here." See the similar lament in Cooper, *The Last of the Mohicans*, 119. "Even the raw natural man": Jansma and Jansma, 233.

157 . . . . "Every intelegent and scientific Traveler": J. C. Jones, Villemont, Chicot Co., Ark. Terr., to Col. A. H. Sevier, Washington, D.C., in Carter, vol. 21, 579–85, 580. By the 1880s, Indian history was more problematic for American boosters, and the perceived history of Indian use of mineral springs in the later-nineteenth-century development of Hot Springs, South Dakota, was very different. See Geores.

Chapter VI, Local Knowledge

159 . . . . "Local knowledge": Warner, *Therapeutic Perspective*, 74; Geertz.

160 . . . . "medical geography": In the nineteenth century and today, the term is used, pragmatically if sloppily, for both the field overall and the writings that constitute it. On the history and sweep of this field, see essays in Rupke, *Medical Geography*, especially Valenčius, "Histories of Medical Geography."

161 . . . . medical geography as a technology of colonialism: Like those described by Headrick and B. Anderson.

161 . . . . Twyman: This initial volume was published in 1845. fledgling medical publications and their audiences: Cassedy, "Flourishing and Character of Early American Medical Journalism"; Shafer, 174–99; Pizer and Steuernagel.

162 . . . . "point of land"; "bottom abounds in sloughs": Twyman, 25. medical geography and agricultural concerns: Stewart, "Let Us Begin with the Weather?"

162 . . . . "in dry seasons the water on the bottom": Twyman, 25.

163 . . . . "rich alluvium" and subsequent descriptions: Ibid., 26. environmental medicine focused on interaction of person and place: As Daniel Drake argued, "the medical topographer is interested in none but peopled countries." Levine, 142.

163 . . . . "continued exposure to the deleterious influence"; "enlargement or structural derangement"; causes of "autumnal fever": Twyman, 29, 26.

163 . . . . "history of the diseases in this county": Ibid., 26. "diarrhoea and cholera morbus": Ibid., 27.

163 . . . . account of "Asiatic cholera": Ibid., 28.

164 . . . . many names for "medical geography": Daniel Drake once termed himself a "medical etiologist." Levine, 139. "medical geology": Drake, "Medical History," 682. Though the meanings of "medical geography" and "medical topography" blurred together, the former was often used as the more general term, while the latter more often referred to the mapping

of health conditions of a defined area. **governmental concern:** Kleinschmidt. **medical ge-ography as focus of scientific investigation:** Warner, *Therapeutic Perspective*, 75–76; Cassedy, "Medical Men," 172.

165 . . . . **Drake,** *Systematic Treatise:* This work has been usefully excerpted in Levine. **in-fluence of Drake's medical geography:** Barrett, "Daniel Drake"; Dorn, "(In)temperate Zones"; Ackerknecht, *Malaria in the Upper Mississippi Valley.* **Drake's leading role in nine-teenth-century medicine and western boosterism:** Szaraz; Shapiro and Miller.

165 . . . . **environmental medicine and colonialism:** Anderson, "Geography, Race, and Nation"; Bewell, Chapter 1, especially 32–34; Curtin, "The Promise and the Terror"; Harrison, "Differences of Degree."

165 . . . . **messy definitions of "science" in the nineteenth century:** Popular usage re-inforced a broad meaning of the term. C. F. M. Noland described his Pete Whetstone charac-ter as "a professional bear-hunter, and a scientific bee-hunter. Pete is no orator; but when it comes to killing a bear, or finding a bee tree, he is *there.*" Noland, *Pete Whetstone of Devil's Fork,* 5. **medical localism and American science:** Numbers and Warner.

166 . . . . **late-eighteenth- and early-nineteenth-century science:** Bowler, Chapter 6; Daniels, Chapter 1. **influence of Alexander von Humboldt:** Cannon; Dettelbach; Rupke, "Adolf Mühry"; ibid., "Humboldtian Medicine." Humboldt's journals were to have a tremendous influence on later-nineteenth-century scientific observers, notably the young Charles Darwin. **new techniques of quantification and visualization:** Rudwick; Rupke and Wonders, "Humboldtian Representations." **instrument portability:** Cannon, 97. **late Enlightenment environmental medicine:** Jordanova; Riley, "Medicine of the Environment."

166 . . . . **impact of quantification on American medicine:** Cassedy, *Medicine and Amer-ican Growth,* and ibid., "Meteorology and Medicine." **broad American interest in statistical description:** Boorstin, 167–73. **dew-point and mortality in epidemics:** Hunt.

167 . . . . **visual representation and medical geography:** Brömer; Camerini; Barrett, "Alfred Haviland"; Rupke and Wonders, "Humboldtian Representations."

167 . . . . **maps in AMA's** *Transactions:* For example, the brilliantly colored and complexly plotted graph of "Climate and Mortality of New Orleans for 1854-'55," in Fenner, "Report on the Epidemics" (1856). Erasmus Fenner was an important figure in the surge of interest in medical geography among medical and scientific professionals in the 1840s and '50s. Cassedy, "Medical Men," 172. Not coincidentally, he was also a staunch advocate of Southern training for Southern physicians.

168 . . . . **early modern interest in the local:** M. A. Cooper; Hannaway, 301; Koerner, *Linneaus.* **utility of scientific investigations of local territory:** Grove; Hendrickson, es-pecially 361–62; Riley, "Medicine of the Environment," 170.

168 . . . . **Science made new lands "American":** Spanagel. Martin Padget (423) argues that the late-nineteenth-century writings of the regional booster Charles Lummis "con-tributed to the process whereby the colonial frontier of the Southwest was claimed by intel-lectual activity and, in tandem with social and economic activities, was transformed into a U.S. national region." Medical and scientific texts functioned in the same way with respect to borderlands regions. **environmental medicine and political thought in the early**

republic: Chinard; Rosen. **"to amalgamate the foreign with the indigenous":** Levine, Drake's preface, v.

168 . . . . **George Hunter:** McDermott, "Western Journals of George Hunter," 71–122; Malone.

169 . . . . **George W. Featherstonhaugh:** Featherstonhaugh, *Excursion through the Slave States*; Berkeley and Berkeley, especially 114–44; Cochran, " 'Low, Degrading Scoundrels.' " **extracts of his report:** Featherstonhaugh, "Geology of Arkansas." **Henry Rowe Schoolcraft:** Rafferty, *Rude Pursuits* (on Schoolcraft's wide reception, see xi). Schoolcraft was to become famous for his six-volume ethnography of American Indians, which was based on his tenure as Indian agent in Michigan Territory during the 1820s; its publication in 1851–57 was funded by Congress. Gillespie, s.v. "Henry Schoolcraft," and Daniels, 222. **Thomas Nuttall:** Gillespie, s.v. "Thomas Nuttall"; Daniels, 218–19; Vaulx. Nuttall's publications include "Collections towards a Flora of the Territory of Arkansas" as well as the more accessible *Journal of Travels into the Arkansas Territory* (Lottinville). **The indomitable Timothy Flint:** Flint, *History and Geography.*

169 . . . . **"sluggish stream" and subsequent conclusions:** C. B. Welch, Fort Smith, to Jos. Lovell, Washington, D.C., 28 Feb. 1834, in Carter, vol. 21, 916–18. **chronic health complaints at Fort Smith:** Martin, 1–11. **surgeon general's directive about weather diaries:** Fleming, 14–19. **Fort Smith weather records:** Martin, 28. **military medical officers as scientific observers:** Brodhead; Stoddard. For example, the commander of Mounted Rangers unit with which Washington Irving completed his "Tour Through the Prairies" was instructed by his commanding officer to "keep a journal, in which you will note the course and distance of each day's march, the character of the soil, timber, water minerals and whatever else you may judge worthy of particular remark." Col. Matthew Arbuckle to Captain Jesse Bean, 5 Oct. 1832, in McDermott, *Western Journals of Washington Irving*, 33. For efforts in the 1840s to enlist state legislators and ordinary citizens to track and record information on population, weather, rainfall, agricultural products, and other aspects of Arkansas counties, see Sherwood, 132.

170 . . . . **"six or seven hundred miles" and subsequent complaints:** Memorial to Congress by the Territorial Assembly, 18 Oct. 1823, in Carter, vol. 19, 554.

170 . . . . **"This is my schooling":** Cooper, *Last of the Mohicans*, 217. **"Experimental knowledge":** Ibid., *The Prairie*, 386.

171 . . . . **"And let me tell you":** Robert F. Henry, Hopkinville, to Dr. J. F. Henry, "On the Wing," 12 Sept. 1819, sixth page, box 2, file 64, HSM. **becoming a physician a route to upward mobility:** McNeilly, 75–77.

171 . . . . **physicians:** Shafer; Shryock, *Medicine and Society in America;* Starr. **Arkansas and Missouri physicians resembled their emigrant contemporaries:** Garrison, 550; Lanser, 32. Many participants were part of the "chain migration" phenomenon whereby immigrants into Arkansas and Missouri had already made a move to the earlier frontier. Andrew Taylor Still, the founder of osteopathy, moved from Virginia to Tennessee with his family in the 1830s, and then on to Missouri in the 1840s. See Hulburt, 25.

171 . . . . **William Armour Cantrell:** Garrison, 551. In 1854, the St. Louis county court licensed the only black physician in antebellum St. Louis. Earlier laws had prohibited black peo-

ple from administering medicine of any kind. Free black and enslaved Missourians and Arkansans provided many kind of healing, but almost every "physician" was white. Bellamy, "Free Blacks," 214; Foley, *Genesis of Missouri*, 154.

172 . . . . **credentials and training from "back East":** Ichabod Sargeant literally carried his training with him when he emigrated to Missouri, carefully preserving his notes from Dartmouth Medical School, which he attended in 1816–17. See ISMN. **"Thornton, a Cherokee who is studying medicine":** Hiram Abiff Whittington, "Dwight Mission, Indian Nation, A.T." (Ark. Terr.), to Granville Whittington, [Boston], 15 Aug. 1828, in Ross, "Letters of Hiram Abiff Whittington," 6.

172 . . . . **"in addition to his practice as a physician":** W.W. Brown, 1. **"Doctoring" on again, off again:** Leo Twyman (28) acknowledged, "During the years 1835 and '36, I was not engaged in practice." **other prosaic skills:** For instance, the Missouri author of one German emigrants' guide, in encouraging artisans to come over, noted that a local blacksmith's "horse-shoeing is so bad that we prefer to ride six miles away to a doctor who shoes a horse very skillfully." Gregory, "Count Baudissin on Missouri Towns," 120. On the more lofty civic engagements of prominent physicians, see Pizer and Steuernagel, 221; Lanser, 45.

172 . . . . **competition and the financial challenges of doctoring:** Adler, *Yankee Merchants*, Chapter 4, especially 68. In 1846, the first volume of the *Missouri Medical and Surgical Journal* tallied 146 professional healers in St. Louis, including "Homeopathists, Botanics, Thompsonians, &c." The journal's editors concluded that each of these practitioners might in theory have "247 persons to attend upon, supposing the whole number to be equally divided; but when we consider the fact, that about one-third of the number have a large practice, we are not surprised that a large number are unable to collect enough to pay their expenses, and the consequence is that many, many, after spending from one to three years, and the means which they brought to the city, leave and settle in the smaller towns in the surrounding country." "The Medical Profession in St. Louis," 96. **"an empiric, or . . . quack":** Hermann Steines, St. Louis, to parents and friends, 8 Nov. 1833, in Bek, "Followers of Duden: First Article," 61, 71–72. **Solingen Emigration Society:** Ibid., "Third Article," 457.

173 . . . . **"washed off"; "ardent spirits"; and subsequent lament:** B. W. Lee, Arkansas Post, to James H. Lucas, St. Louis, 30 April 1844, Box 1, Folder 1, KC.

173 . . . . **barriers to professionalization of regulars:** See Rosenkrantz; Starr. **limited public health activity in Arkansas:** Garrison, 557–60. **"I know, and so does every man of experience and observation":** *Journal of the 7th Session of the General Assembly*, 1831, 289–91; in Baird, *Medical Education in Arkansas*, 7. Pope's veto fit squarely with developments across the United States in the 1830s, as increasing popular skepticism about regular medicine led state legislatures to either repeal or decline to pass statutes mandating physician licensing or registration. Haller, *Medical Protestants*, 52–54.

173 . . . . **medical schools:** The Medical Department of Kemper College and the St. Louis Medical College merged in 1899 to become the Washington University School of Medicine. Pizer and Steuernagel, 222. **medical education broadly:** Ludmerer. **journals:** Pizer and Steuernagel, 255; Lanser, 39. **Medical Society of Missouri:** Pitcock, 336–40. **Missouri State Medical Association:** Pizer and Steuernagel, 255. **"fee bills":** Lanser, 44–45.

174 . . . . **A. W. Webb:** Garrison. Webb was murdered in 1866, in a case that remained unsolved; at his death, his library was valued at $2,000. Baird, *Medical Education in Arkansas*, 327, n. 231. On Webb's career, see ibid., Chapter 1, and Garrison, 530. **notebook discussions:** AWWN, 406 and 626. **therapeutic significance of the stethoscope:** Bynum, 37–41. **"The city physician":** "Madison Tensas, M.D.," "The City Physician versus the Swamp Doctor," in *Odd Leaves from the Life of a Louisiana "Swamp Doctor,"* 1843, in Robb, 23.

174 . . . . **barriers to medical and scientific investigation:** Numbers and Numbers, "Science in the Old South." The first official anatomical dissection in Arkansas—of the "cadaver of a negro"—took place after the Civil War. The dissection of a white person's corpse might have aroused more community opposition. The marker erected to recognize this event names the physicians, but not the person whose corpse was dissected. Lenow; "Dedication of Marker."

175 . . . . **Byrn's book:** Reissued in 1989 (see McNeil). **Byrn's career:** Masterson. **Arkansas as butt of regional fiction:** Cochran, "'Hanged by his Friends'"; ibid., "'Low, Degrading Scoundrels'"; Shea; C. F. Williams.

175 . . . . **"no man there without a title":** Dickens, *Martin Chuzzlewit*, 259. **"the usual number of Judges, Generals, and Colonels":** McDermott, *Western Journals of Washington Irving*, 169.

175 . . . . **no need for "old school training" to be an M.D.:** William A. Falconer to his mother, 10 May 1848, in Martin, 327–28.

176 . . . . **"It is bad enough for a *lawyer* . . . ":** William Mordecai Cooke, St. Louis, to John Coles Rutherfoord, Va., 20 March 1852, in Budd, 359.

176 . . . . **"In the medical skill of this country":** Julia B. Strong, Grand Prairie, Callaway Co., Mo., to "My dear Aunt H.," Mendon, N.Y., 26 Dec. 1838, in McClarty, 341.

176 . . . . **science and the role of the physician:** As John Warner has argued ("Science, Healing, and the Physician's Identity") this was not an easy relationship. Interest in French clinical medicine did animate many nineteenth-century medical professionals, including some from the hinterlands (Warner, "Remembering Paris," and ibid., *Against the Spirit of System*).

177 . . . . **medical geography and popular concerns:** Some practitioners claimed that the many moves and migrations of American society made medical geography of particular relevance to Americans. "Medical Geography." **"A wet summer is a healthy summer":** But beware: "A wet summer and dry fall combined make the most sickly fall." Engelmann, 231. **medicine and agriculture:** Medical journals, especially in borderland regions, often published reports of incipient epidemics or successful cures alongside updates on the newest manuring technique or agricultural machinery. Shafer, Chapter 6. **environmental medicine as a concern of the public:** This has been not well recognized in historical scholarship. One exception is Jones, M.O. 254.

177 . . . . **medical geography and regional self-definition:** Medical geography functioned as an implicit rhetoric of Southern regional self-definition in much the same way as the agricultural orations of antebellum South Carolina analyzed by Drew Gilpin Faust ("Rhetoric and Ritual").

178 . . . . **Goulding's travel for health:** *Arkansas State Gazette* 22 Dec. 1841. **"eligible" site and subsequent discussion of Little Rock:** Goulding, 322, 327, 328. **Goulding**

measured Little Rock's longitude as 15°20': Modern measurements make it between 92° and 93°. Goulding was measuring from Washington, D.C.: only in the 1880s was the Greenwich Meridian established as the international prime meridian. In the antebellum U.S., observers commonly used prime meridians based on the longitude of major cities (Philadelphia, New York, Boston, or for Southern sectionalists, New Orleans) or places like the Harvard Observatory in Cambridge. Pratt, "American Prime Meridians"; personal communication with William J. H. Andrewes, Harvard University Collection of Historical Scientific Instruments, 15 Sept. 1998.

178 . . . . **Goulding's death:** *Arkansas State Gazette*, 22 Dec. 1841.

178 . . . . **similarity of "South" and "West":** Humphreys, *Malaria*, 33.

179 . . . . **movement for Southern medicine:** Breeden; Cassedy, "Medical Men," especially 172; Duffy; Warner, *Therapeutic Perspective*, Chapter 3; ibid., "Idea of Southern Medical Distinctiveness."

179 . . . . **"a successful practitioner":** Twyman, 32.

179 . . . . **"is confirmed by the universal experience":** AWW, 47. **"witnessing"; "the Northern medical man":** Gantt, "A few Reasons," 213, 212. **"witnessing" as integral to scientific truth:** Shapin and Schaffer.

180 . . . . **"I have certainly never seen":** AWW, 13. **"a great fever-doctor":** Skinner, 262. Merrell's assessment echoes a favorable recommendation submitted by an influential Southern physician to the Confederate Army medical examining board; the candidate, although "entirely ignorant of Anatomy, Surgery, Physiology, Pathology and Chemistry," was "a pretty fair practitioner in the ordinary acute diseases of the Country." J. C. Nott to Colonel Beck, 7 Jan. 1862, in Warner, *Therapeutic Perspective*, 14. (See also ibid., Chapter 1, and "Science, Healing, and the Physician's Identity" for Warner's discussion of the role of experience in the formation of practitioner identity.)

180 . . . . **calls for Southern medical education:** Shryock, "Medical Practice in the Old South," especially 168–70; Warner, "A Southern Medical Reform." For a contrasting view, see Kilbride. **"The Southern medical student is well known":** *Savannah Medical Journal* II (1861), 369–70, in Shryock, "Medical Practice in the Old South," 170.

180 . . . . **"if you wish to become familiar":** H. L. Byrd, "Southern Medical Colleges," *Oglethorpe Medical and Surgical Journal* 2 (1859), 57–58, in Breeden, 364. **exodus from medical schools:** Warner, "A Southern Medical Reform," 377–78. Daniel Kilbride (717–19) argues that this was regarded by many participants only as "a Christmas frolic," not a sustained political statement.

181 . . . . **Southern intellectual parochialism:** Faust, *A Sacred Circle*; Rozbicki. Dror Wahrman has argued that in eighteenth-century Britain, choosing between provincial and London-oriented society was "a major formative experience of the 'middling sorts' in the eighteenth century." I contend that American borderland physicians sidestepped this choice by making of provinciality a limited sort of virtue.

181 . . . . **search for ancestors:** Chronicled in more detail in Valenčius, "Histories of Medical Geography."

181 . . . . **Sydenham and "epidemic constitution":** Hannaway, 296–97.

181 . . . . **"The physician, by attentively observing":** Twyman, 28.

182 . . . . **historical uses of Hippocrates:** G. Miller.

182 . . . . *Airs, Waters and Places:* In Lloyd, *Hippocratic Writings.* **interest in Hippocratic corpus:** For example, "McP."

182 . . . . **Greek latitude:** Cassedy, "Medical Men," 176.

182 . . . . **reference to classical glory:** Daniel Drake wrote from Cincinnati, the "Athens of the West." **Engelmann on classical names for slaves:** Bek, "George Engelmann," Part 2, 440. Genovese (447–48) notes that few of these names lasted long after freedom. **"Cato":** this name carried particular irony, for Marcus Porcius Cato the younger, the great-grandson of the agricultural authority and anti-Carthage senator, helped put down the slave revolt led by Spartacus. Albert (120) records one Cato who successfully escaped the South Carolina rice fields.

183 . . . . **politics of regular physicians' citation of Hippocrates:** Warner, "Revolt and Return."

184 . . . . **theses on medical geography:** Warner, *Therapeutic Perspective,* 75; Numbers and Warner, 207. This was particularly true of western medical schools. Many of the theses at Transylvania University, Lexington, Ky., took medical topography as their subject. Personal communication from Charles Boewe, fall of 1997.

184 . . . . **treatise on fevers:** AWW. **intended for publication?:** The first series of the index to the Surgeon General's library (the standard source for medical writings in this era) contains no references to publications by Webb.

184 . . . . **scientific networks and scientific community in the nineteenth century:** Goldstein. The processes documented here of scientific observers' creation of professional alliances complemented and likely overlapped with the economic and familial network formation documented by Adler, *Yankee Merchants.* **cultivating connection with larger professional networks:** Dr. William David Kersch, who moved to northern Arkansas in 1858, corresponded with Alexander Agassiz, Charles Lyell, and other noted scientific leaders. Dixon. **reports on medical geographies of other places:** For instance, Brunel. **interest in medicine of warm climates:** For example, Papillaud.

184 . . . . **Drake's reprinting of Engelmann's data:** Drake, *Systematic Treatise,* 519–25, 531–36; and their correspondence in the GEP. Engelmann also published his own meteorological and mortality reports (see Engelmann) based on the weather diary he kept for almost 50 years. See also Fleming, 135; Elliott, s.v. "Engelmann, George." **"Doctor Borland of Arkansas" and other local physicians:** Drake, *Systematic Treatise,* 133 and 142. Drake quotes Missouri physicians throughout his section on the Missouri River (for example, 169 and 171). **publication of Thompson in the *Boston Medical and Surgical Journal*:** J. E. Thompson.

185 . . . . **Engelmann's request for copies of publications and tables:** Fleming, 135. **bartering information for professional place:** On the "payoffs" enjoyed by volunteer Smithsonian meteorological observers, see ibid., 88, and Goldstein, 588.

185 . . . . **Jacob M. J. Smith:** In C. A. Brown, 3–4.

185 . . . . **capitalizing on knowledge of backwater regions not universally successful:** One scathing 1803 British review of the *Transactions of the American Philosophical Society* dismissed American science precisely because of its preoccupation with meteorological, astronomical, and geographical observation (Cannon, 101). Yet to a large extent the "local" as

described by hinterland scientists was of interest to professionals beyond their regional borders. **courtly or gentlemanly status:** Biagioli; Shapin, *Social History of Truth*. The exchanges documented here also reinforce recent work in the history of science on the vital two-way intellectual interactions between province and metropolis. See Shapin, "Nibbling at the teats of science"; Chambers; Grove.

185 . . . . **William Beaumont's experiments:** Numbers and Orr; Pitcock.

186 . . . . **models for practitioner behavior:** S. M. Stowe. **medical geography as a way of engaging in research in otherwise challenging regions:** Warner, *Therapeutic Perspective*, 75–76. **Nathan D. Smith:** Ball, "Arkansas Weatherman"; W. D. Williams; WPA, *Arkansas*, 217.

186 . . . . **Smith took measurements:** He did this in the same sense that "he" farmed—the grammatical construction elides the labor of other family members and any slaves they owned. In this account, unfortunately, such technicians will remain invisible. Though one source comments that he "trained a staff, including his daughters, to assist him in caring for the overflow of patients" who streamed into their log hospital during warm and sickly months, Smith's own records make no mention of anyone assisting him in his deliberate and demanding routine of measurement. On Smith's daughters, see B. Ball, 68; on scientific practitioners' rendering assistants invisible, see Shapin, "Invisible Technician." **significance of Mitchell's article:** Shaftel, 111; Ludmerer, 25. **"for the satisfaction of myself and family":** N. D. Smith, iii. **knowledge produced in the Arkansas countryside:** James Rodger Fleming (86–87) concludes, "Meteorological observations, especially those taken from remote locations and those taken over many years, were a way for nonelites to contribute to the advancement of science."

187 . . . . **weather records kept by a wide range of observers:** One 1856 document included a table of heat, rainfall, and quality of weather excerpted from "the Meteorological Journal kept by the Young Ladies of the Oakland Institute, at Jackson, Mississippi, for the year ending November 30, 1851" ("Report on the Epidemics" (1855), 605). **weather recording and weather diaries:** Fleming, especially Chapters 1, 3, 4. **medical associations and agricultural societies engaged in similar investigations:** Stewart, "'Let Us Begin with the Weather?,' " 246. The scientific contributions of elite Southerners generally revolved around agriculture. Scarborough.

187 . . . . **"My thermometer has hung all the time":** N. D. Smith, iii. **"I always found the water hot enough":** Featherstonhaugh, "Geology of Arkansas," 11 Aug. 1835. **"hot enough to boil eggs or fish":** Lottinville, 240. One of the upwellings was named "Egg Spring" for just this reason. The use of the hot springs to prepare food and beverages was apparently commonplace, reflecting not only fascination with the heat of the springs, but a preoccupation with getting enough to eat and drink. Dr. Joseph Macrery's 1806 comment (48) that "Meat was boiled in them in a shorter space of time than could be accomplished by a culinary fire; they were made use of to prepare both tea and coffee . . ." reflects satisfaction not only with the extraordinary properties of the local waters, but with a good meal.

187 . . . . **meteorological report reflected domestic setting:** Attention to temperature readings and weather was a practical concern of physicians called to ride out in all seasons to attend patients. Leavitt, "A Worrying Profession," 21. **"observed temperature at sunrise":** N. D. Smith, contents page. It is not inconceivable that Smith might have read Drake's 1836 in-

junction to observe "the temperature of the morning, at or before sun rise, and of the afternoon between two and three o'clock." Drake, "Medical History," 682. **"oaks in bloom"; "Silk-worms spinning":** N. D. Smith, 2.

188 . . . . **"not dependent on the written archives of the profession":** Drake, "Medical History," 681. **observation of nature as political capital:** Spanagel, "When Statesmen Were Opinion Makers."

189 . . . . **anxieties of the era:** A. Douglas. **"fine opportunities for seeing the world" and subsequent description:** Levine, 60–61.

189 . . . . **"I am pretty well reconsiled to the back woods . . . ":** Kirkbride Potts, Galley Creek, Ark., to Ann Potts, [Bordentown, N. J.], 1 July 1830, PFL.

Chapter VII, Cultivation

191 . . . . **"the women are grubbing":** JJB, 16 Jan. 1854. **"a dose of oil and turpentine":** Ibid., 28 Sept. 1857. This language was not unique to how a slave owner might perceive his chattel. Brown similarly commented on 18 June 1857 that a patent medicine had helped heal his son Dick, "his system having been well cleaned beforehand."

191 . . . . **agriculture and identity of self with land:** This environmental holism has deep roots. Wear, 143–44; Sweet.

193 . . . . **Agricultural labor was the central theme:** Raising livestock was an essential part of farm life in early Missouri and Arkansas, yet the metaphorical language of evaluating land gave much less attention to herds and flocks than to the cultivation of crops. This chapter reflects that somewhat skewed focus; although the "agricultural" lifestyle under discussion in these nineteenth-century sources relied on the care and use of domestic animals, contemporary attention and hence this analysis are focused on planting. **"go to farming":** Prof. A. H. Hall, Monticello, Drew Co., Ark., to Col. J. C. Barrow, 15 Nov. 1859, Box "A–B," File 35, JCBP. **"wil be pleased with this contery":** William Bailey, Memphis, to Mrs. Evalina B. Bailey, War Saw, Benton Co., Mo., 29 Aug. 1848, series 2, box 1, file 4, MLC.

193 . . . . **lean and hungry seasons:** Until a recent rain "some really feared a famine" wrote John Brown (JJB, 5 April 1855). When a disease afflicted the plantation's livestock, he worried that "my large family will feel the inconvenience of the want seriously" (ibid., 5 July 1852). **dependence on agriculture:** Gerstäcker (*Wild Sports*) noted that even hunters, who lived on a surprisingly carnivorous diet, needed to be able to exchange occasional sides of venison for fresh buttermilk or furs for salt or cornmeal. See also Gerstäcker, *Wild Sports,* and J. W. Miller, Chapter 5. **"mild plenty":** JJB, 24 April 1855.

193 . . . . **"although they said they had been settled":** McDermott, "Western Journals of Dr. George Hunter," 90.

194 . . . . **"improving" land:** "I rode out to my farm to know from Mʳ Lewis if She concluded to improve it another year." Jensen, Part 7, 9 Jan. 1823, 62. Mart Stewart (*"What Nature Suffers to Groe,"* 104) notes the topographical specificity of "improvement": in the upland south, "improving" land had to do with farming or building on it, while in South Carolina and Georgia plantations, "improving" land implied digging a network of drainage ditches within it. **squatting a common strategy:** McNeilly, 23–24. **extralegal preemption rights:** These

were widely enforced (Faragher, *Sugar Creek*, 53–55), at times with considerable violence. In John S. Robb's 1848 frontier story "The Pre-Emption Right; or, Dick Kelsy's Signature to his Land Claim," a wife-beating would-be land claimant takes advantage of the legal carelessness of a farm's rightful squatter to make a claim to the place. He is brought to justice at the end of a rope, both hanged *and* shot, as the squatter and his neighbors enforce decent behavior against those who would bring "Yankee" ways to the rough but honest frontier. Robb, "Streaks of Squatter Life." **Missouri Preemption Act:** Hurt, *Agriculture and Slavery*, 36. **1841 Pre-emption Act and related policies:** A good review is White, "*It's Your Misfortune,*" 137–45. **"any body can have a farm":** Everard B. Dickinson, Buffalo City, to Mr. and Mrs. Philo Dickinson, Hartford, Conn., 22 Sept. 1848, Box 1, Folder 54, HSM.

194 . . . . **Native American agriculture:** For an introduction, see Hurt, *American Agriculture*, Chapter 1, especially 10–13.

194 . . . . **land use by French colonials:** Ekberg, *French Roots in the Illinois Country;* Foley, *Genesis of Missouri,* 25, 94–5, 187. **farming as an individual effort:** Groups of German emigrants and utopian communities did travel to the region to farm collectively. H. M. Anderson, 153.

195 . . . . **suspicion of seasonal migration:** English scientist George Featherstonhaugh termed areas near the Mississippi "a district where man has not yet permanently occupied the country." Featherstonhaugh, "Geology of Arkansas," 28 July 1835.

195 . . . . **For Cherokees, farming was women's work:** McLoughlin, 43, 64–65. **Indian resistance to inversion of gender roles:** M. Green, 488, 491–9; Park, 143–44. Foley (*Genesis of Missouri,* 108) observes that the preference of many mixed-race Missouri men for river-work, mining, and hunting—rather than the farming of their American contemporaries—may reflect the influence of Indian mothers encouraging more traditionally masculine pursuits. **"are entirely hunters":** Lottinville, 111. Nuttall's criticism of backwoods white men for paying more attention to hunting than farming was consistent with long tradition (Faragher, *Daniel Boone,* 60–61). **Nuttall on cultivation rituals:** Lottinville, 97, 106.

195 . . . . **"an honest livelihood":** Major Stephen H. Long, Belle Fontaine, Missouri Terr., to Brig. Genl. Thomas A. Smith, Belle Fontaine, 30 Jan. 1818, in Carter, vol. 19, 8. **"*good generous living*":** In DeBlack, 168. **"wher people does ther duty by ther crops":** Owen Maguire, Washington Co., Ark., to Samuel and Sally Clark, Montgomery Co., N.C., 18 Sept. 1836, SFM.

196 . . . . **"people whose object it was to make farms":** Flint, *Recollections*, 203. "**here is a Cabbin**": Windell, 39. A similar scorn marks George Hunter's appraisals of Creole settlements along the lower Ouachita River, where "altho the earth would produce very well, yet their want of forethought & industry leaves them in want of almost every comfort, except what is absolutely necessary for subsistence." McDermott, "Western Journals of Dr. George Hunter," 88.

196 . . . . **exaggerated notions of the ease and swiftness of cultivation:** This feature of American boosterism was repeated with respect to successive "frontiers." Dunlop, 179. **"The soil is free from stones":** Flint, *Recollections*, 241; **"speculation and wealth"; "Nothing will grow vigorously":** Ibid., 43. Martin and M. A. Camp similarly encouraged their daughter and son-in-law that "the land is easy cultivated in this country." Martin Camp and

M. A. [?] Camp, [Saline] Co., Ark., to Mary and L. H. Williams, 2 March 1860, series 2, box 1, file 21, MLC.

197 . . . . **"natural state"**: AWW, 7. **"before long the place becomes overgrown"**: J. W. Miller, 65.

197 . . . . **decline of natural resources**: The postbellum writings of Theodore Pease Russell exult in the prowess and sheer magnitude of his hunting in early Missouri but also reflect his sadness that the prodigious hunting and clearing that he so celebrated had largely emptied Missouri of its large game and of many less hardy species during his own lifetime. Keefe and Morrow, *A Connecticut Yankee*. **pigeon extinction**: Price, Chapter 1. **"the richest land you ever seen"**: Lula Taylor, int. Irene Robertson in Rawick, vol. 10, Part 6, 268.

198 . . . . **"Melodious seemed to me"**: Bek, "Followers of Duden, Fifteenth Article: Frederick Muench," 432. **"extraordinary pleasure in laying low with a keen axe"**: Stanley, 148; similarly, Cooper, *The Pioneers*, 205.

198 . . . . **Religious labors**: John Brown welcomed Sundays, when he could draw away from business cares "and cultivate the better parts of my nature." JJB, 2 Sept. 1860. **"We were clearing away the rubbish"**: Park, 106.

198 . . . . **"swing low"**: A deeply romanticized description of plantation life of the 1930s depicts black farm hands in the Arkansas Delta: "a clear tenor rings out, 'Acomin' across Jor-dan, what did Ah see-e?' and the gentle response, 'Comin' for to car-ree me home.' And then they 'swing low' together as they deftly gather the cotton. . . ." WPA, *Arkansas*, 329. The religious imagery, the labor force, and the style of work in that scene from the twentieth century strongly resemble that of the nineteenth, as does white observers' insistence on black contentment and their fascination with black spirituality.

198 . . . . **"green corn dance"**: Park, 179–80. Washburn based his account on conversations with a Cherokee leader, Dick Justice. **marriage ceremonies**: Lottinville, 97; Park, 167.

199 . . . . **nineteenth-century farming**: On farming generally, see Bartlett, Chapter 3; P. W. Gates; Gray (still valuable, though marked by a reliance on the ideas of more elite, well-to-do farmers and agricultural journals); Stewart, *"What Nature Suffers to Groe."* **Missouri**: Hurt, *Agriculture and Slavery*. **Arkansas**: See Bolton, *Territorial Ambition*, Chapter 3. **cotton**: Reports place cotton farms near Helena, on the Mississippi River in the Delta, by 1808, but the main increases in cotton production were to come in the boom decade preceding the Civil War. Holley, 240–41; Woods, 25. **plantations**: The median number of slaves on an Arkansas plantation in 1850 was 18.4, but there was great variation: though almost 33% of the slaves in the state were on farms of 10 or fewer slaves, over 20 percent labored on large plantations of 50 or more slaves. In Louisiana, by contrast, the median plantation had 38.9 slaves; in Missouri, it was 8.6 slaves, and almost 60 percent of the state's slaves were on farms of 10 or fewer. The river valleys of the Missouri and Mississippi rivers, where hemp and tobacco flourished, were cultivated by slave labor. Elsewhere in Missouri, plantation agriculture and plantation culture were much rarer; slave holders held fewer slaves, and many farmers held none. Gray, vol. 2, 530; Hurt.

200 . . . . **hemp and tobacco**: Hemp began to be a substantial product in Missouri from the 1830s, and the state was one of the nation's six largest tobacco producers in the 20 years before the Civil War. Gray, vol. 2, 821, and Chapter 32.

200 . . . . **Brown household foodstuffs and crops:** John Brown does not explicitly mention chickens, but it would be unusual for a household that size not to keep a coop. The Brown holdings were similar in kind to those of larger plantations in southern Arkansas; in 1850, the assets of Lycurgus Johnson's Chicot County plantation were assessed for tax purposes as 95 slaves, 9 horses, 15 mules, 22 cows, 20 oxen, 15 other cattle, 35 sheep, and 200 swine; the year's yield was 3,000 bushels of corn, 100 bushels of sweet potatoes, 40 bushels of Irish potatoes, 60 bushels of peas and beans, 400 pounds of butter, 50 pounds of beeswax and honey, and 100 pounds of wool. DeBlack, 106; also McNeilly, 129. **hog meat and hoecake diet of most slaves:** Kiple and King, 79–95. **physical consequences of this deficient diet:** ibid., 117–33.

200 . . . . **English immigrants:** Erickson, 16–17. **immigrants from German states:** Nicholas Hesse warned German readers of his emigration guide that farm work in new American country—often without servants—was more difficult than many of them might have read in books. Bek, "Nicholas Hesse," Part 3, 285.

200 . . . . **removal of trees:** Sizemore, 13. **"ditching":** Jensen, Part 7, 17 April 1823, 66.

201 . . . . **crop rotation:** Gray, vol. 2, 807–8. **careful agriculture of East Coast elites:** Their experiments and recommendations often had very little relevance to farming in the borderlands. Hurt, *American Agriculture,* 103–4; though see W. D. Williams. On the social meanings of such efforts, see Thornton.

201 . . . . **melons and squash:** For example, J. W. Miller, 190, 198–99. **cotton planting:** Described in fascinating detail in Eakin and Logsdon, 123–30.

201 . . . . **organization of labor:** McNeilly, 139–40.

202 . . . . **heavy work by slave women:** Ibid., 140; testimony of Charlotte Brooks, in Albert, 42. "During slavery times, my father was a farmer. My mother farmed too. She was a hand in the field." Amsy O. Alexander, int. Samuel S. Taylor, in Rawick, vol. 8, 24. "Mama said she druther plough than chop. She was a big woman and they let her plough right along by her two little brothers." Liddie Aiken, Wheatley, Ark., int. Irene Robertson, in Rawick, vol. 8, Part 1, 19. **women in charge of gardens and milk cows:** Martin, 4. But not only women gardened: "Set out . . . my Garden," noted Stephen Hempstead in his diary on April 19, 1813. Jensen, Part 1, 35. **"the weather cleared off into regular spring":** Selina (Wheat) Seay, Camden, Ark., to "Darling Mother," 19 Feb. 1859, TWC. Annette Kolodny (*The Land Before Her*) has argued that American women's response to wilderness in the seventeenth through the nineteenth centuries was to frame the environment as a garden to be made and tended. **Matilda Fulton's many kinds of labor:** Matilda Fulton to William Fulton, 9 Feb. 1832, WSFP, and Bolton, "'A Sister's Consolations.'" Indeed, women ran many agricultural households on their own. Women headed 2 percent of Arkansas households in the territorial period, and were frequently willed estates by husbands. Bolton, *Territorial Ambition,* 83–86.

202 . . . . **relationship between corn, trees, and prairies:** WPA, *Missouri,* 64, and Christisen, 168. **the barrens:** "The 'barrens' are literally what their name imparts," advised *Atkinson's Saturday Evening Post* in 1833 ("Arkansas Territory"). **$2/acre to break prairie:** 1831 emigrants' guide to Missouri, in Christisen, 170.

202 . . . . **work of settlement:** Hurt, *Agriculture and Slavery*, 156–57. **cutting and rolling logs to clear land:** Stanley, 148. **"Cleared up":** Keefe and Morrow, *A Connecticut Yankee*, 88. **"Cleared off":** Lula Taylor, near Brinkley, Ark., int. Irene Robertson, in Rawick, vol. 10, Part 6, 268; and Jervey and Moss, 177. **"taken up":** Flint, *Recollections*, 56 (this phrase was local to the Ohio/Cincinnati regions). **"a high state of cultivation":** ESJ, 3 Oct. 1821; and *Memphis Weekly Appeal*, 18 April 1860, in Woods, "A Promise Unfulfilled," 27. **"in high cultivation":** Flint, *Recollections*, 367.

203 . . . . **"worn out":** Mattie Lee, int. J. Tom Miles, in Rawick, vol. 11, Missouri narratives, 224. **"it sure was rich lan' den":** James Gill, int. Watt McKinney, in Rawick, vol. 9, Part 3, 19–20. **"Strong":** Henry Andrew (Tip) Williams, Biscoe, Ark., int. Irene Robertson (Williams lived as a slave in North Carolina and came to Arkansas after the war), in Rawick, vol. 11, Arkansas narratives, 167. **"poor pine country"; "poor gravelly country":** Noted near Potosi, Missouri, in 1839, by a white physician accompanying Cherokees on the Trail of Tears. Transcription of Dr. W. I. I. Morrow, Diary of Cherokee Removal, April 1839, 6–7, HSM. **"my land is a dark molatto":** Martin Camp and M. A. [?] Camp, [Saline] Co., Ark., to Mary and L. H. Williams, 2 March 1860, series 2, box 1, file 21, MLC.

203 . . . . **seasons of the plantation year:** Eakin and Logsdon, 123–24; McNeilly, 59–60, 138–39; Stampp, 45–46. **"brought out of the cane":** JJB, 8 April 1855. Livestock commonly roamed wild; Matilda Fulton commented to her husband William, "I am glad to inform you our too [two] young yearlings came home a few days since in fine order. I wish our hogs would come home in the sam way." Matilda F. Fulton, Little Rock, to William S. Fulton, Washington, D.C., 1840, box 1, file 12, WSFP. Families would often scatter salt or put out winter forage to encourage cattle and hogs to return periodically to the homestead. John Geiger's diary entry for 9 Jan. 1835, "I spent the day hunting my cattle," was typical of the frustrations of husbandry. JJG. **agricultural cycle of short-staple cotton:** Gray, vol. 2, Chapter 30. **planting, tending, weeding:** DeBlack, 114–15. **"cellered" potatoes:** JJB, 4 Aug. 1852. **harvest work created other seasonal patterns:** Slaves tended to run away from farms most often during periods of strenuous labor. Lack, 275.

203 . . . . **trading and gift exchange:** Foley, *Genesis of Missouri*, 35.

204 . . . . **autumn preparations:** In mid-November 1839, Matilda Fulton wrote her husband, "I have been very much ingaged putting away every thing for the winter." Matilda Fulton, Little Rock, to William Fulton, Washington, D.C., 17 November 1839, WSFP.

204 . . . . **"doing various things":** Journal of Horace Ford, chief overseer for Horace Walworth's Pastoria and Southfield plantations in northern Chicot County, 31 Jan. 1848, in De-Black, 114. **"set round the fire":** Kirkbride Potts [Galley Creek, Ark.], to Ann Potts, Bordentown, N.J., 2 March 1823, PFL.

204 . . . . **seasonality of illness:** In addition to the seasonal patterns of malaria and of epidemic diseases, nutritional deficiencies appeared in midwinter, when diets were poorest in fresh vegetables, and only resolved themselves with the first fruits and vegetables of spring. Kiple and King, 125–26. **"uniform sickliness of every fall season":** Skinner, 250. John Brown resigned himself to a slow cotton harvest: "there has been and is yet so much sickness in the country that if we can all get through the season, even without much work, I shall be satis-

fied." JJB, 20 Aug. 1852. **Frosts:** Frosts did indeed end outbreaks of yellow fever and falciparum malaria. Humphreys, 43.

204 . . . . **soils' characteristics and common knowledge about them:** McNeilly, 22; Stilgoe, 141–47. **"the timbered land":** Blowe, 677, also 671. Timothy Flint agreed, writing that settlers to Kentucky looked for good soil "where pawpaw, cane, and wild clover, marked exuberant fertility." Flint's narrative itself exhibited a certain exuberance of fact with regard to the details of the Boone family's lives, but his comments about agricultural perception indicated common practice. Flint, *First White Man,* 108. In the 1820s and '30s such commonsense ways of judging land were beginning to give way to more scientific approaches, especially in the 1820s and '30s, with the soil chemistry of Justus Liebig, but they nonetheless remained widespread (Stewart, " 'Let Us Begin with the Weather?'" 242; ibid., *"What Nature Suffers to Groe,"*99).

205 . . . . **Slaves' experience of agriculture:** Mart Stewart (*"What Nature Suffers to Groe,"* 135) argues that Georgia low-country slaves "experienced the crop cultures from the ground up," unlike managers or owners. On many smaller Missouri and Arkansas holdings, however, owners worked fields themselves even as they also directed slaves' labor. **Slaves came to know land through agriculture:** Kaye, 72. **"hard work, field work":** Silas Abbott, int. Irene Robertson, in Rawick, vol. 8, 2. **"from can 'til can't":** Henriette Evaline Smith, int. S. S. Taylor, in Rawick vol. 10, Part 6, 194.

205 . . . . **"small lots or patches":** H. Miller, 287. **slaves' planting, hunting, and fishing:** Stewart, *"What Nature Suffers to Groe,"*135–36 (on one astute planter's use of slave plots as the yardstick for slaves' work capacity, see 139). **barter and exchange practices:** One river plantation's slaves' activities are documented in Rawick, vol. 9, Arkansas Narratives, Part 4, 87. **importance of such informal networks of commerce:** Usner, *Indians, Settlers, and Slaves.*

206 . . . . **recounting one's own skill (gained through painful experience with a mule):** Bob Benford, Pine Bluff, Ark. int. Bernice Bowden, in Rawick, vol. 8, 147. **positive views of farm labor:** Fields could also be beautiful, even for those whose labor was coerced. Solomon Northup marveled that "There are few sights more pleasant to the eye than a wide cotton field when it is in the bloom. It presents an appearance of purity, like an immaculate expanse of light, new-fallen snow." He could draw on his life in the North for a comparison unavailable to some of his peers. Eakin and Logsdon, 125.

206 . . . . **James L. Bradley:** Autobiographical letter published in the *Herald of Freedom,* 7 March 1835, in Blassingame, 686–90.

206 . . . . **"task" vs. "gang" systems:** Hurt, 215–16; Gray, vol. 2, 550–56. In the tidewater plantations of the Georgia low-country, a "task" became also a measure of land—about a quarter acre. Stewart, *"What Nature Suffers to Groe,"* 128–29.

207 . . . . **weight of picked cotton:** Northup reported that the average hand on his northern Louisiana plantation picked 200 pounds a day, but an outstanding picker could do 500. Eakin and Logsdon, 125–26. One Mississippi planter estimated that his top cotton pickers averaged 300 pounds a day, while an entire crew of pickers—men, women, and children—averaged 157 pounds per person. DeBlack, 117. Masters in east-central Missouri generally required slaves separating hemp fibers from the rest of the plant to "break" a hundred pounds a day, and punished those who failed to meet this quota. Scarpino, 24. **"half a man's' work":** Drake, *Pioneer Life in Kentucky,* 65, in Levine, vii. **slave women's pride in their physical**

strength and stamina: Fox-Genovese, 172. On Georgia rice plantations, slaves could be classed as a "full hand," or as one quarter, one half, or three quarters of a hand. Stewart, *"What Nature Suffers to Groe,"* 128. **splitting rails:** Drake, *Pioneer Life in Kentucky*, 69, in Levine, vii. "Practiced axmen, and most frontiersmen were that, could cut between 100 and 150 ten-foot rails daily." P. Gates, 186. **learning which woods split well:** J. W. Miller, 179–81. Jobs that were typically women's work do not seem to have had a similarly widespread vocabulary; or perhaps the words for milking, spinning, and cooking were conveyed in conversation and not as often in writing.

207 . . . . **sustenance relative to labor:** "[T]he products of the soil here are raised with less than one half the labor required to raise a tolerable crop on the lands where [prospective emigrants] now reside; and with half the labor here, they would receive double the quantity of grain to the acre." "Arkansas—Her Products—Inviting Emigration." **"nothing could induce me to live in jersey now":** Kirkbride Potts, Galley Creek, Ark., to Ann Potts, Bordentown, N.J., 1 July 1830, PFL. **"Saw 32 men in one field reaping":** Jensen, Part 4, 25 April 1819, 278.

207 . . . . **"[I]t appears to be an improving place":** Tomer and Brodhead, 82. **"some of the . . . healthiest soil":** Flint, *History and Geography* (1832), 280.

208 . . . . **"the stroke is severe":** John J. Walker to Thomas H. Walker, Brownsburgh, Rockbridge Co., Va., 7 Jan. 1832, JJWL.

208 . . . . **"old people are like old trees":** Lucy A. Delaney, *From the Darkness Cometh the Light, or, Struggles for Freedom* (St. Louis: J. T. Smith, ca. 1891), in Gates, *Six Women's Slave Narratives*, 54.

208 . . . . **"red sow took boar":** JJG, 4 March 1835; **"young black sow piged":** Ibid., 12 Feb. 1843; **"One of [the] ewes droped 2 lambs":** Ibid., 13 Feb. 1843.

208 . . . . **significance of seeds:** One former Missouri settler recalled, "I remember distinctly when the seed of sorghum cane was first introduced into our neighborhood." Keefe and Morrow, *White River Chronicles*, 35. **Expertise in cotton seed the mark of an astute planter:** Bartlett, *The New Country*, 207–8; Stewart, *"What Nature Suffers to Groe*, 164. **cotton seeds and cottonseed oil:** Gray, vol. 2, 710.

209 . . . . **"You Yankees":** Keefe and Morrow, *A Connecticut Yankee*, 158.

209 . . . . **"Got to hard cuss gourd seed":** Heat Moon, *Blue Highways*, 30.

209 . . . . **News of gardens:** For example, Matilda Fulton, Little Rock, to William Fulton, [Washington, D.C.?], 6 June 1840, WSFP. **Sending seeds and seedlings:** Vesta P. Stevenson, Jefferson Co., Ark., to "Dear Mother," ca. Jan. 1850, series 2, box 1, file 9, MLC; Hedrick, 266–67.

209 . . . . **"Mrs Mattock gave me something of all she had":** Selina (Wheat) Seay, Camden, Ark., to "Darling Mother," 19 Feb. 1859, TWC.

210 . . . . **"I have about 60 bareing trees":** J. W. Calvert, St. Francis Co., Ark., to John L. Trone, 29 July 1851, JLTC.

210 . . . . **"unless it was some pore place"; "a chance of geting":** Owen and Mary Maguire, Washington Co., Ark., to Samuel and Sally Clark, Montgomery Co., N.C., 18 Sept. 1836, SFM.

210 . . . . **"But if you want to know":** Anderson Wilson, Clay Co., Mo., to Samuel and Ann Wilson Turrentine, Orange Co., N.C., 6 July 1835, in Stokes, 499.

211 . . . . **timing agricultural activities by cycles of the moon:** Stewart, *"What Nature Suffers to Groe,"* 104; ibid., "'Let Us Begin with the Weather?,'" 244. **"fucked over" fields and other sexually related agriculture:** Randolph, *Blow the Candle Out*, 887–89. Contemporary folklore bears witness to the changes in worldview wrought by changes in farming technique. "My grandfather planted his grapes according to the stars and moon," recalled Pete Marvin (formerly Peirangelo Masucci), an Italian emigrant to upstate New York in the late 1970s; "Now the boys out here plant according to Cornell University." Heat Moon, *Blue Highways*, 311.

211 . . . . **women and children:** S. Charles Bolton observes of white women in territorial Arkansas that "Women in their twenties lived with an average of three children, most of them under ten. Women in their thirties lived with five or six youngsters, three or four of them under ten. . . . even those in their fifties had an average of three children in their households, one of whom was sometimes under ten." Bolton, *Territorial Ambition*, especially 80–83. **Brown family fecundity:** John and Clara Brown were married in 1832, which would likely put Clara in her early to mid-forties as she helped her oldest daughter through pregnancy, shepherded several children through adolescence, oversaw several younger ones, and went through what was at least her own ninth pregnancy. In one concurrent mother-daughter set of deliveries, Clara Brown gave birth to a son on April 12, 1857, and Margaret Brown Carleton delivered her first child less than two weeks later, on April 25. John Brown commented on these as well as the two further pregnancies of both Clara and Margaret, and the pregnancies and possible miscarriage of Clara and John's second daughter, Ann, in his journal.

212 . . . . **"rapidly blooming":** Gregory, 114. **"the country bore the appearance":** Featherstonhaugh, "Geology of Arkansas," 28 July 1835. **fertility of land:** Conversely, swamplands profuse with growth could be termed "sterile" by mid-nineteenth-century legislators pushing wetlands drainage because those regions did not grow *crops*. Vileisis, 76. **"through a barren and sterile country":** Transcription of Dr. W. I. I. Morrow, Diary of Cherokee Removal, 1 March 1839, 9, HSM.

212 . . . . **Missouri prairies *too* productive:** Bek, "Nicholas Hesse," Part 2, 181. **"vegetation swelling out so fast":** JJB, 25 April 1856.

212 . . . . **"Such timber, and such bottom land":** T. B. Thorpe, "The Big Bear of Arkansas," in Porter, *The Big Bear of Arkansas*, 21–22.

213 . . . . **"fruit trees grow much faster here":** Bek, "Followers of Duden, Fifteenth Article," 434. **"something . . . almost appalling":** Flint, *Recollections*, 29.

213 . . . . **"The climate here lets everything ripen much quicker":** Dorothea Klein, St. Louis, to unnamed patron in present-day Germany, 8 Aug. 1859, GDKAF.

213 . . . . **"When my Boy was 13 year old":** Charles B. H. Williams, "I'se Much a Man: The Autobiography of Charles Williams," in Rawick, Supplement, series 2, vol. 1, 180–249, 216. **fast growth and rapid decline of children and other living things:** Anderson, *Cultivation of Whiteness*, 20, 27; Chinard, 34; P. W. Gates, 201. **fast-growing but insubstantial vegetation in hot environments:** Kupperman, 230.

214 . . . . **debates over how agriculture would change the young U.S.:** Glacken, 685–93. **"altered the character of the soil":** Morris Birkbeck, *Notes on a Journey in America* (1817), in Dunlop, 42; **"go away altogether":** Ibid., 43 (quoting Thomas Hulme, *Journal of*

a Tour in the Western Countries of America [1820]). **quixotic settlement attempts of Birkbeck and his rival Richard Flowers:** Dunlop, 41–46; P. W. Gates, 188–89.

214 . . . . **"The rose-slips you sent me":** Vesta P. Stevenson Jefferson Co., Ark., to "Dear Mother," ca. Jan. 1850, series 2, box 1, file 9, MLC. **howling wolves:** Cordelia Hambleton, Philips Co., Ark., to John W. Compton, Owensboro, Ky., 4 Dec. 1854, MLC.

215 . . . . **cultivation changes climate:** Chinard, especially 32, 45. **"there is no such thing in Missouri":** Bek, "Travel into Missouri," 41. **"The climate has changed wonderfully":** Keefe and Morrow, *A Connecticut Yankee,* 88. James Fenimore Cooper's consummate nineteenth-century frontier narrative, *The Pioneers,* reflected a similar understanding of human settlement and cultivation (3).

215 . . . . **"rain follows the plow":** Smith, "Rain Follows the Plow"; Tyrell, 90–91. This theory, promoted by western boosters, came to guide and justify positive evaluations of land in the western U.S. in the 1860s and '70s. It was enshrined in federal policy by the Timber Culture Act of 1873, whose purpose was to transform arid lands into humid, cultivable tracts through the planting of trees; it granted quarter-sections of land to heads of household cultivating 40 acres of trees in specified western regions for 10 years. The act was a dismal failure. White, "*It's Your Misfortune,*" 132–33, 150–51; Boorstin, 231–32. **American cultivators forming environment and climate:** One travel guide noted of Illinois Territory in 1818, "The wildness of the country implies an *unformed* climate." Fearon, 264.

215 . . . . **"Not by any magic or enchantment":** Charles Dana Wilber, *The Great Valleys and Prairies of Nebraska and the Northwest* (Omaha, 1881), 70, in Smith, *Virgin Land,* 183.

216 . . . . **"The vapour which issues from fresh earth"; "In the new settlements":** Rush, *An Inquiry,* 34. Similarly, AWW, 4, 12.

216 . . . . **"local causes [of fevers] incident to all new districts":** Goulding, 328.

216 . . . . **"productive and healthy" lands:** "South Arkansas—Our Prospects." **"pleasant, healthy, and fertile country":** Flint, *History and Geography* (1832), 277. **"level, poor and I think sickly":** Jervey and Moss, 176.

217 . . . . **"To breathe the pure healthful air of a farm":** Weems, 130. Weems also created the apocryphal cherry-tree incident (13–14).

217 . . . . **fertility linked with insalubrity:** Goulding, 322. Billy M. Jones (4–5) notes this paradox in western settlement more generally. **"The Land between Saint Francis and Black River":** William Russell, St. Louis, to William Rector, 20 April 1814, in Carter, vol. 14, 755.

217 . . . . **"one of the most desirable places":** James Clemens, Jr., St. Louis, to Isachar Pawling, Danville, Ky., in Clemens. **"The best and richest land":** Nathan Haley, Herculaneum, Jefferson Co., Mo., to Jeremiah Haley, Great Horton, Yorkshire, 20 May 1823, in Erickson, 416. Timothy Flint (*History and Geography* [1833], 36) concurred: "Where the lands are extremely fertile, it seems to be appended to them, as a drawback to that advantage, that they are generally sickly."

218 . . . . **"sections of country":** AWW, 8.

218 . . . . **"causes of the acknowledged sickliness":** Captain John R. Bell, 1820, *Arkansas Territorial Papers,* XIX, 272–75, in Martin, 5. **power of cultivation:** Flint (*Recollections,* 239) reassured his readers that "exposure to the ague" in Missouri "will undoubtedly

lessen with the increase of improvement and cultivation." Similarly, he acknowledged (*History and Geography* [1833], 36) the challenges to health posed by new lands of the region, but insisted that settlement altered the situation: "The rich plains of the Scioto were the graves of the first settlers, [but] they have long since been brought into cultivation, and have lost their character for insalubrity."

218 . . . . **"The forest is levelled" and subsequent dire description:** *Emigrant's Hand-Book*, 46. The author claims to be quoting Timothy Flint in this passage; writers of guides borrowed freely from each other.

218 . . . . **"Yet, where the forest is cleared away":** *Emigrant's Hand-Book*, 46.

218 . . . . **passing of crisis:** Solomon Northup described his recovery from smallpox: "The crisis having passed, I began to revive." Eakin and Logsdon, 55. **bodily understanding:** The notion developed here draws on Rosenberg, notably in "Therapeutic Revolution," and Duden, *Woman Beneath the Skin*.

219 . . . . **childbirth and weaning:** JJB, 22 July 1858 and 25 April 1857. **"an important crisis in my life":** Ibid., 5 Feb. 1854. **crisis as change, for good or ill:** Cooper, *The Prairie*, 335, and *Deerslayer*, 106.

219 . . . . **"give . . . the death blow":** August de Marle, Santa Fe, to Gustavo Wulfing, 6 December 1846, in Bek, "Followers of Duden, Twelfth Article," 498. **"bring the fever to a perfect solution":** AWW, 20, 21. **"I thought her case dangerous":** JJB, 18 Sept. 1852.

219 . . . . **body's maturation:** Puberty and menopause were periods of crisis. Smith-Rosenberg, especially 184. **"ulcerous sore legs":** Gunn, *Domestic Medicine*, 242.

220 . . . . **elephantiasis as "imperfect crisis"; "upon the first appearance of the yaws":** Hillary, 219, 249.

221 . . . . **"clearings":** Cortambert, 213. A. W. Webb similarly warned of "the decay of vegetable matter attendant upon the clearing of new countries" (AWW, 5). **"I'm scared to let in air":** Mary Staton Jones, Federal Writers' Project Papers, SHC, in Humphreys, 120.

221 . . . . **"the fatigue and exposure":** AWW, 7. **Clearing improved land but imperiled laborers:** Cassedy, "Medical Men," 168.

222 . . . . **"land that has been in active cultivation":** Gantt, "Medical Topography," 352. **"more unhealthy within the first five or six years":** AWW, 5.

222 . . . . **"intestines are imperfectly evacuated":** Ibid., 49 and 46. For similar warnings about "half cured" "Scarlatina Canker Rash," see medical recipes at the end of JJG. **"lands in an imperfect state of cultivation":** Currie, 403.

222 . . . . **"being cleared up":** Dr. James Harris noted (478), "it is a well established fact that a country clothed with a dense forest and luxuriant vegetation . . . is *colder* and more *healthy* than one that is being cleared up." **ideal of "agricultural equilibrium":** This ideal also characterized midcentury American aesthetic landscape standards. Stilgoe, 206.

223 . . . . **"The most dangerous period":** Flint, *History and Geography* (1833), 37. Such beliefs also held relevance in older settlements east of the Appalachians; see Cronon, *Changes in the Land*, 125.

223 . . . . **"In a country not cleaned":** ISMN, 26. **sun's power to draw poisons out of the earth:** Kupperman, 217. **"fresh earth":** Rush, *An Inquiry*, 57. Similarly, "exposing [south-

ern Arkansas] marshes to the sun will be very unfavourable to the salubrity of the climate."
AWW, 7.

225 . . . . **"Click! click!":** Porter, "Cupping on the Sternum," in *A Quarter Race in Kentucky*,
186. The sketch employs coarse regional humor as well as gross racial stereotype in its depiction of the interactions of an untrained young physician and an ignorant slave woman. The
"Click! click!" with which the author describes the action of the scarificator's blades, however,
was most likely familiar to a broad section of his audience.

226 . . . . **people referred to land as themselves:** Harington, *Let Us Build Us a City*, 27.

Chapter VIII, Racial Anxiety

229 . . . . **"She will think":** H. A. Whittington, Little Rock, to Granville Whittington,
[Boston], 11 Feb. 1830, in Ross, "Letters of Hiram Abiff Whittington," 14–15.

231 . . . . **racial categories:** The present-day category "African-American" is problematic for
this discussion, since the vast majority of people of African ancestry in the United States before
the Civil War were not regarded by the white majority as being "American" in legal, political,
or even medical terms, and that overwhelming and overpowering fact of American society is
what I am trying to untangle in this chapter. I therefore use the stark "black" and "white," in an
effort to convey the racial frameworks of their time through the contested vocabulary of our
own.

232 . . . . **"To us, West Pennsylvania":** Flint, *Recollections*, 13.

232 . . . . **"White" was a powerful category:** Anderson, *Cultivation of Whiteness;* Ignatiev,
How the Irish Became White; Jacobson, *Whiteness of a Different Color;* Roediger, *Towards the Abolition
of Whiteness;* ibid., *Wages of Whiteness.* **usage unstable:** Reginald Horsman has noted increased
attention to race as indicating inherent, unchanging, and value-laden differences over the first
half of the nineteenth century. The foundational race scholar George Fredrickson has found
much less attention to division among "white" people in the early nineteenth century than in
the immediate prewar decades, but conversations "on the ground" during the period of American expansion beyond the Mississippi River reveal that kinds of whiteness and blackness received significant attention. Fredrickson, Chapter 4. **"These Irish":** JJB, 20 April 1854.
Defense of "whiteness": See Fredrickson, Chapter 1.

233 . . . . **"the Germans sit":** H. Miller, 274.

233 . . . . **national origins reflected in households:** On Germans, Bek, "Followers of
Duden, Fifteenth Article," 432. On French, ibid., "George Engelmann, Man of Science," Part
2, 430. On the regional farming practices of American emigrants, Stilgoe, *Common Landscapes of
America*, 193.

233 . . . . **Flint on "different races":** Flint, *Recollections*, 322; ibid., 228.

233 . . . . **heritage and temperament:** Washington Irving casually concluded of Creole
Arkansas that "poverty and gayety generally go hand-in-hand among the French and their
descendants." McDermott, *Western Journals*, 178. **"her Irish":** Crockett, 65. **"terrible
temper":** Richard Bruner, Nelson, Mo., interviewed by an unidentified woman, in Rawick, *American Slave*, vol. 11, 59. Such linkage between Indianness and temper was common

among the former slaves int. the Federal Writers' Project; see ibid., *Supplement, series* 1, vol. 2, 154.

234 . . . . **"the Germans":** Flint, *Recollections*, 230. **"what is for disposal within":** Ibid., 378.

234 . . . . **slaves from Sierra Leone and Gambia:** Gomez, 38–42; **"Mohammedan" slaves:** Ibid., Chapter 4; also Harms, 160–61. Such notions continued an emphasis on "blood" common to the slave-holding South; see E. Ball, *Slaves in the Family,* Chapter 9.

235 . . . . **"We never mistook":** Flint, *Recollections*, 377.

235 . . . . **climate shaped individual and racial well-being:** Anderson, *Cultivation of Whiteness;* ibid., "Disease, Race, and Empire"; ibid., "Geography, Race and Nation"; ibid., "Immunities of Empire"; Harrison, "Tender Frame of Man"; Kupperman.

235 . . . . **Ham:** The curse itself actually applied to Ham's son Canaan; to this somewhat confusing familial malediction, some theologians added the curse on Cain or a bizarre combination of all of these biblical curses. Fredrickson, 87; Horsman, 124. See Genesis 4:10–15 and 9:20–27.

235 . . . . **monogenesis:** Fredrickson, 72; Horsman, 44–45; Stanton, 1–14.

236 . . . . **polygenesis:** Fredrickson, 73–76; Horsman, Chapter 7; Nott; Stanton, 31, 41–2, 69–72, 100–12, 165; Stewart, "'Let Us Begin with the Weather?'"

236 . . . . **"zoölogical provinces":** Fredrickson, 137–38. See Louis Agassiz, "Sketch of the Natural Provinces of the Animal World and their Relation to the Different Types of Man," in Nott.

236 . . . . **environmental justification for black enslavement:** For instance, Nelson; and on historians' understanding of this conceptual relationship, see Puckrein and Savitt, "Black Health on the Plantation." **"climate is unsuited":** *Emigrant's Hand-Book* 1848, 6.

237 . . . . **African descendants' physiology:** These ideas influenced not only rationalizations for slavery but white arguments for colonization. See Fredrickson, Chapter 1. **"African constitution":** Flint, *Recollections*, 32. **perceived black susceptibility to cold:** Savitt. **"thermal laws":** These climatic doctrines were central in the debate in the late 1840s and '50s over American expansion west into territory that both sides agreed was not particularly fit for cotton cultivation or plantation slavery. The "free soil" advocated by those against extending slavery to the western territories was not a soil on which free black people (or indeed, any black people) were welcome; it was soil with which the free white laborers of the East could cultivate their rightful heritage of dominion over temperate zones. See Fredrickson, Chapter 5.

237 . . . . **Black immunity:** See Kiple and King, Part 2; Wood, Chapter 3. **Perceived black resistance and susceptibility:** Kiple and King, 41–49, 146–47, 137–39, 78; Wood, 81–83, 90–91. Disease and immunity have continued to play an important role in American debates over African American identity; see Humphreys, 14–20; Wailoo, 4–5, 78–9, 145–7, 188–9.

237 . . . . **West Africans' immunity:** On malaria, Humphreys, 17–20, but see 46–47; Kiple and King, 17–23. On yellow fever, Kiple and King, 30 (though see their subsequent discussion of the limitations of acquired immunity in explaining black resistance); Wood, 90–91. Potential links between race and differential immunity are still debated; Cooper and Kiple, 1102.

238 . . . . **"Their internal organization":** Gantt, "A few Reasons," 214. **Black bodies brutish:** Fredrickson, 51–58; Kiple and King, 179; Savitt.

238 . . . . **reports of illness of newly emigrated slaves:** McNeilly, 51. **"got the better of their chills":** Skinner, 262. **"dissatisfied" slaves:** McNeilly, 51.

238 . . . . **Middle Passage:** Later historians of slavery agree that the voyage from Africa was a period of transformation in the identities of captured Africans. Gomez, Chapter 7.

238 . . . . **"In regard to unacclimated negroes":** Letter from Samuel A. Cartwright, 27 June 1844, in Kiple and King, 167.

239 . . . . **slaves' acclimation to a new household:** Gomez, 168–70. Gomez (Chapter 7) argues that learning English was key to Africans' transformative seasoning into slavery. **Northup's "habituation:** Eakin and Logsdon Chapter 3. **"He'd chain a nigger up":** N. R. Yetman, *Life Under the 'Peculiar Institution'* (1970), 18–19, in Hunter, 249.

239 . . . . **"People died in piles":** Warren McKinney, Hazen, Ark., int. Irene Robertson, in Rawick, vol. 10, Arkansas narratives, Part 5, 27. Many freedpeople moved to cities after the war, seeking work or the seeming safety of larger populations. Foner, *Reconstruction*, 81–82.

240 . . . . **whites' fears of acclimation:** On contact with "degenerate" blacks, Stepan, 101. Northerners increasingly argued that living in a system of slave labor degraded and debased free, white men. Foner, *Free Soil*, Chapter 2. Antebellum scientific thinkers explicitly contemplated the consequences of black improvement: those of African descent could become more white, as had one Revolutionary War soldier. Stanton, 5–9; also see Fredrickson, 72.

240 . . . . **attributes handed down:** "For myself I conclude all the Bumppos could shoot," mused James Fenimore Cooper's ever-philosophical backwoodsman Natty Bumppo, "for I have a natural turn with a rifle, which must have been handed down from generation to generation, as, our holy commandments tell us, all good and evil gifts are bestowed." Cooper, *The Last of the Mohicans*, 25. This notion that acquired characteristics could be inherited was rejected by some racial thinkers, particularly Josiah Nott. See Fredrickson, 80. **"There are a number of French":** H. Miller, 228.

241 . . . . **"I have a wife":** B. W. Lee, Post of Arkansas, to James N. Lucas, St. Louis, 30 April 1844, KC.

241 . . . . **"sorrowland" and African American children:** Gomez, 188–89.

241 . . . . **"looked in vain":** Flint, *Recollections*, 373. **bug-based metaphors:** For instance, Flint's comment in his Boone biography (*First White Man,* 111) about the "northern hive of the savages."

242 . . . . **degeneration of mammals and people:** Chinard; Gerbi, 3–6. Arguing the American cause at a dinner with the Abbé Raynal, American emissaries used to great rhetorical advantage the fact that they were all significantly taller than their French hosts. Chinard, 41. **woolly mammoths:** Gerbi, 254, 257; Jefferson, 1999, 51–56.

242 . . . . **danger of hot places:** Kupperman.

242 . . . . **Degeneration:** See Anderson, "Disease, Race, and Empire," "Immunities of Empire," and "The Trespass Speaks"; Pick, especially Chapter 7; and Stepan.

243 . . . . **increasing pessimism about racial change over the nineteenth century:** Anderson, "Disease, Race, and Empire"; ibid., "Immunities of Empire"; Fredrickson; Stepan.

244 . . . . **"blackies"**: Flora Byrne, Byrnham Wood, Mo., to Elizabeth Blackwell Mayer, Baltimore, 4 Aug. 1845, in "Byrnham Wood in Missouri," 86. **"Now I'se a white man!"**: Alexander's life story was written by a Northern abolitionist. These may or may not have been Alexander's words. Eliot, 88. A contemporary wrote of the free black St. Louisan James P. Beckwourth that "So pleasing and agreeable were his characteristics that he was spoken of as the black white man." Quoted in Bellamy, "Free Blacks," 214. Walter Johnson (18–19) and others have recently noted that race definition depended on how a person acted as well as his or her appearance.

244 . . . . **"When negroes were well fed"**: "Recollections of Thomas Beckwith," 36.

244 . . . . **"Swarthiness"**: John Brown noted in 1860 that a sick family member was still "swarthy and lean." JJB, 7 October 1860. **"Frank is a tall mischievous Boy"**: Ann Ball, Pleasant Hills, Ark., to Lucinda Roberson, 9 October 1843, BFP, 1839–56.

244 . . . . **"black" and "white" not self-evident**: Johnson. **rape case**: Stafford, 429–30. Stafford notes that in several such instances of the court's overturning serious criminal sentences for slaves, the concern may have been for the owners' loss of valuable property, rather than for the rights of the slaves. **Abby Guy** : Stafford, 461.

245 . . . . **"poor white man"**: Matilda Fulton, Little Rock, to William Fulton, Washington, D.C., 17 Nov. 1839, box 1, file 12, WSFP. Steamboat captains, too, could be unsure of the race of those they transported: Schafer, 109. On the Fultons as slave owners, see Lack. **"passing" as white to escape**: Franklin and Schweninger, 214–15; Gomez, 238; Schafer, 119. **"White man niggahafied"**: Henry Miller (286), describing the "Grand Nigga Ball" that wound up plantation celebrations in the vicinity of Natchez, in which slaves would dress up and dance cotillions.

245 . . . . **conflict created by masters' fathering of slave children**: Fox-Genovese, 379–80. **change in race label of slave child**: Henry "Happy Day" Green, near Barton and Helena, Ark., int. Irene Robertson, in Rawick, vol. 9, Arkansas narratives, Part 3, 87. **newborns' skin darkening**: Shannan Venable, a pediatric nurse at Arkansas Children's Hospital in Little Rock, confirmed that it is common and unremarkable for African-American babies' skin color to darken, often dramatically, over the first days and weeks of life (personal communication, December 1999). Suzanne Stephens, doula at Barnes-Jewish Hospital in St. Louis, added that the plantation mistress in this account might well have further misperceived the child's "real" color since she likely saw the baby swaddled and diapered, and the ears and genitals are usually the places that are darkest on babies that will ultimately end up dark-skinned (personal communication, February 2002). Such physiological changes were widely noted and widely misunderstood. One 1758 French account reported, "The Indian children are white when they are born; but they darken, because they are rubbed with bear grease when small, in order to expose them to the sun." Layton, 256.

246 . . . . **"superlative of the British"**: Bek, "Nicholas Hesse," Part 3, 297.

246 . . . . "**a new national constitution**": Levine, 701.

246 . . . . **"negroes, or their descendants of mixed blood"**: *Daniel Drake, Letters on Slavery*, 29 (original in italics). **agitation for all-white free U.S.**: See Fredrickson, Chapter 5.

247 . . . . **"may spring up new and mongrel races"**: Washington Irving, *Astoria, or Anecdotes of an Enterprise beyond the Rocky Mountains* (Philadelphia: 1836), quoted in Smith, *Virgin*

Land, 177. Smith puts these images in the context of various fears about the Great Plains, but they existed also in a spectrum of belief about race and region.

247 . . . . **St. Louis wharf:** Typical of travelers' perceptions is the description by Franz von Löher, in Trautmann, 376–77. **cultural interaction of early St. Louis:** Faragher, "More Motley than Mackinaw"; Usner, "An American Indian Gateway." Although Faragher emphasizes the relative decrease in cross-cultural interaction over the period he chronicles, St. Louis remained throughout the antebellum period the site of interaction between American immigrants from across the country, European travelers and emigrants, and Native Americans.

248 . . . . **Free black people:** Bellamy, "Free Blacks." **Legal curtailment of free black rights:** See Stafford, 449–50; and Woods, *Rebellion and Realignment*, 28–29. **calls for black expulsion/colonization:** Bellamy, "Persistency of Colonization"; Fredrickson, Chapters 1 and 5. An 1843 Arkansas law forbade free blacks to immigrate, and those already there who wanted to stay had to post $500 bond. Legislation passed in 1859 attempted to expel all free blacks from the state. Such laws had impact even in nonplantation areas of the state. See Doolin.

249 . . . . **attacks on more independent and skilled urban slaves:** Ignatiev, 100; Stafford, "Slavery and the Arkansas Supreme Court," 449. Work as domestics (for women) and in the building trades (for men) was characteristic of urban slaves, many of whom enjoyed more freedom of movement than rural slaves. Some were even able to run their own households and "rent out" their own time, remitting a set fee to their owners every month or every year. WPA, *Missouri,* 188; Lack; Seematter. **free black Americans moving West:** George Bush, for instance, emigrated to Washington Territory in 1844, carrying along more than $2,000 in silver dollars he had earned as a cattle rancher in Clay County, Mo.; George Washington also left Missouri in the mid-forties to found Centralia, Washington. Bellamy, "Free Blacks," 214–15. **difficulty of migration for most free black people:** In addition to the question of financial resources, many free black people had family members living in slavery whom they would not want to abandon. Jensen, Part 9, 24 May 1849, 416. Families often "bought out" one member at a time. J. L. Morgan; Albert, 124–27.

249 . . . . **decline in status of "mixed bloods":** Foley, *Genesis of Missouri*, 107. **inevitability of Indian decline:** Horsman, 146. James Fenimore Cooper's Chingachgook, famously the "Last of the Mohicans," was "of a fallen race, and belonging to a fallen people." Cooper, *The Deerslayer*, 25.

249 . . . . **"facility with which the French and Indians intermix"; "The lank hair":** Flint, *Recollections*, 158–59. Many Euro-American observers similarly saw mixed Native people as unattractive. Trautmann, 377.

250 . . . . **"a spirit of improvement" and subsequent racial discussion:** HBD, 3 Jan. 1819.

250 . . . . **Amalgamation and deterioration of the white race:** Stanton, 81, 159.

250 . . . . **mixed-race people as threat to white Americans:** "Miscegenation," in Genovese. **recognition of mixed-status families:** Ibid., 418; Elisha Worthington, a southern Arkansas plantation owner whose young wife left him for his adultery, lived openly with a slave woman and recognized and educated their children. Gatewood. Such instances, however, were by far the exception in the slave-holding South. The denial of such dual families continues into the present—see E. Ball.

251 . . . . **white insistence on mixed-race sterility:** Fredrickson, 89; Horsman, 130, 154; Sollors, 226; Stanton, 66–67, 90; Stepan, 100–105. Toward midcentury some thinkers acknowledged at least partial fertility but argued that this did not mean that whites and blacks were in fact the same species. Thus a substantial challenge to contemporary biological understanding of species emerged from the racial dilemmas of the United States. Stanton, 42, 113–15, 148–41; Stepan, "Biological Degeneration," 105–9.

251 . . . . **"aversion to hybridity":** W. W. Wright, "Amalgamation" *Debow's Review* 24 (July 1860) 3, 12–14, quoted in Fredrickson, 89. **"I never had a child":** Sophie D. Belle, Forrest City, Ark., int. Irene Robertson, in Rawick, vol. 8, Part 1, 139.

252 . . . . **"Dutch":** This conflation of national identities caused German immigrants no end of irritation. Friedrich Gerstäcker—himself so frustrated at American pronunciations of his name that he took to calling himself Miller—wrote one story about the lifelong efforts of an immigrant named Ülsicht to have a nearby creek named after him, as was common practice in the borderlands of the U.S., only to find that it was called by his thick-tongued neighbors "Dutchman's Creek." Despondent and disappointed, "finally he died in the unhealthy Mississippi Swamps." See J. W. Miller, Chapter 6. **"Black Dutch"; "Venus of the West":** Cox, and journal, CoxFP, 2 Oct. 1819. Elizabeth McClure's diary reference to an "Old black Dutch Missouri woman" during her own steamboat journey in 1846 suggests that those of German-black or German-Native ancestry may have carried this label more generally. Jervey and Moss, 185.

252 . . . . **enslaved Native Americans:** The last Native American slave in Missouri was reportedly freed by the state in 1834, but many remaining slaves were at least part Indian. Primm, 26. **"her Squaw melato":** Jensen, Part 6, 235. **Mary Hempstead Lisa; Mitain; Rosalie:** Corbett, *In Her Place*, 30–31.

253 . . . . **elaborate language of racial intermixture:** The fictional naturalist of Cooper's *The Prairie* (230) is "indisposed . . . to all admixture of the varieties of species, which only tends to tarnish the beauty and to interrupt the harmony of nature. Moreover, it is a painful innovation on the order of all nomenclatures." Nomenclature was indeed strained by the features and forms created by sexual interaction in the American South and West. **"yellow women":** Flint, *Recollections*, 299. "Mulatto" women fetched high prices at the New Orleans market. See Genovese, 416–17. **"griffe" and related vocabulary:** Schweninger, 113. The son of a prominent Tennessee judge and an enslaved mother who bought her son's freedom with what she earned washing clothes, Thomas became a prominent member of the prewar free black elite in St. Louis, parlaying entrepreneurial savvy into major holdings in cities farther and farther west. **language of race:** Franklin and Schweninger, 215–16. **particularly heightened in New Orleans:** Gomez, 231–32.

253 . . . . **slaves' own language of color:** Kenneth Stampp (Chapter 8) has argued that though to whites, all "blacks" were "black," African Americans themselves were much more attentive to differences of skin tone. On slaves' attention to mixed-race status, see Gomez, 230–39. **"a dark woman," "a ginger cake colored man":** Laura Abromson, Holly Grove, Ark., int. Irene Robertson, in Rawick, vol. 8, Part 1, 8. **"a regular Indian color":** John Williams, Little Rock, int. Samuel S. Taylor, in Rawick, vol. 11, Arkansas narratives, 173. Fannie Alexander of Helena, Ark., recalled, "My papa was a bright color like I am but not near as light as mama." Int. Irene Robertson, in Rawick, vol. 8, Part 1, 31.

253 . . . . **"a Yellowman":** Jensen, Part 7, 17 June 1826, 82. Hempstead's account does not make clear which man died in the fray. **"Mʳ Giddings preached in the forenoon":** Jensen, Part 7, 17 Dec. 1826, 93.

254 . . . . **"yellow" Indians:** Faragher, *Daniel Boone,* 216. "Yellow" also connoted cowardice throughout this period (see p. 218); that meaning likely interacted with racial ideas, especially in the scenes of white-Indian conflict Faragher cites here. Sources on Boone's life—as Faragher makes clear—reflect anything but verisimilitude, but it is still significant that even if Boone himself did not necessarily make these precise remarks, contemporaries would have recorded him as doing so; his hearers, would have found nothing particularly remarkable in remarks about "yellow" Shoshone, and apparently used that language in passing along Boone tales to the many writers who chronicled his life. **"red men":** Faragher, *Daniel Boone,* 299. Boone was in his eighties during the 1810s, when he made this remark. **Americans' perceptions, however, are only half the story:** Nancy Shoemaker argues that self-identification by Cherokee groups in the early eighteenth century as "red men" both served to differentiate between Indians, white interlopers, and black slaves and drew on preexisting Cherokee color symbolism. This color-based identifier served many political and rhetorical purposes in Cherokee political interactions with "whites," just as it served multiple political and rhetorical purposes within American political culture.

254 . . . . **white widow's son sold as a slave:** W. W. Brown, 26. **slave dealers' stealing slaves and kidnapping free black people (especially children):** Eakin and Logsdon; McNeilly, 48. **"purchaser would not buy" and subsequent descriptions:** I. Williams, 54.

255 . . . . **branded in the face:** W. W. Brown, 59. No date is given for the quoted newspaper citation. **branding:** Franklin and Schweninger, 216–19; McNeilly, 154.

256 . . . . **lack of fixity of race in the borderlands:** Noel Ignatiev has posited cities as key sites of the formation of notions of "race" in the nineteenth-century U.S. The present material suggests that what it meant to be "white" developed also in conversations of the rural borderlands and the South.

256 . . . . **tension of frameworks of understanding:** The conflict between implicit recognition of the necessity of racial change and fear of blurred racial boundaries may perhaps be central to American constructions of "people" much in the same way as the tensions Werner Sollors (6) has identified between "consent" and "descent" relations.

Chapter IX, Conclusion

259 . . . . **metaphorical language of body and nation in the nineteenth-century U.S.:** Herschbach, "Fragmentation and Reunion." Also see Burbick, *Healing the Republic.* Similarly enmeshed understanding of bodily process and political life in other eras and places: Barnes, *Making of a Social Disease;* Cooter; Maier; Porter, "Gout."

262 . . . . **"whenever he appeared":** Pope, 228.

263 . . . . **making a vision of the world robust:** C. S. Lewis warns of modern observers' distance from medieval conceptions of the universe that "the planetary characters need to be seized in an intuition rather than built up out of concepts; we need to know them, not to know

about them. . . ." Following that injunction, I have emphasized the experiential quality of nineteenth-century concepts, to give us moderns a hint of the intuition which made ideas like "healthful winds" or "salutary waters" the unquestioned qualities of common sense. At times, as with certain beliefs about the good influence of mountaintops, the potency of change of season, or the health-imparting qualities of bad-tasting things, "Sometimes the old intuitions survive; when they do not, we falter." Lewis, *Discarded Image*, 109.

BIBLIOGRAPHY

_____

Please see pages 271–73 for a list of archives and collections used in the preparation of this book.

Abel, Emily K. "Family Caregiving in the Nineteenth Century: Emily Hawley Gillespie and Sarah Gillespie, 1858–1888." *Bulletin of the History of Medicine* 68 (1994):573–99.

Ackerknecht, Erwin H. *Malaria in the Upper Mississippi Valley, 1760–1900.* Supplements to the Bulletin of the History of Medicine, ed. Henry E. Sigerist. Baltimore: Johns Hopkins Press, 1945.

_____. "Anticontagionism Between 1821 and 1867." *Bulletin of the History of Medicine* 22 (1954):562–93.

Adler, Jeffrey S. *Yankee Merchants and the Making of the Urban West: The Rise and Fall of Antebellum St. Louis.* Interdisciplinary Perspectives on Modern History, ed. Robert Fogel and Stephan Thernstrom. Cambridge: Cambridge University Press, 1991.

Agnew, Brad. "The Cherokee Struggle for Lovely's Purchase." *American Indian Quarterly* 2 (1975–76):347–61.

Albert, Octavia Victoria Rogers. *The House of Bondage, or, Charlotte Brooks and Other Slaves.* 1890. Reprint, Schomburg Library of Nineteenth-Century Black Women Writers, ed. Henry Louis Gates, Jr. New York and Oxford: Oxford University Press, 1988.

Alcott, Louisa M. *Little Women.* 1868. Reprint, New York: Modern Library, 1983.

Allen, Michael. "The Lower Mississippi in 1803: The Travelers' View." *Missouri Historical Review* 77 (1983):253–71.

Allen, Phyllis. "Etiological Theory in America Prior to the Civil War." *Journal of the History of Medicine and the Allied Sciences* 2 (1947):489–520.

Anderson, Benedict. *Imagined Communities: Reflections on the Origin and Spread of Nationalism.* London and New York: Verso, 1983. Rev. ed., London and New York: Verso, 1991.

Anderson, Hattie M. "Missouri, 1804–1828: Peopling a Frontier State." *Missouri Historical Review* 31 (1937):150–80.

Anderson, Warwick. "Climates of Opinion: Acclimatization in Nineteenth-Century France and England." *Victorian Studies* (1992):135–57.

_____. "Disease, Race, and Empire." *Bulletin of the History of Medicine* 70 (1996):62–67.

_____. "Immunities of Empire: Race, Disease, and the New Tropical Medicine, 1900–1920." *Bulletin of the History of Medicine* 70 (1996):94–118.

_____. "Geography, Race and Nation: Remapping 'Tropical' Australia, 1890–1930." *Historical Records of Australian Science* 11 (1997):457–68.

_____. "The Trespass Speaks: White Masculinity and Colonial Breakdown." *American Historical Review* 102 (1997):1343–70.

_____. *The Cultivation of Whiteness: Science, Health and Racial Destiny in Australia.* Melbourne: Melbourne University Press, 2002.

Arese, Count Francesco. *A Trip to the Prairies and in the Interior of North America.* Trans. Andrew Evans. New York: Cooper Square, 1975.

"Arkansas—Her Products—Inviting Emigration." *Arkansas Times,* 23 April 1836, 2.

Arkansas State Gazette. Notice of the Death of John Stuart. 2 Jan. 1839.

Arkansas State Gazette. Obituary of William J. Goulding. 22 Dec. 1841.

"Arkansas Territory." *Atkinson's Saturday Evening Post and Bulletin,* 1 June 1833, 1.

Armitage, Susan. "Through Women's Eyes: A New View of the West." In *The Women's West,* ed. Susan Armitage and Elizabeth Jameson. Norman: University of Oklahoma Press, 1987.

Arnold, David. *Warm Climates and Western Medicine: The Emergence of Tropical Medicine, 1500–1900.* Wellcome Institute Series in the History of Medicine. Amsterdam and Atlanta: Clio Medica, 1996.

Audubon, John James. *Delineations of American Scenery and Character.* Ed. Francis Hobart Herrick. New York: G. A. Baker, 1926.

Bacon, William. "Marsh Miasmata." *New York Journal of Medicine* 10 (1848):370–72.

Baird, Robert. *View of the Valley of the Mississippi, or the Emigrant's and Traveller's Guide to the West . . .* 2nd ed. Philadelphia: H. S. Tanner, 1834.

Baird, W. David. *The Osage People.* Phoenix: Indian Tribal Series, 1972.

_____. "The Reduction of a People: The Quapaw Removal, 1824–1834." *Red River Valley Historical Review* 1 (1974):21–36.

_____. *The Quapaw People.* Phoenix: Indian Tribal Series, 1975.

_____. *Medical Education in Arkansas, 1879–1978.* Memphis: Memphis State University Press, 1979.

_____. *The Quapaw Indians: A History of the Downstream People.* The Civilization of the American Indian Series. Norman: University of Oklahoma Press, 1980.

Ball, Brenda. "Arkansas Weatherman: Dr. Nathan D. Smith." *Arkansas Historical Quarterly* 24 (1965):67–81.

Ball, Edward. *Slaves in the Family.* New York: Ballantine Books, 1998.

Baptist, Edward E. "The Migration of Planters to Antebellum Florida: Kinship and Power." *Journal of Southern History* 62 (1996):527–54.

Barbour, Barton H. "Westward to Health: Gentlemen Health-Seekers on the Santa Fe Trail." *Journal of the West* 28 (1989):39–44.

Barnes, David S. *The Making of a Social Disease: Tuberculosis in Nineteenth-Century France.* Berkeley: University of California Press, 1995.

Barrett, Frank A. "Daniel Drake's Medical Geography." *Social Science and Medicine* 42 (1996):791–800.

———. "Alfred Haviland's Nineteenth-Century Map Analysis of the Geographical Distribution of Diseases in England and Wales." *Social Science and Medicine* 46 (1998):767–81.

Barry, John M. *Rising Tide: The Great Mississippi Flood of 1927 and How It Changed America.* New York: Simon & Schuster, 1997.

Bartlett, Richard A. *The New Country: A Social History of the American Frontier, 1776–1890.* London, Oxford, and New York: Oxford University Press, 1974.

Baur, John E. "The Health Seeker in the Western Movement, 1830–1900." *The Mississippi Valley Historical Review* 46 (1959):91–110.

Baxandall, Roslyn, Linda Gordon, and Susan Reverby, eds. *America's Working Women: A Documentary History 1600 to the Present.* 1976. New York: Norton, 1995.

Bek, William G. "The Followers of Duden." *Missouri Historical Review* 14 (1919–20) "First Article," 29–73; "Second Article," 217–32; "Third Article," 436–58. *Missouri Historical Review* 17 (1923) "Eleventh Article," 339–47; "Twelfth Article," 479–504. *Missouri Historical Review* 18 (1924) "Fourteenth Article," 212–49; "Fifteenth Article," 415–37; "Sixteenth Article," 562–84. *Missouri Historical Review* 19 (1924–25) "Seventeenth Article," 114–29; "Eighteenth Article," 338–52.

———. "George Engelmann, Man of Science." Parts 1–4. *Missouri Historical Review* 23 (1929):167–206, 427–46, 517–35; 24 (1929):66–86.

———. "Nicholas Hesse, German Visitor to Missouri, 1835–1837." Parts 1–6. *Missouri Historical Review* 41 (1946–47):19–44, 164–83, 285–304, 373–90; 42 (1947–48):34–49, 140–52, 241–48.

Bek, William G., ed. and trans. "Travel into Missouri in October, 1838, by Eduard Zimmermann." *Missouri Historical Review* 9 (1914):33–43.

Belkin, Lisa. "Haunted by Mold." *The New York Times Magazine,* 12 August 2001, 29–33, 48, 62–3.

Bell, John. "On Miasm as an Alleged Cause of Fevers." *Philadelphia Journal of the Medical and Physical Sciences,* n.s., 2 (1825):274–316.

Bellamy, Donnie D. "Free Blacks in Antebellum Missouri, 1820–1860." *Missouri Historical Review* 67 (1973):198–226.

———. "The Persistency of Colonization in Missouri." *Missouri Historical Review* 72 (1977):1–24.

Berkeley, Edmund, and Dorothy Smith Berkeley. *George William Featherstonhaugh: The First U.S. Government Geologist.* History of American Science and Technology Series, ed. Lester D. Stephens. Tuscaloosa and London: University of Alabama Press, 1988.

Bewell, Alan. *Romanticism and Colonial Disease.* Baltimore and London: Johns Hopkins University Press, 1999.

Biagioli, Mario. *Galileo, Courtier: The Practice of Science in the Culture of Absolutism.* Science and Its Conceptual Foundations, ed. David Hull. Chicago and London: University of Chicago Press, 1993.

Billon, Frederic L. "Reminiscences of Our Removal to St. Louis." *Missouri Historical Society Bulletin* 12 (1956):278–84.

Bizzell, David W. "A Report on the Quapaw: The Letters of Governor George Izard to the American Philosophical Society, 1825–1827." *Pulaski County Historical Review* 29, no. 4 (1981):66–79.

Blake, Rev. J. L. *American Universal Geography, for Schools and Academies. On the Principles of Analysis and Comparison. . .* Boston: Russell, Odiorne, 1834.

Blassingame, John W., ed. *Slave Testimony: Two Centuries of Letters, Speeches, Interviews, and Autobiographies.* Baton Rouge: Louisiana State University Press, 1977.

[Blowe, Daniel]. *A Geographical, Historical, Commercial, and Agricultural View of the United States of America; Forming a Complete Emigrant's Directory Through every part of the Republic. . .* London: Edwards & Knibb, 1820.

"The Bloyed Family Letters." *Flashback* (Fayetteville, Arkansas) 13, no. 1 (1963):29–33.

Bolsterli, Margaret Jones, ed. *A Remembrance of Eden: Harriet Bailey Bullock Daniel's Memories of a Frontier Plantation in Arkansas, 1849–1872.* Fayetteville: University of Arkansas Press, 1993.

Bolton, Conevery A. [See also "Valencius, Conevery Bolton."] "'A Sister's Consolations': Women, Health, and Community in Early Arkansas, 1810–1860." *Arkansas Historical Quarterly* 50 (1991):271–91.

———. "'The Health of the Country': Body and Environment in the Making of the American West, 1800–1860." Ph.D. thesis, Harvard University, 1998.

Bolton, S. Charles. "Economic Inequality in the Arkansas Territory." *Journal of Interdisciplinary History* 14 (1984):619–33.

———. *Territorial Ambition: Land and Society in Arkansas, 1800–1840.* Fayetteville: University of Arkansas Press, 1993.

———. *Remote and Restless: Arkansas, 1800–1860.* Histories of Arkansas, ed. Elliott West. Fayetteville: University of Arkansas Press, 1998.

Boorstin, Daniel J. *The Americans: The National Experience.* New York: Vintage Books, 1965.

Boutros, David. "The West Illustrated: Meyer's Views of Missouri River Towns." *Missouri Historical Review* 80 (1986):304–20.

Bowler, Peter J. *The Norton History of the Environmental Sciences.* Norton History of Science, ed. Roy Porter. 1992. New York and London: Norton, 1993.

Boyer, Paul S., ed. *The Oxford Companion to United States History.* Oxford and New York: Oxford University Press, 2001.

Brackenridge, Henry Marie. *Views of Louisiana, Together With a Journal of a Voyage up the Missouri River, in 1811.* Pittsburgh, 1814. Facsimile ed., Chicago: Quadrangle Books, 1962.

Braudel, Fernand. *The Mediterranean and the Mediterranean World in the Age of Philip II.* 1949. Trans. Sian Reynolds. Vol. 1. New York: Harper & Row, 1972.

Breeden, James O. "States-Rights Medicine in the Old South." *Bulletin of the New York Academy of Medicine* 52 (1976):348–72.

Bridenbaugh, Carl. "Baths and Watering Places of Colonial America." *William and Mary Quarterly,* 3rd series, 3 (1946):151–81.

Brodhead, Michael J. "Contributions of Medical Officers of the Regular Army to Natural History in the pre-Civil War Era." In *History and Humanities: Essays in Honor of Wilbur S. Shepperson,* ed. Francis X. Hartigan, 3–14. Reno and Nevada: University of Nevada Press, 1986.

Brömer, Rainer. "The First Global Map of the Distribution of Human Diseases: Friedrich Schnurrer's 'Charte über die geographische Ausbreitung der Krankheiten,' 1827." In *Medical Geography in Historical Perspective*, ed. Nicolaas A. Rupke, 176–85. London: Wellcome Trust Centre for the History of Medicine at UCL, 2000.

Bronaugh, Mrs. J. H. "Western Missouri in 1837." *Missouri Historical Quarterly* 20 (1926):388–92.

Brown, C. Allan. "Jacob M. J. Smith, Pioneer Horticulturist." *Flashback* (Fayetteville, Arkansas) 32, no. 2 (1982):1–4.

Brown, William Wells. *The Narrative of William W. Brown, A Fugitive Slave [1848], and a Lecture Delivered Before the Female Anti-Slavery Society of Salem, 1847.* Addison-Wesley's Fugitive Slave Narratives. Reading, Mass.; Menlo Park, Calif.; Don Mills, Ont.: Addison-Wesley, 1969.

Brunel, Adolphus. "Topographical, meteorological, and medical observations made in Rio de la Plata, during the blockade of Buenos Ayres." Review. *Western Journal of Medicine and Surgery* 7 (1843):299–301.

Buchan, William. *Domestic Medicine: Or, a Treatise on the Prevention and Cure of Diseases, by Regimen and Simple Medicine. . .* Boston: Joseph Bumstead, 1809.

Budd, Louis J. "A Virginia Gentleman Moves to Missouri." *Missouri Historical Society Bulletin* 11 (1955):345–63.

Bullard, Loring. "Healing Springs." *Missouri Resources* 19 (2002):4–8.

Burbick, Joan. *Healing the Republic: The Language of Health and the Culture of Nationalism in Nineteenth-Century America.* Cambridge: Cambridge University Press, 1994.

Bynum, W. F. *Science and the Practice of Medicine in the Nineteenth Century.* Cambridge History of Science, ed. George Basalle and Owen Hannaway. Cambridge: Cambridge University Press, 1994.

Bynum, W. F., and Roy Porter, eds. *Companion Encyclopedia of the History of Medicine.* London and New York: Routledge, 1993.

Byrn, Marcus Lafayette. *The Life and Adventures of an Arkansaw Doctor.* Rattlehead's Humorous Series, No. 1. 1851. New York: Hurst & Co., 1879.

"Byrnham Wood in Missouri." *Missouri Historical Society Glimpses of the Past* 4, no. 7–9 (1937):69–118.

"C.C." Review of *The Climate of the United States and its Endemic Influences. Based on the Records of the Medical Department and Adjutant General's Office, United States Army.* By Samuel Forry, M.D. *The Western Journal of Medicine and Surgery* 7 (1843):142–53.

Caldwell, Charles, M.D. "Thoughts on the Means of Preserving Health, in Hot Climates; being an Introductory lecture, Delivered on the 6th day of November, 1832." *Transylvania Journal of Medicine and Allied Sciences* 4 (1833):357–77.

Calloway, Colin G. *First Peoples: A Documentary Survey of American Indian History.* Boston and New York: St. Martin's/Bedford, 1999.

Camerini, Jane R. "Heinrich Berghaus's Map of Human Diseases." In *Medical Geography in Historical Perspective*, ed. Nicolaas A. Rupke, 196–210. London: Wellcome Trust Centre for the History of Medicine at UCL, 2000.

Cannon, Susan Faye. "Humboldtian Science." In *Science in Culture: The Early Victorian Period.* New York: Dawson and Science History Publications, 1978.

Carey, Ken. *Flat Rock Journal: A Day in the Ozark Mountains*. San Francisco: HarperSanFrancisco, 1994.

Carney, Judith. "Landscapes of Technology Transfer: Rice Cultivation and African Continuities." *Technology and Culture* 37 (1996):5–35.

Carter, Clarence Edwin, ed. *The Territorial Papers of the United States*. In 28 vols. Washington, D.C.: United States Government Printing Office, 1934–62. Vol. 13, *The Territory of Louisiana-Missouri, 1803–1806*; vol. 14, *The Territory of Louisiana-Missouri, 1806–1814*; vol. 15, *The Territory of Louisiana-Missouri, 1815–1821*; vol. 19, *The Territory of Arkansas, 1819–1825*; vol. 20, *The Territory of Arkansas, 1825–1829*; vol. 21, *The Territory of Arkansas, 1829–1836*.

Cartwright, Samuel A., M.D. "Proofs of the health-preserving properties of the *Jussieua Grandiflora* or Floating Plant." *The Western Journal of Medicine and Surgery* 1 (1840):428–52.

Cashin, Joan E. *A Family Venture: Men and Women on the Southern Frontier*. Baltimore and London: Johns Hopkins University Press, 1991.

Cassedy, James H. "Meteorology and Medicine in Colonial America: Beginnings of the Experimental Approach." *Journal of the History of Medicine and Allied Sciences* 24 (1969):193–204.

———. "The Flourishing and Character of Early American Medical Journalism, 1787–1860." *Journal of the History of Medicine and Allied Sciences* 38 (1983):135–50.

———. *Medicine and American Growth, 1800–1860*. Madison: University of Wisconsin Press, 1986.

———. "Medical Men and the Ecology of the Old South." In *Science and Medicine in the Old South*, ed. Ronald L. Numbers and Todd L. Savitt, 166–78. Baton Rouge and London: Louisiana State University Press, 1989.

———. *Medicine in America: A Short History*. Baltimore and London: Johns Hopkins University Press, 1991.

"Cautions for the Season." *The Western Medico-Chirurgical Journal (Keokuk)* (1854):112–14.

Chambers, David Wade. "Period and Process in Colonial and National Science." In *Scientific Colonialism: A Cross-Cultural Comparison. Papers from a Conference at Melbourne, Australia, 25–30 May 1981*, ed. Nathan Reingold and Marc Rothenberg, 191–214. Washington and London: Smithsonian Institution Press, 1981.

Chinard, Gilbert. "Eighteenth Century Theories on America as a Human Habitat." *Proceedings of the American Philosophical Society* 91 (1947):27–57.

Chisholm, C. "An Essay towards an Inquiry how far the Effluvia from dead Animal Bodies, passing through the natural process of Putrefaction, are efficient in the production of Malignant Pestilential Fevers; and how far such Effluvia are capable 'of exciting a Putrefactive Emotion in all other' living 'Animal Substances exposed to their action?'." *The Edinburgh Medical and Surgical Journal* 6 (1810):389–420.

Christisen, Donald. "A Vignette of Missouri's Native Prairie." *Missouri Historical Review* 61 (1967):166–86.

"Cholera Epidemics in St. Louis." *Missouri Historical Society Glimpses of the Past* 3, no. 3 (1936):45–76.

Cleary, Patricia. "Contested Terrain: Environmental Agendas and Settlement Choices in Colonial St. Louis." In *Common Fields: An Environmental History of St. Louis*, ed. Andrew Hurley, 58–72. St. Louis: Missouri Historical Society Press, 1997.

Clemens, James, Jr. "Letter of James Clemens, Jr., 1816." *Missouri Historical Society Glimpses of the Past* 3, nos. 7–9 (1936):135–37.

Cochran, Robert. "Hanged by his Friends: The Image of Arkansas in Early Travellers' Reports." In *The Early Republic: The Making of a Nation—The Making of a Culture*, ed. Steve Ickringill, 191–98. Amsterdam: Free University Press, 1988.

————. "'Low, Degrading Scoundrels': George W. Featherstonhaugh's Contribution to the Bad Name of Arkansas." *Arkansas Historical Quarterly* 48 (1989):3–16.

Coleman, William. *Yellow Fever in the North: The Methods of Early Epidemiology.* Wisconsin Publications in the History of Science and Medicine, no. 6, ed. William Coleman, David C. Lindberg, and Ronald L. Numbers. Madison, Wisconsin: University of Wisconsin Press, 1987.

Collins, Ransom Malone. "A Dissertation on the Remote Causes of Fever." *The Transylvania Journal of Medicine and the Associate Sciences* 1 (1828):485–501.

————. "Further Thoughts on Climate, as the remote predisposing cause of Autumnal Diseases." *The Transylvania Journal of Medicine and the Associate Sciences* 2, no. 4 (1829):449–69.

Conard, Howard L., ed. *Encyclopedia of the History of Missouri: A Compendium of History and Biography for Ready Reference.* New York, Louisville, St. Louis: Southern History Company, 1901.

Coolidge, Richard H. (assistant surgeon, U.S.A.). "On the Medical Topography and Diseases of Fort Gibson, Arkansas." In *Southern Medical Reports: Consisting of General and Special Reports on the Medical Topography, Meteorology, and Prevalent Diseases of the Following States: Louisiana, Alabama, Mississippi, South Carolina, Georgia, Florida, Arkansas, Tennessee, Texas, California, to be Published Annually*, ed. E. D. Fenner, M.D., 440–52. New Orleans and New York: D. Davies' Son/Samuel S. & William Wood, 1851.

Cooper, Donald B., and Kenneth F. Kiple. "Yellow Fever." In *Cambridge World History of Human Disease,* ed. Kenneth Kiple. Cambridge: Cambridge University Press, 1993.

Cooper, James Fenimore. *The Pioneers.* 1823. New York: Washington Square Press, 1962.

————. *The Prairie: A Tale.* 1827. New York: Penguin, Signet Classics, 1964.

————. *The Deerslayer.* 1841. New York: Airmont, 1964.

————. *The Last of the Mohicans; A Narrative of 1757.* 1826. Oxford and New York: Oxford University Press, The World's Classics, 1990.

Cooper, Mary Alexandra. "The Local and the Exotic in Late Seventeenth- and Early Eighteenth-Century Dutch and German Natural History." Ph.D. thesis, Harvard University, 1997.

Cooter, Roger. "The Power of the Body: The Early Nineteenth Century." In *Natural Order: Historical Studies of Scientific Culture*, ed. Barry Barnes and Steven Shapin, 73–92. Beverly Hills and London: Sage, 1979.

Corbett, Katharine T. "Draining the Metropolis: The Politics of Sewers in Nineteenth-Century St. Louis." In *Common Fields: An Environmental History of St. Louis*, ed. Andrew Hurley, 107–25. St. Louis: Missouri Historical Society Press, 1997.

————. *In Her Place: A Guide to St. Louis Women's History.* St. Louis: Missouri Historical Society Press, 1999.

Corbin, Alain. *The Foul and the Fragrant: Odor and the French Social Imagination.* Cambridge, Mass., and London: Harvard University Press, 1986.

Corcoran, John. "The Diary of John Corcoran." *Missouri Historical Society Bulletin* 13 (1957):264–74.

Cornet, Florence Doll. "The Experiences of a Midwest Salesman in 1836." *Missouri Historical Society Bulletin* 29 (1973):227–35.

Cortambert, Louis. "Journey to the Land of the Osages 1835–1836." *Missouri Historical Society Bulletin* 19 (1963):199–230.

Cottle, Capt. Warren. "Missouri Wonderland." *Missouri Historical Society Bulletin* 14 (1958):191–93.

Cox, Caleb. "New Orleans to St. Louis and Return, 1819: A Lovelorn Traveler on an Early Steamboat." *Missouri Historical Society Bulletin* 8 (1952):151–74.

Crets, Jennifer A. "'The Land of a Million Smiles': Urban Tourism and the Commodification of the Missouri Ozarks, 1900–1940." In *Common Fields: An Environmental History of St. Louis*, ed. Andrew Hurley, 176–98. St. Louis: Missouri Historical Society Press, 1997.

Crockett, David. *A Narrative of the Life of David Crockett of the State of Tennessee, Written by Himself.* 1834. Reprint, Lincoln and London: University of Nebraska Press, 1987.

Cronon, William. *Changes in the Land: Indians, Colonists, and the Ecology of New England.* New York: Hill & Wang, 1983.

———. *Nature's Metropolis: Chicago and the Great West.* London: Norton, 1991.

Cronon, William, ed. *Uncommon Ground: Rethinking the Human Place in Nature.* New York and London: Norton, 1996.

Currie, William. *An Historical Account of The Climates and Diseases of The United States of America; and of the Remedies and methods of treatment, which have been found most useful and efficacious, particularly in those diseases which depend upon climate and situation. Collected principally from personal observation, and the communications of physicians of talents and experience, residing in the several states.* Philadelphia: T. Dobson, 1792. Facsimile ed., New York: Arno Press and the New York Times, 1972.

Curtin, Philip D. "The Promise and the Terror of a Tropical Environment." In *The Image of Africa: British Ideas in Action, 1780–1950.* Madison: University of Wisconsin Press, 1964.

———. *Death by Migration: Europe's Encounter with the Tropical World in the Nineteenth Century.* Cambridge: Cambridge University Press, 1989.

Dale, Edward E. "Arkansas and the Cherokees." *Arkansas Historical Quarterly* 8 (1949): 95–114.

Dana, Richard Henry. *Two Years Before the Mast: A Personal Narrative.* 1840. Reprint, New York: New American Library, 1964.

Daniel, Pete. *Deep'n as It Come: The 1927 Mississippi River Flood.* Fayetteville: University of Arkansas Press, 1996.

Daniels, George H. *American Science in the Age of Jackson.* New York and London: Columbia University Press, 1968.

Darnton, Robert. *The Great Cat Massacre and Other Episodes in French Cultural History.* New York: Vintage Books, 1985.

Davis, Audrey, and Toby Appel. *Bloodletting Instruments in the National Museum of History and Technology.* Smithsonian Studies in History and Technology, no. 41. Washington, D.C.: Smithsonian Institution Press, 1979.

DeBlack, Thomas A. "A Garden in the Wilderness: The Johnsons and the Making of Lakeport Plantation, 1831–1876." Ph.D. thesis, University of Arkansas, 1995.

De Bow, J. D. B. *The Seventh Census of the United States: 1850. . .* Washington, D.C.: Robert Armstrong, 1853.

"Dedication of Marker to Commemorate First Dissection." *The Journal of the Arkansas Medical Society* 24, 2 (1927):36–37.

"Descriptions of St. Louis." *Missouri Historical Society Glimpses of the Past* 1, no. 4 (1934):20–30.

Dettelbach, Michael. "Humboldtian Science." In *Cultures of Natural History*, ed. Nicholas Jardine, James A. Secord, and Emma Spary, 287–304. Cambridge: Cambridge University Press, 1996.

Dickens, Charles. *Martin Chuzzlewit.* 1844. Hertfordshire: Wordsworth Classics, 1994.

Dickinson, S. D. "Historic Tribes of the Ouachita Drainage System in Arkansas." *Arkansas Archeologist* 21 (1980):1–11.

———. "The Quapaw Journey to Red River." *Pulaski County Historical Review* 34, 1 (1986):14–23.

———. "Health and Death in Early Arkansas, 1541–1803." A History of Medicine Associates Research Award Study. Unpublished manuscript. University of Arkansas for Medical Sciences Historical Research Center, 1987.

Dixon, Mrs. Charles W. "Pioneer Doctors of Lincoln County." *Journal of the Arkansas Medical Society* 39, no. 2 (1942):54–55.

Dobson, Mary J. *Contours of Death and Disease in Early Modern England.* Cambridge Studies in Population, Economy and Society in Past Time, no. 29. Cambridge: Cambridge University Press, 1997.

"Documents: John C. Luttig, Pork Bayou, Arkansas, to Christian Wilt, 16 April 1815." *Arkansas Historical Quarterly* 1 (1942):151–55.

The Domestic Physician; or, Guide to Families: Containing Directions for the Preservation of Health, and the Removal of Disease. Also, a Plain and Accurate Description of the Complaints generally incident to the Human Frame; with an Account of the most Efficacious Remedies, and Directions How to Use Them. Chiefly Selected from the Best Authors, and Made Plain to Persons of Common Understanding. Liverpool: Caxton Press, [1814?].

Doolin, James. "Conditions of Slavery in Washington County." *Flashback* (Fayetteville, Arkansas) 30, no. 1 (1980):5–8, 30–34.

Dorn, Michael L. "(In)temperate Zones: Daniel Drake's Medico-moral Geographies of Urban Life in the Trans-Appalachian American West." *Journal of the History of Medicine and Allied Sciences* 55 (2000):256–91.

Douglas, Ann. *The Feminization of American Culture.* New York, London, Toronto, Sydney, Auckland: Doubleday/Anchor, 1988.

Douglas, Mary. *Purity and Danger: An Analysis of the Concepts of Pollution and Taboo.* 1966. London and New York: Routledge, 1991.

Drake, Daniel. *Natural and Statistical View, or Picture of Cincinnati and the Miami Country, Illustrated by Maps. With an Appendix, Containing Observations on the Late Earthquakes, the Aurora Borealis, and South-west Wind.* Cincinnati: Looker & Wallace, 1815.

———. "To the Physicians of the Western States." *The Western Journal of the Medical and Physical Sciences* 5 (1828):i–vi.

_____. "A Sketch of the Climate of the Valley of the Mississippi." *The Western Journal of the Medical and Physical Sciences* (1833):9–22.

_____. "Medical History of the West." *The Western Journal of the Medical and Physical Sciences* 9, 2nd hexad, vol. 3, (1836):679–85.

_____["D."]. "Summer and Autumn Diseases of 1840." *The Western Journal of Medicine and Surgery* 2, no. 11 (1840):399–400.

_____. "Traveling Editorials: Voyage Up the Mississippi." *The Western Journal of Medicine and Surgery* 8, no. 2 (1843):152–54.

_____. "Traveling Letters from the Senior Editor." *The Western Journal of Medicine and Surgery,* n.s., 1 (June 1844): letter 1, 546–54; 2 (Aug.–Dec. 1844): letter 2, 163–74; letter 3, 174–79; letter 4, 270–79; letter 5, 354–60; letter 6, 360–66; letter 9, 537–54; letter 10, 545–48.

_____. "Dr. Drake's Letter." *The Western Journal of Medicine and Surgery,* n.s., 2 (1844):159–61.

_____. *A Systematic Treatise, Historical, Etiological, and Practical, on the Principal Diseases of the Interior Valley of North America, as they Appear in the Caucasian, African, Indian, and Esquimaux Varieties of its Population.* 2 vols. Philadelphia and New York: Grigg, Elliot/Mason & Law, 1850, 1854.

_____. *A Systematic Treatise, Historical, Etiological, and Practical, on the Principal Diseases of the Interior Valley of North America, as they Appear in the Caucasian, African, Indian, and Esquimaux Varieties of its Population.* 2 vols. vol. 1. Philadelphia and New York: Grigg, Elliot/Mason & Law, 1850.

_____. *Letters on Slavery to Dr. John C. Warren, of Boston, reprinted from the National Intelligencer, Washington, April 3, 5, and 7, 1851.* New York: Schuman's, 1940.

Driver, Felix. "Henry Morton Stanley and his Critics: Geography, Exploration and Empire." *Past and Present* 133 (1991):134–66.

Drumm, Stella, ed. "Letters of Thomas Caute Reynolds." *Missouri Historical Society Glimpses of the Past* 10, nos. 1 and 2 (1943):3–54.

Duden, Barbara. *The Woman Beneath the Skin: A Doctor's Patients in Eighteenth-Century Germany.* Trans. Thomas Dunlap. Cambridge, Mass., and London: Harvard University Press, 1991.

Duden, Gottfried. *Report on a Journey to the Western States of North America and a Stay of Several Years Along the Missouri (During the Years 1824, '25, '26, and 1827).* Elberfeld: Sam Lucas, 1829. Reprint, Columbia and London: State Historical Society of Missouri and University of Missouri Press, 1980.

Duffy, John. "A Note on Ante-Bellum Southern Nationalism and Medical Practice." *Journal of Southern History* 34 (1968):266–76.

Dunlap, Thomas R. "Remaking the Land: The Acclimatization Movement and Anglo Ideas of Nature." *Journal of World History* 8 (1997):303–19.

Dunlop, M. H. *Sixty Miles from Contentment: Traveling the Nineteenth-Century American Interior.* New York: Basic Books, 1995.

Dunn, Frederick L. "Malaria." In *Cambridge World History of Human Disease,* ed. Kenneth Kiple. Cambridge: Cambridge University Press, 1993.

Eakin, Sue, and Joseph Logsdon, eds. *Twelve Years a Slave, by Solomon Northup.* 1853. Baton Rouge: Louisiana State University Press, 1968.

"Editorial: Medical Schools—East, West and South." *St. Louis Medical and Surgical Journal* 13 (1855):469–73.

Ekberg, Carl J. "Antoine Valentin de Gruy: Early Missouri Explorer." *Missouri Historical Review* 76 (1982):136–50.

———. *Colonial Ste. Genevieve: an adventure on the Mississippi frontier.* Tucson: Patrice Press, 1996.

———. *French Roots in the Illinois Country: The Mississippi Frontier in Colonial Times.* Urbana and Chicago: University of Illinois Press, 1998.

Eliot, William G. *The Story of Archer Alexander: From Slavery to Freedom, March 30, 1863.* Boston: Cupples, Upham, 1885.

Elliott, Clark A., ed. *Biographical Dictionary of American Science: The Seventeenth Through the Nineteenth Centuries.* Westport, Conn., and London: Greenwood, 1979.

The Emigrant's Hand-Book; . . . Containing Advice and Directions to . . . those Designing to Settle in the Great Western Valley. And also, a Concise Description of the States of Ohio, Indiana, Illinois, Michigan, Wisconsin, Missouri and Iowa, and the Western Territories; and including a Statement of the Modes and Expenses of Travel from New-York to the Interior, and an Extensive List of Routes in each State by Steamboats, Railroads, Canals and Stages. Accompanied with a Correct Traveling Map of the United States. New York: J. H. Coulton, 1848.

Engelmann, George, M.D. "The Meteorological Causes of our Climatic Diseases." *St. Louis Medical and Surgical Journal* 11 (1853):226–32.

Erickson, Charlotte. *Invisible Immigrants: The Adaptation of English and Scottish Immigrants in Nineteenth-Century America.* Documents in American Social History, ed. Nick Salvatre and Kerby A. Mille. Ithaca and London: Cornell University Press, 1972.

Ewell, Thomas. "Speculations Concerning the Agency of Oxygene in Promoting Conception." *Medical Repository* 10, 2nd hexad, vol. 4 (1807):130–33.

"Exemption of Certain Parts of the Delta of the Mississippi, from Autumnal Diseases." *The Western Journal of the Medical and Physical Sciences* 9, 2nd hexad, vol. 3 (1836):160–61.

Faragher, John Mack. *Women and Men on the Overland Trail.* New Haven, Conn., and London: Yale University Press, 1979.

———. *Sugar Creek: Life on the Illinois Prairie.* New Haven and London: Yale University Press, 1986.

———. *Daniel Boone: The Life and Legend of an American Pioneer.* New York: Henry Holt, 1992.

———. "'More Motley than Mackinaw': From Ethnic Mixing to Ethnic Cleansing on the Frontier of the Lower Missouri, 1783–1833." In *Contact Points: American Frontiers from the Mohawk Valley to the Mississippi, 1750–1830,* ed. Andrew R. L. Cayton and Fredrika J. Teute. Chapel Hill and London: University of North Carolina Press, 1998.

Faragher, John Mack, ed. *Rereading Frederick Jackson Turner: The Significance of the Frontier in American History, and Other Essays.* New York: Henry Holt, 1994.

Faris, Paul. *Ozark Mountain Folks: The Way They Were.* Little Rock: Rose Publishing, 1983.

Faust, Drew Gilpin. *A Sacred Circle: The Dilemma of the Intellectual in the Old South, 1840–1860.* Philadelphia: University of Pennsylvania Press, 1977.

———. "The Rhetoric and Ritual of Agriculture in Antebellum South Carolina." *Journal of Southern History* 45 (1979):541–68.

Fearon, Henry Bradshaw. *Sketches of America. A Narrative of a Journey of Five Thousand Miles through the Eastern and Western States of America; Contained in Eight Reports, addressed to the Thirty-Nine*

English Families by whom the Author was Deputed, in June 1817, to Ascertain Whether Any Part of the United States Would be Suitable for their Residence. . . . London: Hurst, Rees, Orme, & Brown, 1818.

Featherstonhaugh, G. W. "Geology of Arkansas: Extracts from Featherstonhaugh's Report." *Arkansas Gazette*, 21 July 1835; 28 July 1835; 11 Aug. 1835; 25 Aug. 1835; 1 Sept. 1835.

————. *Excursion through the Slave States: from Washington on the Potomac to the Frontier of Mexico; with Sketches of Popular Manners and Geological Notices.* New York: Harper & Bros., 1844.

————. "G. W. Featherstonhaugh to Colonel J. J. Abert: Letters from the First United States Geologist." *Missouri Historical Society Bulletin* 8, 3 (1952):272–91.

Fenner, E. D., M.D. "Report on the Epidemics of Louisiana, Mississippi, Arkansas, and Texas." *Transactions of the American Medical Association* 7 (1854):421–553; 9 (1856):621–720.

Fiege, Mark. *Irrigated Eden: The Making of an Agricultural Landscape in the American West.* Weyerhaeuser Environmental Books, ed. William Cronon. Seattle and London: University of Washington Press, 1999.

Flagg, E. [Edmund]. *The Far West: or, A Tour Beyond the Mountains. Embracing Outlines of Western Life and Scenery; Sketches of the Prairies, Rivers, Ancient Mounds, Early Settlements of the French, Etc., Etc.* Vol. 2. New York: Harper & Bros., 1838.

Fleming, James Rodger. *Meteorology in America, 1800–1870.* Baltimore and London: Johns Hopkins University Press, 1990.

Flint, Timothy. *The History and Geography of the Mississippi Valley. To Which is Appended a Condensed Physical Geography of the Atlantic United States, and the Whole American Continent.* 2 vols. Vol. 1. 2nd ed. Cincinnati: E. H. Flint and L. R. Lincoln, 1832.

————. *The History and Geography of the Mississippi Valley. To Which is Appended a Condensed Physical Geography of the Atlantic United States, and the Whole American Continent.* Vol. 1. 2 vols. 3rd ed. Cincinnati and Boston: E. H. Flint (Cincinnati) and Carter, Hendee, and Co. (Boston), 1833.

————. *The First White Man of the West, or the Life and Exploits of Col. Daniel Boone, The First Settler of Kentucky; Interspersed with Incidents in the Early Annals of the Country.* 1847. Cincinnati: H. M. Rulison, Queen City Publishing House, 1856.

————. *Recollections of the Last Ten Years, Passed in Occasional Residences and Journeyings in the Valley of the Mississippi, from Pittsburg and the Missouri to the Gulf of Mexico, and from Florida to the Spanish Frontier; in a Series of Letters to the Rev. James Flint, of Salem, Massachusetts,* ed. C. Hartley Grattan. Boston: Cummings, Hilliard, 1826. Reprint, New York: Knopf, 1932.

Foley, William E. "Justus Post: Portrait of a Frontier Land Speculator." *Missouri Historical Society Bulletin* 36 (1979):19–25.

————. *The Genesis of Missouri: From Wilderness Outpost to Statehood.* Columbia and London: University of Missouri Press, 1989.

Foner, Eric. *Free Soil, Free Labor, Free Men: The Ideology of the Republican Party Before the Civil War.* New York: Oxford University Press, 1970.

————. *Reconstruction: America's Unfinished Revolution, 1863–1877.* New York: Harper & Row, 1988.

Foreman, Grant, ed. "Journey of a Party of Cherokee Emigrants." *Mississippi Valley Historical Review* 18 (1931):232–45.

BIBLIOGRAPHY 351

Foti, Tom. "The Grand Prairie." *Ozark Society Bulletin [Fayetteville, Arkansas]* 5, 4 (1971):6–11.

————. *Arkansas: Its Land and People*. Little Rock: Arkansas Environmental and Conservation Education Office, Arkansas Department of Education, 1976.

Fox-Genovese, Elizabeth. *Within the Plantation Household: Black and White Women of the Old South*. Chapel Hill and London: University of North Carolina Press, 1988.

"Fragments of Broadhead Collection." *Missouri Historical Society Glimpses of the Past* 2, no. 4 (1935):43–65.

Franklin, John Hope, and Loren Scheninger. *Runaway Slaves: Rebels on the Plantation*. New York and Oxford: Oxford University Press, 1999.

Frapp, Dan, ed. *Encyclopedia of Frontier Biography*. Glendale, Calif.: Arthur H. Clark, 1988.

Fredrickson, George M. *The Black Image in the White Mind: The Debate on Afro-American Character and Destiny, 1817–1914*. New York: Harper & Row, 1971.

Galison, Peter. *How Experiments End*. Chicago and London: University of Chicago Press, 1987.

Gantt, W. H., M.D. "The Medical Topography of some of the Counties of North Alabama." *St. Louis Medical and Surgical Journal* 10 (1852):193–200, 313–26, 401–15.

————. "A few Reasons for Southern and Western Students, attending Medical Lectures in Southern and Western Medical Schools." *St. Louis Medical and Surgical Journal* 9 (1853):211–17.

Garrison, C. W. "The Development of Medicine and Public Health." In *Arkansas and Its People: A History, 1541–1930*, ed. David Y. Thomas, 549–62. New York: American Historical Society, 1930.

Gates, Henry Louis, Jr., ed. *Six Women's Slave Narratives*. With an introduction by William L. Andrews. Schomburg Library of Nineteenth-Century Black Women Writers. Oxford and New York: Oxford University Press, 1988.

Gates, Paul W. *The Farmer's Age: Agriculture, 1815–1860*. Vol. 3, The Economic History of the United States. New York: Holt, Rinehart & Winston, 1960.

Gatewood, Willard B. "Sunnyside: The Evolution of an Arkansas Plantation, 1840–1945." In *Shadows over Sunnyside: An Arkansas Plantation in Transition, 1830–1945*, ed. Jeannie M. Whayne. Fayetteville: University of Arkansas Press, 1993.

Geertz, Clifford. *Local Knowledge: Further Essays in Interpretive Anthropology*. New York: Basic Books, 1983.

Genovese, Eugene D. *Roll, Jordan, Roll: The World the Slaves Made*. 1972. New York: Vintage Books, 1976.

Gentry, North Todd. "William F. Switzler." *Missouri Historical Review* 24 (1930):161–76.

Geores, Martha E. "Surviving on Metaphor: How 'Health = Hot Springs' Created and Sustained a Town." In *Putting Health into Place: Landscape, Identity, and Well-being*, ed. Robin A. Kearns and Wilbert M. Gesler. Syracuse: Syracuse University Press, 1998.

Gerbi, Antonello. *The Dispute of the New World: The History of a Polemic, 1750–1900*. Trans. Jeremy Moyle. Pittsburgh: University of Pittsburgh Press, 1955.

Gerlach, Russel L. *Immigrants in the Ozarks: A Study in Frontier Geography*. Columbia and London: University of Missouri Press, 1976.

Gerstäcker, Friedrich. *Wild Sports in the Far West*. Trans. Harrison Weir. London and New York: Geo. Routledge, 1854.

Gesler, Wilbert M. "Lourdes: Healing in a Place of Pilgrimage." *Health and Place* 2 (1996):95–105.

———. "Bath's Reputation as a Healing Place." In *Putting Health into Place: Landscape, Identity, and Well-being*, ed. Robin A. Kearns and Wilbert M. Gesler. Syracuse: Syracuse University Press, 1998.

Gevitz, Norman. "'But all those authors are foreigners': American Literary Nationalism and Domestic Medical Guides." In *The Popularization of Medicine, 1650–1850*, ed. Roy Porter, 215–31. London and New York: Routledge, 1992.

———. "Unorthodox Medical Theories." In *Companion Encyclopedia of the History of Medicine*, ed. W. F. Bynum and Roy Porter. London and New York: Routledge, 1993.

Gevitz, Norman, ed. *Other Healers: Unorthodox Medicine in America*. Baltimore: Johns Hopkins University Press, 1988.

Gillespie, Charles Coulston, editor in chief. *Dictionary of Scientific Biography*. New York: Charles Scribner's Sons, 1974.

"The Girls of Arkansas." *The Spirit of the Times*, 23 March 1850, 56.

Glacken, Clarence J. *Traces on the Rhodian Shore: Nature and Culture in Western Thought from Ancient Times to the End of the Eighteenth Century*. Berkeley: University of California Press, 1967.

Golan, Tal. "To Serve and Protect—Nuisance Litigation and the Birth of Public Regulation." In "Scientific Expert Testimony in Anglo-American Courts, 1782–1923," 97–125. Ph.D. thesis, University of California at Berkeley, 1997.

Goldstein, Daniel. "'Yours for Science': The Smithsonian Institution's Correspondents and the Shape of Scientific Community in Nineteenth-Century America." *Isis* 85 (1994):573–99.

Gomez, Michael A. *Exchanging our Country Marks: The Transformation of African Identities in the Colonial and Antebellum South*. Chapel Hill and London: University of North Carolina Press, 1998.

Gorn, Elliott J. "Black Magic: Folk Beliefs of the Slave Community." In *Science and Medicine in the Old South*, ed. Ronald L. Numbers and Todd L. Savitt, 295–326. Baton Rouge and London: Louisiana State University Press, 1989.

Goulding, W. J., M.D. "Medical Topography of Central Arkansas; being Observations on the Locality, Climate, and Diseases of the City of Little Rock and vicinity, in the year 1840." *The Western Journal of Medicine and Surgery* 7 (1843):321–28.

Grant, George R., M.D. "The Vital Statistics and Sanitary Conditions of Memphis, Tennessee, an Anniversary Address, delivered by appointment, before the Memphis Medical Society, on the 5th of February, 1852." *The Western Journal of Medicine and Surgery*, 3rd series, 10 (1853?):134–38.

Gray, Lewis Cecil, and Esther Katherine Thompson. *History of Agriculture in the Southern United States to 1860*. Vols. 1 and 2. Carnegie Institution of Washington Publication no. 430; Contributions to American Economic History from the Board of Research Associates in American Economic History. 1933. New York: Peter Smith, 1941.

Green, Barbara L. "Slave Labor at the Meramec Iron Works, 1828–1850." *Missouri Historical Review* 73 (1979):150–64.

Green, Michael D. "The Expansion of European Colonization to the Mississippi Valley, 1780–1880." In *The Cambridge History of the Native Peoples of North America*, ed. Bruce G. Trigger and Wilcomb E. Washburn. Vol. 1, *North America: Part 1.* Cambridge: Cambridge University Press, 1996.

Gregory, Ralph. "Count Baudissin on Missouri Towns." *Missouri Historical Society Bulletin* 27 (1971):111–24.

Grove, Richard H. *Green Imperialism: Colonial Expansion, Tropical Island Edens and the Origins of Environmentalism, 1600–1860.* Studies in Environment and History, ed. Donald Worster and Alfred W. Crosby. Cambridge: Cambridge University Press, 1995.

Gunn, John C. *Gunn's Domestic Medicine, or Poor Man's Friend, in the Hours of Affliction, Pain, and Sickness. This book points out, in plain language, free from doctor's terms the diseases of men, women, and children, and the latest and most approved means used in their cure, and is expressly written for the benefit of families in the western and southern states. It also contains descriptions of the medicinal roots and herbs of the western and southern country, and how they are to be used in the cure of diseases. . .* 1830. Facsimile ed., Knoxville: University of Tennessee Press, 1986.

Hall, David D. *World of Wonder, Days of Judgment: Popular Religious Belief in Early New England.* Cambridge, Mass., and London: Harvard University Press, 1990.

Hall, Leonard. "Wildlife in Missouri History." *Missouri Historical Review* 60 (1966):207–15.

Haller, John S., Jr. *American Medicine in Transition, 1840–1910.* Urbana, Chicago, and London: University of Illinois Press, 1981.

———. *Medical Protestants: The Eclectics in American Medicine, 1825–1939.* Medical Humanities Series, ed. Theodore R. LeBlang. Carbondale and Edwardsville: Southern Illinois University Press, 1994.

Hamlin, Christopher. "Providence and Putrefaction: Victorian Sanitarians and the Natural Theology of Health and Disease." *Victorian Studies* 28 (1985):381–411.

———. "Predisposing Causes and Public Health in Early Nineteenth-Century Medical Thought." *Social History of Medicine* 5 (1992):43–70.

Hannaway, Caroline. "Environment and Miasmata." In *Companion Encyclopedia of the History of Medicine*, ed. W. F. Bynum and Roy Porter. London and New York: Routledge, 1993.

Harington, Donald. *Let Us Build Us a City: Eleven Lost Towns.* San Diego, New York, and London: Harcourt Brace/Helen and Kurt Wolff/ Harvest Books, 1986.

Harms, Robert. *The Diligent: A Voyage Through the Worlds of the Slave Trade.* New York: Basic Books, 2002.

Harris, James C., M.D. "Observations on the Medical Topography, Climate, and Endemic Influences of South Alabama." *The Western Journal of Medicine and Surgery*, n.s., 6, (1846):461–74.

Harrison, Mark. "Differences of Degree: Representations of India in British Medical Topography, 1820–c.1870." In *Medical Geography in Historical Perspective*, ed. Nicolaas A. Rupke, 51–69. London: Wellcome Trust Centre for the History of Medicine at UCL, 2000.

———. "'The Tender Frame of Man': Disease, Climate, and Racial Difference in India and the West Indies, 1760–1860." *Bulletin of the History of Medicine* 70 (1996):68–93.

Hauck, Richard Boyd. "Predicting a Native Literature: William T. Porter's First Issue of the *Spirit of the Times.*" *Mississippi Quarterly* 22 (1969):77–84.

Headrick, Daniel R. "The Tools of Imperialism: Technology and the Expansion of European Colonial Empires in the Nineteenth Century." *Journal of Modern History* 51 (1979):231–63.

"Health and Mortality of New Orleans." *St. Louis Medical and Surgical Journal* 9 (1853):558–60.

"Health of Our City." *St. Louis Medical and Surgical Journal* 3, no. 4 (1845):166.

"Health of St. Louis." *St. Louis Medical and Surgical Journal* 8, no. 1 (1850):45.

"Health of the City." *St. Louis Medical and Surgical Journal* 8 (1850):418.

"Health of the Country." *St. Louis Medical and Surgical Journal* 3, no. 5 (1845):213–14.

"Health of the Season." *Western Medico-Chirurgical Journal* (1851):96.

Heat Moon, William Least. *Blue Highways: A Journey into America*. Boston and Toronto: Little, Brown and Company, 1982.

_____. *PrairyErth (a deep map)*. Boston: Houghton Mifflin/Peter Davison, 1991.

Hedrick, Joan D. *Harriet Beecher Stowe: A Life*. New York and Oxford: Oxford University Press, 1994.

Helman, Cecil G. "'Feed a Cold, Starve a Fever'—Folk Models of Infection in an English Suburban Community, and Their Relation to Medical Treatment." *Culture, Medicine and Psychiatry* 2 (1978):107–37.

Hendrickson, Walter B. "Nineteenth-Century State Geological Surveys: Early Government Support of Science." *Isis* 52 (1961):357–71.

Henry, J. F., M.D. "Medical Topography, Climate and Diseases of Iowa." *The Western Medico-Chirurgical Journal* 1, no. 1 (1850):298–307.

Herschbach, Lisa Marie. "Fragmentation and Reunion: Medicine, Memory and Body in the American Civil War." Ph.D. thesis, Harvard University, 1997.

Hillary, William. *Observations on the Changes of the Air, and the Concomitant Epidemical Diseases in the Island of Barbadoes. To Which is Added, A Treatise on the Putrid Bilious Fever, Commonly Called the Yellow Fever; and Such Other Diseases as are Indigenous or Endemial, in the West India Islands, or in the Torrid Zone. With Notes, by Benjamin Rush, M.D.* Philadelphia: B. & T. Kite, 1811.

Holley, Donald. "The Plantation Heritage: Agriculture in the Arkansas Delta." In *The Arkansas Delta: Land of Paradox*, ed. Jeannie Whayne and Willard B. Gatewood. Fayetteville: University of Arkansas Press, 1993.

Horsman, Reginald. *Race and Manifest Destiny: The Origins of American Racial Anglo-Saxonism*. Cambridge, Mass., and London, England: Harvard University Press, 1981.

Howard, R. Palmer, and Virginia E. Allen. "Stress and Death in the Settlement of Indian Territory." *Chronicles of Oklahoma* 54 (1976):352–59.

Howard-Jones, Norman. "Cholera Therapy in the Nineteenth Century." *Journal of the History of Medicine and Allied Sciences* 27 (1972):373–95.

Huddleston, Duane. "The Cherokee Indians." *Independence County [Arkansas] Chronicle* 11, no. 3 (1970):33–36.

_____. "Some Indian Incidents Along the White River, 1813–1822." *Independence County [Arkansas] Chronicle* 15, no. 14 (1974):36–46.

Hughes, Robert. *The Shock of the New: The Hundred-Year History of Modern Art, Its Rise, Its Dazzling Achievement, Its Fall*. New York: Knopf, 1982.

Hulburt, Ray G. "A. T. Still, Founder of Osteopathy." *Missouri Historical Review* 19 (1924):25–35.

Humphreys, Margaret. *Malaria: Poverty, Race, and Public Health in the United States*. Baltimore and London: Johns Hopkins University Press, 2001.

Hunt, Sanford B., M.D. "The Report of the Committee on the Hygrometrical State of the Atmosphere in Various Localities, and its Influence on Health." *Transactions of the American Medical Association* 8 (1855):327–46.

Hunter, Lloyd A. "Slavery in St. Louis, 1804–1860." *Missouri Historical Society Bulletin* 30 (1974):233–65.

Hurley, Andrew. "Busby's Stink Boat and the Regulation of Nuisance Trades, 1865–1918." In *Common Fields: An Environmental History of St. Louis*, ed. Andrew Hurley, 145–62. St. Louis: Missouri Historical Society Press, 1997.

Hurt, R. Douglas. *Agriculture and Slavery in Missouri's Little Dixie*. Columbia and London: University of Missouri Press, 1992.

————. *American Agriculture: A Brief History*. Ames: Iowa State University, 1994.

Ignatiev, Noel. *How the Irish Became White*. New York and London: Routledge, 1995.

"Influences of the Weather Upon Health." *Missouri Medical and Surgical Journal* 3, no. 9 (1848):200.

Iseminger, William R. "Culture and Environment in the American Bottom: The Rise and Fall of Cahokia Mounds." In *Common Fields: An Environmental History of St. Louis*, ed. Andrew Hurley, 38–57. St. Louis: Missouri Historical Society Press, 1997.

Jacobson, Matthew Frye. *Whiteness of a Different Color: European Immigrants and the Alchemy of Race*. Cambridge, Mass., and London, England: Harvard University Press, 1998.

Jansma, Jerome, and Harriet H. Jansma. "George Engelmann in Arkansas Territory." *Arkansas Historical Quarterly* 50, 3 (1991):225–48.

Jefferson, Thomas. *Notes on the State of Virginia*. Ed Frank Shuffelton. New York: Penguin Books, 1999.

Jefferson, Thomas, and William Dunbar. *Documents Relating to the Purchase and Exploration of Louisiana*. New York: Houghton Mifflin, 1904.

Jensen, Mrs. Dana O., ed. "I at Home, by Stephen S. Hempstead, Sr. The Diary of a Yankee Farmer in Missouri 1811–1814." Parts 1–9. *Missouri Historical Society Bulletin* 13 (1956–57):28–56, 283–317; 14 (1957–58):59–96, 271–88; 15 (1958–59):38–48; 224–47; 22 (1965–66):61–94, 180–206, 410–45.

Jervey, Edward D., and James E. Moss. "From Virginia to Missouri in 1846: The Journal of Elizabeth Ann Cooley." *Missouri Historical Review* 60 (1966):162–206.

Johnson, Walter. "The Slave Trader, the White Slave, and the Politics of Racial Determination in the 1850s." *The Journal of American History* 87 (2000):13–38.

Jones, Billy M. *Health-Seekers in the Southwest, 1817–1900*. Norman: University of Oklahoma Press, 1967.

Jones, Michael Owen. "Climate and Disease: The Traveler Describes America." *Bulletin of the History of Medicine* 41, 3 (1967):254–66.

Jordan, Philip D. "Botanic Medicine in the Western Country." *Ohio State Medical Journal* 40 (1944):143–146, 240–42.

Jordanova, L. J. "Earth Science and Environmental Medicine: The Synthesis of the Late Enlightenment." In *Images of the Earth: Essays in the History of the Environmental Sciences*, ed. L. J. Jordanova and Roy S. Porter. Chalfont, St. Giles: British Journal for the History of Science, 1979.

Kaufmann, Martin. "Medicine and Slavery: An Essay Review." *Georgia Historical Quarterly* 63, 3 (1976):380–90.

Kaye, Anthony E. "The Personality of Power: The Ideology of Slaves in the Natchez District and the Delta of Mississippi, 1830–1865." Ph.D. thesis, Columbia University, 1999.

Keefe, James F., and Lynn Morrow, eds. *A Connecticut Yankee in the Frontier Ozarks: The Writings of Theodore Pease Russell.* Columbia: University of Missouri Press, 1988.

———. *The White River Chronicles of S. C. Turnbo.* Fayetteville: University of Arkansas Press, 1994.

Keeney, Elizabeth Barnaby. "Unless Powerful Sick: Domestic Medicine in the Old South." In *Science and Medicine in the Old South,* ed. Ronald L. Numbers and Todd L. Savitt, 276–94. Baton Rouge and London: Louisiana State University Press, 1989.

Kennedy, Dane. "A Climate of Concern." In *Islands of White: Settler Society and Culture in Kenya and Southern Rhodesia,* 109–27. Durham: Duke University Press, 1987.

———. "The Perils of the Midday Sun: Climatic Anxieties in the Colonial Tropics." In *Imperialism and the Natural World,* ed. John M. MacKenzie, 118–40. Manchester and New York: University of Manchester Press, 1990.

Kennedy, Joseph C. G. *Population of the United States in 1860. . .* Washington, D.C.: GPO, 1864.

Key, Joseph Patrick. "Indians and Ecological Conflict in Territorial Arkansas." *Arkansas Historical Quarterly* 59 (2000):127–46.

Kilbride, Daniel. "Southern Medical Students in Philadelphia, 1800–1861: Science and Sociability in the 'Republic of Medicine.'" *Journal of Southern History* 65 (1999):697–732.

Kiple, Kenneth F., and Virginia Himmelsteib King. *Another Dimension to the Black Diaspora: Diet Disease, and Racism.* Cambridge: Cambridge University Press, 1981.

Klein, Frederick S. "Letters of a Young Surveyor." *Missouri Historical Review* 23, no. 1 (1928):61–84.

Kleinschmidt, Earl E. "Meteorological, Topographical, and Climatological Studies of Early Michigan Sanitarians." *Bulletin of the History of Medicine* 11 (1942):161–73.

Klepp, Susan E. "Lost, Hidden, Obstructed and Repressed: Contraceptive and Abortive Technology in the Early Delaware Valley." In *Early American Technology: Making and Doing Things from the Colonial Era to 1850,* ed. Judith A. McGaw. Chapel Hill and London: University of North Carolina Press and Institute of Early American History and Culture (Williamsburg, Va.), 1994.

———. "Seasoning and Society: Racial Differences in Mortality in Eighteenth-Century Philadelphia." *William and Mary Quarterly,* 3rd series, 51 (1994):473–506.

Koerner, Lisbet. "Linnaeus' Floral Transplants." *Representations* 47 (1994):144–67.

———. *Linnaeus: Nature and Nation.* Cambridge, Mass.: Harvard University Press, 1999.

Kolodny, Annette. *The Lay of the Land: Metaphor as Experience and History in American Life and Letters.* Chapel Hill: University of North Carolina Press, 1975.

———. *The Land Before Her: Fantasy and Experience of the American Frontiers, 1630–1860.* Chapel Hill and London: University of North Carolina Press, 1984.

Kraut, Alan M. *Silent Travelers: Germs, Genes, and the "Immigrant Menace."* New York: Basic Books, 1994.

Kulikoff, Allan. *Tobacco and Slaves: The Development of Southern Cultures in the Chesapeake, 1680–1800.* Chapel Hill and London: University of North Carolina Press and Institute of Early American History and Culture (Williamsburg, Va.), 1986.

Kupperman, Karen Ordahl. "Fear of Hot Climates in the Anglo-American Colonial Experience." *William and Mary Quarterly* 41 (1984):213–40.

Kuriyama, Shigehisa. "Interpreting the History of Bloodletting." *Journal of the History of Medicine* 50 (1995):11–46.

Lack, Paul D. "An Urban Slave Community: Little Rock, 1831–1862." *Arkansas Historical Quarterly* 41 (1982):258–87.

Laduric, Emmanuel Le Roy. *Montaillou: The Promised Land of Error.* Trans. Barbara Bray. New York: Vintage Books, 1979.

Lancaster, Bob. "Malaria's Mark." *Arkansas Times*, Jan. 1988.

Lankford, George E. "Shawnee Convergence: Immigrant Indians in the Ozarks." *Arkansas Historical Quarterly* 58 (1999).

Lanser, Roland. "The Pioneer Physician in Missouri, 1820–1850." *Missouri Historical Review* 44 (1949):31–47.

Layton, Thomas, M.D. "Extracts from an Old History of Louisiana." *New Orleans Medical and Surgical Journal,* n.s., 10 (1882):241–59.

Leake, Chauncey D., ed. *Exercitatio Anatomica De Motu Cordis et Sanguinis in Animalibus by William Harvey, M.D.* Springfield, Ill.: Charles C. Thomas, 1970.

Leavitt, Judith Walzer. "'A Worrying Profession': The Domestic Environment of Medical Practice in Mid-Nineteenth-Century America." *Bulletin of the History of Medicine* 69 (1995):1–29.

Lenow, James A. "Some Facts and the Difficulties that Confronted the Regular Physicians in this State in the Early Seventies and which Led to the Passage of the Law Legalizing Dissection, and Finally to the Establishment of the Arkansas Industrial University Medical Department." *The Journal of the Arkansas Medical Society* 22, no. 11 (1926):231–32.

Levine, Norman D., ed. *Malaria in the Interior Valley of North America: A Selection from A Systematic Treatise, Historical, Etiological, and Practical, on the Principal Diseases of the Interior Valley of North America, as they Appear in the Caucasian, African, Indian, and Esquimaux Varieties of its Population, by Daniel Drake, Cincinnati, Ohio, 1850.* Facsimile reprint, Urbana: University of Illinois Press, 1964.

Lewis, C. S. *The Discarded Image: An Introduction to Medieval and Renaissance Literature.* Cambridge: Cambridge University Press, 1964.

Lightfoot, B. B. "The Cherokee Emigrants in Missouri, 1837–1839." *Missouri Historical Review* 61 (1962):156–67.

Little, Carolyn Yancy. "Samson Gray and the Bayou Meto Settlement, 1820–1836." *Pulaski County [Arkansas] Historical Review* 32, 1 (1984):2–16.

Livingstone, David N. "Human Acclimatization: Perspectives on a Contested Field of Inquiry in Science, Medicine, and Geography." *History of Science* 25 (1987):359–94.

Lloyd, G. E. R. *Hippocratic Writings.* New York: Viking, Penguin Classics, 1983.

Long, Esmond R. "Weak Lungs on the Santa Fe Trail." *Bulletin of the History of Medicine* 8 (1940):1040–54.

Lottinville, Savoie, ed. *A Journal of Travels into the Arkansas Territory During the Year 1819, by Thomas Nuttall, F.L.S.* Norman: University of Oklahoma Press, 1980.

"The Lowell Letter." *Flashback* (Fayetteville, Arkansas), 31, no. 4 (1981):5–9.

Ludmerer, Kenneth M. *Learning to Heal: The Development of American Medical Education.* New York: Basic Books, 1985.

Lupton, David Walker, and Dorothy Ruland Lupton. "A Dragoon in Arkansas Territory in 1833." *Arkansas Historical Quarterly* 45 (1986):217–27.

Macrery, Joseph. "A Description of the Hot Springs and Volcanic Appearances in the Country adjoining the River Ouachitta, in Louisiana." *(New York) Medical Repository* 3, 2nd hexad, (1806):47–50.

Maier, Pauline. "Dr. Thomas Young and the Radicalism of Science and Reason." In *The Old Revolutionaries: Political Lives in the Age of Samuel Adams.* New York: Knopf, 1980.

Malone, Robert J. "The Louisiana Purchase: Exploring Rivers and Boiling Springs," in "Everyday Science, Surveying, and Politics in the Old Southeast: William Dunbar and the Influence of Place on Natural Philosophy." Ph.D. thesis, University of Florida, 1996.

Martin, Amelia Whitaker. *Physicians and Medicine: Crawford and Sebastian Counties, Arkansas, 1817–1976.* Fort Smith, Ark.: Sebastian County Medical Society, 1977.

Masterson, James R. "The Arkansaw Doctor." *Annals of Medical History* 2 (1940):30–51.

Matthew, Patrick. *Emigration Fields. North America, The Cape, Australia, and New Zealand, Describing these Countries, and Giving a Comparative Vew of the Advantages they Present to British Settlers.* Edinburgh and London: Adam and Charles Black/Longman, Orme, Brown, Green & Longmans, 1839.

Maughs, G. M. B., M.D. "The Medical Topography of Kansas City and Adjacent Country." *The Kansas City Surgical and Medical Review* 1 (1860):1–9.

Maury, James A. "Topography of Mercer County, Illinois, and the Diseases Most Common in the Several Districts." *Missouri Medical and Surgical Journal* 1, no. 12 (1846):265–68.

McClarty, Vivian K. "A Missionary's Wife Looks at Missouri: Letters of Julia Barnard Strong, 1836–1839." *Missouri Historical Review* 47 (1953):329–43.

McDermott, John Francis. "A Warning to Emigrants." *Missouri Historical Society Bulletin* 6 (1950):239–45.

————. "The Western Journals of Dr. George Hunter, 1796–1805." *Transactions of the American Philosophical Association* 53 (1963):5–133.

McDermott, John Francis, ed. *The Western Journals of Washington Irving.* Norman: University of Oklahoma Press, 1944.

McGettigan, James William, Jr. "Boone County Slaves: Sales, Estate Divisions and Families, 1820–1865." Parts 1 and 2. *Missouri Historical Review* 72, 2 (1978):176–97, 271–95.

McKivigan, John R., ed. *The Roving Editor, or Talks with Slaves in the Southern States, by James Redpath.* University Park: Pennsylvania State University Press, 1996.

McLaurin, Melton A. *Celia, a Slave.* New York: Avon Books, 1991.

McLear, Patrick E. "The St. Louis Cholera Epidemic of 1849." *Missouri Historical Review* 63 (1969):171–81.

McLoughlin, William G. *Cherokee Renascence in the New Republic.* Princeton: Princeton University Press, 1986.

McMillen, Sally. "Obstetrics in Antebellum Arkansas: Women and Doctors in a New State." In *Contributions to Arkansas Medical History, History of Medicine Associates Research Papers,* No. 1, ed. Edwina Walls, 64–88. Charlotte, N.C.: Delmar Printing Co., 1990.

McNeil, W. K., ed. *The Life and Adventures of an Arkansaw Doctor, by David Rattlehead.* By Marcus Lafayette Byrn. Fayetteville and London: University of Arkansas Press, 1989.

McNeilly, Donald P. *The Old South Frontier: Cotton Plantations and the Formation of Arkansas Society, 1819–1861.* Fayetteville: University of Arkansas Press, 2000.

McP. "Review of *The Writings of Hippocrates and Galen,* Epitomised from the original Latin Translations, by John Redman Coxe, M.D. *St. Louis Medical and Surgical Journal* 4, no. 4 (1847?):259–61.

McRaven, Charles. *Building the Hewn Log House.* Arkansas College Folklore Monograph Series. Hollister, Mo.: Mountain Publishing Services, 1978.

Meanley, Brooke. *Swamps, River Bottoms and Canebrakes.* Barre, Mass.: Barre Publishers, 1972.

"Medical Geography." *The Journal of Health and Recreation [Philadelphia]* 4, no. 1 (1832):1–3.

"The Medical Profession in St. Louis." *Missouri Medical and Surgical Journal* 1, no. 4 (1846):96.

Medicus. "Observations on Fever and Other Diseases of the South and West." *The Western Journal of the Medical and Physical Sciences* 10 (1829):503–13.

"Meet Me in St. Louis–1819." *Missouri Historical Society Bulletin* 7 (1951):182–84.

Merrens, H. Roy. "The Physical Environment of Early America: Images and Image Makers in Colonial South Carolina." *Geographical Review* 59, 4 (1969):530–56.

Merrens, H. Roy, and George D. Terry. "Dying in Paradise: Malaria, Mortality, and the Perceptual Environment in Colonial South Carolina." *Journal of Southern History* 50 (1984):533–50.

Milledoler, Philip E. "Cases of Disease produced by the Poison of Putrid Animal Matter, with Remarks." *New York Medical and Physical Journal,* n.s., 2 (1829–30):39–48.

Miller, Genevieve. "'Airs, Waters, and Places' in History." *Journal of the History of Medicine and Allied Sciences* 8 (1962):129–40.

Miller, Henry. "The Journal of Henry B. Miller." *Missouri Historical Society Collections* 6 (1931):213–87.

Miller, James William, trans., ed. *In the Arkansas Backwoods: Tales and Sketches by Friedrich Gerstäcker.* Columbia and London: University of Missouri Press, 1991.

Mitchell, B. Rush. "Disease Statistics of St. Louis, for 1845." *Missouri Medical and Surgical Review* 1 (1846):269–72.

Mitchell, Samuel L., trans. "Lancisi's Work on the Noxious Exhalations of Marshes: Published in Latin at Rome about one hundred years ago, and translated into English by Samuel L. Mitchell, at Washington, during the second session of the ninth Congress, 1806–7." *Medical Repository* 1, 3rd hexad (1809–10):9–18, 126–35, 237–45, 326–30.

Moffatt, Walter. "Medicine and Dentistry in Pioneer Arkansas." *Arkansas Historical Quarterly* 10 (1951):89–94.

Monette, John W., M.D. "An Essay on the Summer and Autumnal Remittent Fevers of Mississippi." *The Western Journal of Medicine and Surgery* 1 (1840):87–130.

Mooney, James. "The Cherokee Ball Play." *Journal of Cherokee Studies* 7 (1982):10–24.

_____. "The Cherokee River Cult." *Journal of Cherokee Studies* 7 (1982):30–36.

_____. "Cherokee Theory and Practice of Medicine." *Journal of Cherokee Studies* (1982):25–29.

Moore, Waddy William. "Territorial Arkansas, 1819–1836." Ph.D. thesis, University of North Carolina, 1962.

Morgan, Edmund Sears. *American Slavery, American Freedom: The Ordeal of Colonial Virginia*. New York and London: Norton, 1975.

Morgan, James L., Jr. "Biography of a Free Negro." *The Independence County [Arkansas] Chronicle* 5, no. 1 (1963):18–21.

Morrow, Lynn. "New Madrid and Its Hinterland: 1783–1826." *Missouri Historical Society Bulletin* 36 (1980):241–50.

"Mortality in St. Louis, During the Month of January, 1847, Accompanied with Meteorological Observations." *St. Louis Medical and Surgical Journal* 4 (1847):388–90.

Murphy, Michelle. "The 'Elsewhere Within Here' and Environmental Illness; or, How to Build Yourself a Body in a Safe Space." *Configurations* 8 (2000):87–120.

_____. "Sick Buildings and Sick Bodies: The Materialization of an Occupational Illness in Late Capitalism." Ph.D. thesis, Harvard University, 1998.

_____. "Toxicity in the Details: The History of the Women's Office Worker Movement and Occupational Health in the Late-Capitalist Office." *Labor History* 41 (2000):189–213.

Nagel, Paul C. *Missouri: A Bicentennial History*. The States and the Nation Series. New York and Nashville: Norton and the American Association for State and Local History, 1977.

Nash, Linda. "The Changing Experience of Nature: Historical Encounters with a Northwest River." *The Journal of American History* 86 (2000):1600–29.

_____. "Disease," in "Transforming the Central Valley: Body, Identity, and Environment in California, 1850–1970." Ph.D. thesis, University of Washington, Seattle, 2000.

Nash, Roderick. *Wilderness and the American Mind*. 3rd ed. 1967. Reprint, New Haven and London: Yale University Press, 1982.

Nelson, Frank G. "A Danish Account of Missouri in 1839." *Missouri Historical Society Bulletin* 33 (1977):265–68.

Nobles, Gregory H. "Straight Lines and Stability: Mapping the Political Order of the Anglo-American Frontier." *Journal of American History* 80 (1993):9–35.

Noland, C. F. M. *Arkansas Advocate*. "Lawrence County," 9 June 1830; "Jackson County," 20 Oct. 1830; "Crawford County," 12 Jan. 1831.

_____ ["N." of Arkansas]. "Early Settlers of Arkansas." *Spirit of the Times*. Parts 1–5. 15 Dec. 1849; 22 Dec. 1849; 29 Dec. 1849; 12 Jan. 1850; 26 Jan. 1850.

_____. *Pete Whetstone of Devil's Fork: Letters to the "Spirit of the Times,"* ed. Ted R. Worley and Eugene A. Nolte. Van Buren, Ark.: Press-Argus, 1957.

_____. Untitled article on Arkansas Territory. *Arkansas Advocate*, 3 Nov. 1830, 3.

Nott, Josiah. *Types of Mankind: or, Ethnological researches, based upon the ancient monuments, paintings, scultures, and crania of races, and upon their natural, geographical, philological and Biblical history*. 2nd ed. Philadelphia: Lippincott, Grambo & Co., 1854.

Numbers, Ronald L., and Janet S. Numbers. "Science in the Old South: A Reappraisal." *Journal of Southern History* 47 (1982):163–84.

Numbers, Ronald L., and William J. Orr, Jr. "William Beaumont's Reception at Home and Abroad." *Isis* 72 (1981):590–612.

Numbers, Ronald L., and John Harley Warner. "The Maturation of American Medical Science." In *Scientific Colonialism: A Cross-Cultural Comparison,* ed. Nathan Reingold and Marc Rothenberg, 191–214. Washington and London: Smithsonian Institution Press, 1981.

Nuttall, Thomas. "Collections towards a Flora of the Territory of Arkansas. Read before the American Philosophical Society April 4, 1834." *Transactions of the American Philosophical Society* n.s. 5 (1837):139–203.

Nutton, Vivian. "The Seeds of Disease: An Explanation of Contagion and Infection from the Greeks to the Renaissance." *Medical History* 27 (1983):1–34.

_____. "Humoralism." In *Companion Encyclopedia of the History of Medicine*, ed. W. F. Bynum and Roy Porter. London and New York: Routledge, 1993.

"Oh, the Smell of It!" Letter to the editor. *The Washington Post*, 20 May 1992.

"On the Influence of Noxious Effluvia on the Origin and Propagation of Epidemic Disease and On the Influence of Human Effluvia." *St. Louis Medical and Surgical Journal* 9 (1853):555–58.

Ophir, Adi, and Steven Shapin. "The Place of Knowledge: A Methodological Survey." *Science in Context* 4, 1 (1991):3–21.

Osborne, Michael A. "A Collaborative Dimension of the European Empires: Australian and French Acclimatization Societies and Intercolonial Scientific Co-operation." In *International Science and National Scientific Identity*, ed. R. W. Home and S. G. Kohstedt, 97–119. N.p.: Kluwer Academic Publishers, 1991.

Otto, John Solomon, and Ben Wayne Banks. "The Banks Family of Yell County, Arkansas: A 'Plain Folk' Family of the Highlands South." *Arkansas Historical Quarterly* 41 (1982):146–67.

Pabis, George S. "Delaying the Deluge: The Engineering Debate over Flood Control on the Lower Mississippi River, 1846–1861." *Journal of Southern History* 64 (1998):421–54.

Padget, Martin. "Travel, Exoticism, and the Writing of Region: Charles Fletcher Lummis and the 'Creation' of the Southwest." *Journal of the Southwest* 37 (1995):421–49.

Papillaud, L., Dr. "On the Comparative Efficacy of Certain Medicinal Agents in the Treatment of Dysentery, and other Intestinal Fluxes in Warm Climates." *St. Louis Medical and Surgical Journal* 6 (1848):195–98.

Parins, James W. *John Rollin Ridge: His Life and Works.* Lincoln and London: University of Nebraska Press, 1991.

Park, Hugh. *Reminiscences of the Indians by Cephas Washburn.* Van Buren, Ark.: Press-Argus, 1955.

Patterson, K. David. "Disease Environments of the Antebellum South." In *Science and Medicine in the Old South*, ed. Ronald L. Numbers and Todd L. Savitt, 152–65. Baton Rouge and London: Louisiana State University Press, 1989.

Peacock, Leslie Newell. "Deer, Fish . . . and Mososaurs: State's new Grandview acquisition has it all." *Arkansas Times*, 12 June 1998, 12–13.

Pelling, Margaret. "Contagion/Germ Theory/Specificity." In *Companion Encyclopedia of the History of Medicine*, ed. W. F. Bynum and Roy Porter. London and New York: Routledge, 1993.

Pernick, Martin S. "The Calculus of Suffering in 19th-Century Surgery." In *Sickness and Health in America: Readings in the History of Medicine and Public Health*, ed. Judith Walzer Leavitt and Ronald L. Numbers, 98–112. 2nd ed. Madison: University of Wisconsin Press, 1985.

Pick, Daniel. *Faces of Degeneration: A European Disorder, c. 1848–c.1918.* Ideas in Context, ed. Quentin Skinner. Cambridge: Cambridge University Press, 1993.

Pike, Albert ["A Backwoods Lawyer"]. "Sketches of Western Travel, Etc." *The Spirit of the Times,* 2 Sept. 1843, 1.

Pitcock, Cynthia De Haven. "Doctors in Controversy: An Ethical Dispute Between Joseph Nash McDowell and William Beaumont." *Missouri Historical Review* 60 (1966):336–49.

Pizer, Irwin H., and Harriet Steuernagel. "Medical Journals in St. Louis Before 1900." *Missouri Historical Society Bulletin* 20 (1964):221–56.

Pope, Dunbar H., ed. *Early Days in Arkansas, Being for the Most Part the Personal Recollections of an Old Settler. By Judge William F. Pope.* Little Rock: Frederick W. Allsopp, 1895. Reprint, Easley, S.C.: Southern Historical Press, 1978.

Porter, Roy. "Gout: Framing and Fantasizing Disease." *Bulletin of the History of Medicine* 68 (1994):1–28.

Porter, Roy, ed. *The Cambridge Illustrated History of Medicine.* Cambridge: Cambridge University Press, 1996.

Porter, Roy, and Dorothy Porter. *In Sickness and in Health: The British Experience 1650–1850.* New York: Basic Blackwell, 1988.

Porter, William T. "A Quarter Race in Kentucky. And Other Sketches, Illustrative of Scenes, Characters, and Incidents, Throughout the 'Universal Yankee Nation.'" 1846. In *Major Thorpe's Scenes in Arkansaw,* ed. T. B. Thorpe. Philadelphia: T. B Peterson and Brothers, 1858.

Porter, William T., ed. *The Big Bear of Arkansas, and Other Sketches, Illustrative of Characters and Incidents in the South and South-West.* Philadelphia: T. B. Peterson, 1843.

Pratt, Joseph Hyde. "American Prime Meridians." *The Geographical Review* 32 (1942):233–44.

Price, Jennifer. *Flight Maps: Adventures with Nature in Modern America.* New York: Basic Books, 1999.

Primm, James Neal. *Lion of the Valley: St. Louis, Missouri.* Boulder, Co.: Pruett, 1981.

Prince, Mary. *The History of Mary Prince, a West Indian Slave, Related by Herself. With a Supplement by the Editor. To Which is Added, The Narrative of Asa-Asa, A Captured African.* London and Edinburgh: F. Westley and A. H. Davis/Waugh & Innes, 1831.

Puckrein, Gary. "Climate, Health and Black Labor in the English Americas." *Journal of American Studies* 13 (1979):179–93.

Rafferty, Milton D. *Historical Atlas of Missouri.* Norman: University of Oklahoma Press, 1982.

———. *Missouri: A Geography.* Boulder, Co.: Westview Press, 1983.

———. *Rude Pursuits and Rugged Peaks: Schoolcraft's Ozark Journal, 1818–1819.* Fayetteville: University of Arkansas Press, 1996.

Randolph, Vance. *Ozark-Mountain Folks.* New York: Vanguard Press, 1932.

———. *Blow the Candle Out: "Unprintable" Ozark Folksongs and Folklore.* Edited with an introduction by G. Legman. Fayetteville: University of Arkansas Press, 1992.

Randolph, Vance, and George P. Wilson. *Down in the Holler: A Gallery of Ozark Folk Speech.* Norman: University of Oklahoma Press, 1953.

Rawick, George P. *The American Slave: A Composite Autobiography.* Westport, Conn.: Greenwood, 1972, 1977, 1979. Vol. 1, *From Sundown to Sunup: The Making of the Black Community,* Contributions in Afro-American and African Studies, no. 11; vols. 8–10, *Arkansas Narratives,* Parts

1–6; vol. 11, *Arkansas Narratives*, Part 7, and *Missouri Narratives*; Supplement, series 1, vol. 2, *Arkansas, Colorado, Minnesota, Missouri, and Oregon and Washington Narratives;* and series 2, vol. 1, *Alabama, Arizona, Arkansas, District of Columbia, Florida, Georgia, Indiana, Kansas, Maryland, Nebraska, New York, North Carolina, Oklahoma, Rhode Island, South Carolina, and Washington Narratives.*

"Recollections of Thomas Beckwith." *Missouri Historical Society Glimpses of the Past* 2, no. 3 (1935):32–42.

Reed, Silas R. "Observations on Scarlet Fever." *The Western Journal of the Medical and Physical Sciences* 7, 2nd hexad, vol. 1 (1834):9–23.

Reisner, Mark. *Cadillac Desert: The American West and Its Disappearing Water.* New York: Penguin, 1986.

Renbourn, E. T. "Life and Death of the Solar Topi: A Chapter in the History of Sunstroke." *Journal of Tropical Medicine and Hygiene* 65 (1962):203–18.

———. "Seasoning Fluxes and Fevers of Acclimatization. An Introduction to the History of Tropical Adaptation." *Journal of Tropical Medicine and Hygiene* 66 (1963):193–203.

"Report on the Epidemics of Louisiana, Mississippi, Arkansas, and Texas." *Transactions of the American Medical Association* 8 (1855):571–662.

"Rice Delicacies." *Arkansas Gazette*, 9 Dec. 1834, 1.

Ricketson, Shadrach. *Means of Preserving Health, and Preventing Diseases: Founded principally on an attention to Air and Climate, Drink, Food, Sleep, Exercise, Clothing, Passions of the Mind, and Retentions and Excretions.* New York: Collins, Perkins & Co., 1806.

Ridge, John Rollin. "Preface." In *Poems.* San Francisco: Henry Payot, 1868.

Riley, James C. "The Medicine of the Environment in Eighteenth-Century Germany." *Clio Medica* 18 (1983):167–78.

———. *The Eighteenth-Century Campaign to Avoid Disease.* New York: St. Martin's Press, 1987.

Rippere, Vicky. "The Survival of Traditional Medicine in Lay Medical Views: An Empirical Approach to the History of Medicine." *Medical History* 25 (1981):411–14.

Robb, John S. [Solitaire]. *The Swamp Doctor's Adventures in the South-West. Containing the Whole of the Louisiana Swamp Doctor; Streaks of Squatter Life; and Far-Western Scenes; in a Series of Forty-Two Humorous Southern and Western Sketches, Descriptive of Incidents and Character.* Philadelphia: T. B. Peterson, 1853.

Roediger, David R. *The Wages of Whiteness: Race and the Making of the American Working Class.* The Haymarket Series, ed. Mike Davis and Michael Sprinker. London and New York: Verso, 1991.

———. *Towards the Abolition of Whiteness: Essays on Race, Politics, and Working Class History.* London and New York: Verso, 1994.

Rohrbaugh, Malcolm J. *The Trans-Appalachian Frontier: People, Societies, Institutions, 1775–1850.* New York: Oxford University Press, 1978.

Rollings, Willard H. *The Osage: An Ethnohistorical Study of Hegemony on the Prairie-Plains.* Columbia and London: University of Missouri Press, 1992.

Rosen, George. "Political Order and Human Health in Jeffersonian Thought." *Bulletin of the History of Medicine* 26 (1952):32–44.

Rosenberg, Charles. "The Cause of Cholera: Aspects of Etiological Thought in Nineteenth Century America." *Bulletin of the History of Medicine* 34 (1960):331–54.

_____. *The Cholera Years: The United States in 1832, 1849, and 1866*. Chicago and London: University of Chicago Press, 1962.

_____. Introduction, *Gunn's Domestic Medicine*, by John Gunn. Facsimile reprint: Knoxville: University of Tennessee Press, 1986.

_____. "John Gunn: Everyman's Physician." In *Explaining Epidemics and Other Studies in the History of Medicine*, 57–73. Cambridge: Cambridge University Press, 1992.

_____. "Medical Text and Social Context: Explaining William Buchan's *Domestic Medicine*." In *Explaining Epidemics and Other Studies in the History of Medicine*, 32–56. Cambridge: Cambridge University Press, 1992.

_____. "The Therapeutic Revolution: Medicine, Meaning, and Social Change in Nineteenth-Century America." In *Explaining Epidemics and Other Studies in the History of Medicine*. 1978. Cambridge: Cambridge University Press, 1992.

_____. "Catechisms of Health: The Body in the Prebellum Classroom." *Bulletin of the History of Medicine* 69 (1995):175–97.

Rosenkrantz, Barbara Gutman. "The Search for Professional Order in Nineteenth-Century Medicine." In *Sickness and Health in America: Readings in the History of Medicine and Public Health*, ed. Judith Walzer Leavitt and Ronald L. Numbers, 219–32. 2nd ed. Madison: University of Wisconsin Press, 1985.

Ross, Margaret. "The New Madrid Earthquake." *Arkansas Historical Quarterly* 27 (1968):83–104.

Ross, Margaret Smith, ed. "Letters of Hiram Abiff Whittington, An Arkansas Pioneer from Massachusetts, 1827–1834." *Bulletin Series of the Pulaski [Arkansas] County Historical Society* 3 (1956).

Roth, Mitchel. "Cholera Summer: Independence, St. Joseph, and the Path of Contagion." *Gateway Heritage* 15 (1994):20–29.

Rothman, Sheila M. *Living in the Shadow of Death: Tuberculosis and the Social Experience of Illness in American History*. New York: Basic Books, 1994.

Royer-Collard, M. "The Temperaments Considered in Their Relation to Health." *St. Louis Medical and Surgical Journal* 1, no. 9 (1843):138–41.

Rozbicki, Michal J. "The Curse of Provincialism: Negative Perceptions of Colonial American Plantation Gentry." *Journal of Southern History* 63 (1997):727–52.

Rudwick, Martin J. S. "The Emergence of a Visual Language for Geological Science, 1760–1840." *History of Science* 14 (1976):149–95.

Rupke, Nicolaas. "Humboldtian Medicine." *Medical History* 40 (1996):293–310.

_____. "Adolf Mühry (1810–1888): Göttingen's Humboldtian Medical Geographer." In *Medical Geography in Historical Perspective*, ed. Nicolaas A. Rupke, 86–97. London: Wellcome Trust Centre for the History of Medicine at UCL, 2000.

Rupke, Nicolaas, and Karen E. Wonders. "Humboldtian Representations in Medical Cartography." In *Medical Geography in Historical Perspective*, ed. Nicolaas A. Rupke, 163–75. London: Wellcome Trust Centre for the History of Medicine at UCL, 2000.

Rush, Benjamin. "An Enquiry into the Cause of the Increase of Bilious and Intermitting Fevers in Pennsylvania, with Hints for preventing them." *Transactions of the American Philosophical Society* 2 (1786):206–12.

_____. *An Inquiry into the Various Sources of the Usual Forms of Summer & Autumnal Disease in the United States, and the Means of Preventing Them. To Which are Added, Facts, Intended to Prove the Yellow Fever Not to be Contagious.* Philadelphia: J. Conrad, 1805.

Sabin, A. N. "Hot Springs in Arkansas—for the Arkansas Gazette." *Arkansas Gazette* (1832).

Sabo, George, III. "Rituals of Encounter: Interpreting Native American Views of European Explorers." *Arkansas Historical Quarterly* 51 (1992):54–68.

Sargent, Frederick. *Hippocrative Heritage: A History of Ideas About Weather and Human Health.* New York, Oxford: Pergamon Press, 1982.

Savitt, Todd L. "Black Health on the Plantation: Masters, Slaves, and Physicians." In *Sickness and Health in America: Readings in the History of Medicine and Public Health,* ed. Judith Walzer Leavitt and Ronald L. Numbers, 351–68. 3rd ed. Madison: University of Wisconsin Press, 1997.

Scarborough, William K. "Science on the Plantation." In *Science and Medicine in the Old South,* ed. Ronald L. Numbers and Todd L. Savitt. Baton Rouge and London: Louisiana State University Press, 1989.

Scarpino, Philip V. "Slavery in Callaway County, Missouri: 1845–1855." *Missouri Historical Review* 71, 1 (1976):22–43.

Schafer, Judith Kelleher. *Slavery, the Civil Law, and the Supreme Court of Louisiana.* Baton Rouge and London: Louisiana State University Press, 1994.

Schama, Simon. *Landscape and Memory.* New York: Vintage, 1995.

Schlissel, Lillian. *Women's Diaries of the Westward Journey.* New York: Schocken, 1982.

Schneiders, Robert Kelley. *Unruly River: Two Centuries of Change Along the Missouri.* Development of Western Resources, ed. Hal K. Rothman. Lawrence: University Press of Kansas, 1999.

Schnell, J. Christopher, and Katherine B. Clinton. "The New West: Themes in Nineteenth Century Urban Promotion, 1815–1880." *Missouri Historical Society Bulletin* 30 (1974):75–88.

Schroeder, Walter. "Environmental Setting of the St. Louis Region." In *Common Fields: An Environmental History of St. Louis,* ed. Andrew Hurley, 13–37. St. Louis: Missouri Historical Society Press, 1997.

Schweninger, Loren, ed. *From Tennessee Slave to St. Louis Entrepreneur: The Autobiography of James Thomas.* Columbia: University of Missouri Press, 1984.

Scoffern, John. *The Philosophy of Common Life; or, The Science of Health.* London: Ward & Lock, 1857.

Scully, Francis J., M.D. "Across Arkansas in 1844." *Arkansas Historical Quarterly* 13 (1954):31–51.

_____. *Hot Springs, Arkansas and Hot Springs National Park: The Story of a City and the Nation's Health Report.* Little Rock: Hansen/Pioneer Press, 1966.

Sealander, John A. *A Guide to Arkansas Mammals.* Conway, Ark.: River Road Press, 1979.

Seematter, Mary E. "Trials and Confessions: Race and Justice in Antebellum St. Louis." *Gateway Heritage* 12 (1991):36–47.

Sellers, Christopher C. *Hazards of the Job: From Industrial Disease to Environmental Health Science.* Chapel Hill and London: University of North Carolina Press, 1997.

Shafer, Henry Burnell. *The American Medical Profession, 1783 to 1850.* New York: Columbia University Press, 1936.

Shaftel, Norman. "The Evolution of American Medical Literature." In *History of American Medicine*, ed. Felix Marti-Ibanez, 95–118. New York: M.D. Publications, 1958.

Shallat, Todd. *Structures in the Stream: Water, Science, and the Rise of the U.S. Army Corps of Engineers* American Studies Series, ed. William H. Goetzmann. Austin: University of Texas Press, 1994.

Shapin, Steven. "'Nibbling at the teats of science': Edinburgh and the Diffusion of Science in the 1830s." In *Metropolis and Province: Science in British Culture, 1780–1850*, ed. Ian Inkster and Jack Morrell. Philadelphia: University of Pennsylvania Press, 1983.

———. "The House of Experiment in Seventeenth-Century England." *Isis* 79 (1988):373–404.

———. "The Invisible Technician." *American Scientist* 77 (1989):554–63.

———. *A Social History of Truth: Civility and Science in Seventeenth-Century England.* Science and Its Conceptual Foundations, ed. David L. Hull. Chicago and London: University of Chicago Press, 1994.

Shapin, Steven, and Simon Schaffer. *Leviathan and the Air-Pump: Hobbes, Boyle, and the Experimental Life.* Princeton: Princeton University Press, 1985.

Shapiro, Henry D., and Zane L. Miller, eds. *Physician to the West: Selected Writings of Daniel Drake on Science and Society.* Lexington: University Press of Kentucky, 1970.

Shea, William L. "A Semi-Savage State: The Image of Arkansas in the Civil War." *Arkansas Historical Quarterly* 48 (1989):309–28.

Shepherd, Bill, ed. *Arkansas's Natural Heritage.* Little Rock: August House, 1984.

Sherwood, Diana. "Historical Societies in Arkansas." *Arkansas Historical Quarterly* 11 (1952):131–36.

Shoemaker, Nancy. "How Indians Got to Be Red." *American Historical Review* 102 (1997):625–44.

Shortridge, James R. "The Expansion of the Settlement Frontier in Missouri." *Missouri Historical Review* 75, 1 (1980):64–90.

Shryock, Richard H. "Medical Practice in the Old South." *South Atlantic Quarterly* 29 (1930):160–78.

———. *Medicine and Society in America, 1660–1860.* Anson G. Phelps Lectureships in Early American History. New York: New York University Press, 1960.

Silber, Nina. "Sick Yankees in Paradise: Northern Tourism in the Reconstructed South." In *The Romance of Reunion: Northerners and the South, 1865–1900.* Chapel Hill and London: University of North Carolina Press, 1993.

Sizemore, Jean. *Ozark Vernacular Houses: A Study of Rural Homeplaces in the Arkansas Ozarks, 1830–1930.* Fayetteville: University of Arkansas Press, 1994.

Skinner, James L., ed. *The Autobiography of Henry Merrell, Industrial Missionary to the South.* Athens and London: University of Georgia Press, 1991.

Sklar, Kathryn Kish. "All Hail to Pure Cold Water!" In *Women and Health in America: Historical Readings*, ed. Judith Walzer Leavitt. Madison: University of Wisconsin Press, 1984.

Smith, Henry Nash. "Rain Follows the Plow: The Notion of Increased Rainfall for the Great Plains, 1844–1880." *Huntington Library Quarterly* 10 (1947):169–93.

_____. *Virgin Land: The American West as Symbol and Myth*. 1950. Cambridge, Mass.: Harvard University Press, 1978.

Smith, Nathan D., M.D. "Meterological Observations Made Near Washington, Ark., Extending Over a Period of Twenty Years, From 1840 to 1859, Inclusive." In *Smithsonian Contributions to Knowledge*, 12. Washington, D.C.: Smithsonian Institution, 1860.

Smith-Rosenberg, Carroll. "Puberty to Menopause: The Cycle of Femininity in Nineteenth-Century America." In *Disorderly Conduct: Visions of Gender in Victorian America*. New York and Oxford: Oxford University Press, 1985.

Sollors, Werner. *Beyond Ethnicity: Consent and Descent in American Culture*. New York and Oxford: Oxford University Press, 1986.

Sontag, Susan. *"Illness as Metaphor" and "AIDS and its Metaphors."* New York, London, Toronto, Sydney, Auckland: Doubleday/Anchor, 1990.

"South Arkansas—Our Prospects." *Arkansas Democrat*, 18 Nov. 1853.

Southey, Robert, ed. *The Pilgrim's Progress. With a Life of John Bunyan*. 1678. Boston and New York: Crocker and Brewster/Jonathan Leavitt, 1832.

Spanagel, David I. "When Statesmen Were Opinion Makers: Political Patronage and Discourse in Natural Science." Paper delivered at the Annual Meeting of the Organization of American Historians, 2 April 1998.

Sprague, Alden, M.D. "On the Diseases of Arkansas." *Arkansas Gazette* (1832): 27 June 1832, 3; 11 July 1832, 3; 18 July 1832, 1; and 25 July 1832, 1.

St. George, Robert Blair. "'Set Thine House in Order': The Domestication of the Yeomanry in Seventeenth-Century New England." In *Common Places: Readings in American Vernacular Architecture*, ed. Dell Upton and John Michael Vlach. Athens and London: University of Georgia Press, 1986.

Staffords, L. Scott. "Slavery and the Arkansas Supreme Court." *University of Arkansas at Little Rock Law Journal* 19 (1997): 413–64.

Stampp, Kenneth M. *The Peculiar Institution: Slavery in the Ante-Bellum South*. New York: Knopf, 1956.

Stanley, Dorothy, ed. *The Autobiography of Sir Henry Morton Stanley*. Boston and New York: Houghton Mifflin, 1909.

Stanton, William. *The Leopard's Spots: Scientific Attitudes Toward Race in America, 1815–1859*. Chicago: University of Chicago Press, 1960.

Starr, Paul. *The Social Transformation of American Medicine*. New York: Basic Books, 1982.

Stegner, Wallace. *Wolf Willow: A History, a Story, and a Memory of the Last Plains Frontier*. New York: Viking Press, 1966.

Stepan, Nancy. "Biological Degeneration: Races and Proper Places." In *Degeneration: The Dark Side of Progress*, ed. J. Edward Chamberlain and Sander L. Gilman. New York: Columbia University Press, 1985.

Stewart, George R. *Names on the Land: A Historical Account of Place-Naming in the United States*. Boston: Houghton Mifflin, 1967.

Stewart, Maria W. "Productions of Mrs. Maria W. Stewart, Presented to the First African Baptist Church & Society, Of the City of Boston (Published by the Friends of Freedom and Virtue: Boston, 1835)." In *Spiritual Narratives*, ed. with an Introduction by Sue E. Houchins. New York and Oxford: Oxford University Press, 1988.

Stewart, Mart A. "Rice, Water, and Power: Landscapes of Domination and Resistance in the Lowcountry, 1790–1880." *Environmental History Review* 15 (1991):47–64.

———. *"What Nature Suffers to Groe": Life, Labor, and Landscape on the Georgia Coast, 1680–1920.* Wormsloe Foundation Publications, no. 19. Athens and London: University of Georgia Press, 1996.

———. "'Let Us Begin with the Weather?': Climate, Race, and Cultural Distinctiveness in the American South." In *Nature and Society in Historical Context,* ed. Mikuláš Teich, Roy Porter, and Bo Gustafsson. Cambridge: Cambridge University Press, 1997.

Stilgoe, John R. *Common Landscapes of America, 1580 to 1845.* New Haven, Conn.: Yale University Press, 1982.

Stoddard, Amos. "Observations on the Native Salt, Bearded Indians, Earthquakes, and Boundaries of Louisiana. . . " *Medical Repository* 10 (1807):44–50.

Stokes, Durward T. "The Wilson Letters, 1835–1849." *Missouri Historical Review* 60 (1966):495–517.

Stowe, Harriet Beecher. *Dred; A Tale of the Great Dismal Swamp, in Two Volumes.* Boston: Phillips, Sampson & Co., 1856.

———. *Uncle Tom's Cabin or Life Among the Lowly.* Ed. Ann Douglas. 1852. Reprint, New York: Penguin, 1986.

Stowe, Steven M. "Seeing Themselves at Work: Physicians and the Case Narrative in the Mid-Nineteenth-Century American South." *American Historical Review* 101 (1996):41–79.

Sullivan, Robert B. "Sanguine Practices: A Historical and Historiographic Reconsideration of Heroic Therapy in the Age of Rush." *Bulletin of the History of Medicine* 68 (1994):211–34.

Sutton, Keith. "The Age of Discovery and Settlement." *Arkansas Game and Fish* 17, no. 3 (1986):2–12.

Swallow, G. C. "Waters of Missouri." In *Switzler's Illustrated History of Missouri from 1541 to 1877,* 525–27. St. Louis: C. R. Barns, 1879.

Sweet, Victoria. "Hildegard of Bingen and the Greening of Medieval Medicine." *Bulletin of the History of Medicine* 73 (1999):381–403.

Szaraz, Stephen Charles. "History, Character, and Prospects: Daniel Drake and the Life of the Mind in the Ohio Valley, 1785–1852." Ph.D. thesis, Harvard University, 1993.

Tarr, Joel A., and Carl Zimring. "The Struggle for Smoke Control in St. Louis: Achievement and Emulation." In *Common Fields: An Environmental History of St. Louis,* ed. Andrew Hurley, 199–200. St. Louis: Missouri Historical Society Press, 1997.

Taylor, Alan. *William Cooper's Town: Power and Persuasion on the Frontier of the Early American Republic.* New York: Knopf, 1996.

Taylor, Joseph E., III. *Making Salmon: An Environmental History of the Northwest Fisheries Crisis.* Weyerhaeuser Environmental Books, ed. William Cronon. Seattle and London: University of Washington Press, 1999.

Taylor, Orville W. ". . . a good deal of sickness. . . ." In *Negro Slavery in Arkansas.* Durham, N.C.: Duke University Press, 1958.

Temkin, Oswei. "An Historical Analysis of the Concept of Infection." In *The Double Face of Janus and Other Essays in the History of Medicine.* Baltimore and London: Johns Hopkins University Press, 1977.

Terrall, Mary. "Heroic Narratives of Quest and Discovery." *Configurations* 6 (1998):223–42.

Thomas, William L. *History of St. Louis County, Missouri: A Story that Attracts by its Recital of Past Achievements; Its Record of Earnest Endeavor and Sure Development to Present Greatness and its Future filled with Roseate Promises.* Vol. 2. St. Louis, Chicago, and Philadelphia: S. J. Clarke, 1911.

Thompson, Dr. J. E. "Topography and Diseases of Bates County, Missouri." *The Boston Medical and Surgical Journal* 54 (1856):49–53, 269–73, 329–34, 489–95.

Thompson, Kenneth. "Climatotherapy in California." *California Historical Quarterly* 50 (1971):111–30.

———. "Wilderness and Health in the Nineteenth Century." *Journal of Historical Geography* 2 (1976):145–61.

———. "Trees as a Theme in Medical Geography and Public Health." *Bulletin of the New York Academy of Medicine* 54 (1978):517–31.

———. "Forests and Climate Change in America: Some Early Views." *Climatic Change* 3 (1980):47–64.

Thornton, Tamara Plakins. *Cultivating Gentlemen: The Meaning of Country Life Among the Boston Elite, 1785–1860.* New Haven, Conn.: Yale University Press, 1989.

Thorpe, T. B. *Major Thorpe's Scenes in Arkansaw. Containing the Whole of the Quarter Race in Kentucky; and Bob Herring, the Arkansas Bear Hunter. As well as Cupping on the Sternum; Playing Poker in Arkansas; and other Sketches Illustrative of Scenes, Incidents, and Characters, throughout "The Universal Yankee Nation." To Which is Added The Drama in Pokerville; A Night in a Swamp; and other Stories. By J. M. Field, Esq., of the St. Louis Reville.* Philadelphia: T. B Peterson & Bros., 1858.

Ticknor, Caleb. "Climate and Season." In *The Philosophy of Living; or, The Way to Enjoy Life and its Comforts.* New York: Harper & Bros., 1837.

"To the Medical Profession." *Missouri Medical and Surgical Journal* 1, no. 1 (1845):1–3.

Tomer, John S., and Michael J. Brodhead, eds. *A Naturalist in Indian Territory: The Journals of S.W. Woodhouse, 1849–50.* Norman and London: University of Oklahoma Press, 1992.

Trautmann, Frederick. "Missouri Through a German's Eyes: Franz von Löher on St. Louis and Hermann." *Missouri Historical Review* 77 (1983):367–94.

Trials and Confessions of Madison Henderson, alias Blanchard, Alfred Amos Warrick, James W. Seward, and Charles Brown, Murderers of Jesse Baker and Jacob Weaver, as Given by Themselves; and a Likeness of Each, Taken in jail shortly after their arrest. St. Louis: Chambers & Knapp, 1841.

Turrentine, G. R. "Dwight Mission." *Arkansas Valley Historical Papers* (1962):1–11.

Twain, Mark. *Life on the Mississippi.* 1883. New York: Signet, 1980.

Twyman, Leo, M.D. "On the Medical Topography of Saint Charles County, Mo., With some Account of the Prevalent Diseases from 1829 to 1841, inclusive." *Missouri Medical and Surgical Journal* 1 (1845):25–32.

Tyrrell, Ian. *True Gardens of the Gods: Californian-Australian Environmental Reform, 1860–1930.* Berkeley, Los Angeles, and London: University of California Press, 1999.

Ulrich, Laurel Thatcher. *A Midwife's Tale: The Life of Martha Ballard, Based on Her Diary, 1785–1812.* New York: Vintage, 1990.

U.S. Army Corps of Engineers. *The History of the U.S. Army Corps of Engineers.* Alexandria, Va.: Office of History, U.S. Army Corps of Engineers, 1998.

Usner, Daniel H., Jr. "An American Indian Gateway: Some Thoughts on the Migration and Set-
    tlement of Eastern Indians Around Early St. Louis." *Gateway Heritage* 11 (1990–91):42–51.
———. *Indians, Settlers, and Slaves in a Frontier Exchange Economy: The Lower Mississippi Valley Be-
    fore 1783*. Chapel Hill and London: University of North Carolina Press and Institute of Early
    American History and Culture (Williamsburg, Va.), 1992.

Valencius, Conevery Bolton. [See also "Bolton, Conevery A."]. "The Geography of Health and
    the Making of the American West: Arkansas and Missouri, 1800–1860." In *Medical Geography
    in Historical Perspective*, ed. Nicolaas A. Rupke, 121–45. London: Wellcome Trust Centre for
    the History of Medicine at UCL, 2000.
———. "Histories of Medical Geography." In *Medical Geography in Historical Perspective*, ed.
    Nicolaas A. Rupke, 3–30. London: Wellcome Trust Centre for the History of Medicine at
    UCL, 2000.

Vaulx, Julia R. "Another Early Traveler in Arkansas." *Arkansas Historical Quarterly* 5
    (1946):169–78.

Vileisis, Ann. *Discovering the Unknown Landscape: A History of America's Wetlands*. Washington,
    D.C., and Covelo, Calif.: Island Press, 1997.

Wahrman, Dror. "National Society, Communal Culture: An Argument About the Recent His-
    toriography of Eighteenth-Century Britain." *Social History* 17 (1992):43–72.

Wailoo, Keith. *Dying in the City of the Blues: Sickle Cell Anemia and the Politics of Race and Health*.
    Studies in Social Medicine, ed. Allan M. Brandt and Larry R. Churchill. Chapel Hill and
    London: University of North Carolina Press, 2001.

Warner, John Harley. *The Therapeutic Perspective: Medical Practice, Knowledge, and Identity in Amer-
    ica, 1820–1885*. Cambridge, Mass.: Harvard University Press, 1986.
———. "The Idea of Southern Medical Distinctiveness: Medical Knowledge and Practice in
    the Old South." In *Science and Medicine in the Old South*, ed. Ronald L. Numbers and Todd L.
    Savitt, 179–205. Baton Rouge and London: Louisiana State University Press, 1989.
———. "A Southern Medical Reform: The Meaning of the Antebellum Argument for
    Southern Medical Education." In *Science and Medicine in the Old South*, ed. Ronald L. Num-
    bers and Todd L. Savitt, 206–25. Baton Rouge and London: Louisiana State University
    Press, 1989.
———. "Remembering Paris: Memory and the American Disciples of French Medicine in the
    Nineteenth Century." *Bulletin of the History of Medicine* 65, 3 (1991):301–25.
———. "Science, Healing, and the Physician's Identity: A Problem of Professional Character
    in Nineteenth-Century America." *Clio Medica* 22 (1991):65–88.
———. "Revolt and Return: Hippocrates in Antebellum American Medicine." Paper pre-
    sented at "Hippocrates and Modern Medicine," Wood Institute for the History of Medicine,
    Philadelphia, 4–5 May 1996.
———. "From Specificity to Universalism in Medical Therapeutics: Transformation in the
    19th-Century United States." In *Sickness and Health in America: Readings in the History of Medi-
    cine and Public Health*, ed. Judith Walzer Leavitt and Ronald L. Numbers, 87–101. Madison:
    University of Wisconsin Press, 1997.
———. *Against the Spirit of System: The French Impulse in Nineteenth-Century American Medicine*.
    Princeton: Princeton University Press, 1998.

Wear, Andrew, ed. *Medicine in Society: Historical Essays*. Cambridge: Cambridge University Press, 1992.

Webster, Noah. *An American Dictionary of the English Language. . .* Rev. ed. New York: White & Sheffield, 1841.

Weems, Mason L. *The Life of George Washington; with curious anecdotes, equally honourable to himself and exemplary to his young countryment . . .* Philadelphia: Mathew Carey, 1809.

West, Elliott. *The Contested Plains: Indians, Goldseekers, and the Rush to Colorado*. Lawrence, Kans.: University Press of Kansas, 1998.

"Westward Along the Boone's Lick Trail in 1826, the Diary of Colonel John Glover." *Missouri Historical Review* 39 (1945):184–99.

Whayne, Jeannie, and Willard B. Gatewood, eds. *The Arkansas Delta: Land of Paradox*. Fayetteville: University of Arkansas Press, 1993.

Whayne, Jeannie M., ed. *Shadows over Sunnyside: An Arkansas Plantation in Transition, 1830–1945*. Fayetteville: University of Arkansas Press, 1993.

White, Joshua E. "A Report to the Medical Society of Georgia, on the Medical Topography of Savannah and its Vicinity." *Medical Repository* 10, 2nd hexad, vol. 3 (1807):352–63.

White, Richard. *"It's Your Misfortune and None of My Own": A History of the American West*. Norman and London: University of Oklahoma Press, 1991.

———. *The Organic Machine*. New York: Hill & Wang, 1995.

White, Richard, and William Cronon. "Ecological Change and Indian-White Relations." In *Handbook of North American Indians*, ed. Wilcomb E. Washburn. Vol. 4, *History of Indian-White Relations*, 417–29. Washington, D.C.: Smithsonian Institution, 1988.

"Why Epidemics Rage at Night." *The Western Journal of Medicine and Surgery* 6, 3rd ser. (1850?):265–266.

Williams, C. Fred. "The Bear State Image: Arkansas in the Nineteenth Century." *Arkansas Historical Quarterly* 39 (1980):99–111.

Williams, Isaac D. *Sunshine and Shadow of Slave Life: Reminiscences As Told By Isaac D. Williams To "Tege."* East Saginaw, Mich.: Evening News Printing and Binding House, 1885. Reprint, New York: AMS Press, 1975.

Williams, William Donald. "An 1835 Magazine Article by Dr. Nathan D. Smith," *Arkansas Historical Quarterly* 48 (1989):272–77.

Wilson, Sam, and Tom Moritz, eds. *The Sierra Club Wetlands Reader*. San Francisco: Sierra Club Books, 1996.

Windell, Marie George. "The Road West in 1818: The Diary of Henry Vest Bingham." *Missouri Historical Review* 40 (1945):21–54, 174–204.

Winsor, Roger A. "Environmental Imagery of the Wet Prairie of East Central Illinois, 1820–1920." *Journal of Historical Geography* 13 (1987):375–97.

Wood, Peter H. *Black Majority: Negroes in Colonial South Carolina from 1670 Through the Stono Rebellion*. New York: Knopf, 1974.

Woods, James M. *Rebellion and Realignment: Arkansas's Road to Secession*. Fayetteville: University of Arkansas Press, 1987.

Woodson, Carter G., ed. *The Mind of the Negro as Reflected in Letters Written During the Crisis 1800–1860*. Washington, D.C.: Association for the Study of Negro Life and History, 1926.

Worley, Ted R., and Eugene A. Nolte, eds. *Pete Whetstone of Devil's Fork: Letters to the "Spirit of the Times."* Van Buren, Ark.: Press-Argus, 1957.

Worster, Donald. *Rivers of Empire: Water, Aridity, and the Growth of the American West.* New York and Oxford: Oxford University Press, 1992.

WPA. *Missouri: A Guide to the "Show Me" State. Compiled by Workers of the Writers' Program of the Work Projects Administration in the State of Missouri.* American Guide Series. 1941. Reprint, New York: Hastings House, 1954.

WPA. *The WPA Guide to 1930s Arkansas.* 1941. Lawrence: University Press of Kansas, 1987.

Wrigley, Richard, and George Revill. *Pathologies of Travel.* The Wellcome Institute Series in the History of Medicine. Amsterdam and Atlanta: Rodopi, 2000.

Zboray, Ronald J. "The Letter and the Fiction Reading Public in Antebellum America." *Journal of American Culture* 10 (1987):27–34.

PERMISSIONS

I am grateful for permission to use the following material:

Quotations from pages 49, 82, 143–44, and paraphrase of pages 166–200 from *In the Arkansas Backwoods: Tales and Sketches by Friedrich Gerstäcker*, edited by James William Miller are by permission of the University of Missouri Press. Copyright © 1991 by the Curators of the University of Missouri.

Quotations from the John Brown Journal, Heiskell Small Manuscripts, and the letter from Robert F. Henry, Hopkinsville, Arkansas, to Dr. J. F. Henry, "On the Wing," 12 Sept. 1819, Heiskell Small Manuscripts, box 2, file 64, are by permission of the University of Arkansas at Little Rock Archives and Special Collections.

Quotations from "I at Home, by Stephen S. Hempstead, Sr.: The Diary of a Yankee Farmer in Missouri," edited by Mrs. Dana O. Jensen, are by permission of the Missouri Historical Society Press.

Quotations from the Justus Post Papers, the Stephens Family Papers, and the John Geiger Journal, Journals and Diaries Collection, are by permission of the Missouri Historical Society, St. Louis.

Quotations of pages 114, 171–72, and 179, and quotations and paraphrase of pages 101–5 from *Twelve Years a Slave*, by Solomon Northup, edited by Sue Eakin and Joseph Logsdon, are by permission of Louisiana State University Press. Copyright © 1996 by Louisiana State University Press.

I am also grateful to the Wellcome Trust of London for permission to use material from my essays, "Histories of Medical Geography" and "The Geography of Health and the Making of the American West: Arkansas and Missouri, 1800–1860," in *Medical Geography in Historical Perspective* (pp. 3–30 and 121–45), edited by Nicolaas A. Rupke, published by the Wellcome Trust Centre for the History of Medicine (2000). Copyright © 2000 the Trustees of the Wellcome Trust.

INDEX

INDEX 387

Uncle Tom's Cabin, 70

Von Humboldt, Alexander, 166

Walker, John, 77, 105
War of 1812, 42, 44
Washburn, Cephas, 16, 26, 95, 120, 135,
    143, 198
Water
    cleansing power of, 121, 137, 140
    effect of agriculture on, 215
    flooding, 75, 89, 129, 141–145
    healing springs, 152–158
    and health, 89–90, 98, 186–189
    illness caused by, 137–141
    and indoor environments, 94–95
    location and migration, 135–137
    and malaria, 80–81, 138
    and miasma, 114–115, 121, 123–124,
        139–141
    quality, 29
    and slavery, 135
    stagnant, 139, 145–146
    and swamps, 145–152
    therapies, 57, 103–104, 152–158
    See also Springs; Hot Springs
Webb, A. W.
    on ague, 81, 184
    on elevation, 89
    on farming, 197, 217–218, 221–222
    on flow and movement in illness, 60
    on improvements made to the
        environment, 101
    on miasma, 116, 126
    published works by, 174
    on Southern medicine, 179–180
    on temperature effects on health, 75
Webster, Noah, 114, 116
Weems, Mason, 59, 217
Welch, C. B., 107, 123, 169–170
Western Journal of Medicine and Surgery, 178,
    216

Western Medico-Chirurgical Journal, 101
Wheeler, Amos, 100
White, Joshua E., 29
White Americans
    altered characteristics of migrants,
        229–230, 255–258
    beliefs about race differences, 232–240
    and changes in racial characteristics,
        241–243
    and free blacks, 49–52, 239–240,
        248–249
    and malaria, 79–80
    and migration, 238–239
    and race mixing, 245–247, 249–255
    and seasoning, 240–243
    and skin color, 229–231, 241–247
    sold into slavery, 254–255
    and swamps, 149–150
Whittington, Hiram Abiff, 84, 90, 98, 104,
    157, 172, 229
Wilber, Charles Dana, 215
Wilderness, the
    acclimation, 22–34, 231, 238–239,
        238–240
    adventure in, 8–9, 18, 26, 36
    characteristics of migrants to, 37–40,
        229–230
    cultivation and domestication of, 19–20,
        30–31, 127–130
    death in, 18, 31–32, 63–64, 118
    difficulty in traveling through, 20–21,
        147–152
    dynamism of, 20–21
    economic opportunity in, 17–18, 19,
        43–45, 142–143, 151–152,
        207–208
    and farming, 200–202
    literature, 23, 26, 34–37, 103, 128, 134,
        147–152, 161–165, 169, 175,
        177–179, 212, 218–219, 235–236
    missionaries in, 19, 22, 24–25, 98,
        120–121